Java Collections

Java Collections

An Introduction to Abstract Data Types, Data Structures and Algorithms

David A. Watt
University of Glasgow

Deryck F. Brown
The Robert Gordon University

JOHN WILEY & SONS, LTD
CHICHESTER • NEW YORK • WEINHEIM • BRISBANE • SINGAPORE • TORONTO

Other Wiley Editorial Offices

John Wiley & Sons, Inc., 605 Third Avenue,
New York, NY 10158-0012, USA

WILEY-VCH Verlag GmbH
Pappelallee 3, D-69469 Weinheim, Germany

John Wiley & Sons Australia, Ltd, 33 Park Road, Milton,
Queensland 4064, Australia

John Wiley & Sons (Canada) Ltd, 22 Worcester Road
Rexdale, Ontario, M9W 1L1, Canada

John Wiley & Sons (Asia) Pte Ltd, 2 Clementi Loop #02-01,
Jin Xing Distripark, Singapore 129809

British Library Cataloguing in Publication Data

A catalogue record for this book is available from the British Library

ISBN 0 471 89978X

Cover Image – Fondaco dei Turchi, Venice (w/c) by John Ruskin (1819–1900)
Ruskin Musuem, Coniston, Cumbria, UK/Bridgeman Art Library

Contents

Preface

This book has four major themes: *algorithms*, *data structures*, *abstract data types* (*ADTs*), and *object-oriented methods*. All of these themes are of central importance in computer science and software engineering.

The book focuses on a number of important ADTs – stacks, queues, lists (sequences), sets, maps (tables), priority queues, trees, and graphs – that turn up again and again in software engineering. It uses these ADTs to motivate the data structures required to implement them – arrays, linked lists, search trees, hash tables, and heaps – and algorithms associated with these data structures – insertion, deletion, searching, merging, sorting, and traversal. The book shows how to implement these data structures and algorithms in the object-oriented programming language Java.

The book's typical approach is to introduce an ADT, illustrate its use by one or two example applications, develop a 'contract' specifying the ADT's values and operations, and finally consider which data structures are suitable for implementing the ADT. This approach clearly distinguishes between applications and implementations of the ADT, thus reinforcing a key software engineering principle: separation of concerns. The book motivates the study of data structures and algorithms by introducing them on a need-to-know basis. In other words, it adopts a practical (software engineering) approach to the subject, rather than a theoretical one. It does not neglect the important topic of algorithm analysis, but emphasizes its practical importance rather than the underlying mathematics.

Object-oriented methods have emerged as the dominant software technology during the last decade, and Java has become the dominant programming language in computer science education. These developments call for a fresh approach to the teaching of programming and software engineering. This book takes such a fresh approach, using object-oriented methods from the outset to design and implement ADTs. It avoids the mistake of reworking an older book on algorithms and data structures that was written originally for Pascal or C.

Several of the ADTs introduced in this book are directly supported by the Java 2 collection classes. Programmers will naturally prefer to use these collection classes rather than design and implement their own. Nevertheless, choosing the right collection classes for each application requires an understanding of the properties of different ADTs and their alternative implementations. This book aims to give readers the necessary understanding.

Readership

This book can be read by anyone who has taken a first programming course in Java.

The book is designed primarily as a text for a second-level course in algorithms and data structures, in the context of a computer science program in which Java is the main programming language. In terms of the 1991 and 2001 ACM Computing Curricula, the book covers the knowledge units summarized in Table P.1.

The book is also suitable for practicing software engineers who have just learned Java and who now wish to gain (or refresh) the knowledge of algorithms and data structures required to make effective use of the Java 2 collection classes.

The detailed prerequisites of this book are as follows:

- A knowledge of fundamental Java programming topics – expressions, statements, objects, and classes – is essential. A knowledge of more advanced topics – inheritance, exceptions, interfaces, inner classes – is desirable but not essential before reading this book. Readers unfamiliar with the latter topics should refer to Appendix B whenever necessary.
- Certain mathematical topics – powers, logarithms, series summations, and recurrences – are needed to analyze the efficiency of algorithms. Most of these mathematical topics are taught in secondary/high schools. Readers unfamiliar with any of these topics should refer to Appendix A whenever necessary.

Outline

Chapter 1 introduces two of this book's major themes: algorithms and data structures. Chapter 2 takes a closer look at algorithms, showing how we can analyze their efficiency and introducing recursive algorithms.

Chapters 3 and 4 review two simple and ubiquitous data structures – arrays and linked lists – together with their associated insertion, deletion, searching, merging, and sorting algorithms. Later in the book, Chapters 10, 12, 13, and 16 introduce more sophisticated

Table P.1 Coverage of ACM Computing Curricula knowledge units.

ACM/IEEE Computing Curricula 2001	ACM/IEEE Computing Curricula 1991
PF1 (algorithms and problem-solving)	AL1 (basic data structures)
PF3 (basic data structures)	AL2 (abstract data types)
PF4 (recursion)	AL3 (recursive algorithms)
PF5 (abstract data types)	AL4 (complexity analysis)
AL1 (basic algorithmic analysis)	AL6 (sorting and searching)
AL3 (fundamental computing algorithms)	

data structures – binary search trees, hash tables, heaps, AVL-trees, and B-trees – again together with their associated algorithms.

Chapter 5 takes a close look at the idea of an abstract data type (ADT). It introduces the notion of a 'contract' that specifies the values and operations of an ADT without committing to a particular representation. Chapters 6 (stacks), 7 (queues), 8 (lists), 9 (sets), 11 (maps), 13 (priority queues), 14 (trees), and 15 (graphs) introduce a variety of collection ADTs together with alternative implementations of each. The list, set, and map ADTs covered in Chapters 8, 9, and 11 are in fact simplified versions of the corresponding Java 2 collection classes.

Chapter 17 concludes the book. It discusses the role of ADTs in object-oriented design. It also discusses the distinction between heterogeneous and homogeneous collections, and an extension of Java that supports generic homogeneous collections.

Appendix A summarizes the mathematical topics needed to analyze the efficiency of algorithms. Appendix B summarizes the features of Java that are most important in this book, particularly the more advanced features that are likely to be omitted in a first programming course. Appendix C summarizes the Java 2 collection classes.

Ideally, all the chapters of this book should be read in numerical order. Figure P.2 summarizes the dependencies between chapters. Clearly, Chapters 1–5 must be read first, and Chapters 6–9 all rely on this introductory material. Chapter 10 depends on Chapters 6 and 9, and in turn Chapters 11, 13 and 16 all depend on Chapter 10. Readers may vary the order of some of the later chapters, as indicated by Figure P.2. Readers may also omit any of Chapters 13–17 if time is short.

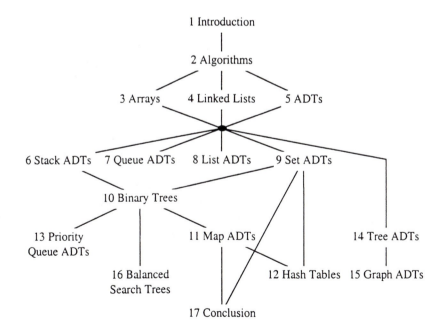

Figure P.2 Dependencies between chapters.

Scope

This book is an *introductory* text. As such, it covers several topics, such as algorithm complexity, hash tables, and graphs, in rather less depth than would be possible in a more advanced text. Moreover, it omits altogether a variety of interesting algorithms, such as compression, encryption, geometric, linear algebra, and scheduling algorithms.

Under Further Reading there is a list of books that do cover these more advanced topics, together with seminal papers on topics covered by this book. There are also bibliographic notes that suggest further reading on the topics covered by each chapter and by the book as a whole.

Java Collections framework

The Java 2 software development kit (SDK) provides a library of classes supporting the most common ADTs: lists, sets, and maps. These are known collectively as the Java *collection classes*, and they fit together in what is called the *Java Collections framework*. Programmers should use these collection classes rather than designing and implementing their own. However, the framework is complex and incomplete, and selecting the correct collection class for a given problem is not always easy.

This book aims to help programmers in the following ways:

- To reduce complexity, we introduce our own contract for each ADT. Our contract captures the fundamental properties of the ADT, and is not biased towards a particular implementation.
- To maintain compatibility, our ADT contract is always a simplified version of the contract of the corresponding Java collection class (if any). The applications presented in this book can all be trivially modified to use the corresponding collection classes. (The only necessary changes are to import the `java.util` package and to modify certain constructor invocations.)
- To guide the selection of the appropriate ADT for a given problem, we present one or more short examples, and a case study, illustrating how to use each ADT.
- To guide the selection of the most appropriate implementation of an ADT, we analyze the efficiency of several alternative implementations, and compare them with the corresponding Java collection class (if any).
- In addition to the list, set, and map ADTs supported by the Java Collections framework, we also cover other important ADTs: stacks, queues, priority queues, trees, and graphs. Our contracts for these ADTs follow the same style as the Java Collections framework, so readers should be able to adapt easily.

Companion Web site

This book is complemented by a Web site, whose URL is

```
www.wiley.co.uk/wattbrown
```

This Web site contains the book's contents and preface, answers to selected exercises, and Java code for all ADTs and case studies. New features will be added from time to time.

Case studies

Case studies are an important feature of this book. They can be found in Chapters 6–9, 11, 13–15, and 17.

Each case study leads the reader through the object-oriented design and implementation of a fair-sized application program. The presentation focuses on the selection of an ADT appropriate for the application, and later on the choice of the most suitable implementation of that ADT (from among those presented earlier in the chapter). The object-oriented design of the application program itself, and the development of algorithms to be employed by the application program, are also discussed. User interface issues are generally omitted here, however.

Complete Java source code for all case studies may be found at the companion Web site. For some case studies, there is an application program that can be downloaded and run. For others, there is an applet that can be run immediately using a Java-enabled Web browser. Where appropriate, each case study comes in two versions, one using the classes developed in this book and the other using the Java collection classes.

Exercises

Each chapter is followed by a set of exercises. Some of these exercises are drill, or simple modifications to designs, algorithms, or implementations presented in the chapter. The more challenging exercises are clearly marked as * (hard) or ** (harder).

Sample answers to selected exercises can be found at the companion Web site.

About the authors

David Watt is a Professor of Computing Science at the University of Glasgow. He has 26 years' experience of teaching undergraduates and graduates, in programming, algorithms, data structures, software engineering, and other topics. He developed the material of Chapters 1–12 for a course in algorithms and data structures, first taught in early 1999. His research interests are design, specification, and implementation of programming languages.

Deryck Brown is a Senior Lecturer in Computing Science at the Robert Gordon University, Aberdeen. He has 6 years' experience of teaching undergraduates and graduates, in object-oriented programming, software engineering, and several other topics. His research interests are specification and implementation of programming languages, and genetic algorithms.

Acknowledgements

Most of the algorithms and data structures described in this textbook have long since passed into computer science folklore, and are almost impossible to attribute to individuals. Instead, we acknowledge those colleagues who have particularly influenced us through discussions on the topics of this book: David Davidson, Rob Irving, Alistair Kilgour, John McCall, and Joe Morris. We wish to thank the Wiley reviewers for reading and providing valuable comments on an earlier draft of this book. In addition, we would like to thank William Teahan for his extensive and detailed comments. Finally, we are delighted to acknowledge the assistance of the staff at John Wiley & Sons, particularly our editors Gaynor Redvers-Mutton and Gemma Quilter.

David A. Watt
Glasgow

Deryck F. Brown
Aberdeen

August 2000

1

Introduction

In this chapter we shall study:

- several simple algorithms, set in a historical context (Section 1.1)
- the relationship between algorithms and programs (Section 1.2)
- static and dynamic data structures, and the concept of an abstract data type (Section 1.3).

1.1 Historical background

Algorithms are procedures for solving stated problems. A very simple example is the problem of multiplying two numbers. Multiplying small numbers such as 7 and 9 is trivial, because we can memorize the answers in advance. But to multiply larger numbers such as 1234 and 789 we need a step-by-step procedure, or algorithm. We all learn such an algorithm in school, using long multiplication or logarithms. (Even if we make an electronic calculator do the work, the calculator uses its own multiplication algorithm.)

Algorithms and computation have a long history, perhaps as long as civilization itself. The achievements of the ancient civilizations of China, Egypt, India, and Mesopotamia leave us in no doubt that their architects, astronomers, engineers, and merchants knew how to perform the computations associated with their professions. Unfortunately we have only fragmentary and indirect knowledge of the algorithms developed by these very ancient civilizations.

(*Note:* Much of the historical information in this chapter was culled from an excellent Web site at the University of St Andrews: www-history.mcs.st-and.ac.uk/ history/.)

The scholars of the Hellenic civilization systematized many of the achievements of their predecessors, and added enormous contributions of their own. Athens, Alexandria, and other Hellenic cities contained 'academies' where scholars worked and taught together – forerunners of modern universities. Scholars such as Euclid (about 325–265 BCE) and Eratosthenes (276–194 BCE), discovered or perfected a variety of algorithms that are still used today.

To find the midpoint of a straight line segment AB:

1. Draw intersecting circles of equal radius centered at points A and B.
2. Let C and D be the two points where the circles intersect.
3. Draw the straight line CD.
4. Let E be the point where AB intersects CD.
5. Terminate with point E as the answer.

Algorithm 1.1   Finding the midpoint of a straight line segment.

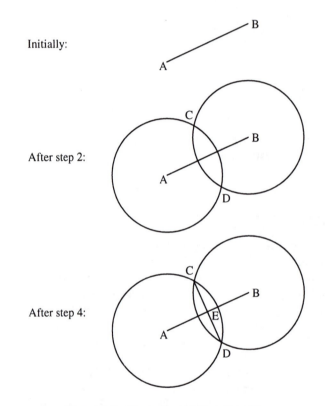

Figure 1.2   Illustration of Algorithm 1.1.

EXAMPLE 1.1   *Finding the midpoint of a straight line segment*

The Hellenic mathematicians systematically studied two- and three-dimensional geometry, motivated by their interests in architecture, astronomy, and geography. Algorithm 1.1 shows a simple geometric construction for finding the midpoint of a given straight line. It consists of several steps, which must be performed one after the other in the order shown. Figure 1.2 illustrates the construction, which needs only simple drawing instruments: a compass (step 1) and a ruler (step 3).

To find the GCD of positive integers m and n:

1. Set p to m, and set q to n.
2. Until q exactly divides p, repeat:
    2.1. Set p to q, and set q to (p modulo q).
3. Terminate with answer q.

Algorithm 1.3   Euclid's algorithm.

To solve the equation $x^2 + bx = c$ (where b and c are known positive numbers):

1. Multiply $b/2$ by itself.
2. Add c to the product.
3. Take the square root of the sum.
4. Let r be the difference of the square root and $b/2$.
5. Terminate with answer r.

Algorithm 1.4   One of al Khwarizmi's algebraic algorithms.

EXAMPLE 1.2   *Computing a greatest common divisor*

The greatest common divisor (GCD) of two positive integers is the largest positive integer that exactly divides both of them. Euclid gave his name to an elegant and efficient algorithm to solve this problem.

Euclid's algorithm is paraphrased as Algorithm 1.3. Note that (p modulo q) is the remainder when we divide p by q.

Step 2 controls a loop. The subsidiary step 2.1 is performed repeatedly until the stated condition arises, i.e., until q exactly divides p.

The Arabic civilization produced a world-renowned center of learning in Baghdad, which drew on the work of Hellenic, Hebrew, and Indian scholars. Muhammad abu Ja'far ibn Musa al Khwarizmi (about 780–850 CE) perfected the Hindu–Arabic decimal system of numbering, which is now universal. He published a famous series of books on algebra, geometry, and astronomy. These books were not just scholarly works, but collections of algorithms for practical use by astronomers, engineers, surveyors, merchants, and the like. In due course these books reached Europe, *via* Spain, where they were translated into Latin. The name al Khwarizmi, translated into Latin as Algorithmus, has given us the modern word *algorithm*.

EXAMPLE 1.3   *Solving quadratic equations*

Al Khwarizmi presented a group of algorithms to solve various quadratic equations (equations involving x^2, where x is unknown), each accompanied by a simple geometric proof of correctness. Algorithm 1.4 paraphrases one of al Khwarizmi's algorithms. (You might recognize the problem as a special case of the general quadratic equation.)

To multiply positive numbers y and z:

1. Convert y and z to their logarithms, log y and log z.
2. Let l be the sum of log y and log z.
3. Let x be the number such that log $x = l$.
4. Terminate with answer x.

Algorithm 1.5   Multiplication using logarithms.

Our story now moves to Europe. The Scots scholar John Napier (1550–1617), observing that computations involving multiplication, division, powers, and roots were slow and error-prone, invented logarithms. The logarithm of a number y is the number of times that 10 must be multiplied by itself to give y; thus $\log_{10}10 = 1$, $\log_{10}100 = 2$ (since $10^2 = 100$), $\log_{10}1000 = 3$ (since $10^3 = 1000$), and so on. Intermediate numbers have fractional logarithms; thus $\log_{10}52 = 1.716$, accurate to 3 decimal places.

EXAMPLE 1.4   *Multiplication using logarithms*

The basic law of logarithms is:

$$\log(y \times z) = \log y + \log z$$

This leads directly to a multiplication algorithm: see Algorithm 1.5.

This algorithm is faster and less error-prone than the long multiplication algorithm. A number can be quickly converted to a logarithm (step 1) or from a logarithm (step 3) by looking up a table of logarithms.

Logarithms (and their mechanical equivalents, slide rules) quickly became essential tools for scientists, engineers, astronomers, and everyone else who had to do complex calculations. They continued to be used routinely until they were superseded by electronic calculators and computers in the 1960s.

The English mathematician and scientist, Isaac Newton (1643–1727), invented the differential calculus. This gave us algorithms for differentiation (determining the slope of a given curve) and integration (determining the area under a given curve). Differential calculus became a keystone of mathematics and physics, and has found a vast array of applications in engineering, weather forecasting, economics, and so on.

EXAMPLE 1.5   *Computing a square root*

Computing the square root of a positive number a is equivalent to finding the side of a square whose area is a. Algorithms for computing square roots approximately have been known since ancient times, but Newton's algorithm is preferred in modern computation.

Newton's algorithm is a by-product of differential calculus, but can be understood intuitively. If we know two different numbers whose product is a, then we can be sure that the square root of a lies somewhere between them; moreover, the mean of these two numbers is a better approximation to the square root than either of the original two numbers. For example, neither 2 nor 3 is a good approximation to the square root of 6, but their mean 2.5 is better, and the mean of 2.5 and 2.4 is even better. (The square root of 6 is in fact 2.4495, accurate to 4 decimal places.)

In step 2.1 of Algorithm 1.6, the two numbers whose product is a are r and a/r. Their mean is a better approximation to the square root of a, so we replace r with this mean. We do this repeatedly, stopping only when we are satisfied that r is sufficiently close to the desired answer. (We can check this by comparing r^2 with a.)

The 17th century saw the development of the first mechanical calculators by Wilhelm Schickard (1592–1635), Blaise Pascal (1623–62), and Gottfried Leibniz (1646–1716).

The abacus (known since ancient times), the slide rule, mechanical calculators, and even electronic calculators are just tools that aid us humans to perform algorithms. Among the outstanding achievements of the modern era has been the development of machines capable of performing algorithms *automatically*.

The first such achievement was in a very different domain from computation. Weaving patterns consist of steps that must be followed exactly, over and over again. For humans, this makes weaving very tedious. The French textile manufacturer Joseph Jacquard (1752–1834) invented an automatic loom that is driven by a pattern encoded on punched cards. In a very real sense, a weaving pattern is an algorithm, and that algorithm is performed by the Jacquard loom.

Returning to computation, the British mathematician Charles Babbage (1791–1871) designed what we would now recognize as a digital computer. His assistant Ada Lovelace (1815–52) is generally recognized to have been the first computer programmer. Unfortunately, Babbage's computer could not actually be built, given the relatively primitive technology of his time.

In the 20th century, the British mathematician Alan Turing (1912–54) studied the very nature of computation. He came up with the remarkable result that there exist problems for which no algorithm exists. For example, no algorithm exists that can prove an arbitrary given theorem in logic. And no algorithm exists that can prove that an arbitrary given computer program is correct or incorrect.

During the Second World War, Turing led a team that discovered how to break the Enigma codes, which the Germans used for encrypting military radio messages. However, their code-breaking algorithm relied on an exhaustive search, which would have been extremely time-consuming, especially since the Germans changed their codes

To compute approximately the square root of a positive real number a:

1. Set r to the mean of 1 and a.
2. Until r^2 is a sufficient good approximation to a, repeat:
   2.1. Set r to the mean of r and a/r.
3. Terminate with answer r.

Algorithm 1.6   Newton's algorithm.

every day. So the team proceeded to build and use a machine, Colossus, that could break the codes hundreds of times faster than mere humans.

The first general-purpose digital computers were built in the USA and Great Britain. You are probably familiar with the story of computers since then. Computers are now ubiquitous, whether as general-purpose computers or as components embedded in devices as diverse as digital watches, kitchen appliances, and aircraft. And every one of these computers is a machine designed to perform algorithms.

We are also surrounded by algorithms intended for performance by humans. Whether or not a device has a computer inside it, it probably comes with a user's manual. Such manuals contain algorithms necessary for us to use the devices effectively: to operate a washing machine, to set a digital watch to give an alarm signal or to record lap times, to change a car wheel, to change a light bulb, to assemble a piece of furniture from a flat-pack, and so on.

1.2 Algorithms and programs

So what exactly *is* an algorithm? We shall attempt a precise definition in Chapter 2. For the time being, we can think of an algorithm as a step-by-step procedure for solving a stated problem. An algorithm may be intended to be performed by a human or a machine. In either case, the algorithm must be broken down into steps that are simple enough to be performed by the human or machine.

Algorithms have many things in common with programs, but there are also important differences between them.

Firstly, algorithms are *more general* than programs. An algorithm may be suitable to be performed by a human, or by a machine, or by both. A program *must* be capable of being performed by a (suitable) machine. In this book, the machine will always be a general-purpose computer (as opposed to a robot or weaving machine, for example).

Secondly, algorithms are *more abstract* than programs. An algorithm can be expressed in any convenient language or notation. A program must be expressed in some programming language. If an algorithm is intended to be performed by a computer, it must first be coded in a programming language. There may be many ways of coding the algorithm and there is a wide choice of programming languages. Nevertheless, all the resulting programs are implementations of the same underlying algorithm. For example, Programs 1.7 and 1.8 are both implementations of Euclid's algorithm, coded in two different programming languages: compare them with Algorithm 1.3.

In this book we will express algorithms in English, and code them as methods in Java. The very same algorithms could be (and undoubtedly have been) equally well expressed in French or Chinese, and coded in C or Pascal or Ada. The point is that we can study these algorithms without paying too much attention to the language in which they are expressed.

Often there exist several different algorithms that solve the same problem. We are naturally interested in comparing such alternative algorithms. Which is fastest? Which needs least memory? Fortunately, we can answer such questions in terms of the qualities of the algorithms themselves, without being distracted by the languages in which they happen to be expressed. We shall study algorithm efficiency in Chapter 2.

```
static int gcd (int m, int n) {
// Return the GCD of positive integers m and n.
   int p = m, q = n;
   while (p % q != 0) {
      int r = p % q;
      p = q;   q = r;
   }
   return q;
}
```

Program 1.7   Implementation of Euclid's algorithm as a Java method.

```
function gcd (m, n: Positive) return Positive is
-- Return the GCD of positive integers m and n.
   p, q, r: Natural;
begin
   p := m;   q := n;
   while p mod q /= 0 loop
      r := p mod q;
      p := q;   q := r;
   end loop;
   return q;
end gcd;
```

Program 1.8   Implementation of Euclid's algorithm as an Ada function.

1.3 Abstract data types and data structures

Complementary to the study of algorithms, and also a major theme of this book, is the study of data structures and abstract data types.

A data structure is a systematic way of organizing a collection of data. A familiar example of a data structure is the array, which you should have met in your first programming course. The array is sometimes called a *static data structure*, because its data capacity is fixed at the time it is created. This book will introduce the more flexible *dynamic data structures*, which are so called because they can freely expand and contract in accordance with the actual amount of data to be stored.

Every data structure needs a variety of algorithms for processing the data contained in it: algorithms for insertion, deletion, searching, and so on. In this book we shall study data structures and algorithms in conjunction.

Often there exist several data structures suitable for representing the same collection of data. Figure 1.9 illustrates this point by showing a character string represented by two different data structures. Figure 1.10 illustrates the point further by showing a set of words represented by three different data structures. We shall explore all these data structures in later chapters.

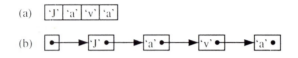

Figure 1.9   Representation of the character string ''Java'' using: (a) an array, (b) a linked list.

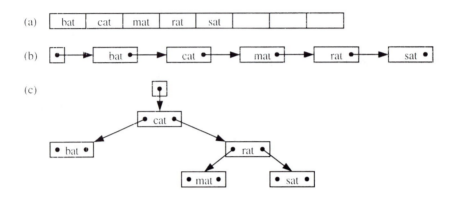

Figure 1.10   Representation of the word set {bat, cat, mat, rat, sat} using: (a) an array, (b) a singly-linked list, (c) a binary search tree.

Of course, when you wish to write a Java program that manipulates character strings, you neither know nor care how strings are represented. You simply declare variables of type `String`, and manipulate them by calling methods provided by the `java.lang.String` class. `String` is a simple example of what we call an *abstract data type*. You are told the name of the abstract data type, and the general properties of objects of that type, and the names of methods for manipulating these objects. But you are *not* told how these objects are represented.

Once an abstract data type has been designed, the programmer responsible for implementing that type is concerned only with choosing a suitable data structure and coding up the methods (without worrying much about the type's future applications). On the other hand, application programmers are concerned only with using that type and calling its methods (without worrying much about how the type is implemented).

This separation of concerns is a fundamental principle of modular software design. An object-oriented programming language typically provides a rich library of predefined abstract data types (classes), but the idea of an abstract data type goes well beyond that. When an application program is being designed, a major part of the designer's job is to identify abstract data types specialized to the requirements of the particular application. A large application program might require tens or even hundreds of abstract data types. Their identification by the designer helps to decompose the program into manageably-sized modules that can be specified, coded, tested, and debugged separately. Such decomposition is essential for successful software development.

Summary

In this chapter:

- We have introduced the idea of an algorithm, illustrating the idea with a variety of algorithms of historical interest, and distinguishing between algorithms and programs.
- We have introduced the idea of a data structure, distinguishing between static and dynamic data structures.
- We have introduced the idea of an abstract data type, distinguishing between the separate concerns of the programmer who implements an abstract data type and the programmers who use it.

In Chapters 2 and 5 we shall study algorithm and abstract data type concepts in greater detail. In other chapters, we shall study a variety of data structures in conjunction with the algorithms that operate on them, and we shall study a variety of abstract data types showing which data structures can be used to implement them.

Exercises

1.1 Use Euclid's algorithm, given in Algorithm 1.3, to find the GCD of the following pairs of numbers: 6 and 9, 12 and 18, 15 and 21, and 11 and 15.

1.2 Consider Newton's algorithm, given in Algorithm 1.6, to calculate the square root of a number.
 (a) Use this algorithm to calculate the square roots of the following numbers: 4, 6, 8 and 9. In each case, use an initial value for r of $a/2$, and calculate your answer to an accuracy of 0.01, i.e., the absolute difference between a and r^2 is less than 0.01.
 (b) Write a Java program to implement the algorithm and use it to check your answers to part (a) above.
 (c) What would happen if step 2 of the algorithm were as follows?

 2. Until $r^2 = a$, repeat:

1.3 Give some examples of algorithms used in everyday life, not requiring a calculator or computer.

1.4 Write an algorithm to perform each of the following tasks:
 (a) Use an automated bank teller to withdraw cash from your account.
 (b) Set the current time on your watch.
 (c) Cook a frozen meal in a microwave oven.
 (d) Match the pairs of socks in a bundle of freshly laundered socks.

1.5 Try to find further examples of early algorithms like the ones given in this chapter.

1.6 Devise an algorithm, similar to Algorithm 1.4, to find the roots of the general quadratic equation $ax^2 + bx + c = 0$. The roots are the two values of the formula $(-b \pm \sqrt{(b^2 - 4ac)})/2a$.

1.7 Consider the algorithms you wrote in Exercise 1.4. How easy would it be for each of these algorithms to be performed by a human? by a suitable machine?

1.8 Consult the documentation for your Java development environment for the list of predefined classes (or consult the on-line documentation at `java.sun.com/products/jdk/1.3/docs/api/index.html`). Consider some of the classes provided from the point of view of abstract data types, and determine the list of operations provided for each class.

2

Algorithms

In this chapter we shall study:

- fundamental principles of algorithms: problems that can or cannot be solved by algorithms, properties of algorithms themselves, and notation for algorithms (Section 2.1)
- analysis of algorithms to determine their time and space efficiency (Section 2.2)
- the notion of complexity of algorithms (Section 2.3)
- recursive algorithms and their complexity (Section 2.4).

2.1 Principles of algorithms

In Section 1.1 we encountered a variety of algorithms. In this section we briefly discuss some fundamental issues concerned with problems, algorithms, and notation.

Problems

Concerning problems, we can state the following principles:

- An algorithm must be designed to solve a stated **problem**, which is a well-defined task that has to be performed.
- The problem must be **solvable** by an algorithm.

We have already (in Section 1.1) encountered a number of problems that can be solved by algorithms. We can also pose some problems that are *not* solvable by algorithms. To say that a problem is unsolvable does not just mean that an algorithm has *not yet* been found to solve it. It means that such an algorithm can *never* be found. A human might eventually solve the problem, but only by applying insight and creativity, not by following a step-by-step procedure; moreover, there can be no guarantee that a solution will be found. Here is an example of a problem that is unsolvable by an algorithm.

EXAMPLE 2.1   *The halting problem*

The problem is to predict whether a given computer program, with given input data, will eventually halt.

This is a very practical problem for us programmers: we all occasionally write a program that gets into a never-ending loop. One of the most famous results in computer science is that this problem cannot be solved by any algorithm. It turns out that any 'algorithm' that purports to solve this problem will itself get into a never-ending loop, for at least some programs that might be given to it. As we shall see later in this section, we insist that every algorithm must eventually terminate.

If we can never find an algorithm to predict whether a given program halts with *given* input data, we clearly can never find an algorithm to prove whether a given program behaves correctly for *all possible* input data.

It may still be possible for a human to prove that a *particular* program is correct. Indeed, this has been done for some important small programs and subprograms. But we can never *automate* such proofs of correctness.

In fact, many problems in mathematics and computer science are unsolvable by algorithms. In a way, this is rather reassuring: we can be sure that mathematicians and computer scientists will never be made redundant by machines!

From now on, we shall consider only problems that are solvable by algorithms.

Algorithms

Concerning algorithms themselves, we can state the following principles:

- The algorithm will be performed by some ***processor***, which may be a machine or a human.
- The algorithm must be expressed in steps that the processor is capable of performing.
- The algorithm must eventually terminate, producing the required answer.

Some algorithms, as we have already seen, are intended to be performed by humans rather than machines. But no algorithm is allowed to rely on qualities, such as insight and creativity, that distinguish humans from machines. This suggests a definition:

An ***algorithm*** is an automatic procedure for solving a stated problem, a procedure that could (at least in principle) be performed by a machine.

The principle that the algorithm must be expressed in steps that can be performed by the processor should now be clear. If the processor has to work out for itself what steps to follow, then what we have is not an algorithm.

The principle that every algorithm must eventually terminate should also be clear. If it never terminates, it never produces an answer, therefore it is not an algorithm! So an algorithm must avoid getting into a never-ending loop.

Notation

Concerning notation, we have one fundamental principle:

- The algorithm must be expressed in a language or notation that the processor 'understands'.

This principle should be self-evident. We cannot expect a weaving machine, or even a computer, to perform an algorithm expressed in natural language. A machine must be programmed in its own language.

On the other hand, an algorithm intended for humans need not necessarily be expressed in natural language. Special-purpose notations are commonly used for certain classes of algorithm. A musical score is an algorithm to be performed by a group of musicians, and is expressed in the standard musical notation. A knitting pattern is an algorithm for either a human or a knitting machine, and is generally expressed in a concise notation invented for the purpose.

Here we restrict our attention to computational algorithms. Even so, we have a variety of possible notations including natural language, programming language, mathematical notation, and combinations of these. In this book we shall express all algorithms in English, occasionally (and where appropriate) augmented by mathematical notation. The choice of a natural language gives us the greatest possible freedom of expression; both programming languages and mathematical notation are sometimes restrictive or inconvenient.

We should remember, however, that expressing an algorithm in a natural language always carries a risk of vagueness or even ambiguity. We must take great care to express the individual steps of the algorithm, and the order in which these steps are to be performed, as precisely as possible.

We have already seen several examples of algorithms, in Section 1.1, which you should now re-examine. Note the use of layout and numbering to show the structure of an algorithm. We number the steps consecutively, and arrange one below another in the intended order, e.g.:

1. Do this.
2. Do that.
3. Do the other.

We use indentation and the numbering system to show when one or more steps are to be performed only if some condition is satisfied:

1. If the condition is satisfied:
   1.1. Do this.
   1.2. Do that.
2. Carry on.

Likewise, we use indentation and the numbering system to show when one or more steps are to be performed repeatedly while (or until) some condition is satisfied:

1. While (or until) the condition is satisfied, repeat:
   - 1.1. Do this.
   - 1.2. Do that.
2. Carry on.

or when one or more steps are to be performed repeatedly as a variable v steps through a sequence of values:

1. For v = sequence of values, repeat:
   - 1.1. Do this.
   - 1.2. Do that.
2. Carry on.

2.2 Efficiency of algorithms

Given an algorithm, we are naturally interested in discovering how efficient it is. Efficiency has two distinct facets:

- *Time efficiency* is concerned with how much (processor) time the algorithm requires.
- *Space efficiency* is concerned with how much space (memory) the algorithm requires for storing data.

Often we have a choice of different algorithms that solve the same problem. How should we decide which of these algorithms to adopt? Naturally we tend to prefer the most efficient algorithm.

Sometimes one algorithm is faster, while an alternative algorithm needs less space. This is a classic space–time tradeoff, which can only be resolved with knowledge of the context in which the chosen algorithm will be used.

In this book we shall tend to pay more attention to time efficiency than to space efficiency. This is simply because time efficiency tends to be the critical factor in choosing between alternative algorithms.

Usually, the time taken by an algorithm depends on its input data. Figure 2.1 shows a hypothetical profile of two alternative sorting algorithms, showing how the time they take depends on n, the number of values to be sorted. Algorithm A is slightly faster for small n, but algorithm B wins more and more easily as n increases.

How should we measure an algorithm's time efficiency? Perhaps the most obvious answer is to use real time, measured in seconds. Real time is certainly important in many practical situations. An interactive program that takes two minutes to respond to a user input will quickly fall into disuse. An aircraft control system that takes 30 seconds to respond to an abnormal altimeter reading will be eliminated by natural selection, along with the unfortunate crew and passengers.

Nevertheless, there are difficulties in using real time as a basis for comparing algorithms. An algorithm's real time requirement depends on the processor speed as well on the algorithm itself. Any algorithm can be made to run faster by using a faster processor,

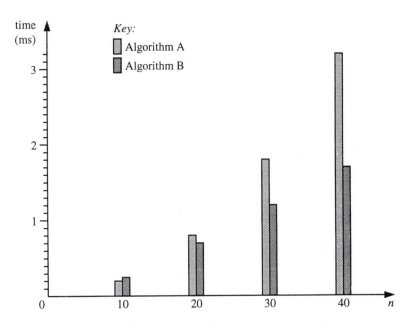

Figure 2.1 Hypothetical profile of two sorting algorithms.

but this tells us nothing about the quality of the algorithm itself. And where the processor is a modern computer, the difficulty is compounded by the presence of software and hardware refinements – such as multiprogramming, pipelines, and caches – that increase the average speed of processing, but make it harder to predict the time taken by an individual algorithm.

We prefer to measure an algorithm's time efficiency in terms of the algorithm itself. One idea is simply to count the number of steps taken by the algorithm until it terminates. The trouble with this idea is that it depends on the granularity of the algorithm steps. Algorithms 2.2(a) and (b) solve the same problem in 3 and 7 steps, respectively. But they are just different versions of the same algorithm, one having course-grained (big) steps, while the other has fine-grained (small) steps.

(a)
To find the area of a triangle with sides a, b, c:

1. Let $s = (a + b + c)/2$.
2. Let $A = \sqrt{(s\,(s-a)\,(s-b)\,(s-c))}$.
3. Terminate with answer A.

(b)
To find the area of a triangle with sides a, b, c:

1. Let $s = (a + b + c)/2$.
2. Let $p = s$.
3. Multiply p by $(s - a)$.
4. Multiply p by $(s - b)$.
5. Multiply p by $(s - c)$.
6. Let A be the square root of p.
7. Terminate with answer A.

Algorithm 2.2 Algorithms to find the area of a triangle.

The most satisfactory way to measure an algorithm's time efficiency is to count *characteristic operations*. Which operations are characteristic depends on the problem to be solved. For an arithmetic algorithm it is natural to count arithmetic operations. For example, Algorithm 2.2(a) takes two additions, three subtractions, three multiplications, one division, and one square root; Algorithm 2.2(b) takes exactly the same number of arithmetic operations. In this book we shall see many examples of algorithms where comparisons or copies or other characteristic operations are the natural choice.

EXAMPLE 2.2 *Power algorithms*

Given a nonnegative integer n, the nth power of a number b, written b^n, is defined by:

$$b^n = b \times \cdots \times b \tag{2.1}$$

(where n copies of b are multiplied together). For example:

$$b^3 = b \times b \times b$$
$$b^2 = b \times b$$
$$b^1 = b$$
$$b^0 = 1$$

Algorithm 2.3 (the 'simple' power algorithm) is based directly on definition (2.1). The variable p successively takes the values 1, b, b^2, b^3, and so on – in other words, the successive powers of b. Program 2.4 is a Java implementation of Algorithm 2.3.

Let us now analyze Algorithm 2.3. The characteristic operations are obviously multiplications. The algorithm performs one multiplication for each iteration of the loop, and there will be n iterations, therefore:

$$\text{No. of multiplications} = n \tag{2.2}$$

Algorithm 2.3 is fine if we want to compute small powers like b^2 and b^3, but it is very time-consuming if we want to compute larger powers like b^{20} and b^{100}.

Fortunately, there is a better algorithm. It is easy to see that $b^{20} = b^{10} \times b^{10}$. So once we know b^{10}, we can compute b^{20} with only one more multiplication, rather than ten more multiplications. This shortcut is even more effective for still larger powers: once we know b^{50}, we can compute b^{100} with only one more multiplication, rather than fifty.

Likewise, it is easy to see that $b^{21} = b^{10} \times b^{10} \times b$. So once we know b^{10}, we can compute b^{21} with only two more multiplications, rather than eleven.

Algorithm 2.5 (the 'smart' power algorithm) takes advantage of these observations. The variable q successively takes the values b, b^2, b^4, b^8, and so on. At the same time, the variable m successively takes the values n, $n/2$, $n/4$, and so on (neglecting any remainders) down to 1. Whenever m has an odd value, p is multiplied by the current value of q. Program 2.6 is a Java implementation of Algorithm 2.5.

This algorithm is not easy to understand, but that is not the issue here. Instead, let us focus on analyzing its efficiency.

First of all, note that steps 2.1 and 2.2 each performs a multiplication, but the multiplication in step 2.1 is conditional. Between them, these steps perform *at most* two multiplications.

Next, note that these steps are contained within a loop, which is iterated as often as we can halve the value of n (neglecting any remainder) until we reach zero. It can be shown (see Appendix A.2) that the number of iterations is $\text{floor}(\log_2 n) + 1$, where $\text{floor}(r)$ is the function that converts a real number r to an integer by discarding its fractional part.

Putting these points together:

$$\begin{aligned}
\text{Maximum no. of multiplications} &= 2\,(\text{floor}(\log_2 n) + 1) \\
&= 2\,\text{floor}(\log_2 n) + 2 \qquad\qquad (2.3)
\end{aligned}$$

The *exact* number of multiplications depends on the value of n in a rather complicated way. For $n = 15$ the actual number of multiplications corresponds to (2.3), since halving 15 repeatedly gives a series of odd numbers; while for $n = 16$ the actual number of multiplications is smaller, since halving 16 repeatedly gives a series of even numbers. Equation (2.3) gives us the *maximum* number of multiplications for any given n, which is a pessimistic estimate.

Figure 2.7 plots (2.2) and (2.3) for comparison. The message should be clear. For small values of n, there is little to choose between the two algorithms. For larger values of n, the smart power algorithm is clearly better; indeed, its advantage grows as n grows.

2.3 Complexity of algorithms

If we want to understand the efficiency of an algorithm, we first choose characteristic operations, and then analyze the algorithm to determine the number of characteristic

To compute b^n (where n is a nonnegative integer):

1. Set p to 1.
2. For $i = 1, \ldots, n$, repeat:
   2.1. Multiply p by b.
3. Terminate with answer p.

Algorithm 2.3   Simple power algorithm.

```
static int power (int b, int n) {
// Return the value of b raised to the n'th power (where n is a nonnegative
// integer).
   int p = 1;
   for (int i = 1; i <= n; i++)
      p *= b;
   return p;
}
```

Program 2.4   Java implementation of the simple power algorithm.

To compute b^n (where n is a nonnegative integer):

1. Set p to 1, set q to b, and set m to n.
2. While m is positive, repeat:
   2.1. If m is odd, multiply p by q.
   2.2. Halve m (neglecting any remainder), and multiply q by itself.
3. Terminate with answer p.

Algorithm 2.5   Smart power algorithm.

```
static int power (int b, int n) {
// Return the value of b raised to the n'th power (where n is a nonnegative
// integer).
    int p = 1, q = b, m = n;
    while (m > 0) {
        if (m%2 != 0)   p *= q;
        m /= 2;   q *= q;
    }
    return p;
}
```

Program 2.6   Java implementation of the smart power algorithm.

operations performed by it. In general, the number of characteristic operations depends on the algorithm's input data.

For some algorithms (like the simple power algorithm in Example 2.2) the analysis is straightforward. For other algorithms (like the smart power algorithm in Example 2.2) the analysis is more complicated. We sometimes have to make simplifying assumptions, and we sometimes have to be content with estimating the maximum (or average) number of characteristic operations rather than the exact number.

The simple power algorithm takes n multiplications, while the smart power algorithm takes at most 2 floor($\log_2 n$) + 2 multiplications. If we double n, the simple power algorithm takes twice as many multiplications, while the smart power algorithm takes at most two extra multiplications. Now this is the heart of the matter. When we compare the efficiencies of alternative algorithms, what is most illuminating is the comparison of *growth rates*. The function 2 floor($\log_2 n$) + 2 grows much more slowly than n. The fundamental reason for this is that $\log_2 n$ grows much more slowly than n, as shown in Figure 2.8.

Of course we are interested in the actual times taken by alternative algorithms, but we are especially interested in the rates at which their time requirements grow with n. This interest in growth rates is easily justified. When n is small, we do not really care which algorithm is fastest, because none of the algorithms will take much time. But when n is large, we certainly do care, because all of the algorithms will take more time, and some

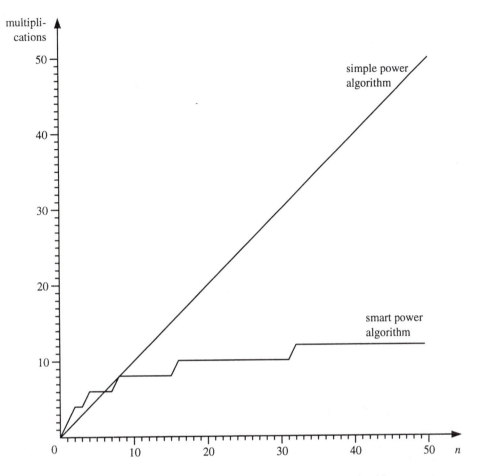

Figure 2.7   Time efficiency of the simple and smart power algorithms.

might take much more time than others. All else being equal, we prefer the algorithm whose time requirement grows most slowly with n.

If we have a formula for an algorithm's time requirement, we can focus on its growth rate as follows:

- Take the fastest-growing term in the formula, and discard all slower-growing terms.
- Discard any constant factor in the fastest-growing term.

The resulting formula is called the algorithm's *time complexity*. We define *space complexity* similarly.

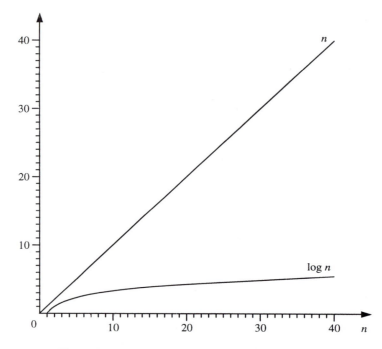

Figure 2.8   Comparison of growth rates of n and log n.

EXAMPLE 2.3 *Time complexity of power algorithms*

The simple power algorithm's efficiency is given by equation (2.2):

No. of multiplications $= n$

The number of multiplications grows proportionately to n. We say that the simple power algorithm's time complexity is *of order n*, and write this as:

$O(n)$

(The analysis in this particular example was trivial, but if the number of multiplications had been $2n + 3$, the time complexity would still have been $O(n)$.)

The smart power algorithm's efficiency is given by equation (2.3):

Maximum no. of multiplications $= 2$ floor($\log_2 n$) $+$ 2

Discarding the slower-growing term ($+$ 2) and the constant factor (2), we get floor($\log_2 n$). We can approximate this as $\log_2 n$. Thus the number of multiplications grows proportionately to $\log_2 n$. We say that the smart power algorithm's time complexity is *of order* log n, and write this as:

$O(\log n)$

Figure 2.8 shows that an $O(\log n)$ algorithm is inherently better than an $O(n)$ algorithm. Regardless of constant factors and slower-growing terms, the $O(\log n)$ algorithm will eventually overtake the $O(n)$ algorithm as n grows.

We have now introduced the **O-notation** for algorithm complexity. The notation $O(X)$ stands for 'of order X', and means that the algorithm's time (or space) requirement grows proportionately to X. X characterizes the algorithm's growth rate, neglecting slower-growing terms and constant factors. In general, X depends on the algorithm's input data.

Table 2.9 summarizes the most common time complexities. These are common enough to have acquired verbal descriptions: for example, we say that the simple power algorithm is a *linear-time* algorithm, while the smart power algorithm is a *log-time* algorithm. The complexities are arranged in order of growth rate: $O(1)$ is the slowest-growing, and $O(2^n)$ is the fastest-growing.

It is important to develop our intuitions about what these complexities tell us, in practical terms, about the time efficiency of algorithms. Table 2.10 shows some numerical information, and Figure 2.11 shows the same information graphically. As we have already noted, $\log n$ grows more gradually than n, so an $O(\log n)$ algorithm is better than an $O(n)$ algorithm that solves the same problem. Of course, the constant 1 does not grow at all, so an $O(1)$ or constant-time algorithm is best of all – if we can find one!

Now study the growth rate of $n \log n$. This grows more steeply than n, so an $O(n)$ algorithm is better than an $O(n \log n)$ algorithm that solves the same problem.

Now study the growth rates of n^2 and n^3. These grow ever more steeply, so an $O(n \log n)$ algorithm is better than an $O(n^2)$ algorithm, which in turn is better than an $O(n^3)$ algorithm, that solves the same problem. One way to look at these algorithms is this: every time n is doubled, $O(n^2)$ is multiplied by four and $O(n^3)$ is multiplied by eight. And every time n is multiplied by 10, $O(n^2)$ is multiplied by 100 and $O(n^3)$ is multiplied by 1000! These numbers are discouraging. If the best algorithm we can find is $O(n^2)$ or $O(n^3)$, we have to accept that the algorithm will rapidly slow down as n increases. Such an algorithm is often too slow to be of practical use.

While n^2 and n^3 grow steeply, 2^n grows at a stupendous rate. Every time n is incremented by 10, $O(2^n)$ is multiplied by over 1000! As n is increased from 10 to 20 to 30 to 40, 2^n grows from a thousand to a million to a billion to a trillion. If the algorithm performs 2^n operations at the rate of a million per second, its time requirement will grow from a millisecond to a second to over 16 minutes to over 11 days! Such an

Table 2.9   Summary of common time complexities.

Complexity	Verbal description	Feasibility
$O(1)$	constant time	feasible
$O(\log n)$	log time	feasible
$O(n)$	linear time	feasible
$O(n \log n)$	log linear time	feasible
$O(n^2)$	quadratic time	sometimes feasible
$O(n^3)$	cubic time	less often feasible
$O(2^n)$	exponential time	rarely feasible

Table 2.10 Comparison of growth rates.

n	10	20	30	40
1	1	1	1	1
$\log n$	3.3	4.3	4.9	5.3
n	10	20	30	40
$n \log n$	33	86	147	213
n^2	100	400	900	1 600
n^3	1 000	8 000	27 000	64 000
2^n	1 024	1.0 million	1.1 billion	1.1 trillion

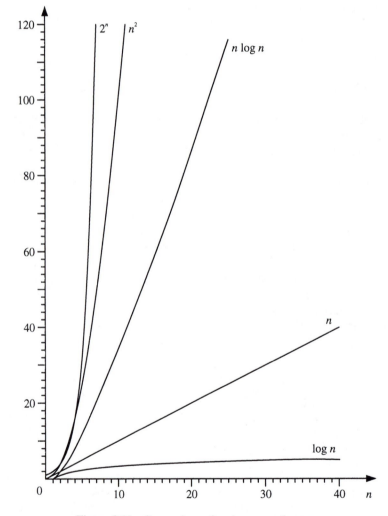

Figure 2.11 Comparison of various growth rates.

algorithm is nearly always far too slow to be used in practice, and even a much faster processor makes hardly any difference (see Example 2.4).

We say that an *algorithm* is *feasible* if it is fast enough to be used in practice. Likewise, we say that a *problem* is *feasible* if it can be solved by a feasible algorithm.

Algorithms of complexity up to $O(n \log n)$ are feasible. Algorithms of complexity $O(n^2)$ or $O(n^3)$ might be feasible, but only for small values of n. Algorithms of complexity $O(2^n)$ are infeasible, except possibly for very small values of n.

EXAMPLE 2.4   *Growth rates*

Suppose that we are given three algorithms that solve the same problem, with complexities $O(n)$, $O(n^2)$, and $O(2^n)$, respectively. Measurement shows that their actual running times on a particular processor are $0.1n$ seconds, $0.01n^2$ seconds, and 0.0001×2^n seconds, respectively, where n is the number of data items to be processed.

The following table shows the largest values of n for which the problem can be solved in a second, a minute, and an hour:

Algorithm	Running time (seconds)	Maximum n in 1 second	Maximum n in 1 minute	Maximum n in 1 hour
A	$0.1n$	10	600	36 000
B	$0.01n^2$	10	77	600
C	0.0001×2^n	10	16	22

In one second, all three algorithms can process the same amount of data (by coincidence). But there the similarity ends. In one minute, Algorithm A can process by far the most data, and Algorithm C the least. If an hour is allowed, Algorithm A is out of sight!

How much difference does it make if we use a processor that is ten times faster? This reduces each algorithm's running time by a factor of ten. The effects are as follows:

Algorithm	Running time (seconds)	Maximum n in 1 second	Maximum n in 1 minute	Maximum n in 1 hour
A	$0.01n$	100	6 000	360 000
B	$0.001n^2$	32	245	1 897
C	0.00001×2^n	13	19	25

Ironically, Algorithm A (already the fastest) benefits the most, and Algorithm C (already the slowest) benefits the least, from using the faster processor! Algorithm A can now process ten times as much data in any given time, Algorithm B about three times as much data, and Algorithm C only three extra data items.

Even if we handicap Algorithm A by leaving it to run on the slower processor, in as little as a minute it beats Algorithm B and outclasses Algorithm C.

The moral of Example 2.4 is this. Constant factors are important only when comparing algorithms of the same time complexity, such as two $O(n)$ algorithms, or two $O(n^2)$ algorithms. But an $O(n)$ algorithm will beat an $O(n^2)$ algorithm, sooner or later, regardless of constant factors. More generally, $O(1)$ beats $O(\log n)$ beats $O(n)$ beats $O(n \log n)$ beats $O(n^2)$ beats $O(n^3)$ beats $O(2^n)$.

2.4 Recursive algorithms

A *recursive algorithm* is an algorithm that calls itself.

When a recursive algorithm calls itself, it performs the same steps over again. This repetition of steps is somewhat similar to the effect we get when the steps are part of a loop. Indeed, often the same algorithm can be expressed either *iteratively* (using a loop) or *recursively*.

Analogously, a *recursive method* is a method that calls itself. Indeed, a recursive algorithm is most naturally coded in Java as a recursive method.

EXAMPLE 2.5 *Recursive simple power algorithm*

Let us return to computing the n'th power of b, i.e., b^n, where n is a nonnegative integer. The definition of b^n in equation (2.1) led naturally to an iterative algorithm (Algorithm 2.3).

Here now is an alternative definition of b^n:

$$b^n = 1 \qquad\qquad \text{if } n = 0 \tag{2.4a}$$
$$b^n = b \times b^{n-1} \qquad \text{if } n > 0 \tag{2.4b}$$

Equation (2.4b) says that we can compute the n'th power of b by taking the $(n-1)$'th power of b and multiplying that by b. On its own, equation (2.4b) would be useless, but equation (2.4a) tells us how to compute the 0'th power of b directly. For example:

$$b^3 = b \times b^2 = b \times (b \times b^1) = b \times (b \times (b \times b^0)) = b \times (b \times (b \times 1))$$

Equations (2.4a–b) together tell us all that we need to know.

These equations lead naturally to Algorithm 2.12. Step 1 deals with the easy case, $n = 0$, when step 1.1 directly gives the answer 1. Step 2 deals with the hard case, $n > 0$, when step 2.1 computes the answer with the help of a recursive call to the same algorithm. Algorithm 2.12 is therefore recursive. (In this section, we shall highlight recursive algorithm calls by underlining.)

Will Algorithm 2.12 terminate, or will it go on calling itself forever? We can reason as follows. When called to compute the n'th power of b, with $n > 0$, the algorithm will call itself to compute the $(n-1)$'th power of b, which is a smaller power of b. In fact it will call itself repeatedly to compute successively smaller powers of b. Eventually it must call itself to compute the 0'th power of b, and at this point it will give a direct answer without calling itself again. Thus Algorithm 2.12 will indeed terminate.

Program 2.13 shows the recursive simple power algorithm coded as a recursive Java method.

Let us now analyze the algorithm's time efficiency. The characteristic operations are multiplications. Let $mults(n)$ be the number of multiplications required to compute b^n.

Then we can immediately write down the following equations:

$$mults(n) = 0 \qquad\qquad \text{if } n = 0 \qquad\qquad\qquad (2.5\text{a})$$
$$mults(n) = 1 + mults(n - 1) \qquad \text{if } n > 1 \qquad\qquad\qquad (2.5\text{b})$$

This is a pair of *recurrence equations*. We shall skip the mathematics and simply state the solution:

$$mults(n) = n \qquad\qquad\qquad\qquad\qquad\qquad\qquad (2.6)$$

The recursive simple power algorithm performs exactly the same number of multiplications as the non-recursive simple power algorithm.

Example 2.5 suggests guidelines for ensuring that a recursive algorithm terminates:

- The problem must have one or more 'easy' cases and one or more 'hard' cases.
- In an 'easy' case, the algorithm must give a direct answer without calling itself.
- In a 'hard' case, the algorithm may call itself, but only to deal with an 'easier' case of the same problem.

In Example 2.5, the problem had one easy case, $n = 0$, and one hard case, $n > 0$. In the hard case, the algorithm called itself to deal with an easier case, $n{-}1$, and used that to compute its answer.

To compute b^n (where n is a nonnegative integer):

1. If $n = 0$:
    1.1. Terminate with answer 1.
2. If $n > 0$:
    2.1. Terminate with answer $b \times \underline{b^{n-1}}$.

Algorithm 2.12   Recursive simple power algorithm.

```java
static int power (int b, int n) {
// Return the value of b raised to the n'th power
// (where n is a nonnegative integer).
   if (n == 0)
      return 1;
   else
      return b * power(b, n-1);
}
```

Program 2.13   Java implementation of the recursive simple power algorithm.

EXAMPLE 2.6 *Recursive smart power algorithm*

The smart power algorithm of Algorithm 2.5 is hard to understand. However, there is an alternative version that is much more lucid. We observed in Example 2.2 that $b^{20} = b^{10} \times b^{10}$ and $b^{21} = b^{10} \times b^{10} \times b$. Generalizing from this example:

$$b^n = 1 \qquad\qquad\qquad \text{if } n = 0 \qquad\qquad\qquad (2.7a)$$
$$b^n = b^{n/2} \times b^{n/2} \qquad\quad \text{if } n > 0 \text{ and } n \text{ is even} \qquad (2.7b)$$
$$b^n = b^{n/2} \times b^{n/2} \times b \quad\; \text{if } n > 0 \text{ and } n \text{ is odd} \qquad (2.7c)$$

(Remember that $n/2$ neglects the remainder if n is odd.)

Equations (2.4a–c) naturally lead to Algorithm 2.14, which is recursive. Step 1 is the easy case, $n = 0$, and gives the answer directly. Step 2 is the hard case, $n > 0$, and works by a recursive call to compute $b^{n/2}$ (highlighted). Computing $b^{n/2}$ is easier than computing b^n, since $n/2$ is smaller than n.

Program 2.15 shows the recursive smart power algorithm coded in Java.

To compute b^n (where n is a nonnegative integer):

1. If $n = 0$:
    1.1. Terminate with answer 1.
2. If $n > 0$:
    2.1. Let $p = \underline{b^{n/2}}$.　　　2.
    2.2. If n is even:
        2.2.1. Terminate with answer $p \times p$.
    2.3. If n is odd:
        2.3.1. Terminate with answer $p \times p \times b$.

Algorithm 2.14　Recursive smart power algorithm.

```
static int power (int b, int n) {
// Return the value of b raised to the n'th power (where n is a nonnegative
// integer).
    if (n == 0)
        return 1;
    else {
        int p = power(b, n/2);
        if (n%2 == 0)      // n is even
            return p * p;
        else               // n is odd
            return p * p * b;
    }
}
```

Program 2.15　Java implementation of the recursive smart power algorithm.

Many algorithms can be expressed using either iteration or recursion. (Compare Algorithms 2.3 and 2.11, and compare Algorithms 2.5 and 2.14.) Typically the recursive algorithm is more elegant and easier to understand, but less efficient, than the corresponding iterative algorithm.

We do not always have a straight choice between iteration and recursion. For some problems an iterative solution would be extremely awkward, and a recursive solution is much more elegant.

EXAMPLE 2.7 *Integer rendering*

Rendering means converting data into a form suitable for printing or display on a screen. Most often, data are rendered as character strings (although some data are suitable for rendering graphically).

The problem is to render a given integer i to a given base (or radix) r between 2 and 10. The rendered integer is to be signed only if negative. For example:

i	r	Rendering
+29	2	"11101"
+29	8	"35"
−29	8	"−35"
+29	10	"29"

We can view this problem in terms of three cases:

- If $i < 0$, we have a negative integer. So we should render a minus-sign '−' and then render $(-i)$ to the base r.
- If $0 \leq i < r$, we have a single-digit nonnegative integer. So we should simply render the required digit. (Note that we must carefully distinguish between the integers 0, 1,...,9 and the corresponding digits '0', '1',...,'9'. A digit is a character, and as such can be printed or displayed on a screen. It is true that each digit has an (integer) internal code, but the internal code of '9' (for example) is *not* 9.)
- If $i \geq r$, we have a multiple-digit nonnegative integer. If we divide i by r, the remainder can be rendered as the rightmost digit, and the quotient can be rendered as the remaining digits. So we should render (i/r) to the base r and then render the single digit corresponding to $(i$ modulo $r)$.

This naturally leads to Algorithm 2.16. Step 2 is the easy case (a small nonnegative integer), which is solved directly. Step 3 is a harder case (a large nonnegative integer), which is solved in part by calling the algorithm recursively to deal with an easier case (a smaller nonnegative integer). Step 1 is also a harder case (a negative integer), which is solved in part by calling the algorithm recursively to deal with an easier case (a nonnegative integer).

Program 2.17 shows the algorithm implemented as a recursive Java method.

EXAMPLE 2.8 *Towers of Hanoi*

Three vertical poles are mounted on a platform. A number of disks are provided, all of different sizes, and each with a central hole allowing it to be threaded on to any of the poles. Initially, all of the disks are on pole 1, forming a tower with the largest disk at the bottom and the smallest disk at the top. Only a single disk may be moved at a time, from the top of any tower to the top of another tower, but no larger disk may be moved on top of a smaller disk. The problem is to move the tower of disks from pole 1 to pole 2.

According to legend, this task was originally set for the monks at the monastery of Hanoi. Sixty-four disks were provided. Once the monks completed their task, the universe would come to an end. How long should this take?

Rather than the particular problem of moving the tower of 64 disks from pole 1 to pole 2, it will prove helpful to address the more general problem of moving a tower of *n* disks from pole *source* to pole *dest*.

To render an integer *i* to the base *r* (where *r* is an integer between 2 and 10):

1. If $i < 0$:
   1.1. Render '−'.
   1.2. Render (−*i*) to the base *r*.
2. If $0 \leq i < r$:
   2.1. Let *d* be the digit corresponding to *i*.
   2.2. Render *d*.
3. If $i \geq r$:
   3.1. Let *d* be the digit corresponding to (*i* modulo *r*).
   3.2. Render (*i*/*r*) to the base *r*.
   3.3. Render *d*.

Algorithm 2.16   Recursive integer rendering algorithm.

```java
static String renderBasedInt (int i, int r) {
// Render i to the base r (where r is an integer between 2 and 10).
  String s;
  if (i < 0) {
    s = '-' + renderBasedInt(-i, r);
  } else if (i < r) {
    char d = (char)('0' + i);
    s = "" + d;
  } else {
    char d = (char)('0' + i%r);
    s = renderBasedInt(i/r, r) + d;
  }
  return s;
}
```

Program 2.17   Java implementation of the recursive integer rendering algorithm.

We immediately see that $n = 1$ is an easy case: just move the single disk from *source* to *dest*.

In the harder case, $n > 1$, we are forced to use the remaining pole (other than *source* and *dest*); let us call it *spare*. If $n = 2$, for example, we can move the smaller disk from *source* to *spare*, then move the larger disk from *source* to *dest*, and then finally move the smaller disk from *spare* to *dest*. (See Figure 2.19.)

This gives us a clue to solving the general case, $n > 1$. Assume for the moment that we have an auxiliary algorithm to move a tower of $(n–1)$ disks from one pole to another. Thus we can proceed as follows: move a tower of $(n–1)$ disks from *source* to *spare* (using the auxiliary algorithm); then move a single disk from *source* to *dest*; then move a tower of $(n–1)$ disks from *spare* to *dest* (again using the auxiliary algorithm). (See Figure 2.20.)

But of course we do not need an auxiliary algorithm to move a tower of $(n–1)$ disks: we just use the same algorithm recursively! Thus we have derived Algorithm 2.18.

To estimate how long the monks of Hanoi will take to move the tower of 64 disks, we need to analyze the algorithm. The characteristic operations are of course single-disk moves. Let *moves*(n) be the number of single-disk moves required to move a tower of n disks from one pole to another. Then we can immediately write down the following equations:

$$moves(n) = 1 \qquad\qquad \text{if } n = 1 \qquad\qquad (2.8a)$$
$$moves(n) = 1 + 2\ moves(n - 1) \quad \text{if } n > 1 \qquad (2.8b)$$

Again we have a pair of recurrence equations. Again we skip the derivation and simply state the solution:

$$moves(n) = 2^n - 1 \qquad\qquad\qquad\qquad (2.9)$$

Thus, for example, *moves*(1) $= 1$, which is obviously correct, and *moves*(2) $= 3$, which we already know from Figure 2.19. If you are mathematically inclined, you should verify the solution (2.9) by induction.

The Towers of Hanoi algorithm has time complexity $O(2^n)$. In fact, it is the first $O(2^n)$ algorithm we have encountered.

To move a tower of n disks from *source* to *dest* (where n is a positive integer):

1. If $n = 1$:
    1.1. Move a single disk from *source* to *dest*.
2. If $n > 1$:
    2.1. Let *spare* be the remaining pole, other than *source* and *dest*.
    2.2. <u>Move a tower of $(n–1)$ disks from *source* to *spare*</u>.
    2.3. Move a single disk from *source* to *dest*.
    2.4. <u>Move a tower of $(n–1)$ disks from *spare* to *dest*</u>.
3. Terminate.

Algorithm 2.18   Recursive algorithm for Towers of Hanoi.

Initially:

After moving a single disk
from *source* to *spare*:

After moving a single disk
from *source* to *dest*:

After moving a single disk
from *spare* to *dest*:

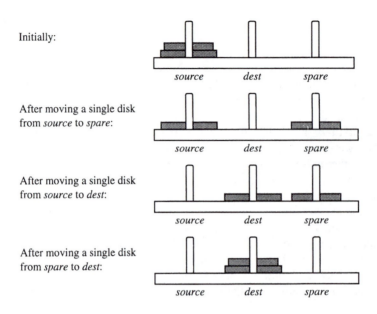

Figure 2.19 Towers of Hanoi with $n = 2$.

Initially:

After moving a tower of 5
disks from *source* to *spare*:

After moving a single disk
from *source* to *dest*:

After moving a tower of 5
disks from *spare* to *dest*:

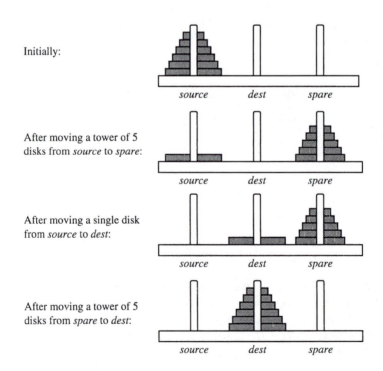

Figure 2.20 Towers of Hanoi with $n = 6$.

The monks of Hanoi would have discovered long ago what this signifies in practice. Their task entails making $2^{64} - 1$ or about 18 million million million moves, an enormous number. At the rate of one move per second, their task would take about 570 billion years, or about 40 times the estimated age of the universe!

Summary

In this chapter:

- We have seen that some problems can be solved by algorithms, but others cannot.
- We have seen that algorithms must be capable of being performed by a processor, one step at a time, and that they must eventually terminate.
- We have introduced a notation, based on English, suitable for expressing algorithms.
- We have seen how we can measure the time efficiency of algorithms in terms of the number of characteristic operations performed.
- We have seen how to determine the time complexity of algorithms, expressed in terms of O-notation, and what this tells us about the growth rate of the algorithms' time requirements.
- We have studied recursive algorithms, how we can ensure that they terminate, and how to determine their time complexity.

Exercises

2.1 Hand-test the simple and smart power algorithms (Algorithms 2.3 and 2.5 respectively). Use the test case $b = 2$, $n = 11$. How many multiplications are performed by each algorithm?

2.2 What is the time complexity of the geometric algorithm given as Algorithm 1.1?

2.3 Create a spreadsheet to reproduce the table of growth rates given in Table 2.10, and extend it to $n = 100$.

2.4 The following Java methods implement matrix addition and multiplication. Each matrix is represented by an $n \times n$ two-dimensional array of **float** numbers.

```
static void matrixAdd (int n, float[][] a,
    float[][] b, float[][] sum) {
// Set sum to the sum of the nxn matrices a and b.
  for (int i = 0; i < n; i++) {
    for (int j = 0; j < n; j++) {
      sum[i][j] = a[i][j] + b[i][j];
    }
  }
}
```

```
static void matrixMult (int n, float[][] a,
    float[][] b, float[][] prod) {
// Set prod to the product of the nxn matrices a and b.
  for (int i = 0; i < n; i++) {
    for (int j = 0; j < n; j++) {
      float s = 0.0;
      for (int k = 0; k < n; k++) {
        s += a[i][k] + b[k][j];
      }
      prod[i][j] = s;
    }
  }
}
```

Analyze these methods in terms of the number of **float** additions and multiplications performed. What is the time complexity of each method?

2.5 Analyze the time complexity of the recursive algorithm to render a given integer i to base r (Algorithm 2.16).

2.6 Devise a non-recursive algorithm to print a given integer i to base r. What is your algorithm's time complexity?

2.7 Devise a recursive version of Euclid's algorithm to calculate the GCD of two numbers. (A non-recursive version of this algorithm was given in Algorithm 1.3.)

2.8 The factorial of a positive integer n can be calculated using the recursive algorithm given in Algorithm 2.21. What is the time complexity of this algorithm?
Devise a non-recursive version of this algorithm.
Implement both algorithms as Java methods.

2.9 The Fibonacci number of a positive integer n can be calculated using the recursive algorithm given in Algorithm 2.22. What is the time complexity of this algorithm?
Devise a better recursive version of this algorithm. What is its time complexity?
Devise a non-recursive version of this improved algorithm.
Implement both algorithms as Java methods.

To calculate the factorial of n:

1. If $n = 0$:
   1.1. Terminate with answer 1.
2. If $n \neq 0$:
   2.1. Let f be the factorial of $n-1$.
   2.2. Terminate with answer $(n \times f)$.

Algorithm 2.21   A recursive factorial algorithm.

2.10   Write a Java program to implement the Towers of Hanoi algorithm given in Algorithm 2.18. Use your program to count the number of moves required and thus verify the time complexity of the algorithm.

* **2.11**   Devise a recursive algorithm to find your way out of a maze from a given starting position.

To calculate the Fibonacci number of n:

1. If $n \leq 0$:
    1.1. Terminate with answer 1.
2. If $n > 0$:
    2.1. Let $f1$ be the Fibonacci number of $n-1$.
    2.2. Let $f2$ be the Fibonacci number of $n-2$.
    2.3. Terminate with answer $(f1 + f2)$.

Algorithm 2.22   A recursive Fibonacci algorithm.

3

The Array Data Structure

In this chapter we shall study:

- arrays, their general properties, and their specific properties in Java (Section 3.1)
- array insertion, deletion, searching, merging, and sorting algorithms (Sections 3.2–6).

3.1 Arrays

Arrays are directly supported by nearly all major programming languages, and are familiar to every programmer. Nevertheless, a brief review of arrays will be useful here, and will serve as an opportunity to disentangle the general properties of arrays from their properties in specific programming languages such as Java. The array algorithms discussed in this chapter are expressed entirely in terms of the general properties of arrays.

An *array* is a sequence of indexed *components*, with the following general properties:

- The *length* of the array (its number of components) is fixed when the array is constructed.
- Each component of the array has a fixed and unique *index*. The indices range from a *lower index bound* through a *higher index bound*.
- Any component of the array can be accessed (inspected or updated) using its index. This is an efficient operation, having time complexity $O(1)$.

Figure 3.1 shows an abstract view of an array, with each box representing a single component.

In this book we shall use the common notation '$a[i]$' to denote the component of array a whose index is i.

Other properties of arrays vary from one programming language to another. In some languages (such as C, C++, and Java) indices are integers, with the lower index bound being zero; in some other languages (such as Pascal and Ada) the programmer is free to choose the lower and upper index bounds, and even to choose the type of the indices. In strongly-typed languages an array must be *homogeneous*, i.e., all its components must

Figure 3.1 Abstract view of an array *a*, with index bounds *low* and *high*.

have the same type; in weakly-typed languages an array may be *heterogeneous*. In different object-oriented languages, arrays are objects (as in Java) or not (as in C++).

Java arrays have the following specific properties:

- For an array of length n, the index bounds are 0 and $n - 1$.
- Every array is homogeneous, the type of its components being stated in the program. The components may be values of some stated primitive type, or objects of some stated class. (Java actually allows a measure of heterogeneity. An array of type $C[\ ]$, where C is an object class, may contain objects of any subclass of C.)
- An array is itself an object. Consequently, an array is allocated dynamically (by means of '**new**'), is manipulated by reference, and is automatically deallocated when no longer referred to.
- The notation for accessing the component with index i in array a is '$a[i]$', and the notation for inspecting the length of array a is 'a.length'.

Figure 3.2 shows a Java array object. The array object contains a class tag (like every object), a length field, and a sequence of indexed components. If the array's component type is T, the class tag is '$T[\ ]$'. The array object is accessed through a reference or pointer (like every object).

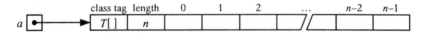

Figure 3.2 Structure of a Java array object (length n and elements of type T).

EXAMPLE 3.1 *Java arrays*

The following Java code allocates and initializes an array of six integers, named `primes`, and the diagram shows this array's structure:

```
int[] primes = {2, 3, 5, 7, 11, 13};
```

class tag	length	0	1	2	3	4	5
int[]	6	2	3	5	7	11	13

primes ●→

The following code prints all the components of `primes`:

```
for (int i = 0; i < primes.length; i++)
    System.out.println(primes[i]);
```

Now assume that a class `Date` has been declared, such that each `Date` object has fields `y`, `m`, and `d`, and is equipped with a method `advance`. The following code allocates (but does not initialize) an array of three `Date` objects, named `holidays`:

```
Date[] holidays = new Date[3];
```

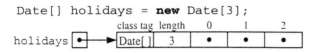

The following code assigns a `Date` object to each component of `holidays`, and then updates one of these objects using the method `advance`:

```
int thisYear = 2000;
...
holidays[0] = new Date(thisYear+1, 1, 1);
holidays[1] = new Date(thisYear+1, 5, 1);
holidays[2] = new Date(thisYear+1, 12, 25);
...
holidays[0].advance(365);
```

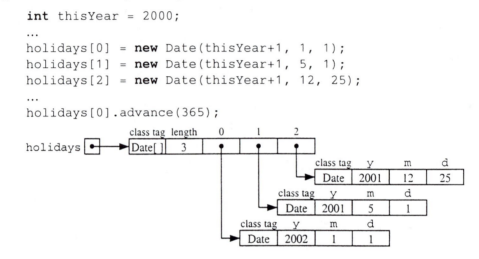

3.1.1 Subarrays

A *subarray* is a sequence of consecutive components forming part of a larger array. Throughout this book we shall use the notation:

$a[l...r]$

to denote a subarray of a consisting of the components $a[l]$ through $a[r]$. This is illustrated in Figure 3.3.

The *length* of a subarray is the number of components in the subarray. The length of subarray $a[l...r]$ is $r - l + 1$.

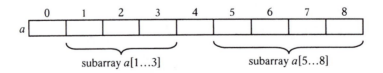

Figure 3.3 Subarrays.

All of the algorithms discussed in this chapter work not only for whole arrays but also for subarrays. We shall generally state the problem to be solved in terms of a (sub)array *a*[*left...right*].

Java, like most programming languages, has no special notation for subarrays. This causes no difficulties in practice: a method that must process the subarray *a*[*left...right*] can be coded with `a`, `left`, and `right` as separate parameters.

3.1.2 Sorted arrays

An array or subarray is ***sorted*** if the values of its components are in ascending order, i.e., the value of each component of the (sub)array is less than or equal to the value of that component's right neighbor. Many of the algorithms discussed in this chapter assume that a (sub)array is sorted.

Figure 3.4 illustrates this definition with sorted and unsorted arrays of words and of integers.

The meaning of '*x* is ***less*** than *y*' (or equivalently '*y* is ***greater*** than *x*') must be defined separately for each data type. For numbers it means that *x* is a smaller number than *y*. For strings, it conventionally means that *x* lexicographically precedes *y*. For dates, it naturally means that *x* is earlier than *y*.

The meanings of ***least*** and ***greatest*** are derived in the obvious way from the meanings of *less* and *greater*. In a sorted array, the leftmost component contains the least value, and the rightmost component the greatest value.

Java 2's `java.lang.Comparable` interface (shown in Program 3.5) captures the notions of *less* and *greater*. This interface requires a `compareTo` method to compare two objects, such that `x.compareTo(y)` returns a negative integer if x is *less* than y, zero if x is *equal* to y, or a positive integer if x is *greater* than y. Comparable is implemented by several Java 2 library classes including `Integer` and `String`. Other

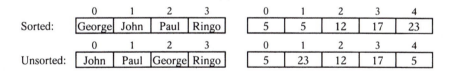

Figure 3.4   Sorted and unsorted arrays.

```
public interface Comparable {

    public int compareTo (Object that);
    // Return a negative integer if this object is less than that,
    // or zero if this object is equal to that,
    // or a positive integer if this object is greater than that.

}
```

Program 3.5   The Java `Comparable` interface.

classes, such as `Date` in Example 3.1, may be declared to implement `Comparable`, in which case they must implement the method `compareTo` appropriately.

3.2 Insertion

Suppose that we are required to insert a new value at a given position in an array. For instance, given the array a[0...8], we might be required to insert *val* at position 3. This can be done only by copying the values in components a[3...7] into their respective right neighbors a[4...8], and then copying *val* into a[3]. The value originally in a[8] will be lost. These effects are a consequence of the rigid structure of an array: it has a fixed number of components, and these components have fixed and consecutive indices.

Algorithm 3.6 inserts *val* at position *ins* in the (sub)array a[*left*...*right*]. The algorithm works correctly even in the boundary cases *ins* = *left* and *ins* = *right*. (Note that step 1 does nothing when *ins* = *right*.)

Figure 3.7 illustrates the algorithm's behavior, one step at a time, as it inserts a word in an array of words.

To insert *val* at position *ins* in a[*left*...*right*] (where *left* ≤ *ins* ≤ *right*):

1. Copy a[*ins*...*right*–1] into a[*ins*+1...*right*].
2. Copy *val* into a[*ins*].
3. Terminate.

Algorithm 3.6   Array insertion algorithm.

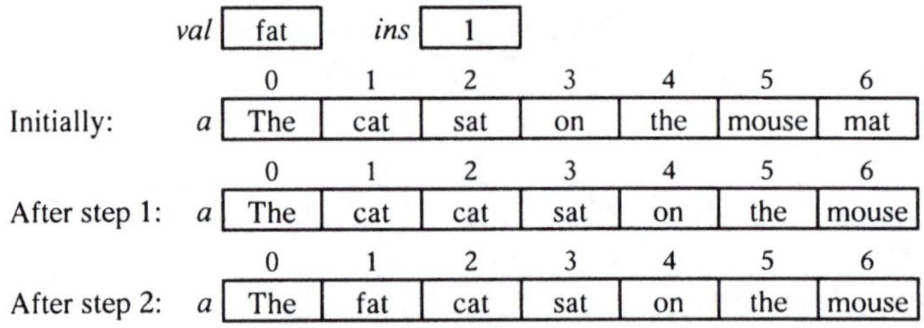

Figure 3.7   Illustration of the array insertion algorithm.

```
static void insert (Object val, int ins,
                    Object[] a, int left, int right) {
// Insert val at position ins in a[left...right]
// (where left ≤ ins ≤ right).
   for (int i = right; i > ins; i--)
      a[i] = a[i-1];
   a[ins] = val;
}
```

Program 3.8   Implementation of the array insertion algorithm as a Java method.

Let us analyze the insertion algorithm's time efficiency. The characteristic operations are copies. Let $n = right - left + 1$ be the length of $a[left...right]$. Step 1 could copy any number from 0 through $n - 1$ components (depending on the value of *ins*). On average, step 1 performs $(n - 1)/2$ copies. Step 2 performs one further copy. In total:

$$\text{Average no. of copies} = (n - 1)/2 + 1 = (n + 1)/2 \tag{3.1}$$

The fastest-growing term is $n/2$, so the insertion algorithm has time complexity $O(n)$.

Program 3.8 shows how the insertion algorithm would be implemented in Java. The algorithm itself works for any array, but the Java code assumes an array of objects. It must be modified slightly if required to handle an array of primitive values (see Exercise 3.5). Note also that step 1 requires careful coding (see Exercise 3.6).

3.3 Deletion

Suppose that we are required to delete the value at a given position in an array. For instance, we might be required to delete the value at position 3 in the array $a[0...8]$. This entails copying the values in components $a[4...8]$ into their respective left neighbors $a[3...7]$. The rightmost component $a[8]$ will become unoccupied.

Algorithm 3.9 deletes the value at position *del* of the (sub)array $a[left...right]$. Figure 3.10 illustrates the algorithm's behavior on an array of words.

Let us analyze the deletion algorithm's time efficiency. The characteristic operations are again copies. Let $n = right - left + 1$ be the length of $a[left...right]$. Step 1 could copy any number from 0 through $n - 1$ components (depending on the value of *del*), therefore:

$$\text{Average no. of copies} = (n - 1)/2 \tag{3.2}$$

The fastest-growing term is $n/2$, so the deletion algorithm has time complexity $O(n)$.

Program 3.11 shows how the deletion algorithm would be implemented in Java.

To delete the value at position *del* of $a[left...right]$ (where $left \leq del \leq right$):

1. Copy $a[del+1...right]$ into $a[del...right-1]$.
2. Make $a[right]$ unoccupied.
3. Terminate.

Algorithm 3.9   Array deletion algorithm.

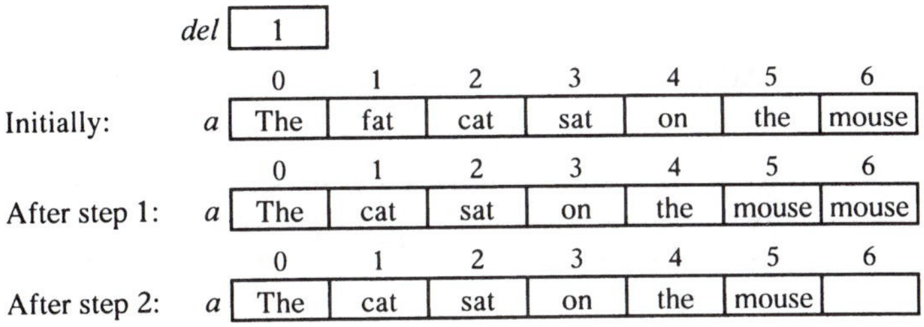

Figure 3.10   Illustration of the array deletion algorithm.

3.4 Searching

In this section we consider the problem of searching an array or subarray a[*left…right*] to find which (if any) component contains a value that equals some target value. In general, the (sub)array could be sorted or unsorted.

3.4.1 Linear search

Unsorted array

For the moment, let us assume that the (sub)array is unsorted. The ***linear search*** (or *sequential search*) algorithm is so called because it compares each array component in turn with the target value: see Algorithm 3.12. As soon as it finds a component that equals the target value, the algorithm terminates and returns that component's index as its answer. If it finds no such component, it returns a special value *none* as its answer.

Figure 3.13 shows the situation between iterations of the linear search algorithm. All components of a[*left…p* − 1] have already been searched and are known not to match *target*. The remaining components a[*p…right*] are still to be searched, and the matching component (if any) must be among them.

```
static void delete (int del,
                 Object[] a, int left, int right) {
// Delete the object at position del of a[left...right]
// (where left ≤ del ≤ right).
   for (int i = del+1; i <= right; i++)
     a[i-1] = a[i];
   a[right] = null;
}
```

Program 3.11   Implementation of the array deletion algorithm as a Java method.

To find which (if any) component of a[*left…right*] equals *target*:

1. For *p* = *left*, …, *right*, repeat:
   1.1. If *target* is equal to a[*p*], terminate with answer *p*.
2. Terminate with answer *none*.

Algorithm 3.12   Unsorted array linear search algorithm.

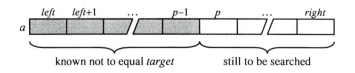

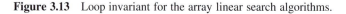

Figure 3.13   Loop invariant for the array linear search algorithms.

A *loop invariant* is a state that pertains before and after every iteration of a particular loop in an algorithm or program. Figure 3.13 is an example of a loop invariant. We shall use loop invariants frequently in this book to assist in understanding algorithms (some of which are rather more complicated than Algorithm 3.12).

Figure 3.14 illustrates linear search of an array of words. At each step, the components known not to equal *target* are highlighted. (Compare with Figure 3.13.)

Let us now analyze the linear search algorithm's time efficiency. For a searching algorithm the characteristic operations are comparisons. Let $n = right - left + 1$ be the length of $a[left...right]$. There are two cases to consider. If the search is *successful*, step 1 could compare *target* with any number of components from 1 through n, so:

$$\text{Average no. of comparisons (successful search)} = (n + 1)/2 \qquad (3.3)$$

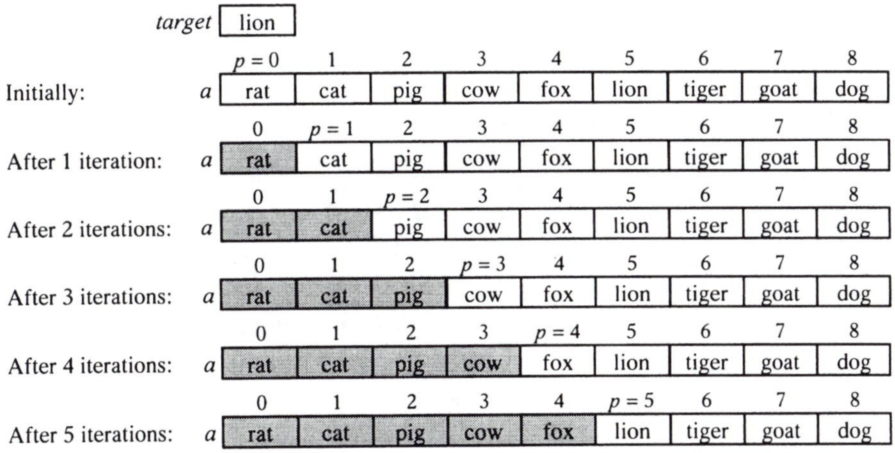

Figure 3.14   Illustration of the unsorted array linear search algorithm.

```
static final int NONE = -1;   // ... distinct from any array index.

static int linearSearch (Object target,
              Object[] a, int left, int right) {
// Find which (if any) component of a[left...right] equals target.
   for (int p = left; p <= right; p++) {
      if (target.equals(a[p]))  return p;
   }
   return NONE;
}
```

Program 3.15   Implementation of the unsorted array linear search algorithm as a Java method.

If the search is *unsuccessful*, on the other hand, all the components will be compared:

$$\text{No. of comparisons (unsuccessful search)} = n \qquad (3.4)$$

In either case, the linear search algorithm has time complexity $O(n)$.

Program 3.15 shows how the linear search algorithm would be implemented in Java.

Sorted array

Now let us assume that the (sub)array is sorted. This enables us to improve the linear search algorithm slightly. In Figure 3.13, if component $a[p]$ contains a value greater than *target*, the search might as well be terminated immediately, because components $a[p + 1...right]$ will be greater still. Algorithm 3.16 shows the sorted array linear search algorithm. Whether the search is successful or unsuccessful, this algorithm's average number of comparisons is $(n + 1)/2$. Its time complexity is still $O(n)$, but on average it requires only half as many comparisons as Algorithm 3.12 when the search is unsuccessful (see Exercise 3.8).

Program 3.17 shows how the sorted array linear search algorithm would be implemented in Java. Note that the array components and `target` are assumed to be objects of a class that implements the `Comparable` interface, and the `compareTo` method is used to compare these objects. Steps 1.1 and 1.2 are implemented with a *single* call to the `compareTo` method.

To find which (if any) component of $a[left...right]$ equals *target* (where a is sorted):

1. For $p = left$, ..., *right*, repeat:
   1.1. If *target* is equal to $a[p]$, terminate with answer p.
   1.2. If *target* is less than $a[p]$, terminate with answer *none*.
2. Terminate with answer *none*.

Algorithm 3.16   Sorted array linear search algorithm.

```
static int linearSearch (Comparable target,
                Comparable[] a, int left, int right) {
// Find which (if any) component of a[left...right] equals target
// (where a is sorted).
    for (int p = left; p <= right; p++) {
        int comp = target.compareTo(a[p]);
        if (comp == 0)  return p;
        else if (comp < 0)  return NONE;
    }
    return NONE;
}
```

Program 3.17   Implementation of the sorted array linear search algorithm as a Java method.

In fact, a much better sorted array searching algorithm is available, which we shall study in the next subsection.

3.4.2 Binary search

Think about how you would search a dictionary for a target word. Would you look at each page in turn, starting at page 1, until you find the page containing the target word? Of course not, but that is exactly what linear search implies. Instead you would probably open the dictionary somewhere in the middle. If by good fortune the target word is on the open page, you are finished. If the target word is less (greater) than the words on the open page, you would focus your attention on the part of the dictionary before (after) that page. Whichever part of the dictionary you have focussed on, you would then search it in the same way, repeatedly dividing the focus of the search until you eventually find the page you are looking for. All this works because the words in a dictionary are sorted.

This idea is the basis of the ***binary search*** algorithm for a sorted array: see Algorithm 3.18.

Figure 3.19 shows the situation between iterations of the binary search algorithm. All components of $a[left...l-1]$ are known to be less than *target*, and all components of $a[r+1...right]$ are known to be greater than *target*. The remaining components $a[l...r]$ are still to be searched, and the matching component (if any) must be among them. Initially all components of $a[left...right]$ remain to be searched, so the algorithm initializes l to *left* and r to *right*.

Figure 3.20(a) illustrates binary search of a sorted array of words. The components known to be less than or greater than *target* are highlighted (compare Figure 3.19).

To find which (if any) component of $a[left...right]$ equals *target* (where a is sorted):

1. Set $l = left$, and set $r = right$.
2. While $l \leq r$, repeat:
    2.1. Let m be an integer about midway between l and r.
    2.2. If *target* is equal to $a[m]$, terminate with answer m.
    2.3. If *target* is less than $a[m]$, set $r = m - 1$.
    2.4. If *target* is greater than $a[m]$, set $l = m + 1$.
3. Terminate with answer *none*.

Algorithm 3.18   Array binary search algorithm.

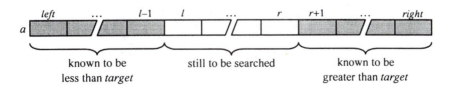

Figure 3.19   Loop invariant for the array binary search algorithm.

Initially $l = 0$ and $r = 8$, so step 2.1 sets $m = 4$. Since *target* is greater than $a[4]$, step 2.4 sets $l = m + 1$. Now $l = 5$ and $r = 8$, so step 2.1 sets $m = 6$ (say). Since *target* is less than $a[6]$, step 2.3 sets $r = m - 1$. Now $l = 5$ and $r = 5$, so step 2.1 sets $m = 5$. Since *target* is equal to $a[5]$, step 2.2 terminates the algorithm with the answer 5. In this case only three iterations are needed; in general, up to four iterations will be needed to search an array of that length.

Figure 3.20(b) illustrates an unsuccessful search. Since no array component equals the target value, the algorithm eventually reaches the state $l > r$, indicating that no part of the array remains to be searched (see Figure 3.19). In that state the algorithm reaches step 3, which gives the answer *none*.

Let us analyze the binary search algorithm's time efficiency. Let $n = right - left + 1$ be the length of $a[left...right]$. The number of iterations is at most the number of times that n can be halved until it reaches zero, i.e., $\text{floor}(\log_2 n) + 1$. (See Appendix A.2.) If we assume that steps 2.2 through 2.4 can be implemented with a single comparison, then we have:

$$\text{Max. no. of comparisons} = \text{floor}(\log_2 n) + 1 \tag{3.5}$$

Thus the binary search algorithm has time complexity $O(\log n)$.

Program 3.21 shows how the binary search algorithm would be implemented in Java.

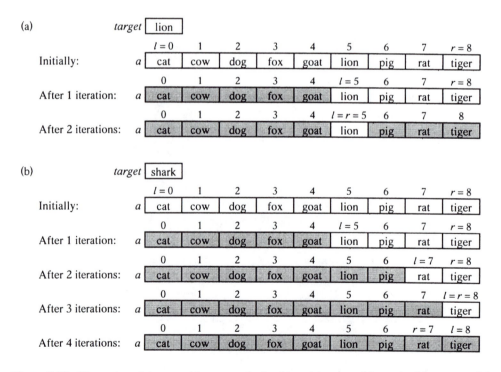

Figure 3.20 Illustration of the array binary search algorithm: (a) successful search; (b) unsuccessful search.

3.4.3 Comparison

Table 3.22 summarizes the efficiency of the three array searching algorithms.

For an unsorted array, we have no alternative but to use linear search.

For a sorted array, binary search is clearly superior to linear search. Our analyses have shown that binary search has time efficiency $O(\log n)$ whereas linear search has time efficiency $O(n)$. Binary search should be preferred unless n is known to be small.

The intuition behind the binary search algorithm's superiority is clear. Compare the subarrays still to be searched (shown unshaded) in Figures 3.14 and Figure 3.20. Each iteration of the linear search algorithm removes only one component from the unsearched subarray, whereas each iteration of the binary search algorithm removes about half of the unsearched subarray's components.

An everyday situation illustrates the point vividly. When we search a 1000-page dictionary or telephone directory using binary search, we will find the target entry in 10 iterations *at most* (the number of pages still to be searched being successively 1000, 500, 250, 125, 62, 31, 15, 7, 3, and 1). If we were foolish enough to use linear search, we

```java
static int binarySearch (Comparable target,
                Comparable[] a, int left, int right) {
// Find which (if any) component of a[left...right] equals target
// (where a is sorted).
   int l = left, r = right;
   while (l <= r) {
      int m = (l + r)/2;
      int comp = target.compareTo(a[m]);
      if (comp == 0)
         return m;
      else if (comp < 0)
         r = m - 1;
      else   // comp > 0
         l = m + 1;
   }
   return NONE;
}
```

Program 3.21   Implementation of the array binary search algorithm as a Java method.

Table 3.22   Efficiency of array searching algorithms.

Algorithm	No. of comparisons (approx.)	Time complexity
Unsorted array linear search	$n/2$ (successful) n (unsuccessful)	$O(n)$
Sorted array linear search	$n/2$	$O(n)$
Sorted array binary search	$\log_2 n$	$O(\log n)$

would need 500 iterations *on average* (the number of pages still to be searched being successively 1000, 999, 998, …).

3.5 Merging

Suppose that we are given two sorted arrays, *a1* and *a2*, and are required to make a third sorted array *a* contain a copy of each value from *a1* and *a2*. This is the **merging** problem.

We should start by comparing the leftmost (least) component of *a1* with the leftmost (least) component of *a2*; whichever value is less, we copy that value into the leftmost component of *a*. We continue in the same way, now ignoring those components of *a1* and

To merge *a1*[*left1*…*right1*] and *a2*[*left2*…*right2*] into *a3*[*left3*…] (where both *a1* and *a2* are sorted):

1. Set *i* = *left1*, set *j* = *left2*, and set *k* = *left3*.
2. While *i* ≤ *right1* and *j* ≤ *right2*, repeat:
   2.1. If *a1*[*i*] is less than or equal to *a2*[*j*]:
      2.1.1. Copy *a1*[*i*] into *a3*[*k*].
      2.1.2. Increment *i* and *k*.
   2.2. If *a1*[*i*] is greater than or equal to *a2*[*j*]:
      2.2.1. Copy *a2*[*j*] into *a3*[*k*].
      2.2.2. Increment *j* and *k*.
3. While *i* ≤ *right1*, repeat:
   3.1. Copy *a1*[*i*] into *a3*[*k*].
   3.2. Increment *i* and *k*.
4. While *j* ≤ *right2*, repeat:
   4.1. Copy *a2*[*j*] into *a3*[*k*].
   4.2. Increment *j* and *k*.
5. Terminate.

Algorithm 3.23   Array merging algorithm.

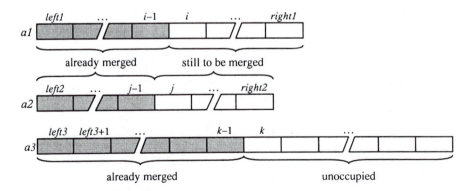

Figure 3.24   Loop invariant for the array merging algorithm.

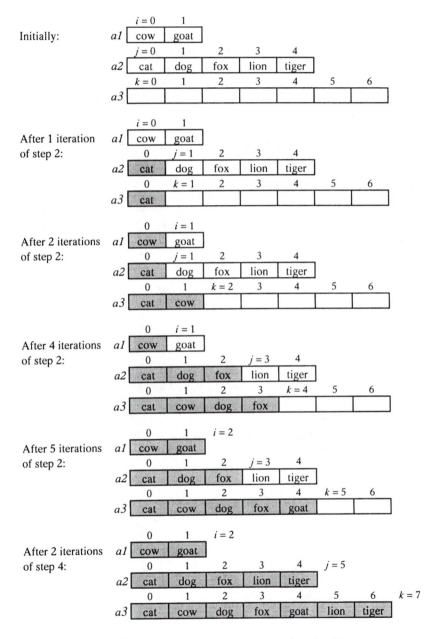

Figure 3.25 Illustration of the array merging algorithm.

a2 that have already been copied into a. When we have copied either all components of a1 or all components of a2, we complete the merge by copying all the remaining components of the other array into a.

Algorithm 3.23 captures this idea. Two points in the algorithm are particularly noteworthy. Firstly, the conditions in steps 2.1 and 2.2 are not mutually exclusive: if a1[i] is *equal* to a2[j], it does not matter whether we perform step 2.1.1 or 2.2.1. Secondly, only one of the loops at steps 3 and 4 will actually do any work: after the loop at step 2 terminates, one of the conditions $i \leq right1$ and $j \leq right2$ will no longer be satisfied.

Figure 3.24 shows the loop invariant for the merging algorithm. (Interestingly, all three loops have the same invariant.) Figure 3.25 illustrates the algorithm's behavior as it merges two arrays of words.

Let us analyze the merging algorithm's time efficiency. Let $n_1 = right1 - left1 + 1$ be the length of $a1[left1...right1]$, let $n_2 = right2 - left2 + 1$ be the length of $a2[left2...right2]$, and let $n = n_1 + n_2$ be the total number of merged components. For the characteristic operations we could choose either copies or comparisons.

Let us first analyze the number of copies. Each component of a1 is copied exactly once, by either step 2.1.1 or step 3.1. Likewise, each component of a2 is copied exactly once, by either step 2.2.1 or step 4.1. Therefore:

$$\text{No. of copies} = n_1 + n_2 = n \tag{3.6}$$

Let us now analyze the number of comparisons. The loop at step 2 is iterated at most $n - 1$ times. If we assume that steps 2.1 and 2.2 can be implemented with a single comparison, then:

```
static void merge
                (Comparable[] a1, int left1, int right1,
                 Comparable[] a2, int left2, int right2,
                 Comparable[] a3, int left3) {
// Merge a1[left1...right1] and a2[left2...right2] into
// a3[left3...] (where both a1 and a2 are sorted).
   int i = left1, j = left2, k = left3;
   while (i <= right1 && j <= right2) {
      int comp = a1[i].compareTo(a2[j]);
      if (comp <= 0)
         a3[k++] = a1[i++];
      else
         a3[k++] = a2[j++];
   }
   while (i <= right1)
      a3[k++] = a1[i++];
   while (j <= right2)
      a3[k++] = a2[j++];
}
```

Program 3.26   Implementation of the array merging algorithm as a Java method.

Max. no. of comparisons $= n - 1$ (3.7)

In terms of either copies or comparisons, the merging algorithm has time complexity $O(n_1 + n_2)$ or $O(n)$.

Program 3.26 shows a Java method implementing the merging algorithm. This method takes all three arrays and their bounds as parameters. It is coded tightly, using the post-increment operator '++' to increment the counters i, j, and k 'on the fly'.

3.6 Sorting

If we have to maintain a large collection of data such as a dictionary or telephone directory, it makes sense to maintain the data in sorted order. We can efficiently search a sorted collection, and we can efficiently merge two sorted collections. But what if the initial collection is unsorted? Or what if we are given an unsorted collection to add to the main collection?

Situations like these give rise to the *sorting* problem: given a collection of data, rearrange the data into ascending order. Sorting is a classical problem in computer science. Numerous algorithms have been devised, varying widely in subtlety and efficiency.

In this section we shall study several array sorting algorithms. In each case, the problem is to sort the (sub)array $a[left...right]$.

3.6.1 Selection sort

Consider the following idea. First, find the least value in the array, and swap it into the leftmost component where it belongs. Henceforth ignore the leftmost component, and repeat the process on the unsorted components to its right. When only one component remains to be sorted, we are finished.

This simple idea is the basis of *selection sort*, and is captured by Algorithm 3.27. Step 1.1 employs an auxiliary algorithm to find the least of a sequence of components. (The auxiliary algorithm is omitted here, but see Exercise 3.10(d).)

Figure 3.28 shows the loop invariant for the selection sort algorithm. The sorted subarray, $a[left...l - 1]$, contains the lesser values. The unsorted subarray, $a[l...right]$, contains the greater values. The algorithm finds the least value in the unsorted subarray, and swaps it into $a[l]$. Now we can claim that the subarray $a[left...l]$ is sorted, so the sorted subarray has expanded by one component at the expense of the unsorted subarray.

To sort $a[left...right]$:

1. For $l = left, ..., right-1$, repeat:
   1.1. Set p such that $a[p]$ is the least of $a[l...right]$.
   1.2. If $p \neq l$, swap $a[p]$ and $a[l]$.
2. Terminate.

Algorithm 3.27   Array selection sort algorithm.

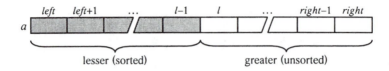

$$a$$

	left	left+1	...	l−1	l	...	right−1	right

lesser (sorted) greater (unsorted)

Figure 3.28 Loop invariant for the array selection sort algorithm.

		l = 0	1	2	3	4	5	6	7	8
Initially:	a	fox	cow	pig	cat	rat	lion	tiger	goat	dog
		0	l = 1	2	3	4	5	6	7	8
After 1 iteration:	a	cat	cow	pig	fox	rat	lion	tiger	goat	dog
		0	1	l = 2	3	4	5	6	7	8
After 2 iterations:	a	cat	cow	pig	fox	rat	lion	tiger	goat	dog
		0	1	2	l = 3	4	5	6	7	8
After 3 iterations:	a	cat	cow	dog	fox	rat	lion	tiger	goat	pig
		0	1	2	3	l = 4	5	6	7	8
After 4 iterations:	a	cat	cow	dog	fox	rat	lion	tiger	goat	pig
		0	1	2	3	4	l = 5	6	7	8
After 5 iterations:	a	cat	cow	dog	fox	goat	lion	tiger	rat	pig
		0	1	2	3	4	5	l = 6	7	8
After 6 iterations:	a	cat	cow	dog	fox	goat	lion	tiger	rat	pig
		0	1	2	3	4	5	6	l = 7	8
After 7 iterations:	a	cat	cow	dog	fox	goat	lion	pig	rat	tiger
		0	1	2	3	4	5	6	7	l = 8
After 8 iterations:	a	cat	cow	dog	fox	goat	lion	pig	rat	tiger

Figure 3.29 Illustration of the array selection sort algorithm.

Figure 3.29 illustrates the selection sort algorithm's behavior as it sorts an array of words. Note that the unsorted subarray shrinks steadily until it is reduced to a single component.

Let us analyze the selection sort algorithm's time efficiency. The characteristic operations in a sorting algorithm are usually held to be comparisons. Let $n = right − left + 1$ be the length of $a[left...right]$. It is easy to see that step 1.1 must perform $right − l$ comparisons. The main loop is performed repeatedly, with l taking the values $left$, $left + 1$, ..., $right − 2$, $right − 1$. Summing these terms we get:

$$
\begin{aligned}
\text{No. of comparisons} &= (right − left) + (right − left − 1) + \cdots + 2 + 1 \\
&= (n − 1) + (n − 2) + \cdots + 2 + 1 \\
&= (n^2 − n)/2
\end{aligned}
\tag{3.8}
$$

(For an explanation of this summation, see Appendix A.3.) The fastest-growing term is $n^2/2$, so the selection sort algorithm has time complexity $O(n^2)$.

It is also possible to analyze a sorting algorithm in terms of copies. Step 1.2 of the selection sort algorithm performs two copies. The main loop is iterated $n - 1$ times, so we get:

$$\text{No. of copies} = 2(n - 1) \tag{3.9}$$

In terms of copies alone, selection sort is $O(n)$. This does not affect its overall time complexity, which is $O(n^2)$.

Program 3.30 shows a Java implementation of the selection sort algorithm.

3.6.2 Insertion sort

Let us briefly consider a slightly different problem: reading a file of values into an array, where the file is unsorted, but the array must be sorted. Of course, we could just copy all the values from the file into the array, and then sort the array. Alternatively, we could keep the array sorted at all times: read one value at a time, and insert it into the array in such a way as to keep the array sorted. This turns out to be a better algorithm (see Exercise 3.15).

We can exploit the same idea to sort values already stored in an array. This is called *insertion sort*, and is shown as Algorithm 3.31. Step 1.2 is a variant of the array insertion algorithm (see Exercise 3.10(c)).

Figure 3.32 shows the loop invariant for the insertion sort algorithm. The left subarray, $a[left...r - 1]$, contains the same values that were originally in this subarray, but by now

```
static void selectionSort
                (Comparable[] a, int left, int right) {
// Sort a[left...right].
  for (int l = left; l < right; l++) {
     int p = l;
     Comparable least = a[p];
     // ... least will always contain the value of a[p].
     for (int k = l+1; k <= right; k++) {
        int comp = a[k].compareTo(least);
        if (comp < 0) {
           p = k;   least = a[p];
        }
     }
     if (p != l) {
        a[p] = a[l];   a[l] = least;
     }
  }
}
```

Program 3.30   Implementation of the array selection sort algorithm as a Java method.

To sort *a*[*left*...*right*]:

1. For *r* = *left*+1, ..., *right*, repeat:
   1.1. Let *val* = *a*[*r*].
   1.2. Insert *val* into *a*[*left*...*r*] in such a way that the subarray is sorted.
2. Terminate.

Algorithm 3.31 Array insertion sort algorithm.

left
left+1
...
r–1
r
...
right–1
right
a
inserted (sorted)
still to be inserted

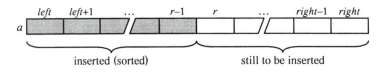

Figure 3.32 Loop invariant for the array insertion sort algorithm.

Initially: a
0 r = 1 2 3 4 5 6 7 8
fox cow pig cat rat lion tiger goat dog
After 1 iteration: a
0 1 r = 2 3 4 5 6 7 8
cow fox pig cat rat lion tiger goat dog
After 2 iterations: a
0 1 2 r = 3 4 5 6 7 8
cow fox pig cat rat lion tiger goat dog
After 3 iterations: a
0 1 2 3 r = 4 5 6 7 8
cat cow fox pig rat lion tiger goat dog
After 4 iterations: a
0 1 2 3 4 r = 5 6 7 8
cat cow fox pig rat lion tiger goat dog
After 5 iterations: a
0 1 2 3 4 5 r = 6 7 8
cat cow fox lion pig rat tiger goat dog
After 6 iterations: a
0 1 2 3 4 5 6 r = 7 8
cat cow fox lion pig rat tiger goat dog
After 7 iterations: a
0 1 2 3 4 5 6 7 r = 8
cat cow fox goat lion pig rat tiger dog
After 8 iterations: a
0 1 2 3 4 5 6 7 8
cat cow dog fox goat lion pig rat tiger

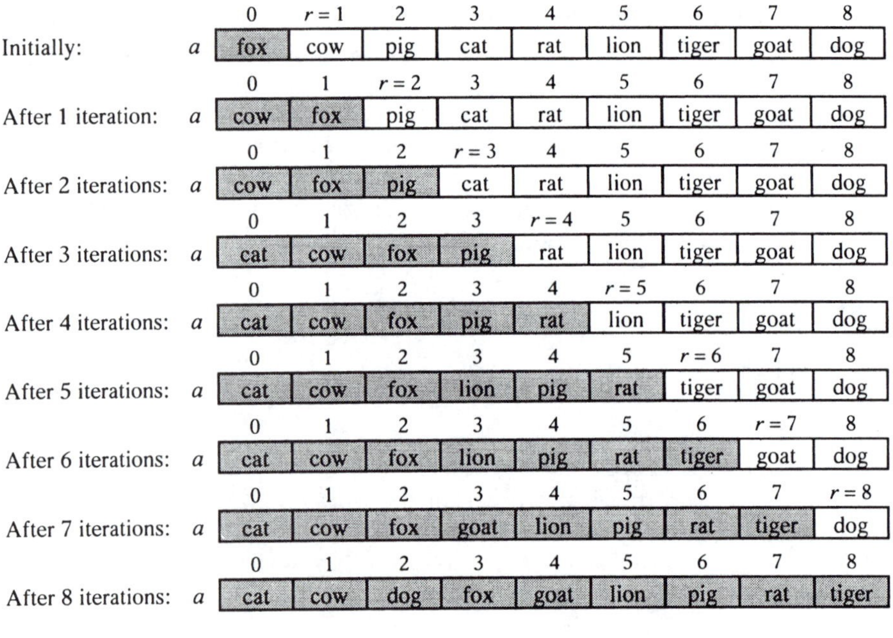

Figure 3.33 Illustration of the array insertion sort algorithm.

sorted. The right subarray, *a*[*r*...*right*], is so far undisturbed. Step 1.2 simply inserts the value of *a*[*r*] into the left subarray. Now *a*[*left*...*r*] is sorted, so the left subarray has expanded by one component at the expense of the right subarray.

Figure 3.33 illustrates the insertion sort algorithm's behavior as it sorts an array of words. Note that the right subarray shrinks steadily until it is reduced to nothing. Compare Figure 3.33 with Figure 3.29.

Let us analyze the insertion sort algorithm's time efficiency. Let $n = right - left + 1$ be the length of $a[left...right]$. Step 1.2 must search a sequence of $(r - left)$ components; this takes on average $(r - left + 1)/2$ comparisons, assuming linear search. The main loop is performed repeatedly, with r taking the values $left + 1$, $left + 2$, ..., $right - 1$, $right$. Summing these terms we get:

Average no. of comparisons
$$= 2/2 + 3/2 + \cdots + (right - left)/2 + (right - left + 1)/2$$
$$= 2/2 + 3/2 + \cdots + (n - 1)/2 + n/2$$
$$= (n^2 + n - 2)/4 \tag{3.10}$$

(For an explanation of this summation, see Appendix A.3.) The fastest-growing term is $n^2/4$, so the insertion sort algorithm has time complexity $O(n^2)$.

Let us also analyze the insertion sort algorithm in terms of copies. Step 1.2 could perform any number of copies from 1 through $r - left + 1$, or $(r - left + 2)/2$ copies on average. The main loop is performed repeatedly, with r taking the values $left + 1$, $left + 2$, ..., $right - 1$, $right$. Summing these terms we get:

Average no. of copies
$$= 3/2 + 4/2 + \cdots + (right - left + 1)/2 + (right - left + 2)/2$$
$$= 3/2 + 4/2 + \cdots + n/2 + (n + 1)/2$$
$$= (n^2 + 3n - 4)/4 \tag{3.11}$$

The fastest-growing term is $n^2/4$.

Thus we see that insertion sort performs only half as many comparisons as selection sort, but it also performs far more copies.

Program 3.34 shows a Java implementation of the insertion sort algorithm.

3.6.3 Merge-sort

A very powerful idea in algorithm design is the ***divide-and-conquer*** strategy: to solve a 'hard' problem, break it down into two or more 'easier' subproblems, solve these subpro-

```
static void insertionSort
          (Comparable[] a, int left, int right) {
// Sort a[left...right].
   for (int r = left+1; r <= right; r++) {
      Comparable val = a[r];   int p = r;
      while (p > left && val.compareTo(a[p-1]) < 0) {
         a[p] = a[p-1];   p--;
      }
      a[p] = val;
   }
}
```

Program 3.34 Implementation of the array insertion sort algorithm as a Java method.

blems separately, and combine their answers. The divide-and-conquer strategy is not suitable for all problems, but it does work very well for sorting.

If we are required to sort an array, we can divide the array into two subarrays of about equal length, sort each subarray separately, and finally merge the two subarrays. This is the basis of the ***merge-sort*** algorithm, which is shown as Algorithm 3.35. Step 1.2 sorts the left subarray; this step could use any sorting algorithm, but it might as well call the merge-sort algorithm recursively. Step 1.3 similarly sorts the right subarray. Step 1.4 then merges the two subarrays into an auxiliary array; this step could use Algorithm 3.23. Finally, step 1.5 overwrites the original array.

As usual with a recursive algorithm, we must ensure that we have at least one easy (non-recursive) case as well as at least one hard (recursive) case. In the merge-sort algorithm, the easy case is *left* $\geq$ *right*, when there is no sorting to do at all; the harder case is *left* < *right*, when there are at least two values to be sorted.

Figure 3.36 illustrates the merge-sort algorithm's behavior as it sorts an array of words.

Let us analyze the merge-sort algorithm's time efficiency. Let $n = right - left + 1$ be the length of $a[left\ldots right]$, and let $comps(n)$ be the number of comparisons required to sort n components. Step 1.1 divides the array into two subarrays each of about $n/2$ components. Thus step 1.2 will have about $n/2$ components to sort, performing $comps(n/2)$ comparisons. Step 1.3 will likewise perform $comps(n/2)$ comparisons. We know from Section 3.5 that the merge in step 1.4 will perform about n comparisons.

To sort $a[left\ldots right]$:

1. If *left* < *right*:
   1.1. Let m be an integer about midway between *left* and *right* (such that
        $left \leq m < right$).
   1.2. Sort $a[left\ldots m]$.
   1.3. Sort $a[m+1\ldots right]$.
   1.4. Merge $a[left\ldots m]$ and $a[m+1\ldots right]$ into an auxiliary array b.
   1.5. Copy all components of b into $a[left\ldots right]$.
2. Terminate.

Algorithm 3.35   Array merge-sort algorithm.

	0	1	2	3	m = 4	5	6	7	8
After step 1.1: a	fox	cow	pig	cat	rat	lion	tiger	goat	dog

	0	1	2	3	m = 4	5	6	7	8
After step 1.2: a	cat	cow	fox	pig	rat	lion	tiger	goat	dog

	0	1	2	3	m = 4	5	6	7	8
After step 1.3: a	cat	cow	fox	pig	rat	dog	goat	lion	tiger

	0	1	2	3	4	5	6	7	8
After step 1.5: a	cat	cow	dog	fox	goat	lion	pig	rat	tiger

Figure 3.36   Illustration of the array merge-sort algorithm.

Summing these terms, and noting that no comparisons at all are needed if $n \leq 1$, we get:

$$comps(n) \approx 2\ comps(n/2) + n \qquad \text{if } n > 1 \qquad (3.12a)$$
$$comps(n) = 0 \qquad\qquad\qquad\ \text{if } n \leq 1 \qquad (3.12b)$$

The solution (see Appendix A.4) is approximately:

$$comps(n) \approx n\ \log_2 n \qquad (3.13)$$

So the merge-sort algorithm has time complexity $O(n \log n)$. This is much superior to the selection sort and insertion sort algorithms.

The major disadvantage of the merge-sort algorithm is its space usage. Let us analyze its space efficiency. We conventionally measure this by counting the total number of *auxiliary* variables, including array components; we do not count the original array. The merge-sort algorithm needs an auxiliary array of length n, plus a few other auxiliary variables that we can ignore here. Therefore its space complexity is $O(n)$. For comparison, the selection sort and insertion sort algorithms need only a fixed number of auxiliary variables, so they have space complexity $O(1)$.

Program 3.37 shows how the merge-sort algorithm could be implemented as a Java method, mergeSort, and an auxiliary method, doMergeSort. The method merge-Sort allocates the auxiliary array, b, required to merge the subarrays, and then calls doMergeSort. The method doMergeSort is an implementation of Algorithm 3.35, and it calls the merge method of Program 3.26.

```java
public static void mergeSort
                (Comparable[] a, int left, int right) {
// Sort a[left...right].
   Comparable[] b = new Comparable[right-left+1];
   doMergeSort(a, left, right, b);
}

private static void doMergeSort(Comparable[] a,
                int left, int right, Comparable[] b) {
// Merge-sort a[left...right] using auxiliary array b.
   if (left < right) {
      int m = (left + right)/2;
      doMergeSort(a, left, m, b);
      doMergeSort(a, m+1, right, b);
      merge(a, left, m, a, m+1, right, b, 0);
      for (int k = left; k <= right; k++)
         a[k] = b[k-left];
   }
}
```

Program 3.37   Implementation of the array merge-sort algorithm as Java methods.

3.6.4 Quick-sort

Quick-sort is another sorting algorithm based on the divide-and-conquer strategy. The idea is as follows. Choose any value from the array, and call that value the *pivot*. Then *partition* the array into three subarrays, such that the left subarray contains values known to be less than (or equal to) the pivot, the middle subarray is a single component containing the pivot itself, and the right subarray contains values known to be greater than (or equal to) the pivot. Now all that remains to be done is to sort the left and right subarrays.

This idea is captured by Algorithm 3.38. Step 1.1 is the partitioning step; this is delegated to an auxiliary partitioning algorithm, which we shall discuss shortly. Steps 1.2 and 1.3 sort the left and right subarrays; each is just a recursive call to the quick-sort algorithm itself. The easy (non-recursive) case is when the array has fewer than two components.

Figure 3.39 shows the state of the array immediately after the partitioning step, and after the two sorting steps. We can see that the partitioning step has moved the pivot into its final position, a[p]. It has also moved all values less than the pivot into the left subarray, a[*left...p* − 1], and all values greater than the pivot into the right subarray, a[p + 1...*right*]. (Any values that happen to be equal to the pivot could end up in either subarray – we do not care which.) Now the left and right subarrays can be sorted separately. Figure 3.39 shows that this makes the whole array sorted.

To sort *a*[*left...right*]:

1. If *left* < *right*:
   1.1. Partition *a*[*left...right*] such that *a*[*left...p*–1] are all less than or equal to *a*[p], and *a*[p+1...*right*] are all greater than or equal to *a*[p].
   1.2. Sort *a*[*left...p*–1].
   1.3. Sort *a*[p+1...*right*].
2. Terminate.

Algorithm 3.38   Array quick-sort algorithm.

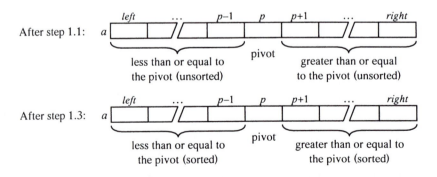

Figure 3.39   Invariants for the array quick-sort algorithm.

Figure 3.40 illustrates the quick-sort algorithm's behavior as it sorts an array of words. This illustration assumes, for simplicity, that the leftmost word is chosen as the pivot.

Now let us study the **partitioning** problem. It is very important to understand that we *need not sort* the array while partitioning it. (That would make steps 1.2 and 1.3 of the quick-sort algorithm redundant!) Nor do we need to pre-select the pivot's final position p. The deliberately loose specification of the partitioning problem turns out to be important, because it allows us to develop an efficient partitioning algorithm whose time complexity is $O(n)$.

Numerous partitioning algorithms have been developed. One idea is as follows. First choose some value as the pivot. Then scan the array from the left looking for a value greater than the pivot, and 'simultaneously' scan the array from the right looking for a value less than the pivot; if we find such values, swap them. Repeat the simultaneous scans until they meet. Finally, put the pivot into the position where the scans met.

We shall adopt a simpler idea, which is captured in Algorithm 3.41. Step 1 chooses the value of the leftmost component as the pivot. Step 2 scans from left to right. Whenever step 2.1 finds a value less than the pivot, step 2.1.1 'rotates' three values: the pivot itself, its right neighbor, and the value just found to be less than the pivot. (This rotation is just a three-way swap.)

Figure 3.42 shows the partitioning algorithm's loop invariant: $a[p]$ contains the pivot, $a[left...p - 1]$ contain values known to be less than $a[p]$, and $a[p + 1...r - 1]$ contain

		0	1	2	3	4	5	6	7	8
Initially:	a	fox	cow	pig	cat	rat	lion	tiger	goat	dog
		0	1	2	$p = 3$	4	5	6	7	8
After step 1.1:	a	cow	cat	dog	fox	rat	lion	tiger	goat	pig
		0	1	2	$p = 3$	4	5	6	7	8
After step 1.2:	a	cat	cow	dog	fox	rat	lion	tiger	goat	pig
		0	1	2	$p = 3$	4	5	6	7	8
After step 1.3:	a	cat	cow	dog	fox	goat	lion	pig	rat	tiger

Figure 3.40 Illustration of the array quick-sort algorithm (assuming that the leftmost component is chosen as the pivot).

To partition $a[left...right]$ such that $a[left...p–1]$ are all less than or equal to $a[p]$, and $a[p+1...right]$ are all greater than or equal to $a[p]$:

1. Let *pivot* be the value of $a[left]$, and set $p = left$.
2. For $r = left+1, ..., right$, repeat:
   2.1. If $a[r]$ is less than *pivot*:
      2.1.1. Copy $a[r]$ into $a[p]$, $a[p+1]$ into $a[r]$, and *pivot* into $a[p+1]$.
      2.1.2. Increment p.
3. Terminate with answer p.

Algorithm 3.41 Quick-sort partitioning algorithm. (See the text for variations on step 1.)

values known to be greater than or equal to $a[p]$. In this state, if $a[r]$ contains a value less than the pivot, step 2.1.1 rotates the values in $a[p]$, $a[p+1]$, and $a[r]$. The result of this rotation is that $a[p]$ now contains the value less than the pivot, $a[p+1]$ contains the pivot itself, and $a[r]$ contains a value greater than the pivot. Step 2.1.2 restores the loop invariant by incrementing p (and the loop itself increments r).

There is a subtle point here: how should the rotation behave when $r = p + 1$, i.e., no values greater than the pivot have yet been found? We could make the algorithm test for this situation and simply swap $a[p]$ with $a[r]$. But this is unnecessary: Figure 3.40 fortuitously works even in this situation (at the expense of a redundant copy).

Figure 3.43 illustrates the algorithm's behavior when partitioning the same array as in Figure 3.40. Figure 3.43 may be seen as an expansion of the first step in Figure 3.40.

Program 3.44 shows implementations of the quick-sort and partitioning algorithms as Java methods.

left ... p–1 p p+1 ... r–1 r ... right
a
less than the pivot (unsorted)
pivot
greater than or equal to the pivot (unsorted)
still to be partitioned

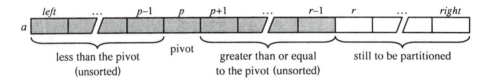

Figure 3.42 Loop invariant for the array partitioning algorithm.

Initially: a
0 1 2 3 4 5 6 7 8
fox cow pig cat rat lion tiger goat dog
Just before step 2: a
p = 0 r = 1 2 3 4 5 6 7 8
fox cow pig cat rat lion tiger goat dog
After 1 iteration of step 2: a
0 p = 1 r = 2 3 4 5 6 7 8
cow fox pig cat rat lion tiger goat dog
After 2 iterations of step 2: a
0 p = 1 2 r = 3 4 5 6 7 8
cow fox pig cat rat lion tiger goat dog
After 3 iterations of step 2: a
0 1 p = 2 3 r = 4 5 6 7 8
cow cat fox pig rat lion tiger goat dog
After 4 iterations of step 2: a
0 1 p = 2 3 4 r = 5 6 7 8
cow cat fox pig rat lion tiger goat dog
After 5 iterations of step 2: a
0 1 p = 2 3 4 5 r = 6 7 8
cow cat fox pig rat lion tiger goat dog
After 6 iterations of step 2: a
0 1 p = 2 3 4 5 6 r = 7 8
cow cat fox pig rat lion tiger goat dog
After 7 iterations of step 2: a
0 1 p = 2 3 4 5 6 7 r = 8
cow cat fox pig rat lion tiger goat dog
After 8 iterations of step 2: a
0 1 2 p = 3 4 5 6 7 8
cow cat dog fox rat lion tiger goat pig

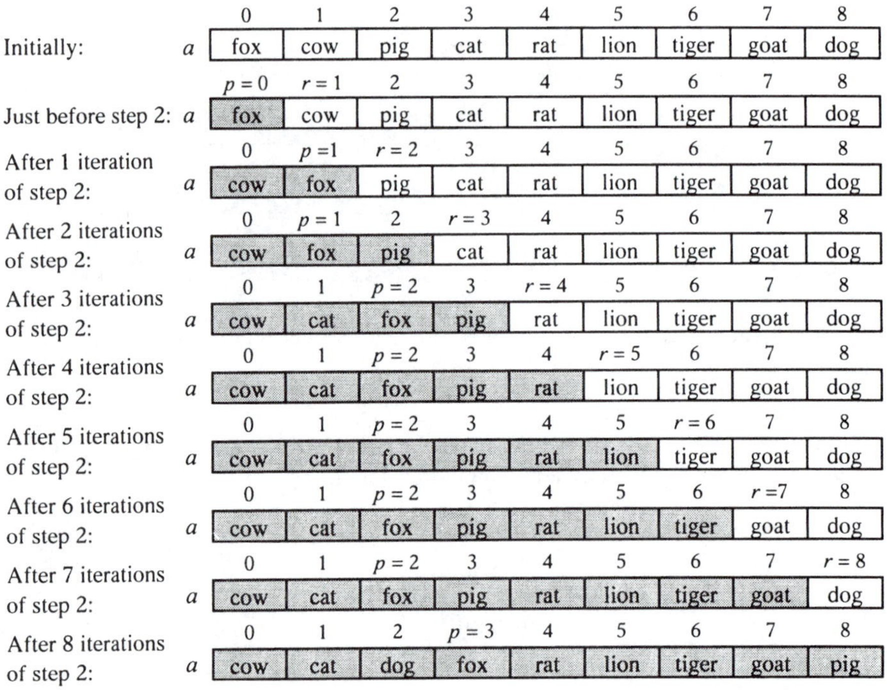

Figure 3.43 Illustration of the array partitioning algorithm.

Now let us analyze the quick-sort algorithm's time efficiency. Let $n = right - left + 1$ be the length of $a[left...right]$, and let $comps(n)$ be the number of comparisons required to sort n components. It is easy to see that the partitioning algorithm will perform about n comparisons. The rest of the analysis depends entirely on the lengths of the left and right subarrays after partitioning. If the left subarray has n' components, step 1.2 will perform $comps(n')$ comparisons. The right subarray will have $n - n' + 1$ components, so step 1.3 will perform $comps(n - n' + 1)$ comparisons. Summing these terms, and noting that no comparisons at all are needed if $n \leq 1$, we get:

$$comps(n) \approx n + comps(n') + comps(n - n' + 1) \qquad \text{if } n > 1 \qquad (3.14a)$$
$$comps(n) = 0 \qquad\qquad\qquad\qquad\qquad\qquad \text{if } n \leq 1 \qquad (3.14b)$$

The quick-sort algorithm's efficiency therefore depends, in a complicated way, on the actual data given to it. To proceed with the analysis, we must make some assumptions.

```java
static void quickSort
                (Comparable[] a, int left, int right) {
   // Sort a[left...right].
   if (left < right) {
      int p = partition(a, left, right);
      quickSort(a, left, p-1);
      quickSort(a, p+1, right);
   }
}

private static int partition
                (Comparable[] a, int left, int right) {
// Partition a[left...right] such that a[left...p-1] are all less than
// or equal to a[p] and a[p+1...right] are all greater than or equal to
// a[p].
   Comparable pivot = a[left];   int p = left;
   for (int r = left+1; r <= right; r++) {
      int comp = a[r].compareTo(pivot);
      if (comp < 0) {
         a[p] = a[r];   a[r] = a[p+1];   a[p+1] = pivot;
         p++;
      }
   }
   return p;
}
```

Program 3.44 Implementation of the array quick-sort algorithm in Java.

Let us start with a *best-case* assumption: that the partitioning step leaves the pivot in the middle of the array. Then n' and $n - n' + 1$ are approximately $n/2$, and we get:

$$comps(n) \approx n + 2\ comps(n/2) \qquad \text{if } n > 1 \tag{3.15a}$$
$$comps(n) = 0 \qquad\qquad\qquad\quad \text{if } n \le 1 \tag{3.15b}$$

The solution (see Appendix A.4) is approximately:

$$comps(n) \approx n\ \log_2 n \tag{3.16}$$

So, on the best-case assumption, the quick-sort algorithm has time complexity $O(n \log n)$. The best-case assumption turns out to be valid if the array is thoroughly unsorted.

Now let us consider a *worst-case* assumption: that the partitioning step leaves the pivot at the left of the array. Then $n' = 0$ and $comps(n') = comps(0) = 0$, so we get:

$$comps(n) = n + comps(n - 1) \qquad \text{if } n > 1 \tag{3.17a}$$
$$comps(n) = 0 \qquad\qquad\qquad\qquad \text{if } n \le 1 \tag{3.17b}$$

The solution (see Appendix A.4) is approximately:

$$comps(n) \approx (n^2 - n)/2 \tag{3.18}$$

So, on the worst-case assumption, the quick-sort algorithm has time complexity $O(n^2)$. The worst-case assumption turns out to be valid if the array is already sorted (or nearly sorted). This is very strange behavior indeed; intuitively we would expect a sorting algorithm to take *less* time when the given array turns out to be already sorted!

Of course, we would never sort an array *known* to be already sorted. But if we are given an unknown array, we do not know whether it is sorted, nearly sorted, or thoroughly unsorted. There is only a tiny probability that an unknown array will happen to be sorted, purely by chance − just as there is only a tiny probability that a shuffled pack of playing cards will happen to be sorted. But in practical data processing things are often not left to chance, and there is quite a high probability that an unknown array will turn out to be sorted (or nearly sorted).

For example, the telephone supervisor responsible for maintaining a business's internal telephone directory might be given a batch of new entries by an assistant. The best way for the supervisor to update the directory is to sort the new entries and then merge them into the directory. But what if the assistant, intending to be helpful, has already sorted the new entries?

If the array is already sorted, $a[left]$ will be the least of $a[left...right]$. But Figure 3.40 chooses the value of $a[left]$ as the pivot, and that pivot will remain at the left end of the array, which is our worst-case assumption. To avoid this situation, the partitioning algorithm should try to choose a pivot that is less likely to be the least value in the array.

One simple idea is to modify Algorithm 3.41 to choose the pivot from the middle of the array:

1. Let *pivot* be the value of $a[m]$ (where m is about midway between *left* and *right*), swap *pivot* into $a[left]$, and set $p = left$.

2. ... (as before).

3. Terminate with answer p.

This works quite well, although there is still a small risk of choosing the least value by chance (or the second-least value, which is almost as bad).

A still better idea is to make the pivot the median of three values taken from the left, middle, and right of the array:

1. Let *pivot* be the median of $a[left]$, $a[m]$, and $a[right]$ (where m is about midway between *left* and *right*), swap *pivot* into $a[left]$ if necessary, and set $p = left$.

2. ... (as before).

3. Terminate with answer p.

This guarantees that the pivot is not the least value, but there is still a small risk of choosing the second-least value by chance.

3.6.5 Comparison

Table 3.45 summarizes the efficiency of the array sorting algorithms we have studied.

The selection sort and insertion sort algorithms both have time complexity $O(n^2)$. However, this simple truth conceals two important points: insertion sort performs only half as many comparisons as selection sort (constant factors do matter when the complexities are the same!), but insertion sort performs far more copies than selection sort. Overall, there is little to choose between them.

The merge-sort and quick-sort algorithms are superior, both having time complexity $O(n \log n)$, at least in the best case. Each has a serious weakness, however. The merge-sort algorithm performs three times as many copies, and needs an auxiliary array of length n, even when the array happens to be sorted. The quick-sort algorithm deteriorates to time complexity $O(n^2)$ in the worst case, which is when the array is sorted or almost sorted and the algorithm is implemented naively. Fortunately, a little care is sufficient to make the worst-case behavior very unlikely to happen in practice, and that makes the quick-sort algorithm a good practical choice.

Table 3.45   Efficiency of array sorting algorithms.

Algorithm	No. of comparisons (approx.)	No. of copies (approx.)	Time complexity	Space complexity
Selection sort	$n^2/2$	$2n$	$O(n^2)$	$O(1)$
Insertion sort	$n^2/4$	$n^2/4$	$O(n^2)$	$O(1)$
Merge-sort	$n \log_2 n$	$2n \log_2 n$	$O(n \log n)$	$O(n)$
Quick-sort (best case)	$n \log_2 n$	$(2n/3) \log_2 n$	$O(n \log n)$	$O(\log n)$
Quick-sort (worst case)	$n^2/2$	0	$O(n^2)$	$O(n)$

Summary

In this chapter:

- We have reviewed the general properties of arrays, and their specific properties in Java.
- We have studied and analyzed array insertion and deletion algorithms.
- We have studied and analyzed the array linear search and binary search algorithms. We found that binary search is significantly faster than linear search.
- We have studied and analyzed the array merging algorithm.
- We have studied and analyzed the array selection sort, insertion sort, merge-sort, and quick-sort algorithms. We found that merge-sort and quick-sort are significantly faster than the others, although quick-sort's performance is variable.

Exercises

3.1 (This exercise is drill for readers unfamiliar with arrays.)

Consider an integer array $a[left...right]$, where $right \geq left$.

(a) Write an algorithm to return the greatest integer in the array.

(b) Write an algorithm to return the position of the greatest integer in the array.

(c) Write an algorithm to sum the integers in the array.

(d) Write an algorithm to count the number of odd and even integers in the array.

(e) Write an algorithm to reverse the order of the integers in the array.

3.2 Write an algorithm to test whether an array $a[left...right]$ is sorted in ascending order.

In terms of the number of comparisons required, determine the time efficiency of your algorithm: in the best case; in the worst case; and on average.

Implement your algorithm as a Java method, assuming that the array elements are `Comparable` objects.

3.3 A *palindrome* is a sequence that is identical to the reverse of itself. For example, the sequence «'m', 'a', 'd', 'a', 'm'» is a palindrome.

Write an algorithm to test whether a character array $a[left...right]$ is a palindrome.

What are the time efficiency and space efficiency of your algorithm?

Implement your algorithm as a Java method.

3.4 Modify the algorithm of Exercise 3.3 to ignore spaces and punctuation. For example, the sentence "Madam, I'm Adam." is a palindrome if we ignore spaces and punctuation.

3.5 Modify Program 3.8 to insert a value `val` of type `double` into an array a of type `double[ ]`.

Repeat this exercise for other Java primitive types: `int` and `char`.

How many methods would you need to cover all possible types in Java?

3.6 Consider Algorithm 3.6 and its implementation in Program 3.8. What would go wrong if step 1 was instead implemented by a for statement that scanned *from left to right* copying each element?

Can you write an algorithm that scans from left to right, but does not have this error? What are its space efficiency and time efficiency?

3.7 Consider the binary search algorithm given in Algorithm 3.16. Hand-test this algorithm with the following array of words:

apple, banana, grape, lime, mango, orange, peach, pear, pineapple, plum

and with each of the following targets: banana; grape; plum; lychees; strawberry. How many comparisons are required in each case?

3.8 Consider Algorithms 3.12 and 3.16. Illustrate each algorithm's behavior as it searches for the target 'lime' in the following array of words:

apple, banana, grape, mango, orange, peach, pear, pineapple, plum.

3.9 Algorithm 3.16 searches the sorted array from left to right. In what circumstances would it be advantageous to search from right to left?

3.10 Devise array algorithms to solve the following problems, and analyze their time complexities:
(a) Delete *val* from an unsorted array *a[left...right]*.
(b) Delete *val* from a sorted array *a[left...right]*.
(c) Insert *val* in a sorted array *a[left...right]*.
(d) Find the least component of an unsorted array *a[left...right]*.

3.11 A simple telephone directory can be represented by an array of objects of the following class:

```
class DirectoryEntry {
    public String name;
    public String number;
}
```

Assume that names are unique but telephone numbers are not unique. The following methods are to be implemented:

```
static String searchByName
                (DirectoryEntry[] dir,
                 String targetName);
// Return the telephone number of the (unique) entry in dir whose
// name equals targetName, or null if there is no such entry.

static String[] searchByNumber
                (DirectoryEntry[] dir,
                 String targetNumber);
// Return an array of all names in dir whose telephone number equals
// targetNumber, or null if there are no such entries.
```

Suppose that searchByName will be called frequently, but searchByNumber will be called only occasionally. How would you organize the directory entries? Implement the two methods accordingly.

3.12 Hand-test the merging algorithm (Algorithm 3.23) to merge the following arrays of names:

James, Tolstoy, Wells

Curie, Einstein, Kelvin, Maxwell

How many name comparisons are required?

3.13 A simple way to represent a *set* of words is by a sorted array of words with no duplicates. You are given two sets of words, s_1 and s_2, represented in this way. By modifying the merging algorithm (Algorithm 3.23), devise algorithms for the following problems:
(a) Compute the *union* of s_1 and s_2. The union is the set of those words found in s_1 or s_2 or both.
(b) Compute the *intersection* of s_1 and s_2. The intersection is the set of those words found in both s_1 and s_2.

3.14 Consider the selection sort algorithm given in Algorithm 3.27.
(a) Hand-test this algorithm with the following array of words:

red, orange, yellow, green, blue, indigo, violet

How many word comparisons and movements are required?
(b) Repeat with the insertion sort algorithm given in Algorithm 3.31.

3.15 Consider the problem of reading a file of (unsorted) values into an array, where the array must be sorted. There are n values in the file.
(a) Write an algorithm to read all of the unsorted values into the array, and then sort the array using the selection sort algorithm given in Algorithm 3.27. What is the time efficiency of your algorithm?
(b) Write an algorithm to read each value in turn, and insert it into a sorted array (initially empty). What is the time efficiency of your algorithm? How does this compare with your answer to part (a)?
(c) Implement your algorithms from parts (a) and (b), and compare them by timing their execution on files with a range of sizes.

3.16 The Dutch national flag problem is as follows. You are given an array of colors (reds, whites, and blues), in no particular order. Sort them into the order of the Dutch national flag (reds followed by whites followed by blues).
(a) Devise an efficient algorithm to solve this problem.
(b) What is your algorithm's time complexity?

3.17 You are given two unsorted arrays of values. You are required to obtain a sorted array containing all these values. Suggest *two* different ways of achieving this. Compare their time efficiency. (*Note:* Assume that suitable merging and sorting algorithms are already available.)

3.18 Devise an algorithm to solve the following problem. Given an array $a[0...n-1]$, and a shorter array $b[0...m-1]$, find the position of the leftmost subarray of a whose elements equal (pairwise) all the elements of b. In other words, if the answer is p, then $a[p]$ must equal $b[0]$, ..., and $a[p+m-1]$ must equal $b[m-1]$.

In the following example, the elements are colors, and the answer should be 3:

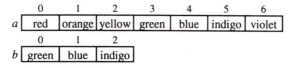

On the other hand, if $b[2]$ were violet, the answer should be *none*, indicating that there is no complete match. Likewise, if the colors in b were in a different order, the answer should be *none*.

What is the time complexity of your algorithm?

* **3.19** Consider the implementations of selection sort (Program 3.30), insertion sort (Program 3.34), merge-sort (Program 3.37), and quick-sort (Program 3.44).

   Modify each of these Java methods to count the number of comparisons and the number of copies. Run the modified sorting methods with a range of array lengths (say 10, 50, 100, 500, 1000, and 5000). Compare your experimental results with the theoretical results given in Table 3.45.

* **3.20** Consider the sorting algorithm given in Algorithm 3.46. This algorithm is known as *bubble sort*. Bubble sort has time complexity $O(n^2)$ and space complexity $O(1)$.
   (a) Hand-test this algorithm with the following array of words:

   red, orange, yellow, green, blue, indigo, violet

   How many word comparisons and copies are required?
   (b) Implement this algorithm as a Java method, then modify your code to count the number of comparisons and the number of copies. Run your method with a range of array lengths. Compare your experimental results with those given in Table 3.45 for other sorting algorithms.

* **3.21** Consider the sorting algorithm given in Algorithm 3.47. This algorithm is known as *Shell sort* (after its inventor, Donald Shell). This version of Shell sort has time complexity $O(n^{1.5})$ and space complexity $O(1)$.
   (a) Hand-test this algorithm with the following array of words:

   red, orange, yellow, green, blue, indigo, violet

   How many word comparisons and copies are required?
   (b) Implement this algorithm as a Java method, then modify your code to count the number of comparisons and the number of copies. Run your method for a range of array lengths.

To sort $a[left...right]$:

1. For $i = 0, ..., right-left+1$, repeat:
   1.1. For $j = left+1, ..., right-i$, repeat:
      1.1.1. If $a[j-1]$ is greater than $a[j]$, swap $a[j-1]$ and $a[j]$.
2. Terminate.

Algorithm 3.46   Array bubble sort algorithm.

Compare your experimental results with those given in Table 3.45 for other sorting algorithms.

To sort *a*[*left*…*right*]:

1. Set *gap* to *right* – *left* + 1.
2. Repeat:
    2.1. Halve *gap* (discarding any remainder).
    2.2. If *gap* is even, increment *gap*.
    2.3. For *i* = *gap*, …, *right*, repeat:
        2.3.1. Copy *a*[*i*] to *current*.
        2.3.2. Set *j* to *i* – *gap*.
        2.3.3. While *j* > *left* and *current* is less than *a*[*j*], repeat:
            2.3.3.1. Copy *a*[*j*] to *a*[*j* + *gap*].
            2.3.3.2. Decrement *j* by *gap*.
        2.3.4. Copy *current* to *a*[*j* + *gap*].
    2.4. If *gap* = 1, terminate.

Algorithm 3.47   Array Shell sort algorithm.

4

Linked-List Data Structures

In this chapter we shall study:

- singly-linked lists and doubly-linked lists (Section 4.1)
- linked-list insertion, deletion, searching, merging, and sorting algorithms (Sections 4.2–6).

This chapter interleaves its explanations of singly-linked lists and doubly-linked lists. If you prefer, on a first reading you can skip the material on doubly-linked lists, namely Sections 4.1.2, 4.2.2, and 4.3.2.

4.1 Linked lists

A *linked list* consists of a sequence of *nodes*, connected by *links*. Each node contains a single element, together with links to one or both neighboring nodes. Figures 4.2 and 4.6 show some examples of linked lists.

A node's *successor* is the next node in the sequence, and its *predecessor* is the previous node in the sequence. The last node in the sequence has no successor, and the first node in the sequence has no predecessor.

By convention, we use a special *null link* wherever there is no node to link to. Thus every node in a linked list contains a link to its successor, but the last node contains a null link instead (indicating that there is no successor).

We routinely use diagrams such as Figures 4.2 and 4.6 to illustrate linked lists. A link is shown as a small black circle at the tail of an arrow, and a null link is shown as a small black circle without an arrow. A node is shown as a box, which contains an element and one or more links. These conventions are summarized in Figure 4.1.

The *length* of a linked list is the number of nodes (elements) in it. A linked list is *empty* if it has length zero, i.e., no nodes at all.

A linked list can be of any length, and can therefore contain any number of elements. We can access the element in any node, provided that we have a link to that node.

Another important property of linked lists is that we can manipulate the links. This makes it possible to achieve a variety of effects. We can insert and delete nodes, thus

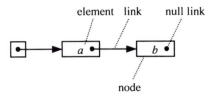

Figure 4.1 Key to diagrams of linked data structures.

varying the linked list's length dynamically. We can change the order of the nodes. In fact, we can make arbitrary changes to a linked list's structure simply by manipulating the links. (Such effects are simply not possible with arrays.)

In linked lists we have a choice between linking each node to one or both of its immediate neighbors. Thus we have two different data structures to study in this chapter:

- singly-linked lists (SLLs)
- doubly-linked lists (DLLs).

4.1.1 Singly-linked lists

A *singly-linked list* (or *SLL*) consists of a sequence of nodes with the following properties:

- Each SLL node contains an element, together with a link to its successor (or a null link if the node has no successor).
- The SLL has a *header*, which contains a link to the SLL's first node (or a null link if the SLL is empty).

Figure 4.2 shows various SLLs. The SLL (a) consists of three nodes, which contain the words 'ant', 'bat', and 'cat', respectively; this SLL's header contains a link to the node containing 'ant', which in turn is linked to the node containing 'bat', which in turn is linked to the node containing 'cat', which being the last node contains a null link. The SLLs (b) and (c) have different numbers of nodes and different elements. The SLL (d) is empty, so its header contains a null link.

In Java, we can represent SLL headers by objects of the class SLL, shown in Program 4.3, and SLL nodes by objects of the class SLLNode, shown in Program 4.4. Each

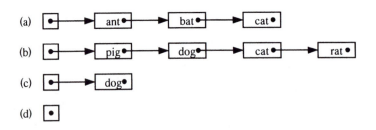

Figure 4.2 Singly-linked lists.

```
public class SLL {

    //  Each SLL object is an SLL header.

    //  This SLL is represented by a reference to its first node (first).
    private SLLNode first;

    public SLL () {
    //  Construct an empty SLL.
        this.first = null;
    }

    ...   //  SLL methods (see below).

}
```

Program 4.3   Java class representing SLL headers.

SLLNode object has two instance variables. The instance variable `element` is of type `Object`. The instance variable `succ` is itself of type `SLLNode`, which means that it will contain either a reference to another `SLLNode` object (the node's successor) or **null** (which refers to no object at all). Each `SLL` object has a single instance variable, `first`, containing a reference to the SLL's first node.

Note that the `SLLNode` class's instance variables and constructor are declared as *protected*, so that they can be accessed by the methods of the `SLL` class.

An SLL, then, will be represented by an `SLL` object (the header) together with a group of `SLLNode` objects (the nodes). The structures of `SLL` and `SLLNode` objects are shown in detail in Figure 4.5. In our diagrams, however, we will generally adopt the uncluttered style of Figure 4.2.

```
public class SLLNode {

    //  Each SLLNode object is an SLL node.

    //  This node consists of an element (element) and a link to its
    //  successor (succ).
    protected Object element;
    protected SLLNode succ;

    protected SLLNode (Object elem, SLLNode succ) {
    //  Construct an SLL node with element elem and successor succ.
        this.element = elem;
        this.succ = succ;
    }

}
```

Program 4.4   Java class representing SLL nodes.

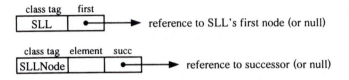

Figure 4.5 Detailed structures of SLL objects and SLLNode objects.

Note the terminology used here. When we talk in general terms about linked-list data structures and algorithms, we talk about *nodes* connected by *links*. When we talk about their implementation in Java, we represent nodes by *objects* connected by *references* to other objects. (In fact, every Java object is accessed through a reference.)

EXAMPLE 4.1 *SLL construction*

The following Java code and diagrams illustrate construction of an SLL:

```
SLLNode c = new SLLNode("cat", null),
SLL zoo1 = new SLL();
```

```
zoo1.first = new SLLNode("ant",
                new SLLNode("bat", c));
```

EXAMPLE 4.2 *SLL traversal*

The following Java method traverses an SLL from its first node to its last node:

```
public void printFirstToLast () {
// Print all the elements in this SLL, in first-to-last order.
   for (SLLNode curr = first; curr != null;
       curr = curr.succ)
     System.out.print(curr.element + " ");
}
```

This would be an instance method of the SLL class.

The local variable `curr` (an abbreviation of 'current') is made to refer to each node of the SLL in turn. Initially it refers to the first node (`curr = first`). Each iteration of the loop accesses the element in the node that `curr` refers to (`curr.element`), and then updates `curr` to refer to that node's successor (`curr = curr.succ`). Iteration continues as long as the end of the SLL has not been reached (`curr != null`).

A typical call to this method would be:

```
zoo1.printFirstToLast();
```

where `zoo1` is the `SLL` object created in Example 4.1. The following diagram shows the method's progress:

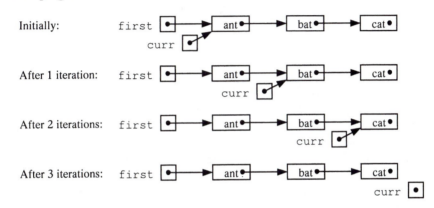

The printed output should be 'ant bat cat '.

If the SLL is empty, `first` is null, and the method prints nothing at all.

Example 4.2 illustrated traversal of an SLL. In general, ***traversal*** of a data structure means visiting some or all of its nodes in some predetermined order. It is straightforward to traverse an SLL in first-to-last order.

EXAMPLE 4.3   *SLL manipulation*

Consider an SLL whose nodes contain 'ant', 'bat', 'cat', etc:

Each of the following code fragments manipulates the above SLL's structure in a different way. Assume that `first` is a link to the SLL's first node.

(a) The following code fragment deletes the SLL's first node:

```
first = first.succ;
```

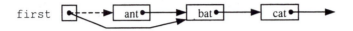

The variable first is simply updated to refer to the first node's successor (i.e., the second node). Now, if we follow the links from first, we see that the SLL's nodes contain 'bat', 'cat', etc. The node containing 'ant' is no longer part of the SLL. (If nothing else refers to that node, Java will automatically deallocate it.)

The above code fragment assumes that the SLL has at least one node initially. If the SLL has exactly one node, first.succ is null and the code fragment makes first null. This is correct behavior.

(b) The following code fragment deletes the SLL's second node:

```
SLLNode second = first.succ;
first.succ = second.succ;
```

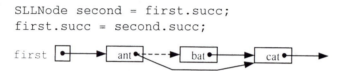

The local variable second is made to refer to the second node, then the first node's successor is updated to be the second node's successor (i.e., the third node). Now, if we follow the links from first, we see that the SLL's nodes contain 'ant', 'cat', etc. The node containing 'bat' is no longer part of the SLL.

The above code fragment assumes that the SLL has at least two nodes initially. If the SLL has exactly two nodes, second.succ is null; the code fragment still works correctly.

(c) The following code fragment swaps the SLL's first and second nodes:

```
SLLNode second = first.succ;
first.succ = second.succ;
second.succ = first;
first = second;
```

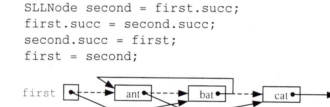

The declaration and first statement unlink the second node, as in (b), but the local variable second still refers to this node. The remaining two statements link this node back into the SLL, this time as the first node. Now, if we follow the links from first, we see that the SLL's nodes contain 'bat', 'ant', 'cat', etc.

The above code fragment assumes that the SLL has at least two nodes initially.

This example has demonstrated how easy it is to restructure an SLL, simply by manipulating links. There is no need to disturb the elements contained in the nodes.

When we restructure a linked list, however, we must take great care to update all the links correctly. Omitting to update even one link would fatally damage the linked list's structure. In practice this is a common programming error.

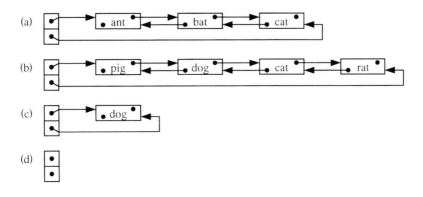

Figure 4.6   Doubly-linked lists.

The characteristic feature of an SLL is that each node contains a link to its successor only. This allows us to visit nodes *from first to last*. This was illustrated in different ways by Example 4.3 (accessing the second node from the first node) and Example 4.2 (traversing the whole SLL first-to-last).

The weakness of SLLs is that there is no easy way to visit nodes *from last to first*. This observation motivates us to consider an alternative data structure.

4.1.2 Doubly-linked lists

A *doubly-linked list* (or *DLL*) consists of a sequence of nodes, with the following properties:

- Each DLL node contains an element, together with a link to its predecessor (or null if it has no predecessor) and a link to its successor (or null if it has no successor).
- The DLL has a *header*, which contains a link to the DLL's first node and a link to the DLL's last node (both links being null if the DLL is empty).

Figure 4.6 shows various DLLs. (Compare with Figure 4.2.) The DLL (a) consists of three nodes, and its header contains links to the first and last (third) nodes. The DLL (c) has a single node, and its header contains two links to that single node. The DLL (d) is empty, and its header contains two null links.

In Java, we can represent DLL headers by objects of class DLL, shown in Program 4.7, and DLL nodes by objects of class DLLNode, shown in Program 4.8. The detailed structures of these objects are shown in Figure 4.9. Compared to an SLLNode object, each DLLNode object has an extra instance variable, pred, and both succ and pred are of type DLLNode.

EXAMPLE 4.4 *DLL construction*

The following Java code and diagrams illustrate construction of a DLL:

```
DLLNode a = new DLLNode("ant", null, null),
         b = new DLLNode("bat", null, null);
DLL zoo2 = new DLL();
zoo2.first = a;   zoo2.last = b;

a.succ = b;   b.pred = a;
```

```
a.succ = b;   b.pred = a;
```

EXAMPLE 4.5 *DLL traversal*

We can trivially modify the method `printFirstToLast` of Example 4.2 to print all the elements in a *DLL* in first-to-last order.

```
public class DLL {

    // Each DLL object is a DLL header.

    // This DLL is represented by a link to its first node (first) and a link
    // to its last node (last).
    private DLLNode first, last;

    public DLL () {
    // Construct an empty DLL.
        this.first = null;   this.last = null;
    }

    ...   // DLL methods (see below).

}
```

Program 4.7 Java class representing DLL headers.

The following method is a mirror-image:

```
public void printLastToFirst () {
// Print all the elements in this DLL, in last-to-first order.
   for (DLLNode curr = last; curr != null;
        curr = curr.pred)
     System.out.print(curr.element + " ");
}
```

This would be an instance method of the DLL class. A typical method call would be:

```
zoo2.printFirstToLast();
```

where zoo2 is the DLL object created in Example 4.4. The printed output should be 'bat ant '.

```
public class DLLNode {

   // Each DLLNode object is a DLL node.

   // This node consists of an element (element), a link to its predecessor
   // (pred), and a link to its successor (succ).
   protected Object element;
   protected DLLNode pred, succ;

   protected DLLNode (Object elem,
                DLLNode pred, DLLNode succ) {
   // Construct a DLL node with element elem, predecessor pred, and
   // successor succ.
      this.element = elem;
      this.pred = pred;
      this.succ = succ;
   }

}
```

Program 4.8 Java class representing DLL nodes.

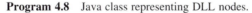

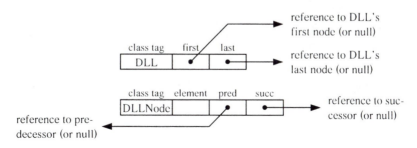

Figure 4.9 Detailed structures of DLL objects and DLLNode objects.

EXAMPLE 4.6   *DLL manipulation*

Consider the following DLL, headed by `first` and `last`:

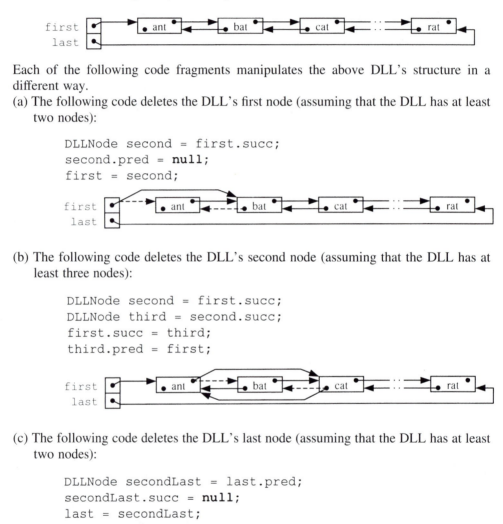

Each of the following code fragments manipulates the above DLL's structure in a different way.

(a) The following code deletes the DLL's first node (assuming that the DLL has at least two nodes):

```
DLLNode second = first.succ;
second.pred = null;
first = second;
```

(b) The following code deletes the DLL's second node (assuming that the DLL has at least three nodes):

```
DLLNode second = first.succ;
DLLNode third = second.succ;
first.succ = third;
third.pred = first;
```

(c) The following code deletes the DLL's last node (assuming that the DLL has at least two nodes):

```
DLLNode secondLast = last.pred;
secondLast.succ = null;
last = secondLast;
```

(d) The following code swaps the DLL's last and second-last nodes (assuming that the

DLL has at least three nodes):

```
DLLNode secondLast = last.pred;
DLLNode thirdLast = secondLast.pred;
thirdLast.succ = last;
last.succ = secondLast;
secondLast.succ = null;
last.pred = thirdLast;
secondLast.pred = last;
last = secondLast;
```

Comparing Example 4.6 with Example 4.3, we see that we can restructure a DLL in much the same way as we restructure an SLL, except that we must update the predecessor links as well as the successor links. Therefore, even greater care is needed to update all the links correctly, and DLL-manipulating code is even more error-prone than SLL-manipulating code. The great advantage of DLLs is their symmetry: we can access any DLL node's predecessor as easily as its successor, and we can access the DLL's last node as easily as its first node.

It is often convenient to view a DLL as a ***backward SLL*** superimposed on a ***forward SLL***, as illustrated in Figure 4.10. If the DLL is headed by the pair of links (*first*, *last*), its forward SLL is headed by *first* and linked by successor links; and its backward SLL is headed by *last* and linked by predecessor links. The forward and backward SLLs share the same nodes.

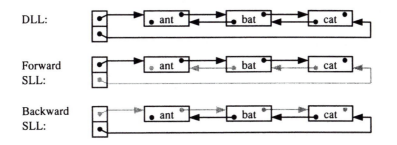

Figure 4.10   A DLL viewed as a backward SLL superimposed on a forward SLL.

4.1.3 Sorted linked lists

A (singly- or doubly-) linked list is ***sorted*** if the elements in its nodes are in ascending order, i.e., the element in each node of the linked list is less than or equal to the element in that node's successor. This definition is analogous to the definition of a sorted array in Section 3.1.2.

Sorted linked lists can be merged, and can be searched a little more efficiently than unsorted linked lists. An unsorted linked list can be sorted. We shall see in this chapter that some (but not all) searching, merging, and sorting algorithms can be adapted to linked lists.

4.2 Insertion

In this section we shall study algorithms for inserting a new node at some point in a linked list. There are potentially four different cases to be handled:

(1) Insertion in an empty linked list.
(2) Insertion before the first node of a nonempty linked list.
(3) Insertion after the last node of a nonempty linked list.
(4) Insertion between nodes of a nonempty linked list.

In general, the insertion algorithm must be given (or must obtain for itself) links to one or both of the new node's future neighbors, in order to allow the new node to be linked properly.

4.2.1 Insertion in a singly-linked list

Algorithm 4.11 inserts a new node at some point in the SLL headed by *first*. Step 1 creates the new node. What follows depends on where the new node is to be inserted.

Step 2 inserts the new node before the first node. The new node's successor becomes *first*, and *first* itself becomes a link to the new node. Step 2 handles case (2) above; fortuitously it also handles case (1), if *first* happens to be null.

Step 3 inserts the new node after some indicated node, given a link *pred* to the indicated node. The new node's successor is set to the former successor of node *pred*, and node *pred*'s successor becomes the new node. Step 3 handles case (4) above; fortuitously it also handles case (3), if *pred* happens to be a link to the last node.

Figure 4.12 illustrates the SLL insertion algorithm's behavior.

To insert *elem* at a given point in the nonempty SLL headed by *first*:

1. Make *ins* a link to a newly-created node with element *elem* and successor null.
2. If the insertion point is before the first node:
   2.1. Set node *ins*'s successor to *first*.
   2.2. Set *first* to *ins*.
3. If the insertion point is after the node *pred*:
   3.1. Set node *ins*'s successor to node *pred*'s successor.
   3.2. Set node *pred*'s successor to *ins*.
4. Terminate.

Algorithm 4.11   SLL insertion algorithm.

The SLL insertion algorithm has time complexity $O(1)$. In other words, it takes a constant amount of time, regardless of the length of the SLL.

An implementation of the SLL insertion algorithm as a Java method, `insert`, is shown in Program 4.13. This would be an instance method of the SLL class of Program 4.3. The method assumes that insertion before the first node is intended if its parameter `pred` is null. The method should be called as follows:

```
zoo1.insert("fox", prev);
```

This inserts a new node after node `prev` in the SLL headed by `zoo1`.

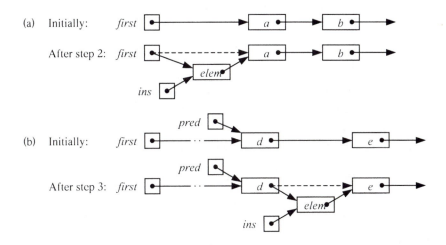

Figure 4.12 Illustration of the SLL insertion algorithm: (a) insertion before first node; (b) insertion after an indicated node.

```
public void insert (Object elem, SLLNode pred) {
    // Insert elem at a given point in this SLL. The insertion point is after the
    // node pred, or before the first node if pred is null.
    SLLNode ins = new SLLNode(elem, null);
    if (pred == null) {              // Insert before first node (if any).
        ins.succ = first;
        first = ins;
    } else {                         // Insert after node pred.
        ins.succ = pred.succ;
        pred.succ = ins;
    }
}
```

Program 4.13 Implementation of the SLL insertion algorithm as a Java method (in class SLL).

4.2.2 Insertion in a doubly-linked list

Algorithm 4.14 inserts a new node at a given point in a DLL headed by (*first*, *last*). Step 1 creates the new node. We divide the rest of the algorithm into two parts: step 2 inserts the new node into the forward SLL headed by *first*; and step 4 inserts the new node into the backward SLL headed by *last*. In the forward SLL, we insert the new node after the given insertion point. In the backward SLL, we insert the new node 'after' the new node's successor.

These two insertion steps are essentially instances of the SLL insertion algorithm given in Algorithm 4.11, but without the creation of a new node in that algorithm. For the backward SLL, however, we must remember that the appropriate links are the mirror image of the forward SLL, i.e., we replace predecessor with successor, *first* with *last*, and *pred* with *succ*. The forward and backward SLL insertion algorithms are shown as auxiliary algorithms in Algorithm 4.14.

To insert *elem* at a given point in a DLL headed by (*first*, *last*):

1. Make *ins* a link to a newly-created node with element *elem*, predecessor null, and successor null.
2. Insert *ins* at the insertion point in the forward SLL headed by *first*.
3. Let *succ* be *ins*'s successor (or null if *ins* has no successor).
4. Insert *ins* after node *succ* in the backward SLL headed by *last*.
5. Terminate.

To insert node *ins* at a given point in the forward SLL headed by *first*:

1. If the insertion point is before the first node:
   1.1. Set node *ins*'s successor to *first*.
   1.2. Set *first* to *ins*.
2. If the insertion point is after the node *pred*:
   2.1. Set node *ins*'s successor to node *pred*'s successor.
   2.2. Set node *pred*'s successor to *ins*.
3. Terminate.

To insert node *ins* after node *succ* in the backward SLL headed by *last*:

1. If *succ* is null:
   1.1. Set node *ins*'s predecessor to *last*.
   1.2. Set *last* to *ins*.
2. If *succ* is not null:
   2.1. Set node *ins*'s predecessor to node *succ*'s predecessor.
   2.2. Set node *succ*'s predecessor to *ins*.
3. Terminate.

Algorithm 4.14   DLL insertion algorithm (with auxiliary forward and backward SLL insertion algorithms).

Figure 4.15 illustrates the DLL insertion algorithm's behavior when the DLL is non-empty.

The DLL insertion algorithm, like the SLL insertion algorithm, has time complexity $O(1)$.

We can implement the DLL insertion algorithm as a Java method, `insert`, and two auxiliary methods, `insertNodeForwards` and `insertNodeBackwards`, as shown in Program 4.16. These would be instance methods of the DLL class of Program 4.7. A typical call to the `insert` method would be:

```
zoo2.insert("fox", prev);
```

This inserts a new node after node `prev` in the DLL headed by `zoo2`.

4.3 Deletion

We have already illustrated the basic ideas for deleting nodes from linked lists (in

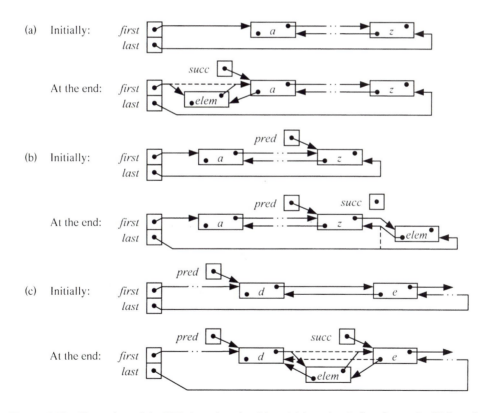

Figure 4.15 Illustration of the DLL insertion algorithm: (a) insertion before first node; (b) insertion after last node; (c) insertion after first or intermediate node.

Examples 4.1 and 4.4). In this section we shall study algorithms for deleting any given node from a nonempty linked list. There are potentially four different cases to be handled:

(1) The node to be deleted is the only node of the linked list.
(2) The node to be deleted is the first (but not the last) node of the linked list.

```java
public void insert (Object elem, DLLNode pred) {
// Insert elem at a given point in this DLL. The insertion point is after the
// node pred, or before the first node if pred is null.
   DLLNode ins = new DLLNode(elem, null, null);
   insertNodeForwards(ins, pred);
   DLLNode succ = ins.succ;
   insertNodeBackwards(ins, succ);
}

private void insertNodeForwards (DLLNode ins,
                  DLLNode pred) {
// Insert the node ins at a given point in the forward SLL of this DLL.
// The insertion point is after the node pred, or before the first node if
// pred is null.
   if (pred == null) {    // Insert before first node (if any).
      ins.succ = first;
      first = ins;
   } else {                 // Insert after node pred.
      ins.succ = pred.succ;
      pred.succ = ins;
   }
}

private void insertNodeBackwards (DLLNode ins,
                  DLLNode succ) {
// Insert the node ins at a given point in the backward SLL of this DLL.
// The insertion point is after the node succ, or before the last node if
// succ is null.
   if (succ == null) {    // Insert before last node (if any).
      ins.pred = last;
      last = ins;
   } else {                 // Insert after node succ.
      ins.pred = succ.pred;
      succ.pred = ins;
   }
}
```

Program 4.16   Implementation of the DLL insertion algorithm as a Java method (in class DLL).

(3) The node to be deleted is the last (but not the first) node of the linked list.

(4) The node to be deleted is an intermediate (neither first nor last) node of the linked list.

The deletion algorithm must be given (or must obtain for itself) links to both neighbors of the node to be deleted, in order to allow the neighbors to be linked to each other.

4.3.1 Deletion in a singly-linked list

Algorithm 4.17 deletes a node from the nonempty SLL headed by *first*. Everything depends on which node is to be deleted.

Step 2 deletes the SLL's first node. The new first node is the former first node's successor. Step 2 handles case (2) above; fortuitously it also handles case (1), if the first node's successor happens to be null.

Step 3 deletes some other node from an SLL. Step 3.1 finds the predecessor of the node to be deleted, and step 3.2 updates the predecessor's successor to be the deleted node's successor. In this way, the deleted node is unlinked from the SLL. Step 3 handles case (4) above; fortuitously it also handles case (3), if the deleted node's successor happens to be null.

Figure 4.18 illustrates the SLL deletion algorithm's behavior.

We can implement the SLL deletion algorithm as a Java method, `delete`, shown in Program 4.19. This would be an instance method of the `SLL` class of Program 4.3. A typical call to the method would be:

```
zoo1.delete(old);
```

which deletes the node `old` in the SLL headed by `zoo1`.

Algorithm 4.17 half-conceals an implementation problem. Step 3.1 needs a link to the node *del*'s predecessor. But an SLL node does not contain a link to its predecessor, and the only way to implement this step is a loop that traverses the SLL from its first node. If the SLL's length is n, this loop could be iterated any number of times from 0 to $n - 1$, or $(n - 1)/2$ times on average. Thus Algorithm 4.17 has time complexity $O(n)$, which in practice is unacceptable.

To delete node *del* in the nonempty SLL headed by *first*:

1. Let *succ* be node *del*'s successor.
2. If *del* = *first*:
   2.1. Set *first* to *succ*.
3. Otherwise (if *del* ≠ *first*):
   3.1. Let *pred* be node *del*'s predecessor.
   3.2. Set node *pred*'s successor to *succ*.
4. Terminate.

Algorithm 4.17   SLL deletion algorithm.

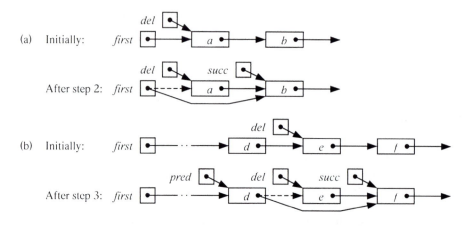

Figure 4.18 Illustration of the SLL deletion algorithm: (a) deletion of first node; (b) deletion of intermediate or last node.

```
public void delete (SLLNode del) {
// Delete node del in this SLL.
   SLLNode succ = del.succ;
   if (del == first)
      first = succ;
   else {
      SLLNode pred = first;
      while (pred.succ != del)
         pred = pred.succ;
      pred.succ = succ;
   }
}
```

Program 4.19 Implementation of the SLL deletion algorithm as a Java method (in class SLL).

4.3.2 Deletion in a doubly-linked list

Algorithm 4.20 deletes a node from the nonempty DLL headed by the pair of links (*first*, *last*). As in the DLL insertion algorithm (Section 4.2.2), we divide the problem into two parts: delete the node from the forward SLL headed by *first*, and delete the node from the backward SLL headed by *last*.

Step 2 deletes the node from the forward SLL headed by *first*. It uses an auxiliary algorithm analogous to the SLL deletion algorithm given as Algorithm 4.17.

Step 3 deletes the node from the backward SLL head by *last*. It uses an auxiliary algorithm that is the mirror-image of the SLL deletion algorithm.

Figure 4.21 illustrates the DLL deletion algorithm's behavior.

To delete node *del* in the nonempty DLL headed by (*first*, *last*):

1. Let *pred* and *succ* be node *del*'s predecessor and successor, respectively.
2. Delete node *del*, whose predecessor is *pred*, from the forward SLL headed by *first*.
3. Delete node *del*, whose successor is *succ*, from the backward SLL headed by *last*.
4. Terminate.

To delete node *del*, whose predecessor is *pred*, from the forward SLL headed by *first*:

1. If *pred* is null:
    1.1. Set *first* to node *del*'s successor.
2. If *pred* is not null:
    2.1. Set node *pred*'s successor to node *del*'s successor.
3. Terminate.

To delete node *del*, whose successor is *succ*, from the backward SLL headed by *last*:

1. If *succ* is null:
    1.1. Set *last* to node *del*'s predecessor.
2. If *succ* is not *null*:
    2.1. Set node *succ*'s predecessor to node *del*'s predecessor.
3. Terminate.

Algorithm 4.20   DLL deletion algorithm (with auxiliary forward and backward SLL deletion algorithms).

The DLL deletion algorithm has time complexity $O(1)$, a huge improvement on the SLL deletion algorithm which is $O(n)$. The difference is that each DLL node contains a link to its own predecessor, so there is no need to traverse the DLL to establish a link to the predecessor.

We can implement the DLL insertion algorithm as a Java method, `delete`, and two auxiliary methods, `deleteNodeForwards` and `deleteNodeBackwards`, as shown in Program 4.22. These would be instance methods of the DLL class of Program 4.7. A typical call to the `delete` method would be:

```
zoo2.delete(old);
```

which deletes the node `old` in the DLL headed by `zoo2`.

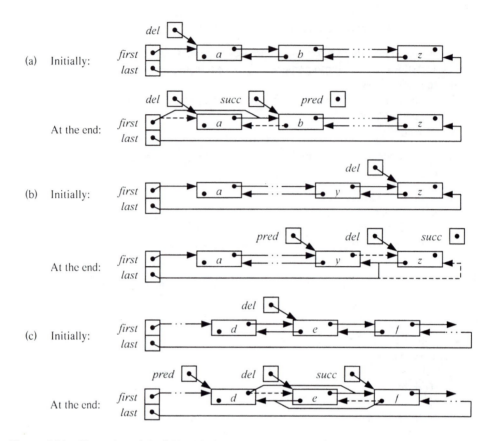

Figure 4.21 Illustration of the DLL deletion algorithm: (a) deletion of first (but not last) node; (b) deletion of last (but not first) node; (c) deletion of intermediate node.

4.4 Searching

We studied array linear search algorithms in Section 3.4.1. Linear search can easily be adapted for linked lists.

Algorithm 4.23 shows the linear search algorithm for an *unsorted* SLL. The algorithm traverses the SLL first-to-last, terminating if it reaches a node that contains an element equal to the target.

The unsorted SLL linear search algorithm performs exactly the same number of comparisons as its array counterpart (Algorithm 3.12): about $n/2$ comparisons (on average) for a successful search, or exactly n comparisons for an unsuccessful search, where n is the SLL's length. The algorithm's time complexity is therefore $O(n)$.

Program 4.24 shows how the SLL linear search algorithm could be implemented as a Java method, `search`. This would be an instance method of the `SLL` class.

If the SLL is known to be sorted, it is possible to speed up the linear search algorithm.

The algorithm would traverse the SLL first-to-last, terminating if it reaches a node that contains an element equal to *or greater than* the target. (See Exercise 4.7.)

Of course, linear search of a DLL is also possible. We have the additional option of searching a DLL last-to-first, and in some circumstances this is advantageous. (See Exercise 4.8.)

```
public void delete (DLNode del) {
   // Delete node del in this DLL.
   deleteNodeForwards(del, del.pred);
   deleteNodeBackwards(del, del.succ);
}

private void deleteNodeForwards (DLLNode del,
                DLLNode pred) {
// Delete node del, whose predecessor is pred, from the forward SLL.
//  If pred is null, then del is the first node in the forward SLL.
   DLLNode succ = del.succ;
   if (pred == null)
      first = succ;
   else
      pred.succ = succ;
}

private void deleteNodeBackwards (DLLNode del,
                DLLNode succ) {
// Delete the node del, whose successor is succ, from the backward SLL.
// If succ is null, then del is the first node in the backward SLL.
   DLLNode pred = del.pred;
   if (succ == null)
      last = pred;
   else
      succ.pred = pred;
}
```

Program 4.22   Implementation of the DLL deletion algorithm as a Java method (in class DLL).

To find which if any node of the SLL headed by *first* contains an element equal to *target*:

1. For each node *curr* of the SLL headed by *first*, repeat:
   1.1. If *target* is equal to node *curr*'s element, terminate with answer *curr*.
2. Terminate with answer *none*.

Algorithm 4.23   Unsorted SLL linear search algorithm.

```
public SLLNode search (Object target) {
  //  Find which if any node of this SLL equals target. Return a link to the
  //  matching node (or null if there is none).
     for (SLLNode curr = first; curr != null;
          curr = curr.succ) {
        if (target.equals(curr.element))
           return curr;
     }
     return null;
}
```

Program 4.24   Implementation of the unsorted SLL search algorithm as a Java method (in class SLL).

Binary search is efficient for arrays, because the middle component of an array can be accessed directly, using simple arithmetic to compute its index. But binary search would be worthless for linked lists, because the middle node of a linked list could be accessed only by counting $n/2$ nodes from the first (assuming that we already know the linked list's length n). Such a traversal would take $O(n)$ time, thus destroying the $O(\log n)$ time complexity that we aim to achieve with binary search.

4.5 Merging

The array merging algorithm of Section 3.5 can easily be adapted for sorted linked lists. Elements from the two given linked lists will be successively appended to a third linked list, which is initially empty.

Algorithm 4.25 merges two given sorted SLLs. It performs a kind of simultaneous traversal of both these SLLs, using variables *cur1* and *cur2* respectively. The variables *first* and *last*, initially null, are links to the first and last nodes of the merged SLL.

Each of the steps 2.1.1, 2.2.1, 3.1, and 4.1 appends an element to the merged SLL, i.e., inserts that element after the node *last*. This is similar to what the SLL insertion algorithm (Algorithm 4.11) does, but with an important new detail: both *first* and *last* must be kept up-to-date. So Algorithm 4.25 is written in terms of a merged SLL whose header is a pair of links (*first*, *last*). An auxiliary algorithm specifically designed to append an element to the merged list is included.

Figure 4.26 shows the SLL merging algorithm's loop invariant. Figure 4.27 illustrates the merging of two linked lists of words.

The SLL merging algorithm performs exactly the same number of comparisons as the array merging algorithm (Algorithm 3.23). Therefore its time complexity is $O(n_1 + n_2)$ or $O(n)$, where n_1 and n_2 are the lengths of the two given SLLs, and $n = n_1 + n_2$ is the length of the merged SLL.

Program 4.28 declares a class AppendableSLL, whose objects are SLL headers with

To merge two sorted SLLs, headed by *first1* and *first2* respectively:

1. Set *cur1* to *first1*, set *cur2* to *first2*, set *first* to null, and set *last* to null.
2. While *cur1* is not null and *cur2* is not null, repeat:
    2.1. If *cur1*'s element is less than or equal to *cur2*'s element:
        2.1.1. Append *cur1*'s element to the SLL headed by (*first*, *last*).
        2.1.2. Set *cur1* to *cur1*'s successor.
    2.2. If *cur1*'s element is greater than or equal to *cur2*'s element:
        2.2.1. Append *cur2*'s element to the SLL headed by (*first*, *last*).
        2.2.2. Set *cur2* to *cur2*'s successor.
3. While *cur1* is not null, repeat:
    3.1. Append *cur1*'s element to the SLL headed by (*first*, *last*).
    3.2. Set *cur1* to *cur1*'s successor.
4. While *cur2* is not null, repeat:
    4.1. Append *cur2*'s element to the SLL headed by (*first*, *last*).
    4.2. Set *cur2* to *cur2*'s successor.
5. Terminate with the SLL headed by *first* as answer.

To append *elem* to the SLL headed by (*first*, *last*):

1. Make *app* a link to a newly-created node with element *elem* and successor null.
2. If *last* is null:
    2.1. Set *first* to *app*.
3. If *last* is not null:
    3.1. Set node *last*'s successor to *app*.
4. Set *last* to *app*.
5. Terminate.

Algorithm 4.25   SLL merging algorithm (with auxiliary appending algorithm).

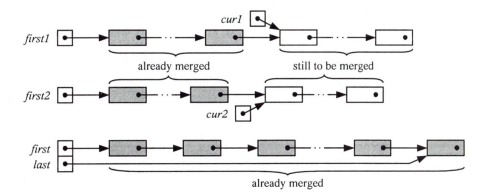

Figure 4.26   Loop invariant for the SLL merging algorithm.

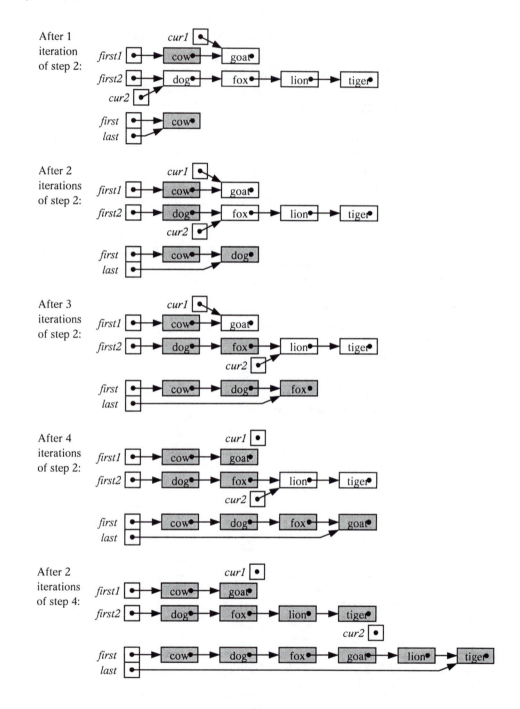

Figure 4.27 Illustration of the SLL merging algorithm.

links to both first and last nodes. AppendableSLL is a subclass of SLL, and is equipped with a method that implements the auxiliary appending algorithm.

Program 4.29 shows how the SLL merging algorithm could be implemented as a Java method, merge. The local variable list3, whose type is AppendableSLL, is used to build up the merged list.

4.6 Sorting

We studied several array sorting algorithms in Section 3.6. Some of these sorting algorithms can be adapted for linked lists.

Algorithm 4.30 shows the SLL *insertion sort* algorithm. It repeatedly removes the unsorted SLL's first node and inserts that node into a second, sorted SLL, which is initially empty. When all nodes have been removed from the unsorted SLL, the algorithm's answer is the sorted SLL.

The auxiliary algorithm inserts an *existing* node into a sorted SLL. It does this entirely by manipulating links: unlike Algorithm 4.11, it copies no element and creates no new node.

Figure 4.31 shows the SLL insertion sort algorithm's loop invariant. The SLL headed by *sorted* consists of the first few nodes from the original SLL, sorted. The SLL headed by *unsorted* consists of the remaining nodes from the original SLL, undisturbed. Figure

```
public class AppendableSLL extends SLL {
    // Each AppendableSLL object is an SLL header, with links to both first
    // and last nodes.

    protected SLLNode last;

    protected AppendableSLL () {
    // Construct an empty SLL.
        this.first = null;  this.last = null;
    }

    protected void append (Object elem) {
    // Append elem to this SLL.
        SLLNode app = new SLLNode(elem, null);
        if (last == null)
            first = app;
        else
            last.succ = app;
        last = app;
    }

}
```

Program 4.28 Java class representing SLL headers equipped with an appending operation.

```
public static SLL merge (SLL list1, SLL list2) {
// Merge two sorted SLLs, list1 and list2. Return the merged SLL.
   AppendableSLL list3 = new AppendableSLL();
   SLLNode cur1 = list1.first, cur2 = list2.first;
   while (cur1 != null && cur2 != null) {
      Comparable elem1 = (Comparable) cur1.element;
      Comparable elem2 = (Comparable) cur2.element;
      int comp = elem1.compareTo(elem2);
      if (comp <= 0) {
         list3.append(elem1);   cur1 = cur1.succ;
      } else {
         list3.append(elem2);   cur2 = cur2.succ;
      }
   }
   while (cur1 != null) {
      list3.append(cur1.element);   cur1 = cur1.succ;
   }
   while (cur2 != null) {
      list3.append(cur2.element);   cur2 = cur2.succ;
   }
   SLL merged = new SLL();
   merged.first = list3.first;
   return merged;
}
```

Program 4.29   Implementation of the SLL merging algorithm as a Java method.

4.32 illustrates the SLL insertion sort algorithm's behavior. (Compare with Figures 3.32 and 3.33.)

The SLL insertion sort algorithm performs exactly the same number of comparisons as the array insertion sort algorithm (Algorithm 3.31), namely $n^2/4$, where n is the number of elements to be sorted. The main disadvantage of the array insertion sort algorithm is that it performs a large number of copies, also $n^2/4$, because it works by inserting each element in turn into an expanding subarray. The SLL insertion sort algorithm performs no copies at all, because it works entirely by manipulating the links. Its time complexity is still $O(n^2)$.

Program 4.33 shows a Java implementation of the SLL insertion sort algorithm.

The selection sort algorithm and the quick-sort algorithm (with the first element as the pivot) can also be adapted for linked lists. (See Exercises 4.14 and 4.15). A linked-list merge-sort algorithm would be more problematic, for the same reason that linked-list binary search is problematic: it would require access to the middle node of a linked list.

To sort the SLL headed by *first*:

1. Make *sorted* empty.
2. Set *unsorted* to *first*.
3. While *unsorted* is not null, repeat:
   3.1. Set *next* to *unsorted*.
   3.2. Set *unsorted* to node *next*'s successor.
   3.3. Insert node *next* into the sorted SLL *sorted*.
4. Terminate with answer *sorted*.

To insert node *next* into the sorted SLL *sorted*:

1. Set *pred* to null, and set *curr* to *sorted*.
2. While *curr* is not null and node *next*'s element is less than or equal to node *curr*'s element, repeat:
   2.1. Set *pred* to *curr*, and set *curr* to node *curr*'s successor.
3. Set node *next*'s successor to *curr*.
4. If *pred* is null, set *sorted* to *next*.
5. If *pred* is not null, set node *pred*'s successor to *next*.
6. Terminate.

Algorithm 4.30   SLL insertion sort algorithm (with auxiliary sorted SLL insertion algorithm).

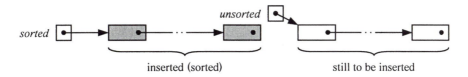

Figure 4.31   Loop invariant for the SLL insertion sort algorithm.

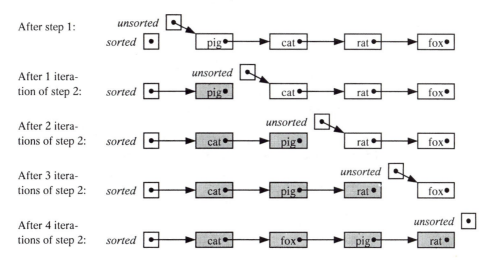

Figure 4.32   Illustration of the SLL insertion sort algorithm.

```
public void insertionSort () {
// Sort this SLL.
  SLL sorted = new SLL();
  SLLNode unsorted = first;
  while (unsorted != null) {
    SLLNode next = unsorted;
    unsorted = next.succ;
    sorted.insertSorted(next);
  }
  first = sorted.first;
}

private void insertSorted (SLLNode next) {
// Insert node next into this SLL (assumed to be sorted).
  Comparable nextElem = (Comparable) next.element;
  SLLNode pred = null, curr = first;
  while (curr != null && nextElem.compareTo(
            (Comparable) curr.element) >= 0) {
    pred = curr;  curr = curr.succ;
  }
  next.succ = curr;
  if (pred == null)
    first = next;
  else
    pred.succ = next;
}
```

Program 4.33 Implementation of the SLL insertion sort algorithm as a Java method (in class SLL).

Summary

In this chapter:

- We have studied singly-linked lists (SLLs) and doubly-linked lists (DLLs).
- We have studied and analyzed insertion and deletion algorithms for both SLLs and DLLs. We found that deletion is much easier in DLLs.
- We have studied and analyzed the linear search algorithm for linked lists. We noted that the binary search algorithm is unsuitable for linked lists.
- We have studied and analyzed the merging algorithm for linked lists.
- We have studied and analyzed the insertion sort algorithm for linked lists. We noted that the selection sort and quick-sort (but not merge-sort) algorithms are also suitable for linked lists.

Exercises

4.1 Devise an algorithm to access the *k*th element of an SLL. What is your algorithm's time complexity?

4.2 Devise an algorithm to access the *k*th element of a DLL. (*Hint:* You can do better than imitating your solution to Exercise 4.1.) What is your algorithm's time complexity?

4.3 Devise an algorithm to reverse the elements of an SLL. What is your algorithm's time complexity and space complexity?

4.4 Devise an algorithm to reverse the elements of a DLL. What is your algorithm's time complexity and space complexity?

4.5 Devise an algorithm to check whether the elements of an SLL of characters is a palindrome. (See Exercise 3.3 for the definition of a palindrome).
   What is the time efficiency of your algorithm?
   Implement your algorithm as a Java method.

4.6 Repeat Exercise 4.5 for a DLL of characters.

4.7 If an SLL is sorted, it is possible to speed up the linear search algorithm. The algorithm traverses the SLL first-to-last, terminating if it reaches a node that contains an element equal to *or greater than* the target.
   (a) Write this modified algorithm, using Algorithm 4.23 as a guide.
   (b) How does this improvement affect the time efficiency of the linear search algorithm when the search is successful? when the search is unsuccessful?
   (c) Write a Java method to implement this algorithm, using Program 4.24 as a guide.

4.8 It is just as easy to search a DLL last-to-first as first-to-last. When might it be advantageous to do so? (*Hint*: Consider a sorted DLL containing a large number of words.)

4.9 Devise a search algorithm that simultaneously searches from both ends of an unsorted DLL.
   How many comparisons would this take to find a given element in the best case? in the worst case? on average?
   What is the time complexity of this algorithm?

4.10 Repeat Exercise 4.9 for a sorted DLL.

4.11 When repeatedly searching an unsorted SLL, it can be advantageous to move an item to the head of the list when it is found, if it is likely that the same item will be searched for again in the near future.
   (a) Write this modified linear search algorithm, using Algorithm 4.23 as a guide.
   (b) How does this modification affect the time efficiency of the algorithm when the same item is searched for 50 times out of the next 100 searches? (*Hint:* Consider the total time taken on average to perform all 100 searches with and without the modification.)
   (c) Write a Java method to implement this algorithm, using Program 4.24 as a guide.

4.12 Devise algorithms to delete the node containing a given element *elem*:
   (a) in an SLL;
   (b) in a DLL.

4.13 Hand-test the merging algorithm (Algorithm 4.25) to merge two SLLs containing the following sequences of names:

James, Tolstoy, Wells

Curie, Einstein, Kelvin, Maxwell

How many name comparisons are required?

4.14 Modify the selection sort algorithm given in Algorithm 3.27 to work with (a) an SLL, and (b) a DLL. In each case, write a Java method to implement the algorithm.

4.15 Modify the quick-sort algorithm given in Algorithm 3.38 to work with (a) an SLL, and (b) a DLL. In each case, write a Java method to implement the algorithm.

* **4.16** Consider the SLL insertion and deletion algorithms given in Algorithms 4.11 and 4.17 respectively. These algorithms must check for the special case when we are inserting or deleting a node at the front of the SLL. These checks can be avoided if we create a *dummy node* at the front of the SLL, i.e., a node that does not contain an element. This ensures that even the first node in the SLL has a predecessor node. This is illustrated in the following diagram:

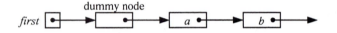

Even an empty SLL contains one node, i.e., the dummy node. When a new SLL is created, *first* is initialized with a link to the dummy node, and thereafter remains unchanged.

Modify the SLL insertion and deletion algorithms to use a dummy node. What changes are required to the other SLL algorithms?

Implement a revised Java class for SLLs that uses your modified algorithms.

Compare the time efficiency of your modified algorithms with the original algorithms.

* **4.17** The DLL insertion and deletion algorithms (given in Algorithms 4.14 and 4.20 respectively) can be improved along the lines of Exercise 4.16 by creating an dummy node at each end of the DLL. Call these the *front* and *rear* dummy nodes. The front dummy node's successor contains the first element of the DLL. The rear dummy node's predecessor contains the last element of the DLL. This is illustrated in the following diagram:

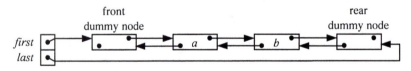

The empty DLL now contains just the two dummy nodes. When a new DLL is created, *first* is initialized with a link to a front dummy node, and *last* is initialized with a link to a rear dummy node. Both of these links remain unchanged thereafter. Initially the successor of the front dummy node is the rear dummy node, and the predecessor of the rear dummy node is the front dummy node. The empty DLL is illustrated in the following diagram:

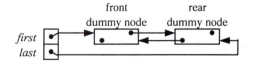

5

Abstract Data Types

In this chapter we shall study:

- data types, which are characterized by their values, operations, and representation (Section 5.1)
- abstract data types, which are characterized by their values and operations only; specification and implementation of abstract data types (Section 5.2)
- design of abstract data types: necessary and sufficient operations; constructors, accessors, and transformers (Section 5.3)
- string abstract data types (Section 5.4)
- a preview of collection abstract data types (Section 5.5)
- a brief survey of abstract data types in the Java class library (Section 5.6).

5.1 Data types

Data are the raw material of computation. For a variety of reasons we find it convenient to classify data into *data types*. For example, we treat booleans (truth values), numbers, and strings as belonging to different data types. We even distinguish between integer (exact) numbers and floating-point (approximate) numbers.

One reason for our interest in data types is that most operations, by their very nature, can be applied only to certain types of data. For example, only booleans can be logically complemented; only numbers can be added, subtracted, multiplied, and so on; only strings can be concatenated.

Another reason for our interest in data types is the issue of data representation. In general, all the values of a given data type have a common representation. For example, the values of the integer data type are typically represented by 32-bit words. This representation is used for all integer values, whether small or large. Any attempt to represent small integers by half-words, and only large integers by words, would be more trouble than it was worth, because small and large integers can be used interchangeably. But it is perfectly sensible to represent all integers by words and all booleans by bytes, provided that booleans cannot be used interchangeably with integers.

Consequently, a ***data type*** is characterized by:

- a set of *values*
- a *data representation*, which is common to all these values
- a set of *operations*, which can be applied uniformly to all these values.

In most programming languages, including Java, the programmer must declare the type of every variable and parameter. The compiler then checks the program to ensure that every operation is applied to data of the expected type.

Every programming language provides some *built-in* data types. The values, representation, and operations of a built-in data type are defined by the language itself. Some of Java's built-in data types are summarized in Table 5.1.

Do not be confused by the fact that different operations sometimes have the same name. For example, '+' denotes several distinct operations in Java: when applied to integers it denotes integer addition; when applied to floating-point numbers it denotes floating-point addition; when applied to strings it denotes concatenation.

We cannot expect any programming language's built-in data types to meet all requirements. Interesting applications demand new data types, so the programming language must provide a means for the programmer to introduce them. From our characterization of a data type above, we see that the programmer must have the means to determine the new data type's values, representation, and operations.

In Java, the means for introducing a new data type is the *class declaration*. The class's instance variables determine the new data type's values and representation; the class's constructors and methods are the new data type's operations.

EXAMPLE 5.1   *A data type for persons*

Suppose that we wish to introduce a new data type, named `Person`, for an application in which the relevant data about a person are his or her name, gender, and year of birth.

Program 5.2 shows a possible class declaration. The four instance variables,

Table 5.1   Principal built-in data types of Java.

Data type	Values	Representation	Principal operations
boolean	false, true	1 byte	`|| && !`
char	Unicode characters (e.g., 'U', '5', '$', '∆', '√')	2 bytes	as for **int**
int	negative, zero, and positive integer numbers	32-bit twos-complement	`+ − * / %` `< <= == >= >`
float	negative, zero, and positive floating-point numbers	IEEE 32-bit floating-point	`+ − * /` `< <= == >= >`
String	sequences of characters (e.g., "", "A", "hullo")	array of characters	`+ length charAt` `substring compareTo`

surname, forename, gender, and yearOfBirth, define the representation of the Person data type. They also implicitly define the data type's set of values: every possible combination of surname, forename, gender, and date. The data type is equipped with just two operations: the Person constructor and the changeName method.

The following code fragment illustrates possible usage of class Person:

```
Person p1 =
    new Person("Curie", "Pierre", false, 1859);
Person p2 =
    new Person("Sklodowska", "Marie", true, 1867);
...
p2.changeName(p1.surname);
```

This code constructs and manipulates two objects of class Person. Figure 5.3 shows what these objects look like after executing this code. Each Person object consists of four instance variables, together with a class tag.

Note that the instance variables surname and forename each contains a reference to an object of class String. The instance variables gender and yearOfBirth each contains a primitive value.

The following example introduces a data type, Date, that will be used as a running example in this chapter.

```
public class Person {

    // Each Person value consists of a person's surname, forename, gender,
    // and year of birth.

    public String surname, forename;
    public boolean female;
    public int yearOfBirth;

    public Person (String surname, String forename,
                   boolean female, int yearOfBirth) {
        this.surname = surname;
        this.forename = forename;
        this.female = female;
        this.yearOfBirth = yearOfBirth;
    }

    public void changeName (String newSurname) {
        this.surname = newSurname;
    }

}
```

Program 5.2   Java class declaration introducing a Person data type.

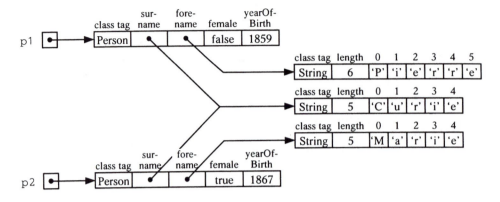

Figure 5.3 Representation of `Person` objects.

EXAMPLE 5.2 *A data type for dates*

Program 5.4 shows a possible class declaration for a new data type named `Date`, and Figure 5.5(a) illustrates the chosen data representation. Each `Date` object consists of three instance variables: the year number `y`, the month number `m`, and the day-in-month number `d`. The class declaration provides two operations: a constructor named `Date` and a method named `advance`. (It also provides two auxiliary methods, `length` and `isLeap`, which are not actually operations on dates.)

The following code fragment illustrates possible usage of class `Date`:

```
Date today = new Date(2000, 12, 25);
today.advance(7);
System.out.println(today.y + "-" + today.m
     + "-" + today.d);
```

This code constructs a date, advances the date by a week, and prints the date in ISO format. It should print '2001-1-1'.

The data representation seems simple and obvious, but it is not free of problems. The combination of the instance variables, `y`, `m`, and `d`, determines not only the data representation but also the potential set of values of the data type. Some of these combinations correspond to proper dates, such as 2000-12-25 and 2001-1-1. Other potential combinations would be improper dates, such as 2001-13-1 (month number out of range), 2002-12-0 (day-in-month number out of range), 2003-2-29 and 2004-4-31 (day-in-month number greater than month length).

We are forced to take special precautions to avoid a discrepancy between the actual set of values of the `Date` data type and the proper set of values. So the `Date` constructor validates its arguments, and throws an exception if an improper date would result. (`IllegalArgumentException` is a predefined Java exception class suitable for use in these circumstances.) Moreover, the `advance` method carefully updates the instance variables to keep the date proper. Application code that uses only these operations to process dates will never compute an improper date.

```java
public class Date {
    // Each Date value is a past, present, or future date.

    // This date is represented by a year number y, a month number m
    // (1 ≤ m ≤ 12), and a day-in-month number d (1 ≤ d ≤ month length ≤ 31).
    public int y;
    public int m;
    public int d;

    public Date (int y, int m, int d) {
    // Construct a date with year y, month m, and day-in-month d.
    // Throw an exception if they constitute an improper date.
        if (m < 1 || m > 12 || d < 1 || d > length(m, y))
            throw new IllegalArgumentException(
                "Improper date");
        this.y = y;   this.m = m;   this.d = d;
    }

    public void advance (int n) {
    // Advance this date by n days (where n ≥ 0).
        int y = this.y, m = this.m, d = this.d + n;
        int last;
        while (d > (last = length(m, y))) {
            d -= last;
            if (m < 12) m++; else { m = 1;   y++; }
        }
        this.y = y;   this.m = m;   this.d = d;
    }

    //////////// Auxiliary methods ////////////

    private static int length (int m, int y) {
    // Return the number of days in month m in year y.
        switch (m) {
            case 1: case 3: case 5: case 7:
            case 8: case 10: case 12:
                return 31;
            case 4: case 6: case 9: case 11:
                return 30;
            case 2:
                return (isLeap(y) ? 29 : 28);
        }
    }

    private static boolean isLeap (int y) {
    // Return true if and only if y is a leapyear.
        return (y%4 == 0 && (y%100 != 0 || y%400 == 0));
    }

}
```

Program 5.4   Java class declaration introducing a Date data type.

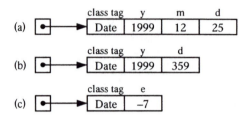

Figure 5.5   Alternative representations of Date objects: (a) year, month, and day-in-month numbers; (b) year and day-in-year numbers; (c) day-in-epoch number (day 0 = 1 January 2000).

Unfortunately, these precautions are not foolproof. The application code is free to update the instance variables directly, e.g.:

```
today.d += 20;
```

The application programmer might write such a statement in a naive attempt to circumvent the advance method (which is admittedly rather slow), but it risks computing an improper date. Careful implementation of the Date operations is in vain if they can simply be circumvented like this.

The fundamental cause of the problems revealed by Example 5.2 is that the data representation is public. This allows application code to manipulate the data representation directly. Logical errors in the application code can then give rise to improper values. Such logical errors tend to be hard to debug.

Even in the absence of logical errors, public data representation leads to a subtler and potentially more serious problem. Any attempt to change the data representation is likely to force many changes to the application code.

EXAMPLE 5.3   *Changing the representation of dates*

The data representation chosen for Date in Example 5.1 allows the Date constructor to be implemented simply and efficiently, but it makes the advance method awkward and slow. If it turns out that the application code calls the advance method much more frequently than the Date constructor, we should look for an alternative data representation that makes the advance method more efficient.

One possibility is to represent a date by a year number and a day-in-year number (with the latter lying in the range 1–366). This is illustrated in Figure 5.5(b). Now we must re-implement the Date constructor and the advance method. The advance method will be simpler and faster, but the Date constructor will be more awkward to implement. (Unfortunately our calendar is inherently awkward. Making one operation smoother is always at the expense of making some other operation more awkward.)

Unfortunately, yet more work remains to be done. The application code might contain statements that directly access instance variables of a `Date` object, e.g.:

```
System.out.println(today.y + "-" + today.m
    + "-" + today.d);
```

Inspecting `today.y` has the same effect as before. Inspecting `today.d` is still possible, but misleadingly yields a day-in-year number rather than a day-in-month number. Most drastic of all, inspecting `today.m` is no longer even possible.

Yet another possibility is to represent a date simply by a day-in-epoch number (i.e., the total number of days since some arbitrary date such as 1 January 2000) e, as illustrated in Figure 5.5(c). This invalidates any application code that directly accesses instance variables of a `Date` object.

Changing the representation of `Date` therefore forces us to examine, and possibly modify, *every* direct reference to an instance variable of a `Date` object. This could be a huge task, because such direct references could be anywhere and everywhere in the application code.

Well-structured software is composed of modules that can be specified, designed, coded, tested, and debugged separately. However, these good things are achieved only if the modules are reasonably independent of each other. We say that a module *P* is **loosely coupled** to a module *Q* if changes to *Q* are likely to force at most minor changes to *P*. Conversely, *P* is **tightly coupled** to *Q* if changes to *Q* are likely to force major changes to *P*. Then we can say that well-structured software is composed of modules that are loosely coupled to one another.

If we write a class declaration with public instance variables, as in Program 5.4, it is all too likely that the application code will become tightly coupled to the class declaration. That is because direct references to the instance variables could be scattered all over the application code. If so, a change to the data representation (i.e., the instance variables) will trigger changes all over the application code.

5.2 Abstract data types

Strong discipline is needed to avoid tight coupling between application code and data representation. The necessary discipline is to deny the application code direct access to the data representation. This leads to the concept of an *abstract* data type.

An **abstract data type** (**ADT**) is characterized by:

- a set of *values*
- a set of *operations*, which can be applied uniformly to all these values.

Data representation plays no part in the characterization of an ADT. Of course, the ADT must have a data representation, but it is *private*. This means that the data representation can be inspected and updated *only* by the ADT's operations. Since the application code cannot access the data representation directly, it can process values of the ADT *only* by calling the operations provided. This ensures that the application code does not become tightly coupled to the data representation.

5.2.1 Specification

Every ADT should have a **contract** (or *specification*) that:

- specifies the set of values of the ADT
- specifies each operation of the ADT (i.e., specifies the operation's name, its parameter types, its result type, if any, and its observable behavior).

The contract does *not* specify the data representation, nor the algorithms used to implement the operations.

The **observable behavior** of an operation is the effect of that operation as 'observed' by the application code. Consider, for example, an operation that sorts a sequence of values. The application code that calls this operation will be able to observe that the sequence has been sorted, but not the detailed steps by which the operation achieves that effect. Thus the fact of sorting is the operation's observable behavior; the choice of sorting algorithm is not.

A contract is so called because it is an agreement between the ADT implementor and the application programmer (who are typically different persons). The ADT implementor undertakes to provide an implementation of the ADT that fully respects the contract. The application programmer undertakes to process values of the ADT using only the specified operations, relying on these operations to have the observable behavior specified in the contract. The application programmer need not be concerned with how the ADT will be implemented; the ADT implementor need not be concerned with how the ADT will be applied. This *separation of concerns* is a key to the modular design and implementation of large software systems.

EXAMPLE 5.4   *Contract for a date ADT*

Let us redesign `Date` as an *abstract* data type. Before we can write a suitable contract, we must identify the application requirements explicitly. Let us assume the following requirements:

1. The values are to be all past, present, and future dates.
2. It must be possible to construct a date from a year number y, a month number m, and a day-in-month number d.
3. It must be possible to compare dates.
4. It must be possible to render a date in the ISO format, i.e., 'y-m-d'.
5. It must be possible to advance a date by a given number of days.

Program 5.6 shows a possible contract for the `Date` ADT, expressed in the form of an outline Java class declaration. Requirements 2–5 above are met by the `Date`, `compareTo`, `toString`, and `advance` operations, respectively.

Note that requirement 4 cannot be met by allowing the application code to inspect the data representation directly. The `toString` operation is the most direct way to meet requirement 4, but there are other ways, as we shall see in Example 5.7.

Program 5.7 is a little application program written against the `Date` contract. This application program is guaranteed to work successfully with any (correct) implementation of the `Date` ADT.

On the other hand, application code like the following:

```
Date today = ...;
System.out.print(today.y);              // illegal!
if (today.d == today.monthLength())     // illegal!
    today.m++;                          // illegal!
```

would *violate* the contract. It assumes that a `Date` object has instance variables named y, m, and d, and is equipped with a method named `monthLength`. But these assumptions are not justified: none of these things is in the contract. Such application code could not be guaranteed to work successfully with all possible implementations of the ADT. This message would be made very clear to the programmer, because the above code would fail to compile!

In Example 5.4, each application requirement was met by exactly one operation. This is not always so: sometimes a single operation might meet several requirements, or several operations might be needed to meet a single requirement.

```
public class Date {

    // Each Date value is a past, present, or future date.

    private ...;   // ... instance variables, not shown here.

    public Date (int y, int m, int d);
    // Construct a date with year y, month m, and day-in-month d.
    // Throw an exception if they constitute an improper date.

    public int compareTo (Date that);
    // Return –1 if this date is earlier than that,
    // or 0 if this date is equal to that,
    // or +1 if this date is later than that.

    public String toString ();
    // Return this date rendered in ISO format.

    public void advance (int n);
    // Advance this date by n days (where n ≥ 0).

}
```

Program 5.6 A possible contract for the `Date` ADT.

```java
public static void main (String[] args) {
// Given a day-name as an argument, print all the dates in year 2000
//  falling on the named day.
  String dayName = args[0];
  int day =
       dayName.equals("Saturday")  ? 1 :
       dayName.equals("Sunday")    ? 2 :
       dayName.equals("Monday")    ? 3 :
       dayName.equals("Tuesday")   ? 4 :
       dayName.equals("Wednesday") ? 5 :
       dayName.equals("Thursday")  ? 6 :
       dayName.equals("Friday")    ? 7 : 0;
  try {
    Date currDate = new Date(2000, 1, day);
    Date lastDate = new Date(2000, 12, 31);
    System.out.println(dayName + "s in 2000:");
    do {
      System.out.println(currDate.toString());
      currDate.advance(7);
    } while (currDate.compareTo(lastDate) <= 0);
  } catch (IllegalArgumentException e) {
    System.out.println("Invalid day-name.");
  }
}
```

Program 5.7 A possible application of the Date ADT.

5.2.2 Implementation

Given a contract for an ADT, an ***implementation*** of the ADT entails:

- choosing a data representation
- choosing a suitable algorithm for each of the operations.

The chosen data representation must represent all possible values of the ADT. The chosen algorithms must be consistent with the chosen representation.

The data representation should be private. Any auxiliary operations (i.e., operations not in the contract) should also be private.

In Java, simply including the keyword **private** in the declaration of a class member (variable, constructor, or method) does the trick. The Java compiler will reject any attempt by application code to refer to a class member declared as private. (In certain cases we will use **protected** rather than **private**.)

EXAMPLE 5.5 *First implementation of the date ADT*

Let us represent a date by a year number, a month number, and a day-in-month number, as illustrated in Figure 5.5(a). Program 5.8 shows this implementation of the Date ADT, in the form of a full Java class declaration. This implementation respects the contract of Program 5.6.

The operations specified in the contract are declared as public: a constructor and three methods. Everything not in the contract is declared as private: the instance variables y, m, and d, and the auxiliary length and isLeap methods (which are present only to facilitate the implementation). As usual, the instance variables define the data representation, but being private they can be inspected and updated only inside the class declaration.

Program 5.7 will work successfully with this implementation of the Date ADT, although that program was written against the ADT's contract and without knowledge of the implementation.

EXAMPLE 5.6 *Second implementation of the date ADT*

Let us now change the implementation so that a date is represented simply by a day-in-epoch number, i.e., the number of days since (say) 1 January 2000, as illustrated in Figure 5.5(c). The new implementation is shown in Program 5.9. The compareTo and advance method are now trivial and fast. (In particular, the time complexity of advance(n) is now $O(1)$, as compared with $O(n)$ for the first implementation.) On the other hand, the Date constructor and the toString method are now nontrivial and slower.

More importantly, this change of implementation has no impact on the application code, since the new implementation still respects the Date contract. The changes to the instance variables do not directly affect the application code, because they are private and the application code cannot directly access them anyway. The public operations (Date, compareTo, toString, and advance) are unchanged as far as the application code is concerned: their names, types, and parameters are unchanged; and crucially their observable behavior is unchanged too. It is true that their detailed behavior is different (inevitably so because they are operating on a different data representation), but the application code cannot tell the difference. For example, Program 5.7 will produce exactly the same results, regardless of the choice of implementation.

On the other hand, application code like the following:

```
Date today = ...;
System.out.print(today.y);              // illegal!
if (today.d == today.monthLength())     // illegal!
    today.m++;                          // illegal!
```

would be rejected by the Java compiler, regardless of the choice of implementation for the ADT. We can now see why this is important. The instance variables y, m, and d do not exist in the second implementation. Moreover, neither implementation has provided a method named monthLength.

```
public class Date {
    //  Each Date value is a past, present, or future date.

    //  This date is represented by a year number y, a month number m
    //  (1 ≤ m ≤ 12), and a day-in-month number d (1 ≤ d ≤ month length ≤ 31).
    private int y, m, d;

    public Date (int y, int m, int d) {
        ...  // as in Program 5.4.
    }

    public int compareTo (Date that) {
    //  Return –1 if this date is earlier than that,
    //  or 0 if this date is equal to that,
    //  or +1 if this date is later than that.
        return
            (this.y < that.y ? -1 :
             this.y > that.y ? +1 :
             this.m < that.m ? -1 :
             this.m > that.m ? +1 :
             this.d < that.d ? -1 :
             this.d > that.d ? +1 : 0);
    }

    public String toString () {
    //  Return this date rendered in ISO format.
        return (this.y + "-" + this.m + "-" + this.d);
    }

    public void advance (int n) {
        ...  // as in Program 5.4.
    }

    ///////////// Auxiliary methods ////////////

    private static int length (int m, int y) {
        ...  // as in Program 5.4.
    }

    private static boolean isLeap (int y) {
        ...  // as in Program 5.4.
    }

}
```

Program 5.8 First implementation of the Date ADT.

```
public class Date {

    // Each Date value is a past, present, or future date.

    // This date is represented by a day-in-epoch number e (0 for 1 January
    // 2000, negative for earlier dates, and positive for later dates).
    private int e;

public Date (int y, int m, int d) {
// Construct a date with year y, month m, and day-in-month d.
// Throw an exception if they constitute an improper date.
    if (m < 1 || m > 12
            || d < 1 || d > length(m, y))
        throw new IllegalArgumentException(
            "Improper date");
    int e = d - 1;
    // Add lengths of months 1 through m–1 in year y ...
    for (int k = 1; k < m; k++)
        e += length(k, y);
    // Add lengths of years 2000 through y–1 ...
    e += 365*(y - 2000);
    // Adjust for leap years ...
    if (y > 2000)
        e += (y - 2001)/4 - (y - 2001)/100
                + (y - 2001)/400 + 1;
    else
        e += (y - 2000)/4 - (y - 2000)/100
                + (y - 2000)/400;
    this.e = e;
}

public int compareTo (Date that) {
// Return –1 if this date is earlier than that,
// or 0 if this date is equal to that,
// or +1 if this date is later than that.
    return
            (this.e < that.e ? -1 :
            this.e > that.e ? +1 : 0);
}
```

Program 5.9 Second implementation of the Date ADT (with changes from the first implementation shown in italics) (*continued on next page*).

```
public String toString () {
//  Return this date rendered in ISO format.
   int y = 2000, m = 1, d = this.e + 1;
   int last;
   if (d > 0) {
     while (d > (last = (isLeap(y) ? 366 : 365))) {
       y++;  d -= last;
     }
   } else {
     do {
       y--;  d += (isLeap(y) ? 366 : 365);
     } while (d <= 0);
   }
   while (d > (last = length(m, y))) {
     m++;  d -= last;
   }
   return (y + "-" + m + "-" + d);
}

public void advance (int n) {
//  Advance this date by n days (where n ≥ 0).
   this.e += n;
}

///////////// Auxiliary methods ///////////////

private static int length (int m, int y) {
   ...   //  as in Program 5.4.
}

   private static boolean isLeap (int y) {
      ...   //  as in Program 5.4.
   }

}
```

Program 5.9 (*continued*)

To summarize, we should implement an ADT by a class whose instance variables are private. This guarantees that application code cannot become tightly coupled to the data representation, for the simple reason that the Java compiler will reject any code that attempts to access an instance variable (or any other class member) declared as private.

5.2.3 Expressing contracts and implementations in Java

There are two alternative conventions for expressing ADT contracts and implementations in Java:

- Express the ADT's contract as an *outline class declaration* (showing only public members, and only headings of constructors and methods); express its implementation as a *completed class declaration*. In this chapter we are expressing contracts as outline class declarations, such as Program 5.6.
- Express the ADT's contract as an *interface*; express its implementation as a *class that implements the interface*. This convention makes the relationship between the contract and the implementation explicit in the source code. The only disadvantage of this convention is that a Java interface does not allow us to specify constructors (although the implementing class can provide constructors). In subsequent chapters we shall express contracts as interfaces.

5.3 Abstract data type design

The discipline of ADTs has major benefits. Because of the high costs of maintenance (which is dominated by change), software should always be designed in such a way as to facilitate future changes. Changes of data representation are common. Often a new data type has several possible representations, and the best choice might not become clear until the application has been in use for some time. Making the data representation private keeps open the option of changing it in future, without having to change the application code too.

When we design an ADT, the outcome should be a contract, in which we specify the set of values of the ADT, and specify each operation in terms of its name, parameter types, result type (if any), and observable behavior.

The contract should leave the implementation open. Of course it is essential that at least one satisfactory implementation exists, otherwise the contract is futile. But the contract should avoid unnecessary bias towards any particular implementation.

5.3.1 Necessary and sufficient operations

The key to good ADT design lies in the choice of operations. A well-designed ADT provides operations that are both sufficient and necessary to meet the requirements of the application.

The operations are **sufficient** if together they meet all the requirements. In other words, the operations must support all processing of the ADT's values required in the application code. (Always remember that the application code cannot process these values directly.)

The operations are **necessary** if none of them is surplus to the requirements. If any operation can be implemented easily and efficiently just by calling other operations, that operation is unnecessary.

An ADT that provides insufficient operations is clearly deficient. On the other hand, an

```
public class Date {

    //  Each Date value is a past, present, or future date.

    private ...;    //  ... instance variables, not shown here.

    public Date (int y, int m, int d);
    //  Construct a date with year y, month m, and day-in-month d.
    //  Throw an exception if they constitute an improper date.

    public int getYear ();
    //  Return this date's year number.

    public int getMonth ();
    //  Return this date's month number.

    public int getDay ();
    //  Return this date's day-in-month number.

    public void advance (int n);
    //  Advance this date by n days (where n ≥ 0).

}
```

Program 5.10   An alternative contract for the Date ADT.

ADT that provides unnecessary operations might still be acceptable, provided that the extra operations make the application programmer's job easier, compensating for the fact that the ADT is more complicated (and therefore costlier to implement and to maintain) than it needs to be.

EXAMPLE 5.7   *Necessary and sufficient operations in the date ADT*

Program 5.6 showed a contract for a Date ADT, providing operations named Date, compareTo, toString, and advance. Example 5.4 showed that these operations are sufficient to meet the requirements of the application. Moreover, all four are necessary. Removal of the Date constructor would make it impossible to construct any dates. Removal of the compareTo method would make it very difficult to compare dates. Removal of the toString method would make it impossible to render a date. Removal of the advance method would make it impossible to change the date.

It does not follow that these particular operations are irreplaceable. Program 5.10 shows an alternative contract in which the compareTo and toString operations have been replaced by getYear, getMonth, and getDay operations. This contract's operations would also be both sufficient and necessary. The application code could format dates itself, e.g.:

```
System.out.println(today.getYear() + "-"
    + today.getMonth() + "-" + today.getDay());
```

The application code could also compare dates itself. In compensation for having more work to do, the application programmer would be able to use the year, month, and day-in-month numbers for a variety of legitimate purposes, e.g.:

```
Date today = ...;
boolean onHoliday = false;
if (today.getMonth() == 1 && today.getDay() == 1)
    onHoliday = true;
```

We could also combine the contracts of Programs 5.6 and 5.10, providing the operations getYear, getMonth, and getDay *as well as* compareTo and toString. This design provides some operations that are not strictly necessary, but nevertheless it would be a good compromise.

Finally, consider adding the following operation to the contract of Program 5.6:

```
public void advance1 ();
// Advance this date by one day.
```

This operation would clearly be unnecessary. The effect of 'today.advance1()' could be achieved just as well by 'today.advance(1)'.

If we *replaced* advance by advance1, the resulting set of operations would be both sufficient and necessary. However, the effect of advancing the date by several days would have to be achieved by a one-day-at-a-time loop in the application code. This would be slower than any reasonable implementation of advance.

5.3.2 Constructors, accessors, and transformers

Another way to assess an ADT design is to classify its operations. Bertrand Meyer has proposed the following classification:

- constructors
- accessors
- transformers.

A *constructor* is an operation that creates a value of the ADT from values of different types. The constructor initializes the components (instance variables) of the ADT value.

An *accessor* is an operation that uses a value of the ADT to compute a value of a different type.

A *transformer* is an operation that uses a value of the ADT to compute a new value of the ADT.

We can subclassify transformers by what they do with the new values they compute. A *mutative transformer* is a transformer that overwrites the old value of the ADT with the new value. An *applicative transformer* is a transformer that returns the new value, without overwriting anything.

The values of an ADT are *mutable* (i.e., could be overwritten) if the ADT provides one or more mutative transformers. Otherwise the ADT values are *immutable*.

A well-designed ADT provides one or more constructors, one or more accessors, and one or more transformers (which may be mutative or applicative). The constructors and transformers between them must be able to generate *all* the intended values of the ADT. The accessors between them must be able to extract any data required by the application from the ADT values.

Constructors are directly supported by Java. Accessors and transformers (both mutative and applicative) can be implemented as Java methods. Mutative transformers are typically implemented as **void** methods.

EXAMPLE 5.8   *Classifying operations in the date ADT*

In the contract of Program 5.6, the operation `Date` is a constructor; `compareTo` and `toString` are accessors; `advance` is a mutative transformer. The presence of this mutative transformer implies that dates are mutable.

The following operation:

```
public Date plus (int n);
// Return this date advanced by n days (where n ≥ 0).
```

would be an applicative transformer. The method call 'today.advance(7)' *overwrites* `today` with a new date, but the method call 'today.plus(7)' would *return* a new date, without overwriting `today`. If `plus` *replaced* `advance` in the `Date` ADT, dates would be immutable.

The distinction between mutative and applicative transformers is important. In the next section we shall see that mutability can influence the choice of implementation.

5.4 String abstract data types

A *string* is a sequence of characters. The characters of a string have consecutive *indices*.

A *substring* is a subsequence of consecutive characters taken from a string.

The *length* of a string is the number of characters in that string. The *empty string* has length zero.

Many commonly-occurring data items can be viewed as strings: words, phrases, names, addresses, diary entries, product descriptions, etc. Strings are therefore ubiquitous in computing.

In this section we shall assume the following requirements for a string ADT:

1. The values are to be character strings of any length.
2. It must be possible to determine the length of a string.
3. It must be possible to obtain an individual character of a string, given the character's index.
4. It must be possible to obtain a substring of a string, given the indices of the characters forming the substring.
5. It must be possible to compare strings lexicographically.
6. It must be possible to concatenate strings.

It turns out that these requirements can be met by very different contracts. In fact we shall design two different string ADTs.

5.4.1 Immutable strings

Program 5.11 shows a possible contract for an ADT named `String`. Note that `substring` and `concat` are applicative transformers. Since none of the operations is a mutative transformer, this contract makes strings immutable.

This contract meets all the requirements stated above. Requirement 1 is met by the `String` constructor, since its argument may be a character array of any length. Require-

```
public class String {

    // Each String value is an immutable string of characters, of any length,
    // with consecutive indices starting at 0.

    private ...;   // ... instance variables, not shown here.

    /////////////// Constructor ///////////////

    public String (char[] cs);
    // Construct a string consisting of all the characters in cs.

    /////////////// Accessors ///////////////

    public int length ();
    // Return the length of this string.

    public char charAt (int i);
    // Return the character at index i in this string.

    public bool equals (String that);
    // Return true if and only if this string is equal to that.

    public int compareTo (String that);
    // Return –1 if this string is lexicographically less than that,
    // or 0 if this string is equal to that,
    // or +1 if this string is lexicographically greater than that.

    /////////////// Transformers ///////////////

    public String substring (int i, int j);
    // Return the substring of this string consisting of the characters whose
    // indices are i through j–1.

    public String concat (String that);
    // Return the string obtained by concatenating this string and that.

}
```

Program 5.11   A possible contract for the `String` ADT.

ments 2–6 are met by the `length`, `charAt`, `substring`, `compareTo`, and `concat` methods, respectively. (Note that the `equals` method is not strictly necessary: the effect of s_1.`equals`(s_2) can be achieved by the test s_1.`compareTo`$(s_2) == 0$.)

Program 5.12 is a simple application of the `String` ADT. Note that a Java string literal is an abbreviation for a call to the `String` constructor with an array of characters as argument:

```
"Mac" ≡ new String(new char[]{'M', 'a', 'c'})
```

Now let us consider possible representations for strings. The most obvious representation, perhaps, is an array of characters, as illustrated in Figure 5.13(a). This indeed permits a simple and efficient representation. In particular, the `charAt` operation has time complexity $O(1)$.

An alternative representation is a singly-linked list (SLL) of characters, preferably with a length field in its header, as illustrated in Figure 5.13(b). The SLL representation is clearly space-consuming: a (Unicode) character occupies two bytes, and a link typically occupies four bytes, so this representation consumes three times as much space as the array representation. The SLL representation also makes some operations more time-consuming. In particular, the `charAt` operation now has time complexity $O(n)$, where n is the string's length. On the other hand, the `concat` operation can be implemented *more* efficiently (see Exercise 5.5).

```
public static String standardize (String surname) {
// Return surname with the prefix "Mc" (if present) replaced by "Mac".
//  (This is needed for sorting Scottish surnames into directory order.)
    int letters = surname.length();
    if (letters > 2
        && surname.substring(0, 2).equals("Mc"))
      return "Mac".concat(
          surname.substring(2, letters));
    else
      return surname;
}
```

Program 5.12   A possible application of the `String` ADT.

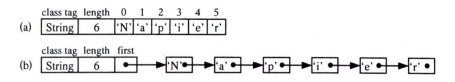

Figure 5.13   Alternative representations of `String` objects: (a) array of characters; (b) SLL of characters.

Table 5.14   Implementation of the `String` ADT using arrays and SLLs: summary of time complexities (where n, n_1, and n_2 are the lengths of the strings involved).

Operation	Time complexity (array representation)	Time complexity (SLL representation)
`length`	$O(1)$	$O(1)$
`charAt`	$O(1)$	$O(n)$
`equals`	$O(\min(n_1, n_2))$	$O(\min(n_1, n_2))$
`compareTo`	$O(\min(n_1, n_2))$	$O(\min(n_1, n_2))$
`substring`	$O(n_2)$	$O(n_1)$
`concat`	$O(n_1 + n_2)$	$O(n_1)$

Table 5.14 summarizes the time complexities of all the operations with both data representations. There is no doubt that the array representation is the better choice for this `String` ADT.

5.4.2 Mutable strings

Immutable strings have important advantages: they are easy to understand, and they can be simply and efficiently represented using arrays. They have an equally important disadvantage: every call to a transformer creates a new `String` object. For this reason alone, applications that frequently transform strings are likely to be very time-consuming.

Program 5.15 shows a possible contract for an ADT named `MutableString`. This contract meets all the requirements stated at the start of Section 5.4. Requirement 1 is met by the `MutableString` constructor in conjunction with the `insert` (or `append`) method, since, starting with an empty string, we can generate any nonempty string by one or more insertions. Requirements 2–6 are met by the `length`, `charAt`, `substring`, `compareTo`, and `append` methods, respectively.

Program 5.16 is a simple application of the `MutableString` ADT. This method might be part of a text editor.

Let us now consider a possible data representation, using an array. (We have already seen that an SLL of characters is unsuitable as a string representation.) If `setCharAt` were the only mutative transformer, the array representation of Figure 5.13(a) would be perfectly adequate; this operation would simply overwrite one of the characters in the array. However, insertion increases the number of characters in the string. With the array representation of Figure 5.13(a), the only way to implement insertion would be to create a new and longer array, copy the original characters and the inserted characters into the new array, and discard the old array. This would be very time-consuming.

It is more efficient simply to insert characters into the original array (using a variant of Algorithm 3.6); this works provided that the original array is long enough. Figure 5.17 shows a suitable data representation. To allow for future insertions, the array has extra components on the right, which are unoccupied for the time being. The length field keeps

```
public class MutableString {
    // Each MutableString value is a mutable string of characters, of
    // any length, with consecutive indices starting at 0.

    private ...;   // ... instance variables, not shown here.

    ///////////// Constructor /////////////

    public MutableString ();
    // Construct an empty mutable string.

    ///////////// Accessors /////////////

    public int length ();
    // Return the length of this mutable string.

    public char charAt (int i);
    // Return the character at index i in this mutable string.

    public int compareTo (MutableString that);
    // Return −1 if this mutable string is lexicographically less than that,
    // or 0 if this mutable string is equal to that,
    // or +1 if this mutable string is lexicographically greater than that.

    public String substring (int i, int j);
    // Return the substring of this mutable string consisting of the characters
    // whose indices are i through j−1.

    ///////////// Transformers /////////////

    public void setCharAt (int i, char c);
    // Set the character at index i in this mutable string to c.

    public void append (String s);
    // Insert the characters of s after the last character of this mutable string.

    public void insert (int i, String s);
    // Insert the characters of s before the character at index i in this mutable
    // string.

    public void delete (int i, int j);
    // Delete the characters of this mutable string whose indices are i through
    // j−1.
}
```

Program 5.15   A possible contract for the MutableString ADT.

track of the length of the string (as opposed to the length of the array); this field is increased by insertion and decreased by deletion.

Of course, there is still a risk that the string will eventually grow too long for the array, a situation that we call an **overflow**. When an overflow occurs, we have no choice but to create a new array, as previously described. But this should not be too time-consuming, on average, provided that we take care to ensure that overflows are infrequent.

This string representation makes both insertion and deletion simple. The main problem is to decide how long to make the array. If we make the array too long, many array components will be unoccupied, wasting space. If we make the array too short, overflows will be frequent. The following alternative strategies are simple and quite effective in practice:

- Whenever an overflow occurs, create a new array that is a fixed number of characters longer than the new string.
- Whenever an overflow occurs, create a new array that is (say) twice as long as the new string.

```
public static void substitute (MutableString line,
                String str1, String str2) {
// Replace every occurrence of str1 by str2 in line.
    int length1 = str1.length(),
        length2 = str2.length();
    int i = 0;
    while (i + length1 <= line.length()) {
      if (str1.equals(
            line.substring(i, i + length1))) {
        line.delete(i, i + length1);
        line.insert(i, str2);
        i += length2;
      } else
        i++;
    }
}
```

Program 5.16 A possible application of the MutableString ADT.

Figure 5.17 Possible representation of MutableString objects.

5.5 Collection abstract data types

In the remainder of this book we shall study a variety of important ADTs:

- *stacks*
- *queues*
- *lists* (or *sequences*)
- *sets*
- *maps* (or *tables*)
- *trees*
- *graphs* (or *networks*).

These ADTs are ubiquitous: at least one of them can be found in almost every software system. Moreover, all have their counterparts in everyday life, for example a *stack* of plates in a diner, a *queue* of passengers at a bus stop, a *list* of places to visit, a *set* of items on a menu, a *table* of countries' economic data, a family *tree*, or a road *network*.

These ADTs are collectively known as collections. A ***collection*** consists of zero or more *elements* (values or objects), and is equipped with operations to add elements to the collection, or to remove elements from the collection. The elements of a given collection are typically all of the same type.

Each kind of collection has its own peculiar properties. For example, the elements of stacks, queues, and lists have a fixed order, while the elements of sets and maps have no particular order.

Consequently, each kind of collection is equipped with its own characteristic operations. A stack allows us to add and remove elements at the same end only. A queue allows us to add and remove elements at opposite ends only. A list allows us to add and remove elements at any given position. A set allows us simply to add and remove elements: its elements have no particular order, so where the elements are to be added and removed is a question that simply does not arise.

We can represent collections by data structures such as:

- *arrays*
- *linked lists*
- *binary trees*
- *hash tables*.

We have already studied arrays and linked lists, which are particularly well suited for representing stacks, queues, and lists. Binary trees and hash tables are particularly well suited for representing sets and maps.

5.6 Abstract data types in the Java class library

The Java class library contains about 2000 classes. For convenience, these classes are grouped into several major *packages*, each package containing classes that are in some way related to one another. A significant proportion of the library classes are ADTs: their data representations (instance variables) are private.

5.6.1 The `java.lang` package

The `java.lang` package provides classes that are essentially parts of the Java language itself.

The `java.lang.String` class is similar to the `String` ADT of Program 5.11, but provides a richer set of operations and consequently meets a larger set of requirements. This class provides a variety of constructors. It also provides methods to search a string, either left-to-right or right-to-left, for a given character or a given substring; to test whether a string has a given prefix (leftmost substring) or suffix (rightmost substring); to edit a string in various useful ways, such as trimming spaces or changing letter case; and so on. The Java language has special syntax for some `String` operations: string literals abbreviate calls to `String` constructors (as explained in Section 5.4.1); the operator '+' abbreviates a call to the `concat` method. In this sense, `String` behaves like a built-in data type of Java.

The oddly-named `java.lang.StringBuffer` class is similar to the `MutableString` ADT of Program 5.15, but again provides a richer set of operations.

5.6.2 The `java.util` package

The `java.util` package provides a number of 'utility' classes. Most programs use some of these classes.

The values of the `java.util.Date` class are specific instants in time, accurate to one millisecond. It provides some operations similar to those of the `Date` ADT of Program 5.6, and more besides. A particularly important operation with no counterpart in Program 5.6 is a parameterless `Date` constructor, which returns the *current* time. Unfortunately, the design of the Java 1.0 `Date` class was found unsuitable for internationalization. (There are many different calendars in use around the world.) Since Java 1.1, most of the `Date` operations have been superseded by operations in the new `java.util.Calendar` class. The current design of Java's date/time classes is messy and confusing: some of the `Calendar` operations would belong more naturally in the `Date` class.

Since Java 2, the `java.util` package has included a number of collection classes, providing lists, sets, and maps. We will study these classes later in this book, in Chapters 8, 9, and 11. Appendix C provides a summary of the Java 2 collection classes.

5.6.3 The `java.awt` package

This package contains a large variety of classes concerned with graphics and graphical user interfaces, including the following.

The values of the `java.awt.Font` class are fonts. This class provides operations to construct a font from its font-name, style, and size; to obtain the font's font-name, style, or size; and so on.

The values of the `java.awt.Graphics` class are essentially pictures. This class provides operations to clear or clip the picture; to add a line or string to the picture; to add a filled or unfilled oval, polygon, or rectangle to the picture; and so on.

The values of the `java.awt.Button`, `Canvas`, `Checkbox`, `Choice`, `Dialog`, `List`, `Scrollbar`, `TextArea`, and `TextField` classes are widgets of various kinds.

5.6.4 The `java.io` package

The `java.io` package supports input–output.

The values of the `java.io.File` class are files. The representation of a file varies from one platform to another. (A *platform* is a combination of processor and operating system.) Keeping the file representation private allows application code to read and write files without becoming tightly coupled to the file representation. In other words, such application code is *portable*: it can be moved with little or no change from one platform to another.

The values of the `java.io.InputStream` class are byte input streams, allowing data to be read byte-by-byte. Similarly, the values of the `java.io.OutputStream` class are byte output streams. An `InputStream` or `OutputStream` object can be constructed by opening a file, for example.

The values of the `java.io.Reader` class are character input streams, allowing data to be read character-by-character. Similarly, the values of the `java.io.Writer` class are character output streams. A `Reader` or `Writer` object can be constructed from an `InputStream` or `OutputStream` object, respectively.

The values of the `java.io.BufferedReader` class are buffered character input streams, allowing text to be read character-by-character or line-by-line. Similarly, the values of the `java.io.BufferedWriter` class are buffered character output streams. A `BufferedReader` or `BufferedWriter` object can be constructed from a `Reader` or `Writer` object, respectively.

Summary

In this chapter:

- We have studied the distinction between data types (characterized by their values, operations, and representation) and ADTs (characterized by their values and operations only).
- We have studied how to specify an ADT by means of a contract, how to implement it, and how to change the implementation without disturbing the application code.
- We have studied how to design an ADT, assessing whether its operations are both necessary and sufficient, and classifying its operations as constructors, accessors, and (mutative and applicative) transformers.
- We have designed immutable and mutable string ADTs.
- We have previewed the collection ADTs that we shall study in subsequent chapters.
- We have surveyed some of the ADTs readily available as Java library classes.

Exercises

5.1 The so-called 'millennium bug' was a major problem for the software industry in the late 1990s. In numerous application programs and databases, each date was represented by a string of decimal digits: two digits for the day-in-month number, two digits for the month number, and two digits for the year number. For example, 31 December 1999 was represented by '311299', the leading digits '19' of the year number being implicit. Thus there was no means to represent dates after (or before) the twentieth century.

In principle, the solution was simple: what? In practice, the problem was enormous: why?

5.2 Re-design and re-implement the class `Person` (Example 5.1) to make it an ADT. Pay particular attention to the choice of operations. Provide sufficient operations to allow application code to manipulate `Person` objects in all reasonable ways – but provide no more operations than necessary.

5.3 Consider the `Date` contract of Program 5.6. Re-implement this contract, representing a date simply by a year number and a day-in-year number, as illustrated in Figure 5.5(b). Compare your implementation with Programs 5.8 and 5.9.

5.4 Enhance the class `Date` (Program 5.10). Provide sufficient operations to allow application code to manipulate `Date` objects in all reasonable ways – but provide no more operations than necessary.

5.5 Consider the `String` contract of Program 5.11.
  (a) Implement this contract, using each of the data representations illustrated in Figure 5.13. Test each of your implementations using a simple application, which you should also test against `java.lang.String`. (*Note:* Your application should avoid using any of Java's special string syntax, such as string literals.)
  (b) Derive each operation's time complexity. Compare with Table 5.14.
  (c) With the SLL representation, how is it possible to implement `concat` with time complexity $O(n_1)$, i.e., independent of the second string's length n_2?

5.6 A *text* is a sequence of characters subdivided into lines. One application of a text is the internal buffer of a text editor.
  (a) Design a text ADT suitable to support a text editor. Assume the usual editing facilities: insertion and deletion of characters, cut, copy, and paste.
  (b) Choose a representation for texts, and implement your ADT in Java.

5.7 Design an ADT to represent a time of day. What operations do you need to provide?
  Implement your ADT in Java in at least two different ways. Which implementation is the easier?

5.8 Design an ADT that combines a date and time-of-day. What operations do you need to provide? (*Hint:* consider the date ADT from Example 5.2 and the time-of-day ADT from Exercise 5.7.)
  Implement your ADT as a Java class. What is the easiest way to do this?

5.9 (For readers familiar with complex numbers.) Design an ADT to represent complex numbers in Java. What operations do you need to provide?
  Implement your ADT in Java using both Cartesian and polar coordinates. Which implementation is the easier?

5.10 Design an ADT to represent a university course. Assume that a course has a course code, a course title, at least one instructor, and one or more teaching assistants. What operations do you need to provide?

   Implement your ADT as a Java class.

5.11 Section 5.5 gave some examples of collection ADTs that occur in everyday life. Can you think of some more examples?

5.12 Locate the on-line documentation for the Java collection classes. You may have a local copy on your computer system, or you may have to find it at Sun's Java Web site (java.sun.com).

   Bookmark the location in your Web browser. You will need to refer to it frequently while reading this book.

6

Stack Abstract Data Types

In this chapter we shall study:

- the concept of a stack (Section 6.1)
- simple applications of stacks (Section 6.2)
- requirements and a contract for a stack abstract data type (Section 6.3)
- alternative implementations of stacks using arrays and linked lists (Sections 6.4–5)
- a case study using stacks (Section 6.6).

6.1 The concept of a stack

Stacks are commonplace in everyday life. A familiar example is a stack of plates in a diner. Staff add newly-washed plates to the top of the stack, and customers take plates from the top of the stack. The last plate to be added is always the first plate to be removed. For this reason, a stack is sometimes called a *last-in-first-out* sequence.

Another example is a stack of books on a table. Figure 6.1 illustrates such a stack, and shows the effects of removing and adding one book at a time. Books can be added and removed only at the top of the stack. We cannot remove a book below the top without first removing all the books above it. Nor can we add a book below other books without first removing these other books.

Let us now define our terms. A *stack* is a sequence of elements, with the property that elements can be added and removed only at one end (the *top* of the stack).

The *depth* of a stack is the number of elements it contains. The *empty stack* has depth zero.

6.2 Applications of stacks

Stacks turn out to be enormously useful in computing, in both application and system programming. The following examples illustrate simple applications of stacks.

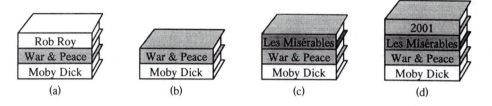

Figure 6.1   A stack of books (illustrating the effect of removing a book and then successively adding two books).

To output the lines in *file* in reverse order:

1. Make *line-stack* empty.
2. For each *line* read from *file*, repeat:
    2.1. Add *line* to the top of *line-stack*.
3. While *line-stack* is not empty, repeat:
    3.1. Remove a line from the top of *line-stack* into *line*.
    3.2. Output *line*.
4. Terminate.

Algorithm 6.2   File reversal algorithm.

EXAMPLE 6.1   *Reversing a text file*

A text file consists of zero or more lines, where each line is a string of characters. Our problem is to output these lines in reverse order.

We can read the file one line at a time, starting with the first line. Since we are required to output the first line last and the last line first, we cannot output any lines until we have read them all. Clearly, therefore, we must store the lines in a last-in-first-out sequence, i.e., a stack.

Algorithm 6.2 reads lines one at a time from the file and adds them to a stack (step 2). It then removes lines one at a time from the stack and outputs them (step 3).

To implement this algorithm in Java, we will need an object to represent a stack of strings. For step 1, let us assume a constructor that creates an empty stack. For step 2.1, let us assume that `s.addLast` (*x*) adds *x* to the top of stack *s*. For step 3, let us assume that `s.isEmpty()` tests whether stack *s* is empty. For step 3.1, let us assume that `s.removeLast()` removes and returns the element at the top of stack *s*.

Program 6.3 shows a Java implementation of the algorithm. This assumes a class `StringStack` whose objects represent stacks of strings, and which is equipped with `addLast`, `removeLast`, and `isEmpty` methods as suggested above.

EXAMPLE 6.2   *Matching brackets*

Bracketing is a feature of many languages, both natural and artificial. In English, for example, round brackets '(' and ')' are used to enclose auxiliary phrases (such as this

```
public static void reverse (BufferedReader input,
                BufferedWriter output)
            throws IOException {
// Copy input to output with lines in reverse order.
   StringStack lineStack = new StringStack();
   for (;;) {
      String line = input.readLine();
      if (line == null)  break;   // ... end of input.
      lineStack.addLast(line);
   }
   input.close();
   while (! lineStack.isEmpty()) {
      String line = lineStack.removeLast();
      output.write(line);
      output.write("\n");
   }
   output.close();
}
```

Program 6.3   Java implementation of the file reversal algorithm.

one) that could just as well be left out. In Java, round brackets '(' and ')' are used for grouping subexpressions and for enclosing arguments in a method call; square brackets '[' and ']' are used for enclosing the index expression in an array access; and curly brackets '{' and '}' are used for grouping statements. In mathematical notation, both round and square brackets are used for grouping subexpressions; curly brackets are used for sets.

Whatever the language, every phrase must be *well-bracketed*. That is to say, all brackets in the phrase must be paired: for each left bracket there must be a later matching right bracket, and for each right bracket there must be an earlier matching left bracket. Moreover, any subphrase enclosed between brackets must itself be well-bracketed. The following mathematical expressions are well-bracketed:

$$s \times (s - a) \times (s - b) \times (s - c)$$
$$(- b \pm \sqrt{[b^2 - 4ac]}) / 2a$$

but the following are ill-bracketed:

$s \times (s - a) \times (s - b \times (s - c)$ (unpaired left bracket)
$s \times (s - a) \times s - b) \times (s - c)$ (unpaired right bracket)
$(- b \pm \sqrt{[b^2 - 4ac})]/2a$ (mismatched brackets)

We can test whether a given phrase is well-bracketed by scanning it from left to right. When we encounter a left bracket, we must store it somewhere until we encounter the corresponding right bracket, since between the left and right brackets there might be many other brackets, which have to be paired in the same way. So we should add each left bracket to a stack, removing it when we encounter the corresponding right bracket.

To test whether *phrase* is well-bracketed:

1. Make *bracket-stack* empty.
2. For each symbol *sym* in *phrase* (scanning from left to right), repeat:
   2.1. If *sym* is a left bracket:
       2.1.1. Add *sym* to the top of *bracket-stack*.
   2.2. If *sym* is a right bracket:
       2.2.1. If *bracket-stack* is empty, terminate with answer false.
       2.2.2. Remove a bracket from the top of *bracket-stack* into *left*.
       2.2.3. If *left* and *sym* are not matched brackets, terminate with answer false.
3. Terminate with answer true if *bracket-stack* is empty, or false otherwise.

Algorithm 6.4   Bracket matching algorithm.

```
public static boolean wellBracketed (String phrase) {
// Test whether phrase is well-bracketed.
   SymbolStack bracketStack = new SymbolStack();
   for (int i = 0; i < phrase.length(); i++) {
      char sym = phrase.charAt(i);
      if (sym == '(' || sym == '[' || sym == '{')
         bracketStack.addLast(sym);
      else if (sym == ')' || sym == ']'
            || sym == '}') {
         if (bracketStack.isEmpty())  return false;
         char left = bracketStack.removeLast();
         if (! matched(left, sym))  return false;
      }
   }
   return (bracketStack.isEmpty());
}

public static boolean matched
                  (char left, char right) {
// Return true if and only if left is a left bracket and right is the matching
// right bracket.
   switch (left) {
      case '(':  return (right == ')');
      case '[':  return (right == ']');
      case '{':  return (right == '}');
      default:   return false;
   }
}
```

Program 6.5   Java implementation of the bracket matching algorithm.

Algorithm 6.4 captures this idea. A left bracket is added to the stack at step 2.1.1, and removed at step 2.2.2 when a right bracket is encountered. Note the care taken to detect all possible symptoms of ill-bracketing: an unpaired left bracket (step 3), an unpaired right bracket (step 2.2.1), and mismatched brackets (step 2.2.3).

Program 6.5 shows a Java implementation. It assumes a class `SymbolStack`, whose objects represent stacks of symbols (characters), and whose methods include `addLast`, `removeLast`, and `isEmpty` as in Example 6.1.

Stacks are useful, not only in application programming, but also in systems such as programming language implementations. For example, a stack lies at the heart of the Java Virtual Machine. This stack is used to store intermediate results during evaluation of complicated expressions. More importantly, it is central to the implementation of method calls. On call, the arguments are added to the top of the stack. On return, they are removed. If one method calls a second method, which in turn calls a third method, all these methods' arguments will be in the stack at the same time. This scheme works just as well when a recursive method calls itself.

6.3 A stack abstract data type

We have seen that the stack is a widely useful concept. Let us therefore design a stack ADT. Let us assume the following requirements:

1. It must be possible to make a stack empty.
2. It must be possible to add an element to the top of a stack.
3. It must be possible to remove the topmost element from a stack.
4. It must be possible to test whether a stack is empty.
5. It should be possible to access the element at the top of a stack without removing it.

We identified requirements 1–4 in Section 6.2. Requirement 5 is a reasonable addition. (We could add further requirements: see Exercise 6.5.)

Program 6.6 shows a possible contract for the stack ADT, in the form of a Java interface named `Stack`. Most of the interface should be self-explanatory. In order to make the ADT as general as possible, the stacked elements will be objects.

In designing this ADT we must decide what should happen if the `getLast` or `removeLast` operation is applied to an empty stack. Since the operation cannot return a nonexistent element, we have chosen to make it throw a suitable exception. It will then be a matter for the application program either to anticipate this situation by catching the exception or (better) to ensure that it never arises. (Programs 6.3 and 6.5 always checked that the stack was nonempty before calling the `removeLast` operation.)

If the names of the operations `addLast`, `removeLast`, and `getLast` seem a little strange, remember that the *last* element added to a stack (and not yet removed) is at the top of the stack, and that is where the operation does its work.

Each class that implements the `Stack` interface must provide all the methods of this interface. The class will declare private instance variables to represent the stack, and its methods will inspect and update these instance variables as appropriate. Thus we can be

```
public interface Stack {

    // Each Stack object is a stack whose elements are objects.

    //////////// Accessors ////////////

    public boolean isEmpty ();
    // Return true if and only if this stack is empty.

    public Object getLast ();
    // Return the element at the top of this stack. Throw a
    // NoSuchElementException if this stack is empty.

    //////////// Transformers ////////////

    public void clear ();
    // Make this stack empty.

    public void addLast (Object elem);
    // Add elem as the top element of this stack.

    public Object removeLast ();
    // Remove and return the element at the top of this stack. Throw a
    // NoSuchElementException if this stack is empty.

}
```

Program 6.6   A contract for a stack ADT.

confident that every Stack object is equipped with the required stack operations. (By a Stack object we mean an object of any class that implements the Stack interface.)

It should be clear now that the StringStack class of Example 6.1 could be written to implement the Stack interface. The SymbolStack class of Example 6.2 is slightly different, because its elements are assumed to be **char** values; however, that example could easily be modified to wrap up the **char** values in Character objects before adding them to the stack, and unwrap them on removing them from the stack.

We now go on to consider, in Sections 6.4 and 6.5, two possible implementations of the Stack contract.

6.4 Implementation of bounded stacks using arrays

A *bounded stack* is one whose depth is limited. If the stack's maximum depth is *maxdepth*, its current depth can vary from 0 through *maxdepth*.

A bounded stack can easily be represented by an array *elems* of length *maxdepth*. When the stack's depth is less than *maxdepth*, some of the array components will be unoccupied, so we must keep track of the stack's current depth, say *depth*. Let us agree that the stacked elements will occupy the subarray *elems*[0…*depth* − 1], in order from bottom to top, and that the value of *depth* will be held in an instance variable. Figure 6.7

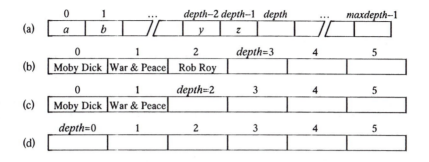

Figure 6.7   Representation of bounded stacks by arrays: (a) general case (z topmost); (b–c) stacks of book titles (with *maxdepth* $=$ 6); (d) empty stack.

shows this representation in the general case, and also illustrates how a stack of book titles would be represented.

The implementation of the stack ADT is now very straightforward, and is shown in Program 6.8. This is a Java class `ArrayStack` that is declared as implementing the `Stack` interface. The instance variable `elems` is an array whose size is fixed when the stack is constructed, and its components are all initially null. The instance variable `depth` keeps track of the stack's depth, and is initially zero. The `addLast` operation increments `depth` and stores the new element in the array. The `removeLast` operation conversely decrements `depth` and returns what was formerly the top element. These stack operations have time complexity $O(1)$: we cannot improve on that!

We must consider the possibility that the `addLast` operation is called when the stack is already full: there are no unoccupied array components. This is an *overflow*. Program 6.8 shows one possible technique for dealing with an overflow. The `addLast` operation calls the auxiliary method `expand`, which copies all the stack elements into a new and longer array and replaces the existing array by that new array. This technique keeps the interface simple, and incidentally gives us an implementation of unbounded stacks. Unfortunately, it is time-consuming.

Another possible technique would be to make the `addLast` operation throw an exception, which the application program can handle as appropriate. Unfortunately, this implies a change in the operation's observable behavior, which must be documented in the `Stack` interface:

```
public void addLast (Object elem);
// Add elem as the top element of this stack, or throw a StackException
// if this stack is already full.
```

Here `StackException` should be declared as a subclass of `RuntimeException`. (See Exercise 6.6.)

The array implementation of stacks would be suitable for the bracket matching application of Example 6.2. Humans have difficulty in understanding expressions with deeply nested brackets, and it is extremely unlikely that any expression will be encountered with brackets nested more than (say) ten deep. So a stack with maximum depth 10 would be satisfactory.

The array implementation of stacks would *not* be suitable for the file reversal application of Example 6.1. The stack depth will equal the number of lines in the file. It would be artificial and unsatisfactory to limit the file to some small number of lines.

6.5 Implementation of unbounded stacks using linked lists

An unbounded stack can easily be represented by a singly-linked list (SLL), with the top element in the first node and the bottom element in the last node. A link to the first node is all we need, since elements will be added and removed at that end only. Figure 6.9 shows this representation in the general case, and also illustrates how a stack of bock titles would be represented.

The implementation of the stack ADT is now very straightforward, and is shown in Program 6.10. This is a Java class `LinkedStack` that is declared as implementing the `Stack` interface. The instance variable `top` is a link to the first node, and is initially null.

```java
public class ArrayStack implements Stack {

    //  Each ArrayStack object is a bounded stack whose elements are
    //  objects.

    //  This stack is represented as follows: its depth is held in depth, and
    //  its elements occupy the subarray elems[0...depth-1].
    private Object[] elems;
    private int depth;

    ///////////// Constructor /////////////

    public ArrayStack (int maxDepth) {
    //  Construct a stack, initially empty, whose depth will be bounded by
    //  maxDepth.
        elems = new Object[maxDepth];
        //  ... All components of elems are initially null.
        depth = 0;
    }

    ///////////// Accessors /////////////

    public boolean isEmpty () {
    //  Return true if and only if this stack is empty.
        return (depth == 0);
    }
```

Program 6.8   Java implementation of bounded stacks using arrays (*continued on next page*).

```java
public Object getLast () {
// Return the element at the top of this stack. Throw a
// NoSuchElementException if this stack is empty.
   if (depth == 0)
     throw new NoSuchElementException();
   return elems[depth-1];
}
```

/////////// Transformers ///////////

```java
public void clear () {
// Make this stack empty.
   for (int i = 0; i < depth; i++)
     elems[i] = null;
   depth = 0;
}

public void addLast (Object elem) {
// Add elem as the top element on this stack.
   if (depth == elems.length)
     expand();
   elems[depth++] = elem;
}

public Object removeLast () {
// Remove and return the element at the top of this stack. Throw a
// NoSuchElementException if this stack is empty.
   if (depth == 0)
     throw new NoSuchElementException();
   Object topElem = elems[--depth];
   elems[depth] = null;
   return topElem;
}
```

/////////// Auxiliary method ///////////

```java
private void expand () {
// Make the elems array longer.
   Object[] newElems = new Object[2*elems.length];
   for (int i = 0; i < depth; i++)
     newElems[i] = elems[i];
   elems = newElems;
}

}
```

Program 6.8   *(continued)*

There is no need to keep track of the stack's depth. The addLast operation simply creates a new node and inserts it before the SLL's first node. The removeLast operation simply deletes the SLL's first node. Both these stack operations have time complexity $O(1)$.

The nodes are of class SLLNode, shown in Program 4.4. Note that the stack implementation is simple enough not to need the more general linked-list insertion and deletion algorithms of Sections 4.2.1 and 4.3.1.

The linked-list implementation of stacks would be suitable in any application, including the file reversal application of Example 6.1 and the bracket matching application of Example 6.2. In particular, the absence of a bound on the stack depth is

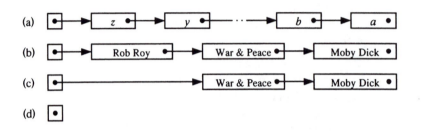

Figure 6.9   Representation of unbounded stacks by SLLs: (a) general case (z topmost); (b–c) stacks of book titles; (d) empty stack.

```
public class LinkedStack implements Stack {

    //  Each LinkedStack object is an unbounded stack whose elements are
    //  objects.

    //  This stack is represented as follows: top is a link to the first node of an
    //  SLL containing the stack's elements, in top-to-bottom order.
    private SLLNode top;

    ///////////// Constructor /////////////

    public LinkedStack () {
    // Construct a stack, initially empty.
       top = null;
    }

    ///////////// Accessors /////////////

    public boolean isEmpty () {
    // Return true if and only if this stack is empty.
       return (top == null);
    }
```

Program 6.10   Java implementation of unbounded stacks using SLLs (*continued on next page*).

```
public Object getLast () {
// Return the element at the top of this stack. Throw a
// NoSuchElementException if this stack is empty.
   if (top == null)
      throw new NoSuchElementException();
   return top.element;
}

//////////// Transformers ////////////

public void clear () {
// Make this stack empty.
   top = null;
}

public void addLast (Object elem) {
// Add elem as the top element on this stack.
   top = new SLLNode(elem, top);
}

public Object removeLast () {
// Remove and return the element at the top of this stack. Throw a
// NoSuchElementException if this stack is empty.
   if (top == null)
      throw new NoSuchElementException();
   Object topElem = top.element;
   top = top.succ;
   return topElem;
}

}
```

Program 6.10 (*continued*)

essential in the file reversal application, because there is no bound on the number of lines in the file.

6.6 Case study: solving and generating mazes

Many people enjoy the challenge of solving a maze, whether it is a maze printed on paper or a real maze constructed from paths and hedges. Solving a maze involves finding a path from a start point to an exit point, if such a path exists. We will assume that a maze has a single start and at least one exit. In this section we shall develop iterative algorithms for solving and generating a maze, each of which uses a stack.

We shall consider only *perfect* mazes. A perfect maze has exactly one path between any two points. This implies that the maze contains no inaccessible areas, no cycles, and no open spaces. Figure 6.11 shows examples of a perfect maze and an imperfect maze. A consequence of our definition is that we should always be able to solve a perfect maze, regardless of the choice of the start and exit points.

We begin by discussing how a maze can be represented in the computer. Then we develop a recursive algorithm for solving a maze. Next, we present an iterative algorithm for solving a maze. Finally, we present an iterative algorithm for generating a maze.

This book's companion Web site contains the complete code for a Java applet that uses our maze generating and solving algorithms repeatedly to generate and solve mazes. Each maze is drawn as it is being generated and as it is being solved. While it is being solved, the current search path and the visited squares are shown in different colors.

(*Note:*Much of the information on mazes in this section was culled from the interesting Web site `www.mazeworks.com/mazegen`.)

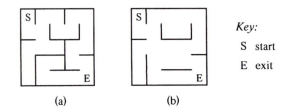

Figure 6.11   Illustrations of (a) a perfect maze and (b) an imperfect maze.

6.6.1 A representation of a maze

We assume that a maze is a rectangular collection of squares. Each square in the maze has four sides, which we will call its north, east, south, and west sides. Each side can be either a wall or a path to an adjacent square. Each square in the maze can be identified by its position, consisting of a column number x and a row number y. One of the squares is designated as the start square, and one or more squares are designated as exit squares.

The obvious implementation of a maze is a two-dimensional array of squares. But how should we represent an individual square? Each side of the square can be either a wall or a path. We could represent each side by a boolean, with true representing a wall and false representing a path. Alternatively we could represent each side by an integer, with 1 representing a wall and 0 representing a path. A square consists of four such values, one for each side. The choice of representation should not affect our design, but it will affect the space required to store the maze, and the time taken to generate and solve it.

While solving a maze, we must also keep track of the *state* of each square. This consists of four pieces of information: whether the square is the start; whether the square is an exit; whether we have already visited this square; and whether this square forms part of a possible path from the start to an exit. Again, we could represent each piece of the state by a boolean or by an integer. And, again, this decision should not affect our design, but it will affect the efficiency of our implementation.

Program 6.12 outlines a Java implementation of a maze, in the form of a class named `Maze`. We have chosen to represent each square by a single byte: four of the bits represent the sides of the square, and the other four bits represent the state of the square.

With this representation, we must use bitwise 'and', 'or' and 'not' operations to access the different pieces of information. This low-level detail, however, can be largely hidden by defining a *flag* for each bit of the byte, and using the names of the flags in our program. We use four flags to represent the sides (NORTH, EAST, SOUTH, and WEST) and four flags to represent the state (START, EXIT, VISITED, and PATH). Each of the four sides of a square is a wall if the corresponding bit is set (i.e., 1), and a path if it is reset (i.e., 0). Similarly, the state of the square has a given property if the corresponding bit is set; for instance, the square is an exit square if the bit determined by the flag EXIT is set.

If we consider only the four bits used to represent the sides of the squares, then in order from right to left, the bits represent the north, east, south, and west sides. For example, for the maze shown in Figure 6.11(a), the north-western square (column number 0, row number 0) would be represented by the binary value 1011. This represents a square with walled sides to the north, east and west, but a path to the south.

When we implement algorithms to process a maze, we require a class of objects to represent positions of squares in the maze. Each position has a column number *x* and a row number *y*. Program 6.13 shows a Java implementation of positions in the form of an inner class named Maze.Position.

Finally, we must consider the auxiliary methods required in the class Maze. Program 6.14 lists these auxiliary methods, which have been carefully chosen to simplify the implementation of the maze solving and generating algorithms. These methods are added to the Maze class of Program 6.12.

6.6.2 A recursive maze solving algorithm

In Exercise 2.11 you were asked to develop a recursive algorithm to find your way out of a maze. You may have developed such an algorithm without regard to its implementation on a computer. Algorithm 6.15 is one such recursive algorithm to find a path from the square at position *start* to an exit square (of which there may be several). It returns the answer true if it finds a path, or false otherwise. To prevent the algorithm from retracing its steps, the path must be constructed entirely from previously unvisited squares.

Algorithm 6.15 has one easy case and one hard case. The easy case is when *start* is itself an exit. Then we have successfully found a path from *start* to an exit, so we can terminate immediately with the answer true (after marking *start* as part of the path). The hard case is when *start* is not an exit. Then we continue our search starting at one of the unvisited neighbors of *start*. This is an easier problem, since the number of squares to search has been reduced by one (*start* having been visited already at step 1). Step 3 searches for a path starting at a neighbor, as long as there are more neighbors to search. If we have at least one unvisited neighbor, then step 3.1 selects one, and step 3.2 recursively calls the algorithm to find a path starting at that neighbor. If we find a path starting at that neighbor, then we have also found a path starting at *start*, so we terminate with the answer true. If we exhaust all of the neighbors of *start* without finding a path, then *start* cannot be on a path to an exit. In this case, we remove *start* from the path and terminate with the answer false.

Program 6.16 shows an implementation of Algorithm 6.15 as a Java method named findAPath. It is a straightforward translation of the algorithm into Java, and uses the

```java
public class Maze {

    // The size of the maze in squares:
    private static final int WIDTH = 50, HEIGHT = 50;

    // The maze itself:
    private byte[][] maze;

    // Flag constants representing the different sides of a square (used by the
    // mark, unmark and isMarked methods, see below):
    private static final byte
        NORTH = 0x01,   EAST = 0x02,
        SOUTH = 0x04,   WEST = 0x08,
        ALL   = 0x0F;

    // Flag constants representing the different states of a square (used by the
    // mark, unmark and isMarked methods, see below):
    private static final byte
        VISITED = 0x10,   PATH  = 0x20,
        EXIT    = 0x40,   START = (byte) 0x80;

    ///////////// Constructor /////////////

    public Maze () {
        maze = new byte[WIDTH][HEIGHT];
    }

    ...   // Methods to generate and solve the maze (Sections 6.6.2–4).

    ...   // Auxiliary methods (Program 6.14).

}
```

Program 6.12   Java implementation of a maze (outline).

```java
private static class Position {

    // Each Maze.Position object represents the position of the square
    // at column number x and row number y in a maze.
    private int x, y;

    private Position (int x, int y) {
        this.x = x;   this.y = y;
    }

}
```

Program 6.13   Java implementation of the position of a square in the maze (as an inner class of class Maze).

`Maze.Position` class of Program 6.13. This method would be part of the Java class `Maze` of Program 6.12.

6.6.3 An iterative maze solving algorithm

Imagine that we are trying to solve a real maze. Naturally we want to avoid getting lost. We can use a long cord to keep track of our path through the maze, and a large bag of pebbles to mark the places we have already visited. We begin our search at the start square, where we fix one end of the cord to a heavy object and drop one of our pebbles on the ground. As we move through the maze, we unroll the cord and leave a pebble in each square that we pass.

```
private void mark (Maze.Position p, byte flag) {
// Mark the square at position p by setting the bit corresponding to flag,
// where flag is one of the flag constants, e.g., NORTH or VISITED.
    ... // See code on the companion Web site.
}

private void unmark (Maze.Position p, byte flag) {
// Unmark the square at position p by resetting the bit corresponding to flag,
// where flag is one of the flag constants, e.g., NORTH or VISITED.
    ... // See code on the companion Web site.
}

private boolean isMarked (Maze.Position p,
                byte flag) {
// Return true if and only if the square at position p has the bit corresponding
// to flag set, where flag is one of the flag constants,
// e.g., NORTH or VISITED.
    ... // See code on the companion Web site.
}

private boolean hasIntactNeighbors (Maze.Position p) {
// Return true if and only if the square at position p has at least one neighbor
// all of whose sides are walled. (Used to generate the maze.)
    ... // See code on the companion Web site.
}

private boolean hasUnvisitedNeighbors
                (Maze.Position p) {
// Return true if and only if the square at position p has at least one unvisited
// neighbor with a path from this square to the neighbor.
    ... // See code on the companion Web site.
}
```

Program 6.14 Auxiliary operations of the class `Maze` (outline) (*continued on next page*).

```
    private void removeWall (Maze.Position p1,
                    Maze.Position p2) {
    // Remove the wall between the squares at positions p1 and p2 (assuming that
    //   these positions are neighbors). (Used to generate the maze.)
        ... // See code on the companion Web site.
    }

    private Maze.Position chooseIntactNeighbor
                    (Maze.Position p) {
    // Choose a neighbor of the square at position p all of whose sides are walled.
    //   Choose the particular neighbor at random. Return the position of the chosen
    //   neighbor. (Used to generate the maze.)
        ... // See code on the companion Web site.
    }

    private Maze.Position chooseUnvisitedNeighbor
                    (Maze.Position p) {
    // Choose an unvisited neighbor of the square at position p such that there is a
    //   path between the square and the neighbor. Choose the particular neighbor
    //   either at random or in a predetermined order. Return the position of the
    //   chosen neighbor.
        ... // See code on the companion Web site.
    }

    private void markAllSidesWalled () {
    // Mark every side of every square of this maze as a wall. (Used to generate the
    //   maze.)
        ... // See code on the companion Web site.
    }

    private Maze.Position randomPosition () {
    // Return a position selected at random in this maze.
        ... // See code on the companion Web site.
    }
```

Program 6.14 (*continued*)

When we get to a junction, we must decide which way to proceed. It would be pointless to choose a path that is already marked by a pebble, since we have already been in that direction, so we should select a path that is unmarked. Sometimes we will walk into a dead end, either because there are no paths, or because all paths are marked by pebbles. When this happens, we *backtrack* through the maze, winding up the cord as we go. We backtrack to the square where either we find an unmarked path or we get back to the start with no paths to explore. In the former case, we continue searching the maze in the new direction. In the latter case, our search has been completely unsuccessful and we are stuck in the maze. Importantly, when we backtrack we never pick up any pebbles, for otherwise we would not know which paths we have already visited.

Consider the sequence of squares in the maze that the cord passes over. We know that the square at the fixed end of the cord is always the start, and the square at the other end of the cord is where we are currently standing. The intermediate squares over which the cord passes represent our current path through the maze. When we explore in a new direction, we unroll the cord, adding new squares to the end of our path. When we have to back-track, we roll up the cord, removing the squares that were previously at the end of our path. So the cord represents a stack: we add and remove squares only at one end of the cord, and we add and remove them in a last-in-first-out order. Also, we have access only to the square at the top of the stack, i.e., the square on which we are currently standing.

Our iterative maze solving algorithm mimics this use of cord and pebbles. It uses a stack of positions in the maze, named *path-stack*, to represent the current search path. Algorithm 6.17 shows the iterative maze solving algorithm. It begins in a similar way to Algorithm 6.15, marking the square at position *start* as visited and as part of the search path.

Next, step 2 initializes the search by making *path-stack* contain only the position *start*. In step 3, if not all possible squares in the maze have been exhausted, the search is continued from the position *current*, which is the topmost position of *path-stack*. If *current* is an exit, the algorithm terminates with answer true. If *current* is not an exit, it considers the neighboring squares of *current*. There are two possibilities:

- If the square at position *current* has at least one unvisited neighbor that is connected to *current* by a path, then step 3.3 selects one such neighbor, updates its state, and makes it part of the current path by adding its position to *path-stack*. The loop is then iterated again, this time with the position *current* being the previous *neighbor*.
- If the square at position *current* has no unvisited neighbors, then it cannot form part of the path to an exit, so step 3.4 removes it from *path-stack* and unmarks it as part of the path. The loop is then iterated again, having backtracked along the path by one square.

On termination, *path-stack* will contain the positions of the squares from the start to the exit for the path that has been found, or will be empty if no such path exists. The squares contained in *path-stack* are also marked in the maze as being part of the path.

> To find and mark a path from the square at position *start* to an exit:
>
> 1. Mark *start* as visited and as part of the path.
> 2. If *start* is an exit, terminate with answer true.
> 3. While *start* has an unvisited neighbor, repeat:
>   3.1. Set *neighbor* to the position of an unvisited neighbor of *start*.
>   3.2. If we find a path from the square at position *neighbor* to an exit, terminate with answer true.
> 4. Unmark *start* as part of the path.
> 5. Terminate with answer false.

Algorithm 6.15 A recursive maze solving algorithm.

```
public boolean findAPath (Maze.Position start) {
// Find and mark a path from the square at position start to an exit in this
// maze. Return true if and only if such a path exists.
   mark(start, VISITED);  mark(start, PATH);
   if (isMarked(start, EXIT))  return true;
   while (hasUnvisitedNeighbors(start)) {
     Maze.Position neighbor =
          chooseUnvisitedNeighbor(start);
     if (findAPath(neighbor))  return true;
   }
   unmark(start, PATH);
   return false;
}
```

Program 6.16 Java implementation of the recursive maze solving algorithm (in class `Maze`).

Program 6.18 is an implementation of Algorithm 6.17 as a Java method named `findAPath`. Like Program 6.16, this uses the `Maze.Position` class of Program 6.13, and would be part of the `Maze` class of Program 6.12.

Consider the example maze shown in Figure 6.11(a). The iterative algorithm would proceed as follows. (Here, we write a position as a pair of coordinates (x, y), with x being the column number and y the row number. Also, we write a stack with the elements listed in order from bottom to top, and enclosed in angle brackets «…».) We begin by initializing *path-stack* to «(0, 0)».

- *current* is (0, 0). This square is not an exit, so we look for an unvisited neighbor. There is only one unvisited neighbor, so we move south to position (0, 1). *path-stack* becomes «(0, 0), (0, 1)».
- *current* is (0, 1). This square is also not an exit, so we look for an unvisited neighbor. Again, there is only one unvisited neighbor, so we move east to position (1, 1). *path-stack* becomes «(0, 0), (0, 1), (1, 1)».
- *current* is (1, 1), which is not an exit. This square has two unvisited neighbors, to the north and south, at positions (1, 0) and (1, 2) respectively. Assume that we choose to move south to position (1, 2). *path-stack* becomes «(0, 0), (0, 1), (1, 1), (1, 2)».
- *current* is (1, 2), which is not an exit. This iteration is shown in Figure 6.19(a). This square has two unvisited neighbors, to the west and east, at positions (0, 2) and (2, 2) respectively. Assume that we choose to move west to position (0, 2). *path-stack* becomes «(0, 0), (0, 1), (1, 1), (1, 2), (0, 2)».

After three more iterations with only a single neighboring square to move to, we get to an iteration with *path-stack* equal to «(0, 0), (0, 1), …, (0, 2), (0, 3), (0, 4)».

- *current* is (0, 4), which is not an exit. This iteration is shown in Figure 6.19(b). This square has no unvisited neighbors. We must backtrack by removing the position at the top of the stack. *path-stack* becomes «(0, 0), (0, 1), (1, 1), (1, 2), (0, 2), (0, 3)».

To find and mark a path from the square at position *start* to an exit:

1. Mark *start* as visited and as part of the path.
2. Make *path-stack* contain only *start*.
3. While *path-stack* is not empty, repeat:
   3.1. Set *current* to the position at the top of *path-stack*.
   3.2. If *current* is an exit, terminate with answer true.
   3.3. If *current* has at least one unvisited neighbor:
      3.3.1. Set *neighbor* to an unvisited neighbor of *current*.
      3.3.2. Mark *neighbor* as visited and as part of the path.
      3.3.3. Add *neighbor* to the top of *path-stack*.
   3.4. If *current* has no unvisited neighbor:
      3.4.1. Remove a position from the top of *path-stack*.
      3.4.2. Unmark *current* as part of the path.
4. Terminate with answer false.

Algorithm 6.17　An iterative maze solving algorithm using a stack.

```java
public boolean findAPath (Maze.Position start) {
// Find and mark a path from the square at position start to an exit.
// Return true if and only if such a path exists.
   mark(start, VISITED);  mark(start, PATH);
   Stack pathStack = new LinkedStack();
   pathStack.addLast(start);
   while (! pathStack.isEmpty()) {
     Maze.Position current =
         (Maze.Position) pathStack.getLast();
     if (isMarked(current, EXIT))  return true;
     if (hasUnvisitedNeighbors(current)) {
       Maze.Position neighbor =
           chooseUnvisitedNeighbor(current);
       mark(neighbor, VISITED);  mark(neighbor, PATH);
       pathStack.addLast(neighbor);
     } else {
       pathStack.removeLast();
       unmark(current, PATH);
     }
   }
   return false;
}
```

Program 6.18　Java implementation of the iterative maze solving algorithm (in class `Maze`).

We continue backtracking until we reach the square at position (1, 2), where we attempt another fruitless search to position (2, 2). Ultimately, we must backtrack to the square at position (1, 1) before we make the correct move north to position (1, 0). After that, we follow a path of forced moves to the only unvisited neighbor until we reach the exit at position (4, 4). Figure 6.19(c) shows the final state of the maze.

6.6.4 An iterative maze generating algorithm

Finally, we consider an iterative algorithm to generate a maze. Algorithm 6.20 shows this algorithm, which has a similar structure to our iterative maze solving algorithm.

We construct the maze by first making all sides of all squares walled. We then select a position in the maze at random, and begin generating the maze. The algorithm uses a stack, *position-stack*, to keep track of the positions reached during a search through the squares of the maze. In this case, however, we are searching for squares that must be connected to this path to make the maze perfect.

At each step, we look for an *intact* neighbor of our current square, i.e., a neighbor all four sides of which are still walled. We then connect this neighbor to the rest of the maze

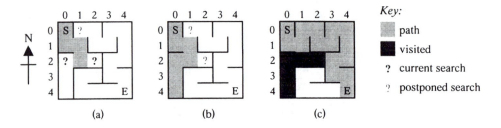

(a)   (b)   (c)

Figure 6.19 Some iterations in the solution of a maze: (a) a choice between two neighbors, west and east; (b) after choosing the west neighbor, the search proves unsuccessful; (c) the final solution.

To generate a maze:

1. Mark all sides of all squares in the maze as walled.
2. Make *position-stack* contain only a random position in the maze.
3. While *position-stack* is not empty, repeat:
    3.1. Set *current* to the position at the top of *position-stack*.
    3.2. If *current* has at least one intact neighbor:
        3.2.1. Set *neighbor* to an unvisited neighbor of *current*, chosen at random.
        3.2.2. Remove the wall between *neighbor* and *current*.
        3.2.3. Add *neighbor* to the top of *position-stack*.
    3.3. If *current* has no intact neighbor:
        3.3.1. Remove the position at the top of *position-stack*.
4. Terminate.

Algorithm 6.20 An iterative maze generating algorithm using a stack.

by removing the wall between it and our current square. The search is then extended to this neighbor by adding its position to the top of *position-stack*. If we have a choice of several intact neighbors, then we simply pick one at random. If the current square has no intact neighbors, then we backtrack to a square that has at least one intact neighbor.

We repeat this process until *position-stack* becomes empty, indicating that we have searched every square in the maze.

Program 6.21 shows the implementation of Algorithm 6.20 as a Java method named `generate`. Again this is a straightforward translation of the algorithm into Java, using the `Maze.Position` class of Program 6.13, and the auxiliary methods of the `Maze` class of Program 6.14. This method is added to the `Maze` class of Program 6.12.

Figure 6.22 shows the order in which the squares are searched to generate the maze of Figure 6.11(a), assuming that the algorithm randomly starts at position (1, 3) and then removes walls as it moves through the maze. (In fact, the algorithm could generate the same maze starting at any square, provided that it makes a suitable sequence of moves.)

```
public void generate () {
// Generate a perfect maze.
   markAllSidesWalled();
   Stack positionStack = new LinkedStack();
   positionStack.addLast(randomPosition());
   while (! positionStack.isEmpty()) {
     Maze.Position current =
          (Maze.Position) positionStack.getLast();
     if (hasIntactNeighbors(current)) {
       Maze.Position neighbor =
            chooseIntactNeighbor(current);
       removeWall(current, neighbor);
       positionStack.addLast(neighbor);
     } else
       positionStack.removeLast();
   }
}
```

Program 6.21   Java implementation of the iterative maze generating algorithm (in class `Maze`).

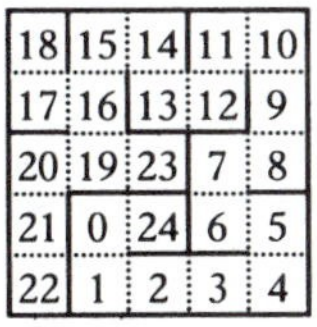

18	15	14	11	10
17	16	13	12	9
20	19	23	7	8
21	0	24	6	5
22	1	2	3	4

Figure 6.22   The generation of the maze from Figure 6.11(a), showing the order in which the squares are visited.

Summary

In this chapter:

- We have studied the concept of a stack, characterized as a last-in-first-out sequence.
- We have seen examples and a case study demonstrating applications of stacks.
- We have designed an ADT for stacks, expressed as a `Stack` interface.
- We have studied how to represent bounded and unbounded stacks by arrays and linked lists, respectively, and how to code these in Java as classes that implement the `Stack` interface.

Exercises

6.1 Section 6.1 gives two examples of stacks in everyday life. Can you think of any more examples?

6.2 Hand-test Algorithm 6.4 with the following phrases:

    (a) `( (4 + 8) * (3 - 2)`
    (b) `{a,b,c} + {d,e,f}`
    (c) `main(String[] args) {System.out.print (arg[0]);}`

6.3 Assuming the array representation of stacks, illustrate the operation of Program 6.5 by drawing the contents of `symbolStack` while each of the phrases in Exercise 6.2 is checked.

6.4 Repeat Exercise 6.3 assuming the SLL representation of stacks.

6.5 Consider the following additional requirements for a stack ADT: it should be possible to obtain a stack's current depth; and it should be possible to access (but not remove) the element at any given depth in the stack.

    (a) Modify the stack contract of Program 6.6 accordingly.
    (b) Modify the array implementation of Program 6.8.
    (c) Modify the SLL implementation of Program 6.10.

6.6 Modify the array implementation of Program 6.8 to deal with an overflow by throwing an exception.

6.7 Write an implementation of the stack ADT as a Java class, `TwinStack`, that allows two stacks to be stored in a single array. You should modify each stack operation to take an extra argument indicating which stack to use.

6.8 Consider the maze case study (Section 6.6). Investigate different implementations of the method `chooseUnvisitedNeighbor` in the class `Maze`. What effect do the different implementations have on the number of squares visited in the maze?

6.9 Modify the maze case study (Section 6.6) to have a randomly selected start and exit square.

6.10 Modify the maze case study (Section 6.6) to have several exit squares.

* **6.11** Develop an algorithm to solve an imperfect maze such as the one shown in Figure 6.11(b).

* **6.12** Extend the maze case study to use a 3-dimensional maze. Each square now has six neighbors: north, south, east, west, up, and down.

** **6.13** Consider the problem of reordering a train of railroad cars using a track layout consisting of a main line and a spur line, as shown in Figure 6.23.

A train consists of n cars, which are numbered 1 through n. The cars of the old train (which are in no particular order) must be individually uncoupled and reordered to produce a new train (in which the cars are in the correct order).

The old train can be viewed as a stack, with its *front* car as its 'top' element, since cars can only be removed at its front. That stack initially contains the whole old train.

Similarly, the new train can be viewed as a stack, with its *rear* car as its 'top' element, since cars can only be added at its rear. That stack is initially empty, but eventually it will contain the whole new train.

The row of cars in the spur can also be viewed as a stack.

With the given track layout, the following movements are possible:

- Move the front car of the old train to the rear of the new train.
- Move the front car of the old train to the spur.
- Move a car from the spur to the front of the old train.
- Move a car from the spur to the rear of the new train.

Devise an algorithm that reorders the train as required. (*Hint:* As well as using the three stacks indicated above, you might also want to remember which stack currently contains each car.)

Implement your algorithm as a Java application. The input should be a sequence of car numbers, one per line, representing the old train with the rear car first. For example, the train «5, 6, 3, 4, 1, 2» would be represented as follows:

```
2
1
4
3
6
5
```

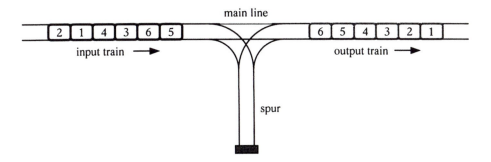

Figure 6.23   Railroad layout consisting of a main line and a spur.

The output should be the sequence of moves required to reorder the train to produce the new train. For example:

```
Move car 5 from old train to spur.
Move car 6 from old train to spur.
Move car 3 from old train to spur.
Move car 4 from old train to spur.
Move car 1 from old train to new train.
Move car 2 from old train to new train.
Move car 4 from spur to old train.
Move car 3 from spur to new train.
...
Finished.
```

** 6.14 Extend your solution to Exercise 6.13 to a track layout with a stated number of spur lines, s, that can be used to reorder the cars. Investigate what happens as the value of s is changed.

7

Queue Abstract Data Types

In this chapter we shall study:

- the concept of a queue (Section 7.1)
- simple applications of queues (Section 7.2)
- requirements and a contract for a queue abstract data type (Section 7.3)
- alternative implementations of queues using arrays and linked lists (Section 7.4–5)
- a case study using queues (Section 7.6).

7.1 The concept of a queue

Queues are a familiar feature of everyday life. Consider a queue of passengers at a bus stop: when a passenger arrives at the bus stop, he or she joins the rear of the queue; when a bus arrives, the passenger at the front of the queue is the first to board. Or consider a queue at an airport check-in desk: when the desk becomes free, the passenger at the front of the queue is the first to be served. Thus the basic principle of a queue is *first-come-first-served*; in other words, it is a *first-in-first-out* sequence.

Let us now define our terms. A ***queue*** is a sequence of elements, with the property that elements can be added only at one end (the ***rear*** of the queue) and removed only at the other end (the ***front*** of the queue).

The ***length*** of a queue is the number of elements it contains. The ***empty queue*** has length zero.

7.2 Applications of queues

Queues turn out to be enormously useful in computing, particularly in system programming. A print server maintains a queue of print jobs; a disk driver maintains a queue of disk access requests; an operating system's scheduler maintains a queue of processes

```
public static void reSortPersons
                (BufferedReader input,
                 BufferedWriter output)
            throws IOException {
// Assuming that input contains a sequence of person records, sorted by
//   name, write the same records to output, females before males, sorted
//   by name within each gender group.
    PersonQueue females = new PersonQueue(),
        males = new PersonQueue();
    for (;;) {
        Person p = readPerson(input);
        if (p == null)  break;   // ... end of input
        if (p.female) females.addLast(p);
        else males.addLast(p);
    }
    while (! females.isEmpty()) {
        Person f = females.removeFirst();
        writePerson(output, f);
    }
    while (! males.isEmpty()) {
        Person m = males.removeFirst();
        writePerson(output, m);
    }
}

private static Person readPerson
                (BufferedReader input)
            throws IOException {
// Read a single person record from input. Assume that each person record
//   occupies a single line, in which the surname, forename, gender ('F'/'M'),
//   and year-of-birth are separated by single spaces. Return null if no person
//   record remains to be read.
    ...   // omitted here.
}

private static void writePerson
                (BufferedWriter output, Person p)
            throws IOException {
// Write a single person record to output.
    output.write(p.surname + " " + p.forename + " "
        + (p.female ? "F" : "M") + " "
        + p.yearOfBirth + "\n");
}
```

Program 7.1   Java implementation of the re-sorting application.

awaiting a slice of processor time. Queues are also useful in application programming, as the following example illustrates.

EXAMPLE 7.1   *Re-sorting*

Suppose that a file contains records about persons, each record consisting of the person's surname, forename, gender, and year of birth (as in the class `Person` declared in Program 5.2). The records are sorted by name. We are required to re-sort the records such that females come before males, such that they remain sorted by name within each gender group.

Notice that a standard sorting algorithm would be much too heavy here. The records are already almost sorted in the required order: the female records are already in the required order, and the male records likewise. The only problem is that the female and male records are merged, so all that we must do is to unmerge them. Recall that merging has time complexity $O(n)$, where n is the total number of elements involved. There is no reason why unmerging should not also have time complexity $O(n)$. This is a lot better than sorting, whose time complexity would be $O(n \log n)$ at best.

Unmerging will create two separate sequences of records, the females and the males. We want to add records to each sequence in the given order (sorted by name), and we want to remove them in the same order. Thus we need a pair of first-in-first-out sequences, i.e., queues.

We will need objects to represent the two queues. Let us assume a class `PersonQueue` whose objects represent queues of `Person` objects. Let us also assume that this class provides a constructor that creates an empty queue; a method such that $q.\mathtt{addLast}(x)$ adds x to the rear of queue q; a method such that $q.\mathtt{removeFirst}()$ removes and returns the element at the front of queue q; and a method such that $q.\mathtt{isEmpty}()$ tests whether queue q is empty.

Program 7.1 shows a Java implementation of the re-sorting application.

7.3 A queue abstract data type

Since the queue is a widely useful concept, let us design a queue ADT. We shall assume the following requirements:

1. It must be possible to make a queue empty.
2. It must be possible to test whether a queue is empty.
3. It must be possible to obtain the length of a queue.
4. It must be possible to add an element at the rear of a queue.
5. It must be possible to remove the element at the front of a queue.
6. It must be possible to access the element at the front of a queue without removing it.

Program 7.2 shows a possible contract for the queue ADT, in the form of a Java interface named `Queue`. The queued elements will be objects. The operations provided are clearly sufficient to meet the above requirements. The `isEmpty` method is not strictly necessary, since the effect of $q.\mathtt{isEmpty}()$ can be achieved by the test

```
public interface Queue {

    //  Each Queue object is a queue whose elements are objects.

    ///////////// Accessors /////////////

    public boolean isEmpty ();
    //  Return true if and only if this queue is empty.

    public int size ();
    //  Return this queue's length.

    public Object getFirst ();
    //  Return the element at the front of this queue. Throw a
    //  NoSuchElementException if this queue is empty.

    ///////////// Transformers /////////////

    public void clear ();
    //  Make this queue empty.

    public void addLast (Object elem);
    //  Add elem as the rear element of this queue.

    public Object removeFirst ();
    //  Remove and return the front element from this queue. Throw a
    //  NoSuchElementException if this queue is empty.

}
```

Program 7.2   A contract for a queue ADT.

q.size() $==$ 0. Nevertheless, isEmpty is more convenient, and might be more efficient, if the implementor chooses to compute rather than store the length of the queue.

It should be clear that the PersonQueue class of Example 7.1 could be written to implement the Queue interface.

We now go on to study, in Sections 7.4 and 7.5, two possible implementations of the Queue interface.

7.4 Implementation of bounded queues using arrays

A *bounded queue* is one whose length is limited. If the queue's maximum length is *maxlength*, its current length can vary from 0 through *maxlength*.

A bounded queue can be represented by an array of length *maxlength*. We must keep track of where the queue's elements are located in the array. This turns out to be less straightforward than in the case of a stack, whose elements naturally occupy the leftmost components of their array (see Figure 6.7). Suppose that the queue's elements initially occupy the leftmost array components (as in Figure 7.3(a)). As long as elements are added to the queue, the only effect is that the rear of the queue moves rightward (Figure

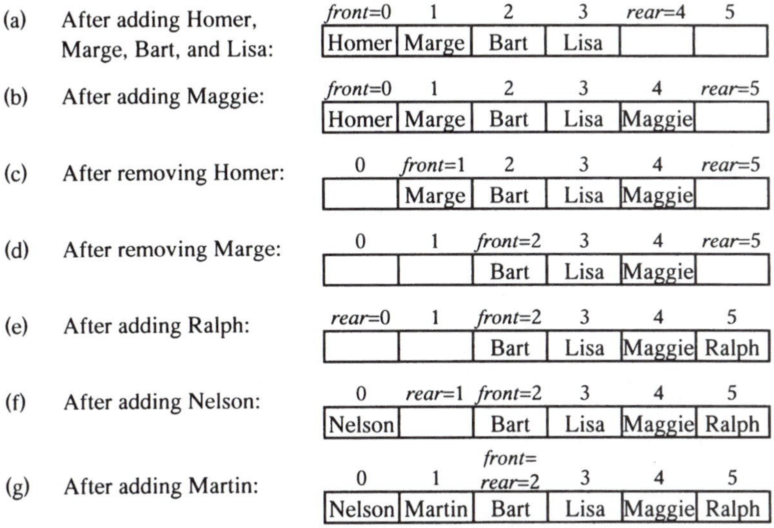

(a) After adding Homer, Marge, Bart, and Lisa:
front=0 1 2 3 rear=4 5
Homer Marge Bart Lisa
(b) After adding Maggie:
front=0 1 2 3 4 rear=5
Homer Marge Bart Lisa Maggie
(c) After removing Homer:
0 front=1 2 3 4 rear=5
Marge Bart Lisa Maggie
(d) After removing Marge:
0 1 front=2 3 4 rear=5
Bart Lisa Maggie
(e) After adding Ralph:
rear=0 1 front=2 3 4 5
Bart Lisa Maggie Ralph
(f) After adding Nelson:
0 rear=1 front=2 3 4 5
Nelson Bart Lisa Maggie Ralph
(g) After adding Martin:
0 1 front= rear=2 3 4 5
Nelson Martin Bart Lisa Maggie Ralph

Figure 7.3 Representation of bounded queues by arrays: adding to and removing from a queue of persons (with *maxlength* = 6).

(a)
0 … front–1 front front+1 … rear–2 rear–1 rear … maxlength–1
a b y z
(b)
0 … rear–2 rear–1 rear … front–1 front front+1 … maxlength–1
s y z a b r

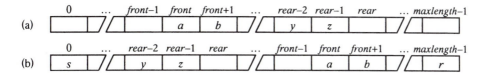

Figure 7.4 Representation of bounded queues by arrays: (a) general case, not wrapped; (b) general case, wrapped.

3
2
4
1
5
0

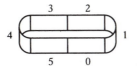

Figure 7.5 Cyclic array (with 6 components).

7.3(b)). But when elements are removed from the queue, its front also moves rightward (Figure 7.3(c–d)). Thus the queue as a whole gradually shifts rightward. Let us agree that the queue's elements will occupy the subarray *elems*[*front*…*rear* − 1], as shown in Figure 7.4(a), where *front* and *rear* are both variables. Adding an element will increment *rear*; removing an element will increment *front*.

There is a further complication. When the queue already occupies the rightmost array components (*rear* = *maxlength*), where should we add a new element? Assuming that there is at least one unoccupied array component, we could make space for the new element by shifting the whole queue leftward. But a much more efficient solution is to store the new element in the *leftmost* array component. In other words, we treat the array as if it were cyclic, wrapped round so that every component has both a left neighbor and a right neighbor (see Figure 7.5). The effect of this refinement is that sometimes the front elements of the queue occupy the rightmost subarray, *elems[front...maxlength* − 1], and

```java
public class ArrayQueue implements Queue {

    // Each ArrayQueue object is a bounded queue whose elements are
    // objects.

    // This queue is represented as follows: its length is held in length;
    // its elements occupy either elems[front...rear-1] or
    // elems[front....maxlength-1] wrapped to elems[0...rear-1].
    private Object[] elems;
    private int length, front, rear;

    /////////// Constructor ///////////

    public ArrayQueue (int maxlength) {
    // Construct a queue, initially empty, whose length will be bounded by
    // maxlength.
        elems = new Object[maxlength];
        length = 0;
        front = rear = 0;
    }

    /////////// Accessors ///////////

    public boolean isEmpty () {
    // Return true if and only if this queue is empty.
        return (length == 0);
    }

    public int size () {
    // Return this queue's length.
        return length;
    }

    public Object getFirst () {
    // Return the element at the front of this queue. Throw a
    // NoSuchElementException if this queue is empty.
        if (length == 0)
            throw new NoSuchElementException();
        return elems[front];
    }
```

Program 7.6   Java implementation of bounded queues using arrays (*continued on next page*).

/////////// Transformers ///////////

```java
public void clear () {
// Make this queue empty.
   for (int i = 0; i < elems.length; i++)
      elems[i] = null;
   length = 0;
   front = rear = 0;
}

public void addLast (Object elem) {
// Add elem as the rear element of this queue.
   if (length == elems.length)  expand();
   elems[rear++] = elem;
   if (rear == elems.length)  rear = 0;
   length++;
}

public Object removeFirst () {
// Remove and return the front element from this queue. Throw a
// NoSuchElementException if this queue is empty.
   if (length == 0)
      throw new NoSuchElementException();
   Object frontElem = elems[front];
   elems[front++] = null;
   if (front == elems.length)  front = 0;
   length--;
   return frontElem;
}
```

/////////// Auxiliary method ///////////

```java
private void expand () {
// Make the elems array longer. Reposition the queue elements if they are
// wrapped around the end of the array.
   ...  // omitted here.
}
```

}

Program 7.6 (*continued*)

the remaining elements occupy the leftmost subarray, *elems*[0...*rear* − 1], as shown in Figure 7.4(b).

We can visualize a cyclic array as shown in Figure 7.5. Although a cyclic array is only a figment of our imagination, it is a useful figment! The difference between ordinary arrays and cyclic arrays is shown up by the index arithmetic:

1. If we view *elems* as an ordinary array, the component *elems*[*i*] has a left neighbor *elems*[*i* − 1] only if *i* > 0, and a right neighbor *elems*[*i* + 1] only if *i* < *maxlength* − 1.

2. If we view *elems* as a cyclic array, every component *elems*[*i*] has both a left neighbor *elems*[(*i* − 1) modulo *maxlength*] and a right neighbor *elems*[(*i* + 1) modulo *maxlength*]. In particular, the component *elems*[0] has a left neighbor *elems*[(− 1) modulo *maxlength*], i.e., *elems*[*maxlength* − 1], and the component *elems*[*maxlength* − 1] has a right neighbor *elems*[*maxlength* modulo *maxlength*], i.e., *elems*[0].

In the representation of a queue, do we need to keep the queue's length in a variable, or can we compute it from *front* and *rear*? It is certainly true that:

$$rear = (front + length) \text{ modulo } maxlength \tag{7.1}$$

But the situation *front* = *rear* has two possible interpretations: either the queue is empty (*length* = 0) or the queue is full (*length* = *maxlength*). So we must keep *length* as a separate variable.

The implementation of the queue ADT is now quite straightforward, and is shown in Program 7.6. This is a Java class `ArrayQueue` that is declared as implementing the `Queue` interface. The instance variable `elems` is an array whose size is fixed when the queue is constructed, and its components are all initially null. The instance variables `length`, `front`, and `rear` keep track of the queue's length, front position, and rear position, and are initially all zero. The `addLast` operation increments `length`, increments `rear` (modulo `elems.length`), and stores the new element in the array. The `removeFirst` operation decrements `length`, increments `front` (modulo `elems.length`), and returns what was the front element. These queue operations have time complexity $O(1)$.

Other possible implementations would be less efficient. For example, if `addLast` shifted the queue to the left, that operation would have time complexity $O(n)$, where n is the queue's length.

The array implementation of queues would *not* be suitable for the re-sorting application of Example 7.1. Any bound on the queue length could easily be exceeded by the number of males or females in the file.

7.5 Implementation of unbounded queues using linked lists

An unbounded queue can easily be represented by a singly-linked list (SLL), with the front element in the first node and the rear element in the last node. We need links to both the first and last nodes, since elements will be added at the rear and removed at the front. Figure 7.7 shows this representation in the general case, and also illustrates how a queue of persons would be represented.

The implementation of the queue ADT is straightforward, and is shown in Program 7.8. This is a Java class `LinkedQueue` that is declared as implementing the `Queue` interface. The instance variables `front` and `rear` are links to the first and last nodes,

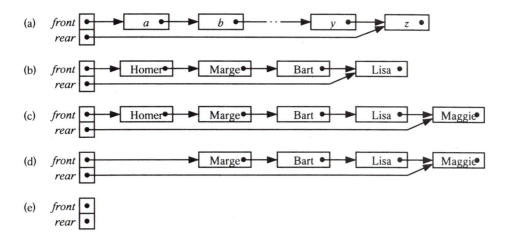

Figure 7.7   Representation of unbounded queues by SLLs: (a) general case; (b–d) queues of persons; (e) empty queue.

respectively, and are initially null. The instance variable `length` keeps track of the queue's length. The nodes are of class `SLLNode` (see Program 4.4). The `addLast` operation creates a new node and inserts it after the SLL's last node. (If the queue was empty, the new node becomes the SLL's first and last node.) The `removeFirst` operation deletes the SLL's first node. All the queue operations have time complexity $O(1)$.

The linked-list implementation of queues would be suitable in any application. In fact, the absence of a bound on the queue length is essential in the re-sorting application of Example 7.1, because there is no bound on the number of records in the file.

7.6 Case study: a traffic simulator

Traffic waiting at a street intersection is a familiar example of queues in real life. In this section we shall develop a simple simulation of a street intersection. The street intersection has four streets and is controlled by traffic signals. We will assume that one street at a time has a green signal (to avoid the problem of turning vehicles being delayed by oncoming vehicles). We will also assume that *all* vehicles must stop at a red signal (unlike some countries where vehicles may turn at a red signal).

We will construct our simulation by first considering the entities we need to simulate: the passage of time, the vehicles, the streets, and the street intersection itself. Then we develop a simple iterative simulation algorithm, which incrementally advances time as it moves the vehicles along the streets and across the intersection.

Our simulation will be concerned not only with these entities, but also with the events that affect them. These events include the arrival of a vehicle in a street, the crossing of the street intersection by a vehicle, and the change of traffic signals between green and red.

We could assume that a vehicle crosses the street intersection instantaneously once it reaches the front of its queue. But it is more interesting if each vehicle takes a certain amount of time to cross the intersection.

Here we will consider only the details of the simulation itself. The complete program is available as a Java applet at the companion Web site, and includes a graphical user interface allowing the user to alter the simulation parameters, and observe the effects, while the simulation is running.

```java
public class LinkedQueue implements Queue {

    // Each LinkedQueue object is a queue whose elements are objects.

    // This queue is represented as follows: its length is held in length;
    // front and rear are links to the first and last nodes of an SLL
    // containing its elements.
    private SLLNode front, rear;
    private int length;

    /////////////// Constructor ///////////////

    public LinkedQueue () {
    // Construct a queue, initially empty.
        front = rear = null;
        length = 0;
    }

    /////////////// Accessors ///////////////

    public boolean isEmpty () {
    // Return true if and only if this queue is empty.
        return (length == 0);
    }

    public int size () {
    // Return this queue's length.
        return length;
    }

    public Object getFirst () {
    // Return the element at the front of this queue. Throw a
    // NoSuchElementException if this queue is empty.
        if (front == null)
            throw new NoSuchElementException();
        return front.element;
    }
```

Program 7.8 Java implementation of unbounded queues using SLLs (*continued on next page*).

```
/////////// Transformers ///////////

public void clear () {
// Make this queue empty.
   front = rear = null;
   length = 0;
}

public void addLast (Object elem) {
// Add elem as the rear element of this queue.
   SLLNode newest = new SLLNode(elem, null);
   if (rear != null)
      rear.succ = newest;
   else
      front = newest;
   rear = newest;
   length++;
}

public Object removeFirst () {
// Remove and return the front element of this queue. Throw a
// NoSuchElementException if this queue is empty.
   if (front == null)
      throw new NoSuchElementException();
   Object frontElem = front.element;
   front = front.succ;
   if (front == null)  rear = null;
   length--;
   return frontElem;
}

}
```

Program 7.8 (*continued*)

7.6.1 Modeling the entities in the simulation

We must decide how to represent the various entities involved. We must consider the street intersection as a whole, the streets that make up the street intersection, and the individual vehicles that are waiting in each street. We also need to decide how to model time in our simulation. Let us now consider these entities in reverse order.

Modeling the passage of time

Using real time in our simulation would be difficult. In fact, that degree of accuracy is unnecessary.

Instead, we can use an abstract notion of time. We let time consist of a series of *clock ticks*, and let each event last for a certain number of ticks. For example, each traffic signal will remain green for some fixed number of ticks, and each vehicle will take a predetermined number of ticks to cross the street intersection. The current time will be zero initially, and will be incremented by one tick on each iteration of the simulation. It does not matter whether a tick represents one second, ten seconds, or even an hour; what does matter is that the actual duration of each event is proportional to the number of ticks assumed.

Modeling vehicles

During the simulation, we are interested in how long each vehicle must wait at the street intersection before proceeding. Clearly, this wait will be affected both by the number of vehicles passing through the intersection and by the duration of the green signal in the street where the vehicle is waiting. We will represent each vehicle by an object that contains the vehicle's arrival time at the intersection. The object will also contain the amount of time that the vehicle will take to cross the intersection. Once the vehicle reaches the front of its queue, this crossing time will be repeatedly decremented (which represents moving across the intersection) until it reaches zero (which represents clearing the intersection).

Program 7.9 shows the Java class `Vehicle`. It is a very simple ADT, with a single constructor, a single accessor (`hasCrossedIntersection`), and a single transformer (`moveAcrossIntersection`).

Modeling streets

We will model each individual street at the intersection by an object that contains a queue of waiting vehicles. The street object will also contain the parameters that affect the simulation: the mean arrival period (i.e., the mean interval between successive arrivals of vehicles at the rear of the queue), and the duration of the green signal in this street. To simplify the simulation algorithm, each street object should also contain the time when the next vehicle is due to arrive, and (for the street whose traffic signal is currently green) the time when the traffic signal is next due to change from green to red.

To determine the next vehicle's arrival time, we could simply add the mean arrival period to the previous vehicle's arrival time. However, it is more interesting to vary the interval between arrivals. So we compute each interval by multiplying the mean arrival period by a random number between 0.5 and 1.5, and add that interval to the previous vehicle's arrival time.

Program 7.10 shows a Java class named `Street`, whose objects will represent streets in the simulation.

Note that some of the methods in the `Street` class are simple 'wrapper' methods for the underlying `Queue` methods. The `Street` methods are more convenient because we know that the queue contains only `Vehicle` objects. For instance, the `getFirstVehicle` method is a wrapper for the `Queue` class's `getFirst` method, but its result is a `Vehicle` object rather than an arbitrary object.

```
public class Vehicle {

    // Each Vehicle object represents a vehicle waiting at the street
    // intersection.

    // A vehicle is described by its arrival time at the street intersection
    // (arrivalTime), and by the amount of time it needs to cross the
    // intersection (crossingTime). Both times are measured in clock ticks.

    private final static int MAX_CROSSING = 5;

    private long arrivalTime;
    private int crossingTime;

    public Vehicle (long arrivalTime) {
    // Create a new vehicle with the given arrival time, and a random
    // crossing time between 1 and MAX_CROSSING.
        this.arrivalTime = arrivalTime;
        this.crossingTime =
            (int) (Math.random()*MAX_CROSSING) + 1;
    }

    public boolean hasCrossedIntersection () {
    // Return true if and only if this vehicle has completely crossed the
    // street intersection.
        return (crossingTime == 0);
    }

    public void moveAcrossIntersection () {
    // Move this vehicle part of the way across the street intersection.
        if (crossingTime > 0)  crossingTime--;
    }
}
```

Program 7.9 Modeling of vehicles by a Java class Vehicle.

Modeling the street intersection

A street intersection is a meeting of several streets. The street intersection object can model these naturally by an array of Street objects. It must also keep track of the current state of the traffic signals (i.e., which street currently has a green signal) and the current time.

Program 7.11 shows an implementation of street intersections using a Java class named StreetIntersection.

This implementation has been complicated by a requirement of our Java applet, which uses the StreetIntersection class. The applet must run in one thread, while performing the simulation of the street intersection in a separate thread. Using threads

```
public class Street {
```

// Each `Street` object represents a single street at a street intersection.

// A street is described by the following data:
// • the mean arrival period (i.e., the mean time between successive
//   vehicle arrivals in this street)
// • the signal duration (i.e., the amount of time that the traffic signal is
//   green in this street)
// • the next vehicle's arrival time in this street
// • the time when this street's traffic signal will next change from green
//   to red
// • the queue of vehicles waiting in this street.
// All times are measured in clock ticks.

```
private int meanArrivalPeriod, signalDuration;
private long nextArrivalTime, nextSignalTime;
private Queue vehicles;
```

//////////// Constructor ///////////

```
public Street (int meanArrivalPeriod,
               int signalDuration,
               int numVehicles) {
```
// Create a new street with the given mean arrival period and signal
// duration, and a queue already containing `numVehicles` waiting
// vehicles.
```
   this.meanArrivalPeriod = meanArrivalPeriod;
   this.signalDuration = signalDuration;
   this.nextArrivalTime = 0;
   this.nextSignalTime = 0;
   this.vehicles = new LinkedQueue();
   for (int i = 0; i < numVehicles; i++)
      vehicles.addLast(new Vehicle(0));
}
```

//////////// Accessors ///////////

```
public boolean arrivalDue (long currentTime) {
```
// Return true if and only if a vehicle is due to arrive in this street at
// or before `currentTime`.
```
   return (currentTime >= nextArrivalTime);
}
```

Program 7.10   Modeling of streets by a Java class `Street` (*continued on next page*).

```
public boolean signalDue (long currentTime) {
// Return true if and only if this street's traffic signal is due to change from
// green to red at or before currentTime. (Assume that this street's
// traffic signal is currently green.)
   return (currentTime >= nextSignalTime);
}

public Vehicle getFirstVehicle () {
// Return the first vehicle waiting in this street.
   return (Vehicle) vehicles.getFirst();
}

public boolean hasVehicles () {
// Return true if and only if at least one vehicle is waiting in this street.
   return ! vehicles.isEmpty();
}

public int numVehicles () {
// Return the number of vehicles waiting in this street.
   return vehicles.size ();
}

///////////// Transformers ////////////

void setNextArrivalTime (long currentTime) {
// Set the arrival time of the next vehicle in this street. That time is to be
// currentTime plus a random number of ticks, between 0.5 and 1.5
// times the mean arrival period.
   nextArrivalTime = currentTime +
       Math.round((Math.random() + 0.5) *
          meanArrivalPeriod);
}
```

Program 7.10 (*continued on next page*)

in Java is relatively straightforward, but requires a few additional methods. Briefly, the steps required to make our StreetIntersection class usable as a Java thread are as follows:

- We indicate that the class may be used as a Java thread by declaring that it implements the Java interface named Runnable. This interface requires the class to implement a method named run, which will be the code executed by the thread when it is running. In our simulation, the thread should be started when the applet becomes active, and stopped when the applet becomes inactivate.
- When the applet becomes active, it calls the start method. This should in turn call the run method.

```
void setSignalDuration (int duration) {
// Set this street's signal duration (i.e., the amount of time at green) to
// duration. Also, adjust the time when the traffic signal will next
// change from green to red.
   nextSignalTime += duration - signalDuration;
   signalDuration = duration;
}

void addVehicle (Vehicle vehicle) {
// Add vehicle behind those waiting in this street.
   vehicles.addLast(vehicle);
}

void removeVehicle () {
// Remove the first vehicle waiting in this street.
   vehicles.removeFirst();
}
}
```

Program 7.10 (*continued*)

- The run method repeatedly calls the simulateOneTick method, which simulates the street intersection for a single clock tick. After each call, the run method pauses for a short time to allow the applet thread to display the new state of the street intersection.
- Just before the applet becomes inactive, it invokes the stop method. This should cause the run method to break out of its loop and terminate.

7.6.2 A traffic simulation algorithm

Having decided how to model the various entities, we now develop an algorithm to simulate the street intersection. This algorithm is the heart of the application.

Our simulation of the street intersection is *iterative*. We simulate the intersection over and over again, one clock tick at a time. At each tick, we have three distinct steps to perform:

- If *green-street* is the street whose traffic signal is currently green, we move the vehicle at the front of *green-street*'s queue across the street intersection. Once it has completely crossed the street intersection, we remove it from the queue.
- In each of the streets meeting at the street intersection, we check if it is time for a vehicle to arrive. If so, we add a new vehicle to the rear of the appropriate queue.
- If it is time for the traffic signals to change, we update *green-street* to be the street whose traffic signal is now changing from red to green.

Algorithm 7.12 shows our algorithm to simulate a street intersection for one clock tick. Steps 2–4 of the algorithm are, respectively, the three steps explained above.

Program 7.13 is an implementation of Algorithm 7.12 as a Java method named simulateOneTick. This method would be added to the StreetIntersection class of Program 7.11.

```java
public class StreetIntersection implements Runnable {

    //  Each StreetIntersection object represents a street intersection.

    //  This street intersection is described by the following data: an array of
    //  streets meeting at the street intersection (streets); the index of the
    //  street whose traffic signal is currently green (greenPos); and the
    //  current time (currentTime). The time is measured in clock ticks.

    private Street[] streets;
    private int greenPos;
    private long currentTime;

    public static final int NUM_STREETS = 4;

    ///////////// Constructor /////////////

    public StreetIntersection () {
    // Create a new street intersection by creating NUM_STREETS streets, each
    //   with 5 ± 2 vehicles initially waiting. Make the mean arrival period for
    //   each street a random number in the interval 20 ± 5. Make all streets have
    //   the same signal duration, a random number in the interval 100 ± 10. Also
    //   set the current time to 0, and set the traffic signal to green in street 0.
        streets = new Street[NUM_STREETS];
        int signalDuration = randomInt(100, 10);
        for (int i = 0; i < streets.length; i++) {
            int meanArrivalPeriod = randomInt(20, 5);
            streets[i] = new Street(meanArrivalPeriod,
                signalDuration, randomInt(5, 2));
            streets[i].setNextArrivalTime(0);
        }
        currentTime = 0;
        greenPos = 0;
        streets[greenPos].setNextSignalTime(
            currentTime);
    }
```

Program 7.11   Modeling of street intersections by a Java class StreetIntersection (using a Java thread) (*continued on next page*).

```
/ / / / / / / / / / /  Thread methods  / / / / / / / / / / /

public void start () {
// Start the simulation of this street intersection. (Make the run method
// start to execute in a new thread.)
    ...   // See code on the companion Web site.
}

public void stop () {
// Stop the simulation of this street intersection. (Make any currently
// executing thread terminate.)
    ... // See code on the companion Web site.
}

public void run () {
// Simulate this street intersection indefinitely, pausing after every clock
// tick to allow the applet thread to display the new state of the intersection.
// Continue the simulation until the simulation thread is stopped.
    while (...) {
        simulateOneTick();
        ...   // pause
    }
}

/ / / / / / / / /  Auxiliary methods  / / / / / / / / / / /

private void simulateOneTick () {
// Simulate this street intersection for a single clock tick.
    ... // See Section 7.6.2.
}

private static int randomInt (int m, int b) {
// Return a random integer chosen uniformly from the interval
// [m-b...m+b].
    return Math.round(Math.random()*b*2) + m - b;
}

}
```

Program 7.11 (*continued*)

Summary

In this chapter:

- We have studied the concept of a queue, characterized as a first-in-first-out sequence.
- We have seen an example and a case study demonstrating applications of queues.
- We have designed an ADT for queues, expressed as a Queue interface.

To simulate a street intersection for a single clock tick:

1. Let *green-street* be the street whose traffic signal is currently green.
2. If at least one vehicle is waiting in *green-street*:
   2.1. Set *vehicle* to the first vehicle waiting in *green-street*.
   2.2. If *vehicle* has now crossed the intersection:
        2.2.1. Remove the first vehicle waiting in *green-street*.
   2.3. If *vehicle* has not yet crossed the intersection:
        2.3.1. Move *vehicle* part of the way across the intersection.
3. For each *street* in the intersection, repeat:
   3.1. If the next vehicle's arrival time in *street* is at or before *current-time*:
        3.1.1. Add a new vehicle behind those waiting in *street*.
        3.1.2. Set the next vehicle's arrival time in *street*.
4. If *green-street*'s traffic signal is due to change from green to red at or before *current-time*:
   4.1. Make the next street's traffic signal green.
   4.2. Set the time when that street's traffic signal will next change from green to red.
5. Increment *current-time* by one clock tick.
6. Terminate.

Algorithm 7.12   Algorithm to simulate a street intersection for a single clock tick.

- We have studied how to represent bounded and unbounded queues by arrays and linked lists, respectively, and how to code these in Java as classes that implement the `Queue` interface.

Exercises

7.1   Section 7.1 gives two examples of queues in everyday life. Can you think of other examples? Try to think of examples that do not involve queues of persons.

7.2   Implement the auxiliary method `expand` in Program 7.6 to deal with the possibility of an overflow. The method should copy all the queue elements into a new and longer new array, and replace the existing array by that new array.

7.3   In the `ArrayQueue` class of Program 7.6, show that one of the three instance variables `length`, `front`, and `rear` can be dropped. Which one? Modify the implementation accordingly.

7.4   Would you implement the queue ADT using a doubly-linked list? Explain your answer.

7.5   Implement a linked implementation of the queue ADT using a SLL that always contains at least one dummy node. (See Exercise 4.16 for an explanation of the data structure to use.)

7.6   (For those familiar with UNIX.) Outline how a UNIX pipe can be implemented by a queue.

```
private void simulateOneTick () {
// Simulate this street intersection for a single clock tick.
   Street greenStreet = streets[greenPos];
   if (greenStreet.hasVehicles()) {
      Vehicle vehicle = greenStreet.getFirstVehicle();
      if (vehicle.hasCrossedIntersection())
        greenStreet.removeVehicle();
      else
        vehicle.moveAcrossIntersection();
   }
   for (int i = 0; i < streets.length; i++) {
      Street street = streets[i];
      if (street.arrivalDue(currentTime)) {
         street.addLast(new Vehicle(currentTime));
         street.setNextArrivalTime(currentTime);
      }
   }
   if (greenStreet.signalDue(currentTime)) {
      greenPos = (greenPos + 1) % NUM_STREETS;
      streets[greenPos].setNextSignalTime(currentTime);
   }
   currentTime++;
}
```

Program 7.13 Implementation of the simulation algorithm as a Java method (in class `Street-Intersection`).

7.7 A *keyboard driver* is a process (generally provided by the operating system) that allows the user to enter characters at any speed, without waiting for the application program to use these characters.

(a) Outline how the keyboard driver can communicate with the application program via a queue.

(b) Write an algorithm for the keyboard driver. It should 'echo' to the screen each graphic character (visible character or space) entered by the user. It should simply ignore any control character.

(c) Suppose now that the DELETE character is to cancel the last graphic character. A sequence of DELETEs is to cancel the same number of graphic characters. What changes are needed to the keyboard driver, and to the communication between the keyboard driver and the application program?

*   **7.8** A *doubly-ended queue* (or *deque*) allows elements to be added or removed at both ends of the queue. In other words, it supports the following operations in addition to the usual queue operations: d.addFirst(x) adds x at the front of deque d; d.removeLast() removes the element at the rear of deque d; d.getLast() retrieves the element at the rear of deque d.

Write a contract, Deque, for a deque as a Java interface using Program 7.2 as a guide.

Write a linked implementation of a deque as a Java class LinkedDeque. Make sure that all deque operations have time complexity $O(1)$.

* **7.9** Consider the railroad problem given as Exercise 6.13. Suppose that the track layout now includes a siding rather than a spur line, as shown in Figure 7.14. The siding can be viewed as a queue, so the following moves are possible:
  - Move a car from the front of the old train to the rear of the new train.
  - Move a car from the front of the old train to the rear of the siding.
  - Move a car from the front of the siding to the rear of the new train.
  - Move a car from the front of the siding to the front of the old train.
    Devise an algorithm to reorder the train.
    Implement your algorithm as part of a Java application. The input and output data are the same as in Exercise 6.13.

** **7.10** Extend your solution to Exercise 7.9 to a track layout with a stated number of sidings, s, that can be used to reorder the cars. Investigate what happens as the value of s is changed.

** **7.11** Modify the traffic simulation case study (Section 7.6) such that facing streets in a four-street intersection have their traffic signals at green simultaneously. Each vehicle now has a designated exit street, and a vehicle must yield to oncoming vehicles if it needs to cross their path. (*Hint:* You may find it useful to have two queues of vehicles in each street.)

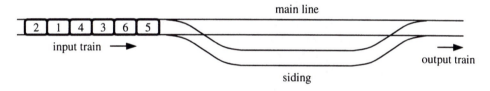

Figure 7.14   Railroad layout consisting of a main line and a siding.

8

List Abstract Data Types

In this chapter we shall study:

- the concept of a list (Section 8.1)
- simple applications of lists (Section 8.2)
- requirements and a contract for a list abstract data type (Section 8.3)
- the concept of an iterator, and iterators over lists (Section 8.4)
- alternative implementations of lists using arrays and linked lists (Section 8.5–6)
- lists in the Java class library (Section 8.7)
- a case study using lists (Section 8.8).

8.1 The concept of a list

A *list* is a sequence of elements, with a fixed order. We can add, remove, inspect, and update elements anywhere in a list. Thus lists are more general than stacks or queues.

The concept of a list or sequence is important in both mathematics and computing. The following are lists of integers. They are expressed in the usual mathematical notation: the list's elements are enumerated between angle brackets «…».

> *fibonacci* = «1, 1, 2, 3, 5, 8, 13, 21, 44, 65»
> *binomial* = «1, 6, 15, 20, 15, 6, 1»

And the following are lists of words:

> *hamlet1* = «'To', 'be', 'or', 'not', 'to', 'be'»
> *hamlet2* = «'That', 'is', 'the', 'question'»
> *sentence* = «'the', 'cat', 'smells', 'a', 'rat'»

The *length* of a list is the number of elements it contains. For example, the length of *hamlet1* is 6 and the length of *hamlet2* is 4.

The *empty list* has length zero. It is expressed in mathematical notation as « ».

The elements in a list have consecutive *indices*. We shall assume that the indices range from 0 through $n - 1$, where n is the list's length. For example, in *hamlet2*, the element at index 0 is 'That', the element at index 1 is 'is', the element at index 2 is 'the', and the element at index 3 is 'question'.

Because of the indices, lists might appear to resemble arrays, but there are important differences. Nevertheless, we shall see later in this chapter that it is possible to *represent* lists by arrays.

We can **inspect** or **update** any element of a list, given its index. For example, in *sentence*, inspecting element 4 gives 'rat', while updating element 4 to 'bat' changes *sentence* to «'the', 'cat', 'smells', 'a', 'bat'».

We can **add** an element anywhere in a list. For example, in *sentence*, adding 'only' before element 0 changes the list to «'only', 'the', 'cat', 'smells', 'a', 'rat'»; adding 'only' before element 2 changes it to «'the', 'cat', 'only', 'smells', 'a', 'rat'»; adding 'only' after the last element changes it to «'the', 'cat', 'smells', 'a', 'rat', 'only'».

Likewise, we can **remove** any element of a nonempty list. For example, in *sentence*, removing element 4 followed by removing element 3 changes the list to «'the', 'cat', 'smells'».

Two lists are **equal** if they have the same length, and each element of the first list equals the corresponding element of the second list. For example, «'the', 'cat', 'smells'» equals «'the', 'cat', 'smells'», but not «'the', 'mat', 'smells'» (because the elements with index 1 are unequal), nor «'the', 'cat', 'smells', 'a', 'rat'» (because the latter list is longer).

The **concatenation** of two lists is a list consisting of all the elements of the first list followed by all the elements of the second list. For example, the concatenation of *hamlet1* and *hamlet2* is «'To', 'be', 'or', 'not', 'to', 'be', 'That', 'is', 'the', 'question'». Note that the concatenation of any list *l* with the empty list is equal to *l*.

8.2 Applications of lists

Lists are ubiquitous in computing. The following example illustrates a simple application of lists.

EXAMPLE 8.1 *Text editor*

Consider a very simple text editor, the kind of editor that might be used to compose an e-mail message. Our editor will provide commands to insert, delete, and replace lines anywhere in the text. It will also provide commands to save and load text held in files.

Our editor will be equipped with a suitable user interface to issue these commands, but the user interface is not our concern here. We merely assume that the user is able to *select* any line of the text, either directly (by a mouse-click, for example) or by searching for a line containing some substring. When the user issues a deletion or replacement command, it is the selected line that is deleted or replaced. When the user issues an insertion command, the new line is inserted either just before or just after the selected line, as the user wishes. When the user issues a search command, the search starts at the selected line.

We can view the text essentially as a list of lines. The basic editing operations of insertion, deletion, and replacement are very easily implemented in terms of the list operations outlined in Section 8.1. Let us assume a class `StringList` whose objects represent lists of strings (here lines of text). Let us also assume that this class provides a constructor that creates an empty list, and methods such that: l.`isEmpty()` tests whether list l is empty; l.`size()` returns the length of list l; l.`get($i$)` inspects element i of list l; l.`set($i$, $x$)` updates element i of list l to x; l.`add($i$, $x$)` adds x before element i of list l; l.`add($x$)` adds x after the last element of list l; and l.`remove($i$)` removes element i of list l.

Program 8.1 shows a Java implementation of the text editor. This is a class, `TextEditor`, that provides methods corresponding directly to the user commands. The text is represented by a list of lines, `text`, together with the number of the currently-selected line, `sel`. The text editor's `select` method updates `sel` only. The `find` method inspects successive lines from the text until it finds a line that contains the given substring, and updates `sel` accordingly. The `insertBefore`, `insertAfter`, `delete`, and `replace` methods simply call the appropriate `StringList` methods to operate on `text`, and update `sel` as required. The `load` method reads lines from the given file and adds each after the last line of the text. The `save` and `display` methods will write all the lines of the text, to a file and to the screen, respectively. (We defer the implementation of these methods to Program 8.6.)

8.3 A list abstract data type

Let us design a list ADT. The requirements for stack and queue ADTs in Chapters 6 and 7 were quite clear-cut, but the requirements for a list ADT could vary considerably from one application to another. For the purposes of this chapter, let us assume the following requirements:

1. It must be possible to make a list empty.
2. It must be possible to test whether a list is empty.
3. It must be possible to obtain the length of a list.
4. It must be possible to add an element anywhere in a list.
5. It must be possible to remove an element anywhere in a list.
6. It must be possible to inspect or update an element anywhere in a list.
7. It must be possible to concatenate lists.
8. It must be possible to test lists for equality.
9. It must be possible to traverse a list (i.e., visit each list element in turn).

Program 8.2 shows a possible contract for the list ADT, in the form of a Java interface named `List`. Each `List` object is a list of elements that are themselves objects. The operations of the `List` interface are sufficient to meet all the above requirements. For example, requirement 6 is met by the `get` and `set` operations, and requirement 7 by the `addAll` operation.

The `List` interface contains two operations named `add`. These operations are distinguished by the number and types of their parameters. One operation adds a new element

```java
public class TextEditor {
  // Each TextEditor object represents a text to be edited. The text
  // consists of lines numbered 0, 1, 2, .... If the text is nonempty, one line is
  // always selected; initially line 0 is selected.

  // This text is represented as a list of lines, text. The number of the
  // currently-selected line (or -1 if the text is empty) is held in sel.
  // Invariant: -1 ≤ sel < text.size().
  private StringList text;
  private int sel;

  public TextEditor () {
  // Construct a text, initially empty.
    text = new StringList();
    sel = -1;
  }

  public void select (int ln)
                throws EditException {
  // Select the line numbered ln in this text.
    if (ln < 0 || ln >= text.size())
      throw new EditException();   // no such line
    sel = ln;
  }

  public void find (String s)
                throws EditException {
  // Find the first line, between the selected line and the end of this text, that
  // has a substring s, and select that line.
    if (sel < 0)
      throw new EditException();   // no text to search
    int length = text.size();
    for (int ln = sel; ln < length; ln++) {
      String line = text.get(ln);
      if (line.indexOf(s) >= 0) {   // substring found
        sel = ln;
        return;
      }
    }
    throw new EditException();   // no line has this substring
  }
```

Program 8.1   Java implementation of the text editor (*continued on next page*).

```
public void insertBefore (String line)
                throws EditException {
// Insert line immediately before the selected line in this text.
   if (sel < 0)
     throw new EditException();   // no line to insert before
   text.add(sel++, line);
}

public void insertAfter (String line) {
// Insert line immediately after the selected line in this text, and select the
//  inserted line.
   text.add(++sel, line);
}

public void delete ()
                throws EditException {
//  Delete the selected line in this text, and select the following line (or the
//  previous line, if the last line was deleted).
   if (sel < 0)
     throw new EditException();   // no text to delete
   text.remove(sel);
   if (sel == text.size())
     sel--;
}

public void replace (String line)
                throws EditException {
//  Replace the selected line in this text by line, and select the replacement
//  line.
   if (sel < 0)
     throw new EditException();   // no text to replace
   text.set(sel, line);
}

public void load (BufferedReader input)
                throws IOException {
//  Insert the text contained in input after the last line of this text, and
//  select the last line inserted.
   for (;;) {
     String line = input.readLine();
     if (line == null)  break;
     text.add(line);
   }
   sel = text.size()-1;
}
```

Program 8.1 (*continued on next page*)

```
public void save (BufferedWriter output)
                  throws IOException {
// Write this text to output.
   ...   //  See Program 8.6.
}
public void display () {
// Display this text, highlighting the selected line.
   ...   //  See Program 8.6.
}

}
```

Program 8.1 (*continued*)

at a given index in the list, and the other adds a new element at the end of the list. In Java, these operations are said to be ***overloaded***. (See Appendix B.2.)

Requirement 9 is met by the `iterator` method. An *iterator* over a list enables application code to visit each element of the list in turn, without knowing how the list is represented. The iterator is an important concept, which we are encountering for the first time here, so we shall devote the whole of Section 8.4 to iterators.

In Sections 8.5 and 8.6 we shall study two possible implementations of the `List` interface, including implementations of their iterators.

8.4 Iterators

We are all familiar with the following code pattern, which visits all components of an array `a`:

```
for (int i = 0; i < a.length; i++)
   ...   // code that inspects and/or updates a[i]
```

This code pattern is a loop that makes a variable (`i`) range over the indices of the array components, and uses the array indexing notation (`a[i]`) to access each component. We say that this code pattern ***traverses*** (or ***iterates over***) the array. In other words, it ***visits*** (accesses) each array component in turn.

We can easily adapt this code pattern to traverse a list `list`, visiting each element of the list in order from left to right:

```
for (int i = 0; i < list.size(); i++)
   ...   // code that calls list.get(i) and/or list.set(i)
```

This code pattern is a loop that makes a variable (`i`) range over the indices of the list elements, and uses the `get` and/or `set` methods to visit each element. This code pattern was used in the implementation of method `find` in Program 8.1 (although in that case only some of the list elements were visited).

```
public interface List {
```

// Each List object is an indexed list (sequence) whose elements are
// objects.

/////////// Accessors ///////////

```
public boolean isEmpty ();
```
// Return true if and only if this list is empty.

```
public int size ();
```
// Return this list's length.

```
public Object get (int i);
```
// Return the element with index i in this list. Throw an
// IndexOutOfBoundsException if i is out of range.

```
public boolean equals (List that);
```
// Return true if and only if this list and that have the same length, and
// each element of this list equals the corresponding element of that.

/////////// Transformers ///////////

```
public void clear ();
```
// Make this list empty.

```
public void set (int i, Object elem);
```
// Replace by elem the element at index i in this list. Throw an
// IndexOutOfBoundsException if i is out of range.

```
public void add (int i, Object elem);
```
// Add elem as the element with index i in this list. Throw an
// IndexOutOfBoundsException if i is out of range.

```
public void add (Object elem);
```
// Add elem after the last element of this list.

```
public void addAll (List that);
```
// Add all the elements of that after the last element of this list.

```
public Object remove (int i);
```
// Remove and return the element with index i in this list. Throw an
// IndexOutOfBoundsException if i is out of range.

/////////// Iterator ///////////

```
public Iterator iterator ();
```
// Return an iterator that will visit all elements of this list, in left-to-right
// order.

```
}
```

Program 8.2   A contract for a list ADT.

Unfortunately, traversing a list in this way is likely to be inefficient. Accessing an array component has time complexity $O(1)$, so traversing the whole array has time complexity $O(n)$, where n is the array's length. But accessing a single list element using get or set could have time complexity $O(n)$ (as we shall see in Section 8.6), in which case traversing the whole list would have time complexity $O(n^2)$, where n is the list's length.

Besides, there are other kinds of collections – stacks, queues, sets, maps, and so on – whose elements are not indexed. The above code pattern cannot be adapted for such collections.

Fortunately, there is a more general means of traversing a collection, such as a list. The idea is to construct an ***iterator*** from the collection. Think of the iterator as an invisible thread, and think of the collection's elements as beads. To *construct the iterator*, we thread the elements together in the desired order. To *perform the traversal*, we unthread the elements, one at a time.

Figure 8.3 illustrates a left-to-right traversal of a list. To construct the required iterator, we thread the list elements together in left-to-right order. (The thread is shown as a dashed line.) The first step of the traversal is to unthread (visit) the first element on the thread. As the traversal progresses, the elements are unthreaded, one at a time, until eventually no elements are left on the thread.

A variety of iterators can be constructed on the same list. Figure 8.4(a) shows the left-to-right iterator we have already met. Figure 8.4(b) shows a right-to-left iterator, which will allow the same elements to be visited in reverse order. An iterator does not necessarily include every element: Figure 8.4(c) shows an iterator that will allow only every second element to be visited.

The concept of an iterator is captured by Java 2's java.util.Iterator interface, outlined in Program 8.5. In terms of our thread metaphor, the hasNext method tests whether any elements remain on the thread, and (if so) the next method unthreads the next element and returns that element.

The code pattern for traversing a list list, expressed in terms of Iterator operations, is as follows:

```
Iterator elems = list.iterator();
while (elems.hasNext()) {
    Object elem = elems.next();
    ...  // code that inspects elem
}
```

First, we construct an iterator using the appropriate List operation (elems = list.iterator()). Next, we repeatedly fetch the next element on the thread (elems.next()), as long as an element remains to be fetched (elems.hasNext()).

This code pattern allows the list elements to be inspected, but not updated (unless they happen to be mutable). In the code pattern above, 'elem = ...' would update the local variable elem, but would have no effect on the element in the list.

Program 8.6 shows how iterators would be used in the text editor introduced in Example 8.1.

In Sections 8.5 and 8.6, we shall see how iterators are implemented for lists represented in two different ways.

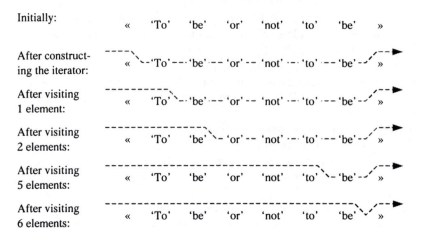

Figure 8.3   Left-to-right iterator over a list of words (conceptual view).

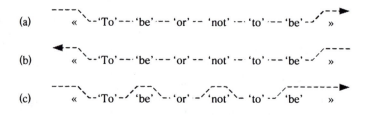

Figure 8.4   Several possible iterators over a list of words: (a) left-to-right; (b) right-to-left; (c) alternate words left-to-right.

```
public interface Iterator {
    // Each Iterator object represents an iterator over some collection, i.e.,
    // a series of elements in that collection.

    public boolean hasNext ();
    // Return true if and only if this iterator has a next element.

    public Object next ();
    // Return the next element in this iterator, or throw a
    // NoSuchElementException if there is no such element.

    ...   // The remove method is omitted here.
}
```

Program 8.5   The Java 2 `Iterator` interface.

```
public class TextEditor {

  private List text;
  private int sel;

  ...//    Constructor and methods as in Program 8.1.

  public void save (BufferedWriter output)
            throws IOException {
  // Write this text to output.
    Iterator lines = text.iterator();
    while (lines.hasNext()) {
      String line = (String) lines.next();
      output.write(line);
      output.write("\n");
    }
  }

  public void display () {
  //  Display this text, highlighting the selected line.
    int ln = 0;   // ... line number
    Iterator lines = text.iterator();
    while (lines.hasNext()) {
      String line = (String) lines.next();
      boolean selected = (ln == sel);
      ...    // Display line on the screen, highlighting it if selected.
      ln++;
    }
  }

}

...    //   Constructor and methods as in Program 8.1.
```

Program 8.6   Implementation of text editor methods using iterators.

8.5 Implementation of bounded lists using arrays

A **bounded list** is one whose length is limited. If the list's maximum length is *maxlength*, its current length can vary from 0 through *maxlength*.

A bounded list can be represented by an array *elems* of length *maxlength*. When the list's length is less than *maxlength*, some of the array components will be unoccupied. Let us agree that the list elements will occupy the subarray *elems*[0...*length* − 1], in order from left to right, with the list's length *length* being held in an instance variable. Figure 8.7 shows this representation in the general case, and also illustrates how a list of words would be represented.

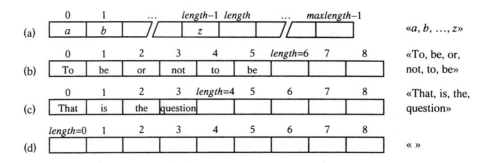

Figure 8.7 Representation of bounded lists by arrays: (a) general case; (b–c) lists of words (with *maxlength* = 8); (d) empty list.

Table 8.8 Implementation of lists using arrays: summary of algorithms (where n, n_1, and n_2 are the lengths of the lists involved).

Operation	Algorithm	Time complexity
get	array indexing	$O(n)$
equals	element-wise equality test	$O(n_2)$
set	array indexing	$O(n)$
add (2 parameters)	array insertion	$O(n)$
add (1 parameter)	array insertion after last element	$O(1)$
addAll	repeated array insertion after last element	$O(n_2)$
remove	array deletion	$O(n)$

The implementation of the list ADT is now quite straightforward. Table 8.8 summarizes the algorithms that would be used, together with their complexities.

The implementation itself is shown in Program 8.9. This is a Java class ArrayList that is declared as implementing the List interface. The instance variable elems is an array whose size is fixed when the list is constructed, and its components are all initially null. The instance variable length keeps track of the list's length, and is initially zero. The get and set operations use simple array indexing, and have time complexity $O(1)$. The remove operation employs the array deletion algorithm (Algorithm 3.9), and therefore has time complexity $O(n)$, where n is the list's length. Likewise, the 2-parameter add operation employs the array insertion algorithm (Algorithm 3.6), and also has time complexity $O(n)$. However, the 1-parameter add operation has no need to shift elements, and so has time complexity $O(1)$.

The array implementation of lists could be suitable for the text editor application of Example 8.1, provided that a bound on the number of lines in a text is an acceptable restriction.

The iterator operation in Program 8.9 constructs a left-to-right iterator over the ArrayList object. This iterator is an object of the class ArrayList.LRIterator shown in Program 8.10. This would be an *inner class* of the `ArrayList` class. (For an explanation of inner classes see Appendix B.6.) Thus the iterator has an implicit reference to the `ArrayList` object that creates the iterator object. The iterator is represented by a place-marker, `place`, which is initially zero, but which will be incremented each time an element is visited. Figure 8.11 shows an `ArrayList` object together with an `ArrayList.LRIterator` object that has just been constructed from

```
public class ArrayList implements List {

    // Each ArrayList object is an indexed list (sequence) whose elements
    // are objects.

    // This list is represented as follows: its elements occupy
    // elems[0...length-1].
    private Object[] elems;
    private int length;

    ///////////// Constructor /////////////

    public ArrayList (int maxlength) {
    // Construct a list, initially empty, whose length will be bounded by
    // maxlength.
        elems = new Object[maxlength];
        length = 0;
    }

    ///////////// Accessors /////////////

    public boolean isEmpty () {
    // Return true if and only if this list is empty.
        return (length == 0);
    }

    public int size () {
    // Return this list's length.
        return length;
    }

    public Object get (int i) {
    // Return the element with index i in this list. Throw an
    // IndexOutOfBoundsException if i is out of range.
        if (i < 0 || i >= length)
            throw new IndexOutOfBoundsException();
        return elems[i];
    }
```

Program 8.9 Java implementation of bounded lists using arrays (*continued on next page*).

```java
public boolean equals (List that) {
// Return true if and only if this list and that have the same length,
// each element of this list equals the corresponding element of that.
   ArrayList other = (ArrayList) that;
   if (length != other.length)
     return false;
   for (int i = 0; i < length; i++) {
     if (! elems[i].equals(other.elems[i]))
       return false;
   }
   return true;
}

/////////////// Transformers ///////////////

public void clear () {
// Make this list empty.
   for (int i = 0; i < length; i++)
     elems[i] = null;
   length = 0;
}

public void set (int i, Object elem) {
// Replace by elem the element at index i in this list. Throw an
// IndexOutOfBoundsException if i is out of range.
   if (i < 0 || i >= length)
     throw new IndexOutOfBoundsException();
   elems[i] = elem;
}

public void add (int i, Object elem) {
// Add elem as the element with index i in this list. Throw an
// IndexOutOfBoundsException if i is out of range.
   if (i < 0 || i > length)
     throw new IndexOutOfBoundsException();
   if (length == elems.length)  expand();
   for (int j = length; j > i; j--)
     elems[j] = elems[j-1];
   elems[i] = elem;
   length++;
}
```

Program 8.9 (*continued on next page*)

```java
public void add (Object elem) {
// Add elem after the last element of this list.
   if (length == elems.length)  expand();
   elems[length++] = elem;
}
public void addAll (List that) {
// Add all the elements of that after the last element of this list.
   ArrayList other = (ArrayList) that;
   for (int i = 0; i < other.length; i++)
     add(other.elems[i]);
}

public Object remove (int i) {
// Remove and return the element with index i in this list. Throw an
// IndexOutOfBoundsException if i is out of range.
   if (i < 0 || i >= length)
     throw new IndexOutOfBoundsException();
   Object oldElem = elems[i];
   for (int j = i+1; j < length; j++)
     elems[j-1] = elems[j];
   length--;
   elems[length] = null;
   return oldElem;
}

/////////// Iterator ///////////

public Iterator iterator () {
// Return an iterator that will visit all elements of this list, in left-to-right
// order.
   return new ArrayList.LRIterator();
}

/////////// Auxiliary method ///////////

private void expand () {
// Make the elems array longer.
   ...   // Code omitted here.
}

}
```

Program 8.9 *(continued)*

it (including the implicit reference between the two). Each call to the iterator's `next` method simply returns the list element indexed by `place`, and also increments `place`.

Observe that the `ArrayList` class's instance variables `elems` and `length` were declared as private in Program 8.9. The methods in the `ArrayList.LRIterator` class can still access these instance variables, since an inner class can access all parts of the class that contains it.

```java
private class LRIterator implements Iterator {
    // An ArrayList.LRIterator object is a left-to-right iterator over a
    // list represented by an ArrayList object.
    // This iterator is represented by the array index of the next element to be
    // visited, place.
    private int place;

    private LRIterator () {
        place = 0;
    }

    public boolean hasNext () {
        return (place < length);
    }

    public Object next () {
        if (place >= length)
            throw new NoSuchElementException();
        return elems[place++];
    }

    ...    // The remove method is omitted here.

}
```

Program 8.10 Iterator for the implementation of bounded lists using arrays (as an inner class of `ArrayList`).

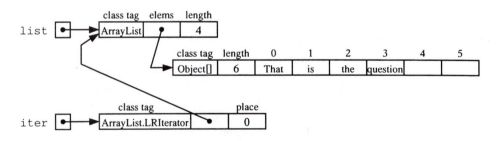

Figure 8.11 An `ArrayList` object `list`, and an iterator object `iter` constructed from it by: `iter = list.iterator()`.

It is important to note that the iterator *shares* the list object. In particular, the iterator does *not* copy the list elements. It does not need its own data structure. All the information needed by the iterator is contained in the list's own data structure, apart from the place-marker. This is typical of most iterators over most collections: a place-marker and a reference to the underlying collection (which may be implicit) are quite sufficient to implement them.

8.6 Implementation of unbounded lists using linked lists

An unbounded list can easily be represented by a singly-linked list (SLL). We will need links to both the first and last nodes, since elements will sometimes be added at the end of the list. Figure 8.12 shows this representation in the general case, and also illustrates how a list of words would be represented.

The implementation of the list ADT is again straightforward. Table 8.13 summarizes the SLL algorithms that would be used, together with their complexities.

The implementation itself is shown in Program 8.14. This is a Java class named `LinkedList` that is declared as implementing the `List` interface. The instance vari-

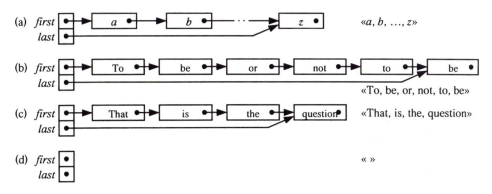

Figure 8.12 Representation of unbounded lists by SLLs: (a) general case; (b–c) lists of words; (d) empty list.

Table 8.13 Implementation of lists using SLLs: summary of algorithms (where n, n_1, and n_2 are the lengths of the lists involved).

Operation	Algorithm	Time complexity
get	node counting	$O(n)$
equals	element-wise equality test	$O(n_2)$
set	node counting	$O(n)$
add (2 parameters)	node counting followed by SLL insertion	$O(n)$
add (1 parameter)	SLL insertion after last node	$O(1)$
addAll	repeated SLL insertion after last node	$O(n_2)$
remove	node counting followed by SLL deletion	$O(n)$

ables `first` and `last` are links to the first and last nodes, respectively, and are initially null. The instance variable `length` keeps track of the list's length. The nodes themselves are of class `SLLNode` (see Program 4.4).

The 1-parameter `add` operation has time complexity $O(1)$, because a direct link to the last node is available. However, the `get`, `set`, 2-parameter `add`, and `remove` operations each has to locate the node with a given index. Unless that node happens to be the first or last node, no direct link to that node is available, so the operation must count out nodes from the start of the SLL. The index could be anything between 0 and n, where n is

```java
public class LinkedList implements List {
    // Each LinkedList object is an unbounded list whose elements are
    // objects.
    // This list is represented as follows: first and last are links to the first
    //   and last nodes of an SLL containing its elements; length is the number
    //   of elements.
    private SLLNode first, last;
    private int length;

    /////////////// Constructor ////////////////

    public SLLList () {
    // Construct a list, initially empty.
        first = last = null;
        length = 0;
    }

    /////////////// Accessors ////////////////

    public boolean isEmpty () {
    // Return true if and only if this list is empty.
        return (first == null);
    }

    public int size () {
    // Return this list's length.
        return length;
    }

    public Object get (int i) {
    // Return the element with index i in this list. Throw an
    // IndexOutOfBoundsException if i is out of range.
        if (i < 0 || i >= length)
            throw new IndexOutOfBoundsException();
        SLLNode curr = node(i);
        return curr.element;
    }
```

Program 8.14 Java implementation of unbounded lists using SLLs (*continued on next page*).

```
public boolean equals (List that) {
//  Return true if and only if this list and that have the same length, and
//  each element of this list equals the corresponding element of that.
    LinkedList other = (LinkedList) that;
    if (length != other.length)
      return false;
    for (SLLNode curr1 = first,
          curr2 = other.first;
        curr1 != null;
        curr1 = curr1.succ, curr2 = curr2.succ) {
      if (! curr1.element.equals(curr2.element))
        return false;
    }
    return true;
}

///////////// Transformers ////////////

public void clear () {
//  Make this list empty.
    first = last = null;
    length = 0;
}

public void set (int i, Object elem) {
//  Replace by elem the element at index i in this list. Throw an
//  IndexOutOfBoundsException if i is out of range.
    if (i < 0 || i >= length)
        throw new IndexOutOfBoundsException();
    SLLNode curr = node(i);
    curr.element = elem;
}
```

Program 8.14 (*continued on next page*)

the list's length, and will be about $n/2$ on average. Thus these four operations all have time complexity $O(n)$.

The linked-list implementation of lists could be used in any application (including the text editor of Example 8.1). The fact that it supports unbounded lists is a major advantage. On the other hand, the $O(n)$ time complexity of several operations would slow down any application that uses these operations frequently (such as the text editor). In practice, this implementation is not suitable for applications that process very long lists.

The iterator operation in Program 8.14 constructs a left-to-right iterator over the LinkedList object. This iterator is an object of the class LinkedList. LRIterator shown in Program 8.15 (which would be an inner class of the LinkedList class). The iterator is represented by a place-marker, place. This

```java
public void add (int i, Object elem) {
// Add elem as the element with index i in this list. Throw an
// IndexOutOfBoundsException if i is out of range.
   if (i < 0 || i > length)
       throw new IndexOutOfBoundsException();
   SLLNode newest = new SLLNode(elem, null);
   if (i == 0) {
     newest.succ = first;
     first = newest;
   } else {
     SLLNode pred = node(i-1);
     newest.succ = pred.succ;
     pred.succ = newest;
   }
   if (newest.succ == null)
     last = newest;
   length++;
}

public void add (Object elem) {
// Add elem after the last element of this list.
   SLLNode newest = new SLLNode(elem, null);
   if (first == null)
     first = newest;
   else
     last.succ = newest;
   last = newest;
   length++;
}

public void addAll (List that) {
// Add all the elements of that after the last element of this list.
   LinkedList other = (LinkedList) that;
   for (SLLNode curr = other.first;
       curr != null; curr = curr.succ)
     add(curr.element);
}
```

Program 8.14 (*continued on next page*)

place-marker is initially a link to the first node of the SLL, but will later be a link to the other nodes in turn. Figure 8.16 shows a `LinkedList` object together with a `LinkedList.LRIterator` object that has just been constructed from it (including the implicit reference between the two). Each call to the iterator's `next` method simply returns the list element in the node to which `place` is a link, and also advances `place` to the successor node (which may be null).

```java
public Object remove (int i) {
// Remove and return the element with index i in this list. Throw an
// IndexOutOfBoundsException if i is out of range.
    if (i < 0 || i >= length)
        throw new IndexOutOfBoundsException();
    Object oldElem;
    if (i == 0) {
        oldElem = first.element;
        if (first == last)
            last = null;
        first = first.succ;
    } else {
        SLLNode pred = node(i-1);
        SLLNode old = pred.succ;
        oldElem = old.element;
        pred.succ = old.succ;
        if (old == last)
            last = pred;
    }
    length--;
    return oldElem;
}

/////////// Iterator ///////////

public Iterator iterator () {
// Return an iterator that will visit all elements of this list, in left-to-right
// order.
    return new LinkedList.LRIterator();
}

/////////// Auxiliary method ///////////

private SLLNode node (int i) {
// Return a link to the node containing the element with index i in this list.
    SLLNode curr = first;
    for (int j = 0; j < i; j++)
        curr = curr.succ;
    return curr;
}

}
```

Program 8.14 (*continued*)

```
private class LRIterator implements Iterator {
    // A LinkedList.LRIterator object is a left-to-right iterator over a
    // list represented by a LinkedList object.

    // This iterator is represented by a link to the node containing the next
    // element to be visited, place.
    private SLLNode place;
    private LRIterator () {
        place = first;
    }

    public boolean hasNext () {
        return (place != null);
    }

    public Object next () {
        if (place == null)
            throw new NoSuchElementException();
        Object nextElem = place.element;
        place = place.succ;
        return nextElem;
    }

        ...    // The remove method is omitted here.

}
```

Program 8.15 Iterator for the implementation of unbounded lists using SLLs (as an inner class of LinkedList).

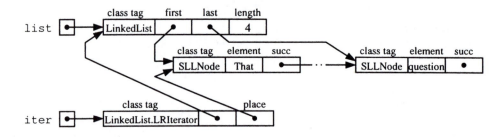

Figure 8.16 A LinkedList object list, and an iterator object iter constructed from it by: iter = list.iterator().

8.7 Lists in the Java class library

The Java 2 class library includes several classes that support lists of objects. The class library similarly supports sets and maps (tables). The classes that support lists, sets, and maps are known as the *collection classes*, and are surveyed in Appendix C.

The list ADT contract is embodied by the `java.util.List` interface, which is shown in Appendix C.2. This interface is similar to the simpler `List` interface of Program 8.2. The `java.util.List` interface differs mainly in that:

- Its `equals` method accepts an arbitrary object as argument. This is because it overrides the `equals` method of the ancestor `Object` class. Of course, the `equals` method in any `List` class must return false if its argument is not a `List` object.
- Its `addAll` method accepts an arbitrary collection as argument, not necessarily a list. The motivation here is to make the collection classes inter-operable, as far as possible. Thus l.`addAll`(c) adds all the elements of collection c to list l. We can view this as first forming a list of all the elements of c, then concatenating the lists as usual.
- It provides several additional methods such as `indexOf` and `lastIndexOf` (which search the list for a given element), `contains` (which tests whether the list contains a given element), `containsAll` (which tests whether the list contains all the elements in a given collection), `removeAll` and `retainAll` (which remove from the list all the elements in, or not in, a given collection).
- It provides additional iterators (discussed below).

Several library classes implement the `java.util.List` interface, representing lists in different ways.

The `java.util.ArrayList` class represents a list by an array, as described in Section 8.5. If addition of an element causes an overflow, all elements are copied into a new and longer array. As well as the operations required by the `java.util.List` interface, this class provides an operation that allows application code to expand the array in anticipation of future additions.

The `java.util.Vector` class is a Java 1 legacy that has been retrospectively adapted to implement the `java.util.List` interface. This class is very similar to `java.util.ArrayList`, but the latter was specifically designed to fit into the collection classes framework and should be preferred.

The `java.util.LinkedList` class represents a list by a doubly-linked list (DLL). This class provides additional operations `getFirst`, `getLast`, `addFirst`, `addLast`, `removeFirst`, and `removeLast`, which allow a `LinkedList` object to mimic a stack or queue. It is not clear why these useful operations were left out of the `java.util.List` interface, as they can be implemented efficiently with any reasonable list representation (see Exercise 8.12). The choice of a DLL representation is easily justified (see Exercise 8.13).

We have already encountered the `java.util.Iterator` interface, in Section 8.4. This interface provides not only the `hasNext` and `next` operations shown in Program 8.5, but also a `remove` operation (which removes from the underlying collection the element most recently returned by `next`). For example, the following code pattern:

```
Iterator elems = list.iterator();
while (elems.hasNext()) {
  Object elem = elems.next();
  ...  // code that inspects elem
  elems.remove();
}
```

iterates over the list `list`, inspecting *and then removing* each element in turn.

The `java.util.ListIterator` interface has additional operations that are specific to iteration over lists. It extends the `java.util.Iterator` interface with operations `hasPrevious` and `previous` (which are analogous to `hasNext` and `next`, and allow right-to-left iteration over the underlying list), `set` (which replaces, in the underlying list, the element most recently returned by `next` or `previous`), and `add` (which adds a new element to the underlying list just before the place-marker). The `java.util.LinkedList` class provides a `listIterator` operation, which constructs a `ListIterator` object from a `LinkedList` object.

8.8 Case study: a videotape manager

It is awkward for users to keep track of the contents of their videotapes. Indeed, the latest 'smart' video recorders offer to do this automatically. A particular problem is to find a gap on a videotape where we can record a video program without overwriting another program.

In this section we will develop a simple system to keep track of the contents of a videotape. We will think of a videotape as being divided into *segments* of varying length, where each segment is either recorded (containing a video program) or blank. The videotape's contents will be a list of segments.

To make things slightly more complicated, a video program can be recorded in either standard-play mode or long-play mode. A video program recorded in long-play mode occupies half as much space on the tape as one recorded in standard-play mode.

We will assume that our videotape manager must satisfy the following requirements:

- It must be possible to view the list of segments on the videotape.
- It must be possible to add a new video program to the videotape. The new video program should occupy the first sufficiently-long blank segment on the videotape. If no sufficiently-long segment can be found, a suitable message should be displayed. Note that adding a video program may involve splitting an existing blank segment into the new recorded segment and a shorter blank segment.
- It must be possible to erase a video program from the videotape. The segment containing the video program should become blank. This blank segment should be combined with adjacent blank segments to prevent the videotape's contents from becoming *fragmented* (see Section 8.8.3).

The complete system is available as a Java application on the companion Web site, and includes a suitable user interface. In this section we will confine our attention to the representation of a videotape and the algorithms needed to add and erase programs.

8.8.1 Representing a videotape's contents

Our first task in the design of our video manager is to decide how to represent the various entities.

Representing video programs

A recorded video program has attributes such as its title, its channel, its duration, and whether it has been recorded in standard-play or long-play mode.

Program 8.17 shows a Java class named `VideoProgram`, whose objects will repre-

```java
public class VideoProgram {

    // Each VideoProgram object represents a recorded video program.

    // This video program is represented by its title, its channel name, its
    // duration (in seconds), and a flag indicating whether it is recorded in
    // long-play mode.
    private String title, channel;
    private int duration;
    private boolean isLongPlay;

    ///////////// Constructor /////////////

    public VideoProgram (String title, String channel,
                    int duration, boolean isLongPlay) {
    // Create a new video program with the given details.
        this.title = title;
        this.channel = channel;
        this.duration = duration;
        this.isLongPlay = isLongPlay;
    }

    ///////////// Accessors /////////////

    // One simple accessor per attribute: getTitle, getChannel,
    // getDuration, isLongPlay.

    ...    // See code on the companion Web site.

}
```

Program 8.17   Representation of recorded video programs by a Java class `VideoProgram`.

sent video programs recorded on a videotape. Note that this class needs no transformers: our system allows the user no means to change the details of a video program once recorded.

Representing segments

We have already decided that a videotape's contents will be a list of segments, but what attributes and operations are needed for each segment?

Clearly, each segment has a certain length that indicates how much of the videotape it occupies. Recall that there are two kinds of segments: the content of a recorded segment is a video program; the content of a blank segment is nothing.

We will use a class named Segment to represent videotape segments, shown in Program 8.18.

Representing videotapes

We now consider the representation of a videotape. Clearly, a videotape object should contain the videotape's contents as a list of segments. It should also contain the videotape's title and its overall length in seconds.

Apart from some simple accessor methods to retrieve the values of these attributes, a videotape object must also be equipped with two transformers: one to add a new video program, and one to erase an existing video program. We shall develop these transformers in Sections 8.8.2 and 8.8.3 respectively.

Program 8.19 shows the implementation of videotapes by a Java class named Videotape. Note that, when we create a new videotape, its initial content is a single blank segment with the same length as the entire videotape.

8.8.2 Adding a new video program to a videotape

Adding a new video program to a videotape needs several steps. We first search for a sufficiently-long blank segment. If such a segment exists, we create a new recorded segment containing the video program, add it to the contents list before the blank segment, and reduce the length of the blank segment by the length of the new recorded segment. If the new recorded segment happens to be exactly as long as the old blank segment, the recorded segment simply replaces the blank segment.

Program 8.20 implements this idea as a Java method named record, which belongs to the Videotape class of Program 8.19.

8.8.3 Erasing a video program from a videotape

Erasing a video program from a videotape's contents list basically entails replacing an old recorded segment with a new blank segment of the same length. If we did nothing more, however, the contents of the videotape would become *fragmented*.

Fragmentation occurs when segments are successively added and removed. Over time, the contents list accumulates more and more short blank segments. If this happens, it

```java
public class Segment {

    // Each Segment object represents a videotape segment.

    // This segment is represented by a length (in seconds) and a reference to a
    // VideoProgram object, or null if the segment is blank.
    private int length;
    private VideoProgram program;

    ////////////// Constructors //////////////

    public Segment (int length) {
    // Construct a blank segment of the given length.
        this.length = length;
        this.program = null;
    }

    public Segment (VideoProgram program) {
    // Construct a recorded segment with the given video program. This
    // segment's length is determined by the video program's duration and
    // recording mode.
        int duration = program.getDuration();
        this.length = (program.isLongPlay() ?
            (duration+1)/2 : duration);
        this.program = program;
    }

    ////////////// Accessors //////////////

    // One simple accessor per attribute: getLength, getProgram.

    ...    // See code on the companion Web site.

    public boolean isBlank () {
    // Return true if and only if this segment is blank.
        return (program == null);
    }

    ////////////// Transformer //////////////

    public void setLength (int length) {
    // Change the length of this segment to length, but only if this
    // segment is blank (otherwise the recorded video program's duration
    // would become inconsistent with the segment's length).
        if (program == null)
            this.length = length;
    }

}
```

Program 8.18   Representation of videotape segments by a Java class Segment.

```
public class Videotape {

    // Each Videotape object represents a videotape.

    // This videotape is represented by its title, its overall length (in seconds),
    // and a list of segments into which it has been divided.
    private String title;
    private int length;
    private List contents;    // Elements are Segment objects.

    ///////////// Constructor /////////////

    public Videotape (String title, int length) {
    // Create a new videotape with the details given, containing a single
    // blank segment of the same length as the videotape.
        this.title = title;
        this.length = length;
        this.contents = new LinkedList();
        this.contents.add(new Segment(length));
    }

    ///////////// Accessors /////////////

    // One simple accessor method per attribute: getTitle, getLength,
    // getContents, and getContentsSize.

    ...    // See code on the companion Web site.

    ///////////// Transformers /////////////

    public int record (VideoProgram program) {
    // Add program to this videotape's contents list. Place it in a new
    // recorded segment, either before or in place of the first sufficiently-long
    // blank segment. Return the index of the new recorded segment, or NONE
    // if there is no sufficiently-long blank segment on this videotape.
        ...    // See Section 8.8.2.
    }

    public void erase (int i) {
    // Erase the video program at index i from this videotape's contents list,
    // and coalesce adjacent blank segments.
        ...    // See Section 8.8.3.
    }

}
```

Program 8.19   Representation of videotapes by a Java class Videotape (outline).

```java
public int record (VideoProgram program) {
// Add program to this videotape's contents list. Place it in a new
// recorded segment, either before or in place of the first sufficiently-long
// blank segment. Return the index of the new recorded segment, or NONE
// if there is no sufficiently-long blank segment on this videotape.
    boolean gapFound = false;
    Segment newSeg = new Segment(prog);
    int newLength = newSeg.getLength();
    Segment seg;
    int index = 0;
    Iterator segments = contents.iterator();
    while (segments.hasNext()) {
        seg = (Segment) segments.next();
        index++;
        if (seg.isBlank()
            && seg.getLength() >= newLength) {
            gapFound = true;
            break;
        }
    }
    if (gapFound) {
        int remainder = seg.getLength() - newLength;
        if (remainder == 0)
            contents.set(index, newSeg);
        else { // (remainder > 0)
            contents.add(index, newSeg);
            seg.setLength(remainder);
        }
        return index;
    } else
        return NONE;
}
```

Program 8.20   Implementation of the addition algorithm as a Java method (in class `Videotape`).

becomes more and more difficult to find a sufficiently-long blank segment to record a new video program (even if the videotape is largely blank!).

To reduce fragmentation, we should coalesce adjacent blank segments into a single blank segment. (The only way to eliminate fragmentation completely would be periodically to move all of the recorded segments to the beginning of the videotape, and so coalesce all of the blank segments into a single blank segment at the end of the videotape. But this is impractical, since it would require two video recorders!)

The auxiliary method `coalesceBlanks` of Program 8.21 coalesces all the adjacent blank segments in a videotape's contents list. This method iterates over the contents list looking for adjacent blank segments. Whenever it finds a pair of adjacent blank segments, it updates the length of the first segment to be sum of their lengths, and removes the second segment.

The `erase` method of Program 8.22 is a method that erases a recorded segment from a videotape's contents list, given that segment's index. It replaces the recorded segment by a blank segment of the same length, and then coalesces any adjacent blank segments.

Both the `erase` and `coalesceBlanks` methods would be added to the `Video-tape` class of Program 8.19.

```java
private void coalesceBlanks () {
// Coalesce adjacent blank segments in this videotape's contents list.
    Iterator segs = contents.iterator();
    Segment prev = (Segment) segs.next();
    while (segs.hasNext()) {
        Segment curr = (Segment) segs.next();
        if (prev.isBlank() && curr.isBlank()) {
            int totalLength = prev.getLength() +
                curr.getLength();
            prev.setLength(totalLength);
            segs.remove();
        } else
            prev = curr;
    }
}
```

Program 8.21   Implementation of the coalescence algorithm as a Java method (in class `Videotape`).

```java
public void erase (int i) {
// Erase the video program at index i from this videotape's contents list,
//  and coalesce adjacent blank segments.
    Segment seg = (Segment) contents.get(i);
    if (! seg.isBlank()) {
        Segment newSeg = new Segment(seg.getLength());
        contents.set(i, newSeg);
        coalesceBlanks();
    }
}
```

Program 8.22   Implementation of the erasure algorithm as a Java method (in class `Videotape`).

Summary

In this chapter:

- We have studied the concept of a list, an indexed sequence in which elements can be added, removed, inspected, and updated anywhere.
- We have seen an example and a case study demonstrating applications of lists.
- We have designed an ADT for lists, expressed as a `List` interface.
- We have studied how to represent bounded and unbounded lists by arrays and linked lists, respectively, and how to code these in Java as classes that implement the `List` interface.
- We have studied the concept of an iterator, and how to implement left-to-right iterators over lists.

Exercises

8.1 Give some examples of lists (or sequences) in everyday life. Remember that the order of items in a list is significant: a shopping 'list' is genuinely a list only if it specifies the order in which you are going to buy things!

8.2 Compare the `Stack` and `Queue` ADTs of Programs 6.6 and 7.6, respectively, with the `List` ADT of Program 8.2.
  (a) Show that the `Stack` ADT is a special case of the `List` ADT. Which list operations correspond to `addLast`, `removeLast`, and `getLast`?
  (b) Show that the `Queue` ADT is a special case of the `List` ADT. Which list operations correspond to `addLast`, `removeFirst`, and `getFirst`?

8.3 Using the `List` ADT of Program 8.2, write the following method:

```
static List reorder (List persons) {
    //  Assume that persons is a list of Person objects, ordered by name.
    //  Return a similar list of Person objects, ordered such that all
    //  children (aged under 18) come before all adults (aged 18 or over), but
    //  otherwise preserving the ordering by name.
    ...
}
```

Assume that each `Person` object has public instance variables `name` and `age`.

8.4 Use an iterator to extend the simple text editor given in Program 8.1 with the following methods: `findFirst(s)` selects the first line in the text that has a substring s; `findNext()` selects the next line in the text that has the substring s that was last supplied as an argument to `findFirst`. If there are no further occurrences of s, the currently selected line is unchanged. To search the entire list, call `findFirst` once, then call `findNext` as often as necessary.

* 8.5 Extend the `List` interface of Program 8.2 with an operation `listIterator` that returns a

ListIterator object that is capable of traversing this list in both directions. (See Section 8.7 and the java.util.ListIterator interface for details.)
(a) Modify the ArrayList class of Program 8.9 to include a ListIterator.
(b) Modify the LinkedList class of Program 8.14 to include a ListIterator.
What is the time complexity of each operation in the ListIterator?

8.6 Suppose that the following operations are to be added to the List interface of Program 8.2. The operation *l*.contains(*x*) returns true if and only if object *x* is an element of list *l*. The operation *l*.indexOf(*x*) returns the index of object *x* in *l* if it is an element, or −1 otherwise. (See the java.util.List interface in Appendix C.2 for a detailed description of these operations).
(a) Modify the ArrayList class of Program 8.9 to implement these operations.
(b) Modify the LinkedList class of Program 8.14 to implement these operations.

8.7 Suppose that the following operation is to be added to the List interface of Program 8.2. The operation *l*.subList(*i*, *j*) is to return a new list that contains all of the elements in *l* with indices *i* through *j* − 1.
(a) Modify the ArrayList class of Program 8.9 to implement this operation.
(b) Modify the LinkedList class of Program 8.14 to implement this operation.

* **8.8** Modify your solution to Exercise 6.13 to use the List ADT instead of the Stack ADT. Use the contains method described in Exercise 8.6 to eliminate the need for a separate record of which stack contains each railroad car.

* **8.9** Repeat Exercise 8.8 for your solution to Exercise 7.9.

8.10 Implement the auxiliary method expand in Program 8.9 to deal with the possibility of an overflow. The method should copy all the list elements into a new and longer new array, and replace the existing array by that new array.

8.11 In the linked-list implementation of lists (Program 8.14), what are the advantages and disadvantages of using instance variable length to keep track of the list's length? Modify the implementation to dispense with this variable.

8.12 Suppose that getFirst, getLast, addFirst, addLast, removeFirst, and removeLast operations were added to the List interface of Program 8.2.
(a) Modify the ArrayList class of Program 8.9 to implement these operations.
(b) Modify the LinkedList class of Program 8.14 to implement these operations.
Modify the data representations if you think fit.

8.13 The java.util.LinkedList class represents a list by a DLL, rather than an SLL as in Program 8.14. Justify this decision. Show how you would modify Program 8.14 to use a DLL.

8.14 Program 8.20 uses a *first-fit* strategy to select which blank segment to use for recording a video program: it selects the *first* sufficiently-long blank segment that it encounters. There are two other common strategies that could be employed:
- *Best-fit* strategy: select the shortest sufficiently-long blank segment.
- *Worst-fit* strategy: select the longest blank segment.
(a) Write two new algorithms that use the best-fit and worst-fit strategies, respectively.
(b) Write two new Java methods to implement your algorithms from part (a).
(c) Replace the record method in the Videotape class of Program 8.19 with each of

your revised methods from part (b), and observe the results when adding programs to a videotape's contents list.

8.15 Consider the video manager system from Section 8.8.

(a) Extend the application to allow the videotape's contents list to be loaded from a file at the start, and saved to the same file at the end. Assume that the filename is supplied as a command-line argument when the application is started.

(b) Extend the application to allow the user interactively to save and load a videotape's contents list to or from a file. The filename should be selected from a menu using the standard file open and save dialogs.

9

Set Abstract Data Types

In this chapter we shall study:

- the concept of a set (Section 9.1)
- simple applications of sets (Section 9.2)
- requirements and a contract for a set ADT (Section 9.3)
- simple implementations of sets using arrays and linked lists (Section 9.4–6)
- sets in the Java class library (Section 9.7)
- a case study using sets (Section 9.8).

9.1 The concept of a set

A *set* is a collection of distinct values, whose order has no significance. The values contained in a set are called its *members*.

The concept of a set is fundamental in both mathematics and computing. The following are examples of sets of integers. They are expressed in the usual mathematical notation, the members being enumerated between curly brackets {...}:

$$
\begin{array}{ll}
evens & = \{0, 2, 4, 6, 8\} \\
odds & = \{1, 3, 5, 7, 9\} \\
squares & = \{1, 4, 9\}
\end{array}
$$

Note that *squares* could just as well be written as {4, 1, 9} or {9, 4, 1}, since the order of the members has no significance.

The following are examples of sets of characters:

$$
\begin{array}{ll}
digits & = \{ \text{'0', '1', '2', '3', '4', '5', '6', '7', '8', '9'} \} \\
letters & = \{ \text{'a', 'b', 'c', 'd', 'e', 'f', 'g', 'h', 'i', 'j', 'k', 'l', 'm',} \\
& \quad \text{'n', 'o', 'p', 'q', 'r', 's', 't', 'u', 'v', 'w', 'x', 'y', 'z'} \}
\end{array}
$$

And the following are examples of sets of countries:

$$EU \quad = \{AT, BE, DE, DK, ES, FI, FR, GR, IE, IT, LU, NL, PT, SE, UK\}$$
$$NAFTA = \{CA, MX, US\}$$
$$NATO \quad = \{BE, CA, CZ, DE, DK, ES, FR, GR, HU, IS, IT, LU, NL, NO, PL,$$
$$\quad\quad\quad\quad PT, TR, UK, US\}$$

The **cardinality** of a set is the number of (distinct) members of that set. In mathematics, the cardinality of s is written as $\#s$. For example, $\#EU$ is 15, $\#NAFTA$ is 3, and $\#NATO$ is 19.

The **empty set** has cardinality zero, i.e., it has no members at all. In mathematics, the empty set is written as $\{\ \}$ or $\emptyset$.

We can test whether x is a member of a set s; this is called a **membership test**. For example, DK and NO are members of *NATO*, but SE is not. In mathematics, the assertion that x is a member of s is written as $x \in s$.

We can **add** a value x to a set s. If x is already a member of s, adding x has no effect, since a set has no duplicate members. Otherwise adding x increases $\#s$ by one. For example, adding CU to $\{CA, MX, US\}$ would change this set to $\{CA, CU, MX, US\}$, but adding MX to this set would have no effect.

We can **remove** a value x from a set s. If x is a member of s, removing x decreases $\#s$ by one. Otherwise removing x has no effect. For example, removing CU from $\{CA, CU, MX, US\}$ would change this set to $\{CA, MX, US\}$, but removing BR from this set would have no effect.

The above operations test, add, or remove a single member. The true power of sets is revealed by operations that work on whole sets.

Two sets are **equal** if they contain exactly the same members. For example, $\{CA, MX, US\}$ equals $\{MX, US, CA\}$, since the order of the members has no significance. But this set does not equal $\{CA, US\}$ nor $\{CA, UK, US\}$ nor $\{CA, CU, MX, US\}$.

Two sets are **disjoint** if they have no members in common. For example, *EU* and *NAFTA* are disjoint, but neither *EU* nor *NAFTA* is disjoint from *NATO*.

A set s_1 **subsumes** another set s_2 (or s_1 is a **superset** of s_2) if every member of s_2 is also a member of s_1. For example, *NATO* subsumes $\{CA, US\}$, but does not subsume *NAFTA*. In mathematics, set subsumption is written as $s_1 \supseteq s_2$. Note that every set subsumes itself ($s \supseteq s$), and every set subsumes the empty set ($s \supseteq \{\}$).

The **union** of two sets, s_1 and s_2, is the set containing just those values that are members of s_1 or s_2 or both. For example, the union of $\{DK, NO, SE\}$ and $\{IS, NO\}$ is $\{DK, IS, NO, SE\}$. In mathematics, set union is written as $s_1 \cup s_2$.

The **intersection** of two sets, s_1 and s_2, is the set containing just those values that are members of both s_1 and s_2. For example, the intersection of *NATO* and *NAFTA* is $\{CA, US\}$, whereas the intersection of *EU* and *NAFTA* is the empty set. In mathematics, set intersection is written as $s_1 \cap s_2$.

The **difference** of two sets, s_1 and s_2, is the set containing just those values that are members of s_1 but not of s_2. In mathematics, set difference is written as $s_1 - s_2$. For example, the difference $NATO - EU$ is $\{CA, CZ, HU, IS, NO, PL, TR, US\}$, whereas the difference $EU - NATO$ is $\{AT, FI, IE, SE\}$.

9.2 Applications of sets

Sets are not just an elegant mathematical abstraction: they have a variety of applications in computing. Indeed, they often enable us to formulate very elegant and concise algorithms. The following examples illustrate such applications.

EXAMPLE 9.1 *Eratosthenes' sieve algorithm*

The problem is to compute all the primes less than a given integer m. (A **prime** is an integer greater than 1 that is divisible only by itself and 1. The set of primes less than 20 is {2, 3, 5, 7, 11, 13, 17, 19}.)

The Hellenic mathematician Eratosthenes devised an elegant and efficient algorithm to solve this problem: see Algorithm 9.1. This algorithm starts with the set of integers {2, 3, ..., $m - 1$}, and then progressively removes integers that are found to be multiples of other integers.

To implement Eratosthenes' algorithm in Java, we will need an object to represent the set of integers. For step 2.1 of the algorithm, let us assume a method such that `s.contains(i)` tests whether integer i is a member of set s. For step 2.1.1, let us assume a method such that `s.remove(i)` removes i from set s. Step 1 requires us to construct the set {2, 3, ..., $m - 1$}. Rather than assuming a constructor or method that performs that rather specialized function, let us assume a method such that `s.add(i)` adds a single integer i to set s; this method can be called for each of the integers 2, 3, ..., $m - 1$ in turn.

Program 9.2 shows a Java method that implements Eratosthenes' algorithm. The set is an object of class `IntSet`. This class (not shown) is assumed to provide methods `add`, `remove`, and `contains`, as suggested above. It is also assumed to provide a constructor whose argument defines the range of integers that may be added to the constructed set.

> To compute the set of primes less than m (where $m > 0$):
> 1. Set *sieve* = {2, 3, ..., m–1}.
> 2. For $i = 2, 3, ...$, while $i^2 < m$, repeat:
>   2.1. If i is a member of *sieve*:
>   2.1.1. Remove all multiples of i from *sieve*.
> 3. Terminate with answer *sieve*.

Algorithm 9.1   Eratosthenes' sieve algorithm.

EXAMPLE 9.2 *Information retrieval*

A document base is a collection of documents. Given a document base, information retrieval is the process of discovering which of these documents satisfy a query entered by the user. At its simplest, a query is just a (small) set of key words, say *keywords*, to be compared with the set of words found in each document, say *docwords*. The user might want to know:

```
public static IntSet primesLessThan (int m) {
// Return the set of primes less than m.
   IntSet sieve = new IntSet(m);
   for (int i = 2; i < m; i++)
      sieve.add(i);
   for (int i = 2; i*i < m; i++) {
      if (sieve.contains(i)) {
         for (int mult = 2*i; mult < m; mult += i)
            sieve.remove(mult);
      }
   }
   return sieve;
}
```

Program 9.2   Implementation of Eratosthenes' sieve algorithm.

- Does the document contain all of the key words? This amounts to asking whether *docwords* subsumes *keywords* (i.e., *docwords* $\supseteq$ *keywords*).
- Does the document contain any of the key words? This amounts to asking whether *docwords* and *keywords* are disjoint (i.e., *docwords* $\cap$ *keywords* = {}).

Program 9.3 shows extracts from a very simple information retrieval system. This assumes that a WordSet object represents a set of words. It also assumes that class WordSet provides the following methods: s.add(w) adds word w to set s; s_1.containsAll(s_2) returns true if and only if s_1 subsumes s_2; and s.iterator() is an iterator that will visit all words in set s (in no particular order).

The score method crudely scores a named document against a given set, keywords. It first reads all words in the documents into a set, docwords. Then it uses set operations to determine whether the document contains all of the key words (docwords.containsAll(keywords)) or none (disjoint(docWords, keywords)).

The readAllWords method returns the set of all words found in a given document. It starts by creating an empty set (docwords = **new** WordSet()). Then it reads words one at a time, and adds each word (in lower case) to the set (docwords.add (word.toLowerCase())).

The disjoint method uses an iterator over one set to determine whether any member of that set is contained in the other set.

9.3 A set abstract data type

Given that the set is such a useful abstraction, it is natural to capture the essence of sets by

```
public static final int
    NONE = 0,  SOME = 1,  ALL = 2;

public static int score (String docname,
                WordSet keywords) {
// Return a score reflecting whether the document named docname contains
// all, some, or none of the words in keywords.
    BufferedReader doc =
        new BufferedReader(
            new InputStreamReader(
                new FileInputStream(docname)));
    WordSet docwords = readAllWords(doc);
    doc.close();
    if (docwords.containsAll(keywords))
        return ALL;
    else if (disjoint(docWords, keywords))
        return NONE;
    else
        return SOME ;
}

private static WordSet readAllWords
                (BufferedReader doc)
                throws IOException {
// Return the set of all words occurring in the document inputDoc.
    WordSet docwords = new WordSet();
    for (;;) {
        String word = readWord(doc);
        if (word == null)  break;   // end of doc
        docwords.add(word.toLowerCase());
    }
    return docwords;
}

private static String readWord
                (BufferedReader doc)
                throws IOException {
// Read and return the next word from doc, skipping any preceding white
// space or punctuation. Return null if no word remains to be read.
    ...    // Code omitted here.
}
```

Program 9.3 A simple information retrieval program (extracts) (*continued on next page*).

```
private static boolean disjoint (WordSet docwords,
                WordSet keywords) {
// Return true if and only if the sets docwords and keywords have no
// common words.
    Iterator iter = keywords.iterator();
    while (iter.hasNext()) {
        String keyword = (String) iter.next();
        if (docwords.contains(word))  return false;
    }
    return true;
}
```

Program 9.3 (*continued*)

an ADT. For the purposes of this chapter, let us assume the following requirements (most of which were foreshadowed by Section 9.1):

1. It must be possible to make a set empty.
2. It must be possible to test whether a set is empty.
3. It must be possible to obtain the cardinality of a set.
4. It must be possible to test whether a value is a member of a set.
5. It must be possible to add or remove a member of a set.
6. It must be possible to test whether two sets are equal.
7. It must be possible to test whether one set subsumes another.
8. It must be possible to compute the union, intersection, or difference of two sets.
9. It must be possible to traverse a set (i.e., visit each of its members in turn).

Program 9.4 shows a possible contract for this ADT, expressed as a Java interface named Set. The methods of this Set interface are sufficient to meet all of the above requirements.

The addAll method computes a set union. To be precise, s_1.addAll(s_2) updates s_1 to be the union of s_1 and s_2. The retainAll and removeAll methods similarly compute a set intersection and a set difference, respectively. These three methods, together with clear, add, and remove, are mutative transformers. Consequently Set objects are mutable.

If we wanted Set objects to be immutable, we would have to replace all these methods by applicative transformers with Set objects as their results, for example:

```
public Set union (Set that);
// Return the union of this set and that.
```

For example, s_1.union(s_2) would simply return the union of s_1 and s_2, without overwriting s_1. Unfortunately, it would have to copy all members of both sets involved. Exercise 9.6 explores this alternative contract, but we shall not pursue it further here.

The Set interface of Program 9.4 allows the set members to be arbitrary objects. In

```
public interface Set {

    // Each Set object is a set whose members are objects.

    ///////////// Accessors /////////////

    public boolean isEmpty ();
    // Return true if and only if this set is empty.

    public int size ();
    // Return the cardinality of this set.

    public boolean contains (Object obj);
    // Return true if and only if obj is a member of this set.

    public boolean equals (Set that);
    // Return true if and only if this set is equal to that.

    public boolean containsAll (Set that);
    // Return true if and only if this set subsumes that.

    ///////////// Transformers /////////////

    public void clear ();
    // Make this set empty.

    public void add (Object obj);
    // Add obj as a member of this set. (Throw a ClassCastException
    // if this set cannot contain an object with the class of obj.)

    public void remove (Object obj);
    // Remove obj from this set.

    public void addAll (Set that);
    // Make this set the union of itself and that.

    public void removeAll (Set that);
    // Make this set the difference of itself and that.

    public void retainAll (Set that);
    // Make this set the intersection of itself and that.

    ///////////// Iterator /////////////

    public Iterator iterator();
    // Return an iterator that will visit all members of this set, in no particular
    // order.

}
```

Program 9.4   A contract for a set ADT.

some implementations of the `Set` interface, however, we shall restrict the set members to be `Comparable` objects. In Sections 9.4 and 9.5 we shall see that this restriction facilitates efficient implementations of sets, by enabling the members to be kept sorted. In practice, this restriction does not reduce the generality of the implemented sets very much.

It should now be clear that class `WordSet` in Example 9.2 could be written to implement the `Set` interface. (Class `IntSet` in Example 9.1 is slightly different, because its members are integers rather than objects.)

In accordance with the ADT philosophy, we have designed an interface but avoided any premature consideration of how sets might be represented. In fact, sets are particularly interesting in that they can be represented by a wide variety of data structures. In the next three sections of this chapter we study how sets can be represented using the familiar data structures of arrays and linked lists. In later chapters we shall explore more sophisticated representations.

9.4 Implementation of bounded sets using arrays

A ***bounded set*** is one whose cardinality is bounded. If the set's maximum cardinality is *maxcard*, its actual cardinality can vary from 0 through *maxcard*.

A simple and obvious way to represent a bounded set is to store its members in an array *members* of length *maxcard*. When the set's cardinality *card* is less than *maxcard*, some of the array components will be unoccupied. Let us assume that the set members occupy the subarray *members*$[0 \ldots card - 1]$.

Having made this basic decision, we still have several choices:

- How should we keep track of the set's cardinality *card*? We could store *card* in an instance variable. Alternatively, we could assign null values to all unoccupied array components, and count the occupied array components whenever required. The latter would be time-consuming.
- Should we allow duplicates to be stored in the array? *Avoiding* duplicates has a cost: every time a value is added to the set, the array must be searched to check whether it is already present. *Allowing* duplicates has several costs: slowing down the membership test, wasting space, and increasing the risk of overflow (and when overflow occurs, duplicates must be eliminated after all).
- Should we keep the array sorted? An *unsorted* array would slow down the search for an existing member. A *sorted* array would slow down adding or removing a member, since some of the existing members must be shifted. It also restricts the set members to be `Comparable` objects.

The best compromise is to store the set's cardinality explicitly, to avoid duplicates, and to keep the array sorted. Figure 9.5 shows this representation in the general case, and also illustrates the representation of some sets of countries.

This representation allows us to use efficient array algorithms for all of the set operations. In particular:

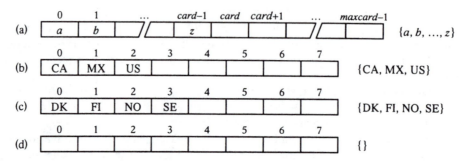

Figure 9.5 Representation of bounded sets by sorted arrays: (a) general case; (b–c) sets of countries (with *maxcard* = 8); (d) empty set (with *maxcard* = 8).

- The `contains` operation should use binary search (Algorithm 3.18). Its time complexity is $O(\log n)$, where n is the set's cardinality.
- The `add` operation should use binary search to locate where the new member should be added, and then if necessary shift some members to the right. For example, consider adding IE to an array containing members {BE, DE, FR, IT, LU, NL}: first search the array to determine that IE should be inserted between FR and IT, then insert IE by shifting IT, LU, and NL to the right. The search stage is $O(\log n)$. The insertion stage is $O(n)$, but is skipped if the value to be added is already a member. So the operation as a whole is $O(n)$ in general, but $O(\log n)$ in the best case.
- The `remove` operation similarly should use binary search to locate the member to be removed, and then if necessary shift some members to the left. Like the insert operation, the remove operation has time complexity $O(n)$ in general, but $O(\log n)$ if the value to be deleted is not a member of the set.
- The `equals` operation should simply compare the members of the two sets pairwise. The answer is known as soon as a pair of unequal members is found or the end of either set is reached. A useful refinement is first to check whether the two sets' cardinalities are unequal; if so, the answer must be false. For example, {DK, FI, NO, SE} and {DK, FI, IS, NO, SE} are immediately found to be unequal because of their different cardinalities; whereas {DK, FI, NO, SE} and {DK, FI, IS, SE} are found to be unequal only after comparing the first three pairs of members. The operation as a whole is $O(n)$ if both sets have cardinality n.
- The `containsAll` operation should compare the members of the two sets pairwise, ignoring any members of the first set that are not also members of the second set. A useful refinement here is first to check whether the second set's cardinality exceeds the first set's; if so, the answer must be false.
- The `addAll` operation should use the standard array merging algorithm (Algorithm 3.23). Every member of either set is copied to the result array, but a member common to both sets is copied only once.
- The `retainAll` operation should use a variant of the array merging algorithm, whereby only members common to both sets are copied to the result array.

The algorithms and their time complexities are summarized in Table 9.6.

Note that binary search, merging, and pairwise comparisons all rely on the members being sorted. The efficiency of these algorithms justifies our decision to keep the array sorted, although it restricts the set members to be `Comparable` objects.

Program 9.7 outlines a Java implementation. This is a class `ArraySet` that is declared as implementing the `Set` interface. The instance variable `members` is an array of `Comparable` objects, whose length is fixed when the set is constructed. Unoccupied components of `members` are null. The instance variable `card` keeps track of the set's cardinality, and is initially zero. Only selected methods are shown; the remaining methods can be found at this book's companion Web site.

The `iterator` operation of Program 9.7 constructs an iterator over the `ArraySet` object. This iterator is an object of the class `ArraySet.LRIterator` shown in Program 9.8. This is an inner class that would be added to Program 9.7. The iterator is represented by a place-marker `place`, which is initially zero. Each call to the `next` method increments `place`. Thus the set's members will be visited in ascending order, because the array is sorted. So the `iterator` operation of Program 9.7 does more than satisfy the terms of the `Set` contract of Program 9.4 (which specifies no particular order for visiting the set's members).

Note that, since `ArraySet.LRIterator` is an inner class, the iterator *shares* the `ArraySet` object through an implicit reference; it does not need its own data structure.

9.5 Implementation of unbounded sets using linked lists

We can represent an unbounded set straightforwardly by a singly-linked list (SLL). As in Section 9.4, we have several choices:

- How should we keep track of the set's cardinality? One option is to store the cardinality in an instance variable. Another option is just to count the list nodes whenever required.
- Should we allow duplicates to be stored in the SLL? Avoiding duplicates has a cost:

Table 9.6 Implementation of bounded sets using arrays: summary of algorithms (where n, n_1, and n_2 are the cardinalities of the sets involved).

Operation	Algorithm	Time complexity
`contains`	binary search	$O(\log n)$
`equals`	pairwise comparison	$O(n_2)$
`containsAll`	variant of pairwise comparison	$O(n_2)$
`add`	binary search combined with insertion	$O(n)$
`remove`	binary search combined with deletion	$O(n)$
`addAll`	array merge	$O(n_1 + n_2)$
`removeAll`	variant of array merge	$O(n_1 + n_2)$
`retainAll`	variant of array merge	$O(n_1 + n_2)$

every time a value is added to the set, the SLL must be searched to check whether the value is already present. On the other hand, allowing duplicates wastes space.

- Should we keep the SLL sorted? An unsorted SLL would slow down the search for an existing member – on average, about twice as many nodes must be visited. A sorted SLL forces us to restrict the set members to be Comparable objects.

```java
public class ArraySet implements Set {

    // Each ArraySet object is a bounded set whose members are
    // Comparable objects.

    // This set is represented as follows: its cardinality is held in card, and
    // its members (which are sorted and distinct) occupy the subarray
    // members[0...card-1].
    private Comparable[] members;
    private int card;

    ///////////// Constructor /////////////

    public ArraySet (int maxcard) {
    // Construct a set, initially empty, whose cardinality will be bounded by
    // maxcard.
        members = new Comparable[maxcard];
        card = 0;
    }

    ///////////// Accessors /////////////

    public boolean isEmpty () {
    // Return true if and only if this set is empty.
        return (card == 0);
    }

    public int size () {
    // Return the cardinality of this set.
        return card;
    }

    public boolean contains (Object obj) {
    // Return true if and only if obj is a member of this set.
        if (obj instanceof Comparable) {
            Comparable it = (Comparable) obj;
            int pos = search(it);
            return it.equals(members[pos]);
        else
            return false;
    }
```

Program 9.7 Java implementation of bounded sets using arrays (outline) (*continued on next page*).

```
public boolean equals (Set that) {
// Return true if and only if this set is equal to that.
   ArraySet other = (ArraySet) that;
   if (this.card != other.card)  return false;
   for (int i = 0; i < this.card; i++) {
      if (! this.members[i].equals(other.members[i]))
         return false;
   }
   return true;
}

...   // Other accessors are omitted here. See the companion Web site.

///////////// Transformers ////////////

public void clear () {
// Make this set empty.
   for (int i = 0; i < card; i++)
      members[i] = null;
   card = 0;
}

public void add (Object obj) {
// Add obj as a member of this set. (Throw a ClassCastException
// if this set cannot contain an object with the class of obj.)
   Comparable it = (Comparable) obj;
   int pos = search(it);
   if (! it.equals(members[pos])) {
      // it is not already a member.
      if (card == members.length)  expand();
      for (int i = card; i > pos; i--)
         members[i] = members[i-1];
      members[pos] = it;
      card++;
   }
}
```

Program 9.7 (*continued on next page*)

These choices are similar to the choices affecting the array representation in Section 9.4, but the decision is less clear-cut. In particular, binary search is no longer a possibility: we must use linear search, whether the members are sorted or not. Nevertheless, we choose to store the cardinality explicitly, to avoid duplicates, and to keep the SLL sorted. Figure 9.9 shows this representation in the general case, and also illustrates the representation of some sets of countries. (Compare these with Figure 9.5.)

```java
public void retainAll (Set that) {
// Make this set the intersection of itself and that.
   ArraySet other = (ArraySet) that;
   Comparable[] newMembers =
        new Comparable[this.members.length];
   int i = 0, j = 0, k = 0;
   while (i < this.card && j < other.card) {
     int comp = this.members[i].compareTo(
         other.members[j]);
     if (comp < 0)
        i++;          // Discard a member of this set not in that.
     else if (comp > 0)
        j++;          // Discard a member of that not in this set.
     else {  // (comp == 0)
        newMembers[k++] = this.members[i++];
        j++;          // Retain a member common to both sets.
     }
   }
   this.members = newMembers;
   this.card = k;
}

...    // Other transformers are omitted here. See the companion Web site.

///////////// Iterator /////////////

public Iterator iterator () {
// Return an iterator that will visit all members of this set, in no particular
// order.
   return new ArraySet.LRIterator();
}

///////////// Auxiliary methods /////////////

private void expand () {
// Make the members array longer.
   ...   // Code omitted here.
}
```

Program 9.7 (*continued on next page*)

This representation allows us to use standard SLL algorithms for all of the set operations. In particular:

- The `contains` operation should use the sorted SLL linear search algorithm (similar to Algorithm 4.24). Its time complexity is $O(n)$, where n is the set's cardinality.

```
private int search (Comparable target) {
// Return the index of the leftmost component of members that is not
// less than target.
    int l = 0, r = card-1;
    while (l <= r) {
        int m = (l + r)/2;
        int comp = target.compareTo(members[m]);
        if (comp == 0)
            // Here target is equal to members[m].
            return m;
        else if (comp < 0)
            r = m - 1;
        else  // comp > 0
            l = m + 1;
    }
    // Here target is greater than members[0...l-1] and less than
    // members[l...card-1].
    return l;
}

}
```

Program 9.7 (*continued*)

- The add operation should use linear search to locate where the new member should be added, and then if necessary insert a new node.
- The remove operation similarly should use linear search to locate the member to be removed, and then delete the node (if any) containing that member.
- The equals and containsAll operations should first compare the two sets' cardinalities, and then compare the two SLLs node by node, along the same lines as Section 9.4.
- The addAll operation should use the standard SLL merging algorithm (Algorithm 4.25), and retainAll a variant of that merging algorithm, along the same lines as Section 9.4.

The algorithms and their time complexities are summarized in Table 9.10.

Compare Tables 9.6 and 9.10. For the important contains operation, the array representation wins against the linked-list representation ($O(\log n)$ vs. $O(n)$), because binary search is possible. However, the add and remove operations are $O(n)$ in both representations. These time complexities make both array and linked-list representations suitable only for small sets (up to about 50 members, say). For a large set, the array representation is suitable only if the set is static (i.e., additions and removals happen rarely or never), but the linked-list representation is unlikely to be suitable.

Program 9.11 outlines a Java implementation of sets represented by SLLs. This is a class `LinkedSet` that implements the `Set` interface. The `SLLNode` class was defined in Program 4.4.

The `iterator` operation of Program 9.11 constructs a `LinkedSet.LRIterator` object, which will be an iterator over the set represented by an SLL. The `Linked-Set.LRIterator` class would be very similar to the `LinkedList.LRIterator` class of Program 8.15.

```java
private class LRIterator implements Iterator {

    // An ArraySet.LRIterator object is an iterator over a set
    // represented by an ArraySet object.

    // This iterator is represented by the array index of the next member to be
    // visited, place.
    private int place;

    private LRIterator () {
        place = 0;
    }

    public boolean hasNext () {
        return (place < card);
    }

    public Object next () {
        if (place >= card)
            throw new NoSuchElementException();
        return members[place++];
    }

    ...    // The remove method is omitted here.

}
```

Program 9.8 Iterator for the implementation of bounded sets using arrays (as an inner class of `ArraySet`).

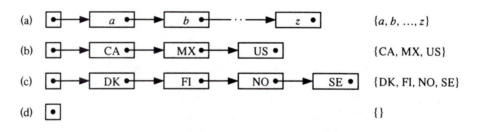
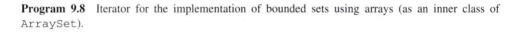
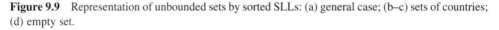

Figure 9.9 Representation of unbounded sets by sorted SLLs: (a) general case; (b–c) sets of countries; (d) empty set.

Table 9.10   Implementation of unbounded sets using SLLs: summary of algorithms (where n, n_1, and n_2 are the cardinalities of the sets involved).

Operation	Algorithm	Time complexity
contains	sorted SLL linear search	$O(n)$
equals	node-wise comparison	$O(n_2)$
containsAll	variant of node-wise comparison	$O(n_2)$
add	sorted SLL linear search combined with insertion	$O(n)$
remove	sorted SLL linear search combined with deletion	$O(n)$
addAll	SLL merge	$O(n_1 + n_2)$
removeAll	variant of SLL merge	$O(n_1 + n_2)$
retainAll	variant of SLL merge	$O(n_1 + n_2)$

9.6 Implementation of small-integer sets using boolean arrays

Consider a set whose members are known to be small integers, lying in the range 0 through $m - 1$. Then we can represent the set by a boolean array b of length m; $b[i]$ will be true if and only if i is a member of the set. This representation is shown in Figure 9.12.

This representation is efficient in time. The contains, add, and remove operations each accesses a single array component, so they have time complexity $O(1)$. The whole-set operations equals and containsAll each compares m pairs of array components, so they have time complexity $O(m)$. The other whole-set operations, addAll, retainAll, and removeAll, each performs a logical operation on m pairs of array components, so they also have time complexity $O(m)$. Table 9.13 summarizes the operations and their time complexities.

This representation is also efficient in space: m bytes for a whole set. It can even be compressed to m bits for the set, if we replace the boolean array by a bit-string.

Program 9.14 outlines a Java implementation of class IntSet. Note that IntSet does *not* implement the Set interface: the set members (and therefore the arguments of contains, add, and remove) are of type **int** rather than Object. Nevertheless, IntSet does conform to the spirit of the Set interface: it provides all the corresponding set operations.

Note that the contains, add, and remove methods must take some appropriate action if their arguments are out-of-range integers. Note also that the whole-set methods (such as equals and retainAll) must allow for the possibility that the two sets are represented by boolean arrays of different lengths. (This possibility was neglected in the analysis summarized in Table 9.13.)

This class IntSet can be used to complete Program 9.2. Another possible application of IntSet would be to represent sets of characters, since characters are essentially small integers. More generally, IntSet objects can be used to represent sets of any values that can be translated to small integers.

The iterator operation of Program 9.11 constructs an iterator over the IntSet object. This iterator is an object of the class IntSet.LRIterator shown in Program

```
public class LinkedSet implements Set {
// Each LinkedSet object is an unbounded set whose members are
// Comparable objects.
// This set is represented as follows: its cardinality is held in card, and
// first is a link to the first node of an SLL containing its members
// (which are sorted and distinct).
private SLLNode first;
private int card;

///////////// Constructor /////////////

public LinkedSet () {
// Construct a set, initially empty.
   first = null;
   card = 0;
}

///////////// Accessors /////////////

public boolean isEmpty () {
// Return true if and only if this set is empty.
   return (card == 0);
}

public int size () {
// Return the cardinality of this set.
   return card;
}

public boolean contains (Object obj) {
// Return true if and only if obj is a member of this set.
   if (obj instanceof Comparable) {
      Comparable it = (Comparable) obj;
      for (SLLNode curr = first; curr != null;
           curr = curr.succ) {
         int comp = it.compareTo(
              (Comparable) curr.element);
         if (comp == 0)
            return true;
         else if (comp < 0)
            break;
      }
   }
   return false;
}
```

Program 9.11 Java implementation of unbounded sets using SLLs (outline) (*continued on next page*).

...   // Other accessors are omitted here. See the companion Web site.

//////////// Transformers ////////////

```java
public void clear () {
// Make this set empty.
   first = null;
   card = 0;
}

public void add (Object obj) {
//  Add obj as a member of this set. (Throw a ClassCastException
//  if this set cannot contain an object with the class of obj.)
   Comparable it = (Comparable) obj;
   SLLNode prev;
   for (SLLNode curr = first; curr != null;
        curr = curr.succ) {
     int comp = it.compareTo(
          (Comparable) curr.element);
     if (comp == 0)
       return;   // it is already a member.
     else if (comp < 0)
       break;     // it is smaller than curr.
     prev = curr;
   }
   SLLNode ins = new SLLNode(it, curr);
   if (prev == null)
      first = ins;
   else
      prev.succ = ins;
   card++;
}
```

...   // Other transformers are omitted here. See the companion Web site.

//////////// Iterator ////////////

```java
public Iterator iterator() {
// Return an iterator that will visit all members of this set, in no particular
// order.
   return new LinkedSet.LRIterator();
}

}
```

Program 9.11 (*continued*)

9.15. It is represented by a place-marker, `place`. In other respects this iterator differs from the ones we have seen before. The `IntSet.LRIterator` constructor sets `place` to the smallest integer in the set, by searching the array b from the left until it finds a component that is true. The `next` method returns this value of `place`, but also updates `place` to the next smallest integer in the set. If there is no next smallest integer, `place` is set to `b.length`. The `hasNext` method simply compares `place` with `b.length`.

9.7 Sets in the Java class library

The Java 2 class library provides a `java.util.Set` interface, which is shown in Appendix C.3. This interface is similar to the simpler `Set` interface of Program 9.4. The `java.util.Set` interface differs mainly in that:

- Its `equals` method accepts an arbitrary object as argument. Of course, the `equals` method in any `Set` class must return false if its argument is not a `Set` object.
- Its `containsAll`, `addAll`, `retainAll`, and `removeAll` methods all accept arbitrary collections as arguments, not necessarily sets. For example, $s.addAll(c)$

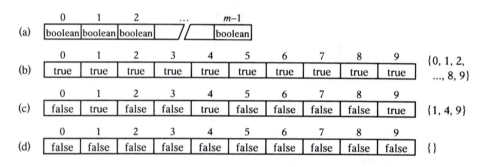

Figure 9.12 Representation of small-integer sets by boolean arrays: (a) general case (with members in range 0 through $m - 1$); (b–c) sets of integers (with $m = 10$); (d) empty set.

Table 9.13 Implementation of small-integer sets using boolean arrays: summary of algorithms (where set members are in the range 0 through $m - 1$).

Operation	Algorithm	Time complexity
`contains`	test array component	$O(1)$
`equals`	pairwise equality test	$O(m)$
`containsAll`	pairwise implication test	$O(m)$
`add`	make array component true	$O(1)$
`remove`	make array component false	$O(1)$
`addAll`	pairwise disjunction	$O(m)$
`removeAll`	pairwise negation and conjunction	$O(m)$
`retainAll`	pairwise conjunction	$O(m)$

```
public class IntSet {

   // Each IntSet object is a set whose members are small nonnegative
   // integers.

   // This set is represented as follows: b[i] is true if and only if integer i
   // is a member of the set.
   private boolean[] b;

   /////////////// Constructor ////////////////

   public IntSet (int m) {
   // Construct a set, initially empty, whose members will be integers in the
   // range 0 through m-1.
      b = new boolean[m];   // ... All components are initially false.
   }

   /////////////// Accessors ////////////////

   public boolean isEmpty () {
   // Return true if and only if this set is empty.
      for (int i = 0; i < b.length; i++) {
        if (b[i])  return false;
      }
      return true;
   }

   public int size () {
   // Return the cardinality of this set.
      int card = 0;
      for (int i = 0; i < b.length; i++) {
        if (b[i])  card++;
      }
      return card;
   }

   public contains (int i) {
   // Return true if and only if i is a member of this set.
      if (i < 0 || i >= b.length)  return false;
      return b[i];
   }
```

Program 9.14 Java implementation of small-integer sets using boolean arrays (outline) (*continued on next page*).

```
public boolean equals (IntSet that) {
// Return true if and only if this set is equal to that.
   int minLength =
       Math.min(this.b.length, that.b.length);
   for (int i = 0; i < minLength; i++) {
     if (this.b[i] != that.b[i])  return false;
   }

   for (int i = minLength; i < this.b.length; i++) {
     if (this.b[i])  return false;
   }
   for (int i = minLength; i < that.b.length; i++) {
     if (that.b[i])  return false;
   }
   return true;
}

...   // Other accessors are omitted here. See the companion Web site.

////////////// Transformers //////////////

public void clear () {
// Make this set empty.
   for (int i = 0; i < b.length; i++)
     b[i] = false;
}

public add (int i) {
// Add i as a member of this set.
   if (i < 0 || i >= b.length)
     throw new IllegalArgumentException();
   b[i] = true;
}
```

Program 9.14 (*continued on next page*)

adds all the elements of collection *c* to set *s*. We can view this as first forming the set of all (distinct) elements of *c*, then uniting the sets as usual.

The class library also provides a java.util.SortedSet interface, which extends the java.util.Set interface as follows:

- All members of a SortedSet object normally must be Comparable objects. Alternatively, a SortedSet object must contain its own comparator, in which case the SortedSet implementation uses that comparator instead of compareTo. (A ***comparator*** is a function that compares two objects and returns a negative, zero, or

```
   public void remove (int i) {
   //  Remove i from this set.
      if (i >= 0 && i < b.length)
         b[i] = false;
   }

   public retainAll (IntSet that) {
   //  Make this set the intersection of itself and that.
      int minLength =
          Math.min(this.b.length, that.b.length);
      for (int i = 0; i < minLength; i++)
         this.b[i] &= that.b[i];
      for (int i = minLength; i < this.b.length; i++) {
         this.b[i] = false;
      }
   }

   ...   //  Other transformers are omitted here. See the companion Web site.

   ///////////// Iterator /////////////

   public Iterator iterator() {
   //  Return an iterator that will visit all members of this set, in no particular
   //  order.
      return new IntSet.LRIterator();
   }

}
```

Program 9.14 (*continued*)

positive result, reflecting some total ordering of the objects concerned. The standard `compareTo` is itself an example of a comparator.)

- The `java.util.SortedSet` interface provides additional methods such as `first` and `last`, which return the least and greatest members of the set, respectively.

- Its `iterator` method returns an iterator that guarantees to visit all the set members *in ascending order*.

9.8 Case study: an interactive spell-checker

To check the spelling of words in a document, we check each word against a given vocabulary. The *vocabulary* (also called a *dictionary*) is a large collection of correctly spelled words. If the vocabulary contains a word, we say that the word is *recognized*: it is known to be correctly spelled. If the vocabulary does not contain a word, we say that the word is *unrecognized*. That does not necessarily mean that the word is incorrectly

```
private class LRIterator implements Iterator {
  // An IntSet.LRIterator object is an iterator over a small-integer set
  // represented by an IntSet object.

  // This iterator is represented by the value of the next member to be visited,
  // place.
  private int place;

  private LRIterator () {
    place = 0;
    while (place < b.length && ! b[place])
      place++;
  }

  public boolean hasNext () {
    return (place < b.length);
  }

  public Object next () {
    if (place >= b.length)
      throw new NoSuchElementException();
    int nextMember = place;
    place++;
    while (place < b.length && ! b[place])
      place++;
    return new Integer(nextMember);
  }

  ...   // The remove method is omitted here.

}
```

Program 9.15   Iterator for the implementation of small-integer sets using boolean arrays (as an inner class of IntSet).

spelled: it might simply be an uncommon word that was omitted from the vocabulary. (There is no such thing as a complete vocabulary.) In the latter case, the user might want to add the unrecognized word to the vocabulary, so that it will be recognized in future. So a vocabulary is just a set of words, and the main operations on the vocabulary are to test whether it contains a given word and to add a given word.

In this section we will develop a simple, interactive spell-checker that uses a set of words for its vocabulary. Actually, it will use three separate vocabularies:

- The *main vocabulary* will contain the majority of the words.
- The *user vocabulary* will contain only those words recognized by a particular user.

- The *ignored vocabulary* will contain words (or, more likely, acronyms or such like) that are to be ignored by the spell-checker during the current session only.

A word is recognized if it is in any of these vocabularies.

The interactive spell-checker must check all words in an input document. For each unrecognized word, it must allow the user to select one of the following five options:

- *Ignore* just this occurrence of the unrecognized word.
- *Ignore all* (present and future) occurrences of the unrecognized word, i.e., add the word to the ignored vocabulary.
- *Add* the unrecognized word to the *main* vocabulary.
- *Add* the unrecognized word to the *user* vocabulary.
- *Replace* the unrecognized word with another word entered by the user.

The interactive spell-checker must generate an output document containing the same text as the input document, except for any replacements made by the user. Note that it is not required to *suggest* replacements for an unrecognized word: that would be a much harder problem.

When the interactive spell-checker starts, it must load the main and user vocabularies from two text files. When the spell-checker terminates, it must save the (possibly updated) main and user vocabularies to two new text files. Each of these files must contain a set of words, one word per line, in no particular order.

9.8.1 Representing a spell-checker

We can easily choose a suitable representation for a spell-checker: it will consist of three vocabularies. Each vocabulary is a set of words, where a word is just a string of lowercase letters. The spell-checker should be equipped with a method to check a given word against the vocabularies (`recognizes`), and methods to add a new word to any of the vocabularies (`addToMainVocabulary`, `addToUserVocabulary`, and `addToIgnoredVocabulary`, respectively).

Program 9.16 is an implementation of a spell-checker as a Java class named `Spell-Checker`. As well as the methods to check and add words, it also provides methods to load and save the main and user vocabularies. These are used to initialize the vocabularies before spell-checking, and to remember the words added to the vocabularies after spell-checking. Note that the ignored vocabulary is initially empty, and is discarded after spell-checking.

9.8.2 A batch spell-checker

Our goal is an interactive spell-checker. For the moment, however, let us consider a simpler application: a batch spell-checker that reads the input document and prints out every unrecognized word that it encounters.

The algorithm to spell-check a document is straightforward: we read the document one word at a time, and print the word if it is unrecognized. Program 9.17 shows the

```java
public class SpellChecker {

    // Each SpellChecker object represents a spell-checker.

    // This spell-checker consists of a main vocabulary, a user vocabulary, and
    // an ignored vocabulary. Each vocabulary is represented by a set of
    // lowercase words.
    private Set mainVocabulary, userVocabulary,
        ignoredVocabulary;

    /////////////// Constructor ///////////////

    public SpellChecker (String mainFilename,
                    String userFilename) {
    // Create a new spell-checker in which the main vocabulary and the user
    // vocabulary are loaded from files named mainFilename and
    // userFilename, but the ignored vocabulary is empty.
        mainVocabulary = new LinkedSet();
        userVocabulary = new LinkedSet();
        ignoredVocabulary = new LinkedSet();
        loadVocabulary(mainVocabulary, mainFilename);
        loadVocabulary(userVocabulary, userFilename);
    }

    /////////////// Accessors ///////////////

    public boolean recognizes (String word) {
    // Return true if and only if the given word, in lowercase, is contained in
    // one of this spell-checker's vocabularies.
        String lcWord = word.toLowerCase();
        return (mainVocabulary.contains(lcWord)
                || userVocabulary.contains(lcWord)
                || ignoredVocabulary.contains(lcWord));
    }

    public void saveMainVocabulary (String filename) {
    // Write the set of words in this spell-checker's main vocabulary to a file
    // with the given filename.
        saveVocabulary(mainVocabulary, filename);
    }

    public void saveUserVocabulary (String filename) {
    // Write the set of words in this spell-checker's user vocabulary to a file
    // with the given filename.
        saveVocabulary(userVocabulary, filename);
    }
```

Program 9.16   Java implementation of a spell-checker (*continued on next page*).

`/ / / / / / / / / / /` Transformers `/ / / / / / / / / / /`

```
public void addToMainVocabulary (String word) {
// Add the given word, in lowercase, to this spell-checker's main
// vocabulary.
   mainVocabulary.add(word.toLowerCase());
}

public void addToUserVocabulary (String word) {
// Add the given word, in lowercase, to this spell-checker's user
// vocabulary.
   userVocabulary.add(word.toLowerCase());
}

public void addToIgnoredVocabulary (String word) {
// Add the given word, in lowercase, to this spell-checker's ignored
// vocabulary.
   ignoredVocabulary.add(word.toLowerCase());
}

public void loadMainVocabulary (String filename) {
// Read a set of words from the file with the given filename, and load them
// into this spell-checker's main vocabulary.
   loadVocabulary(mainVocabulary, filename);
}

public void loadUserVocabulary (String filename) {
// Read a set of words from the file with the given filename, and load them
// into this spell-checker's user vocabulary.
   loadVocabulary(userVocabulary, filename);
}
```

`/ / / / / / / / / / /` Auxiliary methods `/ / / / / / / / / / /`

```
private static void loadVocabulary (Set vocabulary,
                  String filename) {
// Read a set of words from the file named filename, and load them
// into vocabulary. Assume that the file contains one word per line.
   ...   // See code on the companion Web site.
}
private static void saveVocabulary (Set vocabulary,
                  String filename) {
// Save the set of words in vocabulary to the file named filename.
// The file will contain one word per line.
   ...   // See code on the companion Web site.
}

}
```

Program 9.16 (*continued*)

```
public class BatchSpellChecker {

    private static String readWord
            (BufferedReader input) {
    // Return the next word read from input, or null if there is no word. A
    // word is a sequence of letters. The word may be preceded by zero or more
    // non-letters, which are skipped.
        ...  // See code on the companion Web site.
    }

    public static void main (String[] args) {
    // Read the words of the document whose filename is args[0]. Print any
    // unrecognized words.
        SpellChecker checker =
            new SpellChecker("main.voc", "user.voc");

      try {
        BufferedReader inputDoc =
            new BufferedReader(
              new InputStreamReader(
                new FileInputStream(args[0])));
        for (;;) {
          String word = readWord(inputDoc);
          if (word == null)  break;  // end of inputDoc
          if (! checker.recognizes(word))
            System.out.println(word);
        }
        inputDoc.close();
      } catch (IOException e) {
        System.out.println(e.getMessage());
      }
    }

}
```

Program 9.17   Implementation of a batch spell-checker.

implementation of this algorithm. Note that, in this application, we never add new words to a vocabulary.

9.8.3 An interactive spell-checker

Algorithm 9.18 is an interactive spell-checking algorithm that satisfies the requirements stated in Section 9.8.1. In outline it resembles the algorithm used in Program 9.17, but on each unrecognized word it interacts with the user.

The implementation of Algorithm 9.18 as a Java application with a graphical user

To check the spelling in an input document:

1.   Set *current-word* to null.
2.   Repeat:
    2.1.   If *current-word* is not null, write it to the output document.
    2.2.   Set *current-word* to the next word in the input document.
    2.3.   While *current-word* is not null and it is recognized, repeat:
        2.3.1.   Write *current-word* to the output document.
        2.3.2.   Set *current-word* to the next word in the input document.
    2.4.   If *current-word* is null, terminate.
    2.5.   Prompt the user for how to handle *current-word*.
    2.6.   If the user decides to ignore just this occurrence of the word.
        2.6.1.   Do nothing.
    2.7.   If the user decides to ignore all occurrences of the word.
        2.7.1.   Add *current-word* to *ignored-vocabulary*.
    2.8.   If the user decides to add the word to the main vocabulary.
        2.8.1.   Add *current-word* to *main-vocabulary*.
    2.9.   If the user decides to add the word to the user vocabulary.
        2.9.1.   Add *current-word* to *user-vocabulary*.
    2.10.   If the user decides to replace the word:
        2.10.1. Set *current-word* to the replacement text entered by the user.

Algorithm 9.18   Interactive spell-checking algorithm.

interface is complicated by event-driven interaction with the user. This requires certain parts of the algorithm to be placed in certain methods. Program 9.19 shows an outline of the implementation.

Most of the processing is performed by the `actionPerformed` method, which is invoked whenever the user clicks on a button. Our user interface will include five buttons, corresponding to the five user options for dealing with an unrecognized word: *ignore* just this occurrence of the word; *ignore all* occurrences of the word; *add* the word to the *main* vocabulary; *add* the word to the *user* vocabulary; and *replace* the word with another word. The `actionPerformed` method must first identify the button that has been clicked, and then take the required action. The possible actions correspond to steps 2.6–2.10 in Algorithm 9.18.

The next unrecognized word is then read using the auxiliary method `getNext-UnrecognizedWord`, which reads words from the input document until it finds a word that is not recognized. This corresponds to steps 2.1–2.4 in Algorithm 9.18. This method 'terminates' by disabling all of the buttons on the user interface, leaving the user with no option but to quit the application by closing its window. When the window is closed, the modified vocabularies are saved before the application exits.

Punctuation and other non-letter characters are copied to the output document verbatim when a word is read. In the application, the input document is also copied to a text area on the screen to provide the user with some context for an error.

```
public class InteractiveSpellChecker
    extends JFrame
    implements ActionListener {

  private SpellChecker checker;
  private String currentWord;
  private BufferedReader inputDoc;
  private BufferedWriter outputDoc;

  public SpellCheckerApplication
                (BufferedReader input,
                 BufferedWriter output) {
// Create a new spell-checker application.
    checker =
        new SpellChecker("main.voc", "user.voc");
    inputDoc = input;
    outputDoc = output;
    currentWord = null;
    createGUI();
  }

  private JButton[] buttons;
  private JTextField correctedText;

  // Button ids:
  private static final int
      IGNORE = 0,  IGNORE_ALL = 1,  ADD_MAIN = 2,
      ADD_USER = 3,  REPLACE = 4;

  private void createGUI () {
// Create the graphical user interface by creating and initializing all of the
//  interface components and enabling the event listeners.
      ...   // See code on the companion Web site.
  }
```

Program 9.19 Implementation of an interactive spell-checker as a Java application (*continued on next page*).

Summary

In this chapter:

- We have reviewed the concept of a set, characterized by operations such as membership test, addition and removal of a member, equality test, subsumption test, union, intersection, and so on.
- We have seen examples and a case study demonstrating practical applications of sets.
- We have designed an ADT for sets, expressed as a Set interface.

```
public void actionPerformed (ActionEvent e) {
// Handle the user clicking on a button. The button clicked determines the
// action to be performed on currentWord. Then continue with the next
// unrecognized word.
   JButton button = (JButton) e.getSource();
   int id;
   for (id = 0; id < buttons.length; id++)
     if (button == buttons[id])  break;
   switch (id) {
     case IGNORE:        // Ignore this occurrence of the word.
       break;
     case IGNORE_ALL:   // Ignore all occurrences of the word.
       checker.addToIgnoredVocabulary(currentWord);
       break;
     case ADD_MAIN:     // Add the word to the main vocabulary.
       checker.addToMainVocabulary(currentWord);
       break;
     case ADD_USER:     // Add the word to the user vocabulary.
       checker.addToUserVocabulary(currentWord);
       break;
     case REPLACE:      // Replace the word with entered text.
       currentWord = correctedText.getText();
       ...  // Display the correction (omitted here).
       break;
   }
   try {
     getNextUnrecognizedWord();
   } catch (IOException e) {
     System.out.println(e.getMessage());
   }
}
```

Program 9.19 *(continued on next page)*

- We have studied how to represent unbounded and bounded sets by sorted arrays and sorted SLLs, respectively, and how to implement these in Java as classes that implement the Set interface. We have also studied how to represent sets of small integers by boolean arrays, an interesting special case.

Although the sorted-array representation makes the contains operation efficient, the array and SLL representations are really suitable only for small sets. Fortunately there exist several representations of sets for which the contains, add, and remove operations are all efficient, making these representations suitable for large sets. In later chapters we shall study these representations: binary search trees (Chapter 10), hash tables (Chapter 12), AVL-trees and B-trees (Chapter 16).

```
private String readWord ()
      throws IOException {
// Return the next word read from inputDoc, or null if there is no such
// word. Copy non-letters between words to outputDoc.
   ...   // See code on the companion Web site.
}

private void getNextUnrecognizedWord ()
      throws IOException {
// Set currentWord to the next unrecognized word from inputDoc.
// Copy recognized words to outputDoc.
   if (currentWord != null)
     outputDoc.write(currentWord);
   currentWord = readWord();
   while (currentWord != null
        && checker.recognizes(currentWord)) {
     outputDoc.write(currentWord);
     currentWord = readWord();
   }
   if (currentWord != null)
     correctedText.setText(currentWord);
   else {
     ...   // Display a message that spell-checking is finished.
     ...   // Disable the buttons.
   }
}
}
```

Program 9.19 (*continued*)

Exercises

9.1 (This exercise is drill for readers unfamiliar with sets.)

(a) Using {...} notation, write down the set of primary colors, the set of colors of the rainbow, and the set of colors in your country's national flag. Call these sets *primary*, *rainbow*, and *flag* respectively. What are their cardinalities?

(b) In terms of the sets *primary*, *rainbow*, and *flag*, and the set operations ⊆, ∪, ∩, and −, write down expressions representing:

(i) the set of rainbow colors in your national flag;

(ii) the set of rainbow colors not in your national flag;

(iii) the assertion that all colors in your national flag occur in the rainbow;

(iv) the assertion that your national flag contains exactly the primary colors.

Evaluate each of these expressions.

9.2 Can you think of any examples of sets in everyday life? Remember that a 'chess set', i.e., a 'set of chess pieces', is not a set (since some pieces are duplicated); but a 'set of playing cards' really is a set.

9.3 In Eratosthenes' sieve algorithm (Algorithm 9.1), show that removing step 2.1 would make the algorithm less efficient, but still correct.

9.4 Modify Eratosthenes' sieve algorithm (Algorithm 9.1) to compute the set of *non-primes* less than m.

9.5 A real information retrieval program would use a more elaborate scoring system than that of Program 9.3.
(a) Write a `score` method that returns the *percentage* of the key words that actually occur in the document.
(b) Suggest changes to the `Set` interface that would allow you to write your `score` method more efficiently.

9.6 In the `Set` interface of Program 9.4, suppose that the mutative transformers `addAll`, `removeAll`, and `retainAll` are to be replaced by applicative transformers that return the set union, difference, and intersection, respectively (without updating the sets to which the operations are applied). The other mutative transformers are to be replaced likewise.
(a) Modify the `Set` interface accordingly.
(b) Modify the array implementation of Program 9.7 accordingly.

9.7 In the `Set` interface of Program 9.4, the effect of s.`add`(x) could be specified formally by:

$$s' = s \cup \{x\}$$

where s is the set before the operation, and s' is the set after the operation. In similar fashion, specify the remaining `Set` operations formally.

9.8 Consider the array representation of bounded sets shown in Program 9.7.
(a) Draw diagrams showing how the set of words in each of the following sentences would be represented, assuming that *maxcard* $= 12$ and making no distinction between upper and lower case:

To be, or not to be.
The moon is a balloon.
The rain in Spain falls mainly on the plain.

(b) Write the missing methods.

9.9 Modify the array representation of bounded sets shown in Program 9.7, such that the set members are left unsorted.
(a) Draw diagrams showing *several* possible representations of the set of words in the following sentence, assuming that *maxcard* $= 6$ and making no distinction between upper and lower case:

To be, or not to be.

(b) Modify the Java implementation as required.
(c) Summarize your algorithms and their complexities, in the same manner as Table 9.6. Comment on your results.

9.10 Modify the array representation of bounded sets outlined in Program 9.7, such that the cardinality is not stored explicitly. What are the consequences?

9.11 Suggest a suitable representation for sets of colors (as in Exercise 9.1). Assume that color values are of type `java.awt.Color`.

9.12 Suggest suitable representations for:
(a) sets of ISO-LATIN-1 (8-bit) characters;
(b) sets of Unicode (16-bit) characters.
   Given suitable sets of ISO-LATIN-1 characters, how would you test whether a given character is a digit? a letter? a letter or digit?

9.13 Suggest a suitable representation for sets of countries (as in Section 9.1).

9.14 Consider the `IntSet` implementation of small-integer sets (Program 9.14).
(a) What is the complexity of the `size` operation?
(b) Modify the implementation by providing an instance variable that keeps track of the set's cardinality (like `card` in Programs 9.7 and 9.11).

* **9.15** Do you think that the spell-checker in your favorite word processor uses a set implementation like the ones in this chapter? What particular properties of the set of words could the spell-checker use to minimize the space required to store it?
   Try to design a suitable data structure that would minimize the storage space required for the set of words.

9.16 (For UNIX users.) The UNIX `spell` command has its own vocabulary that is normally stored in a text file called `/usr/dict/words`. (If this file does not exist in your version of UNIX, the manual page for `spell` should tell you what the correct file is.)
   Examine this file using a text editor. What do you notice about the list of words? (*Hint:* Look for the words 'abandon', 'abandons', and 'abandoned'.)
   What does this tell you about the implementation of the `spell` command?

9.17 Consider the `recognizes` method from Program 9.16. Analyze its worst-case, best-case, and average-case time efficiency when the word is contained:
(a) in the main vocabulary only
(b) in the user vocabulary only
(c) in the ignored vocabulary only.

* **9.18** In the spell-checker case study, we use a single set to store all of the words in the main vocabulary. With the implementations of sets given in this chapter, how would this application behave with a real vocabulary containing many thousands of words?
   How might you improve the application without modifying the set implementation used? (*Hint:* Is there an easy way to represent the main vocabulary by more than one set?) What effect would this have on the application when searching for particular words?
   Implement your modification in the interactive spell-checker application.

** **9.19** Consider the maze case study given in Section 6.6. Another way to represent each square in the maze would be as a *set of walls*. A suitable representation for such a set would be the `IntSet` class given in Program 9.14.
   Use the `IntSet` class to implement the maze case study.

* **9.20** A *bag* (or *multiset*) is similar to a set, but it may contain several instances of the same member. For example, {'to', 'be', 'or', 'not', 'to', 'be'} is a bag of words, which is equal

to {'be', 'be', 'not', 'or', 'to', 'to'} (since order of members is insignificant), but is unequal to {'be', 'not', 'or', 'to'} (since the number of instances is significant). Adding (removing) a member increases (decreases) the number of instances in the bag by one. The member is deleted from the bag when it has no instances.

(a) Design a bag ADT. Provide set-like operations, including bag union and bag subsumption (but not bag intersection or difference). In addition, provide an operation that returns the number of instances of a given member.

(b) How would you represent a bag without actually storing multiple instances of the same member?

(c) Implement a bag ADT using a sorted array implementation similar to Program 9.7.

(d) Implement a bag ADT using a sorted SLL implementation similar to Program 9.11.

10

Binary Tree Data Structures

In this chapter we shall study:

- binary trees, balanced binary trees, and binary search trees (Section 10.1)
- searching, insertion, deletion, traversal, and merging algorithms for binary search trees (Sections 10.2–6)
- implementation of unbounded sets using binary search trees (Section 10.7).

10.1 Binary trees

We are all familiar with the notion of a *family tree*, which represents parent–child relationships. The branches of a family tree connect parents to their children, children to grandchildren, and so on: see Figure 10.1. (Real family trees are complicated by the fact that every child has two parents. This complication is ignored in Figure 10.1.)

Trees are also extremely important in computing. We shall explore the tree concept fully in Chapter 14. In this chapter, however, we shall study a restricted form of tree, the binary tree, a dynamic data structure that is suitable for representing sets. This is defined as follows.

A *binary tree* is a group of nodes such that:

- Each node contains an *element* (value or object), together with links to at most two other nodes (its *left child* and its *right child*).
- The tree has a *header*, which contains a link to a designated node (the *root* node).
- Every node other than the root node is the left or right child of exactly one other node (its *parent*). The root node has no parent – the only link to it is the header.

We use a null link wherever there is no node to link to. Every binary tree node contains both a left link and a right link, but the left link is null if the node has no left child, and the right link is null if the node has no right child.

A *leaf* node is one that has no children (i.e., both its links are null). Continuing the arboreal terminology, links in trees are often called **branches**.

Figure 10.2(a) shows an example of a binary tree. The node containing *a* is the root node. The nodes containing *e* and *f* are the left and right children of the node containing *c*, and conversely the node containing *c* is the parent of these two nodes. The node containing *b* has a right child but no left child. The nodes containing *d*, *e*, and *g* have no children at all, so they are leaf nodes.

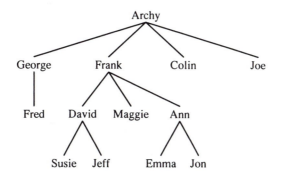

Figure 10.1   A family tree.

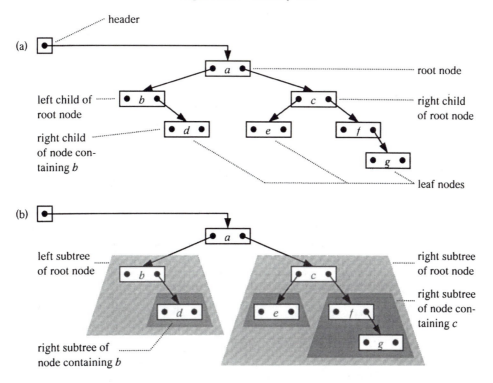

Figure 10.2   A binary tree, showing: (a) header, root node, child nodes, and leaf nodes; (b) subtrees.

The *size* of a tree is the number of nodes (elements) in that tree.

An *empty* binary tree has size zero. It has no nodes at all; its header is null.

Every binary tree node has both a left subtree and a right subtree. The node's *left subtree* consists of the node's left child together with the left child's own children, grandchildren, etc. The node's *right subtree* analogously consists of the node's right child together with the right child's own children, grandchildren, etc. Either subtree or both may be empty.

Subtrees are illustrated in Figure 10.2(b). The node containing *a* has a left subtree of size 2 and a right subtree of size 4. The node containing *b* has a right subtree of size 1 but its left subtree is empty.

Note that each subtree is itself a binary tree. This gives rise to an alternative recursive definition. A *binary tree* is:

(i) empty, *or*
(ii) nonempty, in which case it has a root node containing an element, a link to a left subtree, and a link to a right subtree (where the left and right subtrees are themselves binary trees).

This view of a binary tree is pictured in Figure 10.3. We shall find this view useful for designing recursive algorithms over binary trees.

Trees, like linked lists, are dynamic data structures. By manipulating the links, we can achieve a variety of effects. We can insert and delete nodes, thus expanding and contracting a tree dynamically. We can change a tree's structure by moving nodes from one part of the tree to another.

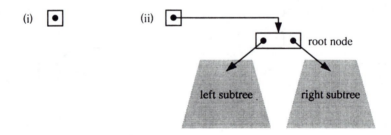

Figure 10.3   Recursive view of a binary tree: (i) empty binary tree; (ii) nonempty binary tree.

10.1.1 Balanced binary trees

Consider the three binary trees of Figure 10.4. They are similar in size, but very different in shape. Binary tree (a) is said to be *well-balanced*: the root node's left and right subtrees are similar in size. Binary tree (b) is *ill-balanced*: the root node's left subtree is much larger and deeper than the root node's right subtree. Binary tree (c) is extremely ill-balanced: every node has an empty left subtree. The following definitions make the concept of balance more precise.

Note that there is exactly one sequence of links from the root to any given node in a tree. The ***depth*** of a *node* in a tree is the number of links that must be followed to reach that node from the root node. The ***depth*** of a *tree* is the depth of the deepest node in the tree.

For example, the binary trees of Figure 10.4 have depths 2, 3, and 5, respectively. A tree consisting of a single node has depth 0. We adopt the convention that an empty tree has depth -1.

A binary tree of depth d is ***balanced*** if every node at depths 0, 1, ..., $d - 2$ has two children. Each node at depth $d - 1$ may have two, one, or no children. (By definition, each node at depth d has no children.)

Depth and balance are illustrated in Figure 10.4. Binary tree (a) is balanced. Binary tree (b) is ill-balanced, because its depth is 3 but it has a node at depth 1 with no children. Binary tree (b) is extremely ill-balanced, because its depth is 5 but it has nodes at depths 0–3 with less than two children.

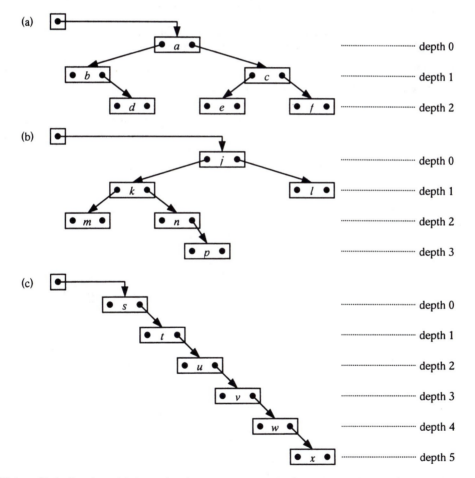

Figure 10.4 Depth and balance in binary trees: (a) balanced; (b) ill-balanced; (c) extremely ill-balanced.

A balanced binary tree of depth d has at least 2^d and at most $2^{d+1} - 1$ nodes. Conversely:

$$\text{Depth of a balanced binary tree of size } n = \text{floor}(\log_2 n) \qquad (10.1)$$

An ill-balanced binary tree of depth d could have as few as $d + 1$ nodes. Conversely:

$$\text{Maximum depth of an ill-balanced binary tree of size } n = n - 1 \qquad (10.2)$$

We shall use these equations to analyze the complexity of binary tree algorithms later in this chapter.

10.1.2 Binary search trees

A *binary search tree* (or *BST*) is a binary tree with the following property. For every node in the binary tree, if that node contains element *elem*:

* the node's left subtree contains only elements less than *elem* (or is empty)
* the node's right subtree contains only elements greater than *elem* (or is empty).

(Our definition of a BST prohibits duplicate elements. An alternative definition that does allow duplicate elements is also possible: allow the node's left subtree to contain elements less than *or equal to elem*.)

Figure 10.5 illustrates two BSTs, in which the nodes contain words. For example, consider the node containing 'lion' in BST (a): its left subtree contains words less than 'lion'; its right subtree contains words greater than 'lion'. Or consider the node containing 'fox': its left subtree contains words less than 'fox'; its right subtree is empty.

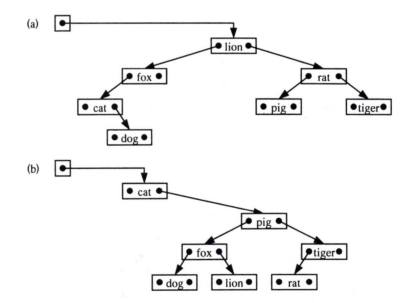

Figure 10.5 Illustrative binary search trees.

An equivalent recursive definition is also possible. A ***binary search tree*** is:

(i) empty, *or*

(ii) nonempty, in which case it has a root node containing an element *elem*, a link to a left subtree containing only elements less than *elem*, and a link to a right subtree containing only elements greater than *elem* (where the left and right subtrees are themselves binary search trees).

In Java, we can represent the BST as a whole by an object of class BST, shown in Program 10.6; and we can represent each BST node by an object of class BSTNode, shown in Program 10.7. Each BSTNode object has three instance variables. The instance variable element is here declared with type Comparable; this allows elements to be compared using the compareTo method. The instance variable left is itself of type BSTNode, and will contain either a reference to another BSTNode object (the node's left child) or null. The instance variable right is analogous. A BST object has a single instance variable, root, which will contain either a reference to the BST's root node or null.

Note that the instance variables left and right in the BSTNode class are declared as *protected*, so that they can be accessed by the BST methods.

A BST, then, will be represented by a BST object (the header) together with a group of BSTNode objects (the nodes). The structures of BST and BSTNode objects are shown in detail in Figure 10.8. In our diagrams of BSTs, however, we will generally adopt the uncluttered style of Figure 10.5.

The rest of this chapter (except Section 10.5) concentrates on BSTs. We shall see in Sections 10.2–4 that searching, insertion, and deletion in a BST are very fast, provided that the BST is well-balanced. This makes BSTs a very good way to represent sets, as we shall see in Section 10.7.

```
public class BST {

    //  Each BST object is a binary search tree (BST) header.

    //  This BST is represented by a link to its root node (root).
    private BSTNode root;

    public BST () {
    //  Construct an empty BST.
        root = null;
    }

    ...    //  BST methods (see below).

}
```

Program 10.6 Java class representing BSTs.

```
public class BSTNode {
```

// Each BSTNode object is a binary search tree (BST) node.

// This node consists of an element (element), a link to its
// left child (left), and a link to its right child (right).
// For every element x in the left subtree:
//   x.compareTo(element) < 0
// For every element y in the right subtree:
//   y.compareTo(element) > 0
```
protected Comparable element;
protected BSTNode left, right;
protected BSTNode (Comparable elem) {
```
// Construct a BST node with element elem and no children.
```
    this.element = elem;
    this.left = null;
    this.right = null;
}
```

   ...   // BSTNode methods (see below).

```
}
```

Program 10.7   Java class representing BST nodes.

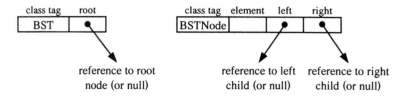

Figure 10.8   Detailed structures of BST and BSTNode objects.

10.2 Searching

Consider the BST of Figure 10.5(a). Suppose that we have to search this BST for the target word 'pig'. We start at the root node (the only node to which we have a direct link). The root node contains the word 'lion'; comparison with the target word shows that the target word is greater, so we follow the link from the root node to its right child. (Recall the defining property of a BST: the root's left (right) subtree contains only elements less (greater) than the root's element.) This node contains the word 'rat'; comparison with the target word shows that the target word is less, so we follow the link from this node to its left child. That node contains the word 'pig'; comparison with the target word shows that the target word is equal, so the search is declared successful. This search is illustrated in Figure 10.9(a), highlighting the links followed during the search. (This sequence of links is called the *search path*.)

Figures 10.9(b) and (c) illustrate two other searches, one successful, the other unsuccessful. The search is declared unsuccessful if we try to follow a null link. In Figure 10.9(c), this happens when we find that the node containing 'dog' has no right child.

The BST search algorithm is easily formulated: see Algorithm 10.10. The loop at step 2 searches the BST from the root node downward, with the variable *curr* being a link to the node currently being inspected. When *curr* is null (step 2.1), the algorithm terminates the search unsuccessfully. When *target* equals node *curr*'s element (step 2.2), the algorithm terminates the search successfully. Otherwise (step 2.3 or 2.4), it updates *curr* to node *curr*'s left or right child, depending on whether *target* is less than or greater than node *curr*'s element.

BST search is potentially very efficient. Every comparison eliminates a complete subtree. In Figure 10.9, for example, the very first comparison is enough to eliminate four of the seven nodes. It should be clear that *any* search in this particular BST will

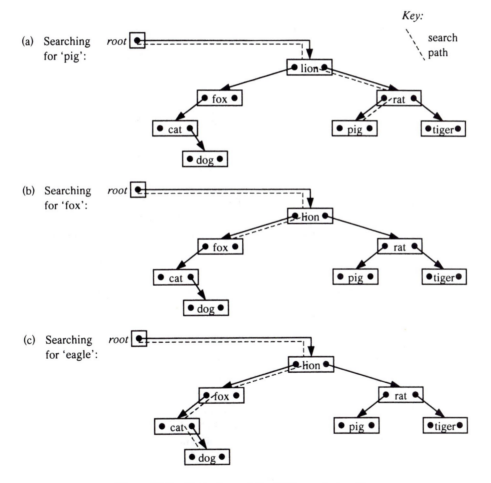

Figure 10.9 Illustrations of the BST search algorithm.

require at most four comparisons, since the BST's depth is 3. Often fewer comparisons will be needed, if the search terminates at a node whose depth is less than the BST's depth, as in Figures 10.9(a) and (b).

Consider searching a *balanced* BST of size n. From equation (10.1), the BST's depth is floor($\log_2 n$). The required number of comparisons is one more than the depth of the node where the search terminates. Consequently:

$$\text{Maximum no. of comparisons} = \text{floor}(\log_2 n) + 1 \qquad (10.3)$$

It can be shown (although the analysis is more difficult) that the *average* number of comparisons is half the maximum number. Either way, the BST search algorithm's time complexity is $O(\log n)$, provided that the BST is well-balanced. A slightly unbalanced BST entails slightly more comparisons than a perfectly balanced BST, but the time complexity is still $O(\log n)$.

Compare equation (10.3) with equation (3.5) for the binary search algorithm. The number of comparisons is exactly the same, and the reason is the same: each comparison halves the number of elements still to be searched. Indeed, this is why *binary search* trees are so called.

But now consider searching an *ill-balanced* BST of size n. From equation (10.2), the BST's depth is at most $n - 1$, and consequently:

$$\text{Maximum no. of comparisons} = n \qquad (10.4)$$

The *average* number of comparisons is half the maximum number. Either way, the BST search algorithm's time complexity is $O(n)$, if the BST is ill-balanced.

Compare equation (10.4) with equation (3.3) for the linear search algorithm. The number of comparisons is exactly the same, and again the reason is the same: each comparison eliminates only one element from the search. Indeed, an extremely ill-balanced BST is no better than a sorted singly-linked list.

Summarizing, the BST search algorithm has time complexity $O(\log n)$ when the BST is well-balanced, but degenerates to $O(n)$ when it is ill-balanced. This is an interesting practical matter, to which we shall return frequently.

To find which if any node of a BST contains an element equal to *target*:

1. Set *curr* to the BST's root.
2. Repeat:
    2.1. If *curr* is null:
        2.1.1. Terminate with answer *none*.
    2.2. Otherwise, if *target* is equal to node *curr*'s element:
        2.2.1. Terminate with answer *curr*.
    2.3. Otherwise, if *target* is less than node *curr*'s element:
        2.3.1. Set *curr* to node *curr*'s left child.
    2.4. Otherwise, if *target* is greater than node *curr*'s element:
        2.4.1. Set *curr* to node *curr*'s right child.

Algorithm 10.10　BST search algorithm.

The BST search algorithm is easily implemented as a Java method: see Program 10.11. This method would be added to the BST class of Program 10.6.

A recursive formulation of the BST search algorithm is also possible: see Exercise 10.2.

10.3 Insertion

Let us consider how to insert a new element into a BST. It turns out that we can always do this by replacing an existing null link by a link to a new node containing the new element. We need not change any of the BST's existing non-null links; in other words, we need not change the BST's existing structure.

For example, consider inserting a new word into the BST of Figure 10.5(a). If the new word is less than 'cat', the new node will become the left child of the 'cat' node. If the new word is greater than 'cat' but less than 'dog', the new node will become the left child of the 'dog' node. If the new word is greater than 'dog' but less than 'fox', the new node will become the right child of the 'dog' node. And so on.

The only problem is to decide which node will be the new node's parent. In fact, this is similar to BST search (Algorithm 10.10). Suppose that 'monkey' is to be inserted in the BST of Figure 10.5(a). As usual, we start at the root node. The root node contains the word 'lion'; comparison with the new word shows that the new word is greater, so we follow the link from the root node to its right child. This node contains the word 'rat'; comparison with the target word shows that the target word is less, so we follow the link from this node to its left child. That node contains the word 'pig'; comparison with the

```java
public BSTNode search (Comparable target) {
// Find which if any node of this BST contains an element equal to target.
// Return a link to that node (or null if there is none).
    int direction = 0;  // ... 0 for here, < 0 for left, > 0 for right
    BSTNode curr = root;
    for (;;) {
      if (curr == null)
        return null;
      direction = target.compareTo(curr.element);
      if (direction == 0)
        return curr;
      else if (direction < 0)
        curr = curr.left;
      else  // direction > 0
        curr = curr.right;
    }
}
```

Program 10.11   Implementation of the BST search algorithm as a Java method (in class BST).

target word shows that the target word is less. But that node has no left child, so we make its left child a newly-created node containing 'monkey'.

Algorithm 10.12 uses this idea to insert the element *elem* into a BST. The loop at step 2 searches the BST from the root node downward, and is similar in outline to the loop in Algorithm 10.10. The main difference is that here two links are needed: *curr* is a link to the node currently being inspected, while *parent* is a link to that node's parent (if any). When *curr* is null (step 2.1), the algorithm creates a new node containing *elem*, and makes this node either the root node or *parent*'s left child or *parent*'s right child, depending on where the null link was found during the search. When *elem* equals *curr*'s element (step 2.2), the algorithm simply terminates, to avoid inserting a duplicate element. Otherwise (step 2.3 or 2.4), it updates *parent* to *curr,* and *curr* to *curr*'s left or right child.

Figure 10.13 illustrates the BST insertion algorithm's behavior as words are successively added to an initially empty BST. Note that the first word to be added occupies the root node thereafter; words added later occupy nodes deeper and deeper in the BST.

Figure 10.14 illustrates the algorithm's behavior as the same words are successively added to an initially empty BST, but this time the words happen to be added in ascending order. Every new word occupies a node that is its parent's right child. The result is an extremely ill-balanced BST.

The BST insertion algorithm performs the same number of comparisons as the BST search algorithm, which we analyzed in Section 10.2. The BST insertion algorithm therefore has time complexity $O(\log n)$ if the BST is well-balanced, or $O(n)$ if the BST is ill-balanced.

An implementation of the BST insertion algorithm as a Java method, `insert`, is shown in Program 10.15. This method would be added to the `BST` class of Program 10.6.

A recursive formulation of the BST insertion algorithm is also possible: see Exercise 10.3.

To insert the element *elem* into a BST:

1. Set *parent* to null, and set *curr* to the BST's root.
2. Repeat:
    2.1. If *curr* is null:
        2.1.1. Let *ins* be a newly-created node with element *elem* and no children.
        2.1.2. Replace the null link from which *curr* was taken (either the BST's root or *parent*'s left child or *parent*'s right child) by *ins*.
        2.1.3. Terminate.
    2.2. Otherwise, if *elem* is equal to node *curr*'s element:
        2.2.1. Terminate.
    2.3. Otherwise, if *elem* is less than node *curr*'s element:
        2.3.1. Set *parent* to *curr*, and set *curr* to node *curr*'s left child.
    2.4. Otherwise, if *elem* is greater than node *curr*'s element:
        2.4.1. Set *parent* to *curr*, and set *curr* to node *curr*'s right child.

Algorithm 10.12 BST insertion algorithm.

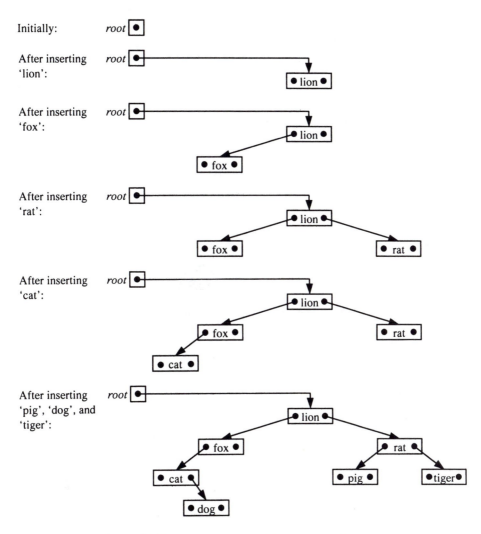

Figure 10.13   Illustration of the BST insertion algorithm.

10.4 Deletion

Consider the problem of deleting a given element in a BST. Finding the node containing this element is straightforward, but actual deletion of the element sometimes forces some restructuring of the BST.

We shall approach this problem in three stages. In Sections 10.4.1 and 10.4.2 we study the simpler problems of deleting the leftmost and topmost elements, respectively, in a BST or subtree. In Section 10.4.3 we return to the original problem of deleting an arbitrary given element in a BST.

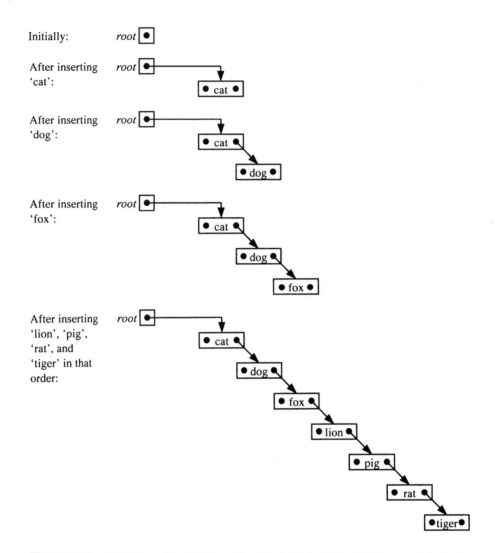

Figure 10.14   Illustration of the BST insertion algorithm: inserting already-sorted elements.

10.4.1 Deleting the leftmost element in a subtree

Let us first study the simpler problem of how to delete the *leftmost* element in a BST – in other words, the element in its leftmost node.

There are two cases to consider:

(a) The BST's root node has no left child. In this case the root node itself is the leftmost node. We replace the BST by the root node's right subtree.

(b) The root node has a left child. In this case we inspect the left child, the left child's

```java
public void insert (Comparable elem) {
// Insert the element elem into this BST.
    int direction = 0;   // ... 0 for here, < 0 for left, > 0 for right
    BSTNode parent = null, curr = root;
    for (;;) {
        if (curr == null) {
            BSTNode ins = new BSTNode(elem);
            if (root == null)
                root = ins;
            else if (direction < 0)
                parent.left = ins;
            else  // direction > 0
                parent.right = ins;
            return;
        }
        direction = elem.compareTo(curr.element);
        if (direction == 0)
            return;
        parent = curr;
        if (direction < 0)
            curr = curr.left;
        else  // direction > 0
            curr = curr.right;
    }
}
```

Program 10.15 Implementation of the BST insertion algorithm as a Java method (in class BST).

left child, and so on until we find a node with no left child. That node is the leftmost node. We replace its parent node's left subtree by the leftmost node's right subtree.

Each case is illustrated in Figure 10.16.

Algorithm 10.17 generalizes this, showing how to delete the leftmost element in an arbitrary given subtree (not necessarily a complete BST). Step 1 covers case (a) above, and step 2 covers case (b). Since the algorithm modifies the given subtree, its answer is a link to the topmost node of the modified subtree. (The answer will be the original topmost node in case (b), but a different node in case (a).)

The algorithm is implemented by the Java method of Program 10.18, which would be added to the BSTNode class of Program 10.7.

10.4.2 Deleting the topmost element in a subtree

Now let us study the related problem of how to delete the *topmost* element in a given BST – in other words, the element in its root node. Of course, we cannot just delete the root

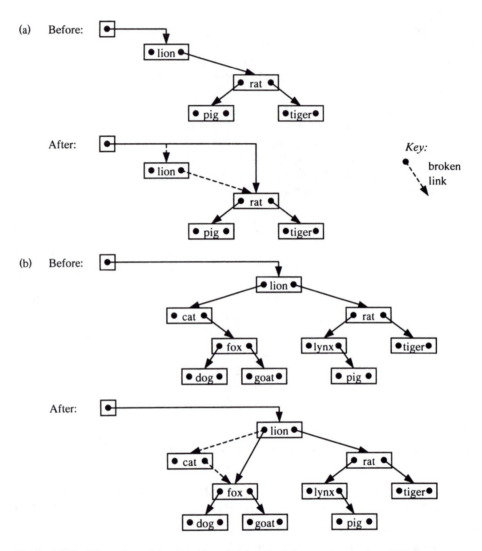

Figure 10.16   Illustration of the algorithm to delete the leftmost element in a BST or subtree.

node itself: it might have nonempty subtrees, which will contain elements that must *not* be deleted.

Each of the BST's two subtrees might be empty or nonempty. This gives us four cases to consider:

(a) The root node has two empty subtrees.
(b) The root node has an empty left subtree but a nonempty right subtree.
(c) The root node has an empty right subtree but a nonempty left subtree.
(d) The root node has two nonempty subtrees.

To delete the leftmost element in the (nonempty) subtree whose topmost node is *this*:

1. If node *this* has no left child:
    1.1.   Terminate with node *this*'s right child as answer.
2. If *this* has a left child:
    2.1.   Set *parent* to *this*, and set *curr* to node *this*'s left child.
    2.2.   While node *curr* has a left child, repeat:
        2.2.1.   Set *parent* to *curr*, and set *curr* to node *curr*'s left child.
    2.3.   Set *parent*'s left child to node *curr*'s right child.
    2.4.   Terminate with *this* as answer.

Algorithm 10.17   Algorithm to delete the leftmost element in a subtree.

```
private BSTNode deleteLeftmost () {
// Delete the leftmost element in the (nonempty) subtree whose topmost node is
// this node. Return a link to the modified subtree.
   if (this.left == null)
      return this.right;
   else {
      BSTNode parent = this, curr = this.left;
      while (curr.left != null) {
         parent = curr;   curr = curr.left;
      }
      parent.left = curr.right;
      return this;
   }
}
```

Program 10.18   Implementation of Algorithm 10.17 as a Java method (in class `BSTNode`).

Each case is illustrated in Figure 10.19.

Case (a) is easy: replace the BST by an empty BST.

Case (b) is also easy: replace the BST by its right subtree. Its left subtree is empty, so nothing is lost.

Case (c) is analogous: replace the BST by its left subtree.

Case (d) is more tricky. Simply deleting the root node would leave us with two disconnected nonempty subtrees. Fortunately we can solve this problem neatly. Simply copy the leftmost element in the right subtree into the root node, and then delete the leftmost element in the right subtree (as shown in Section 10.4.1). (The leftmost element in the right subtree is (by definition of a BST) the least element greater than the element in the root node.)

In Figure 10.19(d), the right subtree's leftmost element is 'lynx', so we copy 'lynx' into the root node and then delete 'lynx' from the right subtree.

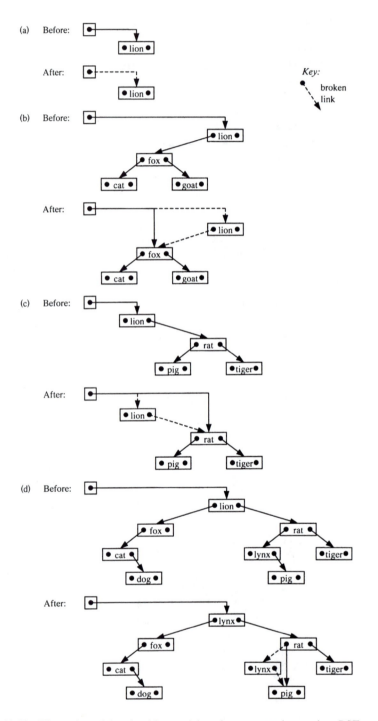

Figure 10.19 Illustration of the algorithm to delete the topmost element in a BST or subtree.

To delete the topmost element in the subtree whose topmost node is *top*:

1. If node *top* has no left child:
    1.1. Terminate with node *top*'s right child as answer.
2. If node *top* has no right child:
    2.1. Terminate with node *top*'s left child as answer.
3. If node *top* has both a left child and a right child:
    3.1. Set *top*'s element to the leftmost element in node *top*'s right subtree.
    3.2. Delete the leftmost element in node *top*'s right subtree.
    3.3. Terminate with *top* as answer.

Algorithm 10.20   Algorithm to delete the topmost element in a subtree.

To determine the leftmost element in the (nonempty) subtree whose topmost node is *this*:

1. Set *curr* to *this*.
2. While node *curr* has a left child, repeat:
    2.1. Set *curr* to node *curr*'s left child.
3. Terminate with node *curr*'s element as answer.

Algorithm 10.21   Algorithm to determine the element in the leftmost node of a subtree.

Algorithm 10.20 generalizes all this, showing how to delete the topmost element in an arbitrary subtree (not necessarily a complete BST). Step 1 covers case (b) above, step 2 covers case (c), and both of these steps also cover case (a). Step 3 covers case (d). Since the algorithm modifies the given subtree, its answer is a link to the topmost node in the modified subtree (which might be either the original topmost node or a different one).

Algorithm 10.20 employs two auxiliary algorithms. One is Algorithm 10.21, which finds the leftmost (least) element in a given nonempty subtree. The other is Algorithm 10.17.

These algorithms are implemented by the Java methods of Program 10.22, which would be added to the `BSTNode` class of Program 10.7.

10.4.3 Deleting a given element in a binary search tree

Now let us return to the original problem of deleting an arbitrary given element *elem* in a BST. Finding the node containing *elem* is similar to BST search (Algorithm 10.10). Actual deletion of the element in that node amounts to deleting the topmost element in a subtree, and is therefore similar to the problem we studied in Section 10.4.2.

Algorithm 10.23 shows the solution. The loop at step 2 searches the BST from the root node downward, and is similar in outline to the loops of the BST search and insertion algorithms. Algorithm 10.23 maintains two variables: *curr* is a link to the node currently

```
public BSTNode deleteTopmost () {
// Delete the topmost element in the subtree whose topmost node is this node.
// Return a link to the modified subtree.
    if (left == null)
        return right;
    else if (right == null)
        return left;
    else {   // this node has both a left child and a right child
        element = right.getLeftmost();
        right = right.deleteLeftmost();
        return this;
    }
}

private Comparable getLeftmost () {
// Return the leftmost element in the (nonempty) subtree whose topmost node
// is this node.
    BSTNode curr = this;
    while (curr.left != null)
        curr = curr.left;
    return curr.element;
}
```

Program 10.22 Implementation of Algorithms 10.20 and 10.21 as Java methods (in class `BSTNode`).

To delete the element *elem* in a BST:

1. Set *parent* to null, and *curr* to the BST's root node.
2. Repeat:
    2.1. If *curr* is null:
        2.1.1. Terminate.
    2.2. Otherwise, if *elem* is equal to node *curr*'s element:
        2.2.1. Delete the topmost element in the subtree whose topmost node is node *curr*, and let *del* be a link to the modified subtree.
        2.2.2. Replace the link to node *curr* by *del*.
        2.2.3. Terminate.
    2.3. Otherwise, if *elem* is less than node *curr*'s element:
        2.3.1. Set *parent* to *curr*, and set *curr* to node *curr*'s left child.
    2.4. Otherwise, if *elem* is greater than node *curr*'s element:
        2.4.1. Set *parent* to *curr*, and set *curr* to node *curr*'s right child.

Algorithm 10.23 BST deletion algorithm.

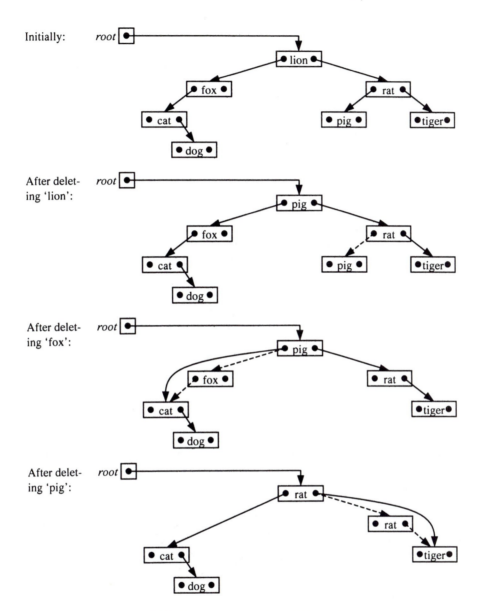

Figure 10.24 Illustration of the BST deletion algorithm.

being inspected, and *parent* is a link to that node's parent. When *curr* is null (step 2.1), the algorithm just terminates, since the BST contains no element equal to *elem*. When *elem* equals node *curr*'s element (step 2.2), the algorithm modifies the subtree whose topmost node is *curr*: first it deletes the element in that topmost node (step 2.2.1); then it makes the modified subtree replace the original subtree in the BST (step 2.2.2).

```
public void delete (Comparable elem) {
// Delete the element elem in this BST.
   int direction = 0;   // ... 0 for here, < 0 for left, > 0 for right
   BSTNode parent = null, curr = root;
   for (;;) {
     if (curr == null)
       return;
     direction = elem.compareTo(curr.element);
     if (direction == 0) {
       BSTNode del = curr.deleteTopmost();
       if (curr == root)
         root = del;
       else if (curr == parent.left)
         parent.left = del;
       else  // curr == parent.right
         parent.right = del;
       return;
     }
     parent = curr;
     if (direction < 0)
       curr = parent.left;
     else  // direction > 0
       curr = parent.right;
   }
}
```

Program 10.25 Implementation of the BST deletion algorithm as a Java method (in class BST).

Figure 10.24 illustrates the BST deletion algorithm's behavior as words are successively deleted from a BST.

We can implement the BST deletion algorithm as a Java method, delete, shown in Program 10.25. This method would be added to the BST class of Program 10.6.

A recursive formulation of the BST deletion algorithm is also possible: see Exercise 10.4.

10.5 Traversal

Traversal of a binary tree consists of visiting each node in turn. There are many possible reasons for such a traversal: to count the nodes, to print the elements in the nodes, and so on.

EXAMPLE 10.1 *Determining the size of a binary tree*

A Java method that determines the size of a given subtree is shown as Program 10.26.

This method traverses the subtree, simply counting the nodes. Of course, it need not inspect the elements in the nodes.

Note, in particular, the expression in the second return statement. The term 1 represents the visit to the node `top`. The term `size(top.left)` represents a traversal of the left subtree, and similarly `size(top.right)` represents a traversal of the right subtree. The latter two terms are recursive method calls.

For counting nodes, the order of traversal is not significant. For many other purposes, such as printing the elements, the order in which we visit the nodes of the binary tree clearly is significant.

In the following subsections we shall study three basic traversal orders:

- *in-order traversal*: left–root–right (or its mirror-image right–root–left)
- *pre-order traversal*: root–left–right (or its mirror-image root–right–left)
- *post-order traversal*: left–right–root (or its mirror-image right–left–root).

10.5.1 In-order traversal

In-order traversal of a binary tree consists of traversing the left subtree, then visiting the root node, then traversing the right subtree (in short, left–root–right). Each subtree is itself traversed in in-order, so this definition is recursive. In-order traversal is shown schematically in Figure 10.27.

An important application is in-order traversal of a binary *search* tree. The effect is to

```
public static int size (BSTNode top) {
// Determine the size of the subtree whose topmost node is top.
   if (top == null)    // the subtree is empty
      return 0;
   else                // the subtree is nonempty
      return 1 + size(top.left) + size(top.right);
}
```

Program 10.26   Java method to determine the size of a BST (in class `BSTNode`).

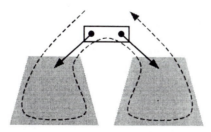

Figure 10.27   In-order traversal of a binary tree.

visit all the nodes in ascending order of elements. This is illustrated in Figure 10.28, which shows in-order traversal of a BST whose nodes contain words.

Algorithm 10.29 captures the idea of in-order traversal. It is a recursive algorithm, formulated in terms of traversing an arbitrary subtree, and directly follows from our definition of in-order traversal.

Algorithm 10.29 is said to be *generic*, because the step 'Visit node *top*' is unspecific about what is done when the node is visited. Any particular implementation of Algorithm 10.29 must be more specific. The printInOrder method of Program 10.30 prints an element when it visits a node. The size method of Program 10.26 simply adds 1 to a node count when it visits a node.

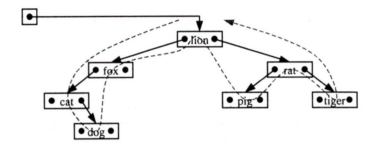

Figure 10.28 In-order traversal of a BST containing words.

To traverse, in in-order, the subtree whose topmost node is *top*:

1. If *top* is not null:
    1.1.   Traverse, in in-order, node *top*'s left subtree.
    1.2.   Visit node *top*.
    1.3.   Traverse, in in-order, node *top*'s right subtree.
2. Terminate.

Algorithm 10.29 Binary tree in-order traversal algorithm.

```
public static void printInOrder (BSTNode top) {
// Print all the elements in the subtree whose topmost node is top, in
// ascending order.
    if (top != null) {
        printInOrder(top.left);
        System.out.println(top.element);
        printInOrder(top.right);
    }
}
```

Program 10.30 Java method to print the elements in a BST.

EXAMPLE 10.2 *Printing the elements in a BST*

Program 10.30 is a Java method that prints all the elements in a given subtree of a BST, in ascending order. It does this by performing an in-order traversal; when it visits a node, it simply prints the element in that node.

10.5.2 Pre-order traversal

Pre-order traversal of a binary tree consists of visiting the root node, then traversing the left subtree, then traversing the right subtree (in short, root–left–right). Each subtree is itself traversed in pre-order, so this definition is recursive. Pre-order traversal is shown schematically in Figure 10.31, and illustrated in Figure 10.32.

Algorithm 10.33 directly follows from our definition of pre-order traversal. It is a recursive algorithm, formulated in terms of traversing an arbitrary subtree.

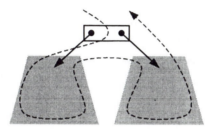

Figure 10.31   Pre-order traversal of a binary tree.

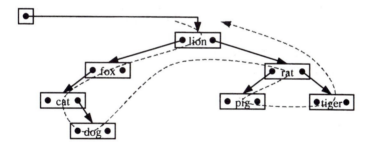

Figure 10.32   Pre-order traversal of a BST containing words.

To traverse, in pre-order, the subtree whose topmost node is *top*:

1. If *top* is not null:
    1.1. Visit node *top*.
    1.2. Traverse, in pre-order, node *top*'s left subtree.
    1.3. Traverse, in pre-order, node *top*'s right subtree.
2. Terminate.

Algorithm 10.33   Binary tree pre-order traversal algorithm.

EXAMPLE 10.3 *Saving the elements in a BST*

Suppose that an application program maintains a collection of data in a BST. The user may update the collection by inserting and deleting data. When the user quits the application, the data must be saved in a file until the application is restarted.

There is a very simple way to save a BST in a file: we just write the elements in the BST to a file, in some suitable order. (There is no need to save the links.) To restore the BST subsequently, we read one element at a time from the file, and insert each element into an initially empty BST. This idea is captured by the algorithms given in Algorithm 10.34.

To save the elements in the BST we must traverse the BST, but in which order? Recall, from Section 10.3, that the very first element inserted in a BST will thereafter occupy the root node. If we want to save the BST in such a way that it can be restored exactly, we must save the element in the root node first. This suggests a pre-order traversal.

As we see in Figure 10.32, pre-order traversal of that particular BST will visit the words in the following order:

   lion, fox, cat, dog, rat, pig, tiger.

If we start with an empty BST, and then insert these words in this order, the resulting BST will have exactly the same shape as the original. (See also Exercise 10.6.)

10.5.3 Post-order traversal

Post-order traversal of a binary tree consists of visiting the root node, then traversing the left subtree, then traversing the right subtree (in short, left–right–root). Each subtree is itself traversed in post-order, so this definition is recursive. Post-order traversal is shown schematically in Figure 10.35, and illustrated in Figure 10.36.

Algorithm 10.37 directly follows from our definition of post-order traversal. It is a recursive algorithm, formulated in terms of traversing an arbitrary subtree.

To save a BST *tree* to *file*:

1. Traverse *tree* in pre-order; at each node, write the node's element to *file*.
2. Terminate.

To restore a BST from *file*:

1. Make *tree* an empty BST.
2. While there is still an element to read from *file*, repeat:
    2.1. Read the next element from *file* into *elem*.
    2.2. Insert *elem* in *tree*.
3. Terminate with answer *tree*.

Algorithm 10.34 Algorithms to save and restore a BST.

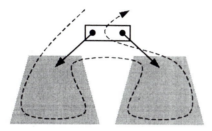

Figure 10.35   Post-order traversal of a binary tree.

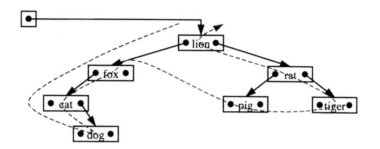

Figure 10.36   Post-order traversal of a BST containing words.

To traverse, in post-order, the subtree whose topmost node is *top*:

1. If *top* is not null:
    1.1.   Visit node *top*.
    1.2.   Traverse, in post-order, node *top*'s left subtree.
    1.3.   Traverse, in post-order, node *top*'s right subtree.
2. Terminate.

Algorithm 10.37   Binary tree post-order traversal algorithm.

10.6 Merging

Given two BSTs, consider merging the second BST into the first BST. After the merge, the first BST will contain just the elements that were in either BST or both.

This problem can be solved easily by traversing the second BST. At each node of the second BST, insert the node's element into the first BST. This is shown as Algorithm 10.38. We choose pre-order traversal because this order is most likely to keep the first BST well-balanced (assuming that it is initially well-balanced).

Let us assume that the first BST remains well-balanced throughout the merge. Let n_1 be the *initial* size of the first BST, and let n_2 be the size of the second BST. Each insertion entails at most floor($\log_2 n_1'$) + 1 comparisons, where n_1' is the *current* size of the first

BST. Thus $n_1' = n_1$ in the first insertion, and $n_1' = n_1 + n_2 - 1$ in the last insertion. In total:

Maximum no. of comparisons
$$= (\text{floor}(\log_2 n_1) + 1) + \cdots + (\text{floor}(\log_2(n_1 + n_2 - 1)) + 1)$$
$$< n_2(\log(n_1 + n_2) + 1) \tag{10.5}$$

since the summation has n_2 terms, each term being smaller than $\log(n_1 + n_2) + 1$. It follows that the BST merging algorithm has time complexity $O(n_2 \log(n_1 + n_2))$ when the first BST is well-balanced.

Let us now assume that the first BST remains ill-balanced throughout the merge. Each insertion entails at most $n_1' + 1$ comparisons. In total:

Maximum no. of comparisons
$$= (n_1 + 1) + \cdots + (n_1 + n_2)$$
$$= n_2(2n_1 + n_2 + 1)/2 \tag{10.6}$$

It follows that the BST merging algorithm has time complexity $O(n_2(n_1 + n_2))$ when the first BST is ill-balanced.

A possible implementation of the BST merging algorithm is shown as the method `addAll` in Program 10.41.

To merge the BST *tree2* into the BST *tree1*:

1. Traverse *tree2* in pre-order; at each node, insert the node's element into *tree1*.
2. Terminate.

Algorithm 10.38 BST merging algorithm.

10.7 Implementation of unbounded sets using binary search trees

As we have already hinted, a BST makes an effective representation for a set. The BST combines an unbounded representation with potentially efficient search, insertion, and deletion algorithms.

Figure 10.5 illustrates BSTs representing sets of words, and Figure 10.39 illustrates BSTs representing sets of countries. Note that the BST representation is non-unique: the same set can be represented by several different BSTs. (Compare Figure 10.39(c) and (d).)

Recall the Set contract of Program 9.4. If we choose a BST representation, we would implement the operations using BST algorithms as follows:

- The `size` operation should count the nodes in the BST, as in Example 10.1. Its time complexity is $O(n)$, where n is the set's cardinality. (Exercise 10.9 explores the possibility of storing the cardinality explicitly.)

- The `contains` operation should use the BST search algorithm (Algorithm 10.10). Its time complexity is $O(\log n)$ if the BST is well-balanced, or $O(n)$ if it is ill-balanced.
- The `add` and `remove` operations should use the BST insertion and deletion algorithms, respectively (Algorithms 10.12 and 10.23). Each has time complexity $O(\log n)$ if the BST is well-balanced, or $O(n)$ if the BST is ill-balanced.
- The `containsAll` operation should traverse the second BST (in any order); at each node visited, it should check that the element is also in the first BST. Its time complexity is $O(n_2 \log n_1)$ if the first BST is well-balanced, or $O(n_1 n_2)$ if it is ill-balanced, where n_1 and n_2 are the cardinalities of the first and second sets, respectively.
- The `equals` operation must take into account the fact that the same set can be represented by different BSTs: a simple node-by-node comparison would be incorrect. Fortunately, this problem can be neatly solved using the law that, for any sets s_1 and s_2:

$$s_1 = s_2 \text{ if and only if } \#s_1 = \#s_2 \text{ and } s_1 \supseteq s_2 \qquad (10.7)$$

So the operation should first check that the two sets have equal cardinalities, and then proceed as for `containsAll`.

- The `addAll` operation should use the BST merging algorithm (Algorithm 10.38).
- The `removeAll` operation should use a variant of the BST merging algorithm that deletes rather than inserts in the first BST.
- The `retainAll` operation should construct a new BST, inserting into it just those elements common to both BSTs. It can do this by traversing one BST (preferably pre-order), testing whether each element is also in the other BST.

The algorithms and their time complexities are summarized in Table 10.40.

Program 10.41 outlines the implementation, in the form of a Java class `BSTSet` that implements the `Set` interface. The `BSTSet` class is similar to the `BST` class developed earlier in this chapter, but the `search`, `insert`, and `delete` methods of Sections 10.2–4 have been demoted to auxiliary methods, assisting in the implementation of the methods mandated by the `Set` interface.

The `preOrderIterator` operation in Program 10.41 returns an iterator of class `BSTSet.PreOrderIterator`. This iterator should traverse the BST representing the set, in pre-order. Several other operations in Program 10.41 (including `addAll` and `retainAll`) create and use pre-order iterators for their own internal purposes. These operations could be programmed directly, along the lines of Algorithm 10.33, but it is arguably better to implement them in terms of iterators.

Admittedly, a BST traversal algorithm (such as Algorithm 10.33) is simple and elegant, at least when expressed recursively. But consider what happens when we implement this algorithm as a method. When called, that method takes control, visiting all the nodes at times of its own choosing. When we use a BST iterator, on the other hand, the *application code* retains control, visiting the next node at a time of *its* own choosing (and possibly interleaving other tasks with visiting the nodes). Moreover, the iterator can be implemented once, and subsequently used over and over again.

Like any other iterator, a BST pre-order iterator must remember how far it has proceeded with the traversal. But, unlike an array or linked-list iterator, it cannot work with a simple place-marker. After visiting a node, the pre-order iterator must be ready to

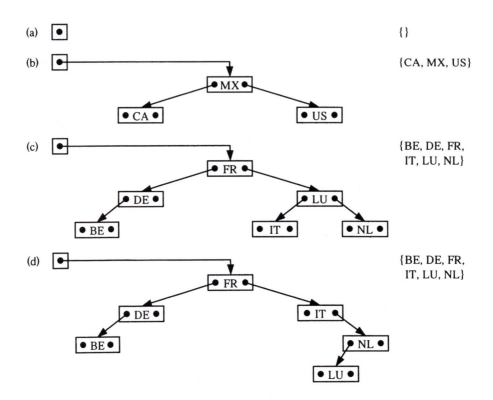

Figure 10.39 Representations of unbounded sets by BSTs: (a) empty set; (b–d) sets of countries.

Table 10.40 Implementation of unbounded sets using BSTs: summary of algorithms (where n, n_1, and n_2 are the cardinalities of the sets involved).

Operation	Algorithm	Time complexity (well-balanced)	Time complexity (ill-balanced)
size	BST node count	$O(n)$	$O(n)$
contains	BST search	$O(\log n)$	$O(n)$
equals	check for equal size, thereafter as for contains All	$O(n_2 \log n_1)$	$O(n_1 n_2)$
containsAll	traversal of second BST, checking that each element is in first BST	$O(n_2 \log n_1)$	$O(n_1 n_2)$
add	BST insertion	$O(\log n)$	$O(n)$
remove	BST deletion	$O(\log n)$	$O(n)$
addAll	BST merge	$O(n_2 \log(n_1 + n_2))$	$O(n_1 n_2)$
removeAll	variant of BST merge	$O(n_2 \log n_1)$	$O(n_1 n_2)$
retainAll	traversal of second BST, inserting each element into a new BST only if it is a member of first BST	$O(n_2 \log(n_1 + n_2))$	$O(n_1 n_2)$

traverse that node's left subtree, then its right subtree, then its parent's right subtree, then its grandparent's right subtree, and so on. Evidently the iterator must remember all the subtrees to be traversed in future.

Program 10.42 shows the implementation. The instance variable `track` is a general-

```
public class BSTSet implements Set {
    // Each BSTSet object is an unbounded set whose members are
    // Comparable objects.

    // This set is represented as follows: root is a link to the root node of a
    // BST containing its members.
    BSTNode root;

    /////////////// Constructor ///////////////

    public BSTSet () {
    // Construct a set, initially empty.
        root = null;
    }

    /////////////// Accessors ///////////////

    public boolean isEmpty () {
    // Return true if and only if this set is empty.
        return (root == null);
    }

    public int size () {
    // Return the cardinality of this set.
        return BSTNode.size(root);
    }

    public boolean contains (Object obj) {
    // Return true if and only if obj is a member of this set.
        if (obj instanceof Comparable)
            return (search((Comparable) obj) != null);
        else
            return false;
    }

    public boolean equals (Set that) {
    // Return true if and only if this set is equal to that.
        BSTSet other = (BSTSet) that;
        return (this.size() == other.size()
            && this.containsAll(other));
    }
```

Program 10.41 Java implementation of unbounded sets using BSTs (outline) (*continued on next page*).

ized place-marker: it is a stack of references to the topmost nodes of nonempty subtrees that will be traversed in future, in the correct order from top to bottom of the stack. Initially the stack contains just the BST's root node, if any. The hasNext operation simply tests whether the stack is empty. The next operation does most of the work. It starts by removing a node from the stack. The element in this node is the one due to be visited next, and will be returned by next. Before returning, however, next adds the node's right and left children, if any, to the stack. It adds the left child last, so that the left child will be visited next.

```java
public boolean containsAll (Set that) {
// Return true if and only if this set subsumes that.
   BSTSet other = (BSTSet) that;
   Iterator iter = other.preOrderIterator();
   while (iter.hasNext()) {
     Comparable obj = (Comparable) iter.next();
     if (! this.contains(obj))
       return false;
   }
   return true;
}

...   // Other accessors are omitted here – see the companion Web site.

///////////// Transformers /////////////

public void add (Object obj) {
// Add obj as a member of this set.
   insert((Comparable) obj);
}

public void remove (Object obj) {
// Remove obj from this set.
   if (obj instanceof Comparable)
     delete((Comparable) obj);
}

public void addAll (Set that) {
// Make this set the union of itself and that.
   BSTSet other = (BSTSet) that;
   Iterator iter = other.preOrderIterator();
   while (iter.hasNext()) {
     Comparable obj = (Comparable) iter.next();
     this.insert(obj);
   }
}
```

Program 10.41 (*continued on next page*)

```java
public void retainAll (Set that) {
// Make this set the intersection of itself and that.
   BSTSet result = new BSTSet();
   BSTSet other = (BSTSet) that;
   Iterator iter = other.preOrderIterator();
   while (iter.hasNext()) {
      Comparable obj = (Comparable) iter.next();
      if (this.contains(obj))
         result.insert(obj);
   }
   this.root = result.root;
}
```

... // Other transformers are omitted here – see the companion Web site.

/////////// Iterators ///////////

```java
public Iterator iterator() {
// Return an iterator that visits all members of this set, in ascending
// order.
   return new BSTSet.InOrderIterator();
}
```

```java
public Iterator preOrderIterator() {
// Return an iterator that visits all members of this set, in pre-order.
   return new BSTSet.PreOrderIterator();
}
```

/////////// Auxiliary methods ///////////

```java
private BSTNode search (Comparable target) {
// Find which if any node of this BST contains an element equal to
// target. Return a link to that node (or null if there is none).
   ...
}
```

```java
private void insert (Comparable elem) {
// Insert the element elem into this BST.
   ...
}
```

```java
private void delete (Comparable elem) {
// Delete the element elem in this BST.
   ...
}
```

```java
}
```

Program 10.41 (*continued*)

```java
private class PreOrderIterator implements Iterator {

  // A BSTSet.PreOrderIterator object is an iterator that will
  // traverse, in pre-order, the BSTSet object representing a set.

  // This iterator is represented by a stack of references to nonempty subtrees
  // still to be traversed, track.
  private Stack track;

  private PreOrderIterator () {
    track = new LinkedStack();
    if (root != null)
      track.addLast(root);
  }

  public boolean hasNext () {
    return (! track.isEmpty());
  }

  public Object next () {
    if (track.isEmpty())
      throw new NoSuchElementException();
    BSTNode place = (BSTNode) track.removeLast();
    if (place.right != null)
      track.add(place.right);
    if (place.left != null)
      track.add(place.left);
    return place.element;
  }
  ...  // The remove method is omitted here.

}
```

Program 10.42 Pre-order iterator for the implementation of unbounded sets using BSTs (as an inner class of BSTSet).

The `iterator` operation in Program 10.41 returns an iterator of class `BSTSet.InOrderIterator`. This iterator should traverse, in in-order, the BST representing the set. The `iterator` operation is not required by the set contract of Program 9.4 to traverse the elements in ascending order, but is useful nevertheless for applications such as printing the set's members. (See Program 10.44.) It is also consistent with the `java.util.SortedSet` interface, which requires the iterator over a set of `Comparable` objects to return the elements in ascending order.

To remember how far it has proceeded with the traversal, the in-order iterator must remember which nodes remain to be visited in future. For each node that remains to be visited, it is implicit that its right subtree also remains to be traversed (by definition of in-order traversal).

```
private class InOrderIterator implements Iterator {
    // A BSTSet.InOrderIterator object is an iterator that will traverse,
    // in in-order, the BSTSet object representing a set.

    // This iterator is represented by a stack of references to nodes still to be
    // visited, track.
    private Stack track;

    private InOrderIterator () {
        track = new LinkedStack();
        for (BSTNode curr = root; curr != null;
                curr = curr.left)
            track.addLast(curr);
    }

    public boolean hasNext () {
        return (! track.isEmpty());
    }

    public Object next () {
        if (track.isEmpty())
            throw new NoSuchElementException();
        BSTNode place = (BSTNode) track.removeLast();
        for (BSTNode curr = place.right; curr != null;
                curr = curr.left)
            track.addLast(curr);
        return place.element;
    }

    ...    // The remove method is omitted here.

}
```

Program 10.43   In-order iterator for the implementation of unbounded sets using BSTs (as an inner class of BSTSet).

Program 10.43 shows the implementation. The instance variable track is a stack of references to nodes that will be visited in future, in the correct order from top to bottom of the stack. Initially the stack contains the BST's root node, the root node's left child, that child's own left child, and so on down to the first such node that has no left child. The hasNext operation simply tests whether the stack is empty. The next operation starts by removing a node from the stack. The element in this node is the one due to be visited next, and will be returned by next. Before returning, however, next adds to the stack the node's right child, that child's own left child, that child's own left child, and so on down to the first such node that has no left child.

```
public static void printInOrder (Set set) {
// Print all members of the given set, in ascending order.
   Iterator iter = set.iterator();
   while (iter.hasNext()) {
      Object member = iter.next();
      System.out.println(member);
   }
}
```

Program 10.44   Java method to print the members of a set (using an in-order iterator).

Summary

In this chapter:

- We have studied binary trees, and particularly BSTs.
- We have studied algorithms for search, insertion, and deletion in a BST, and found that all these algorithms have time complexity $O(\log n)$ if the BST is well-balanced, deteriorating to $O(\log n)$ if the BST is ill-balanced.
- We have studied algorithms for in-order, pre-order, and post-order traversal of binary trees.
- We have studied how to represent sets by BSTs, respectively, and how to implement this representation in Java as a class that implements the Set interface.

Although the BST search, insertion, and deletion algorithms are potentially $O(\log n)$, we must be careful to keep the BST reasonably well-balanced. Inserting a sorted sequence of elements makes a BST ill-balanced. This situation could arise through carelessness (see Exercise 10.7) or by bad luck. Some possible solutions to this problem are:

- Periodically *rebalance* the BST, i.e., restructure the BST to make it well-balanced (see Exercises 10.10 and 10.11). For example, rebalancing the BST of Figure 10.5(b) would give us a BST similar to Figure 10.5(a).
- Modify the insertion and deletion algorithms to preserve balance. This gives us a special form of BST called an *AVL tree*, which we shall meet in Section 16.1.
- Abandon BSTs altogether in favor of trees that are inherently balanced. A good choice is a *B-tree*, which we shall meet in Section 16.2.

Exercises

10.1   Consider a binary search tree (BST) whose elements are abbreviated names of chemical elements.
(a) Starting with an empty BST, show the effect of successively adding the following elements: H, C, N, O, Al, Si, Fe, Na, P, S, Ni, Ca.
(b) Show the effect of successively deleting Si, N, O from the resulting BST.

10.2   Algorithm 10.45 is a recursive formulation of the BST search algorithm. Implement this as a Java method as follows:

```
public static BSTNode search (BSTNode top,
                    Comparable target);
// Find which if any node of the subtree whose topmost node is top
// contains an element equal to target. Return a link to that node (or
// null if there is none).
```

10.3   Algorithm 10.46 is a recursive formulation of the BST insertion algorithm. Note that its answer is a link to the modified subtree. Implement this algorithm as a Java method as follows:

```
public static BSTNode insert (BSTNode top,
                    Comparable elem);
// Insert the element elem in the subtree whose topmost node is top.
// Return a link to the modified subtree.
```

* **10.4**   Consider a recursive formulation of the BST deletion algorithm.
    (a) Devise a recursive algorithm that deletes the element *elem* in the subtree whose topmost node is *top*. Its answer should be a link to the modified subtree.
    (b) Implement your algorithm in Java.

10.5   Consider Program 10.26 to return the size of a given BST. Similarly, write Java methods to:
    (a) return the depth of a given BST;
    (b) return the p'th element from the left in a given BST.

    To find which if any node of the subtree whose topmost node is *top* contains an element equal to *target*:

1.   If *top* is null:
    1.1.   Terminate with answer *none*.
2.   If *top* is not null:
    2.1.   If *target* is equal to node *top*'s element:
        2.1.1.   Terminate with answer *top*.
    2.2.   Otherwise, if *target* is less than node *top*'s element:
        2.2.1.   Find which if any node of the subtree whose topmost node is node *top*'s left child contains an element equal to *target*.
        2.2.2.   Terminate with that node as answer.
    2.3.   Otherwise, if *target* is greater than node *top*'s element:
        2.3.1.   Find which if any node of the subtree whose topmost node is node *top*'s right child contains an element equal to *target*.
        2.3.2.   Terminate with that node as answer.

Algorithm 10.45   Recursive BST search algorithm.

To insert the element *elem* in the subtree whose topmost node is *top*:

1. If *top* is null:
    1.1. Make *ins* a link to a newly-created node with element *elem* and no children.
    1.2. Terminate with answer *ins*.
2. If *top* is not null:
    2.1. If *elem* is equal to node *top*'s element:
        2.1.1. Terminate with answer *top*.
    2.2. Otherwise, if *elem* is less than node *top*'s element:
        2.2.1. Insert *elem* in the subtree whose topmost node is node *top*'s left child.
        2.2.2. Terminate with answer *top*.
    2.3. Otherwise, if *elem* is greater than node *top*'s element:
        2.3.1. Insert *elem* in the subtree whose topmost node is node *top*'s right child.
        2.3.2. Terminate with answer *top*.

Algorithm 10.46   Recursive BST insertion algorithm.

10.6   Verify that pre-order traversal of the BST of Figure 10.5(b), followed by inserting the words one by one into an initially empty BST, will reproduce the original BST exactly.

10.7   What happens if the BST save algorithm, given in Algorithm 10.34, instead traverses the BST in *in-order*?

10.8   Write Java methods to implement the BST save and restore algorithms given in Algorithm 10.34.

10.9   Modify the set implementation of Program 10.41 such that the set's cardinality is stored in an instance variable. What are the advantages and disadvantages of this modification?

10.10   Write a Java method that tests whether a given BST is well-balanced.

*   **10.11**   Write a Java method that balances a given BST if necessary.

*   **10.12**   It is possible to represent a BST using an array of nodes. The nodes in the BST are stored in the array as follows:

- The root node of the BST is stored in position 0.
- A node stored in position p has its left child stored in position $2p + 1$, and its right child stored in position $2p + 2$ (so the children of the root node are in positions 1 and 2 respectively).

To represent a tree of depth d, the array must contain 2^d nodes. A nonexistent element is represented by null.

(a) Implement versions of the BST search, insertion, and deletion algorithms using an array.

(b) Modify the `BSTSet` class given in Program 10.41 to use an array.

(c) What happens to the space efficiency of the array representation when the tree is ill-balanced?

10.13   Repeat Exercise 10.1 using the array implementation of a BST described in Exercise 10.12.

10.14   Repeat Exercise 10.2 using the array implementation of a BST described in Exercise 10.12.

10.15   Repeat Exercise 10.3 using the array implementation of a BST described in Exercise 10.12.

10.16   Repeat Exercise 10.5 using the array implementation of a BST described in Exercise 10.12.

* **10.17**   Consider an experiment to study the efficiency of the BST insertion and deletion algorithms on a BST constructed at random. Assume that the elements in the BST are integers.
   (a) Design an algorithm to generate an element at random that *is not* already contained in the BST (such elements will be used to test the insertion algorithm). What is the efficiency of your algorithm?
   (b) Design an algorithm to generate an element at random that *is* already contained in a given BST (such elements will be used to test the deletion algorithm). What is the efficiency of your algorithm?
   (c) Implement your algorithms from parts (a) and (b) as Java methods.
   (d) Use your Java methods from part (c) to test the efficiency of a BST constructed from 1000 random elements. In other words, starting with an empty tree, make 1000 insertions followed by 1000 deletions. Count the number of comparisons required to perform each insertion and deletion operation.

* **10.18**   Modify the spell-checker case study from Section 9.8 to use the `BSTSet` class given in Program 10.41. Compare the time efficiency of this modified version with the original version when spell-checking a simple document.

10.19   Repeat Exercise 9.17 for the modified spell-checker application from Exercise 10.18.

** **10.20**   Design an algorithm to draw a BST graphically in a `java.awt` window.
   Implement your algorithm in Java, and test it using the example trees shown in this chapter.

11

Map Abstract Data Types

In this chapter we shall study:

- the concept of maps (Section 11.1)
- applications of maps (Section 11.2)
- requirements and contract for a map abstract data type (Section 11.3)
- implementations of maps using arrays, linked lists, and binary search trees (Sections 11.4–7)
- maps in the Java class library (Section 11.8)
- a case study using maps (Section 11.9).

In the next chapter, we shall study another implementation of maps, using hash tables (Section 12.5).

11.1 The concept of a map

A *map* (or *table*) is a collection of entries, whose order is of no significance, and which have distinct keys.

Each *entry* is a tuple, one of whose fields is designated as the *key* field. No two entries in a given map may have equal keys, but there is no such restriction on the other field(s) in a map. In this book, for the sake of simplicity, we shall assume that every entry is a pair, consisting of a key k and a value v. We shall often write such an entry using the notation ⟨k, v⟩.

(Note that there is no loss of generality in assuming that each entry consists of a key and a value: the value may itself be a tuple of fields.)

Here are some examples of maps. They are presented in tabular form, with keys in the left column and values in the right column, and with one row for each entry.

The following is a map of letters to their numerical values in Roman numerals:

$Roman =$

letter	value
I	1
V	5
X	10
L	50
C	100
D	500
M	1000

In each entry of this map, the key is a letter and the value is an integer.

Each of the following is a map from countries to their currencies:

$NAFTA =$

country	currency
CA	dollar
US	dollar
MX	peso

$EC =$

country	currency
DE	mark
FR	franc
IT	lira
NL	guilder
BE	franc
LU	franc

In each entry of these maps, the key is a country and the value is a currency.

These examples show that the values in a given map are not necessarily unique, although the keys are necessarily unique.

The **cardinality** of a map is the number of entries in that map. For example, the cardinality of EC is 6.

An **empty map** has cardinality zero, i.e., it has no entries at all.

The most fundamental operation on a map is to **look up** the value (if any) corresponding to a given key. For example, looking up the value corresponding to FR in EC would give franc; attempting to look up the value corresponding to US in EC would be unsuccessful.

We can **add** a new entry ‹k, v› to a map. For example, adding ‹BM, dollar› to $NAFTA$ would change it to:

$NAFTA' =$

country	currency
CA	dollar
US	dollar
MX	peso
BM	dollar

We can **remove** the entry with key k from a map. For example, removing the entry with key BM from *NAFTA'* would change it back to *NAFTA*, but attempting to remove the entry with key CU from *NAFTA'* would have no effect.

We can **overlay** one map m_1 with another map m_2. If m_1 and m_2 both contain entries with the same key, the entry from m_2 replaces the entry from m_1. Otherwise the resulting map contains all entries from m_1 and m_2. For example, overlaying *EC* with the following map:

country	currency
UK	pound
IE	pound
DK	krone

results in the following map:

$$EC' =$$

country	currency
DE	mark
FR	franc
IT	lira
NL	guilder
BE	franc
LU	franc
UK	pound
IE	pound
DK	krone

11.2 Applications of maps

Maps are used frequently in all application areas of computing.

In relational databases, for example, each relation must have a designated key field, and no two entries in the same relation may have the same key. Relations are in fact maps. In Section 11.9 we shall study a database-type application, a student record system. Here we look at a simpler example of maps.

EXAMPLE 11.1   *Mobile telephone directory*

Suppose that a mobile telephone is equipped with a memory, a keypad, and a display. The memory can be used to store a personalized telephone directory, containing a collection of telephone numbers, each identified by a name. The user can enter a name using the keypad, find the corresponding telephone number from the directory, and finally call that number with a further key-press. (Of course, the user can also enter a telephone number directly.) The directory is initially empty, but the user can add and remove entries using the keypad.

We might also suppose that a top-of-the-range telephone has the additional capability of downloading directory entries from another telephone and adding them to its own directory.

This application can be seen as a simple combination of a map (the directory) with a textual user interface (the keypad and display). In the directory, the keys are names (strings) and the values are telephone numbers (strings of decimal digits).

We will need an object to represent the directory. Let us assume a class `Directory-Map` equipped with the following methods: d.get (n) returns the telephone number corresponding to name n in directory d (or null if there is no such name); d.remove (n) removes the entry with name n from directory d, returning the corresponding telephone number (or null if there was no such name); d.put (n, t) adds an entry ⟨n, t⟩ to directory d; d.putAll (d_2) adds all entries of directory d_2 to directory d, replacing any existing entries with the same names; d.keySet () returns the set of all names used as keys in directory d.

Programs 11.1 and 11.2 outline the application code. The download method overlays the directory with another directory, using the putAll method, but not before it has warned the user if any of the old entries will be lost. To anticipate this eventuality, it first determines the set of names in each directory, using the keySet method, and then tests whether these sets are disjoint, using a method disjoint similar to that of Program 9.3.

11.3 A map abstract data type

Let us now design a map ADT. As usual, we start by identifying requirements. Most of the following requirements were foreshadowed in the previous two sections.

1. It must be possible to make a map empty.
2. It must be possible to test whether a map is empty.
3. It must be possible to test whether a map contains an entry with a given key.
4. It must be possible to look up the value corresponding to a given key in a map.
5. It must be possible to add a new entry to a map or to replace an existing entry.
6. It must be possible to remove an entry from a map, given its key.
7. It must be possible to test whether two maps are equal.
8. It must be possible to compute the overlay of two maps.
9. It must be possible to traverse a map.

Program 11.3 shows a possible contract, expressed as a Java interface named Map. The methods of this interface are sufficient to meet all the above requirements. Note, in particular, that the get method meets both requirements 3 and 4. Also, the keySet

```
public class DirectoryMap {
    // A DirectoryMap object is a map from names to telephone numbers,
    // where a telephone number consists of a string of decimal digits.
    ...   // Code omitted here.
}
```

Program 11.1   Class declaration for the mobile telephone directory application.

```java
public class TelephoneDirectorySystem {

    DirectoryMap directory;

    String name;      // current name (most recently entered by the user)
    String number;    // current number (most recently entered by the
                      // user or looked up in directory)

    public void lookup () {
    // Look up the number corresponding to the current name.
        display.write(name);
        number = directory.get(name);
        if (number != null)
            display.write(" " + number + ".");
        else
            display.write(" NOT FOUND.");
    }

    public void addEntry () {
    // Add an entry consisting of the current name and number.
        display.write(name);
        display.write(number);
        directory.put(name, number);
        display.write(" ADDED.");
    }

    public void removeEntry () {
    // Remove the entry corresponding to the current name.
        display.write(name);
        number = directory.remove(name);
        if (number != null)
            display.write(" REMOVED.");
        else
            display.write(" NOT FOUND.");
    }

    public void download () {
    // Add entries downloaded from another mobile telephone:
        DirectoryMap newEntries = line.download();
        if (! disjoint(directory.keySet(),
                newEntries.keySet())) {
            display.write("SOME ENTRIES WILL BE LOST.");
            display.write("PRESS CANCEL TO AVOID THIS.");
            if (keypad.read() == CANCEL)  return;
        }
        directory.putAll(newEntries);
    }

}
```

Program 11.2 A mobile telephone directory application (outline).

method meets requirement 9: we can call `keySet` to determine the set of keys, then iterate over the set of keys, using each key to look up and visit the corresponding map entry.

```
public interface Map {
```
    // Each Map object is a map in which the keys and values are arbitrary
    // objects.

    ///////////// Accessors /////////////

```
    public boolean isEmpty ();
```
    // Return true if and only if this map is empty.

```
    public int size ();
```
    // Return the cardinality of this map, i.e., the number of entries.

```
    public Object get (Object key);
```
    // Return the value in the entry with key in this map, or null if there is no
    // such entry. (Throw a ClassCastException if this map cannot
    // contain a key with the class of key.)

```
    public boolean equals (Map that);
```
    // Return true if this map is equal to that.

```
    public Set keySet ();
```
    // Return the set of all keys in this map.

    ///////////// Transformers /////////////

```
    public void clear ();
```
    // Make this map empty.

```
    public Object remove (Object key);
```
    // Remove the entry with key (if any) from this map. Return the value
    // in that entry, or null if there was no such entry.

```
    public Object put (Object key, Object val);
```
    // Add the entry ‹key, val› to this map, replacing any existing entry
    // whose key is key. Return the value in that entry, or null if there was no
    // such entry. (Throw a ClassCastException if this map cannot
    // contain a key with the class of key.)

```
    public void putAll (Map that);
```
    // Overlay this map with that, i.e., add all entries of that to this map,
    // replacing any existing entries with the same keys.

```
}
```

Program 11.3   A contract for a map ADT.

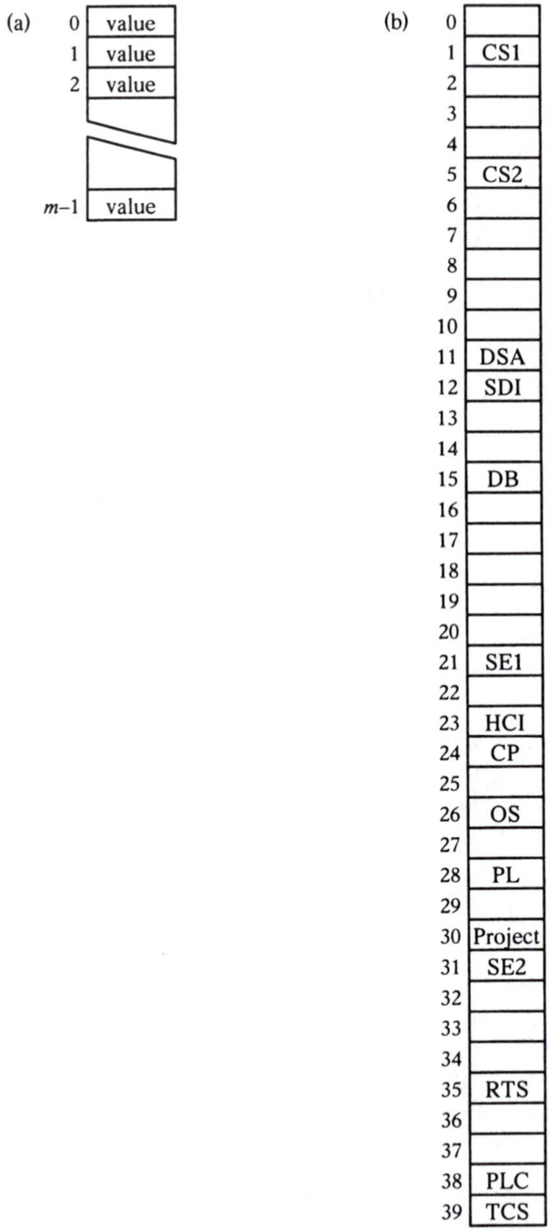

(a)

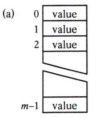

(b)

0	
1	CS1
2	
3	
4	
5	CS2
6	
7	
8	
9	
10	
11	DSA
12	SDI
13	
14	
15	DB
16	
17	
18	
19	
20	
21	SE1
22	
23	HCI
24	CP
25	
26	OS
27	
28	PL
29	
30	Project
31	SE2
32	
33	
34	
35	RTS
36	
37	
38	PLC
39	TCS

code	title
1	CS1
5	CS2
11	DSA
12	SDI
15	DB
21	SE1
23	HCI
24	CP
26	OS
28	PL
30	Project
31	SE2
35	RTS
38	PLC
39	TCS

Figure 11.4 Representation of small-integer-key maps by key-indexed arrays: (a) general case (with keys ranging from 0 through $m - 1$); (b) map from course codes to titles (with $m = 40$).

The `clear`, `remove`, `put`, and `putAll` methods are mutative transformers. Consequently `Map` objects are mutable. In this respect our design of the `Map` ADT is consistent with our design of the `Set` ADT in Program 9.4. An alternative design in which `Map` objects are immutable is also possible, but would be less efficient (see Exercise 11.5).

Our design assumes that both keys and values will be arbitrary objects. However, it is often more efficient if the keys in the map can be ordered, i.e., if they are `Comparable` objects. To allow for this, the `put` and `get` operations accept arbitrary objects as keys, but may throw an exception if the object is not of a suitable class. This restriction, however, still leaves open a large choice of implementations, as we shall see in the next few sections.

11.4 Implementation of small-integer-key maps using key-indexed arrays

In this section we shall assume that the keys are small integers. This assumption is not as restrictive as it might seem. For example, manufacturers assign numeric identifiers to the components they supply, allowing themselves (and their customers) to identify particular components uniquely and reliably. Similarly, banks assign numeric identifiers to their customers; universities assign numeric (or alphanumeric) identifiers to their staff, students, departments, and courses; and so on. Such numeric identifiers are of course chosen to be unique. (In contrast, names are not necessarily unique, and are easily misspelled.)

To be concrete, let us suppose that the keys in a given map are known to be integers in the range 0 through $m - 1$. Then we can represent the map by an array $vals[0 \ldots m - 1]$; $vals[k]$ will contain the value corresponding to key k, or null if there is no such value. This representation is shown in Figure 11.4.

This representation is efficient in both space and time (unless the map happens to be very sparse, i.e., its cardinality is very small compared to m). The `get`, `remove`, and `put` methods are easily implemented with a single array access, and so have time complexity $O(1)$. However, the `equals`, `clear`, and `putAll` methods must iterate over the whole array, and so have time complexity $O(m)$. Table 11.5 summarizes the time complexities of the principal map operations.

Program 11.6 outlines a Java implementation, expressed as a class named `IntKey-`

Table 11.5 Implementation of small-integer-key maps using arrays: summary of algorithms (where keys are in the range 0 through $m - 1$).

Operation	Algorithm	Time complexity
get	inspect one array component	$O(1)$
remove	make one array component null	$O(1)$
put	update one array component	$O(1)$
equals	pairwise comparison	$O(m)$
putAll	update all array components	$O(m)$

```java
public class IntKeyMap {
   // Each IntKeyMap object is a map in which the keys are small integers
   // and the values are arbitrary objects.

   // This map is represented as follows: vals[k] contains the value
   // corresponding to key k, or null if there is no such value.
   private Object[] vals;

   /////////////// Constructor ///////////////

   public IntKeyMap (int m) {
   // Construct a map, initially empty, whose keys will be integers in the
   // range 0 through m-1.
      vals = new Object[m];
   }

   /////////////// Accessors ///////////////

   public Object get (int key) {
   // Return the value in the entry with key in this map, or null if there is no
   // such entry.
      if (key < 0 || key >= vals.length)
        return null;
      return vals[key];
   }

   ...    // Other accessors omitted here – see the companion Web site.

   /////////////// Transformers ///////////////

   public Object put (int key, Object val) {
   // Add the entry ‹key, val› to this map, replacing any existing entry
   // whose key is key. Return the value in that entry, or null if there was no
   // such entry.
      if (key < 0 || key >= vals.length)
        throw new IllegalArgumentException();
      Object oldval = vals[key];
      vals[key] = val;
      return oldval;
   }

   ...    // Other transformers omitted here – see the companion Web site.

}
```

Program 11.6 Java implementation of small-integer-key maps using arrays (outline).

Map. This class does not actually implement the Map interface, since the keys have type **int** rather than Object, but it does adhere to the spirit of that interface.

11.5 Implementation of bounded maps using arrays

A ***bounded map*** is one whose cardinality is bounded. If the map's maximum cardinality is *maxcard*, its actual cardinality *card* ranges from 0 through *maxcard*.

We can represent such a map by storing its entries in an array *entries*, of length *maxcard*. When *card* is less than *maxcard*, only the subarray *entries*[0...*card* − 1] is occupied. Let us choose to store *card* explicitly, and to keep the entries sorted in ascending order of keys. Figure 11.7 illustrates this representation of maps.

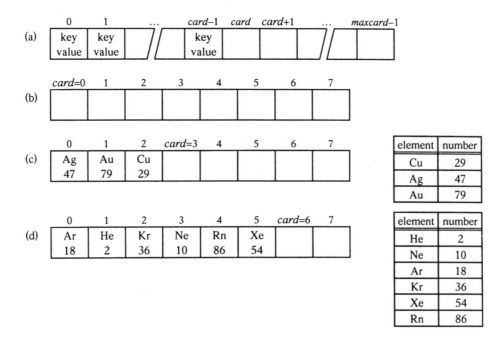

Figure 11.7 Representation of bounded maps by arrays: (a) general case; (b) empty map (with *maxcard* = 8); (c–d) maps from chemical elements to atomic numbers (with *maxcard* = 8).

Table 11.8 Implementation of bounded maps using arrays: summary of algorithms (where n, n_1, and n_2 are the cardinalities of the maps involved).

Operation	Algorithm	Time complexity
get	binary search	$O(\log n)$
remove	binary search plus deletion	$O(n)$
put	binary search plus insertion	$O(n)$
equals	pairwise comparison	$O(n_2)$
putAll	array merge	$O(n_1 + n_2)$

```
public class ArrayMap implements Map {
  // Each ArrayMap object is a bounded map in which the keys are
  // Comparable objects and the values are arbitrary objects.

  // This map is represented as follows: its cardinality is held in card;
  // its entries (sorted by key) occupy the subarray entries[0...card-1].
  private ArrayMap.Entry[] entries;
  private int card;

  /////////////// Constructor ////////////

  public ArrayMap (int maxcard) {
  // Construct a map, initially empty, whose cardinality will be bounded by
  // maxcard.
    entries = new ArrayMap.Entry[maxcard];
    card = 0;
  }

  /////////////// Accessors ////////////

  public Object get (Object key) {
  // Return the value in the entry with key in this map, or null if there is no
  // such entry. (Throw a ClassCastException if this map cannot
  // contain a key with the class of key.)
    int pos = search((Comparable) key);
    if (key.equals(entries[pos].key))
      return entries[pos].value;
    else
      return null;
  }

  ...   // Other accessors omitted here – see the companion Web site.
```

Program 11.9 Java implementation of bounded maps using arrays (outline) *(continued on next page)*.

This representation allows us to implement the map operations as follows:

- The get operation can be implemented using the binary search algorithm, adapted to compare only keys (i.e., ignoring the corresponding values). The use of binary search exploits the fact that the entries are sorted, and makes this operation's time complexity $O(\log n)$, where n is the map's cardinality.
- The put operation should use binary search to locate where the new entry should be inserted. Similarly, the remove operation should use binary search to locate where the old entry should be deleted. Both operations must still shift entries in the array, so they have time complexity $O(n)$ in general. However, the put operation is $O(\log n)$ if the new entry simply replaces an existing entry.

```
//////////// Transformers ////////////
public Object remove (Object key) {
// Remove the entry with key (if any) from this map. Return the value
// in that entry, or null if there was no such entry.
   if (key instanceof Comparable) {
      int pos = search((Comparable) key);
      if (key.equals(entries[pos].key)) {
         Object oldVal = entries[pos].value;
         for (int i = pos+1; i < card; i++)
            entries[i-1] = entries[i];
         entries[card] = null;
         card--;
         return oldVal;
      }
   }
   return null;
}

public Object put (Object key, Object val) {
// Add the entry <key, val> to this map, replacing any existing entry
// whose key is key. Return the value in that entry, or null if there was no
// such entry. (Throw a ClassCastException if this map cannot
// contain a key with the class of key.)
   Comparable compKey = (Comparable) key;
   ArrayMap.Entry newEntry =
         new ArrayMap.Entry(compKey, val);
   int pos = search(compKey);
   if (compKey.equals(entries[pos].key)) {
      Object oldVal = entries[pos].value;
      entries[pos] = newEntry;
      return oldVal;
   } else {
      // No entry matches key. Insert newEntry at position pos ...
      if (card == entries.length)  expand();
      for (int i = card; i > pos; i--)
         entries[i] = entries[i-1];
      entries[pos] = newEntry;
      card++;
      return null;
   }
}
...    // Other transformers omitted here – see the companion Web site.
```

Program 11.9 (*continued on next page*)

```
///////////  Auxiliary methods  ///////////

private void expand () {
// Make entries longer.
    ...   // Code omitted here – see the companion Web site.
}

private int search (Comparable targetKey) {
// Return the index of the leftmost component of entries whose key
// is not less than targetKey.
    ...   // Code omitted here – see the companion Web site.
}

///////////  Inner class for map entries  ///////////

private static class Entry {
    // Each ArrayMap.Entry object is a map entry consisting of a key,
    // which is a Comparable object, and a value, which is an arbitrary
    // object.

    private Comparable key;
    private Object value;

    ...   // Constructor and methods omitted here.

}

}
```

Program 11.9 (*continued*)

- The `equals` operation should first check that the two maps have equal cardinalities. Then it should compare the entries pairwise, terminating if it comes upon unequal entries in corresponding array components.
- The `putAll` operation can use the array merge algorithm, adapted to discard any entry in the first map that has the same key as an entry in the second map.

Table 11.8 summarizes the algorithms and their time complexities.

Program 11.9 outlines a Java implementation of maps, in the form of a class named `ArrayMap` that implements the `Map` interface. The map is represented by an array `entries`, whose components are of type `ArrayMap.Entry`, together with an integer variable `card`. The `get` and `put` methods use an auxiliary method, `search`, which uses the binary search algorithm.

The inner class `ArrayMap.Entry` represents an entry by a `Comparable` object paired with an arbitrary object.

11.6 Implementation of unbounded maps using linked lists

The simplest representation for an unbounded map is a singly-linked list (SLL) in which each node contains a single entry. Let us choose to keep the entries sorted by key (since this speeds up some of the map operations), and to store the map's cardinality explicitly (rather than computing it when required). Figure 11.10 illustrates this representation of maps.

Table 11.11 summarizes the algorithms that would be used in the principal map operations, together with their time complexities.

Program 11.12 outlines a Java implementation. This is a class named `LinkedMap`, which implements the `Map` interface.

The inner class `LinkedMap.Entry` is a modified version of the `SLLNode` class given in Program 4.4. It represents an entry by a `Comparable` object paired with an arbitrary object, and includes the link to the successor of this entry in the SLL.

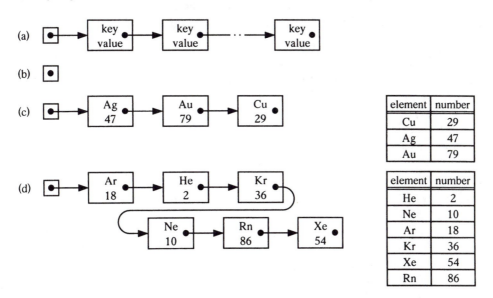

Figure 11.10   Representation of unbounded maps by SLLs: (a) general case; (b) empty map; (c–d) maps from chemical elements to atomic numbers.

Table 11.11   Implementation of unbounded maps using SLLs: summary of algorithms (where n, n_1, and n_2 are the cardinalities of the maps involved).

Operation	Algorithm	Time complexity
get	sorted SLL linear search	$O(n)$
remove	sorted SLL linear search plus deletion	$O(n)$
put	sorted SLL linear search plus insertion	$O(n)$
equals	node-wise comparison	$O(n_2)$
putAll	SLL merge	$O(n_1 + n_2)$

11.7 Implementation of unbounded maps using binary search trees

We saw in Section 10.7 that a binary search tree (BST) makes an excellent representation for a set (provided that the BST is kept well-balanced). Similarly, a BST makes an excellent representation for a map. Figure 11.13 illustrates the BST representation of maps.

A BST representing a map has one entry in each node, and it must satisfy the following property. For every node in the BST, if that node contains the entry ⟨k, v⟩:

```java
public class LinkedMap implements Map {
    // Each LinkedMap object is a map in which the keys are Comparable
    // objects and the values are arbitrary objects.

    // This map is represented as follows: its cardinality is held in card;
    // first is a link to the first node of an SLL containing the entries.
    private LinkedMap.Entry first;
    private int card;

    /////////////// Constructor ///////////////

    public LinkedMap () {
    // Construct a map, initially empty.
        first = null;
        card = 0;
    }

    /////////////// Accessors ///////////////

    public Object get (Object key) {
    // Return the value in the entry with key in this map, or null if there is no
    // such entry. (Throw a ClassCastException if this map cannot
    // contain a key with the class of key.)
        Comparable compKey = (Comparable) key;
        for (LinkedMap.Entry curr = first; curr != null;
            curr = curr.succ) {
          int comp = compKey.compareTo(curr.key);
          if (comp == 0)
            return curr.value;
          else if (comp < 0)
            break;
        }
        return null;
    }
```

Program 11.12 Java implementation of unbounded maps using SLLs (outline) (*continued on next page*).

... // Other accessors omitted here – see the companion Web site.

/////////// Transformers ////////////

```java
public Object put (Object key, Object val) {
// Add the entry ‹key, val› to this map, replacing any existing entry
// whose key is key. Return the value in that entry, or null if there was no
// such entry. (Throw a ClassCastException if this map cannot
// contain a key with the class of key.)
   Comparable compKey = (Comparable) key;
   LinkedMap.Entry prev = null, curr;
   for (curr = first; curr != null;
        curr = curr.succ) {
     int comp = compKey.compareTo(curr.key);
     if (comp == 0) {
       Object oldVal = curr.value;
       curr.value = val;
       return oldVal;
     } else if (comp < 0)
       break;
     prev = curr;
   }
   LinkedMap.Entry ins =
       new LinkedMap.Entry(key, val, curr);
   if (prev == null)
     first = ins;
   else
     prev.succ = ins;
}
```

... // Other transformers omitted here – see the companion Web site.

/////////// Inner class for map entries ////////////

```java
private static class Entry {

   // Each LinkedMap.Entry object is a map entry consisting of a key,
   // which is a Comparable object, a value, which is an arbitrary
   // object, and a link to the successor entry in the SLL.

   private Comparable key;
   private Object value;
   private Entry succ;

   ... // Constructor and methods omitted here.

}

}
```

Program 11.12 (*continued*)

- the node's left subtree contains only entries whose keys are less than *k* (or the subtree is empty);
- the node's right subtree contains only entries whose keys are greater than *k* (or the subtree is empty).

We can use the BST algorithms introduced in Sections 10.2–6 to implement the map operations. In particular:

- The `get`, `put`, and `remove` operations should use the BST search, insertion, and deletion algorithms, respectively, adapted to compare keys only.
- The `putAll` operation should traverse the second BST, inserting each entry into the first BST.
- The `equals` operation should first check that the two maps have equal cardinalities. Then it should traverse one BST, comparing each entry in that BST with the corresponding (same-key) entry in the other BST.

Table 11.14 summarizes these algorithms and their time complexities.

Program 11.15 outlines a Java implementation, in the form of a class named `BSTMap` that implements the `Map` interface.

The inner class `BSTMap.Entry` is a modified version of the `BSTNode` class given in Program 10.7. It represents an entry by a `Comparable` object paired with an arbitrary object, and includes the links to the left and right children of this entry in the BST.

11.8 Maps in the Java class library

The Java class library provides a `java.util.Map` interface, which is shown in Section C.4. This interface is similar to the simple `Map` interface of Program 11.3, except that:

- It allows keys to be arbitrary objects. Methods like `get`, `put`, and `remove` do not throw an exception when their key argument is not a `Comparable` object.
- Its `equals` method accepts an arbitrary object as argument (but the answer is false if that object is not a map).
- It provides a `containsKey` method that tests whether the map contains an entry with a given key (without retrieving the corresponding value). It also provides a `containsValue` method that tests whether the map contains at least one entry with a given value.
- In addition to the `keySet` method, it provides `entrySet` and `values` methods (see below).

The Java class library also provides a `java.util.SortedMap` interface, which requires keys to be `Comparable` objects. The `java.util.SortedMap` interface provides a few useful methods in addition to those of the `java.util.Map` interface. For example, `firstKey` and `lastKey` return the least and greatest keys, respectively, in the map.

Surprisingly, neither of these map interfaces provides an `iterator` method, so it is not possible directly to iterate over the entries of a map. Instead, the `keySet` method returns a *set view* of the map's keys. This set view shares the keys with the underlying map. (It does *not* contain separate copies of the keys.) This implies that adding or removing map entries will immediately change any existing set view of the map's keys. Likewise, the `entrySet` method returns a set view of the map's entries, and the `values` method returns a *collection view* of the map's values (not a set view, since values may be duplicated in a map).

The `java.util.SortedMap` interface is implemented by the `java.util.TreeMap` class. In this class a map is represented by a special form of balanced BST called a *red-black tree*.

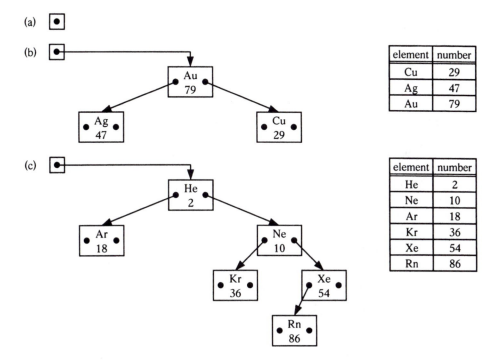

Figure 11.13 Representations of unbounded maps by BSTs: (a) empty map; (b–c) maps from chemical elements to atomic numbers.

Table 11.14 Implementation of unbounded maps using BSTs: summary of algorithms (where n, n_1, and n_2 are the cardinalities of the maps involved).

Operation	Algorithm	Time complexity (well-balanced)	Time complexity (ill-balanced)
get	BST search	$O(\log n)$	$O(n)$
remove	BST deletion	$O(\log n)$	$O(n)$
put	BST insertion	$O(\log n)$	$O(n)$
equals	traversal of one BST combined with searches of the other BST	$O(n_2 \log n_1)$	$O(n_1 n_2)$
putAll	BST merge	$O(n_2 \log(n_1 + n_2))$	$O(n_1 n_2)$

```
public class BSTMap implements Map {
```

// Each BSTMap object is a map in which the keys are Comparable
// objects and the values are arbitrary objects.

// This map is represented as follows: root is a link to the root node of a
// BST containing the entries.
```
private BSTMap.Entry root;
```

/////////// Constructor ///////////

```
public BSTMap () {
```
// Construct a map, initially empty.
```
   root = null;
}
```

/////////// Accessors ///////////

```
public Object get (Object key) {
```
// Return the value in the entry with key in this map, or null if there is no
// such entry. (Throw a ClassCastException if this map cannot
// contain a key with the class of key.)
```
   BSTMap.Entry node = search((Comparable) key);
   if (node != null)
      return node.value;
   else
      return null;
}
```

... // Other accessors omitted here – see the companion Web site.

/////////// Transformers ///////////

```
public Object put (Object key, Object val) {
```
// Add the entry ‹key, val› to this map, replacing any existing entry
// whose key is key. Return the value in that entry, or null if there was no
// such entry. (Throw a ClassCastException if this map cannot
// contain a key with the class of key.)
```
   Comparable compKey = (Comparable) key;
   BSTMap.Entry node = search(compKey);
   if (node == null) {
      insert(compKey, val);
      card++;
      return null;
```

Program 11.15 Java implementation of unbounded maps using BSTs (outline) (*continued on next page*).

```
    } else {
      Object oldValue = node.value;
      node.value = val;
      return oldValue;
    }
  }

  ...   // Other transformers omitted here – see the companion Web site.

  ///////////// Auxiliary methods ////////////

  private BSTMap.Entry search
                  (Comparable targetKey) {
  // Find which if any node of this BST contains an element whose key is
  // equal to targetKey. Return a link to that node (or null if there is
  // none).
      ...   // Code omitted here – see the companion Web site.
  }

  private void insert (Comparable key,
                    Object val) {
  // Insert an entry consisting of key and val into this BST.
      ...   // Code omitted here – see the companion Web site.
  }

  ///////////// Inner class for map entries ////////////

  private static class Entry {

    // Each BSTMap.Entry object is a map entry consisting of a key,
    // which is a Comparable object, a value, which is an arbitrary object,
    // and links to its left and right children.

    private Comparable key;
    private Object value;
    private Entry left, right;

      ...   // Constructor and methods omitted here.

  }

}
```

Program 11.15 (*continued*)

11.9 Case study: a student record system

In this section we shall design a simple student record system. The system is to keep track of the students in a single university department that offers several degree programs. Each degree program consists of a collection of courses. A student is registered for a single degree program, and may be enrolled on a number of different courses. A prototype system is required that can load details about students, degree programs, and courses from text files, and thereafter display a sorted list of the students pertaining to a number of degree programs or courses selected by the user.

We assume that the following data are provided:

- Each student has a student identifier (which is unique), a name, an address – which are strings – and a birth date.
- A degree program has a degree program identifier (which is unique) and a title – which are strings – and the collection of students registered for that degree program.
- A course has a course identifier (which is unique) and a name – which are strings – and the grades obtained by all students enrolled on that course.

The system must keep track of students, degree programs, and courses. Each of these will be a map whose keys are the identifiers of the respective entities, and whose values

```java
public class Student {

    // A Student object contains the details of an individual student.

    // Each student record consists of a student identifier, a name, an address,
    // and a birth date.
    private String studentID, name, address;
    private Date birthDate;

    ///////////// Constructor /////////////

    public Student (String studentID,
                    String name, String address,
                    int birthYear, int birthMonth,
                    int birthDay) {

    // Construct a new student record with the given details.
        this.studentID = studentID;
        this.name = name;
        this.address = address;
        this.birthDate =
            new Date(birthYear, birthMonth, birthDay);
    }

    ///////////// Accessors /////////////

    public String getStudentID () {
    // Return this student's identifier.
        return studentID;
    }
```

Program 11.16   Implementation of students as a Java class Student (*continued on next page*).

```
public String getName () {
// Return this student's name.
   return name;
}

public String sortKey () {
// Return a key suitable for sorting student records alphabetically by
// surname. Treat a Scottish surname prefixed by "Mc" as if it were
// prefixed by "Mac". A key consists of the student's (modified) surname,
// initials, and identifier.
   ... // See code on the companion Web site.
}

/////////// Transformer ///////////

public static Student read
                (BufferedReader input)
                throws Exception {
// Create a new student record using data read from input.
// Return the new student record, or null if there is no record to read.
// Throw an exception if the input data is ill-formed.
   ... // See code on the companion Web site.
}

}
```

Program 11.16 (*continued*)

are objects representing those entities. For example, the students in the system are represented by a map from student identifiers to student objects.

11.9.1 Representing the data

Program 11.16 shows the representation of students using a Java class named `Student`. This class is straightforward. It has instance variables for the required data, along with an appropriate constructor and accessors. It has a single applicative transformer that creates a new object based on data read from a text file. A student's birth date is represented using the `Date` class from Program 5.8.

Program 11.17 shows the representation of degree programs using a Java class named `Degree`. The representation of the degree program identifier and title are straightforward. We must decide, however, how to represent the collection of students registered for a particular degree program. The natural choice is a set of student identifiers. The degree program class contains an appropriate constructor, accessors, and an applicative transformer to create a new object from data read from a text file. It also contains a mutative transformer to add a new student to this degree program.

Program 11.18 shows the implementation of courses using a Java class named

```java
public class Degree {

    // A Degree object contains the details of a degree program.

    // Each degree program record consists of a degree program identifier, a
    // title, and a set of registered students.
    private String degreeID, title;
    private Set studentIDs;

    ///////////// Constructor /////////////

    public Degree (String degreeID, String title) {
    // Construct a new degree program record from the given details.
        this.degreeID = degreeID;
        this.title = title;
        this.studentIDs = new BSTSet();
    }

    ///////////// Accessors /////////////

    public String getDegreeID () {
    // Return this degree program's identifier.
        return degreeID;
    }

    public String getTitle () {
    // Return this degree program's title.
        return title;
    }

    public Set getStudentIDs () {
    // Return the set of identifiers of students registered for this degree
    // program.
        return studentIDs;
    }

    ///////////// Transformers /////////////

    public static Degree read (BufferedReader input)
                    throws Exception {
    // Create a new degree program record using data read from input.
    // Return the new degree program record, or null if there is no record to
    // read. Throw an exception if the input data is ill-formed.
        ...  // See code on the companion Web site.
    }

    public void addStudent(Student student) {
    // Register the given student for this degree program.
        studentIDs.add(student.getStudentID());
    }
}
```

Program 11.17 Implementation of degree programs as a Java class Degree.

Course. The most important decision is how to represent the grades of the students enrolled on this course. We must record a grade for each student, so we choose to use a map `grades`, whose keys are student identifiers and whose values are strings. A grade consists of a letter followed by an optional sign, e.g., ''A'', ''B+'' or ''C−''. We use a special value, NO_GRADE, when a student currently has no grade recorded for this course. The `getStudentIDs` accessor returns the students enrolled on a course, which it finds by taking the set of keys of the `grades` map. The class has two mutative transformers: one to add a new student to the results (initially with no grade), and the other to record a grade for a given student.

11.9.2 Implementing queries on the data

The prototype system requires only two queries to be supported:

- Find all students registered for a selection of degree programs.
- Find all students enrolled on a selection of courses.

Since each degree program and course record contains only a collection of student identifiers, we must combine data from a particular degree program or course record with data from the records of the corresponding students in order to answer the query.

```
public class Course {

    // A Course object contains the details of a particular course.

    // Each course record consists of a course identifier, a name, and a grades
    // map (which maps student identifiers to grades).
    private String courseID, name;
    private Map grades;

    // Constant indicating that no grade has yet been recorded for a student:
    public static final String NO_GRADE = "NO GRADE";

    ///////////// Constructor /////////////

    public Course (String courseID, String name) {
        this.courseID = courseID;
        this.name = name;
        this.grades = new BSTMap();
    }

    ///////////// Accessors /////////////

    public String getCourseID () {
    // Return this course's identifier.
        return courseID;
    }
```

Program 11.18   Implementation of courses as a Java class `Course` (*continued on next page*).

```java
public String getName () {
// Return this course's name.
   return name;
}

public Set getStudentIDs () {
// Return the set of identifiers of students enrolled on this course.
   return grades.keySet();
}

/////////// Transformers ///////////

public void addStudent (Student student) {
// Enroll the given student on this course. Throw an exception if the
// student is already enrolled.
   String studentID = student.getStudentID();
   if (grades.get(studentID) == null)
     grades.put(studentID, NO_GRADE);
   else
     throw new IllegalArgumentException("student "
           + studentID
           + " is already enrolled on course "
           + name);
}

public void recordGrade (Student student,
                 String grade) {
// Record the given grade for the given student taking this course.
// Throw an exception if the student is not enrolled on this course.
   String studentID = student.getStudentID();
   if (grades.get(studentID) != null)
     grades.put(studentID, grade);
   else
     throw new IllegalArgumentException("student "
           + studentID
           + " is not enrolled on course "
           + name);
}

public static Course read (BufferedReader input)
                 throws Exception {
// Create a new course record using data read from input.
// Return the new course record, or null if there is no record to read.
// Throw an exception if the input data is ill-formed.
   ... // See code on the companion Web site.
}
}
```

Program 11.18 (*continued*)

```java
private Map select (Map map, Set keys) {
// Return the map obtained by selecting only those entries from map whose
// keys are in keys.
   Map result = new BSTMap();
   Iterator iter = keys.iterator();
   while (iter.hasNext()) {
      Object key = iter.next();
      Object val = map.get(key);
      if (val != null)
         result.put(key, val);
   }
   return result;
}
```

Program 11.19   Implementation of the select algorithm as a Java method.

In this application, we can combine the data as follows: select the course (or degree program) records from a map of all courses (or degree programs); retrieve the set of student identifiers contained within these course (or degree program) records; and select the students with these student identifiers.

Program 11.19 shows a generic method named `select` that is given a map and a set

```java
public interface StudentCollection {
    public Set getStudentIDs ();
}

/////////////////////////////////////////////////////////

private Set getAllStudents (Map map) {
// Return the set of all student identifiers contained in the given map of
// StudentCollection objects.
   Set result = new BSTSet();
   Iterator iter = map.keySet().iterator();
   while (iter.hasNext()) {
      Object key = iter.next();
      StudentCollection record =
           (StudentCollection) map.get(key);
      result.addAll(record.getStudentIDs());
   }
   return result;
}
```

Program 11.20   Implementation of the Java method `getAllStudents`.

of keys, and returns a map that contains only those entries whose keys are in the set. We can use this method to select course or degree program records, and to select all of the students to be displayed.

To compute the results of a query, we also need a method to retrieve the set of student

```java
public class StudentRecordSystem {

    // This is a prototype student record system.

    // The system contains three maps: students records all of the students
    // by student id; degrees records all of the degree programs by degree
    // program id; courses records all of the courses by course id.
    private Map students, degrees, courses;

    /////////// Constructor ///////////

    public StudentRecordSystem () {
        students = new BSTMap();
        degrees = new BSTMap();
        courses = new BSTMap();
    }

    /////////// File reading methods ///////////

    private static Map readStudents (String filename) {
    // Read student data from the file with the given filename. Return a map of
    //   student records constructed from the data.
        Map students = new BSTMap();
        try {
          BufferedReader input =
              new BufferedReader(
                new InputStreamReader(
                  new FileInputStream(filename)));
          for (;;) {
            Student s = Student.read(input);
            if (s == null)  break;   // end of input
            students.put(s.getStudentID(), s);
          }
        } catch (IOException e) {
            System.out.println(e.getMessage());
        }
        return students;
    }
```

Program 11.21   Implementation of a student records system as a Java application (in outline) (*continued on next page*).

```
private static Map readDegrees (String filename) {
// Read degree program data from the file with the given filename. Return
// a map of degree program records constructed from the data.
    ... // See code on the companion Web site.
}

private static Map readCourses (String filename) {
// Read course data from the file with the given filename. Return a map of
// course records constructed from the data.
    ... // See code on the companion Web site.
}

/////////// Database-like operations ///////////

private Map select (Map map, Set keys) {
// Return the map obtained by selecting only those entries from map whose
// keys are in keys.
    ... // See Program 11.19.
}

private Set getAllStudents (Map map) {
// Return the set of all student identifiers contained in the given map of
// StudentCollection objects.
    ... // See Program 11.20.
}

/////////// Report methods ///////////

public void displayCourses (JTextArea output,
                Set courseIDs) {
// Display on output the identifiers and names of all students enrolled
// on any of the courses whose identifiers are in courseIDs.
    Set students =
        getAllStudents(select(courses, courseIDs));
    Map sorted = selectSortedStudents(students);
    displayMap(output, sorted);
}

public void displayDegrees (JTextArea output,
                Set degreeIDs) {
// Display on output the identifiers and names of all students registered
// for any of the degree programs whose identifiers are in degreeIDs.
    ... // See code on the companion Web site.
}
```

Program 11.21 (*continued on next page*)

identifiers contained in a map of course or degree program records. Note that each of the `Course` and `Degree` classes contains a method named `getStudentIDs` that returns the set of student identifiers contained in a given course or degree program record. The answer to the query is just the union of these sets for all the selected courses or degree programs.

Program 11.20 shows a Java method named `getAllStudents` that returns the set of student identifiers contained in a given map of course or degree program records. It

```java
private Map selectSortedStudents (Set ids) {
// Return a map containing all of the students with identifiers in the set
// ids, but using their sort-keys as keys.
   Map result = new BSTMap();
   Iterator iter = ids.iterator();
   while (iter.hasNext()) {
      String id = (String) iter.next();
      Student s = (Student) students.get(id);
      result.put(s.sortKey(), s);
   }
   return result;
}

private void displayMap (JTextArea output,
                Map map) {
// Display in output the identifiers and names of all students in map.
   Iterator iter = map.keySet().iterator();
   output.setText("");
   while (iter.hasNext()) {
      String key = (String) iter.next();
      Student s = (Student) map.get(key);
      output.append(s.getStudentID() + " " +
          s.getName() + "\n");
   }
}

public static void main (String[] args) {
   StudentRecordSystem system =
       new StudentRecordSystem();
   system.students = readStudents("students.txt");
   system.degrees = readDegrees("degrees.txt");
   system.courses  = readCourses("courses.txt");
   ...   // Create a graphical user interface and display it.
}

}
```

Program 11.21 (*continued*)

uses a Java interface named `StudentCollection` to represent objects equipped with a `getStudentIDs` method (such as course and degree program records). By making the `Course` and `Degree` classes implement this interface, we can make the `getAllStudents` method work for maps of both course and degree program records.

11.9.3 A simple student record system

Program 11.21 outlines an implementation of a simple student record system as a Java class named `StudentRecordSystem`. It satisfies the requirements given in Section 11.9.1.

Three maps are used to store the data: `students`, `degrees`, and `courses`. These maps are initialized, using data read from text files, by the methods `readStudents`, `readDegrees`, and `readCourses`, respectively.

The graphical user interface for this application (not shown) allows the user to select one or more courses (or degree programs), and have the set of students taking these courses (or degree programs) displayed in a text area. The user interface interacts with the record system by invoking the method `displayCourses` or `displayDegrees` as appropriate.

To display a *sorted* set of students we use an auxiliary method named `select-SortedStudents`. This is similar to the `select` method from Program 11.19, but the key for each student is a special sort key, rather than the student identifier. This key consists of the student's surname, initials and student identifier. If we iterate through these keys in ascending order, we will select students sorted by surname. The selected students are displayed using the method `displayMap`, which assumes that the set of keys for this map can be iterated in ascending order using the `ascendingIterator` of the `BSTSet` class from Program 10.41.

At first sight this application may seem rather inefficient, since it creates new maps of student, course, and degree program records all the time. However, these maps contain only *references* to the records, so only a single copy of each student, degree program, or course record is created. Likewise, the keys in each map might seem at first sight to be duplicated in the entries. For example, a `Student` object contains a student identifier, but this is also the key in the `students` map. However, the key and the field in the student record are actually *references* to the same (string) object, so no duplication of data actually takes place.

Summary

In this chapter:

- We have studied the concept of a map, a collection of entries in which each entry has a unique key and a value.
- We have seen an example and a case study demonstrating practical applications of maps.
- We have designed an ADT for maps, expressed as a `Map` interface.

- We have studied how to represent maps by sorted arrays, by sorted SLLs, and by BSTs, and how to implement them in Java as classes that implement the `Map` interface. We have also studied how to represent a useful special case: maps with small-integer keys.

Exercises

11.1   Can you think of any examples of maps (or tables) in everyday life?

11.2   Consider the array representation of bounded maps explained in Section 11.5.
   (a) Draw diagrams showing how the example maps *Roman*, *NAFTA*, and *EC* shown in Section 11.1 would be represented by arrays, assuming that *maxcard* = 10.
   (b) Figure 12.3 shows two maps of chemical elements to atomic numbers. Draw diagrams showing how these maps would be represented by arrays, assuming that *maxcard* = 12.

11.3   Repeat Exercise 11.2 using the linked-list representation of unbounded maps explained in Section 11.6.

11.4   Repeat Exercise 11.2 using the BST representation of unbounded maps explained in Section 11.7.

11.5   In the `Map` interface of Program 11.3, suppose that the mutative transformers `remove`, `put`, and `putAll` operations are to be replaced by applicative transformers, each of which is to return a new map (rather than overwriting the maps to which the operation is applied).
   (a) Modify the `Map` interface accordingly.
   (b) Modify the array implementation of Program 11.9 accordingly.
   (c) Modify the linked-list implementation of Program 11.12 accordingly.
   (d) Modify the BST implementation of Program 11.15 accordingly.

11.6   Complete the implementation of the Java class `IntKeyMap` given in Program 11.6.
   Test the class by constructing the map from course codes to titles shown in Figure 11.4(b).

11.7   In the array representation of bounded maps shown in Program 11.9, suppose that the keys are to be arbitrary objects and are to be left unsorted.
   (a) Modify the Java implementation accordingly.
   (b) Summarize your algorithms and their complexities, in the same manner as Table 11.8. Comment on your results.

11.8   Modify the array representation of bounded maps outlined in Program 11.9, such that the cardinality is not stored explicitly. What are the consequences?

11.9   Repeat Exercise 11.7 using the linked-list representation of unbounded maps shown in Program 11.12.

11.10 Suggest a suitable representation for a map of font names (i.e., strings) to fonts. Assume that font values are of type `java.awt.Font`.
   If a font is identified by a font name, a size, and a style (e.g., 'Times', 12, 'bold'), suggest two possible representations that would allow a font to be selected on the basis of

this information. (*Hint:* Consider either a single map with a special class of keys, or a *nested map*, where the values stored in the entries of one map are themselves maps.)

11.11 The implementation of the interface java.util.Set given by the Java class java.util.TreeSet uses a map to represent a set.
(a) How would the set operations be implemented in terms of the map operations in the interface java.util.Map?
(b) What are the advantages and disadvantages of this decision?

* **11.12** Consider the List interface given in Program 8.2.
(a) Design an implementation of the List interface using only the operations of the Map interface. What is the time complexity of each of the list operations?
(b) Implement your answer to part (a) as a Java class.

11.13 Suppose that the following operations were added to the Map interface of Program 11.3. The operation m.containsKey(k) returns true if and only if map m contains an entry with key k, and the operation m.containsValue(v) returns true if and only if map m contains an entry with value v. (See the java.util.Map interface for a detailed description of these operations).
(a) Modify the ArrayMap class of Program 11.9 to implement these operations.
(b) Modify the LinkedMap class of Program 11.12 to implement these operations.
(c) Modify the BSTMap class of Program 11.15 to implement these operations.

11.14 Consider the following operation: m.subMap(k1, k2) returns a new map that contains all of the entries in map m whose keys are not less than k1 and not greater than k2.
(a) Modify the ArrayMap class of Program 11.9 to implement this operation.
(b) Modify the LinkedMap class of Program 11.12 to implement this operation.
(c) Modify the BSTMap class of Program 11.15 to implement this operation.

11.15 A *multimap* is similar to a map, except there may be several entries with the same key.
(a) How would you represent a multimap without storing multiple copies of the same key?
(b) Implement a multimap ADT using a sorted array implementation similar to Program 11.9.
(c) Implement a multimap ADT using a sorted SLL implementation similar to Program 11.12.
(d) Implement a multimap ADT using a BST implementation similar to Program 11.15.

* **11.16** Design an algorithm that takes an input text file and generates a report listing, in lexicographic order, all words that appear in the file. Each word must be followed by the line numbers where it appears in the file.
For example, given the input file:

```
To be, or not to be,
That is the question.
Whether it is nobler
To die, or to live
And bear the slings and arrows
Of outrageous misfortune.
```

The first few lines of the output should be:

```
and: 5
arrows: 5
be: 1
bear: 5
die: 4
is: 2, 3
it: 3
...
```

Implement your algorithm as a Java program.

* **11.17** Extend your program from Exercise 11.16 to implement a simple file indexer. The output should contain only those words given in a separate set of index words (rather than all words in the file).

Consider two ways of solving this problem. Which way is more efficient?

12

Hash-Table Data Structures

In this chapter we shall study:

- the principles of hash tables (Section 12.1)
- closed-bucket hash tables, their searching, insertion, and deletion algorithms, and their design issues (Sections 12.2)
- open-bucket hash tables, their searching, insertion, and deletion algorithms, and their design issues (Sections 12.3)
- implementations of sets and maps by hash tables (Sections 12.4–5).

12.1 Hash tables

In Section 11.4 we saw that a map whose keys are small integers can be represented efficiently by an array indexed by keys. With this representation the critical searching, insertion, and deletion algorithms all have the ideal time complexity $O(1)$.

Of course, a map with small-integer keys is a special case. More generally, we need representations that will work with keys of any type. The best general representation that we have encountered so far is the binary search tree (BST). With a BST representation the critical searching, insertion, and deletion algorithms all have time complexity $O(\log n)$, but that performance deteriorates to $O(n)$ if the BST is ill-balanced.

Surprisingly, we can approach the ideal $O(1)$ time complexity without unduly restricting the type of the keys. The basic idea is *hashing*: translate each key to a small integer, and use that integer to index an array.

A *hash table* is an array of *buckets*, together with a *hash function* that translates keys to bucket indices. This is illustrated in Figure 12.1. Given a hash function *hash*, insertion, search, and deletion work as follows:

- To insert a new entry with key k in the hash table, assign that entry to a particular bucket by computing its index $hash(k)$. That bucket is called the entry's *home bucket*.

- To search for (or delete) the entry with key k in the hash table, determine its home bucket by computing $hash(k)$, and search there.

The searching, insertion, and deletion algorithms cooperate smoothly, provided that the hash function *hash* is *consistent*, i.e., if $k_1 = k_2$ then $hash(k_1) = hash(k_2)$.

Ideally, the hash function would be a one-to-one function, assigning every key to a different home bucket. In general, this is not possible. In many applications, the number of possible keys far exceeds the number of buckets. So we must be content with a many-to-one function. The hash table can therefore contain entries with different keys but with the same home bucket: $k_1 \neq k_2$ but $hash(k_1) = hash(k_2)$. This situation is called a **collision**. For reasons that will become clear, we should try to choose a hash function that minimizes the probability of collisions.

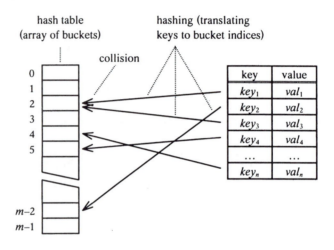

Figure 12.1   Hash table concepts.

EXAMPLE 12.1   *A naive hash function for words*

Suppose that the keys are words or, more generally, alphabetic strings. A particularly simple hash function is one that translates each word to its initial letter's alphabetic position. This gives us a hash table with 26 buckets.

The effect of this hash function is that all words with initial letter 'A' are assigned to bucket 0, all words with initial letter 'B' to bucket 1, and so on. Collisions occur when two or more words with the same initial letter occur as keys in the same hash table.

The initial-letter hash function is easy to understand, and we will often use it for illustration in this chapter. However, it is too naive to be used in real applications, since it tends to give rise to many collisions.

(*Note:* We are using the representation of maps to motivate hash tables. But hash tables can also be used to represent sets, in analogous fashion: for *map* you may read *set*, and for *key* or *entry* you may read *member*.)

In this chapter we shall study two different kinds of hash tables:

- *Closed-bucket hash tables:* Each bucket may be occupied by several entries; the buckets are completely separate from one another.
- *Open-bucket hash tables:* Each bucket may be occupied by at most one entry; collisions are resolved by displacing colliding entries to other buckets.

12.1.1 Hashing in Java

Java directly supports hashing. Every object is equipped with the following instance method:

```
public int hashCode ();
// Translate this object to an integer such that x.equals(y) implies
// x.hashCode () = y.hashCode ().
```

Note that a hashCode method must be consistent. Its result is not necessarily a small integer, however. In order to translate a key k to a bucket index b, for a hash table with m buckets, we take the method's result modulo m:

```
int b = Math.abs(k.hashCode()) % m;   // 0≤b<m
```

(Inconveniently, hashCode can return any integer – negative, zero, or positive. Math.abs is used here to ensure that the left operand of % is nonnegative, and thus ensure that the result of % is nonnegative.)

The hashCode method is defined in the ancestor Object class, but may be overridden by any subclass. Table 12.2 summarizes the hashCode methods of some Java library classes.

12.2 Closed-bucket hash tables

In a *closed-bucket hash table* (or *CBHT*) the buckets are completely separate from one another. Every entry occupies its home bucket.

In the presence of collisions, a bucket will be occupied by several entries, whose keys are different but are translated by the hash function to the same bucket index. The simplest way to deal with this situation is to organize all the entries in a bucket into a singly-linked list (SLL). The CBHT is then an array of such SLLs.

Table 12.2 Behavior of hashCode methods of selected Java library classes.

Class of x	Result of x.hashCode()
Date	(ms / 2^{32}) exclusive-or (ms modulo 2^{32}), where ms = x expressed in milliseconds since 1970-01-01
Integer	integer value of x
List	weighted sum of hash-codes of elements of list x
Set	sum of hash-codes of members of set x
String	weighted sum of characters of x

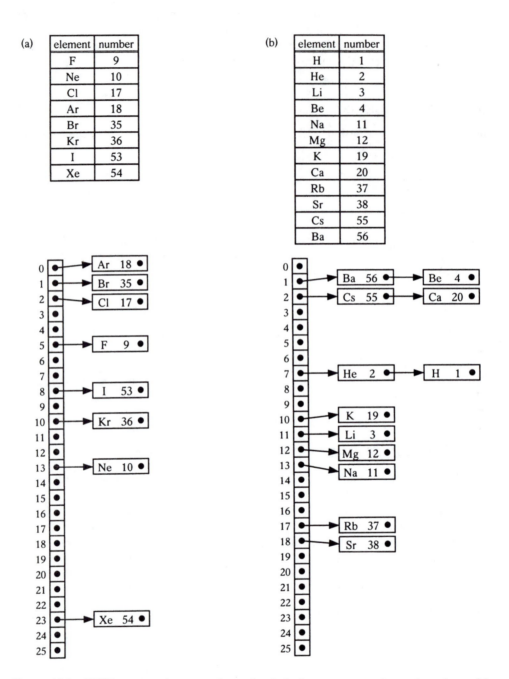

Figure 12.3 CBHTs representing maps from chemical elements to atomic numbers ($m = 26$; $hash(elem) = elem$'s initial letter $-$ 'A').

Figure 12.3 shows two examples of CBHTs, representing maps whose keys are chemical elements. The hash function translates each chemical element to its initial letter's alphabetical position. In Figure 12.3 no bucket is occupied by more than two entries. In general, however, the number of entries per bucket is unbounded.

A CBHT may be seen as partitioning its entries into buckets according to the results of hashing their keys. Each bucket is occupied by a subset of the entries. If we assume that each bucket is occupied by only a small number of entries, we can efficiently search, insert, and delete in any bucket even when the latter is a simple data structure such as an unsorted SLL.

In Java, we can represent a CBHT by an object of the class CBHT, shown in Program 12.4. This class has one instance variable, `buckets`, an array of links to bucket nodes.

```java
public class CBHT {

    // An object of class CBHT is a closed-bucket hash table, in which each
    // entry consists of a key and a value.

    private BucketNode[] buckets;

    public CBHT (int m) {
    // Construct an empty CBHT with m buckets.
        buckets = new BucketNode[m];
    }

    ...   // CBHT methods (see below)

    private int hash (Object key) {
    // Translate key to an index of the array buckets, such that
    // x.equals(y) implies hash(x) = hash(y).
        return Math.abs(key.hashCode()) % buckets.length;
    }

    ///////////// Inner class for CBHT nodes ////////////

    private static class BucketNode {

        private Object key, value;
        private BucketNode succ;

        private BucketNode (Object key, Object val) {
            this.key = key;  this.value = val;
            this.succ = null;
        }

    }

}
```

Program 12.4 Java class representing CBHTs.

The CBHT class is also equipped with a private `hash` method. Finally, the objects of the inner class `CBHT.BucketNode` are bucket nodes, which are singly-linked.

12.2.1 Searching

Searching a CBHT is simple, as shown in Algorithm 12.5. Step 1 hashes the target key; this tells us immediately which bucket is (potentially) occupied by an entry with that key. Step 2 searches that bucket's SLL to find which node (if any) contains that entry; this step is similar to Algorithm 4.23.

Program 12.6 shows how the CBHT search algorithm could be implemented as a Java method. Note that this method does not assume that the SLLs in the hash table are sorted. Since we hope that all these SLLs will be short, it is not worthwhile to keep them sorted.

To find which if any node of a CBHT contains an entry whose key is equal to *target-key*:

1. Set *b* to *hash(target-key)*.
2. Find which if any node of the SLL of bucket *b* contains an entry whose key is equal to *target-key*, and terminate with that node as answer.

Algorithm 12.5 CBHT search algorithm.

```
public BucketNode search (Object targetKey) {
// Find which if any node of this CBHT contains an entry whose key is equal
// to targetKey. Return a link to that node (or null if there is none).
   int b = hash(targetKey);
   for (BucketNode curr = buckets[b]; curr != null;
      curr = curr.succ) {
     if (targetKey.equals(curr.key))
       return curr;
   }
   return null;
}
```

Program 12.6 Implementation of the CBHT search algorithm as a Java method (in class CBHT).

12.2.2 Insertion

Insertion in a CBHT is also simple, as shown in Algorithm 12.7. Step 1 hashes the new entry's key, to determine which bucket the new entry will occupy. Step 2 inserts the new entry into that bucket's SLL. If the new entry has the same key as an existing entry, the new entry must *replace* the existing entry. Otherwise the new entry must be stored in a newly-constructed node of the SLL.

To insert the entry ‹*key*, *val*› into a CBHT:

1. Set *b* to *hash*(*key*).
2. Insert the entry ‹*key*, *val*› into the SLL of bucket *b*, replacing any existing entry with *key*.
3. Terminate.

Algorithm 12.7   CBHT insertion algorithm.

```
public void insert (Object key, Object val) {
// Insert the entry ‹key, val› into this CBHT.
    int b = hash(key);
    for (BucketNode curr = buckets[b]; curr != null;
        curr = curr.succ) {
      if (key.equals(curr.key)) {
        // Make val replace the existing value:
        curr.value = val;
        return;
      }
    }
    // Insert the new entry at the front of bucket b's linked list:
    buckets[b] = new BucketNode(key, val, buckets[b]);
}
```

Program 12.8   Implementation of the CBHT insertion algorithm as a Java method (in class CBHT).

Program 12.8 shows how the CBHT insertion algorithm could be implemented as a Java method, insert. This method inserts the new node at the front of the appropriate bucket's SLL, making no attempt to keep the SLL sorted. This is consistent with the search method of Program 12.6, which also does not assume that the SLL is sorted.

12.2.3 Deletion

Deletion in a CBHT is shown in Algorithm 12.9. Step 1 hashes the given key, to determine which bucket is (potentially) occupied by the entry with that key. Step 2 deletes that entry from that bucket's SLL. If no such entry is found, nothing more is done.

To delete the entry (if any) whose key is equal to *key* from a CBHT:

1. Set *b* to *hash*(*key*).
2. Delete the entry (if any) whose key is equal to *key* from the SLL of bucket *b*.
3. Terminate.

Algorithm 12.9   CBHT deletion algorithm.

```java
public void delete (Object key) {
// Delete the entry (if any) whose key is equal to key from this CBHT.
   int b = hash(key);
   for (BucketNode pred = null, curr = buckets[b];
        curr != null;
        pred = curr, curr = curr.succ) {
     if (key.equals(curr.key)) {
       if (pred == null)
          buckets[b] = curr.succ;
       else
          pred.succ = curr.succ;
       return;
     }
   }
}
```

Program 12.10   Implementation of the CBHT deletion algorithm as a Java method (in class CBHT).

Program 12.10 shows how the CBHT deletion algorithm could be implemented as a Java method, `delete`.

12.2.4 Analysis

Let us analyze the time complexity of the CBHT search algorithm. Let n be the number of entries. We shall assume that the hash function takes a constant amount of time, small enough to neglect. We shall count only comparisons as characteristic operations.

In Algorithm 12.5, step 2 is a linear search of the home bucket's SLL. So the average number of comparisons is the number of entries in the home bucket if the search is unsuccessful, or about half that number if the search is successful.

The *best-case* assumption is that no bucket is occupied by more than (say) two entries, therefore:

Maximum no. of comparisons $= 2$

In this case the search algorithm's time complexity is the ideal $O(1)$. (See also Exercise 12.4(a).)

The *worst-case* assumption is that all n entries are in the same bucket, therefore:

Maximum no. of comparisons $= n$

In fact, the CBHT has degenerated to a single linked list. In this case the search algorithm's time complexity is $O(n)$. (See also Exercise 12.4(b).)

The analyses for the CBHT insertion and deletion algorithms are identical: best case $O(1)$, worst case $O(n)$.

The best-case assumption might seem unrealistic, but we can justify this assumption provided that we design the CBHT with care. Thus we can actually approach the ideal $O(1)$ time complexity for searching, insertion, and deletion.

12.2.5 Design

The design of a CBHT entails deciding the number of buckets m and the hash function *hash*. Before making these design decisions, we should study the characteristics of the data likely to be stored in the CBHT.

We have seen that CBHT searching, insertion, and deletion algorithms have $O(1)$ time complexity in the best case, but $O(n)$ time complexity in the worst case. The worst case arises when there are many collisions, so our fundamental aim is to minimize the probability of collisions. We should try to ensure that the entries are distributed evenly over the buckets, with few or no buckets occupied by more than (say) two entries.

Choice of number of buckets

We define the ***load factor*** of a hash table to be n/m, where n is the current number of entries and m is the number of buckets. For example, the hash tables of Figure 12.3 have load factors of 0.31 (8/26) and 0.46 (12/26), respectively. Note that the load factor does not depend on the choice of hash function.

As a rule of thumb, we should choose the number of buckets m such that the load factor is likely to be not less than 0.5 and not more than 0.75. If the load factor is too high, many buckets are likely to have more than two entries; if the load factor is too low, the CBHT will be unreasonably space-consuming.

Since the hash function typically performs modulo-m arithmetic, it is a good idea to make m a prime number, for the following reason. Suppose that the keys are integers and the hash function is simply $hash(k) = k$ modulo m. If, for example, m is a multiple of ten, and it turns out that most of the keys are also multiples of ten, then most of the entries will be assigned to only one-tenth of the buckets! This is an example of a pattern in the keys, which we should try to avoid replicating in the distribution of entries among buckets. If we choose m to be a large prime number, it is more likely that the entries will be distributed evenly over the buckets, regardless of any pattern in the keys.

Choice of hash function

The hash function should be efficient, performing only a small number of arithmetic operations.

Even more important, the hash function should distribute the entries evenly over the buckets. An even distribution, together with a sufficiently low load factor, is the only way to minimize the probability of collisions. Uneven distribution leads to many collisions and $O(n)$ time complexity.

There is often a tradeoff between efficiency and even distribution. If we speed up the hash function by making it use only part of the key, we must take care to use a part of the key that is distributed evenly. (See Examples 12.2 and 12.4, and Exercise 12.5.)

EXAMPLE 12.2   *Design of a hash table for an English vocabulary*

Consider a vocabulary to be used by a spell-checker, as in Section 9.8. Such a vocabulary is just a set of words. We will assume a small vocabulary consisting of about a thousand of the most common words in English.

If the vocabulary is to be represented by a hash table, we must choose a hash function over words. We could make the hash function depend on any or all of the word's letters. We could also make it depend on the word's length.

A hash function that simply returned the word's length would be a poor choice. This hash function would give us only about 20 buckets – far too few. (The corresponding load factor would be 50 = 1000/20, very much greater than 0.75!) Moreover, the distribution would be very uneven: English has many common words with 3–10 letters, but very few with more than 12 letters.

A hash function that simply selected the word's initial letter would also be a poor choice. This hash function would give us 26 buckets – far too few. Again, the distribution would be very uneven: some letters (such as X and Z) occur very infrequently as initial letters of English words.

A hash function that combined the length and initial letter, such as:

$$hash(word) = 26 \times (\text{length of } word - 1) + (\text{initial letter of } word - \text{`A'})$$

would still be unsatisfactory. Few words would be hashed to buckets 0–51 (since few words have length 1 or 2). Few words would be hashed to buckets 25, 51, 77, 103, and so on (since few words have initial letter Z).

A better idea is to compute a weighted sum of the word's letters modulo m (the number of buckets):

$$hash(word) = (c_1 \times \text{1st letter of } word + c_2 \times \text{2nd letter of } word + \cdots) \text{ modulo } m$$

Commonly we choose $c_i = i$, i.e.:

$$hash(word) = (\text{1st letter of } word + 2 \times \text{2nd letter of } word + \cdots) \text{ modulo } m$$

We can then choose m to be a prime number such as 1499. This will give us a load factor of 0.67 if the vocabulary consists of 1000 words.

12.3 Open-bucket hash tables

We have seen that, in an CBHT where buckets are completely separated from one another, we often get multiple entries in each bucket. By way of contrast, in an **open-bucket hash table** (or **OBHT**) each bucket is occupied by *at most one* entry. This works very well as long as no collision occurs. But what if a collision does occur? If a new entry's home bucket is already occupied by another entry, we must displace the new entry into another (unoccupied) bucket. This idea might seem paradoxical, but it works correctly provided that the searching, insertion, and deletion algorithms all agree where displaced entries will be located.

EXAMPLE 12.3 *Populating an OBHT*

Figure 12.11 shows two OBHTs, populated with entries whose keys are chemical

(a)

element	number
F	9
Ne	10
Cl	17
Ar	18
Br	35
Kr	36
I	53
Xe	54

(b)

element	number
H	1
He	2
Li	3
Be	4
Na	11
Mg	12
K	19
Ca	20
Rb	37
Sr	38
Cs	55
Ba	56

0	Ar	18
1	Br	35
2	Cl	17
3		
4		
5	F	9
6		
7		
8	I	53
9		
10	Kr	36
11		
12		
13	Ne	10
14		
15		
16		
17		
18		
19		
20		
21		
22		
23	Xe	54
24		
25		

0		
1	Be	4
2	Ca	20
3	Cs	55
4	Ba	56
5		
6		
7	H	1
8	He	2
9		
10	K	19
11	Li	3
12	Mg	12
13	Na	11
14		
15		
16		
17	Rb	37
18	Sr	38
19		
20		
21		
22		
23		
24		
25		

Figure 12.11 OBHTs representing maps from chemical elements to atomic numbers ($m = 26$; $hash(elem) = elem$'s initial letter $-$ 'A'; $step = 1$).

elements. The hash function translates each chemical element to its initial letter's alphabetical position.

Figure 12.11(a) illustrates the effect of populating an OBHT with a set of entries in which, fortuitously, all the entries have different home buckets; there are no collisions.

Figure 12.11(b) illustrates the effects of collisions. Assume that, on a collision, we displace the new entry into the *next* unoccupied bucket. If we insert the following entries into the OBHT in the order shown, the effects are as follows:

‹H, 1›	*hash*(H) = 7, so this entry occupies bucket 7.
‹He, 2›	*hash*(He) = 7, but bucket 7 is already occupied, so this entry occupies bucket 8.
‹Li, 3›	*hash*(Li) = 11, so this entry occupies bucket 11.
‹Be, 4›	*hash*(Be) = 1, so this entry occupies bucket 1.
‹Na, 11›	*hash*(Na) = 13, so this entry occupies bucket 13.
‹Mg, 12›	*hash*(Mg) = 12, so this entry occupies bucket 12.
‹K, 19›	*hash*(K) = 10, so this entry occupies bucket 10.
‹Ca, 20›	*hash*(Ca) = 2, so this entry occupies bucket 2.
‹Rb, 37›	*hash*(Rb) = 17, so this entry occupies bucket 17.
‹Sr, 38›	*hash*(Sr) = 18, so this entry occupies bucket 18.
‹Cs, 55›	*hash*(Cs) = 2, but bucket 2 is already occupied, so this entry occupies bucket 3.
‹Ba, 56›	*hash*(Ba) = 1, but buckets 1–3 are already occupied, so this entry occupies bucket 4.

Summarizing, we were able to make most of these entries occupy their home buckets. However, we were forced to displace ‹He, 2› from bucket 7 to bucket 8, and later ‹Cs, 55› from bucket 2 to bucket 3, because their home buckets were already occupied. Even more drastically, we were forced to displace ‹Ba, 56› from bucket 1 to bucket 4, because not only bucket 1 but also the following buckets 2 and 3 were already occupied.

In general, if we cannot make an entry occupy its home bucket because the latter is already occupied, we displace it to the next unoccupied bucket. For this purpose we treat the bucket array as cyclic: if we find that the last bucket is occupied, we go on to test whether bucket 0 is occupied.

So far we have pretended that each bucket is either occupied or unoccupied. In fact, each bucket in an OBHT has three possible states:

- *never-occupied*
- *occupied* (by an entry)
- *formerly-occupied* (by an entry that has since been deleted, and not yet replaced).

We shall explain the need for the *formerly-occupied* state in Section 12.3.3. For the time being, you should ignore all references to formerly-occupied buckets in the searching and insertion algorithms of Sections 12.3.1–2.

Study Figure 12.11 carefully: it shows a pattern that is typical of an OBHT. The entries form several **clusters**, i.e., sequences of consecutive occupied buckets. The cluster comprising buckets 10–13 is coincidental: it just so happens that four of the entries have consecutive home buckets. The cluster comprising buckets 1–4 is not coincidental: it is a by-product of the way that collisions are resolved in an OBHT. Once a cluster has formed, displacing an entry into the *next* unoccupied bucket makes the cluster longer. As more entries are inserted, clusters tend to coalesce, as illustrated in Figure 12.17. Thus clusters tend to get longer very quickly.

In Java, we can represent an OBHT by an object of the class OBHT, shown in Program 12.12. The instance variable buckets is an array of entries, some of which may be null (representing never-occupied buckets).

```java
public class OBHT {

    // An object of class OBHT is an open-bucket hash table, containing entries
    // of class BucketEntry.

    private BucketEntry[] buckets;
    // buckets[b] is null if bucket b has never been occupied.
    // buckets[b] is BucketEntry.FORMER if bucket b is formerly-
    // occupied by an entry that has since been deleted (and not yet replaced).

    public static final int
        NONE = -1;   // ... distinct from any bucket index.

    public OBHT (int m) {
    // Construct an empty OBHT with m buckets.
        buckets = new BucketEntry[m];
    }

    ...   // OBHT methods (see below)

    private int hash (Object key) {
    // Translate key to an index of the array buckets, such that
    // x.equals(y) implies hash(x) = hash(y).
        return Math.abs(key.hashCode()) % buckets.length;
    }

    ///////////// Inner class for OBHT entries /////////////

    private static class BucketEntry {

        private Object key, value;

        private BucketEntry (Object key, Object val) {
            this.key = key;   this.value = val;
        }

        private static final BucketEntry FORMER =
            new BucketEntry(null, null);

    }

}
```

Program 12.12   Java class representing OBHTs.

12.3.1 Searching

Now that we understand how an OHBT is populated, and in particular how collisions are resolved, we are in a position to formulate an algorithm to search an OHBT for a given key, *target-key*. This is shown as Algorithm 12.13.

Step 1 translates *target-key* to a bucket number, b. What follows depends on the state of bucket b. If bucket b is never-occupied (step 2.1), the search is unsuccessful. If bucket b is occupied by an entry whose key matches *target-key* (step 2.2), the search is successful. If bucket b is occupied by an entry whose key does not match *target-key* (step 2.3), the search continues, since the entry we are seeking might have been displaced into another bucket. So we increment b (modulo the number of buckets, m, since the bucket array is cyclic) and repeat step 2.

Figure 12.14 illustrates several searches in the same OBHT, showing the search path in each case. (In an OBHT, a **search path** is the sequence of buckets visited during a search.) Search (a) computes $hash(\text{Mg}) = 12$, and finds a matching key immediately in bucket 12. Search (b) computes $hash(\text{He}) = 7$, finds a non-matching key in bucket 7, and then finds a matching key in bucket 8; in other words, the search path is 7–8. Search (c) is similar, but has a longer search path: 1–2–3–4. In search (d), the search path 17–18–19 reaches the unoccupied bucket 19; there would be no point in searching further, so this search is unsuccessful.

We must be very careful to ensure that the OBHT search algorithm terminates. In the case of an unsuccessful search, the loop at step 2 repeats itself until it finds a never-occupied bucket. If there are no such buckets, the search algorithm will never terminate. The OBHT insertion algorithm must therefore ensure that this situation never arises.

Program 12.15 shows how the OBHT search algorithm could be implemented as a Java method, `search`. This method would be added to the OBHT class of Program 12.12. Note the assumption that a never-occupied bucket is null.

12.3.2 Insertion

Algorithm 12.16 shows how to insert a new entry ⟨*key*, *val*⟩ into an OHBT.

To find which if any bucket of an OBHT is occupied by an entry whose key is equal to *target-key*:

1. Set b to $hash(\text{target-key})$.
2. Repeat:
    2.1. If bucket b is never-occupied:
        2.1.1. Terminate with answer *none*.
    2.2. If bucket b is occupied by an entry whose key is equal to *target-key*:
        2.2.1. Terminate with answer b.
    2.3. If bucket b is formerly-occupied, or is occupied by an entry whose key is not equal to *target-key*:
        2.3.1. Increment b modulo m.

Algorithm 12.13   OBHT search algorithm.

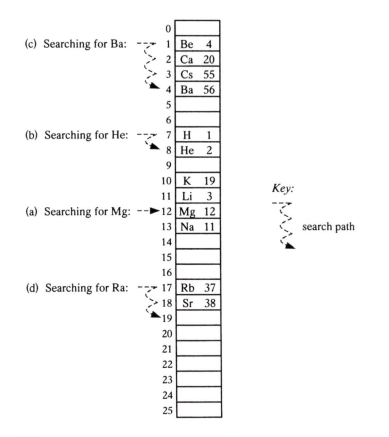

Figure 12.14   Illustration of the OHBT searching algorithm ($m = 26$; $hash(elem) = elem$'s initial letter $-$ 'A'; $step = 1$).

As usual, step 1 translates *key* to a bucket number, *b*, and what follows depends on the state of bucket *b*. If bucket *b* is never-occupied (step 2.1), or is occupied by an entry with the same key (step 2.2), the new entry can be made to occupy this bucket. If bucket *b* is occupied by an entry with a different key (step 2.3), the new entry must be displaced into another bucket, so we increment *b* (modulo the number of buckets, *m*) and repeat step 2.

Note that OBHT insertion entails visiting a sequence of buckets, which constitutes a search path. In this respect OBHT insertion resembles OBHT search.

Figure 12.17 illustrates several consecutive insertions into an OBHT, showing the search path in each case. Insertion (b) immediately finds an unoccupied bucket for the new entry. Insertion (c) follows the search path 17–18–19, eventually finding an unoccupied bucket for the new entry. Insertion (d) is similar, but the search path 1–2–3–4–5–6 is longer.

Program 12.18 shows how the OBHT insertion algorithm could be implemented as a Java method, `insert`. This method would be added to the `OBHT` class of Program 12.12.

In Section 12.3.1 we noted that the OBHT search algorithm terminates only if there is at least one never-occupied bucket in the OBHT. This explains step 2.1.1 in the OBHT insertion algorithm: if the last never-occupied bucket is about to become occupied, the OBHT is effectively full. In these circumstances, the number of buckets must be expanded. (See Exercise 12.6.)

```
public int search (Object targetKey) {
// Find which if any bucket of this OBHT is occupied by an entry whose key is
// equal to targetKey. Return the index of that bucket , or NONE if there is
// no such bucket.
    int b = hash(targetKey);
    for (;;) {
      BucketEntry oldEntry = buckets[b];
      if (oldEntry == null)
        return NONE;
      else if (oldEntry != BucketEntry.FORMER
          && targetKey.equals(oldEntry.key))
        return b;
      else
        b = (b + 1) % buckets.length;
    }
}
```

Program 12.15   Implementation of the OBHT search algorithm as a Java method (in class OBHT).

To insert the entry ‹*key, val*› into an OBHT:

1. Set *b* to *hash*(*key*).
2. Repeat:
    2.1. If bucket *b* is never-occupied:
        2.1.1.   If bucket *b* is the last never-occupied bucket:
            2.1.1.1.   Expand the number of buckets.
            2.1.1.2.   Set *b* to *hash*(*key*).
            2.1.1.3.   Repeat from step 2.
        2.1.2.   Make bucket *b* occupied by ‹*key, val*›.
        2.1.3.   Terminate.
    2.2. If bucket *b* is formerly-occupied, or is occupied by an entry whose key is equal to *key*:
        2.2.1.   Make bucket *b* occupied by ‹*key, val*›.
        2.2.2.   Terminate.
    2.3. If bucket *b* is occupied by an entry whose key is not equal to *key*:
        2.3.1.   Increment *b* modulo *m*.

Algorithm 12.16   OBHT insertion algorithm.

In order to implement the test in step 2.1.1, the `insert` method uses a private instance variable, `load`, which is initially zero. The `insert` method increments this variable every time it makes a new entry occupy a bucket that was never-occupied.

We assume the presence of an auxiliary method, `expand`, that will create a new, longer array when the old array becomes full. However, this operation is more complicated than previous `expand` methods, for two reasons. First, it must choose a new number of buckets, which should be a larger prime number. Second, it must rehash all the entries in the hash table when moving them to the new array, effectively performing an insert operation for each entry. This makes the `expand` method much more expensive than previous similar operations, and so it is important that it is not called frequently. (See Exercise 12.6.)

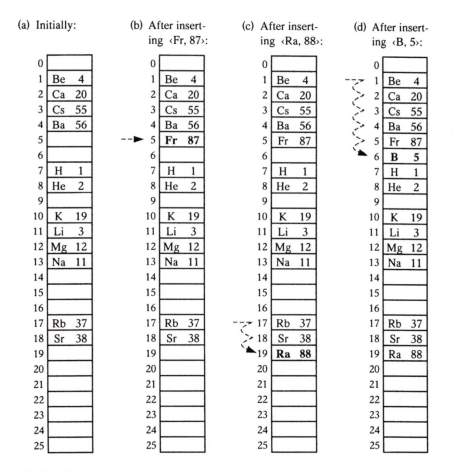

Figure 12.17 Illustration of the OHBT insertion algorithm ($m = 26$; *hash(elem)* = *elem*'s initial letter $-$ 'A'; *step* = 1).

```java
private int load = 0;
// ... number of occupied or formerly-occupied buckets in this OBHT.

public void insert (Object key, Object val) {
// Insert the entry <key, val> into this OBHT.
   BucketEntry newEntry = new BucketEntry(key, val);
   int b = hash(key);
   for (;;) {
      BucketEntry oldEntry = buckets[b];
      if (oldEntry == null) {
         if (++load == buckets.length) {
            expand();
            b = hash(key);
            continue;
         }
         buckets[b] = newEntry;
         return;
      } else if (oldEntry == BucketEntry.FORMER
            || key.equals(oldEntry.key)) {
         buckets[b] = newEntry;
         return;
      } else
         b = (b + 1) % buckets.length;
   }
}

private void expand () {
// Expand the number of buckets, rehashing all existing entries.
   ...    // code omitted here.
}
```

Program 12.18   Implementation of the OBHT insertion algorithm as a Java method (in class OBHT).

12.3.3 Deletion

Algorithm 12.19 shows how to delete an entry from an OHBT, given that entry's key *key*. This algorithm is rather similar to OBHT search, since we must first find the entry before we can delete it.

As usual, step 1 translates *key* to a bucket number, *b*, and what follows depends on the state of bucket *b*. If bucket *b* is never-occupied (step 2.1), there is no matching entry to delete. If bucket *b* is occupied by an entry whose key matches *key* (step 2.2), we delete that entry by making bucket *b* formerly-occupied. If bucket *b* is occupied by an entry whose key does not match *key* (step 2.3), the search continues, since the entry we are seeking might have been displaced into another bucket. So we increment *b* (modulo the number of buckets, *m*) and repeat step 2.

Figure 12.20 illustrates several consecutive deletions from an OBHT, showing the search path in each case. Deletion (b) immediately finds the matching entry in bucket 12, and deletion (c) immediately finds the matching entry in bucket 2. Deletion (d) follows the search path 1–2–3–4, eventually finding the matching entry in bucket 4.

Deletions (c) and (d) illustrate a very important point. If deletion (c) simply reset bucket 2 to its original never-occupied state, deletion (d) would incorrectly terminate on reaching the unoccupied bucket 2. So we must make a clear distinction between a *never-occupied* bucket and a *formerly-occupied* bucket. The distinction is that a search may continue past a formerly-occupied bucket, but not past a never-occupied bucket. This distinction is reflected in the search, insertion, and deletion algorithms. Study them again in this light. In our diagrams (such as Figure 12.20), never-occupied buckets are shown blank, whereas formerly-occupied buckets are marked *former*. In Programs 12.12, 12.15, 12.18, and 12.21, never-occupied buckets are represented by **null**, whereas formerly-occupied buckets are represented by a special `BucketEntry` object, `FORMER`.

Program 12.21 shows how the OBHT deletion algorithm could be implemented as a Java method, `delete`. This method would be added to the OBHT class of Program 12.12.

12.3.4 Analysis

Let us analyze the time complexity of the OBHT search, insertion, and deletion algorithms. (They are all the same.) Let n be the number of entries. Let us assume that we can neglect the time taken by the hash function, so we need count only comparisons as characteristic operations.

Step 2 of the OBHT search algorithm is a linear search, in which the target key is compared with consecutive entries in the cluster that includes its home bucket. The search could start anywhere in the cluster.

To delete the entry (if any) whose key is equal to *key* from an OBHT:

1. Set b to *hash(key)*.
2. Repeat:
    2.1. If bucket b is never-occupied:
        2.1.1. Terminate.
    2.2. If bucket b is occupied by an entry whose key is equal to *key*:
        2.2.1. Make bucket b formerly-occupied.
        2.2.2. Terminate.
    2.3. If bucket b is formerly-occupied, or is occupied by an entry whose key is not equal to *key*:
        2.3.1. Increment b modulo m.

Algorithm 12.19 OBHT deletion algorithm.

The *best-case* assumption is that no cluster consists of more than (say) four entries:

Maximum no. of comparisons = 4

In this case the search algorithm's time complexity is $O(1)$.

The *worst-case* assumption is all n entries form a single cluster:

Maximum no. of comparisons = n

In this case the search algorithm's time complexity is $O(n)$.

The analyses for the OBHT insertion and deletion algorithms are identical: best case $O(1)$, worst case $O(n)$.

The worst case is all too likely to arise in practice: clusters form whenever entries have the same *or adjacent* home buckets. To justify the best-case assumption, and thus achieve the ideal $O(1)$ time complexity for searching, insertion, and deletion, we must design the OBHT very carefully.

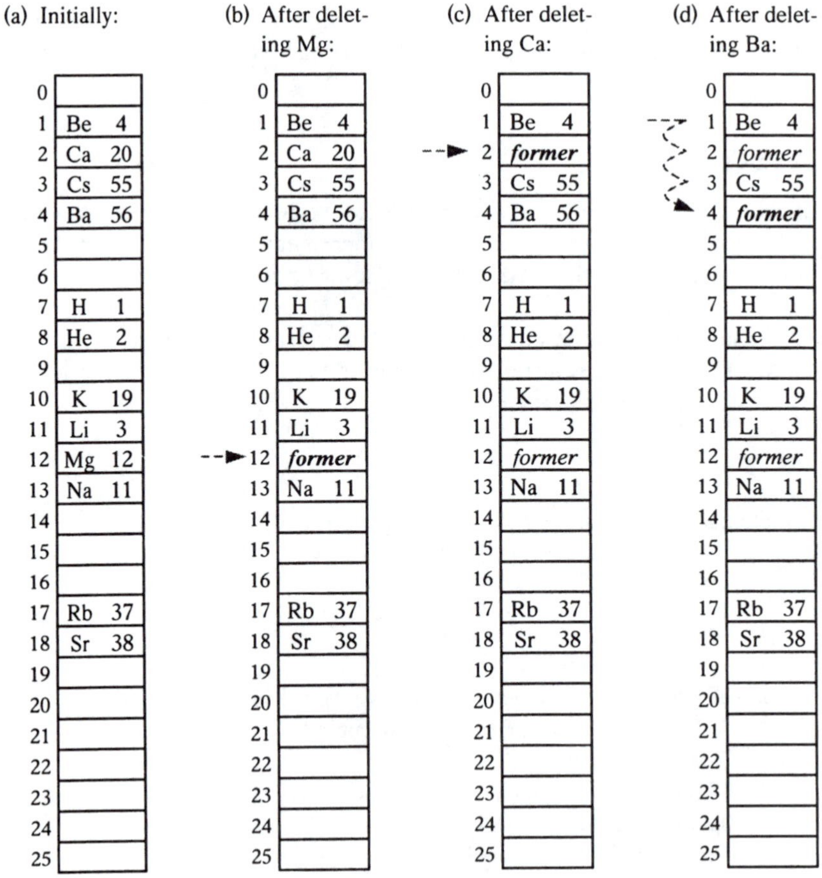

(a) Initially:	(b) After deleting Mg:	(c) After deleting Ca:	(d) After deleting Ba:
0	0	0	0
1 Be 4	1 Be 4	1 Be 4	1 Be 4
2 Ca 20	2 Ca 20	2 *former*	2 *former*
3 Cs 55	3 Cs 55	3 Cs 55	3 Cs 55
4 Ba 56	4 Ba 56	4 Ba 56	4 *former*
5	5	5	5
6	6	6	6
7 H 1	7 H 1	7 H 1	7 H 1
8 He 2	8 He 2	8 He 2	8 He 2
9	9	9	9
10 K 19	10 K 19	10 K 19	10 K 19
11 Li 3	11 Li 3	11 Li 3	11 Li 3
12 Mg 12	12 *former*	12 *former*	12 *former*
13 Na 11	13 Na 11	13 Na 11	13 Na 11
14	14	14	14
15	15	15	15
16	16	16	16
17 Rb 37	17 Rb 37	17 Rb 37	17 Rb 37
18 Sr 38	18 Sr 38	18 Sr 38	18 Sr 38
19	19	19	19
20	20	20	20
21	21	21	21
22	22	22	22
23	23	23	23
24	24	24	24
25	25	25	25

Figure 12.20 Illustration of the OHBT deletion algorithm ($m = 26$; *hash*(elem) = elem's initial letter − 'A'; *step* = 1).

```
public void delete (Object key) {
// Delete the entry (if any) whose key is equal to key from this OBHT.
   int b = hash(key);
   for (;;) {
      BucketEntry oldEntry = buckets[b];
      if (oldEntry == null)
         return;
      else if (oldEntry != BucketEntry.FORMER
            && key.equals(oldEntry.key)) {
         buckets[b] = BucketEntry.FORMER;
         return;
      } else
         b = (b + 1) % buckets.length;
   }
}
```

Program 12.21   Implementation of the OBHT deletion algorithm as a Java method (in class OBHT).

12.3.5 Design

The design of an OBHT entails deciding the number of buckets m and the hash function *hash*, as before, and also the step length (which will be defined shortly). The design issues are broadly similar to those we discussed in Section 12.2.5 for CBHTs. However, the design decisions are even more critical because of the OBHT's limited capacity (at most $m - 1$ entries) and the phenomenon of clustering.

Choice of number of buckets

As before, we should choose the number of buckets m such that the load factor is likely to be not less than 0.5 and not more than 0.75. As the load factor increases towards 1, the effect of clustering rapidly increases the time required for searching, insertion, or deletion. A high load factor affects an OHBT's performance even more seriously than a CBHT's.

As before, it is a good idea to make m a prime number.

Choice of hash function

As before, the hash function should be efficient.

It is particularly important that the hash function should distribute the entries evenly over the buckets. A cluster will form when several entries fall into the same *or adjacent* home buckets. For example, suppose that the keys are integers and the hash function is simply $hash(k) = k$ modulo m. If the entries are likely to include groups with consecutive keys (such as 11, 12, 13, 14, and 15), the home buckets of these entries will be adjacent (regardless of the value of m). This is another example of a pattern in the keys, which we should try to avoid replicating in the distribution of entries among buckets. One way to avoid such a situation would be to incorporate multiplication into the hash function, e.g., $hash(k) = (c \times k)$ modulo m, where the constant c is also a prime number.

Collision resolution

Clustering in an OBHT is a consequence of the manner in which Algorithm 12.16 resolves collisions: it simply uses the next unoccupied bucket. If, for example, bucket 13 is occupied by an entry, any further entries whose home bucket is also 13 will actually be stored in buckets 14, 15, and so on. These entries form a cluster. If this cluster continues to grow, moreover, it will sooner or later coalesce with a nearby cluster.

The OBHT search, insertion, and deletion algorithms contain a step 'Increment b modulo m'. So far we have interpreted this step as incrementing b by 1. In actual fact, we could increment b by any positive integer, which we shall call the ***step length***. Suppose, for example, that we have chosen a step length of 3. Then, once bucket 13 is occupied by an entry, any further entries whose home bucket is also 13 will actually be stored in buckets 16, 19, and so on. This is a slight improvement, since this cluster will not coalesce with a cluster of entries whose home bucket is 14 or 15.

A much better idea, however, is to let the step length depend on the key! Of course, the search, insertion, and deletion algorithms must still cooperate: for any given key, all three algorithms must follow the same search path. However, different keys may have different search paths. In particular, different keys may have different step lengths, provided that each key always has the same step length. To compute a key's step length we can use a second hash function, which we shall call *step*. This idea is therefore called ***double hashing***.

Algorithm 12.22 shows the OBHT insertion algorithm modified to use double hashing. (The OBHT search and deletion algorithms can be modified similarly.)

The modified insertion algorithm's behavior is illustrated in Figure 12.23. Compare this with the corresponding illustration of the unmodified insertion algorithm's behavior in Figure 12.17. The effect of clustering is less pronounced. Insertions (c) and (d) are both achieved with shorter search paths than before. This is despite the fact that the number of buckets has been reduced from 26 to the prime number 23, thus increasing the load factor.

More generally, a careful statistical analysis shows that double hashing should achieve about a 26% reduction in the length of the average search path when the load factor is 0.75, and even greater reductions as the load factor increases.

Whatever collision resolution strategy we adopt, we must ensure that every search path eventually reaches an unoccupied bucket. Here is an example of what can go wrong. Suppose that there are 21 buckets and that the step length is 3. If a new entry's home bucket, 5, is already occupied, the insertion algorithm will then try buckets 8, 11, 14, 17, 20, and 2. (Note that 2 = (20 + 3) modulo 21.) If all these seven buckets are already occupied, there would be nowhere to store the new entry, even if all 14 remaining buckets are unoccupied! Suppose instead that there are 17 buckets and that the step length is 3. If

To insert the entry ‹*key*, *val*› into an OBHT:

1. Set *b* to *hash*(*key*), <u>and set *s* to *step*(*key*)</u>.
2. Repeat:
    2.1. If bucket *b* is never-occupied:
        2.1.1. If bucket *b* is the last never-occupied bucket:
            2.1.1.1. Expand the number of buckets.
            2.1.1.2. Repeat from step 1.
        2.1.2. Make bucket *b* occupied by ‹*key*, *val*›.
        2.1.3. Terminate.
    2.2. If bucket *b* is formerly-occupied, or is occupied by an entry whose key is equal to *key*:
        2.2.1. Make bucket *b* occupied by ‹*key*, *val*›.
        2.2.2. Terminate.
    2.3. If bucket *b* is occupied by an entry whose key is not equal to *key*:
        2.3.1. Increment *b* <u>by *s*</u>, modulo *m*.

Algorithm 12.22   OBHT insertion algorithm with double hashing.

a new entry's home bucket, 5, is already occupied, the insertion algorithm will then try buckets 8, 11, 14, 0, 3, 6, 9, 12, 15, 1, 4, 7, 10, 13, 16, and 2 – i.e., *all* the remaining buckets.

In general, we must ensure that the number of buckets and the step length have no common factors. The easiest way to ensure this is to make the number of buckets, *m*, a prime number, and to make the *step* function compute an integer in the range 1 through $m - 1$. This is the case in Figure 12.23.

Choice between closed-bucket and open-bucket hash tables

CBHTs rely on dynamic allocation of nodes. OBHTs, being simple arrays, do not. As a consequence, CBHTs can be used to represent unbounded maps (and sets). OBHTs are bounded; when an OBHT becomes full, a time-consuming operation is needed to expand the number of buckets, rehashing all the existing entries.

Both CBHTs and OBHTs suffer from reducing efficiency as the load factor increases. This effect is particularly marked in OBHTs because entries rapidly coalesce into longer and longer clusters.

CBHTs are nearly always preferable to OBHTs. An OBHT should be chosen only if memory is scarce, dynamic memory management is infeasible, and the number of entries is naturally bounded.

EXAMPLE 12.4   *Design of a hash table for student records*

Suppose that the entries are a university's current student records. Each student has a unique student identifier, which serves as a key. Student identifiers are of the form *yydddd*, where *yy* are the last two digits of the year in which the student first registered,

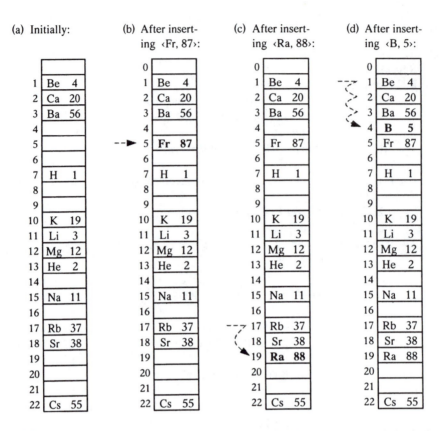

Figure 12.23 Illustration of OHBT insertion algorithm with double hashing ($m = 23$; $hash(elem) =$ (1st letter of $elem$ − 'A') modulo 23; $step(elem) = 1$ if $elem$ is a single letter, otherwise (2nd letter of $elem$ − 'a') modulo 21 + 2.

and *dddd* are four digits allocated serially. Typically students enroll for about four years, and about 6000 students are registered at any given time.

A hash function that simply selected the leading two digits of the student identifier would be a poor choice. This hash function would give us 100 buckets – far too few. Moreover, the distribution of entries among buckets would be very uneven. In the year 2001, for example, nearly all current students would have student identifiers with leading digits 98, 99, 00, or 01.

A hash function that simply selected the last four digits of the student identifier would also be a poor choice. The number of buckets (10000) would be about right, resulting in a load factor of about 0.6. But these four digits are allocated serially each year, starting with 0000 and running up to about 1500 (the average number of new registrations). Again, the distribution of entries among buckets would be very uneven.

A reasonable design would be to let the number of buckets, m, be about 10000, and let $hash(k) = k$ modulo m, where k is the numerical value of the student identifier. But we must choose the exact value of m carefully. If m = 10000 exactly, for example, we have the same hash function as in the previous paragraph. It is much better to make m a prime number, such as 9997.

For this application the fact that an OBHT is bounded would cause no difficulty, since we know roughly how many entries will be stored. (A CBHT would also be satisfactory, of course.)

Finally we need to choose a step length. If we choose a constant step length of 1, the OBHT will contain clusters of 1500 entries! To avoid such a disaster, we should either choose a constant step length greater than 1500, or use double hashing.

12.4 Implementations of sets using hash tables

Hash tables make excellent representations for both sets and maps, provided that we carefully address the design issues discussed in Sections 12.2.5 and 12.3.5.

When a set is represented by a hash table, the keys are the set members themselves; there are no corresponding values.

Figure 12.24 illustrates both a CBHT and an OBHT representing a set of countries. Note that neither representation is unique: the representation of a set depends on the order in which members were added (and also, in the case of an OBHT, the order in which members were removed).

Recall the `Set` contract of Program 9.4. If we choose a CBHT representation, we would implement the set operations using CBHT algorithms as follows:

- The `size` operation should count the nodes in the CBHT. Its time complexity is $O(n)$, where n is the set's cardinality. (Of course, we could make this $O(1)$ by storing the cardinality explicitly.)
- The `contains` operation should use the CBHT search algorithm (Algorithm 12.5). Its time complexity is $O(1)$ if the load factor is low, or $O(n)$ if the load factor is high.
- The `add` and `remove` operations should use the CBHT insertion and deletion algorithms, respectively (Algorithms 12.7 and 12.9). Each has time complexity $O(1)$ if the load factor is low, or $O(n)$ if the load factor is high.
- Operations that operate on whole sets (such as `equals`) should exploit the fact that each whole set is partitioned by the CBHT into an array of little sets (one little set per bucket). These little sets can be operated upon independently (provided that both whole sets are represented by CBHTs with the same number of buckets). For instance, the `equals` operation should test whether the little set in bucket b of the first CBHT equals the little set in bucket b of the second CBHT, for all bucket indices b. The little-set comparison must allow for the fact that each little set is represented by an *unsorted* SLL. (We could speed up the comparison by using *sorted* SLLs, but this would scarcely be worthwhile if, as we hope, most of the little sets have two or fewer members.) The `containsAll`, `addAll`, `removeAll`, and `retainAll` operations should be implemented along similar lines.

Table 12.25 summarizes the algorithms, together with each operation's best- and worst-case time complexities. The time complexities in Table 12.25 take into account the number of buckets as well as the number of members.

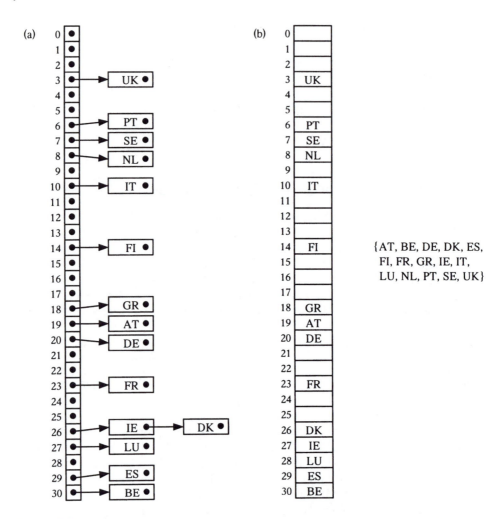

Figure 12.24   Representation of a set of countries by (a) a CBHT, and (b) an OBHT ($m = 31$; $hash(elem) = (26 \times (\text{1st letter} - \text{'A'}) + (\text{2nd letter} - \text{'A'}))$ modulo 31; $step = 1$).

12.5 Implementations of maps using hash tables

Figure 12.3 illustrates CBHTs, and Figure 12.11 OBHTs, representing maps from chemical elements to atomic numbers. For maps as well as sets, neither representation is unique.

Recall the Map contract of Program 11.3. If we choose a CBHT representation, we would implement the map operations using CBHT algorithms as follows:

- The get operation should use the CBHT search algorithm (Algorithm 12.5).
- The put and remove operations should use the CBHT insertion and deletion

algorithms, respectively (Algorithms 12.7 and 12.9). Note that these algorithms must be slightly modified to return the previous value in the map.

- Operations that operate on whole maps (`equals` and `putAll`) should exploit the fact that the CBHT partitions each map into an array of little maps (one little map per bucket), which can be operated upon independently. The `equals` operation should test whether the little map in bucket b of the first CBHT equals the little map in bucket b of the second CBHT, for all bucket indices b. The `putAll` operation should be implemented along similar lines.

Table 12.26 summarizes the algorithms. It also shows each operation's best- and worst-case time complexities, in terms of the number of buckets as well as the number of entries.

Table 12.25 Implementation of unbounded sets using CBHTs: summary of algorithms (where n, n_1, and n_2 are the cardinalities of the sets involved, and m is the number of buckets).

Operation	Algorithm	Time complexity (best case)	Time complexity (worst case)
`contains`	CBHT search	$O(1)$	$O(n)$
`equals`	equality test on corresponding buckets of both CBHTs	$O(m)$	$O(n_1 \, n_2)$
`containsAll`	subset test on corresponding buckets of both CBHTs	$O(m)$	$O(n_1 \, n_2)$
`add`	CBHT insertion	$O(1)$	$O(n)$
`remove`	CBHT deletion	$O(1)$	$O(n)$
`addAll`	'merge' on corresponding buckets of both CBHTs	$O(m)$	$O(n_1 \, n_2)$
`removeAll`	variant of 'merge' on corresponding buckets of both CBHTs	$O(m)$	$O(n_1 \, n_2)$
`retainAll`	variant of 'merge' on corresponding buckets of both CBHTs	$O(m)$	$O(n_1 \, n_2)$

Table 12.26 Implementation of unbounded maps using CBHTs: summary of algorithms (where n, n_1, and n_2 are the cardinalities of the maps involved, and m is the number of buckets).

Operation	Algorithm	Time complexity (best case)	Time complexity (worst case)
`get`	CBHT search	$O(1)$	$O(n)$
`remove`	CBHT deletion	$O(1)$	$O(n)$
`put`	CBHT insertion	$O(1)$	$O(n)$
`equals`	equality test on corresponding buckets of both CBHTs	$O(m)$	$O(n_1 \, n_2)$
`putAll`	'merge' on corresponding buckets of both CBHTs	$O(m)$	$O(n_1 \, n_2)$

Summary

In this chapter:

- We have studied the basic principles of hashing.
- We have studied both closed-bucket and open-bucket hash tables, together with their searching, insertion, and deletion algorithms.
- We have analyzed these algorithms, and found that their time complexity is $O(1)$ in the best case, but deteriorates to $O(n)$ if the load factor is high or the entries are unevenly distributed over the buckets.
- We have seen that careful design of hash tables, taking into account the likely characteristics of the data, makes best-case performance achievable in practice.
- We have studied how hash tables can be used to represent sets and maps.

Exercises

12.1 Consider a CBHT in which the keys are student identifiers (strings of 6 digits). Assume the following number of buckets and hash function:

$$m = 100; \quad hash(id) = \text{first two digits of } id$$

(a) Starting with an empty hash table, show the effect of successively adding the following student identifiers: 000014, 990021, 990019, 970036, 000015, 970012, 970023.

(b) What is the average number of comparisons when the resulting hash table is searched for each of these keys?

(c) Show the effect of deleting 000014 from the hash table.

12.2 Repeat Exercise 12.1 with an OBHT with double hashing, assuming the following second hash function:

$$step(id) = \text{last digit of } id$$

12.3 Consider a flight timetable whose keys are flight codes. A flight code consists of an airline code (2 letters) and a serial number (3 or 4 digits).

Design a hash table to suit this application. Assume that the number of entries is not expected to exceed about 200.

12.4 Consider the analysis of the CBHT search algorithm in Section 12.2.1.

(a) The best-case assumption was that no bucket is occupied by more than two entries. Suppose instead that we allow for up to *five* entries in a bucket. How does this affect the analysis?

(b) The worst-case assumption was that one bucket is occupied by all the entries. Suppose instead that the entries are concentrated in *ten* buckets, the remaining buckets being empty. How does this affect the analysis?

12.5 Consider a hash table in which the keys are the names of Web servers (such as 'www.wiley.co.uk' and 'www.dcs.gla.ac.uk').

(a) Suppose that the hash function uses only the first six characters of the Web server name. Why is this a bad choice?

(b) Suggest a more suitable hash function.

12.6 Consider how Program 12.18 deals with an almost-full OBHT.

(a) Implement the auxiliary method `expand`. The method should create a new array with more buckets, insert all existing entries into the new array, and make the new array replace the old one. Note that the expansion of the array changes the behavior of the hash function!

(b) Modify the method `insert` so that it prevents the load factor from exceeding 0.75 (rather than allowing the load factor to approach 1.0).

12.7 Given a known set of keys, a ***perfect hash function*** is one that translates every key to a different bucket index. For example, given the set of keys {'alpha', 'beta', 'gamma', 'delta'}, the following is a perfect hash function:

$$m = 4; \quad hash(k) = \text{(initial letter of } k - \text{'}a\text{')} \text{ modulo } 4$$

(a) Under what circumstances does it make sense to seek a perfect hash function?

(b) How can a perfect hash function be exploited in implementing a hash table?

(c) Given the following set of keys:

  {CA, MX, US}

find a perfect hash function with $m = 3$.

(d) Given the following set of keys:

  {AT, BE, DE, DK, ES, FI, FR, GR, IE, IT, LU, NL, PT, SE, UK}

find a perfect hash function with $m < 20$.

12.8 Design an iterator for a CBHT that visits the elements of the CBHT in no particular order. Implement your design as a Java iterator class.

12.9 Repeat Exercise 12.8 using an OBHT.

* **12.10** Design an iterator for a CBHT that visits the elements of the CBHT in ascending order. (*Hint:* You may use an auxiliary structure to sort the keys.)
Implement your design as a Java iterator class.

** **12.11** Repeat Exercise 12.10 using an OBHT.

12.12 Consider representations of sets by hash tables:

(a) Write a Java class `CBHTSet` that implements the `Set` interface of Program 9.4, representing sets by CBHTs as outlined in Section 12.4.

(b) Write a Java class `OBHTSet` that implements the `Set` interface of Program 9.4, representing *bounded* sets by OBHTs.

* **12.13** Consider the representation of a *bag* (or *multiset*) by a hash table. (See Exercise 9.20 for the definition of a bag.)

(a) How would you represent a bag using a hash table without storing multiple instances of each member?

(b) Implement bags using a CBHT implementation similar to your answer to Exercise 12.12(a).

(c) Implement bags using an OBHT implementation similar to your answer to Exercise 12.12(b).

12.14 Consider the representation of maps by hash tables.
   (a) Write a Java class CBHTMap that implements the Map interface of Program 11.3, representing maps by CBHTs as outlined in Section 12.5.
   (b) Write a Java class OBHTMap that implements the Map interface of Program 11.3, representing *bounded* maps by OBHTs.

12.15 Repeat Exercise 11.13 using the CBHTMap class from Exercise 12.14(a).

12.16 Repeat Exercise 11.13 using the OBHTMap class from Exercise 12.14(b).

12.17 Repeat Exercise 11.14 using the CBHTMap class from Exercise 12.14(a). What is the time efficiency of this operation?

12.18 Repeat Exercise 11.14 using the OBHTMap class from Exercise 12.14(b). What is the time efficiency of this operation?

* **12.19** Modify the spell-checker case study from Section 9.8 to use the CBHTSet class from Exercise 12.12(a). Compare the time efficiency of this modified version with the original version when spell-checking a simple document.

12.20 Repeat Exercise 9.17 for the modified spell-checker application from Exercise 12.19.

* **12.21** Repeat Exercise 12.19 using the OBHTSet class from Exercise 12.12(b).

12.22 Repeat Exercise 9.17 for the modified spell-checker application from Exercise 12.21.

* **12.23** Modify your answer to Exercise 11.16 to use the OBHTMap class from Exercise 12.14(b). Compare the time efficiency of this modified version with the original version.

* **12.24** Repeat Exercise 11.17 using your answer to Exercise 12.23.

** **12.25** We can visualize the occupancy of an OBHT graphically as follows. Bucket numbers form the horizontal axis, at intervals of 1 pixel (say). If bucket b is occupied, a 1-pixel-wide vertical line is drawn at position b on the horizontal axis. For example, Figure 12.27 visualizes the OBHTs shown in Figure 12.11. Note that a solid black rectangle indicates the presence of a cluster, and the width of the rectangle indicates the size of that cluster.
   Write a program in Java that visualizes an OBHT every time an entry is inserted or removed.
   Use your program, with various sets of input data, to investigate the effects of clustering with different OBHT designs (including double hashing).

Figure 12.27   Visualizing the occupancy of the OBHTs of Figure 12.11.

13

Priority-Queue Abstract Data Types

In this chapter we shall study:

- the concept of a priority queue (Section 13.1)
- simple applications of priority queues (Section 13.2)
- requirements and a contract for a priority-queue abstract data type (Section 13.3)
- implementations of priority queues using linked lists (Section 13.4)
- a special kind of binary tree called a heap (Section 13.5)
- an alternative implementation of priority queues using heaps (Section 13.6)
- a case study using priority queues (Section 13.7).

13.1 The concept of a priority queue

A priority queue differs from an ordinary queue in one significant respect: the elements in a priority queue are *prioritized*, such that the *least* element in the priority queue is always the first element to be removed. An ordinary queue is a first-in-first-out sequence; a priority queue is a *least-first-out* sequence.

Thus a **priority queue** is a sequence of elements, with the property that elements are removed least first.

If the priority queue contains several equal least elements, we must decide which one to remove first. There are two common approaches: either we select any one of the equal elements, or we select the one that was added first.

The **length** of a priority queue is the number of elements it contains. The **empty priority queue** has length zero.

13.2 Applications of priority queues

For an everyday example, consider a bus company whose policy is to allow elderly passengers to board before other passengers. Then the queue at a bus stop is actually a priority queue. Note that it does not matter whether the elderly passengers actually stand in front of the other passengers at the bus stop; they still board in front.

Another application of priority queues is sorting. This is illustrated in the following example by a method that sorts data held in a file. (The same idea works equally well for sorting data held in an array or linked list.)

EXAMPLE 13.1 *File sorting*

Suppose that a file contains records about persons, each record consisting of the person's surname, forename, gender, and year of birth. The records are in no particular order. We are required to write the records to a second file, in ascending order by year of birth.

A simple solution to this problem is to read the records, one at a time, and add them to a priority queue, prioritized by year of birth. Then we remove the records from the priority queue, one at a time, and write them to the second file.

We will need a class of objects representing persons. A suitable Person class is shown in Program 13.1. This is similar to Program 5.2, but additionally provides a compareTo method for comparing Person objects. In this application, the 'least' Person object (and therefore the first to be removed from the priority queue) is the one with the earliest year of birth.

We will also need an object to represent the priority queue itself. Let us assume a class SeniorityQueue whose objects represent priority queues of Person objects, prioritized by year of birth. Let us also assume that this class provides a constructor that creates an empty priority queue, and the following methods: *pq*.add(*x*) adds *x* to

```
public class Person implements Comparable {

    // Each Person object consists of a person's surname, forename, gender,
    // and year of birth.

    public String surname, forename;
    public boolean female;
    public int yearOfBirth;

    ...  // Person constructor and methods (see Program 5.2).

    public int compareTo (Object that) {
    // Return a negative (zero, positive) integer if this person was born in an
    // earlier (same, later) year than that person.
        Person other = (Person) that;
        return (this.yearOfBirth - other.yearOfBirth);
    }

}
```

Program 13.1 Java class declaration introducing a Person data type.

priority queue *pq*; *pq*.removeLeast() removes and returns the least element in priority queue *pq*; and *pq*.isEmpty() tests whether priority queue *pq* is empty.

Program 13.2 shows the solution, in which the variable people is the priority queue.

13.3 A priority-queue abstract data type

Let us now design a priority-queue ADT. We shall assume the following requirements:

1. It must be possible to make a priority queue empty.
2. It must be possible to test whether a priority queue is empty.

```
public static void sortPersons
                (BufferedReader input,
                 BufferedWriter output)
                throws IOException {
// Assuming that input contains a sequence of person records, write the same
// records to output, in ascending order by year of birth.
   SeniorityQueue people = new SeniorityQueue();
   for (;;) {
      Person p = readPerson(input);
      if (p == null)  break;   // end of input
      people.add(p);
   }
   while (! people.isEmpty()) {
      Person p = people.removeLeast();
      writePerson(output, p);
   }
}

private static Person readPerson
                (BufferedReader input)
                throws IOException {
// Read a single person record from input, and return the corresponding
// Person object.
   ...   // Code omitted here.
}

private static void writePerson
                (BufferedWriter output, Person p)
                throws IOException {
// Write to output a single person record corresponding to p.
   ...   // Code omitted here.
}
```

Program 13.2   Java implementation of the file sorting application.

3. It must be possible to obtain the length of a priority queue.
4. It must be possible to add an element to a priority queue.
5. It must be possible to remove the least element in a priority queue.
6. It must be possible to access the least element in a priority queue without removing it.

Program 13.3 shows a possible contract for the priority-queue ADT, in the form of a Java interface named `PriorityQueue`. Note that the queued elements are restricted to be `Comparable` objects.

It should be clear that the `SeniorityQueue` class of Example 13.1 could be written to implement the `PriorityQueue` interface.

In Sections 13.4 and 13.6 we shall study some very different implementations of the `PriorityQueue` interface.

```java
public interface PriorityQueue {
    // Each PriorityQueue object is a priority queue whose elements are
    // Comparable objects.

    ///////////// Accessors /////////////

    public boolean isEmpty ();
    // Return true if and only if this priority queue is empty.

    public int size ();
    // Return this priority queue's length.

    public Comparable getLeast ();
    // Return the least element in this priority queue, or throw a
    // NoSuchElementException if this priority queue is empty.
    // (If there are several equal least elements, return any one of them.)

    ///////////// Transformers /////////////

    public void clear ();
    // Make this priority queue empty.

    public void add (Comparable elem);
    // Add elem to this priority queue.

    public Comparable removeLeast ();
    // Remove and return the least element in this priority queue, or throw
    // a NoSuchElementException if this priority queue is empty.
    // (If there are several equal least elements, remove the same element
    // that would be returned by getLeast.)

}
```

Program 13.3 A contract for a priority-queue ADT.

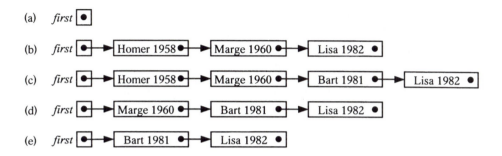

Figure 13.4 Representation of priority queues by sorted SLLs: (a) empty queue; (b–e) queues of persons prioritized by year of birth, showing the effects of one addition followed by two removals.

13.4 Implementations of priority queues using linked lists

A priority queue can easily be represented by a singly-linked list (SLL). In fact we have a choice of two such representations:

- a *sorted* SLL, in which the elements are listed in ascending order
- an *unsorted* SLL, in which the elements are listed in no particular order.

These two representations have completely different behaviors and performance characteristics.

13.4.1 Implementation using a sorted linked list

Figure 13.4 illustrates how a priority queue of persons would be represented by a sorted SLL, and how the add and removeLeast operations would work.

This implementation of the priority-queue ADT is fairly straightforward, and is shown in Program 13.5. This is a Java class SortedLinkedPriorityQueue that is declared as implementing the PriorityQueue interface. The instance variable first is a link to the first node (i.e., the node containing the least element), and is initially null. The instance variable length keeps track of the priority queue's length. The nodes are of class SLLNode (see Program 4.4). The add operation inserts the new element at the appropriate position in the SLL, keeping it sorted. All the other operations are trivial to implement. The removeLeast operation simply deletes the SLL's first node.

All the priority-queue operations have time complexity $O(1)$, except the add operation which is $O(n)$.

13.4.2 Implementation using an unsorted linked list

Figure 13.6 illustrates how a priority queue of persons would be represented by an unsorted SLL.

This implementation of the priority-queue ADT is also quite straightforward (see

```java
public class SortedLinkedPriorityQueue
        implements PriorityQueue {
    // Each SortedLinkedPriorityQueue object is a priority queue
    // whose elements are Comparable objects.

    // This priority queue is represented as follows: length is the number of
    // elements; first is a link to the first node of an SLL containing the
    // elements in ascending order.
    private SLLNode first;
    private int length;

    /////////// Constructor ///////////

    public SortedLinkedPriorityQueue () {
    // Construct a priority queue, initially empty.
        first = null;
        length = 0;
    }

    /////////// Accessors ///////////

    public boolean isEmpty () {
    // Return true if and only if this priority queue is empty.
        return (length == 0);
    }

    public int size () {
    // Return this priority queue's length.
        return length;
    }

    public Comparable getLeast () {
    // Return the least element in this priority queue, or throw a
    // NoSuchElementException if this priority queue is empty.
    // (If there are several equal least elements, return any one of them.)
        if (first == null)
            throw new NoSuchElementException();
        return (Comparable) first.element;
    }

    /////////// Transformers ///////////

    public void clear () {
    // Make this priority queue empty.
        first = null;
        length = 0;
    }
```

Program 13.5 Java implementation of unbounded priority queues using sorted SLLs (*continued on next page*).

Exercise 13.4). The add operation inserts the new node (say) after the last node of the SLL. The removeLeast operation must delete the node containing the least element; this entails traversing the entire SLL. Even the getLeast operation must traverse the entire SLL.

The add operation therefore has time complexity $O(1)$, but the removeLeast and getLeast operations are $O(n)$.

13.4.3 Comparison

Table 13.7 summarizes the time complexities of the most important priority-queue operations, for both sorted and unsorted linked-list representations of the priority queue. Note that, whichever of these two representations we choose, one of the add and removeLeast operations has time complexity $O(n)$.

```
public void add (Comparable elem) {
// Add elem to this priority queue.
   SLLNode pred = null, curr = first;
   while (curr != null
         && elem.compareTo(curr.element) >= 0) {
     pred = curr;  curr = curr.succ;
   }
   SLLNode newNode = new SLLNode(elem, curr);
   if (pred == null)
     first = newNode;
   else
     pred.succ = newNode;
   length++;
}

public Comparable removeLeast () {
// Remove and return the least element in this priority queue, or throw
// a NoSuchElementException if this priority queue is empty.
// (If there are several equal least elements, remove the same element
// that would be returned by getLeast.)
   if (first == null)
     throw new NoSuchElementException();
   Comparable least = (Comparable) first.element;
   first = first.succ;
   length--;
   return least;
}

}
```

Program 13.5 (*continued*)

A priority queue can analogously be represented by a sorted or unsorted *array*. Table 13.7 shows the time complexities of the priority-queue operations for these array representations also. These performance characteristics are quite similar to those for linked lists.

Consider a program, such as Program 13.2, that adds n elements to a priority queue and subsequently removes all these elements. If this program uses a priority-queue implementation in which either `add` or `removeLeast` has time complexity $O(n)$, the program has time complexity $O(n^2)$. Clearly we need a more efficient priority-queue implementation.

13.5 The heap data structure

Fortunately, priority queues can be implemented more efficiently, if we represent them using a special form of binary tree called a *heap*.

We shall introduce heaps in this section. But first we shall find it convenient to study an array representation of binary trees.

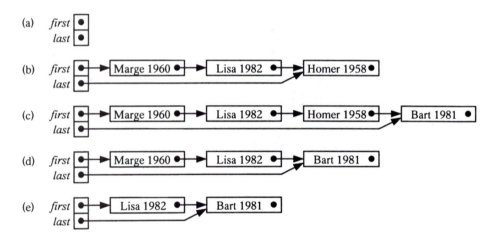

Figure 13.6 Representation of priority queues by unsorted SLLs: (a) empty queue; (b–e) queues of persons prioritized by year of birth, showing the effects of one addition followed by two removals.

Table 13.7 Implementation of priority queues using sorted and unsorted linked-list and arrays: summary of time complexities (where n is the length of the priority queue).

Operation	Time complexity (sorted SLL)	Time complexity (unsorted SLL)	Time complexity (sorted array)	Time complexity (unsorted array)
add	$O(n)$	$O(1)$	$O(n)$	$O(1)$
removeLeast	$O(1)$	$O(n)$	$O(1)$	$O(n)$
getLeast	$O(1)$	$O(n)$	$O(1)$	$O(n)$

13.5.1 Array representation of binary trees

Consider the positions that are *potentially* occupied by the nodes of a binary tree. We can think of these positions in family terms: the root, the root's left child, the root's right child, the root's left child's left child, and so on. We can assign a unique index to each position:

0: root
1: root's left child
2: root's right child
3: root's left child's left child
4: root's left child's right child
5: root's right child's left child
6: root's right child's right child
7: root's left child's left child's left child
8: root's left child's left child's right child

...

Figure 13.8 illustrates several binary trees, showing each node's position index. The elements in these particular binary trees are letters.

In any given binary tree, only some of the positions are actually occupied. In the binary tree of Figure 13.8(e), for example, the root has no left child, so position 1 is vacant. Consequently, positions 3 and 4 are also vacant (since these positions would be occupied by the left child's own children).

We can represent any binary tree by an array $elems[0...m - 1]$, in which $elems[p]$ represents the node at position p. The component $elems[p]$ contains the element at position p, or is unoccupied if that position is vacant. It is assumed that positions m, $m + 1, ...$ are all vacant. Figure 13.8 shows an array representation of each binary tree.

The array representation of a binary tree eliminates the need for explicit parent–child links. These relationships are implicit in the position indices:

- The left child of $elems[p]$ is $elems[2p + 1]$ (unless $2p + 1 \geq m$, implying that $elems[p]$ has no left child).
- The right child of $elems[p]$ is $elems[2p + 2]$ (unless $2p + 2 \geq m$, implying that $elems[p]$ has no right child).
- The parent of $elems[p]$ is $elems[(p - 1)/2]$ (unless $p = 0$, implying that $elems[p]$ is the root and has no parent). (As usual, we assume that integer division by 2 ignores any remainder.)

The array representation of binary trees has two advantages and one disadvantage over the conventional linked representation:

- It is just as easy to move from a child to its parent as *vice versa*.
- The elimination of explicit links saves space.
- Unoccupied components in the array waste space.

Overall, the array representation is preferable to the linked representation if the binary tree is known to be well-balanced (since that implies relatively few unoccupied positions). The particular kinds of binary trees introduced in the next section (complete binary trees and heaps) are indeed best represented by arrays.

13.5.2 Complete binary trees and heaps

A *complete binary tree* is a binary tree with no vacancies in the positions 0 through $n - 1$, where n is the size (number of nodes) of the binary tree.

In a complete binary tree of depth d, there are no vacancies at depths 0 through $d - 1$; any vacancies at depth d are in the rightmost positions. In Figure 13.8, binary trees (a–c) are complete. But binary tree (d) is not complete, because it has a vacancy to the left of an

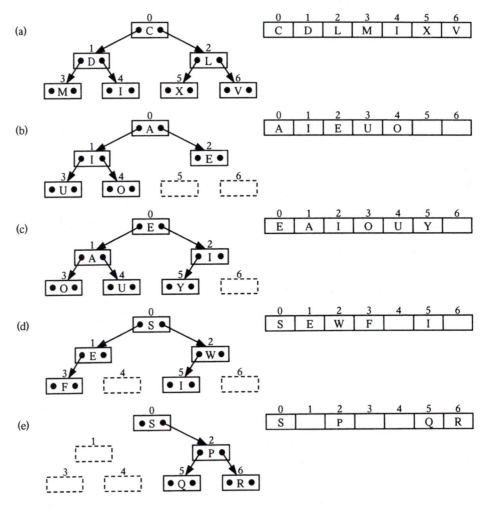

Figure 13.8 Binary trees with position indices, and their array representations: (a–c) are complete binary trees, and (a–b) are heaps.

occupied position at depth 2. Binary tree (e) is also not complete, because it has a vacancy at depth 1 (its own depth being 2).

Complete binary trees are interesting for two reasons:

- A complete binary tree is balanced, by definition.
- A complete binary tree is efficiently represented by a subarray $elems[0...n-1]$, where n is its size. *All* components of this subarray will be occupied.

A **heap** is a complete binary tree with the following *heap property*: the element at every position is less than or equal to the element(s) at its child position(s), if any.

(Unfortunately, the term *heap* is also used to mean the memory region in which objects are stored while a program is running. Take care not to confuse these completely different meanings.)

In Figure 13.8, binary trees (a–b) are heaps. But binary tree (c) is not a heap, because the element E at position 0 is greater than the element A at the left child position 1. Binary trees (d–e) are also not heaps, because they are not complete binary trees.

13.5.3 Heap insertion

How can we insert an element *elem* into a given heap? It would be incorrect simply to store *elem* at the next vacant position: the resulting structure would still be a complete binary tree, but the heap property would be lost if the element at the parent position happened to be greater than *elem*.

The correct idea is as follows. We expand the heap into the next vacant position, but temporarily leave a 'hole' at that position. Then we compare *elem* with the element at the hole's parent position. If the parent element is less than or equal to *elem*, we simply copy *elem* into the hole and terminate. But if the parent element is greater than *elem*, we copy the parent element into the hole, thus creating a new hole at the parent position – which we will fill in the same manner. If we eventually create a hole at the root position

To insert the element *elem* into a heap:

1. Expand the heap by one position, and set *hole* to the new position.
2. Repeat:
   - 2.1. If *hole* is the root position:
      - 2.1.1. Store *elem* at position *hole*.
      - 2.1.2. Terminate.
   - 2.2. Set *parent* to the position of *hole*'s parent.
   - 2.3. If the element at position *parent* is less than or equal to *elem*:
      - 2.3.1. Store *elem* at position *hole*.
      - 2.3.2. Terminate.
   - 2.4. If the element at position *parent* is greater than *elem*:
      - 2.4.1. Copy the element at position *parent* into position *hole*.
      - 2.4.2. Set *hole* to *parent*.

Algorithm 13.9 Heap insertion algorithm.

(because every element in the heap is greater than *elem*), we simply copy *elem* into that hole and terminate. Algorithm 13.9 captures this idea.

Figure 13.10 illustrates the algorithm's behavior as it inserts the element C into a heap of letters. (For clarity, the heap is shown in its binary tree form rather than its array representation.) Notice that the elements L and then D are copied downwards by step 2.4.1, and finally the new element C is placed at the root position by step 2.1.1 – three iterations of the loop.

If the element to be inserted in the same heap had been E, then L would have been copied downwards by step 2.4.1, and finally E would have been placed at position 2 by step 2.3.1 – two iterations. If the element to be inserted had been N, then N would have been placed immediately at position 6 by step 2.3.1 – one iteration only.

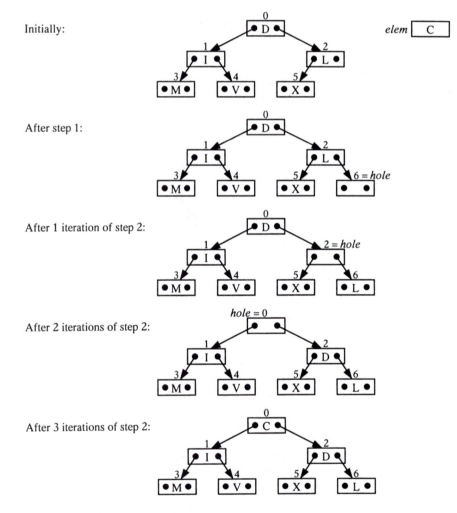

Figure 13.10 Illustration of the heap insertion algorithm.

Let us analyze the heap insertion algorithm's time complexity. Let n be the size (number of nodes) of the heap. Assuming that steps 2.3 and 2.4 are implemented with a single comparison, the maximum number of comparisons is equal to the depth of the heap. Since the heap is a balanced binary tree, its depth is given by equation (10.1). Therefore:

$$\text{Maximum no. of comparisons} = \text{floor}(\log_2 n) \qquad (13.1)$$

The algorithm's time complexity is $O(\log n)$. It is very important to note that the logarithmic performance of heap insertion is *guaranteed*. (This is unlike binary search tree insertion, whose performance deteriorates to $O(n)$ if the tree becomes ill-balanced.)

We shall see a Java implementation of the heap insertion algorithm later, in Program 13.15.

13.5.4 Heap deletion

Let us consider the problem of deleting the *least* element in a given heap. (This is because we are interested in heaps as a representation of priority queues.)

It is easy to locate the least element: by the definition of a heap, it is the element at the root position. However, we must take care to rearrange the other elements in such a way as to preserve the heap property.

The correct idea is as follows. We contract the heap by deleting the last occupied position, but only after noting the element at that position, say *last*. We temporarily leave

To delete the least element in a heap:

1. Set *least* to the element at the root position, and set *hole* to the root position.
2. Set *last* to the element at the last position, and contract the heap by eliminating that position.
3. Repeat:
    3.1. If *hole* has no child:
        3.1.1. Store *last* at position *hole*.
        3.1.2. Terminate with answer *least*.
    3.2. If *hole* has a left child only:
        3.2.1. Set *child* to the position of *hole*'s left child.
    3.3. If *hole* has two children:
        3.3.1. Set *child* to the position of whichever child of *hole* contains the lesser element.
    3.4. If *last* is less than or equal to the element at position *child*:
        3.4.1. Store *last* at position *hole*.
        3.4.2. Terminate with answer *least*.
    3.5. If *last* is greater than the element at position *child*:
        3.5.1. Copy the element at position *child* into position *hole*.
        3.5.2. Set *hole* to *child*.

Algorithm 13.11   Heap deletion algorithm.

a hole at the root position. Then we compare *last* with either the element at the hole's left child position (if there is only a left child) or the lesser of the elements at the two child positions (if there are two children). If *last* is less than or equal to the child element, we simply copy *last* into the hole and terminate. But if *last* is greater than the child element, we copy the child element into the hole, thus creating a new hole at the child position – which we will fill in the same manner. If we eventually create a hole at a leaf position, we simply copy *last* into that hole and terminate. Algorithm 13.11 captures this idea.

Figure 13.12 illustrates the algorithm's behavior as it deletes the least element in a heap of letters. Notice that the elements D and then I are copied upwards by step 3.5.1, and finally the *last* element V is stored in a leaf position by step 3.1.1 – three iterations of the loop.

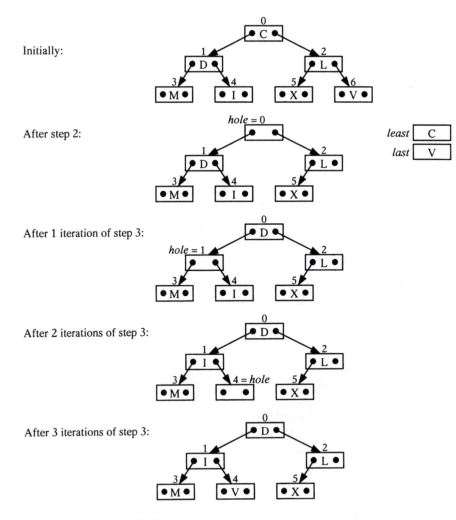

Figure 13.12   Illustration of the heap deletion algorithm.

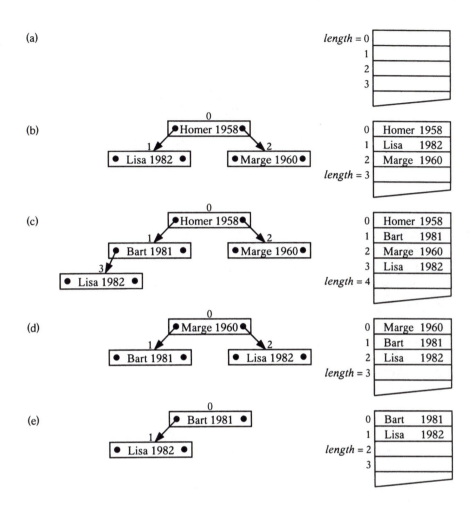

Figure 13.13   Representation of priority queues by heaps: (a) empty queue; (b–e) queues of persons prioritized by year of birth, showing the effects of one addition followed by two removals.

Table 13.14   Implementation of priority queues using heaps: summary of algorithms (where n is the length of the priority queue).

Operation	Algorithm	Time complexity
add	heap insertion	$O(\log n)$
removeLeast	heap deletion	$O(\log n)$
getLeast	access root element	$O(1)$

Let us analyze the heap deletion algorithm's time complexity. Let n be the size (number of nodes) of the heap. Assuming that steps 3.4 and 3.5 are implemented with a single comparison, the maximum number of comparisons is equal to the depth of the heap. Therefore:

$$\text{Maximum no. of comparisons} = \text{floor}(\log_2 n) \tag{13.2}$$

The algorithm's time complexity is $O(\log n)$.

We shall see a Java implementation of the heap deletion algorithm later, in Program 13.15.

```java
public class HeapPriorityQueue
              implements PriorityQueue {
// Each HeapPriorityQueue object is a priority queue whose elements
// are Comparable objects.

// This priority queue is represented as follows: the subarray elems[0...
// ...length-1] contains the priority queue's elements, arranged in such a
// way that elems[(p-1)/2] is less than or equal to elems[p] for every
// p > 0.
private Comparable[] elems;
private int length;

/////////// Constructor ///////////

public HeapPriorityQueue (int maxlength) {
// Construct a priority queue, initially empty, whose length will be bounded
// by maxlength.
   elems = new Comparable[maxlength];
   length = 0;
}

/////////// Accessors ///////////

public boolean isEmpty () {
// Return true if and only if this priority queue is empty.
   return (length == 0);
}

public int size () {
// Return this priority queue's length.
   return length;
}
```

Program 13.15 Java implementation of bounded priority queues using heaps (*continued on next page*).

```java
public Comparable getLeast () {
// Return the least element in this priority queue, or throw a
// NoSuchElementException if this priority queue is empty.
// (If there are several equal least elements, return any one of them.)
   if (length == 0)
     throw new NoSuchElementException();
   return elems[0];
}
///////////// Transformers ////////////

public void clear () {
// Make this priority queue empty.
   for (int p = 0; p < length; p++)
     elems[p] = null;
   length = 0;
}

public void add (Comparable elem) {
// Add elem to this priority queue.
   if (length == elems.length)  expand();
   int hole = length++;
   for (;;) {
     if (hole == 0) {
       elems[hole] = elem;
       return;
     }
     int parent = (hole-1)/2;
     if (elems[parent].compareTo(elem) <= 0) {
       elems[hole] = elem;
       return;
     } else {
       elems[hole] = elems[parent];
       hole = parent;
     }
   }
}
```

Program 13.15 (*continued on next page*)

```java
public Comparable removeLeast () {
// Remove and return the least element in this priority queue, or throw
// a NoSuchElementException if this priority queue is empty.
// (If there are several equal least elements, remove the same element
// that would be returned by getLeast.)
  if (length == 0)
    throw new NoSuchElementException();
  int hole = 0;
  Comparable least = elems[0];
  Comparable last = elems[--length];
  for (;;) {
    int left = 2*hole + 1, right = 2*hole + 2;
    int child;
    if (left > length) {          // hole has no child
      elems[hole] = last;
      return least;
    }
    else if (right > length)   // hole has a left child only
      child = left;
    else                          // hole has two children
      child = (elems[left].compareTo(elems[right])
                  <= 0 ? left : right);
    if (last.compareTo(elems[child]) <= 0) {
      elems[hole] = last;
      return least;
    } else {
      elems[hole] = elems[child];
      hole = child;
    }
  }
}

/////////////// Auxiliary method ///////////////

private void expand () {
// Expand the heap array.
  ...
}

}
```

Program 13.15 (*continued*)

13.6 Implementation of priority queues using heaps

It is now a straightforward matter to represent a priority queue by a heap. The least element in the priority queue will occupy the heap's root position.

Figure 13.13 illustrates how a priority queue of persons would be represented by a heap, how the heap would in turn be represented by an array, and how the add and removeLeast operations would work.

Table 13.14 summarizes the algorithms and their time complexities. The most important point to observe is that the add and removeLeast operations have time complexity $O(\log n)$.

The implementation of the priority-queue ADT is shown as Program 13.15. This is a Java class HeapPriorityQueue that implements the PriorityQueue interface. The add operation uses the heap insertion algorithm, and the removeLeast operation uses the heap deletion algorithm.

Consider a program, such as Program 13.2, that adds n elements to a priority queue and subsequently removes all these elements. If this program uses the heap implementation of priority queues, in which both add and removeLeast have time complexity $O(\log n)$, the program has complexity $O(n \log n)$. Thus the heap representation of priority queues is a substantial improvement on the linked-list representations discussed in Section 13.4.

The idea of using a heap to sort a sequence of elements gives rise to the ***heap-sort*** algorithm, shown as Algorithm 13.16.

13.7 Case study: an improved traffic simulator

Recall the traffic simulator presented in Section 7.6. It simulates a street intersection iteratively. At each clock tick, it must process the possible arrival of a vehicle in each street of the intersection; advance the frontmost car in the street whose traffic signal is currently green; and check for the traffic signal changing. It spends a lot of the processing time just checking to see whether one of these events has occurred, rather than actually

To sort a sequence of elements *input* into a sequence *output*:

1. Create an empty heap.
2. For each element *elem* of *input*, repeat:
   2.1. Insert *elem* into the heap.
3. Make *output* empty.
4. While the heap is nonempty, repeat:
   4.1. Remove the least element from the heap into *elem*.
   4.2. Append *elem* to *output*.
5. Terminate.

Algorithm 13.16   Heap-sort algorithm.

advancing the simulation. Fortunately, there is a much better way to organize the simulation, using a technique known as ***discrete event simulation***.

In discrete event simulation, the simulation models the events that actually occur. Rather than advancing time by a single clock tick on each iteration, the simulation proceeds directly from one event to the next event. By eliminating the need to check whether an event has occurred, this makes the simulation faster. Moreover, discrete event simulation can handle a large number of interacting processes, whereas the iterative approach of Section 7.6 quickly becomes unmanageable.

13.7.1 Events in the traffic simulation

In our simulation of a street intersection, three kinds of event can arise:

- A new vehicle arrives in a street (a *vehicle-arrival* event).
- The frontmost vehicle in the street whose traffic signal is green clears the intersection and departs (a *vehicle-departure* event).
- The traffic signals change from green to red in one street, and from red to green in the next street (a *signal-change* event).

Every event occurs at a given time. We must take care to process the events in the order in which they occur. We can achieve this by adding them to a priority queue of events prioritized by time. The least element of the priority queue is the next event to be processed. The simulation algorithm itself becomes trivial: simply remove the least element from the priority queue, and process it. This is repeated until there are no further events.

Clearly, if the simulation is going to run for any length of time, new events must be generated, but how does this happen? The answer is simple: when an event is processed, it may generate new events, which are then added to the priority queue.

We shall model events in general using the Java abstract class, `TrafficEvent`, given in Program 13.17. Each event contains a timestamp, and the `compareTo` method prioritizes events according to their timestamps. Each implementation of the `performAction` abstract method must process one kind of event appropriately.

We shall model the three kinds of event using three subclasses of `TrafficEvent`. These classes are `VehicleArrivalEvent` (shown in Program 13.18), `Vehicle-DepartureEvent` (Program 13.19), and `SignalChangeEvent` (Program 13.20). A `VehicleArrivalEvent` contains a reference to the street in which the vehicle arrives. Similarly, a `VehicleDepartureEvent` contains a reference to the street from which the vehicle departs. A `SignalChangeEvent` contains references to two streets: the street whose traffic signal is about to change from green to red, and the next street whose traffic signal is about to change to green. All three contain references to the street intersection.

We shall consider how to process each class of event in the next subsection.

13.7.2 Processing events in the traffic simulation

The discrete event simulation is driven entirely by performing the actions associated with

```
public abstract class TrafficEvent
                implements Comparable {

    // Each TrafficEvent object represents an event in the simulation.

    // This simulation event contains a timestamp.

    long timestamp;

    public TrafficEvent (long timestamp) {
    // Construct a new simulation event containing timestamp.
        this.timestamp = timestamp;
    }

    public int compareTo (Object that) {
    // Compare this simulation event with that. Return a result that is
    // negative (zero, positive) if this event's timestamp is earlier than
    // (equal to, later than) that's timestamp.
        TrafficEvent other = (TrafficEvent) that;
        return (int) (this.timestamp - other.timestamp);
    }

    public abstract void performAction
                (PriorityQueue events);
    // Perform the action associated with this event, adding new events
    // to the events queue.

}
```

Program 13.17   Java class modeling simulation events in general.

the various events. When a particular action is performed, it alters the state of the simulation and creates new (future) events.

When a vehicle-arrival event occurs, we must create a new vehicle and add it behind the waiting vehicles in the given street. However, we must also decide what new events will result from this arrival. First, if the new vehicle is the only vehicle in the street (i.e., there were no vehicles in the street before its arrival) and the street's traffic signal is currently green, we must create a vehicle-departure event for the new vehicle. The new event's timestamp is the current event's timestamp plus the new vehicle's crossing time (i.e., the time it will take to clear the intersection). Second, we must create a vehicle-arrival event for the next vehicle to arrive in this street. The new event's timestamp is the timestamp of the current event plus a random interval based on the mean arrival period of vehicles in this street.

When a vehicle-departure event occurs, we must check that the given street still has its traffic signal at green. If not, the vehicle-departure event is simply ignored. If so, we remove the frontmost vehicle in this street, and if there are still vehicles in this street, we create a new vehicle-departure event for the next vehicle (which is now the frontmost

```
public class VehicleArrivalEvent
                extends TrafficEvent {

    // Each VehicleArrivalEvent represents the arrival of a new vehicle
    // in a street of the intersection.

    // This vehicle-arrival event contains references to the street in which
    // the new vehicle arrives and the street intersection. It inherits a timestamp.

    private Street arrivalStreet;
    private StreetIntersection intersection;

    public VehicleArrivalEvent (long timestamp,
                StreetIntersection intersection;
                Street street) {
    // Construct a new vehicle-arrival event containing the given data.
        ... // See code on the companion Web site.
    }

    public void performAction (PriorityQueue events) {
    // Perform the action associated with this vehicle-arrival event,
    // adding new events to the events queue.
        ...    // See Program 13.22.
    }

}
```

Program 13.18 Java class modeling vehicle-arrival events.

vehicle). The new event's timestamp is the current event's timestamp plus the next vehicle's crossing time.

When a signal-change event occurs, the street with a green traffic signal must change to red, and the next street's traffic signal must change to green. If there are vehicles in the next street, we must create a new vehicle-departure event for the frontmost vehicle in the next street. The new event's timestamp is the current event's timestamp plus the crossing time of the frontmost vehicle. Finally, we must create a signal-change event for the next change of the traffic signals. The new event's timestamp is the current event's timestamp plus the next street's signal duration (i.e., the amount of time the traffic signal will be green).

The implementation of these algorithms is straightforward, and the corresponding performAction methods are shown in Programs 13.21–13.23. These methods would be added to the appropriate subclasses of TrafficEvent.

13.7.3 Modeling the entities in the traffic simulation

The Java classes representing of the entities in the simulation remain largely unchanged from those given in Section 7.6.1. A few minor changes are summarized here:

- The `Vehicle` class no longer updates the crossing time that determines when the vehicle has crossed the street intersection. The methods `hasCrossedInter-section` and `moveAcrossIntersection` are removed. A simple accessor method, `getCrossingTime`, is added.
- The `Street` class no longer records when the next vehicle will arrive, and when the traffic signals will next change. The methods `arrivalDue`, `signalDue`, `setNextArrivalTime`, and `setNextSignalTime` are removed, along with the instance variables `nextArrivalTime` and `nextSignalTime`.
- The `StreetIntersection` class no longer keeps track of the current time. Instead, it creates the priority queue of events, and adds to it the initial events that start the simulation. It requires a new accessor method, `getGreenStreet`, that returns the street whose traffic signal is currently green, and a corresponding transformer method, `setGreenStreet`. We shall consider the simulation algorithm in more detail in the next section.

```
public class VehicleDepartureEvent
             extends TrafficEvent {

// Each VehicleDepartureEvent represents the departure of
// the frontmost vehicle in a street of the intersection.

// This vehicle-departure event contains a reference to the street from which
// the vehicle departs and a reference to the street intersection. It inherits a
// timestamp.

private Street departureStreet;
private StreetIntersection intersection;

public VehicleDepartureEvent (long timestamp,
               StreetIntersection intersection;
               Street street) {
// Construct a new vehicle-departure event containing the given data.
    ... // See code on the companion Web site.
}

public void performAction (PriorityQueue events) {
// Perform the action associated with this vehicle-departure event, possibly
// adding new events to the events queue.
    ...  // See Program 13.22.
}

}
```

Program 13.19 Java class modeling vehicle-departure events.

```
public class SignalChangeEvent
                extends TrafficEvent {

    //  Each SignalChangeEvent represents the change of the traffic signal
    //  in the current street from green to red, and the change of the traffic signal
    //  in the next street from red to green.

    //  This signal-change event contains a reference to the street whose traffic
    //  signal is about to change from green to red, a reference to the street
    //  whose traffic signal is about to change to green, and a reference to the
    //  street intersection. It inherits a timestamp.

    private Street greenStreet, nextStreet;
    private StreetIntersection intersection;

    public SignalChangeEvent (long timestamp,
                StreetIntersection intersection,
                Street greenStreet,
                Street nextStreet) {
    //  Construct a new signal-change event with the given data.
        ...  //  See code on the companion Web site.
    }

    public void performAction (PriorityQueue events) {
    //  Perform the action associated with this signal-change event, possibly
    //  adding new events to the events queue.
        ...    //  See Program 13.23.
    }

}
```

Program 13.20   Java class modeling signal-change events.

13.7.4 An event-based traffic simulation algorithm

As in the iterative simulation, the event-based simulation of the street intersection is handled by the StreetIntersection class. The simulation algorithm, however, is greatly simplified. The method simulateOneTick is no longer needed: all of the processing of the simulation is now handled by the actions associated with events.

To simulate the street intersection, the run method (given in Program 7.11) simply removes the least event from the priority queue, and performs the associated action.

Creating the initial events in the simulation turns out to be straightforward. We create an initial vehicle-arrival event for each street in the intersection, and an initial signal-change event for the first street. From these initial events, the rest of the simulation follows.

```java
public void performAction (PriorityQueue events) {
// Perform the action associated with this vehicle-arrival event,
//  adding new events to the events queue.
   Vehicle vehicle = new Vehicle(timestamp);
   arrivalStreet.addVehicle(vehicle);
   if (arrivalStreet.numVehicles() == 1
       && arrivalStreet ==
             intersection.getGreenStreet()) {
     long nextDepartTime =
         timestamp + vehicle.getCrossingTime();
     VehicleDepartureEvent nextDepartureEvent =
         new VehicleDepartureEvent(nextDepartTime,
             intersection, arrivalStreet);
     events.add(nextDepartureEvent);
   }
   long nextArrivalTime =
       timestamp + Math.round((Math.random() + 0.5) *
           arrivalStreet.getMeanArrivalPeriod());
   VehicleArrivalEvent nextArrivalEvent =
       new VehicleArrivalEvent(nextArrivalTime,
           intersection, arrivalStreet);
   events.add(nextArrivalEvent);
}
```

Program 13.21 Method to perform the action associated with a vehicle-arrival event (in class `VehicleArrivalEvent`).

Summary

In this chapter:

- We have studied the concept of a priority queue, characterized as a least-first-out sequence.
- We have seen an example and a case study demonstrating applications of priority queues.
- We have designed an ADT for priority queues, expressed as a `PriorityQueue` interface.
- We have studied a special kind of binary tree called a heap, and how a heap can be efficiently represented by an array.
- We have studied how to represent priority queues by sorted and unsorted linked lists, and most efficiently by heaps, and how to code these in Java as classes that implement the `PriorityQueue` interface.

```
public void performAction (PriorityQueue events) {
// Perform the action associated with this vehicle-departure event,
//  adding new events to the events queue.
   if (departureStreet ==
          intersection.getGreenStreet()) {
      departureStreet.removeVehicle();
      if (departureStreet.hasVehicles()) {
         Vehicle vehicle =
             departureStreet.getFirstVehicle();
         long nextDepartTime =
             timestamp + vehicle.getCrossingTime();
         VehicleDepartureEvent nextDepartureEvent =
             new VehicleDepartureEvent(nextDepartTime,
                 intersection, departureStreet);
         events.add(nextDepartureEvent);
      }
   }
}
```

Program 13.22 Method to perform the action associated with a vehicle-departure event (in class VehicleDepartureEvent).

```
public void performAction (PriorityQueue events) {
// Perform the action associated with this signal-change event,
//  adding new events to the events queue.
   intersection.setGreenStreet(nextStreet);
   if (nextStreet.hasVehicles()) {
      Vehicle vehicle = nextStreet.getFirstVehicle();
      long nextDepartTime =
          timestamp + vehicle.getCrossingTime();
      VehicleDepartureEvent nextDepartureEvent =
          new VehicleDepartureEvent(nextDepartTime,
              intersection, nextStreet);
      events.add(nextDepartureEvent);
   }
   long nextSignalTime =
       timestamp + nextStreet.getSignalDuration();
   SignalChangeEvent nextSignalChange =
       new SignalChangeEvent(nextSignalTime,
           intersection, nextStreet,
           intersection.getStreetAfter(nextStreet));
   events.add(nextSignalChange);
}
```

Program 13.23 Method to perform the action associated with a signal-change event (in class SignalChangeEvent).

Exercises

13.1 Section 13.2 gives an example of a priority queue in everyday life. Can you think of any more examples?

13.2 Draw diagrams to show the effects of adding the letters D, G, A, E, B, C, and F (in that order) to a priority queue represented by:
(a) a sorted SLL (Figure 13.4)
(b) an unsorted SLL (Figure 13.6)
(c) a heap with *maxlength* = 7 (Figure 13.13).

13.3 Using your answers to Exercise 13.2, show the effects of performing the `removeLeast` operation three times on the resulting priority queue, for each of the representations (a–c).

13.4 Write a Java implementation of the unsorted SLL representation of a priority queue (outlined in Section 13.4.2). Does your implementation achieve the time complexities shown in Table 13.7?

13.5 Modify the `PriorityQueue` interface to support a `getGreatest` operation (*instead* of the `getLeast` operation).
Modify the Java implementations accordingly.

13.6 Modify the `PriorityQueue` interface to support *both* the `getLeast` and `getGreatest` operations.
Modify the Java implementations accordingly. What are the time complexities of the two operations?

13.7 By using suitable priorities, use a priority queue to implement a *last-in-first-out* sequence.

13.8 By using suitable priorities, use a priority queue to implement a *first-in-first-out* sequence.

13.9 Rather than restrict the elements of a priority queue to be `Comparable` objects, we can allow them to be arbitrary objects, provided that we equip the priority queue with a `java.util.Comparator` object to compare them.
Modify the `PriorityQueue` interface (Program 13.3) and the `HeapPriority-Queue` class (Program 13.15) to allow a priority queue to contain arbitrary objects, which are compared using a given `Comparator` object.
Use this modified implementation in Example 13.1, where `Person` objects are compared using a `PersonByYearComparator` object rather than using the `compareTo` method.

* 13.10 Extend your answer to Exercise 13.9 to allow a priority queue to contain *either* arbitrary objects that are compared using a given `Comparator` object, *or* `Comparable` objects that are compared using their `compareTo` method.
The modified `HeapPriorityQueue` class should provide two constructors:

```
public HeapPriorityQueue (int maxlength);
// Construct a priority queue, initially empty, whose length will be
// bounded by maxlength. Its elements will be Comparable objects
// ordered using compareTo.

public HeapPriorityQueue (int maxlength,
                Comparator comp);
// Construct a priority queue, initially empty, whose length will be
// bounded by maxlength. Its elements will be arbitrary objects
// ordered using the comparator comp.
```

13.11 Repeat Exercise 3.19 using the heap-sort algorithm (Algorithm 13.16).

** **13.12** Devise your own discrete event simulation using the techniques of Section 13.7. Implement it in Java.

** **13.13** One common application of a priority queue is the scheduling of processes in a computer operating system. At each scheduling decision, the 'least' process according to some criterion is selected and executed in its entirety.

A process includes the following data: a creation time, a duration, and a priority. When a process is executed, it is also given a start time and a stop time.

Create a simulation of process scheduling in a simple operating system. Generate processes at random. When each process is executed, show its creation time, start time, and stop time. (*Note:* A process cannot be executed before it is created.)

Use your simulation to compare the following scheduling strategies:

(a) *First-come, first-served:* the process with the least creation time is executed next.

(b) *Shortest-job first:* the process with the least duration is executed next.

(c) *Priority-based scheduling:* the process with the least priority is executed next.

For each strategy, calculate the average waiting time and the average turnaround time. (The *waiting time* of a process is the difference between its start time and its creation time. The *turnaround time* of a process is the difference between its stop time and its creation time.)

13.14 In a computer operating system, the priority of a process may change over time. For example, a low-priority process may have its priority periodically increased to ensure that it is eventually executed.

Modify the PriorityQueue interface to allow an element in the queue to be replaced using the following operation:

```
public void setElement (Comparable oldElem,
                Comparable newElem);
// Replace the element in this priority queue equal to oldElem by
// newElem. Throw a NoSuchElementException if this priority
// queue contains no such element.
```

Similarly modify the HeapPriorityQueue implementation. What is the time complexity of this operation?

** **13.15** Repeat Exercise 7.11 using the modified traffic simulator in Section 13.7.

** **13.16** Extend the traffic simulation of Section 13.7 to model a pair of four-street intersections at opposite ends of a city block. The two intersections are connected to each other by a (two-way) street. A vehicle departing from one intersection along that particular street will arrive (after a short interval) at the other intersection.

14

Tree Abstract Data Types

In this chapter we shall study:

- the concept of a tree, ordered and unordered trees (Section 14.1)
- applications of trees (Section 14.2)
- requirements and contract for a tree abstract data type (Section 14.3)
- a linked implementation of unordered trees (Section 14.4)
- specialized tree abstract data types (Section 14.5)
- a case study using trees (Section 14.6).

14.1 The concept of a tree

In Chapter 10 we studied binary search trees, which are data structures useful for representing sets and maps.

In this chapter we shall study trees as an abstract data type (ADT) in their own right. A tree is a *hierarchical* collection of elements (values). This characteristic property distinguishes trees from lists and other ADTs. Figures 14.1–14.3 are examples of trees.

More precisely, a *tree* is a collection of nodes such that:

- Each *node* contains an *element*, and has *branches* leading to a number of other nodes (its *children*).
- The tree has a unique *root* node.
- Every node other than the root node is a child of exactly one other node (its *parent*). The root node has no parent.

Note that a node may have any number of children.

A *leaf* node is one that has no children. The *size* of a tree is the number of nodes (elements) in that tree. An *empty tree* has size zero.

A node's *descendants* are its children, its grandchildren (children's children), and so on down to the leaf nodes. A node's *ancestors* are its parent, its grandparent (parent's parent), and so on up to the root node.

The **subtree rooted at** a given node consists of that node and all its descendants.

An **ordered tree** is one in which each node's children have a particular order (i.e., each node has a *list* of children). An **unordered tree** is one in which each node's children have no particular order (i.e., each node has a *set* of children).

14.2 Applications of trees

Trees occur frequently in real life:

- An *organization tree* records the structure of a hierarchical organization, such as the divisional structure within a business or university. (See Figure 14.1.)
- A *taxonomy* is a classification of organisms such as animals or plants. (See Figure 14.2.)
- A *family tree* records human parent–child relationships. (See Figure 14.3.) Our strict definition of a tree limits us to one parent per child, but we could model a complete family history by a pair of trees, one for mother–child relationships and one for father–child relationships.

Note that organization trees and taxonomies are unordered trees, whereas family trees are ordered (by date of birth).

Trees also occur frequently in computer applications. The following example illustrates an application of trees found in every modern computer system.

EXAMPLE 14.1 *File hierarchies*

A modern file system supports both documents and folders. A *document* (or *plain file*) is a named data file, which might contain text or pictures or spreadsheets. A *folder* (or *directory*) is a named group of documents and other folders. Since a folder may contain other folders, to any depth, we have a file hierarchy.

We can model a file hierarchy by a tree in which documents are modeled by leaf nodes and (nonempty) folders are modeled by parent nodes. Figure 14.4 illustrates a possible file hierarchy.

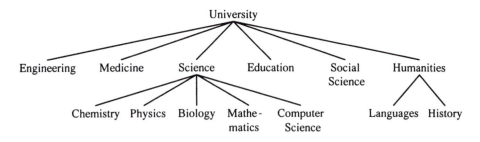

Figure 14.1   An organization tree for a typical university (simplified).

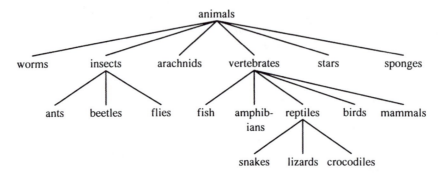

Figure 14.2 A taxonomy of animals (simplified).

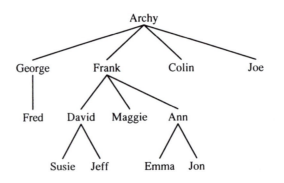

Figure 14.3 A family tree.

Program 14.5 shows part of the application code, in the form of a class named `FileHierarchy`. The variable `fileTree` represents the file hierarchy. The `create` method is a typical operation on the file hierarchy, creating a new document in a given folder. The find method is another typical operation, finding all documents with a given name in the file hierarchy. This method calls an auxiliary method, `findAll`, that recursively searches a given folder and all its subfolders for all documents with a given name.

Program 14.6 shows an inner class, `Descriptor`, whose objects describe documents and folders. For the purposes of this example, the most relevant instance variables are `name` and `isFolder`.

The application code assumes various operations on trees that behave as follows: t.`root()` returns the root node of tree t; t.`parent(n)` returns the parent of node n in tree t; t.`children(n)` returns an iterator that will visit all the children of node n in tree t; t.`addChild(n, e)` adds a node containing element e, making it a child of node n in tree t; n.`getElement()` returns the element contained in node n.

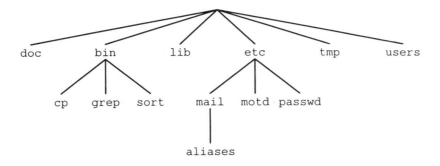

Figure 14.4   A hierarchical file system.

14.3 A tree abstract data type

Let us now design a tree ADT. As usual, we start by identifying requirements. Some of the following requirements were foreshadowed in the previous two sections.

1. It must be possible to access the root of a tree.
2. It must be possible to access all the ancestors of any node in a tree.
3. It must be possible to access all the descendants of any node in a tree.
4. It must be possible to add a new node to a tree, either as the root node or as the child of an existing node.
5. It must be possible to remove a given node from a tree, together with all its descendants.
6. It must be possible to traverse a tree.

Program 14.7 shows a possible contract, expressed as a Java interface named `Tree`, which includes an inner interface named `Tree.Node`. The methods of the `Tree` interface are sufficient to meet all the above requirements. In particular, requirement 2 is met by repeated applications of the `parent` operation, and requirements 3 and 6 are met by repeated applications of the `children` operation.

14.4 A linked implementation of trees

Trees can be represented in a variety of ways. Here we shall consider just one possible representation, based on singly-linked lists (SLLs). The children of a parent are linked together in an SLL, with the parent containing a link to the first child. In addition, each child is linked to its parent. This representation is illustrated in Figure 14.8.

14.4.1 Unordered trees

In an unordered tree, each parent has a *set* of children. We have already seen, in Section

```java
public class FileHierarchy {

    // Each FileHierarchy object describes a hierarchical collection of
    // documents and folders, in which a folder may contain any number of
    // documents and other folders. Within a given folder, all documents and
    // folders have different names.

    // This file hierarchy is represented by a tree, fileTree, whose elements
    // are Descriptor objects.
    private Tree fileTree;

    public final String DELIMITER = "/";
    public final String ROOTPATHNAME = "";

    /////////////// Constructor ///////////////

    public FileHierarchy () {
    // Construct a new, empty file hierarchy.
        fileTree = new LinkedUnorderedTree();
    }

    /////////////// File hierarchy operations ///////////////

    public void create (String localName,
                    Tree.Node folder) {
    // Create a new document, named localName, inside folder in this
    // file hierarchy, or throw an exception if this the name is already used.
        if (used(localName, folder))
            throw new IllegalArgumentException(localName
                + " already used");
        Descriptor descr = new Descriptor(localName,
            false, Descriptor.DEFAULT_PERMISSIONS,
            new File());
        fileTree.addChild(folder, descr);
    }

    public List find (String targetName) {
    // Return a list of the complete path-names of all documents named
    // targetName in this file hierarchy.
        List pathnames = new LinkedList();
        findAll(targetName, fileTree.root(), pathnames);
        return pathnames;
    }
```

Program 14.5 A file hierarchy application (*continued on next page*).

... // Other file hierarchy operations, omitted here.

/////////// Auxiliary methods ///////////

```
private boolean used (String name,
              Tree.Node folder) {
// Return true if and only if name is the name of a document or folder
// within folder in this file hierarchy.
    Iterator children = fileTree.children(folder);
    while (children.hasNext()) {
      Tree.Node child = (Tree.Node) children.next();
      Descriptor childDescr =
          (Descriptor) child.getElement();
      if (name.equals(childDescr.name))
        return true;
    }
    return false;
}


private void findAll (String targetName,
              Tree.Node folder, List pathnames) {
// Add to pathnames the complete pathnames of all documents named
// targetName in folder, and all of its sub-folders, in this file
// hierarchy.
    Iterator children = fileTree.children(folder);
    while (children.hasNext()) {
      Tree.Node child = (Tree.Node) children.next();
      Descriptor childDescr =
          (Descriptor) child.getElement();
      if (childDescr.isFolder)
        findAll(targetName, child, pathnames);
      else if (targetName.equals(childDescr.name))
        pathnames.add(pathName(child));
    }
}
```

Program 14.5 (*continued on next page*)

9.5, that a set can be represented by an unsorted SLL. In typical applications of trees this simple set representation is perfectly adequate, since the number of children per parent tends to be quite small.

We shall analyze the principal tree operations in terms of the number of nodes visited.

Since each child contains a link to its parent, the `parent` operation's time complexity is $O(1)$.

```
    private String pathName (Tree.Node node) {
// Return the full pathname of the file at node in this file hierarchy.
    if (node == fileTree.root())
      return ROOTPATHNAME;
    else {
      Descriptor descr =
          (Descriptor) node.getElement();
      return pathName(fileTree.parent(node))
          + DELIMITER + descr.name;
    }
  }
}

//////////  Inner class for document/folder descriptors.  //////////

...   //  See Program 14.6.

}
```

Program 14.5 (continued)

```
private static class Descriptor {

    // Each Descriptor object describes a document or folder.

    // This description contains the document or folder's local name (name); a
    // flag indicating whether it is a folder (isFolder); a flag whose least
    // significant bits indicate whether it is readable, writable, and executable
    // (permissions); and a reference to its underlying file in the case of a
    // document (file).
    private String name;
    private boolean isFolder;
    private byte permissions;
    private File file;   // null for a folder

    private static final byte
            DEFAULT_PERMISSIONS = 0x07;

    private Descriptor (String name, boolean isFolder,
                byte permissions, File file) {
      this.name = name;  this.isFolder = isFolder;
      this.permissions = permissions;
      this.file = file;
    }

}
```

Program 14.6   Representation of document/folder descriptors (inner class of `FileHierarchy`).

```
public interface Tree {

    //  Each Tree object is a tree whose elements are arbitrary objects.

    ///////////// Accessors /////////////

    public Tree.Node root ();
    //  Return the root node of this tree, or null if this tree is empty.

    public Tree.Node parent (Tree.Node node);
    //  Return the parent of node in this tree, or null if node is the root node.

    public int childCount (Tree.Node node);
    //  Return the number of children of node in this tree.

    ///////////// Transformers /////////////

    public void makeRoot (Object elem);
    //  Make this tree consist of just a root node containing element elem.

    public Tree.Node addChild (Tree.Node node,
                    Object elem);
    //  Add a new node containing element elem as a child of node in this
    //  tree, and return the new node. The new node has no children of its own.

    public void remove (Tree.Node node);
    //  Remove node from this tree, together with all its descendants.

    ///////////// Iterator /////////////

    public Iterator children (Tree.Node node);
    //  Return an iterator that will visit all the children of node in this tree.

    ///////////// Inner interface for tree nodes /////////////

    public interface Node {

        //  Each Tree.Node object is a node of a tree, and contains a single
        //  element.

        public Object getElement ();
        //  Return the element contained in this node.

        public void setElement (Object elem);
        //  Change the element contained in this node to be elem.

    }

}
```

Program 14.7 A contract for a tree ADT.

The addChild operation might as well insert the new node at the front of the SLL, since the order of children within the SLL is insignificant. This operation's time complexity is therefore $O(1)$.

The remove operation can be implemented by a variant of SLL deletion. Unless the node to be removed happens to be its parent's first child, it is necessary to access the node's predecessor in the SLL, by following links from the first child. If the maximum number of children per node is c, the remove operation visits at most c nodes, and its time complexity is $O(c)$.

Table 14.9 summarizes the algorithms and their time complexities. In theory $O(c)$ could mean $O(n)$, because a tree of size n could consist of a root with $n - 1$ children. In practical applications of trees, however, c typically does not grow in proportion to n.

Program 14.10 outlines a Java implementation of unordered trees. This consists of a class named LinkedUnorderedTree, which includes a private inner class named LinkedUnorderedTree.Node. These classes implement the Tree and Tree.Node interfaces respectively.

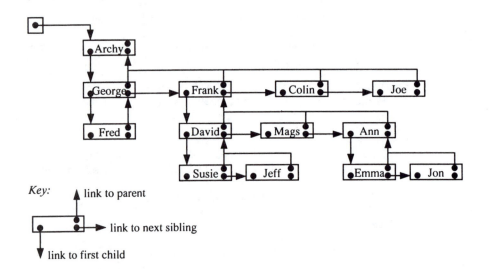

Figure 14.8   Linked representation of a tree (corresponding to Figure 14.3).

Table 14.9   Implementation of unordered trees using linked data structures: summary of algorithms (where c is the maximum number of children per parent).

Operation	Algorithm	Time complexity
parent	trivial	$O(1)$
addChild	SLL insertion before first node	$O(1)$
remove	SLL deletion	$O(c)$

```
public class LinkedUnorderedTree implements Tree {

    //  Each LinkedUnorderedTree object is an unordered tree whose
    //  elements are arbitrary objects.

    //  This tree is represented by a reference to its root node (root), which is
    //  null if the tree is empty. Each tree node contains links to its first child, to
    //  its parent, and to its next sibling.
    private LinkedUnorderedTree.Node root;

    ///////////// Constructor ////////////

    public LinkedUnorderedTree () {
    //  Construct a tree, initially empty.
        root = null;
    }

    ///////////// Accessors ////////////

    public Tree.Node root () {
    //  Return the root node of this tree, or null if this tree is empty.
        return root;
    }

    public Tree.Node parent (Tree.Node node) {
    //  Return the parent of node in this tree, or null if node is the root node.
        return node.parent;
    }

    public int childCount (Tree.Node node) {
    //  Return the number of children of node in this tree.
        LinkedUnorderedTree.Node parent =
            (LinkedUnorderedTree.Node) node;
        int count = 0;
        for (LinkedUnorderedTree.Node child =
                parent.firstChild;
            child != null; child = child.nextSib)
            count++;
        return count;
    }
```

Program 14.10 Java implementation of unordered trees using linked data structures (outline) (*continued on next page*).

```
///////////  Transformers  ///////////

public void makeRoot (Object elem) {
// Make this tree consist of just a root node containing element elem.
  root = new LinkedUnorderedTree.Node(elem);
}


public Tree.Node addChild (Tree.Node node,
            Object elem) {
// Add a new node containing element elem as a child of node in this
// tree, and return the new node. The new node has no children of its own.
  LinkedUnorderedTree.Node parent =
          (LinkedUnorderedTree.Node) node;
  LinkedUnorderedTree.Node newChild =
          new LinkedUnorderedTree.Node(elem);
  newChild.parent = parent;
  newChild.nextSib = parent.firstChild;
  parent.firstChild = newChild;
  return newChild;
}


public void remove (Tree.Node node) {
// Remove node from this tree, together with all its descendants.
  if (node == root) {
    root = null;
    return;
  }
  LinkedUnorderedTree.Node parent = node.parent;
  if (node == parent.firstChild)
    parent.firstChild = node.nextSib;
  else {
    LinkedUnorderedTree.Node prevSib =
      parent.firstChild;
    while (prevSib.nextSib != node)
      prevSib = prevSib.nextSib;
    prevSib.nextSib = node.nextSib;
  }
}
///////////  Iterator  ///////////

...   // Omitted here.
```

Program 14.10 (*continued on next page*)

```
private static class Node implements Tree.Node {

    // Each LinkedUnorderedTree.Node object is a node of an
    // unordered tree, and contains a single element.

    // This tree node consists of an element (element), a link to its first
    // child (firstChild) a link to its parent (parent), and a link to its
    // next sibling (nextSib).
    private Object element;
    private LinkedUnorderedTree.Node firstChild,
        parent, nextSib;

    private Node (Object elem) {
    // Construct a tree node, containing element elem, that has no children,
    // no parent, and no siblings.
        this.element = elem;  this.firstChild = null;
        this.parent = null;   this.nextSib = null;
    }

    public Object getElement () {
    // Return the element contained in this node.
        return this.element;
    }

    public void setElement (Object elem) {
    // Change the element contained in this node to be elem.
        this.element = elem;
    }

    }

}
```

Program 14.10 (*continued*)

14.4.2 Ordered trees

The linked representation of trees in Figure 14.8 is also suitable for ordered trees. The only difference is that the order of nodes in each SLL of children *is* significant; the addChild operation must add the new node at the end of the SLL. This makes the addChild operation's time complexity $O(c)$ rather than $O(1)$, unless we modify the representation such that each tree node contains a link to its last child as well as its first child.

14.5 Specialized tree abstract data types

The tree ADT designed in Section 14.3 (and implemented in Section 14.4) is very general: it allows nodes to contain arbitrary elements, and it allows each node to have an arbitrary number of children. It is quite common, however, for a particular application to feature trees with a specialized structure. In such an application it might be preferable to design and implement a specialized tree ADT. The following example illustrates this possibility.

EXAMPLE 14.2 *Arithmetic expression trees*

We are all familiar with arithmetic expressions, such as:
(a) $10 - 3$
(b) $2 \times 3.1416 \times 5.0$
(c) $2 \times (0.3 + 0.4)$
(d) $1/2 + 1/3$

Such expressions are conventionally presented as strings of symbols. But when we attempt to develop algorithms to interpret such expressions (e.g., to evaluate them), the string representation turns out to be very inconvenient. Consider expression (d) above: the algorithm must take care to interpret it as $(1/2) + (1/3)$, as intended, and not as $((1/2) + 1)/3$ or $1/(2 + 1)/3$.

Much better is a tree representation, in which each leaf node contains a numeral (such as 2 or 3.1416) and each non-leaf node contains an operator ($+$, $-$, $\times$, or $/$). Expression trees for the above expressions are shown in Figure 14.11. Consider Figure 14.11(d): the tree's structure makes it absolutely clear that the operands of '+' are 1/2 and 1/3.

It is simple to devise a recursive algorithm to evaluate an expression tree. For instance, if the tree's topmost node contains '+', evaluate the left operand (i.e., left subtree), evaluate the right operand (i.e., right subtree), and add the results. The other operators are analogous. If the tree has a single leaf node, it is evaluated immediately.

We can represent expression trees by objects of the class `Expression` shown in Program 14.12. `Expression` is an abstract class, so a tree actually consists of a collection of objects of the subclasses of `Expression`, namely `Numeral`, `Sum`, `Difference`, `Product`, and `Quotient`. Each of these objects represents a tree node. Moreover, each `Sum`, `Difference`, `Product`, or `Quotient` object contains references to two other `Expression` objects, its left and right operands. Figure 14.13 shows the detailed structure of the `Expression` tree corresponding to Figure 14.11(c).

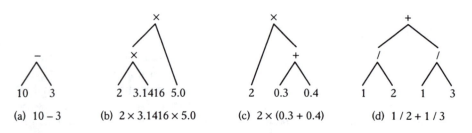

Figure 14.11 Some expression trees.

```
public abstract class Expression {

    // Each Expression object describes an arithmetic expression.

    public abstract float evaluate ();
    // Return the result of evaluating this expression.

}

///////////////////////////////////////////////////////

public class Numeral extends Expression {

    // Each Numeral object describes an expression consisting simply of a
    // numeric literal.

    private float literalValue;

    public float evaluate () {
    // Return the result of evaluating this expression.
        return literalValue;
    }

}

///////////////////////////////////////////////////////

public class Sum extends Expression {

    // Each Sum object describes an expression consisting of the sum of two
    // operands, which are themselves expressions.

    private Expression leftOperand, rightOperand;

    public float evaluate () {
        return leftOperand.evaluate()
             + rightOperand.evaluate();
    }

}
```

Program 14.12 Class declarations for expression trees (*continued on next page*).

```
//////////////////////////////////////////////////////////

public class Difference extends Expression {

    //  Each Difference object describes an expression consisting of the
    //  difference of two operands, which are themselves expressions.

    ...   // Analogous to Sum.

}


//////////////////////////////////////////////////////////

public class Product extends Expression {

    //  Each Product object describes an expression consisting of the product
    //  of two operands, which are themselves expressions.

    ...   // Analogous to Sum.

}


//////////////////////////////////////////////////////////

public class Quotient extends Expression {

    //  Each Quotient object describes an expression consisting of the
    //  quotient of two operands, which are themselves expressions.

    ...   // Analogous to Sum.

}
```

Program 14.12 (*continued*)

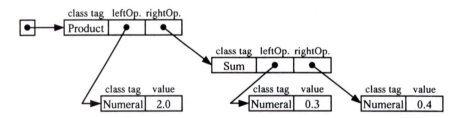

Figure 14.13 Detailed structure of objects in an Expression tree (corresponding to Figure 14.11(c)).

In Program 14.12 we have equipped each `Expression` object with an `evaluate` method, which returns the result of evaluating the corresponding expression. For a `Numeral` expression the evaluation is trivial. For a `Sum` expression the `evaluate` method simply evaluates the two operands and adds the results. The other cases are analogous.

14.6 Case study: game playing

How do computers play chess and other games of skill? At the center of every game-playing program is a ***game tree***. A game tree records the current position in the game, some of the possible future positions, and the moves required to reach each future position. It allows the program to assess the effects of playing different moves, and thus decide which is the best move in a given position.

For example, *chess* is a game played by two players, conventionally known as White and Black. The root node of a chess game tree contains the initial position. The children of the root node contain the positions that can be reached after White's first move. (There are twenty possible moves.) Each of these child nodes in turn has its own children, which contain the positions reached after Black's reply. (Again there are twenty possible moves, so there are already 400 possible positions.) We can grow the tree further, representing positions reached after further moves by White and Black.

The leaf nodes of a complete game tree represent the ***terminal positions*** in the game. For example, the terminal positions in a chess game tree would be the checkmate and stalemate positions. A terminal position can be assigned a score, representing a win, loss, or draw.

Given a complete game tree, a game-playing program can select the best moves simply by following a path from the root node that leads to the best outcome, i.e., a win for the computer. Unfortunately, the complete game tree for many games is extremely large. For example, a complete chess game tree consists of approximately 10^{100} nodes, and so its construction is infeasible.

Even when a complete game tree cannot be constructed, we can make do with an incomplete game tree. Typically we expand the tree to only a certain depth below the current position. The chosen depth is called the ***ply***. But how do we evaluate the leaf nodes of this incomplete game tree, which no longer necessarily represent terminal positions? We develop an ***evaluation function***, which takes a position and produces a score that represents the 'goodness' of that position, i.e., how likely it is to lead to a winning terminal position. We then use the scores of the leaf nodes to select the best sequence of moves to follow (given the current ply). The scores are usually integers, with increasingly positive values representing increasingly better positions for the computer, and increasingly negative values representing increasingly better positions for the human.

In this case study, we will look at the use of a game tree in a program to play the relatively simple game of *tic-tac-toe* (or *noughts and crosses*). Our implementation of the game tree, however, will be largely independent of the particular game being played, and could be adapted to other game-playing programs. (See Exercise 14.19.)

14.6.1 Representing tic-tac-toe positions

To construct a tic-tac-toe game tree, we first require a representation of a position in the game. We shall record the following data for each tic-tac-toe position:

- the board, indicating which squares are occupied and which are empty
- the player who will make the next move
- the last move, i.e., the move played to reach this position (except for the initial position)
- the score for this position.

Figure 14.14 shows the layout of the board in a tic-tac-toe game. The squares are numbered 0 (top-left corner) through 8 (bottom-right corner). Program 14.15 is an implementation of a Java class, GamePosition, that represents a tic-tac-toe position. The board is represented by an array of nine bytes, and a move is just an index of the array. For efficiency, we also record whether or not a position is terminal.

14.6.2 A tic-tac-toe evaluation function

To evaluate a position in tic-tac-toe we should consider both players' chances of winning. To win, a player must complete a line of three 'X's or three 'O's (as the case may be). There are eight possible lines (three horizontal, three vertical, two diagonal) on the board.

Let a *blocked line* be a line containing both 'X's and 'O's. A blocked line is worthless, since it can never lead to a win.

Let an *open line* be a line consisting entirely of 'X's and empty squares, or consisting entirely of 'O's and empty squares. The *length* of an open line is the number of 'X's or 'O's it contains; this can be 1, 2, or 3. To evaluate a position in tic-tac-toe, we count the open lines of length 1, 2, and 3 for each player.

Consider a position resulting from a move by the computer. One of the following situations must apply:

- The human has already completed a line of length 3, and so has won the game. (The computer's move is irrelevant.) The score should be the largest negative integer, representing a loss for the computer.
- The computer has completed a line of length 3, and so has won. The score should be the largest positive integer, representing a win for the computer.
- The computer plays a move, but no lines of length 3 have been completed, and so neither player has won. In this situation, we should consider the likely outcome of the game, and the score should reflect the threats and opportunities available to both players.

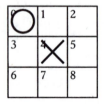

Figure 14.14   The tic-tac-toe board, showing the nine positions (0–8).

```
public class GamePosition {

    // Each GamePosition object represents a position in a tic-tac-toe game.

    // This game position consists of the board, the player to move next,
    // the last move played, the score for this position, and whether or not this
    // position is terminal.

    private byte[] board;
    private byte nextPlayer;
    private int lastMove;
    private int score;
    private boolean isTerminal;

    // Constants representing (i) the states of the squares on the board, and
    // (ii) the players:
    public static final byte EMPTY = 0,
        COMPUTER_PLAYER = 1,  HUMAN_PLAYER = 2;

    ///////////// Constructors /////////////

    public GamePosition (byte player) {
    // Create a new game position representing the initial position, with
    // player to move first.
        this.board = new byte[9]; // ... all EMPTY
        this.nextPlayer = player;  this.lastMove = 0;
        this.score = 0;  this.isTerminal = false;
    }

    private GamePosition (byte[] board,
                    byte nextPlayer, int lastMove) {
    // Create a new game position representing a position with the given board,
    // next player, and last move (used only inside this class).
        this.board = board;
        this.nextPlayer = nextPlayer;
        this.lastMove = lastMove;
        this.evaluate();
        this.isTerminal = hasWon(COMPUTER_PLAYER) ||
            hasWon(HUMAN_PLAYER) || numMovesLeft() == 0;
    }
}
```

Program 14.15 Java implementation of tic-tac-toe positions (*continued on next page*).

```
///////////  Accessors  ///////////

public static byte other (byte player) {
// Given player, return the other player.
   return (player == COMPUTER_PLAYER ?
      HUMAN_PLAYER : COMPUTER_PLAYER);
}

public int getNextPlayer () {
// Return the next player to play from this position.
   return this.nextPlayer;
}

public int getScore () {
// Return the score for this position.
   return this.score;
}

public int getLastMove () {
// Return the last move played to reach this position.
   return this.lastMove;
}

public boolean isValidMove (int move) {
// Return true if and only if move is valid in this position.
   return (move >= 0 && move <= 8
      && board[move] == EMPTY);
}

public boolean isTerminalPosition () {
// Return true if and only if this position is terminal, i.e., either a win
// for one player or a draw.
   return this.isTerminal;
}

public void drawBoard (Panel panel) {
// Draw a representation of the board on the given window panel.
   ... // See code on the companion Web site.
}

///////////  Transformers  ///////////

public void setScore (int score) {
// Set the score of this game position to score.
   this.score = score;
}
```

Program 14.15 (*continued on next page*)

```java
public GamePosition playMove (int move) {
// Return a new game position that results from playing move in this
// game position.
   return new GamePosition (
        createBoard(nextPlayer, move),
        other(nextPlayer), move);
}


public GamePosition[] playAllMoves () {
// Return an array of new game positions that result from all possible
// moves in this game position.
    ... // See code on the companion Web site.
}


public boolean isWinner (byte player) {
// Return true if and only if player is the winner of the game.
    ... // See code on the companion Web site.
}

/////////////// Auxiliary methods ///////////////

private void evaluate () {
// Evaluate this game position, and set its score accordingly.
    ... // See Section 14.6.2.
}


private int numMovesLeft () {
// Return the number of empty squares on the board.
    ... // See code on the companion Web site.
}


private byte[] createBoard (byte player,
                int move) {
// Create the board that results from player playing move in this game
// position.
    ... // See code on the companion Web site.
}

}
```

Program 14.15 (*continued*)

Consider this last case in more detail. If the human has an open line of length 2, then he or she is threatening to win the game on the next move. This threat should receive a very large and negative value, say -1000 (bad for the computer). If the computer has an open line of length 2, then it has an opportunity to win the game on its next move, but only if the human does not block it. This opportunity should receive a large and positive value, say $+100$ (good for the computer); this is not as large as the negative value of the human's threat, since the win for the computer is not certain. If the human has an open line of length 1, he or she may extend this line to length 2, and so move closer to winning the game. This indirect threat should receive a small and negative value, say -10 (bad for the computer). Finally, if the computer has on open line of length 1, it may similarly extend it to a line of length 2. This opportunity should receive a very small and positive value, say $+1$ (good for the computer).

In general, the position will contain multiple threats or opportunities. We determine its score by summing the values for the individual threats and opportunities.

The values attached to the individual threats and opportunities must be chosen carefully. For example, even if the computer has two open lines of length 2, their contribution to the score must not exceed a single open line of length 2 for the human, since the human can win before the computer has a chance to exploit its open lines. The values we have chosen are decreasing powers of 10 with alternating signs, i.e., $-1000, +100, -10$, and $+1$.

Now consider a position resulting from a move by the human. The situation we have just described is reversed: for the human, negative values are good and positive values are bad. So we reverse the signs of the values attached to the opportunities and threats: $+1000, -100, +10, -1$. The simplest way to do this is to compute the score as above and then reverse its sign.

Program 14.16 shows the implementation of our tic-tac-toe evaluation function as a Java method, `evaluate`, and an auxiliary method, `countLines`. These would be added to the `GamePosition` class of Program 14.15.

14.6.3 A tic-tac-toe game tree

The nodes in the tic-tac-toe game tree contain positions in the game. The game tree of Figure 14.17 shows some possible early positions in the game.

Figure 14.17 omits positions that are symmetrically similar. For example, there are nine possible opening moves, but only three of the resulting positions are distinct: an 'X' in the center square, in a corner square, or in a square in the middle of an edge. Similarly, only twelve of the possible moves by the other player lead to distinct positions.

However, our simple tic-tac-toe program does not exploit symmetry. The game tree contains all nine opening positions at depth 1, and each of these nine positions has eight subsequent positions at depth 2. The game tree therefore has seventy-two nodes at depth 2, rather than just twelve.

The main operations required on the game tree are:

- It must be possible for the computer to calculate the score for a given position by looking several moves ahead.

```
private static final int
       LOSS = - Integer.MAX_VALUE + 1,
       WIN  = + Integer.MAX_VALUE - 1;

private void evaluate () {
// Evaluate this game position, and set its score accordingly.
   byte playerLines[] = countLines(nextPlayer);
   byte opponentLines[] =
       countLines(other(nextPlayer));
   if (opponentLines[3] > 0)
     score = LOSS;
   else if (playerLines[3] > 0)
     score = WIN;
   else
     // Score the opportunities and threats:
     score = - 1000 * opponentLines[2]
           + 100 * playerLines[2]
           - 10 * opponentLines[1]
           + playerLines[1];
   // Reverse the sign of the score if the next player is the human:
   if (nextPlayer == HUMAN_PLAYER)
     score = -score;
}


private byte[] countLines (byte player) {
// Count the number of open lines of length 1, 2, and 3 for player.
// Return an array a such that a[i] is the number of open lines of length i.
// (a[0] is unused.)
   ... // See code on companion Web site.
}
```

Program 14.16   A tic-tac-toe evaluation function (in class `GamePosition`).

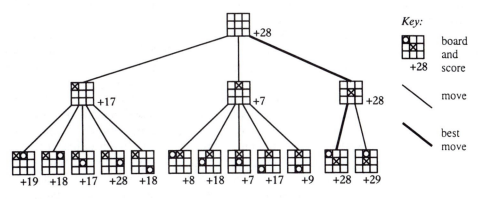

Figure 14.17   The initial tic-tac-toe game tree, with the computer to move (simplified). The ply is 2.

- It must be possible for the computer to play the best move found in a given position.
- It must be possible for the human to play any valid move.

Given the current position, we must calculate its score. If it is a terminal position, then its score is known immediately. If is not terminal, we must consider the possible moves from this position in the game tree. In fact, we must propagate the best score from the leaf nodes of the tree up to the current node. We do this with the ***minimax*** algorithm, which we now explain.

At each depth in the game tree, the best move depends on which player is to move. If it is the computer's turn, the best move is the one with the maximum score, whereas if it is the human's turn, the best move is the one with the minimum (most negative) score. To calculate the score for a particular non-leaf node, we take the maximum score of its children if it is the computer's turn, and we take the minimum score of its children if it is the human's turn. The minimax algorithm is named after the alternating minimizing and maximizing of the scores at different depths in the tree.

Program 14.19 gives the implementation of a game tree as a Java class, `GameTree`. A game tree consists of two instance variables: a tree whose nodes contain `GamePosition` objects, and a reference to the current node, i.e., the node containing the current position. The root of the game tree contains the initial position in the game. The path from the root to the current node contains only a single node at each depth, and represents the sequence of moves already played. Below the current node, the tree is used to search for moves, and the current node has as many children as there are possible moves resulting from that position. The depth of the subtree rooted at the current node is the ply. When a move is made, we update the current node to be the new position, and remove all of its sibling nodes. We then expand the tree by searching further ahead.

The construction of the tree is performed by the auxiliary method `calculateScore`. This method proceeds as follows. If the given node contains a terminal position, the method terminates. Otherwise, if the given node has no children, the method expands the tree by generating all possible moves from the current position (using `playAllMoves`). If the ply is greater than 1, it continues the construction of the game tree by recursively calculating the score for each child node, but for the other player and with the ply reduced by one. Finally, it determines the score for the given node by taking either the maximum or the minimum score of its children, depending on the player. This is the minimax step.

The methods `makeBestMove` and `makeOpponentsMove` update the game tree with the computer's and the human's move, respectively. In both cases, once a move has been played, the sibling positions in the game tree are removed, as they are no longer needed.

In method `makeBestMove`, a best move is a child of the current node with the same score as the current node. We must proceed with care, however, as it is possible that several children may share the same best score. For example, they might all represent a win for the computer. Some of these children might contain terminal positions, i.e., they represent an immediate win, while others contain nonterminal positions. When we select the best move, we should prefer an immediate win to a delayed win (not because the outcome will be different, but because it is annoying for the human if the computer does not finish the game quickly). If none of the best children contain terminal positions, we can choose any one of them. All sibling nodes of the chosen move should be removed from the tree.

In method `makeOpponentsMove`, the new current node is determined by the move entered by the human. Since the tree should contain all possible moves, we should simply remove the nodes corresponding to different moves, and update the current node accordingly. However, if the human is moving first, or if the ply is very small, it is possible that the tree has not yet been expanded to give the current node any children, so we must create a new node to contain the new position.

Figure 14.18(a) shows the game tree for a tic-tac-toe game after four moves, with the computer due to play next. (The computer is 'X' and the human is 'O'.) From the position in the current node, the game tree has been expanded to a ply of 2. The computer has a choice of five possible moves. Four of these moves fail to block a line of length 2 belonging to the human, so the resulting positions have a losing score for the computer. (Positions resulting from the human omitting to play the winning move have been omitted in Figure 14.18(a).)

If the computer does block the human's open line, by the move that leads to position a, the human will have four possible moves in reply, leading to positions b, c, d, and e. The scores for these four positions are calculated using the evaluation function, and are shown

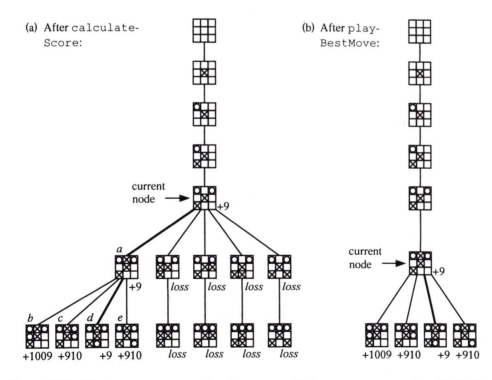

Figure 14.18 The tic-tac-toe game tree after four moves, with the computer to move (simplified). The ply is 2.

```java
public class GameTree {

    // Each GameTree object represents the sequence of moves in the game
    // so far, and the possible future moves from the current position.

    // A game tree consists of a tree of GamePosition objects, and a tree
    // node containing the current position.

    private Tree gameTree;
    private Tree.Node currentNode;

    ///////////// Constructor /////////////

    public GameTree (byte player) {
    // Construct a new game tree containing the opening position with
    // player due to move first.
        this.gameTree = new LinkedUnorderedTree();
        GamePosition pos = new GamePosition(player);
        gameTree.makeRoot(pos);
        this.currentNode = gameTree.root();
    }

    ///////////// Accessors /////////////

    public boolean isOver () {
    // Return true if and only if the game is over, i.e., the current position is a
    // terminal position.
        ...  // See code on companion Web site.
    }


    public byte getWinner () {
    // Return the identity of the winning player, or 0 if the game is a draw.
    // (Assume that the current position is terminal.)
        ...  // See code on companion Web site.
    }


    public boolean isValidMove (int move) {
    // Return true if and only if move is valid in the current position.
        ...  // See code on companion Web site.
    }
```

Program 14.19 Java implementation of tic-tac-toe game trees (*continued on next page*).

```
public void drawBoard (Panel panel) {
// Draw a representation of the board in the current position on the
// given window panel.
   ... // See code on companion Web site.
}


//////////// Transformers ///////////


public void calculateScore (int ply) {
// Set the score for the current position to the best score found by
// searching for a move by the next player using a look-ahead of ply.
// (Assume that ply ≥ 1.)
   calculateScore(currentNode, ply);
}


public void makeBestMove () {
// Play the best move from the current node, update the current node, and
// remove siblings of the new current node.
   GamePosition currentPos =
        (GamePosition) currentNode.getElement();
   int bestScore = currentPos.getScore();
   boolean foundEndMove = false;
   Iterator children =
        gameTree.children(currentNode);
   currentNode = null;
   // ... will eventually be updated according to the chosen move.
   while (children.hasNext()) {
     Tree.Node nextNode =
          (Tree.Node) children.next();
     GamePosition nextPos =
          (GamePosition) nextNode.getElement();
     if (nextPos.getScore() == bestScore
         && ! foundEndMove) {
       // nextPos has the best score.
       if (nextPos.isTerminalPosition()) {
         // We have found a move to end the game, so choose it.
         if (currentNode != null)
            gameTree.remove(currentNode);
         currentNode = nextNode;
         foundEndMove = true;
       } else {
         // We have found a best move, so choose it provisionally
         // (unless we have already chosen another move).
```

Program 14.19 (*continued on next page*)

```
                    if (currentNode == null)
                        currentNode = nextNode;
                    else
                        children.remove();
                }
            } else {
                // Either nextPos does not have the best score, or we have
                // already found a move to end the game.
                children.remove();
            }
        }
    }
}

public void makeOpponentsMove (int move) {
// Play move in the current position, update the current node, and remove
// siblings of the new current node. If move is not already present in the
// tree, add it.
    ...     // See code on companion Web site.
}

//////////// Auxiliary methods ////////////

private void calculateScore (Tree.Node node,
                int ply) {
// Set the score for the position in node to the best score found by
// searching for a move by the next player using a look-ahead of ply.
// (Assume that ply ≥ 1.)
    GamePosition pos =
        (GamePosition) node.getElement();
    if (pos.isTerminalPosition())  return;
    if (gameTree.childCount(node) == 0) {
        // Expand this node by adding its children.
        GamePosition[] positions = pos.playAllMoves();
        for (int i = 0; i < positions.length; i++)
            gameTree.addChild(node, positions[i]);
    }
    // If required, expand the tree further:
    if (ply > 1) {
        Iterator children = gameTree.children(node);
        while (children.hasNext()) {
            Tree.Node newNode =
                (Tree.Node) children.next();
            calculateScore(newNode, ply-1);
        }
    }
}
```

Program 14.19 (*continued on next page*)

```
    //  Set the score of this position to the best score found:
    byte player = pos.getNextPlayer();
    int bestScore =
        (player == GamePosition.COMPUTER_PLAYER ?
            getMaximum(node)  : getMinimum(node));
    pos.setScore(bestScore);
}


  private int getMaximum (Tree.Node node) {
  //  Return the largest score of all the children of node.
    int maxScore = Integer.MIN_VALUE;
    //  ... smaller than any valid score.
    Iterator children = gameTree.children(node);
    while (children.hasNext()) {
      Tree.Node curr = (Tree.Node) children.next();
      GamePosition pos =
          (GamePosition) curr.getElement();
      int score = pos.getScore();
      if (score > maxScore)  maxScore = score;
    }
    return maxScore;
  }


  private int getMinimum (Tree.Node node) {
  //  Return the smallest score of all the children of node.
    ... //  Analogous to getMaximum.
  }


}
```

Program 14.19 (*continued*)

beside each position in Figure 14.18(a). To calculate the score for position *a*, we take the *minimum* of the scores of positions *b*, *c*, *d*, and *e*, since it is the human's turn to move. This results in a score of +9 for position *a*.

At the current node, we take the *maximum* of the scores of its children, since it is the computer's turn to move. Since +9 is greater than *loss* (which is negative), the score for the position in the current node is +9. Now the computer will play the best move ('X' in square 2), update the current node, and remove the siblings of the new current node. This leads to the situation shown in Figure 14.18(b).

14.6.4 A simple tic-tac-toe program

It is now straightforward to design a program to play tic-tac-toe. Algorithm 14.20 shows how a tic-tac-toe game is played by a computer against a human opponent.

To play a tic-tac-toe game with *starting-player* to make the first move:

1. Set *current-player* to *starting-player*.
2. Set *game-tree* to contain only the opening position for *starting-player*.
3. While the game is not over, repeat:
   3.1. Display the current position.
   3.2. If *current-player* is the computer:
      3.2.1. Search *game-tree* for the best move from the current node.
      3.2.2. Play the best move found in *game-tree*.
   3.3. If *current-player* is the human:
      3.3.1. Get a valid move from the human.
      3.3.2. Play the given move in *game-tree*.
   3.4. Set *current-player* to the other player.
4. Terminate.

Algorithm 14.20   A tic-tac-toe algorithm.

A tic-tac-toe applet can be found at the companion Web site. This applet plays games indefinitely, with the computer and human players making the first move in alternating games. The human player enters a move by clicking the mouse over the desired square.

Most of the difficulty in implementing the tic-tac-toe applet comes from the structure imposed on the program by the event-driven graphical user interface. Some of these problems were discussed in Section 9.6.3. The applet must also use a separate thread to play the game, as the main thread is used to update the display. This problem was discussed in Section 7.6.1.

As you will know, a tic-tac-toe game ends in a draw if both players play the best moves. With a ply of 2, the computer does always play the best move, so it never loses!

Summary

In this chapter:

- We have studied the concept of a tree, characterized as a hierarchical collection of elements.
- We have seen examples and a case study demonstrating applications of trees.
- We have designed an ADT for trees, expressed as a `Tree` interface.
- We have studied how to represent trees by linked structures, and how to code this representation in Java as a class that implements the `Tree` interface.
- We have seen that specialized tree ADTs, such as expression trees, can be designed for particular applications.

Exercises

14.1   Section 14.2 gives three examples of trees. Can you think of any other examples?

14.2   Draw your own family tree, using Figure 14.3 as a guide. Remember that in a proper tree, each child only has one parent. Draw an alternative version of your family tree by selecting a different parent for each child.

14.3   Implement the Java classes for a file hierarchy given in Example 14.1, and test them using the directory tree given in Figure 14.4. What other file hierarchy operations would be useful?

14.4   The *class hierarchy* of a Java program represents the subclass relationship between classes. (See Appendix B.2.) The class hierarchy can be represented by a tree.
(a) For any Java program, what is the root node of the class hierarchy tree?
(b) What property of the Java language makes the class hierarchy a tree?
(c) Draw the class hierarchy for the Java classes given in Program 14.12.
(d) If Java interfaces are included, why is the 'hierarchy' no longer a tree?

14.5   Implement an ordered tree ADT as a Java class, `LinkedOrderedTree`, using the unordered implementation (Program 14.10) as a guide.

14.6   Using only the methods of the `Tree` interface (Program 14.7), write a Java method, `preOrderTraversal`, that visits, in pre-order, all of the nodes in a given tree.

14.7   Suppose that the `Tree` interface (Program 14.7) is to be extended with the following method:

> **public** Iterator nodesPreOrder ();
> // Return an iterator that will visit all nodes of this tree, in pre-order
> // (i.e., each node is visited before its children).

Write a Java class, `TreePreOrderIterator`, and use it to implement this method.

14.8   Repeat Exercise 14.6 for a post-order traversal of the tree.

14.9   Repeat Exercise 14.7 for the following method:

> **public** Iterator nodesPostOrder ();
> // Return an iterator that will visit all nodes of this tree, in post-order
> // (i.e., each node is visited after its children).

* 14.10   Devise an algorithm to visit the nodes of a tree ordered by depth. So the root node (at depth 0) is visited before its children (all at depth 1), which are all visited before their children (all at depth 2), and so on.
   Implement your algorithm as a Java method, `nodesDepthOrder`.

14.11   Implement an unordered tree ADT where the child nodes are stored in an array rather than an SLL. What are the time complexities of the `addChild` and `remove` operations?

14.12   Repeat Exercise 14.7 using your answer to Exercise 14.11.

14.13   Repeat Exercise 14.9 using your answer to Exercise 14.11.

14.14 Consider the linked implementation of an unordered tree (Program 14.10). The explicit reference to a node's parent can be removed at the expense of making the parent operation slower.

Modify the unordered tree implementation accordingly. What is the time complexity of the parent operation now?

* **14.15** Implement a specialized tree ADT for Java expressions. For simplicity, include only the arithmetic and relational operators, and literals of the primitive types **boolean**, **int**, and **double**.

Equip your ADT with an evaluate method that returns the result of evaluating the Java expression. (*Hint:* Make the method return an object of class Boolean, Integer, or Double.)

** **14.16** Extend your answer to Exercise 14.15 with a method, typecheck, that checks whether an operator is applied to operands of the correct type. For example, it should reject the trees corresponding to the expressions '1 + false', 'false < true', and '6 == true'. Note that the result of an arithmetic operation is of type **double** if any of its operands are of type **double**, otherwise its result is of type **int**.

* **14.17** Modify the tic-tac-toe program of Section 14.6 to exploit information about symmetrical board positions when expanding the game tree. Measure the number of nodes created at each depth, and compare this with the original program.

* **14.18** Modify the tic-tac-toe program of Section 14.6 as follows:
(a) Use a 4 × 4 grid and a winning line of length 4.
(b) Use an $m \times n$ grid and a winning line of length 4, where $m > 4$ and $n > 4$.
(c) Implement the game of *Connect Four*, which is played on a 7 × 6 grid and has a winning line of length 4. The valid moves in a position are restricted to the empty squares nearest to the bottom of the seven columns.

** **14.19** Use the GameTree class of Program 14.19 to write a different game program, e.g., othello, checkers, or backgammon.

** **14.20** Design an algorithm to draw a tree graphically in a java.awt window.

Implement your algorithm as a Java method, and test it using the example trees shown in this chapter.

15

Graph Abstract Data Types

In this chapter we shall study:

- the concept of a graph, directed and undirected graphs (Section 15.1)
- applications of graphs (Section 15.2)
- requirements and contracts for directed and undirected graph abstract data types (Section 15.3)
- implementations of directed graphs using the edge-set representation (Section 15.4), the adjacency-set representation (Section 15.5), and the adjacency-matrix representation (Section 15.6)
- graph traversal algorithms (Section 15.7)
- the graph topological sort algorithm (Section 15.8)
- a case study using graphs (Section 15.9).

15.1 The concept of a graph

In this chapter we shall study graph abstract data types (ADTs). A graph is an *interconnected* collection of elements (values). This characteristic property distinguishes graphs from lists, trees, and other ADTs. See Figures 15.1–15.3 for examples of graphs.

More precisely, a **graph** is a collection of nodes and edges such that:

- Each **node** (or *vertex*) contains an **element**.
- Each **edge** (or *arc*) connects two nodes together, and optionally contains an **edge attribute**.

A node may be connected by any number of edges to other nodes. If two nodes are connected by an edge, these nodes are said to be **neighbors**. The **degree** of a node is its number of connecting edges. In Figure 15.1, for example, Glasgow has degree 2, and its neighbors are Edinburgh and Carlisle.

The *size* of a graph is the number of nodes (elements) in the graph. The *empty graph* has size zero.

An *undirected graph* is one in which edges have no direction. A *directed graph* (or *digraph*) is one in which each edge has a direction. For example, Figure 15.1 is an undirected graph, whereas Figures 15.2 and 15.3 are directed graphs.

In a *directed* graph, if *e* is an edge from node *v* to node *w*, we say that *v* is the *source* of *e* and that *w* is the *destination* of *e*. We also say that *e* is an *in-edge* of *w*, that *e* is an *out-edge* of *v*, that *w* is a *successor* of *v*, and that *v* is a *predecessor* of *w*. The *in-degree* of a node is its number of in-edges, and the *out-degree* of a node is its number of out-edges.

The concepts we have just introduced are used throughout this chapter. In Sections 15.7 and 15.8 we shall study algorithms that move around a graph from node to node, following the edges. This leads us to define the important concepts of paths and cycles in graphs.

A *path* in a graph is a list of nodes such that each node and its successor in the list are connected by an edge in the graph. In Figure 15.1, for example, «Glasgow, Carlisle, Manchester, Birmingham, London» is a path, as are «Swansea, Bristol, Exeter» and «Exeter, Bristol, Swansea». But «Carlisle, Glasgow, Perth» is *not* a path, since no edge connects Glasgow and Perth.

In a *directed* graph, a path must follow the directions of the edges. In Figure 15.3, for example, «Software Engineering, Software Design, Algorithms & Data Structures, Programming» is a path. But «Programming, Computer Architecture, Computer Fundamentals» is *not* a path, since it goes against the direction of the edge from Computer Architecture to Programming.

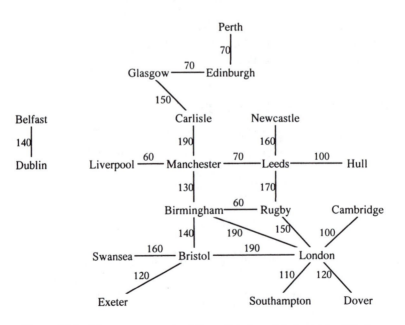

Figure 15.1 Motorway network of Great Britain and Ireland (simplified).

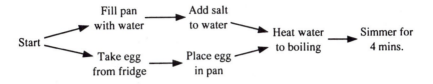

Figure 15.2   An activity chart to make a boiled egg.

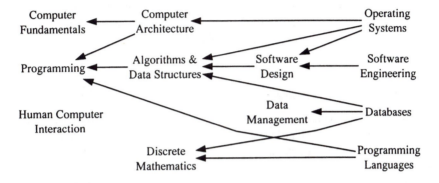

Figure 15.3   A possible University CS curriculum, with prerequisites.

A *cycle* in a graph is a path whose first and last nodes are the same. In Figure 15.1, for example, «London, Birmingham, Bristol, London» is a cycle.

A *cyclic graph* is one in which there is at least one cycle. An *acyclic graph* is one in which there is no cycle. For example, Figure 15.1 is a cyclic graph, whereas Figures 15.2 and 15.3 are acyclic graphs.

15.2 Applications of graphs

Graphs occur frequently both in real life and in computing:

- A *road network* is a graph whose nodes are cities and whose edges are roads connecting these cities. The edge attributes are typically distances. (See Figure 15.1.) Similarly we have *rail networks* (whose nodes are rail stations) and *flight networks* (whose nodes are airports). Such networks, collectively known as *transportation networks*, are usually undirected graphs, since each edge allows movement in both directions. One exception is a city street map, whose nodes are street intersections: if we wish to allow for one-way streets, we must make this a directed graph.
- A *pipeline network* is a directed graph whose nodes are pumping stations and whose edges are pipelines connecting them. The edge attributes could be either pipeline lengths or capacities. A pipeline network is a directed graph because the direction of water or oil flow in each pipeline is fixed.
- An *activity chart* is a directed graph whose nodes are activities and whose edges signify the order in which these activities must be performed. An edge from activity

A to activity B signifies that A must be completed before B is started. (See Figure 15.2.) Edge attributes are unnecessary in an activity chart.

- A *curriculum* at a university is a collection of courses, where each course identifies other courses as its prerequisites. A curriculum may be viewed as a directed graph whose nodes are courses and whose edges signify prerequisites. An edge from course A to course B signifies that B is a prerequisite of A. (See Figure 15.3 and Example 15.1.) Edge attributes are unnecessary in a curriculum graph.
- The *Internet* is a graph whose nodes are computers and whose edges are communication links. It is an undirected graph because a communication link can transmit data in both directions. The transmitted data are e-mail messages, Web pages, files, and such like. The edge attributes could be communication-link capacities.

EXAMPLE 15.1 *University course prerequisites*

Suppose that we are given a directed graph representing a university curriculum. Then we can check whether a student is qualified to take a particular course, given the set of courses already passed by the student. Let us insist that the student has passed, not only the given course's prerequisites, but also *their* prerequisites and so on.

In Figure 15.3, for example, a student wishing to take Databases must have passed not only that course's prerequisites Data Management, Discrete Mathematics, and Algorithms & Data Structures, but also the last course's own prerequisite Programming.

Program 15.4 shows a Java method `qualified` that performs this check. This method iterates over the prerequisites (i.e., successors) of `course`. It checks that each prerequisite is a member of `coursesPassed`. It calls itself recursively to check that each prerequisite's own prerequisites are members of `coursesPassed`. Only if all checks are satisfied does it return the answer true.

Program 15.5 shows a Java method `readCurriculum` that builds a directed graph representing a curriculum, given suitable input data. It starts by constructing an empty directed graph. Then, for each course, it adds a node to represent that course, together with an edge from that course to each of its prerequisites. Since the input data consists of course-codes (strings), the method uses an auxiliary map, `coursesMap`, that maps each course-code to the corresponding node in the graph.

The application code in this example assumes the following operations on directed graphs: `g.addNode(x)` adds to graph g a node containing element x, and returns that node; `g.addEdge(v, w)` adds to graph g an edge from node v to node w; and `g.successors(v)` returns an iterator that will visit all successors of node v in graph g. Finally, `v.getElement()` returns the element contained in node v.

15.3 Graph abstract data types

Let us now design an ADT for graphs. We shall assume the following requirements (covering both directed and undirected graphs):

1. It must be possible to make a graph empty.
2. It must be possible to add a new node, or to add a new edge connecting two existing nodes, to a graph.
3. It must be possible to remove a given node (together with all its connecting edges), or to remove a given edge, from a graph.
4. It must be possible to test whether a graph has an edge connecting two given nodes.
5. It must be possible to access all nodes, or all edges, of a graph.
6. It must be possible to access all neighbors, or all connecting edges, of a given node in a graph.
7. It must be possible to inspect or update the element contained in a given node, or to inspect or update the attribute (if any) contained in a given edge, of a graph.

Program 15.6 shows a possible contract that meets all the above requirements. It is expressed as a Java interface, `Graph`. This has two inner interfaces, `Graph.Node` and `Graph.Edge`, which are shown in Figures 15.7 and 15.8, respectively.

For *directed* graphs, we shall assume an additional requirement:

8. It must be possible to access all successors, or all out-edges, of a given node in a directed graph.

```
public static boolean qualified
                  (Graph.Node courseNode,
                   Set coursesPassed,
                   Digraph curriculum) {
// Return true if and only if a student who has passed all courses in
// coursesPassed is qualified to take the course contained in
// courseNode in curriculum. Every course that is (directly or indirectly)
// a prerequisite of course must be in coursesPassed. Assume that the
// members of coursesPassed and the elements of curriculum are
// course-codes.
   Iterator prereqs =
        curriculum.successors(courseNode);
   while (prereqs.hasNext()) {
     Graph.Node prereqNode =
          (Graph.Node) prereqs.next();
     if (! coursesPassed.contains(
            prereqNode.getElement()))
       return false;
     if (! qualified(prereqNode, coursesPassed,
            curriculum))
       return false;
   }
   return true;
}
```

Program 15.4 Method to check a student's passes against a course's prerequisites.

```
public static Digraph readCurriculum
            (BufferedReader input)
            throws IOException {
// Read a curriculum from input. Assume that the input data for each course
// are on a line of the form:
//    course-code prerequisite-code ... prerequisite-code
// and that each course is input after all its prerequisites.
    Digraph curriculum = new ASDigraph();
    Map coursesMap = new BSTMap();
    for (;;) {
      String courseCode = readCourseCode(input);
      if (courseCode == null)  break;   // end of input
      Graph.Node courseNode =
            curriculum.addNode(courseCode);
      coursesMap.put(courseCode, courseNode);
      for (;;) {
        String prereqCode = readPrereqCode(input);
        if (prereqCode == null)  break;   // end of line
        Graph.Node prereqNode =
              (Graph.Node) coursesMap.get(prereqCode);
        if (prereqNode == null)
          throw new IOException();
        curriculum.addEdge(courseNode, prereqNode);
      }
    }
    return curriculum;
}

private static String readCourseCode
            (BufferedReader input)
            throws IOException {
// Read a course-code from input. Return the course-code, or null if all
// input data have already been read.
    ...
}

private static String readPrereqCode
            (BufferedReader input)
            throws IOException {
// Read a prerequisite code from input. Return the prerequisite code, or null
// if all the current course's prerequisite codes have already been read.
    ...
}
```

Program 15.5 Methods to build a directed graph representing a curriculum.

```
public interface Graph {
```

// Each `Graph` object is a (directed or undirected) graph whose elements
// and edge attributes are arbitrary objects.

/////////////// Accessors ///////////////

```
public int size ();
```
// Return the number of nodes in this graph.

```
public int degree (Graph.Node node);
```
// Return the number of edges connecting node in this graph.

```
public boolean containsEdge (Graph.Node node0,
                  Graph.Node node1);
```
// Return true if and only if there is an edge connecting node0 and
// node1 in this graph. (If the graph is directed, node0 is the edge's
// source and node1 is its destination.)

/////////////// Transformers ///////////////

```
public void clear ();
```
// Make this graph empty.

Program 15.6   A contract for a graph ADT (*continued on next page*).

Program 15.9 shows a contract that meets this additional requirement. It is expressed as a Java interface, `Digraph`, that extends `Graph` with a few additional methods.

15.4 Edge-set representation of graphs

We can represent any directed graph by a node set together with an edge set, where each edge is linked to the two nodes that it connects. This is called the ***edge-set representation***.

We can represent the node set in various ways. A good choice is a doubly-linked list (DLL), to facilitate node deletion. For the same reason, we can represent the edge set by a DLL. Thus we obtain the data structure illustrated (for a directed graph) in Figure 15.10.

In the following analysis, let n be the number of nodes of the graph, and let e be the number of edges.

The space occupied by the node set is $O(n)$, and the space occupied by the edge set is $O(e)$. The total space occupied by the data structure is therefore $O(n + e)$.

If the `size` operation had to count the nodes, it would have time complexity $O(n)$. But we can easily make it $O(1)$ by storing the graph's size in the graph object (and incrementing or decrementing the size every time a node is added or removed, respectively).

The `containsEdge` operation must perform a linear search of the edge-set DLL, looking for an edge connecting the two given nodes. This operation therefore has time complexity $O(e)$.

```
public Graph.Node addNode (Object elem);
// Add to this graph a new node containing element elem, but with no
// connecting edges, and return the new node.

public Graph.Edge addEdge (Graph.Node node0,
                 Graph.Node node1);
// Add to this graph a new edge connecting node0 and node1, but
// containing no attribute, and return the new edge. (If the graph is directed,
// node0 is the edge's source and node1 is its destination.)

public Graph.Edge addEdge (Graph.Node node0,
                 Graph.Node node1, Object attr);
// Add to this graph a new edge connecting node0 and node1, and
// containing attribute attr, and return the new edge. (If the graph is
// directed, node0 is the edge's source and node1 is its destination.)

public void removeNode (Graph.Node node);
// Remove node from this graph, together with all its connecting edges.

public void removeEdge (Graph.Edge edge);
// Remove edge from this graph.

///////////// Iterators /////////////

public Iterator nodes ();
// Return an iterator that will visit all nodes of this graph, in no particular
// order.

public Iterator edges ();
// Return an iterator that will visit all edges of this graph, in no particular
// order.

public Iterator neighbors (Graph.Node node);
// Return an iterator that will visit all neighbors of node in this graph,
// in no particular order.

public Iterator connectingEdges (Graph.Node node);
// Return an iterator that will visit all connecting edges of node in this
// graph, in no particular order.

///////////// Inner interface for graph nodes /////////////

...   // See Program 15.7.

///////////// Inner interface for graph edges /////////////

...   // See Program 15.8.

}
```

Program 15.6 (*continued*)

The addNode operation might as well insert the new node at the front of the node-set DLL. Similarly, the addEdge operation might as well insert the new edge at the front of the edge-set DLL. Both operations therefore have time complexity $O(1)$.

The removeEdge operation simply deletes the given edge from the edge-set DLL; this has time complexity $O(1)$. (But it would be $O(n)$ if the node set were represented by a singly-linked list.)

The removeNode operation must remove not only the given node but also all connecting edges. Deletion of the node from the node-set DLL has time complexity $O(1)$. Deletion of all connecting edges requires traversal of the entire edge set, and therefore has time complexity $O(e)$. Overall, the removeNode operation has time complexity $O(e)$.

Table 15.11 summarizes the algorithms used to implement representative graph operations, together with their time complexities.

```
public interface Node {

    // Each Graph.Node object is a graph node, and contains a single
    // element.

    public Object getElement ();
    // Return the element contained in this node.

    public void setElement (Object elem);
    // Change the element contained in this node to elem.

}
```

Program 15.7   A contract for nodes in the graph ADT (inner interface of Graph).

```
public interface Edge {

    // Each Graph.Edge object is a graph edge, and optionally contains
    // an attribute.

    public Graph.Node[] getNodes ();
    // Return an array containing the two nodes connected by this edge. (If
    // the graph is directed, the array will contain the edge's source and
    // destination nodes, in that order.)

    public Object getAttribute ();
    // Return the attribute contained in this edge, or null if there is none.

    public void setAttribute (Object attr);
    // Change the attribute contained in this edge to attr.

}
```

Program 15.8   A contract for edges in the graph ADT (inner interface of Graph).

The edge-set representation has the advantage of simplicity. Its major disadvantage is that the `containsEdge` and `removeNode` operations (which must search and traverse the edge set) are slow. Exercise 15.6 explores some variations on the edge-set representation.

15.4.1 Directed graphs

In the edge-set representation of *directed* graphs, the only special consideration is that we must distinguish between each edge's source and destination nodes.

The `outEdges` iterator must traverse the entire edge set to find all of the given node's out-edges. Its time complexity is therefore $O(e)$. For the same reason, the `successors` iterator also has time complexity $O(e)$.

Program 15.12 very briefly outlines a Java implementation. This consists of a class, `ESDigraph`, that implements the `Digraph` interface of Program 15.9. This class contains two inner classes, `ESDigraph.Node` and `ESDigraph.Edge`, that implement the inner interfaces of Figures 15.7 and 15.8, respectively. Program 15.12 shows the data representation but omits most of the constructors and methods. (Complete code can be found at the companion Web site.)

15.4.2 Undirected graphs

In the edge-set representation of *undirected* graphs, the only special consideration is that we must take care *not* to distinguish between the two nodes connected by an edge. For example, `g.containsEdge(v, w)` must give the same result as `g.contains-Edge(w, v)`, regardless of the order in which *v* and *w* are stored in the edge object.

```java
public interface Digraph extends Graph {
    // Each Digraph object is a directed graph whose elements and edge
    // attributes are arbitrary objects.

    /////////////// Accessor ///////////////

    public int outDegree (Graph.Node node);
    // Return the number of out-edges of node in this directed graph.

    /////////////// Iterators ///////////////

    public Iterator successors (Graph.Node node);
    // Return an iterator that will visit all successors of node in this
    // directed graph, in no particular order.

    public Iterator outEdges (Graph.Node node);
    // Return an iterator that will visit all out-edges of node in this
    // directed graph, in no particular order.

}
```

Program 15.9 A contract for a directed graph ADT. (See also Program 15.6.)

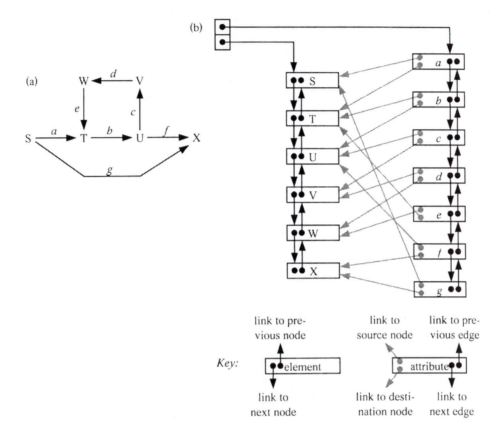

Figure 15.10 (a) A directed graph. (b) Edge-set representation of the directed graph.

Table 15.11 Edge-set representation of graphs: summary of algorithms (where e is the number of edges).

Operation	Algorithm	Time complexity
containsEdge	linear search of edge-set DLL	$O(e)$
addNode	insertion at front of node-set DLL	$O(1)$
addEdge	insertion at front of edge-set DLL	$O(1)$
removeNode	deletion in node-set DLL, plus multiple deletions in edge-set DLL	$O(e)$
removeEdge	deletion in edge-set DLL	$O(1)$

15.5 Adjacency-set representation of graphs

We have seen that a single large edge set is inefficient. It makes sense to divide it into smaller sets, called *adjacency sets*, each of which contains only edges connecting a particular node. We can then represent the graph as a whole by its node set, with each node being linked to its own adjacency set. This is called the *adjacency-set representation*.

```java
public class ESDigraph implements Digraph {

// Each ESDigraph object is a directed graph whose elements and edge
// attributes are arbitrary objects.

// This directed graph is represented by a node set and edge set as follows.
// firstNode is a link to the first node of a DLL of ESDigraph.Node
// objects, each of which contains an element. firstEdge is a link to the
// first node of a DLL of ESDigraph.Edge objects, each of which
// contains an edge attribute and is linked to the edge's source and
// destination nodes. size contains the graph's size.

    private ESDigraph.Node firstNode;
    private ESDigraph.Edge firstEdge;
    private int size;

    public ESDigraph () {
    // Construct a directed graph, initially empty.
        firstNode = null;
        firstEdge = null;
        size = 0;
    }

    public boolean containsEdge (Graph.Node node0,
                    Graph.Node node1) {
    // Return true if and only if there is an edge connecting node0 to
    // node1 in this graph.
        ESDigraph.Node source = (ESDigraph.Node) node0,
            dest = (ESDigraph.Node) node1;
        for (ESDigraph.Edge e = firstEdge;
            e != null; e = e.nextEdge) {
          if (e.source == source && e.dest == dest)
            return true;
        }
        return false;
    }

    ...   // For other methods, see the companion Web site.
```

Program 15.12 Edge-set representation of directed graphs in Java (outline) (*continued on next page*).

We shall represent the node set by a DLL, as before. We can reasonably represent the adjacency sets by singly-linked lists (SLLs), since they are likely to be short. Thus we obtain the data structure illustrated (for a directed graph) in Figure 15.13.

In the following analysis, let n be the number of nodes of the graph, and let e be the number of edges. Also, let d be the maximum degree of each node.

The total space occupied by the data structure is $O(n + e)$, as in the edge-set representation.

In a directed graph, the `containsEdge` operation must search the appropriate adjacency-set. This has to be linear search in an SLL of up to d nodes, which performs up to d comparisons. So this operation has time complexity $O(d)$. In an undirected graph, the `containsEdge` operation may need to search two adjacency-sets, again using linear search of an SLL. This may require up to $2d$ comparisons, but still has time complexity $O(d)$.

The `addEdge` operation must insert the new edge in the appropriate adjacency set. It can insert it at the front of the adjacency-set SLL. This operation has time complexity $O(1)$.

/////////// Inner class for graph nodes ///////////

```
private static class Node implements Graph.Node {

    //  Each ESDigraph.Node object is a directed graph node, and
    //  contains a single element.

    private Object element;
    private int outDegree;
    private ESDigraph.Node prevNode, nextNode;

    ...   // For constructor and methods, see the companion Web site.

}
```

/////////// Inner class for graph edges ///////////

```
private static class Edge implements Graph.Edge {

    //  Each ESDigraph.Edge object is a directed graph edge, and
    //  optionally contains an attribute.

    private Object attribute;
    private ESDigraph.Node source, dest;
    private ESDigraph.Edge prevEdge, nextEdge;

    ...   // For constructor and methods, see the companion Web site.

}

}
```

Program 15.12 (*continued*)

The `removeEdge` operation must remove the given edge from the appropriate adjacency set. This is SLL deletion, which takes up to d steps. So this operation has time complexity $O(d)$.

The `removeNode` operation must remove not only the given node but also all its connecting edges. Deletion of the node from the node-set DLL automatically deletes the node's adjacency set too. There might also be connecting edges in its neighbors' adjacency sets, however, so the operation must traverse all other adjacency sets, to find and delete these connecting edges, thus inspecting all e edge objects. So this operation has time complexity $O(e)$.

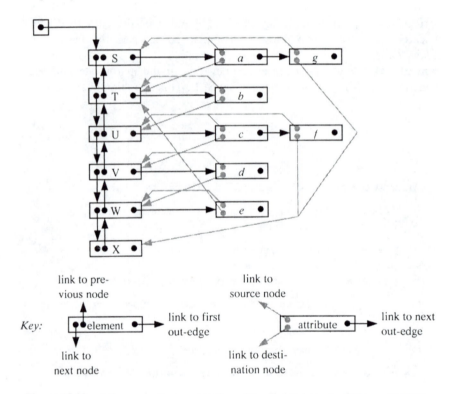

Figure 15.13 Adjacency-set representation of the directed graph of Figure 15.10(a).

Table 15.14 Adjacency-set representation of graphs: summary of algorithms (where e is the number of edges and d is the maximum degree of each node).

Operation	Algorithm	Time complexity
`containsEdge`	linear search of adjacency-set SLL	$O(d)$
`addNode`	insertion at front of node-set DLL	$O(1)$
`addEdge`	insertion at front of adjacency-set SLL	$O(1)$
`removeNode`	deletion in node-set DLL, plus traversal of all adjacency-set SLLs to find and delete connecting edges	$O(e)$
`removeEdge`	deletion in adjacency-set SLL	$O(d)$

Table 15.14 summarizes the algorithms used to implement representative graph operations, together with their time complexities.

The adjacency-set representation is nearly as simple and space-efficient as the edge-set representation, and it significantly speeds up the `containsEdge` and `successors` operations. It does not speed up the `removeNode` operation, which has to traverse the entire edge set in order to locate the old node's in-edges. (Exercise 15.7 explores an important alternative, which is to link each node to its set of in-edges as well as its set of out-edges.)

```java
public class ASDigraph implements Digraph {

  // Each ASDigraph object is a directed graph whose elements and
  // edge attributes are arbitrary objects.

  // This directed graph is represented by adjacency sets as follows.
  // firstNode is a link to the first node of a DLL of ASDigraph.Node
  // objects, each of which contains an element and is linked to an SLL of
  // ASDigraph.Edge objects representing the node's out-edges. Each
  // ASDigraph.Edge object contains an attribute and is linked to the
  // edge's source and destination nodes. size contains the graph's size.

  private ASDigraph.Node firstNode;
  private int size;

  public ASDigraph () {
  // Construct a directed graph, initially empty.
    firstNode = null;
    size = 0;
  }

  public boolean containsEdge (Graph.Node node0,
                 Graph.Node node1) {
  // Return true if and only if there is an edge connecting node0 to
  // node1 in this graph.
    ASDigraph.Node source = (ASDigraph.Node) node0,
        dest = (ASDigraph.Node) node1;
    for (ASDigraph.Edge edge = source.firstOutEdge;
        edge != null; edge = edge.nextOutEdge) {
      if (edge.dest == dest)
        return true;
    }
    return false;
  }

  ...    // For other methods, see the companion Web site.
```

Program 15.15 Adjacency-set representation of directed graphs in Java (outline) (*continued on next page*).

15.5.1 Directed graphs

In the adjacency-set representation of *directed* graphs, we can make each node's adjacency set contain that node's out-edges only. The containsEdge, addEdge, and removeEdge operations then confine their attention to the source node's adjacency set. The removeNode operation finds all of the old node's out-edges in its own adjacency set, but to find and delete all in-edges the operation must traverse all other adjacency sets too. The time complexities in Table 15.14 are still correct, if we take d to be the maximum *out*-degree of each node.

The outEdges and successors iterators traverse only the given node's adjacency set. So their time complexity is $O(d)$.

Program 15.15 very briefly outlines a Java implementation, consisting of a class, ASDigraph, that implements the Digraph interface of Program 15.9, together with two inner classes.

```
/////////// Inner class for graph nodes ///////////

private static class Node implements Graph.Node {

    // Each ASDigraph.Node object is a directed graph node, and
    // contains a single element.

    private Object element;
    private int outDegree;
    private ASDigraph.Edge firstOutEdge;
    private ASDigraph.Node prevNode, nextNode;

    ...    // For constructor and methods, see the companion Web site.

}

/////////// Inner class for graph edges ///////////

private static class Edge implements Graph.Edge {

    // Each ASDigraph.Edge object is a directed graph edge, and
    // optionally contains an attribute.

    private Object attribute;
    private ASDigraph.Node source, dest;
    private ASDigraph.Edge nextOutEdge;

    ...    // For constructor and methods, see the companion Web site.

}

}
```

Program 15.15 (*continued*)

15.5.2 Undirected graphs

In the adjacency-set representation of *undirected* graphs, it makes sense to include each edge in the adjacency sets of *both* the nodes connected by the edge. Thus a node's adjacency set includes *all* of its connecting edges. The `containsEdge` operation can search *either* of the given nodes' adjacency sets (preferably the smaller). On the other hand, the `addEdge` and `removeEdge` operations must work on the adjacency sets of *both* nodes.

15.6 Adjacency-matrix representation of graphs

In the previous two sections we represented the graph's node set by a DLL. Here we shall adopt a completely different representation. We assume that each node is arbitrarily assigned a distinct position number, in the range 0 through $m - 1$ (say). We represent the node set by an array a, of length m, and indexed by the nodes' position numbers: the node in position p occupies the array component $a[p]$. Moreover, we represent each node's adjacency set by an array, also of length m, and also indexed by the nodes' position numbers. Thus the data structure is essentially an $m \times m$ square matrix (array of arrays). If the graph has an edge e connecting nodes v and w, where these nodes have position numbers p and q, then the matrix component $a[p][q]$ refers to the edge object e; if the graph has no such edge, then $a[p][q]$ is null. This is called the ***adjacency-matrix representation***.

This representation is illustrated (for a directed graph) in Figure 15.16. The nodes S–X have been assigned position numbers 0–5, respectively.

The total space occupied by the data structure is $O(m^2)$.

The `containsEdge` operation simply tests the matrix component corresponding to the two given nodes. Provided that we know these nodes' position numbers (which can be arranged by storing each node's position number in the node itself), this is simple array indexing. This operation therefore has time complexity $O(1)$.

The `addEdge` and `removeEdge` operations simply update the matrix component corresponding to the nodes connected by the edge. Both operations have time complexity $O(1)$.

The `removeNode` operation can be implemented simply by clearing the old node's row and column in the matrix. (Gaps in the matrix are harmless.) This operation has time complexity $O(m)$.

The `addNode` operation can be implemented simply by assigning an unused position number. This operation has time complexity $O(m)$, because of the need to search for an unused position number. (Exercise 15.8(b) explores an alternative.)

Table 15.17 summarizes the algorithms used to implement representative directed-graph operations, together with their time complexities.

The adjacency-matrix representation makes the `containsEdge`, `addEdge`, and `removeEdge` operations very fast. But it also makes the `addNode` operation relatively slow. It is also space-consuming, especially if the graph has few edges relative to its size. Finally, it restricts the represented graph in two ways:

- The graph's size is limited to *m*. (A Java implementation can get round this problem by expanding the arrays when necessary, but this is time-consuming.)
- The graph is restricted to at most one edge connecting any pair of nodes.

15.6.1 Directed graphs

In the adjacency-matrix representation of *directed* graphs, the matrix must represent the direction of each edge. If an edge's source and destination nodes have position numbers p and q, respectively, then a reference to the edge object is placed in $a[p][q]$ but *not* in $a[q][p]$.

The outEdges and successors iterators must traverse a whole row of the matrix. So their time complexity is $O(m)$, which is slow.

Program 15.18 very briefly outlines a Java implementation, consisting of a class,

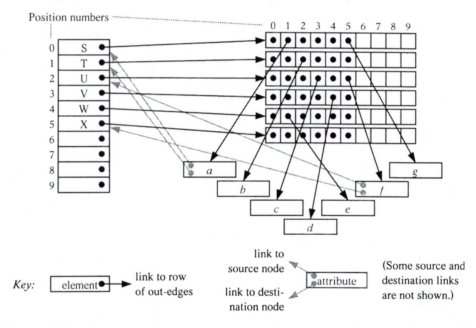

Figure 15.16   Adjacency-matrix representation of the directed graph of Figure 15.10(a) ($m = 10$).

Table 15.17   Adjacency-matrix representation of graphs: summary of algorithms.

Operation	Algorithm	Time complexity
containsEdge	matrix indexing	$O(1)$
addNode	finding a cleared matrix row and column	$O(m)$
addEdge	matrix indexing	$O(1)$
removeNode	clearing a matrix row and column	$O(m)$
removeEdge	matrix indexing	$O(1)$

AMDigraph, that implements the Digraph interface of Program 15.9, together with two inner classes.

15.6.2 Undirected graphs

In the adjacency-matrix representation of *undirected* graphs, if an edge connects the nodes with position numbers p and q, a reference to the edge object should be placed in both $a[p][q]$ and $a[q][p]$, thus reflecting the edge's lack of direction.

An alternative is to store the reference to the edge object only in $a[p][q]$, where p is the larger of the two position numbers and q is the smaller. This implies that half the matrix is unused and can be dispensed with, leaving us with a *triangular* matrix. More precisely, row p of the matrix has length $p + 1$. (In particular, row 0 has length 1, and row $m - 1$ has length m.) This refinement approximately halves the total space occupied by the data structure, but its space requirement is still $O(m^2)$.

15.7 Graph traversal

In this and the following section we shall study a number of important graph algorithms. They can all be implemented in terms of the Graph ADT of Program 15.6, or the Digraph ADT of Program 15.9. See Exercise 15.10.

```
public class AMDigraph implements Digraph {

    // Each AMDigraph object is a directed graph whose elements and
    // edge attributes are arbitrary objects.

    // This directed graph is represented by an adjacency matrix as follows.
    // nodes is an array of AMDigraph.Node objects, each of which
    // contains an element, the node's position number, and a link to an array of
    // AMDigraph.Edge objects. The latter array represents the node's
    // possible out-edges (with null indicating the absence of a particular out-
    // edge). Each AMDigraph.Edge object contains an attribute and is
    // linked to the edge's source and destination nodes. size contains the
    // graph's size.

    private AMDigraph.Node[] nodes;
    private int size;

    public AMDigraph (int maxsize) {
    // Construct a directed graph, initially empty, whose size will be bounded
    // by maxsize.
        nodes = new AMDigraph.Node[maxsize];
        size = 0;
    }
```

Program 15.18 Adjacency-matrix representation of directed graphs in Java (outline) (*continued on next page*).

Consider problems like the following:

- Given a transportation network, enumerate all nodes that be reached by following paths from a given starting node. In Figure 15.1, for example, the cities that can be reached by motorway from Glasgow are all other cities in the motorway network, except Belfast and Dublin.

```java
public boolean containsEdge (Graph.Node node0,
                Graph.Node node1) {
// Return true if and only if there is an edge connecting node0 to
// node1 in this graph.
   AMDigraph.Node source = (AMDigraph.Node) node0,
       dest = (AMDigraph.Node) node1;
   int p = source.position, q = dest.position;
   return (nodes[p].outEdges[q] != null);
}

...   // For other methods, see the companion Web site.

///////////// Inner class for graph nodes ///////////

private static class Node implements Graph.Node {

   // Each AMDigraph.Node object is a directed graph node, and
   // contains a single element.

   private Object element;
   private int outDegree;
   private AMDigraph.Edge[] outEdges;
   private int position;

   ...   // For constructor and methods, see the companion Web site.

}

///////////// Inner class for graph edges ///////////

private static class Edge implements Graph.Edge {

   // Each AMDigraph.Edge object is a directed graph edge, and
   // optionally contains an attribute.

   private Object attribute;
   private AMDigraph.Node source, dest;

   ...   // For constructor and methods, see the companion Web site.

}

}
```

Program 15.18 (*continued*)

- Given a curriculum, enumerate all (direct and indirect) prerequisites of a given course. In Figure 15.3, for example, the direct and indirect prerequisites of Operating Systems are Algorithms & Data Structures, Computer Architecture, Computer Fundamentals, Programming, and Software Design.

Algorithms to solve such problems must *traverse* the graph, following all possible paths from the starting node, and visiting each node reached along these paths.

Consider also problems like the following:

- Given a transportation network, determine whether a given target node can be reached by following a path from a given starting node. In Figure 15.1, for example, London can be reached from Glasgow, but Dublin cannot be reached from Glasgow.
- Given a curriculum, determine whether one course is a (direct or indirect) prerequisite of another course. In Figure 15.3, for example, Programming is an (indirect) prerequisite of Operating Systems, but Discrete Mathematics is not.

Algorithms to solve such problems must *search* the graph, following paths from the starting node, and terminating when it reaches a target node.

Any graph traversal algorithm can be specialized to a graph searching algorithm, by the simple expedient of making it terminate as soon as it reaches a target node. (See Exercise 15.9.) Bearing this in mind, from now on we shall study only graph traversal algorithms.

A graph traversal algorithm may be able to reach the same node by several different paths from the starting node. For example, in Figure 15.3 there are three possible paths from Operating Systems to Programming.

A graph traversal algorithm should 'mark' each node on the first occasion that it reaches it, in order to avoid visiting the same node more than once. An implementation of the algorithm can mark nodes in various ways, for example:

- Declare a boolean field (initially false) in each node object. Mark a node by changing this field to true.
- Declare a set of nodes (initially empty), separately from the graph. Mark a node by adding it to the set.

It is also important to realize that a graph traversal algorithm does not necessarily visit all nodes of the graph. For example, the undirected graph of Figure 15.1 consists of two disconnected subgraphs (one for Great Britain, one for Ireland), so a traversal starting in one subgraph cannot reach any of the nodes in the other subgraph. The directed graph of Figure 15.2 has no disconnected subgraphs, but a traversal starting at 'Fill pan with water' cannot reach 'Place egg in pan' without going against the direction of the edges.

Any graph traversal algorithm can be made to test whether it has visited every node. It need only count the nodes that it visits, and finally compare this count with the graph's size.

15.7.1 Depth-first traversal

Suppose that we wish to traverse the directed graph of Figure 15.19(a), starting at Operating Systems. One way to proceed is as follows. After visiting Operating Systems itself, we visit one of its successors, say Computer Architecture (Figure 15.19(b)). Then we visit one of *that* node's successors, say Computer Fundamentals (Figure 15.19(c)). Computer Fundamentals has no successors, so we go back to Computer Architecture and then visit its other successor, Programming (Figure 15.19(d)). Programming has no successors, and Computer Architecture's successors have all been visited, so we go back to Operating Systems and then visit another of its successors, say Algorithms & Data Structures (Figure 15.19(e)). That node has a successor, Programming, but we have visited it already and do not wish to visit it again. So we go back to Operating Systems and then visit its remaining successor, Software Design (Figure 15.19(f)). Software Design has a successor, Algorithms & Data Structures, but we have visited it already. Now we have exhausted all possible paths from the starting node.

Every time we visit a node, we mark it in order to avoid visiting it again.

The procedure we have just illustrated first explores one possible path as far as possible, before it considers any alternative paths. It is called ***depth-first traversal***.

We can formulate depth-first traversal by the recursive algorithm shown as Algorithm 15.20.

We can see now that the `qualified` method of Example 15.1 employed a variant of the recursive depth-first traversal algorithm, specialized as follows: whenever it visited a node of a curriculum graph, it checked the course in that node for membership of the set `coursesPassed`. (However, the `qualified` method naively omitted to mark nodes as it reached them.)

We can also formulate depth-first traversal by a nonrecursive algorithm if we use a stack, as shown in Algorithm 15.21. The stack contains the unvisited successors of already-visited nodes, such that the successors of recently-visited nodes are near the top of the stack. After visiting a node, the algorithm stacks that node's successors and at the same time marks them. However, if any successor has already been marked, that successor must have been stacked previously, so there is no need to stack it again. The algorithm starts by stacking the starting node, and terminates when the stack is empty.

Finally, note that Algorithms 15.20 and 15.21 can easily be adapted to perform a depth-first traversal of an *undirected* graph. Simply replace 'For each unreached successor …' by 'For each unreached neighbor …'.

15.7.2 Breadth-first traversal

Suppose again that we wish to traverse the directed graph of Figure 15.22(a), starting at Operating Systems. Another way to proceed is as follows. After visiting Operating Systems itself, we visit in turn all of its successors, namely Computer Architecture, Algorithms & Data Structures, and Software Design (Figure 15.22(b)). Then we visit in turn each of *these* node's successors (other than those already visited), namely Computer Fundamentals and Programming (Figure 15.22(c)). Now we have exhausted all possible paths from the starting node.

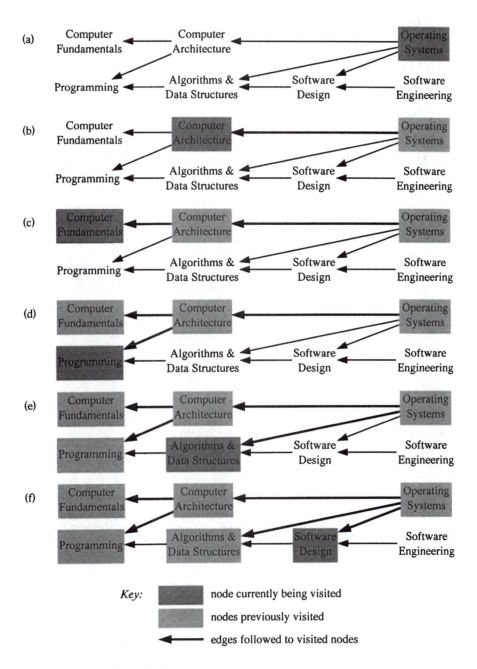

Figure 15.19   Depth-first traversal of a directed graph.

To traverse graph *g* in depth-first order, starting at node *start*:

1. Visit node *start*, and mark *start* as reached.
2. For each unreached successor *w* of *start*, repeat:
    2.1. Traverse *g* in depth-first order, starting at node *w*.
3. Terminate.

Algorithm 15.20   Depth-first traversal algorithm for a directed graph (recursive).

To traverse graph *g* in depth-first order, starting at node *start*:

1. Make *node-stack* contain only node *start*, and mark *start* as reached.
2. While *node-stack* is not empty, repeat:
    2.1. Remove the top element of *node-stack* into *v*.
    2.2. Visit node *v*.
    2.3. For each unreached successor *w* of node *v*, repeat:
        2.3.1. Add node *w* to *node-stack*, and mark *w* as reached.
3. Terminate.

Algorithm 15.21   Depth-first traversal algorithm for a directed graph (iterative).

The procedure we have just illustrated visits all the starting node's successors before it visits their successors, and so on. It is called ***breadth-first traversal***.

We can formulate breadth-first traversal by an algorithm that uses a queue, as shown in Algorithm 15.21. The queue contains the unvisited successors of already-visited nodes, such that the successors of earlier-visited nodes are near the front of the queue. After visiting a node, the algorithm queues its successors and at the same time marks them. However, if any successor has already been marked, that successor must have been queued previously, so there is no need to queue it again. The algorithm starts by queuing the starting node, and terminates when the queue is empty.

The similarity of Algorithms 15.21 and 15.23 is striking. Indeed, the only difference is that depth-first traversal uses a *stack* (so successors of *recently*-visited nodes will be visited next), whereas breadth-first traversal uses a *queue* (so successors of *earlier*-visited nodes will be visited next).

Finally, note that Algorithm 15.23 can easily be adapted to perform a breadth-first traversal of an *undirected* graph. Simply replace 'For each unreached successor ...' by 'For each unreached neighbor ...' in step 2.3.

15.8 Topological sort

Consider an activity chart such as Figure 15.2. This is a directed graph whose nodes are activities, with an edge from node A to node B signifying that activity A must be performed before activity B. Using such an activity chart, we can choose an order for performing all the activities. Redraw the graph with all the nodes lined up from left to right, in such a way that every edge is directed from left to right. The result is a *topological ordering* of the activity chart. This particular activity chart has several different topological orderings, two of which are shown in Figure 15.24.

Every directed *acyclic* graph has one or more topological orderings. Algorithm 15.25 is a *topological sort* algorithm, which finds a topological ordering of a given directed acyclic graph. The algorithm sorts the nodes into a list, *node-list*, such that an edge from node *v* to node *w* ensures that *v* appears before *w* in *node-list*. The algorithm uses an auxiliary queue, *node-queue*, which initially contains only those nodes that have no

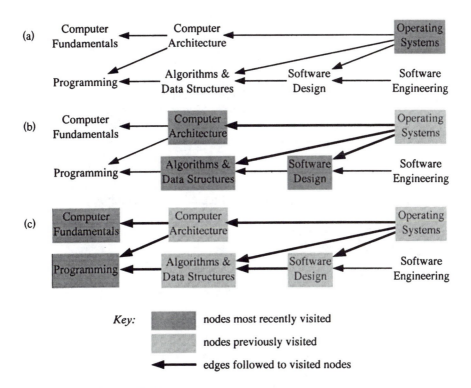

Figure 15.22   Breadth-first traversal of a directed graph.

To traverse graph *g* in breadth-first order, starting at node *start*:

1. Make *node-queue* contain only node *start*, and mark *start* as reached.
2. While *node-queue* is not empty, repeat:
    2.1. Remove the front element of *node-queue* into *v*.
    2.2. Visit node *v*.
    2.3. For each unreached successor *w* of node *v*, repeat:
        2.3.1. Add node *w* to *node-queue*, and mark *w* as reached.
3. Terminate.

Algorithm 15.23   Breadth-first traversal algorithm for a directed graph.

in-edges. As the algorithm proceeds, it progressively adds each of the other nodes to *node-queue*, but only when all that node's predecessors have already been added to *node-list*. The idea is to associate an integer in_v with each node v, initialize in_v to the in-degree of v, and decrement in_v every time a predecessor of v is added to *node-list*. When in_v reaches zero, we know that v is ready to be added to *node-list*. Nodes removed from *node-queue* are added to the end of *node-list*. Figure 15.26 illustrates how this algorithm works.

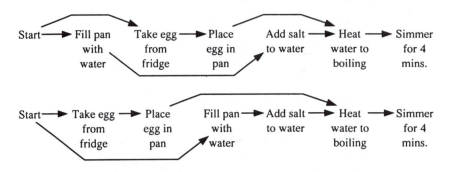

Figure 15.24 Two possible topological orderings of the directed graph of Figure 15.2.

To find a topological ordering of directed acyclic graph g:

1. Make *node-list* empty.
2. Make *node-queue* empty.
3. For each node v of g, repeat:
    3.1. Set in_v to the in-degree of node v.
    3.2. If $in_v = 0$, add node v to *node-queue*.
4. While *node-queue* is not empty, repeat:
    4.1. Remove the front element of *node-queue* into v.
    4.2. Add node v as the last element of *node-list*.
    4.3. For each successor w of node v, repeat:
        4.3.1. Decrement in_w.
        4.3.2. If $in_w = 0$, add node w to *node-queue*.
5. Terminate with answer *node-list*.

Algorithm 15.25 Topological sort algorithm for a directed acyclic graph.

15.9 Case study: material requirements planning

In manufacturing, a manufacturer receives orders for its products from customers. Each order specifies how much of a particular product must be manufactured, and when it is to be shipped to the customer. A ***production schedule*** is created by taking all of the orders for a given week, and calculating the total amount of each product required. (Sometimes the production schedule is based on estimated orders rather than actual orders, but this does not alter the problem.)

Material requirements planning involves using the production schedule to calculate how much raw material is needed to manufacture the required amount of finished products, and when this raw material must be obtained from the suppliers. This planning

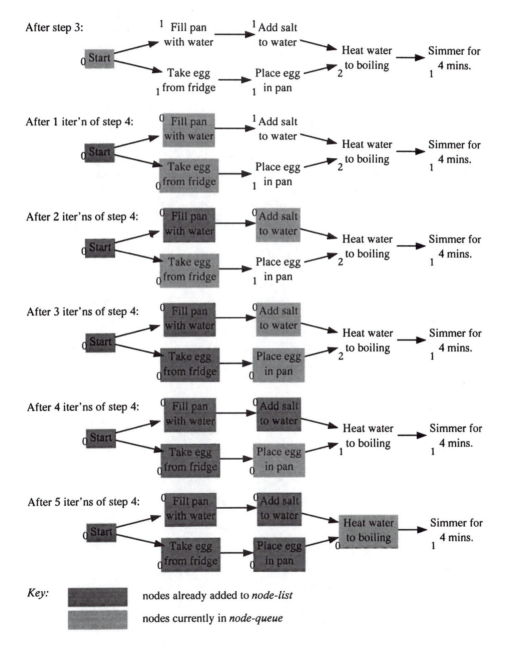

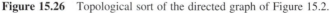

Figure 15.26 Topological sort of the directed graph of Figure 15.2.

process relies on information about how products are constructed from their raw materials, and how long it takes to manufacture each product.

Material requirements planning becomes more complicated when each product is assembled from a number of parts, each part is itself assembled from sub-parts, and so on. It is also possible for several products to share one or more parts. For example, consider a manufacturer whose products are personal computer systems, which it manufactures from bought-in parts such as CPUs, memory modules, and keyboards. It might sell several products with different specifications, e.g., different CPU speeds, memory capacities, monitor sizes, and so on. These different products might share parts, such as keyboards, mice, disk drives, motherboards, and so on.

In general, we define a *part* to be either a *raw material* (which is bought in), an *intermediate part* (which is manufactured), or a *product* (which is manufactured and will be sold).

The information about products and their construction can be represented by a directed graph. The nodes of the graph are parts. Each part is manufactured from the parts that are its successors in the graph. In particular, an edge from part P to part Q indicates that part Q is directly used in the manufacture of part P, and the edge attribute is the quantity of part Q required to manufacture a single part P. A product has no in-edges; a raw material has no out-edges.

In addition, each part has a stated *lead time*. For a raw material, the lead time is the time required to obtain the raw material from a supplier. For any other part, the lead time is the time required to manufacture the part.

Figure 15.27 shows a graph representing the parts used to manufacture two different products, described as a 'standard computer system' and a 'professional computer system'. The intermediate parts are those described as 'standard base unit', 'standard system assembly', and so on. The raw materials are those described as 'mouse', 'keyboard', 'hard disk drive', and so on. (In this example, our manufacturer's raw materials are another manufacturer's products.)

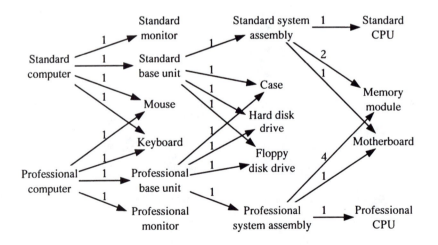

Figure 15.27   A directed graph showing the parts used in two different personal computers.

Material requirements planning generates a report for each part. This report shows the following four quantities on a weekly basis:

- The *required quantity* is the amount of a part required each week. If the part is a product, this is the amount to be shipped to customers. If the part is an intermediate part or raw material, this is the amount required to manufacture other parts.
- The *available quantity* is the amount of a part held in stock each week. The available quantity is either used to satisfy the required quantity or held in stock until the following week.
- The *delivered quantity* is the amount of a part that is to be delivered each week. If the part is a raw material, this is the amount to be delivered by the supplier. If the part is an intermediate part or product, this is the amount that must have been manufactured by this week. The delivered quantity is the remainder of the required quantity that could not be satisfied by the available quantity.
- The *ordered quantity* is the amount of a part that must be ordered each week. If the part is a raw material, this is the amount that must be ordered from a supplier. If the part is an intermediate part or product, this is the amount whose manufacture must start in this week.

An example of a material requirements report for a single part ('standard computer system') is shown in Table 15.28. In this example, the required quantity in week 4 (25 units) exceeds the available quantity (20 units), so the delivered quantity is 5 units. Assuming that the lead time for this part is one week, these 5 units must appear in the ordered quantity in week 3. Once the available quantity has been exhausted, the required quantity must be satisfied entirely from the delivered quantity, as in weeks 5, 6, and 8. This results in further ordered quantities in weeks 4, 5, and 7.

We adopt the following convention:

- Week 1 is the current week.
- Weeks 2–9 are the coming eight weeks. The total number of weeks over which we plan is arbitrary, and can be adjusted to suit the total time required to manufacture the products.
- Week 0 represents the past. If a production schedule requires parts to be delivered or ordered before the current week, a nonzero delivered quantity or ordered quantity will appear in week 0. This implies that the production schedule is infeasible, since it requires events to happen in the past. The initial available quantity of a part appears in week 0.

Table 15.28 A material requirements report for one part. (Zero entries are left blank.)

| Part: standard computer system | | | | | | | | | | |
Week number	0	1	2	3	4	5	6	7	8	9
Required quantity					25	200	75		100	
Available quantity	20	20	20	20	20					
Delivered quantity					5	200	75		100	
Ordered quantity				5	200	75		100		

15.9.1 An algorithm for material requirements planning

In this section we consider an algorithm to perform material requirements planning. This algorithm will help us to identify the data that we must store about each part, which we will consider in more detail in the next section.

Algorithm 15.29 gives an algorithm to perform material requirements planning, given a directed acyclic graph, *parts-graph*, representing the parts and their manufacturing dependencies. We assume that the required quantity of each product in each week has been initialized according to the production schedule, and that the initial available quantity of each part has been entered in week 0. All other quantities are initially zero.

The algorithm performs a depth-first traversal of *parts-graph* for each product. Since *parts-graph* is acyclic, we need not mark the graph nodes during the traversal. As in Algorithm 15.21, we use a stack, *parts-stack*, to hold the nodes still to be visited. To

To calculate the materials required for a production schedule, given *parts-graph*:

1. Make *part-stack* contain all products in *parts-graph*.
2. While *part-stack* is not empty, repeat:
   2.1. Remove the topmost element of *part-stack* into *current-part*.
   2.2. Calculate the requirements for *current-part*.
   2.3. For each successor, *part*, of *current-part* in *parts-graph*, repeat:
      2.3.1. Set *qty* to the quantity of *part* used to manufacture *current-part*.
      2.3.2. For $t = 1, \ldots,$ number of weeks, repeat:
         2.3.2.1. Add *qty* times the ordered quantity of *current-part* in week t to the required quantity of *part* in week t.
      2.3.3. Add *part* to the top of *part-stack*.
3. Terminate.

To calculate the requirements for *part*:

1. For $t = 1, \ldots,$ number of weeks, repeat:
   1.1. Set the available quantity of *part* in week t to the difference between the available quantity in week $t-1$ and the required quantity in week $t-1$, or to 0 if that difference is negative.
   1.2. Set the delivered quantity of *part* in week t to the difference between the required quantity in week t and the available quantity in week t, or to 0 if that difference is negative.
   1.3. If the delivered quantity of *part* in week t is nonzero:
      1.3.1. Set t_0 to the difference between t and the lead time of *part*, or to 0 if that difference is negative.
      1.3.2. Add the delivered quantity of *part* in week t to the ordered quantity of *part* in week t_0.
2. Terminate.

Algorithm 15.29   A material requirements planning algorithm (with auxiliary algorithm).

perform a depth-first traversal for all products, we begin by adding all product nodes to *parts-stack*.

On each iteration of the algorithm, we remove the topmost part node, *current-part*, from *parts-stack*, and calculate the available, delivered, and ordered quantities for each week based on the corresponding required quantity (the calculation is specified in the auxiliary algorithm). Next, for each part, *part*, used to construct *current-part*, we update its required quantity for each week, based on the ordered quantity of *current-part*. We then add *part* to the top of *parts-stack*, and continue with the next iteration.

Once the algorithm terminates, we can generate a report for each part similar to the one given in Table 15.28.

15.9.2 Representing the data

Given the requirements of Algorithm 15.29, choosing a representation for a part is straightforward. Program 15.30 shows the representation expressed as a Java class named `Part`. Each `Part` object contains a unique part identifier, a description of the part, and the lead time. In addition, each part contains the four planning quantities for each week, which we choose to represent using four arrays of integers indexed by the week number. There is also a flag indicating whether or not this part is a product.

15.9.3 A material requirements planning application

In this section, we present an application to perform material requirements planning. The application is shown as Program 15.31. It proceeds in three stages: reading the input data; calculating the planning quantities; and generating the report.

Traditionally, the input to material requirements planning is in three parts: the *parts list* contains all of the parts (i.e., the nodes of the parts graph); the *bill of materials* contains all of the manufacturing dependencies between parts (i.e., the edges of the parts graph); and the *production schedule* contains the required amount of each product in a given week. We shall assume that the data are provided in three separate input files.

The first stage of the application is the construction of the parts graph by reading the data held in the input files. This is performed by the method `readGraph`, which uses three auxiliary methods (not shown) to read the three input files. This method uses an auxiliary map that maps part identifiers to the corresponding graph nodes. (A similar idea was used in Example 15.1.) The separation of the parts list and the bill of materials means that the parts need not be input in any particular order.

The second stage of the application is the calculation of the planning quantities. This is performed by the method `calculatePlan`, and is an implementation of Algorithm 15.29.

The third stage of the application is the generation of the planning report. This is performed by the method `printReport`, and involves simply iterating over the nodes in the graph, generating a report for the part contained in each node. This report should resemble Table 15.28.

```java
public class Part {

    // Each Part object represents a part.

    // This part contains a part identifier, a description, a lead time, a flag
    // indicating whether this part is a product, and the four planning quantities
    // for each week.

    private String partId, description;
    private int leadTime;   // in weeks
    private int[] required, available, delivered,
        ordered;
    private boolean isProduct;

    public final static int NUM_WEEKS = 10;

    ///////////// Constructors /////////////

    public Part (String partId, String description,
                  int leadTime, int available) {
    // Create a new part with the given part identifier, description, lead time,
    // and initial available quantity.
        this.partId = partId;
        this.leadTime = leadTime;
        this.description = description;
        this.isProduct = false;
        this.required  = new int[NUM_WEEKS];   // initially all 0
        this.available = new int[NUM_WEEKS];   // initially all 0
        this.delivered = new int[NUM_WEEKS];   // initially all 0
        this.ordered   = new int[NUM_WEEKS];   // initially all 0
        this.available[0] = available;
    }

    ///////////// Accessors /////////////

    public String getPartId () {
    // Return the part identifier for this part.
        return this.partId;
    }

    public boolean isProduct () {
    // Return true if and only if this part is a product.
        return this.isProduct;
    }
```

Program 15.30 Java implementation of parts (*continued on next page*).

```java
public String generateReport () {
// Generate a planning report for this part.
   ... // See code on the companion Web site.
}

/////////////// Transformers ////////////////

public static Part readPart (BufferedReader input)
               throws IOException {
// Read the details for a part from input, and return a new part created
// using this information.
   ... // See code on the companion Web site.
}

public void setRequirements (int t, int qty) {
// Set the required quantity in week t for this part to qty.
   this.required[t] = qty;
}

public void updateRequirements (Part other,
                int qty) {
// Update the required quantity in each week for this part, using the
// ordered quantities of part other, and the quantity qty of this part
// required to manufacture other.
   for (int t = 0; t < NUM_WEEKS; t++)
     this.required[t] += other.ordered[t] * qty);
}

public void markAsProduct () {
// Mark this part as a product. (Assume that a part is a product if it
// appears in the production schedule.)
   this.isProduct = true;
}

public void calculateQuantities () {
// Calculate the planning quantities in each week for this part.
   for (int t = 1; t < NUM_WEEKS; t++) {
     available[t]= Math.max(0,
         available[t-1] - required[t-1]);
     delivered[t] = Math.max(0,
         required[t] - available[t]);
     if (delivered[t] > 0) {
       int t0 = Math.max(0, t - leadTime);
       ordered[t0] += delivered[t];
     }
   }
}

}
```

Program 15.30 (*continued*)

```
public class MaterialRequirementsPlanning {
    ... // Auxiliary methods to read the input files – see the companion
        // Web site.
    private static void readGraph (Digraph partsGraph,
                       String partsFileName,
                       String bomFileName,
                       String scheduleFileName) {
    // Construct partsGraph from the data held in the following three files:
    // the parts list in the file named partsFileName; the bill of materials in
    // the file named bomFileName; and the production schedule in the file
    // named scheduleFileName.
        ... // See code on the companion Web site.
    }
    private static void calculatePlan (
                    Digraph partsGraph) {
    // Calculate the material requirements plan for all of the products contained
    // in partsGraph.
        Stack partsStack = new LinkedStack();
        Iterator nodes = partsGraph.nodes();
        while (nodes.hasNext()) {
            Graph.Node node = (Graph.Node) iter.next();
            Part part = (Part) node.getElement();
            if (part.isProduct())
                partsStack.addLast(node);
        }
        while (! partsStack.isEmpty()) {
            Graph.Node currentNode =
                (Graph.Node) partsStack.removeLast();
            Part currentPart =
                (Part) currentNode.getElement();
            currentPart.calculateQuantities();
            Iterator outEdges =
                partsGraph.outEdges(currentNode);
            while (outEdges.hasNext()) {
                Graph.Edge edge =
                    (Graph.Edge) outEdges.next();
                Graph.Node destNode = edge.getNodes()[1];
                Integer qty = (Integer) edge.getAttribute();
                Part part = (Part) destNode.getElement();
                part.updateRequirements(
                    currentPart, qty.intValue());
                partsStack.addLast(destNode);
            }
        }
    }
```

Program 15.31 A material requirements planning application as a Java class (*continued on next page*).

```
private static void printReport (
                Digraph partsGraph) {
// Print a report for each part in partsGraph showing the planning
// quantities in each week.
   Iterator nodes = partsGraph.nodes();
   while (nodes.hasNext()) {
      Graph.Node node = (Graph.Node) nodes.next();
      Part part = (Part) node.getElement();
      System.out.println(part.generateReport());
   }
}

public static void main (String[] args) {
// Generate a material requirements plan for each part. Assume that args
// contains the filenames of the parts list, bill of materials, and production
// schedule.
   Digraph partsGraph = new ESDigraph();
   readGraph(partsGraph, args[0], args[1], args[2]);
   calculatePlan(partsGraph);
   printReport(partsGraph);
}
}
```

Program 15.31 (*continued*)

Summary

In this chapter:

- We have studied the concept of a graph, characterized as an interconnected collection of elements, and we have distinguished between directed and undirected graphs.
- We have seen examples and a case study demonstrating applications of graphs.
- We have designed ADTs for graphs, expressed by Graph and Digraph interfaces.
- We have studied the edge-set, adjacency-set, and adjacency-matrix representations of graphs, and outlined how to code these representations in Java as classes that implement either the Graph or Digraph interface.
- We have studied algorithms for graph depth-first and breadth-first traversal, and for graph topological sort.

Exercises

15.1 Section 15.2 gives some examples of graphs in both computing and everyday life. Can you think of any others? Are your examples directed or undirected graphs?

15.2   Consider the motorway network in Figure 15.1. Find all of the paths in the graph connecting the following cities:
(a) Perth and Exeter
(b) Dover and Leeds
(c) Liverpool and Cambridge.
For each path, calculate its length in terms of (i) the number of edges, and (ii) the total distance.

15.3   Construct a road, rail, or flight network, similar to the one in Figure 15.1, for your own country or state.
Repeat Exercise 15.2 for pairs of cities selected from your graph.

15.4   Trace the `qualified` method of Example 15.1 as it checks whether a student is qualified to take Operating Systems. In what respect is it unnecessarily inefficient? Modify the method to avoid this inefficiency.

15.5   Consider the directed graph of Figure 15.3. Draw diagrams showing how this graph would be represented:
(a) using the edge-set representation
(b) using the adjacency-set representation
(c) using the adjacency-matrix representation.

15.6   In the edge-set representation of graphs (Section 15.4), consider the following alternatives:
(a) Represent the node set by an *SLL*.
(b) Represent the edge set by a *hash table*.
For each alternative, state what algorithms would be used to implement the graph operations, and determine their time complexities.

15.7   In the adjacency-set representation of graphs (Section 15.5), consider the following alternatives:
(a) Represent the adjacency sets by *DLLs*.
(b) For a directed graph, provide each node with *two* adjacency sets, one for its in-edges and one for its out-edges.
For each alternative, state what algorithms would be used to implement the graph operations, and determine their time complexities.

15.8   Consider the adjacency-matrix representation of directed graphs (Section 15.6).
(a) Show the effect of removing node V in Figure 15.16.
(b) Modify the implementation such that `removeNode` keeps the matrix compact by shifting rows and columns. (For example, removing node V in Figure 15.16 would reassign nodes W and X to position numbers 3 and 4.) How would this change affect the time complexities of `removeNode` and the other graph operations?

15.9   Modify both graph traversal algorithms (Algorithms 15.21 and 15.23) to make them graph *searching* algorithms. Each should search the graph for a node whose element is equal to *target-elem*.

15.10 Implement the graph traversal algorithms of Section 15.7 in Java, using the `Graph` and `Digraph` interfaces of Figures 15.6 and 15.9.

15.11 The maze solving algorithms in Section 6.6 (Algorithms 6.15 and 6.17) perform a depth-first traversal of the squares of the maze. Verify this by comparing them with Algorithms 15.20 and 15.21.

Devise an iterative maze solving algorithm that use a breadth-first traversal, and implement this as a Java method. Compare its maze-solving ability with the depth-first traversal.

15.12 Devise an algorithm to determine whether there is a path between two given nodes, *v* and *w*, in a given directed graph. (*Hint:* This is just a special case of a graph traversal algorithm.) Implement your algorithm as a Java method.

* **15.13** Define the *distance* along a path to be the total number of edges on that path. Consider the problem of finding the distance along the *shortest* path between a given node, *start*, and every other node in a graph.

You can solve this problem by using a variant of the breadth-first traversal algorithm: see Algorithm 15.32. As well as marking each node *v* as reached, you must also record an integer $dist_v$ for each node *v*. This will be either the distance along some path from *start* to *v*, or (if no such path has yet been found) infinity. You can record the distances $dist_v$ in alternative ways:

- Record each $dist_v$ directly by an integer field in the node object *v*. Initially the field is infinity (represented by a very large integer). On finding a path to *v* along which the distance is *d*, store *d* in the field. On finding a shorter path, update the field.
- Record all the $dist_v$ in a map, separately from the graph. Initially the map is empty. On finding a path of *d* edges to node *v*, add an entry ‹*v, d*› to the map, indicating that $dist_v = d$. On finding a shorter path, replace that entry in the map. The absence of an entry for node *v* in the map indicates that $dist_v$ is infinity.

Implement Algorithm 15.32 as a Java method, and test it with the graph of Figure 15.1.

* **15.14** Consider a graph where the edge attributes are positive numbers (such as the road network of Figure 15.1). The problem is to find the path with the smallest sum of its edge attributes between a given node, *start*, and every other node in the graph.

This is just a modified version of Algorithm 15.32, with the *distance* along any path redefined to be the sum of the attributes of the edges on that path. (In particular, the distance between two neighbors is the attribute of the edge connecting them, rather than 1.)
(a) Modify Algorithm 15.32 accordingly.
(b) Implement your algorithm as a Java method. Test it with the graph of Figure 15.1.

To find the shortest path in graph *g* from node *start* to every other node:

1. Make *node-queue* contain only node *start*.
2. Set $dist_{start}$ to 0, and set $dist_v$ for all other nodes *v* to infinity.
3. While *node-queue* is not empty, repeat:
   3.1. Remove the front element of *node-queue* into *v*, and mark node *v* as reached.
   3.2. For each unreached neighbor *w* of node *v*, repeat:
        3.2.1. Let *d* be $dist_v + 1$.
        3.2.2. If $d < dist_w$, set $dist_w$ to *d*.
        3.2.3. Add node *w* to *node-queue*.
4. Terminate.

Algorithm 15.32 Shortest-path algorithm for an undirected graph.

** **15.15** *Dijkstra's algorithm* is another way to find the shortest path between a given node, *start*, and every other node in a graph. It is similar to the algorithm in the answer to Exercise 15.14(a), except that the ordinary queue of nodes is replaced by a *priority queue*, in which nodes are prioritized by their distance from *start* (smallest distance first).
(a) Write Dijkstra's algorithm by modifying your answer to Exercise 15.14.
(b) Implement Dijkstra's algorithm as a Java method. Test it with the graph of Figure 15.1.

15.16 Consider the topological sort algorithm (Figure 15.25).
(a) How will the algorithm behave if the directed graph *g* is cyclic?
(b) Modify the algorithm to issue a warning message if *g* is cyclic.
(c) Modify the algorithm to work without *node-queue*.

15.17 Implement the topological sort algorithm (Figure 15.25) in Java, using the `Digraph` interface of Program 15.9.

15.18 Suppose that the `Digraph` interface (Program 15.9) is to be extended with the following method:

```
public Iterator depthFirstIterator
            (Graph.Node node);
// Return an iterator that will visit all nodes of this graph that are
// reachable from node, in a depth-first traversal.
```

Choose one of the `Digraph` implementations (Program 15.12, 15.15, or 15.18). Write an inner class, named `DepthFirstIterator`, and use it to implement the above method.

15.19 Suppose that the `Digraph` interface (Program 15.9) is to be extended with the following method:

```
public Iterator breadthFirstIterator
            (Graph.Node node);
// Return an iterator that will visit all nodes of this graph that are
// reachable from node, in a breadth-first traversal.
```

Choose one of the `Digraph` implementations (Program 15.12, 15.15, or 15.18). Write an inner class, named `BreadthFirstIterator`, and use it to implement the above method.

15.20 Implement the `calculatePlan` method of the material requirements planning application given in Program 15.31, using your answer to Exercise 15.18.

15.21 Repeat Exercise 15.20 using your answer to Exercise 15.19. Compare the results with your answer to Exercise 15.20.

* **15.22** Extend the material requirements planning case study as follows. Assume that each part is given a *reorder quantity*. When a part's order quantity is calculated, it must be rounded up to a multiple of the reorder quantity. When a part is delivered, any difference between the part's required quantity and ordered quantity is held in stock, and added to the available quantity.

** **15.23** Devise an algorithm to draw a graph graphically in a `java.awt` window.
    Implement your algorithm as a Java method, and test it using the graphs in Figures 15.1–15.3. Compare your results with the hand-drawn diagrams.

16

Balanced Search Tree Data Structures

In this chapter we shall study:

- AVL-trees, which are binary search trees equipped with special insertion and deletion algorithms that keep them well-balanced (Section 16.1)
- B-trees, which are balanced search trees with multiple elements per node, and which are shallower than binary search trees (Section 16.2).

16.1 AVL-trees

We have seen that binary search trees (BSTs) are an effective representation for sets and maps. The BST search, insertion, and deletion algorithms have $O(\log n)$ time complexity, provided that the BST remains well-balanced. The weakness of BSTs is that all these algorithms degenerate to $O(n)$ time complexity if the BST becomes ill-balanced.

In some applications it is possible, with care, to ensure that the BST remains well-balanced. In general this is not possible. Consider the information retrieval application of Example 9.2, in which the method `readAllWords` accumulates the set of all words found in a given document. Assume that the word set is represented by a BST. If we are lucky, the words will be inserted in random alphabetical order, in which case the BST will probably be reasonably well-balanced. If we are unlucky, the first few words in the document might be 'African aardvarks and antelopes', in which case the BST will become, and remain, very ill-balanced!

One idea for dealing with such eventualities is to rebalance the BST periodically. Unfortunately, any algorithm to rebalance an arbitrary BST must have time complexity $O(n \log n)$ or worse, and this is even slower than the worst-case performance of the search, insertion, and deletion algorithms. If the application is an interactive program, rebalancing a large BST might cause a noticeable and unexpected pause, irritating for the user.

A better idea is to keep the tree well-balanced at all times. This turns out to be feasible.

We can make the insertion and deletion algorithms rebalance the tree locally, when necessary. This slows down insertion and deletion only by a constant factor, so their time complexity remains $O(\log n)$.

16.1.1 Concept

The *height* of a *node* in a tree is the number of links that must be followed from that node to reach its remotest descendant. The *height* of a *(sub)tree* is the height of its topmost node.

These definitions have the following consequences. The height of a leaf node is 0. The height of a non-leaf node is one greater than the maximum height of its subtrees. Likewise, the height of a nonempty tree is one greater than the maximum height of its subtrees. By convention, an empty tree or subtree is deemed to have height -1.

(*Note:* The concepts of height and depth are related. The height and depth of a *(sub)tree* are always equal. However, the height and depth of a *node* are complementary: the height of a node is counted from its remotest descendant, whereas the depth of a node is counted from its remotest ancestor.)

A *node* is **height-balanced** if the heights of its subtrees differ by at most one. (If it has only one subtree, the latter must have height 0, i.e., it must have a single node.) A *tree* is **height-balanced** if all its nodes are height-balanced.

It is useful to quantify this notion of height-balance. A node's **balance factor** is the difference between its left subtree's height and its right subtree's height. A node is therefore height-balanced if and only if its balance factor is -1, 0, or $+1$.

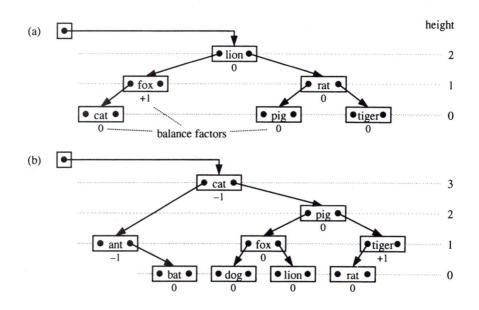

Figure 16.1   Illustrative AVL-trees (showing heights and balance factors).

An ***AVL-tree*** is a BST that is height-balanced. AVL-trees are named after the mathematicians G. M. Adel'son Vel'skii and Y. M. Landis, who invented them.

Figure 16.1 illustrates two AVL-trees, showing the heights and balance factors of all nodes. Tree (a) is not only height-balanced but also strictly balanced (i.e., balanced in the sense of Section 10.1.1). Tree (b) is not strictly balanced, but it is height-balanced.

Every strictly balanced BST is an AVL-tree, but not every AVL-tree is strictly balanced. The important point, however, is that AVL-trees are *sufficiently* balanced to guarantee that the AVL-tree search, insertion, and deletion algorithms are all $O(\log n)$.

16.1.2 Search

The AVL-tree search algorithm is identical to the BST search algorithm (Algorithm 10.10). The only difference – but a crucial difference – is that the height-balanced property guarantees that the AVL-tree search algorithm's time complexity is $O(\log n)$. We shall analyze this in detail in Section 16.1.5.

16.1.3 Insertion

AVL-tree insertion consists of an ordinary BST-insertion, followed by a local restructuring ('rotation') of the tree if necessary to restore height-balance.

Suppose that we are given an AVL-tree. Consider what happens when we perform an ordinary BST-insertion, using Algorithm 10.12. The BST-insertion replaces a null link by a newly-created leaf node containing the new element. This could increase the heights, and change the balance factors, of the new node's ancestors (its parent, grandparent, etc.). Some of these ancestors could become height-unbalanced.

Figure 16.2 illustrates this effect. The BST-insertion of 'dog' changes the balance factors of the ancestor nodes containing 'cat', from 0 to -1, 'fox', from $+1$ to $+2$, and 'lion', from 0 to $+1$. So the node containing 'fox' is now height-unbalanced. This situation can be remedied by *rotating* the nodes containing 'dog', 'cat', and 'fox' such that the median of these elements ('dog') is in the topmost node, the least element ('cat') is in the topmost node's left child, and the greatest element ('fox') is in the topmost node's right child.

Figure 16.3 illustrates another case. The BST-insertion of 'goat' changes the balance factor of the node containing 'cat' from -1 to -2, making it height-unbalanced. This situation can be remedied by rotating the nodes containing 'fox', 'pig', and 'cat' such that the median element ('fox') is in the topmost node, the least element ('cat') is in the topmost node's left child, and the greatest element ('pig') is in the topmost node's right child. The other subtrees (shaded in Figure 16.3) are left intact by this rotation.

Rotation focuses on three of the newly-inserted node's ancestors: a child, its parent, and its grandparent, where the grandparent is the nearest ancestor that has become height-unbalanced. A little thought should convince you that such a group of three nodes can always be found if any node has become height-unbalanced. (The newly-inserted node has height 0. Only a node of height 2 or more can possibly be height-unbalanced.)

Of these three nodes, let a be the node containing the least element, let b be the node containing the median element, and let c be the node containing the greatest element.

Also, let *T1*, *T2*, *T3*, and *T4* be the four free subtrees of *a*, *b*, and *c* (i.e., the subtrees whose top nodes are not *a*, *b*, and *c* themselves). In general, there are four cases to consider:

(1) Node *a* is the left child of *b*, which is the left child of *c*. In this case we move *c* downward to become *b*'s right child, and we move *b*'s right subtree (*T3*) to becomes *c*'s left subtree. (See Figure 16.4.)

(2) Node *b* is the right child of *a*, which is the left child of *c*. In this case we move *b* upward 'between' *a* and *c*, which become its left and right children, and move *b*'s two subtrees (*T2* and *T3*) to become *a*'s right subtree and *c*'s left subtree. (See Figure 16.5.)

(3) Node *c* is the right child of *b*, which is the right child of *a*. This is the mirror image of case (1). (This case was illustrated in Figure 16.3.)

(4) Node *b* is the left child of *c*, which is the right child of *a*. This is the mirror image of case (2).

Case (1) is shown in Figure 16.4. The subtree as a whole was initially height-balanced, with the heights of *T3* and *T4* exceeding by 1 the heights of *T1* and *T2*. However, the BST-insertion has increased the height of either *T1* or *T2*, and consequently the heights of its ancestors *a*, *b*, and *c*. Nodes *a* and *b* are still height-balanced, but node *c* is now height-unbalanced, its balance factor having changed from +1 to +2. The rotation of nodes *a*, *b*,

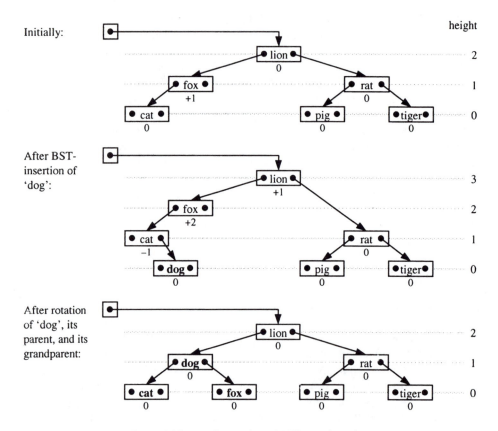

Figure 16.2 An illustration of AVL-tree insertion.

and c makes all three nodes height-balanced. Moreover, the rotated subtree has exactly the same height as the initial subtree (before the BST-insertion), so all ancestor nodes of the rotated subtree are now height-balanced once more. (In fact, they have exactly the same balance factors as they did initially.)

Case (2) is shown in Figure 16.5. The subtree as a whole was initially height-balanced, with the heights of *T1* and *T4* exceeding by 1 the heights of *T2* and *T3*. However, the BST-insertion has increased the height of either *T2* or *T3*, and consequently the heights of its ancestors b, a, and c. Nodes b and a are still height-balanced, but node c is now height-unbalanced, its balance factor having changed from $+1$ to $+2$. The rotation of nodes a, b, and c makes all three nodes height-balanced. Moreover, the rotated subtree has exactly the same height as the initial subtree, so all ancestor nodes of the rotated subtree are now height-balanced once more.

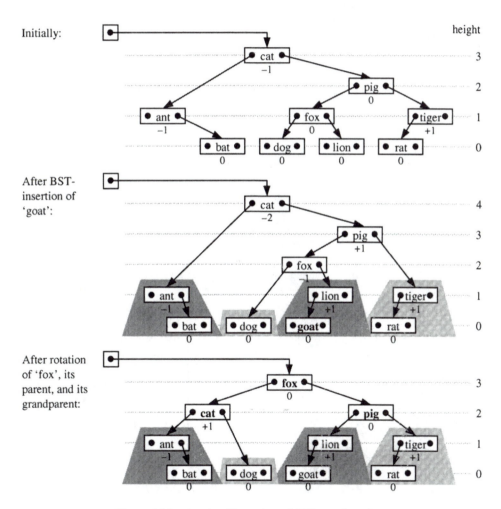

Figure 16.3   Another illustration of AVL-tree insertion.

Note that, in every case:

- The rotation moves node b to the top of the subtree; node a becomes node b's left child; and node c becomes node b's right child. Moreover, the four free subtrees ($T1$, $T2$, $T3$, and $T4$) retain their left-to-right order.
- After the rotation, the nodes a, b, and c are all height-balanced. Moreover, the rotated subtree (with top node b) has the same height as the original subtree. Thus the tree as a whole is once again an AVL-tree.

Algorithms 16.6 and 16.7 capture the above idea. Algorithm 16.6 is the AVL-tree insertion algorithm itself: step 1 is an ordinary BST-insertion, and step 2.2 is a rotation. The latter is performed by the auxiliary Algorithm 16.7.

Figure 16.8 illustrates the effect of inserting a sequence of words into an initially-empty AVL-tree. Although these words happen to arrive in ascending order, the final tree is still height-balanced. Compare this with Figure 10.14, where the effect of inserting the same sequence of words into an initially-empty BST was to build an extremely ill-balanced BST.

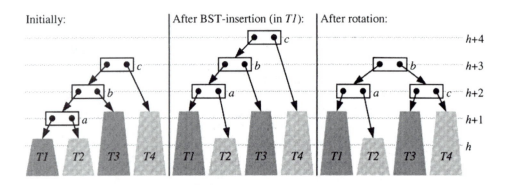

Figure 16.4 AVL-tree insertion and rotation: case (1). (*Note:* BST-insertion in *T2* has a similar effect.)

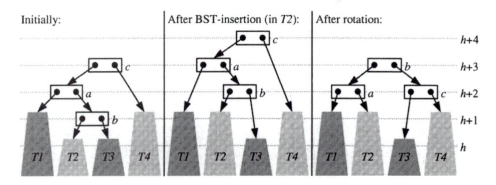

Figure 16.5 AVL-tree insertion and rotation: case (2). (*Note:* BST-insertion in *T3* has a similar effect.)

To insert element *elem* into the AVL-tree *tree*:

1. Perform a BST-insertion of *elem* into *tree*, and let *ins* be the newly-created node containing *elem*.
2. If *ins* or any ancestor of *ins* is now height-unbalanced:
   2.1. Let *child* be either *ins* or an ancestor of *ins* such that *child*'s grandparent is the nearest height-unbalanced ancestor of *ins*.
   2.2. Let *rotated-subtree* be the subtree obtained by rotating *child*, its parent, and its grandparent.
   2.3. Make *rotated-subtree* replace the subtree of *tree* whose top node is *child*'s grandparent.
3. Terminate.

Algorithm 16.6   AVL-tree insertion algorithm.

To rotate the nodes *child*, *parent*, and *grandparent*:

1. Let (a, b, c) be a left-to-right enumeration of *child*, *parent*, and *grandparent*.
2. Let $(T1, T2, T3, T4)$ be a left-to-right enumeration of the four free subtrees of a, b, and c (i.e., the subtrees whose top nodes are not a, b, and c themselves).
3. Let *rotated-subtree* be a subtree constructed as follows: (i) its top node is b; (ii) b's left and right children are a and c; (iii) a's left and right subtrees are $T1$ and $T2$; (iv) c's left and right subtrees are $T3$ and $T4$.
4. Terminate with answer *rotated-subtree*.

Algorithm 16.7   AVL-tree rotation (auxiliary algorithm for Algorithms 16.6 and 16.12).

16.1.4 Deletion

AVL-tree deletion consists of an ordinary BST-deletion, followed by local rotations where necessary to restore height-balance. Compared with AVL-tree insertion, there are two important differences: (i) sometimes there is a choice of rotations; and (ii) multiple rotations might be needed to restore height-balance.

When we perform an ordinary BST-deletion, using Algorithm 10.17, some node is deleted from the tree. (Remember that the deleted node is not necessarily the node that contained the element to be deleted; it is sometimes a descendant of that node.) The BST-deletion could decrease the heights, and change the balance factors, of some of the deleted node's ancestors. Some of these ancestors could become height-unbalanced.

Figure 16.9 illustrates this effect. The BST-deletion of 'bat' changes the balance factors of the ancestor node containing 'ant', from -1 to 0, and 'cat', from -1 to -2. Thus the node containing 'cat' is now height-unbalanced. This situation can be remedied *either* by rotating the nodes containing 'cat', 'pig', and 'fox' *or* by rotating the nodes

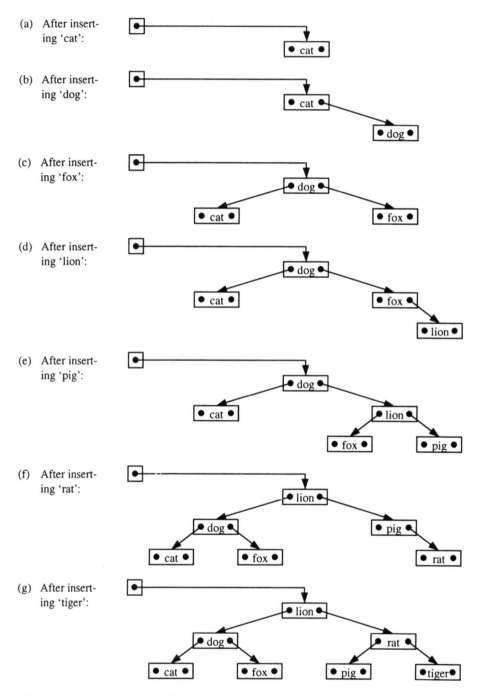

Figure 16.8 Illustration of the AVL-tree insertion algorithm, when used to insert a sequence of elements in ascending order.

containing 'cat', 'pig', and 'tiger'. These alternative rotations lead to different trees, but both are height-balanced.

To decide which nodes to rotate, we start with the deleted node's parent v. If v and all of its ancestors are still height-balanced, there is nothing to do. Otherwise we take the

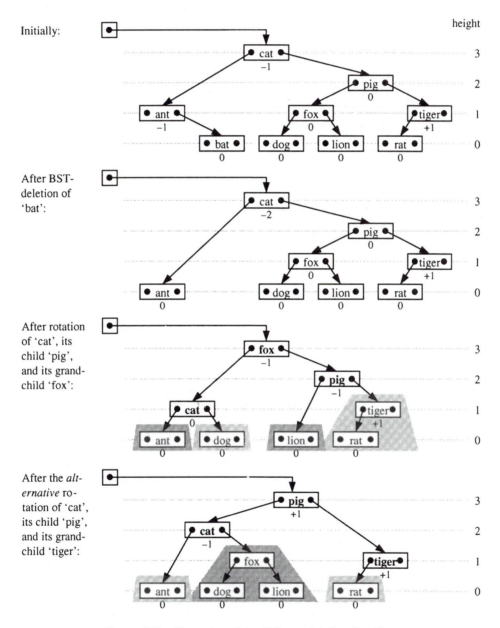

Figure 16.9   Illustration of the AVL-tree deletion algorithm.

height-unbalanced node nearest to *v* (call it *grandparent*). We also choose the child of *grandparent* with the greater height (call it *parent*), and similarly choose the child of *parent* with the greater height (call it *child*). Then we rotate the nodes *grandparent*, *parent*, and *child*, exactly as described in Section 16.1.3.

Note that *parent* and *child* are always in the opposite subtree of *grandparent* from *v*.

To determine which child of node *w* has the greater height, we simply use node *w*'s balance factor. If it is positive, we choose the left child; if it is negative, we choose the right child; and if it is zero, we choose either child.

Of the three nodes *grandparent*, *parent*, and *child*, let *a* be the node containing the least element, let *b* be the node containing the median element, and let *c* be the node containing the greatest element. As in Section 16.1.3, there are four cases to consider:

(1) Node *a* is the left child of *b*, which is the left child of *c*.
(2) Node *b* is the right child of *a*, which is the left child of *c*.
(3) Node *c* is the right child of *b*, which is the right child of *a*.
(4) Node *b* is the left child of *c*, which is the right child of *a*.

Case (1) is shown in Figure 16.10. The subtree of interest was initially height-balanced, but the BST-deletion has decreased the height of subtree *T4*. Node *c* is now height-unbalanced, its balance factor having changed from $+1$ to $+2$. The rotation of nodes *a*, *b*, and *c* makes all three nodes height-balanced. Moreover, the rotated subtree has exactly the same height as the initial subtree, so all ancestor nodes of the rotated subtree are now height-balanced once more.

Case (2) is shown in Figure 16.11(a). The subtree of interest was initially height-balanced, but the BST-deletion has decreased the height of subtree *T4*. Node *c* is now height-unbalanced, its balance factor having changed from $+1$ to $+2$. The rotation of nodes *a*, *b*, and *c* makes all three nodes height-balanced. Moreover, the rotated subtree has exactly the same height as the initial subtree, so all ancestor nodes of the rotated subtree are now height-balanced once more.

But now consider Figure 16.11(b), which is similar to Figure 16.11(a) except that the height of subtree *T1* is one less than before. Rotation of the same three nodes makes the whole subtree height-balanced, but unfortunately it also reduces the overall height of that subtree. The same phenomenon would have been observed in Figure 16.10 if the height of subtree *T3* had been one less.

In every case:

- The rotation moves node *b* to the top of the subtree; node *a* becomes node *b*'s left child; and node *c* becomes node *b*'s right child. Moreover, the four free subtrees (*T1*, *T2*, *T3*, and *T4*) retain their left-to-right order.
- After the rotation, the nodes *a*, *b*, and *c* are all height-balanced. Moreover, the height of the rotated subtree (with top node *b*) is either the same as or one less than the initial subtree.

If the height of the rotated subtree is indeed one less than the initial subtree, some of node *b*'s ancestors might have become height-unbalanced as a consequence of the rotation. The remedy then is to perform a further rotation higher up in the tree. This procedure must eventually terminate, for example when it turns out that (after the rotation) *b* is the root node of the whole tree.

Algorithm 16.12 captures the above idea. Step 1 is an ordinary BST-deletion, and step 2.4 is a rotation. The latter is performed by Algorithm 16.7.

16.1.5 Analysis

Search

Let us analyze the efficiency of AVL-tree search in terms of comparisons. Just as for BST search, the maximum number of comparisons is one more than the depth (or height) of the tree.

The best case is when the AVL-tree is strictly balanced (in the sense of Section 10.1.1).

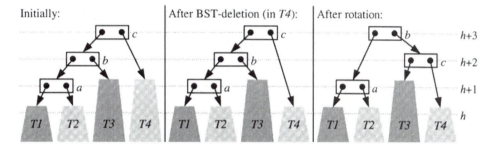

Figure 16.10   AVL-tree deletion and rotation: case (1).

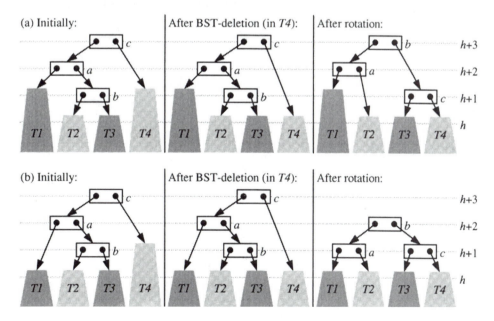

Figure 16.11   AVL-tree deletion and rotation: case (2).

To delete element *elem* from the AVL-tree *tree*:

1. Perform a BST-deletion of *elem* from *tree*, and let *v* be the parent of the node that was actually deleted.
2. While either *v* or an ancestor of *v* is height-unbalanced, repeat:
   2.1. Let *grandparent* be either *v* or an ancestor of *v* that is height-unbalanced, choosing the one that is nearest to *v*.
   2.2. Let *parent* be the child of *grandparent* with the greater height, choosing either child if they have equal height.
   2.3. Let *child* be the child of *parent* with the greater height, choosing either child if they have equal height.
   2.4. Let *rotated-subtree* be the subtree obtained by rotating *child*, *parent*, and *grandparent*.
   2.5. Make *rotated-subtree* replace the subtree of *tree* whose top node is *grandparent*.
   2.6. Set *v* to the top node of *rotated-subtree*.
3. Terminate.

Algorithm 16.12 AVL-tree deletion algorithm.

Then we get the same answer as for a balanced BST:

$$\text{Maximum no. of comparisons} = \text{floor}(\log_2 n) + 1 \tag{16.1}$$

The worst case is when the AVL-tree is not strictly balanced. An AVL-tree of height h can have one subtree of height $h - 1$ and one subtree of height $h - 2$. Let $size(h)$ be the number of nodes in this tree. Allowing for the root node, we obtain the following equation:

$$size(h) = 1 + size(h - 1) + size(h - 2)$$

The mathematics is difficult, so we simply give an approximate solution to this equation:

$$n = size(h) \approx 2^{(h+1.33)/1.44} - 2$$

Therefore:

$$h \approx 1.44 \log_2(n + 2) - 1.33$$

Since the search performs at most $h + 1$ comparisons, it follows that:

$$\text{Maximum no. of comparisons} \approx 1.44 \log_2(n + 2) - 0.33 \tag{16.2}$$

Therefore, in both best and worst cases, AVL-tree search has time complexity $O(\log n)$. Moreover, it is only about 44% slower in the worst case than in the best case.

Insertion

Let us now analyze the time complexity of AVL-tree insertion (Algorithm 16.6). The BST-insertion in step 1 entails at most $1.44 \log_2(n + 2) - 0.33$ comparisons, by the same argument as above. The preparation for rotation in step 2 (when necessary to restore height-balance) entails 3 comparisons. Adding these numbers:

$$\text{Maximum no. of comparisons} \approx 1.44 \log_2(n + 2) + 2.67 \qquad (16.3)$$

Therefore the time complexity of AVL-tree insertion is also $O(\log n)$.

Deletion

Let us now analyze the time complexity of AVL-tree deletion (Algorithm 16.12). The BST-deletion in step 1 entails at most $1.44 \log_2(n + 2) - 0.33$ comparisons, by the same argument as above. The preparation for rotation in step 2 (when necessary to restore height-balance) entails 3 comparisons. The rotation is repeated at most $\text{floor}(\log_2 n)/3$ times. Putting all these numbers together:

$$\text{Maximum no. of comparisons} \approx 1.44 \log_2(n + 2) + \text{floor}(\log_2 n) - 0.33 \qquad (16.4)$$

Therefore the time complexity of AVL-tree deletion is also $O(\log n)$.

16.2 B-trees

A balanced search tree is an efficient data structure for representing a set or map for one fundamental reason: its depth increases slowly as the tree grows. Another way of saying the same thing is this: the tree's size grows rapidly as the tree gets deeper.

We can easily quantify this phenomenon. The size of a *binary tree* grows with the tree's depth as shown by the following equation:

$$\text{Maximum size of a binary tree of depth } d = 2^{d+1} - 1 \qquad (16.5)$$

(See Section 10.1.1.) For example, a binary tree of depth 4 has up to 31 elements, and a binary tree of depth 8 has up to 511 elements.

A tree's maximum size is even greater if we let it have more elements and more children per node. In a *k-ary tree*, each node contains up to $k - 1$ elements and has up to k children. By generalizing equation (16.5) we obtain:

$$\text{Maximum size of a } k\text{-ary tree of depth } d = k^{d+1} - 1 \qquad (16.6)$$

Table 16.13 gives some illustrative figures. It shows that a 5-ary tree has a much greater maximum size than a binary (2-ary) tree of the same depth. A 64-ary tree (even a very shallow one) has an enormous maximum size.

16.2.1 Concept

In this section we shall study *B-trees*. A B-tree is a restricted form of *k*-ary tree, equipped with insertion and deletion algorithms that guarantee that the B-tree remains both shallow and well-balanced as it grows and shrinks.

Figure 16.14 illustrates two 5-ary B-trees, whose elements are country-codes.

B-tree (a) has depth 1. Its root node has three elements and four children. All four children are leaf nodes, each node having three or four elements.

B-tree (b) has depth 2. Its root node has one element and two children. Each of these children has two elements and three children of its own. All the grandchildren are leaf nodes, each having two, three, or four elements.

Every node of a 5-ary B-tree contains 2–4 elements, except the root node which may contain 1–4 elements.

In general, every B-tree non-leaf node containing e elements has links to $e + 1$ children. We picture these links and elements arranged from left to right as follows: link, element, link, …, element, link. Each element has both a left child link (the link immediately to its left) and a right child link (the link immediately to its right). Note that each element's right child is also its right neighbor's left child.

Table 16.13 Maximum sizes of trees.

k	Maximum size of k-ary tree			
	of depth 1	of depth 2	of depth 3	of depth 4
2	3	7	15	31
5	24	124	624	3124
64	4095	262143	16.8 million	1.1 billion

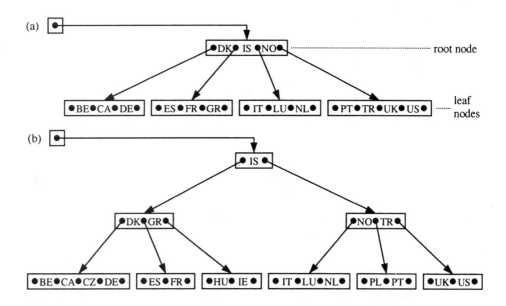

Figure 16.14 Illustrative 5-ary B-trees.

In a B-tree (as in any tree), a leaf node has no children.

We can also think of *subtrees* in a B-tree. Each non-leaf node in a 5-ary B-tree has up to five subtrees. Each element in a non-leaf node has both a left subtree and a right subtree.

Every B-tree is *sorted*. This means that the elements in any node and the elements in that node's subtrees (if any) are arranged in ascending order. For example, consider B-tree (a) in Figure 16.14. Its root node contains DK, IS, and NO, in that order. The left subtree of DK contains elements (BE, CA, DE) that are less than DK. The right subtree of DK / left subtree of IS contains elements (ES, FR, GR) that are greater than DK but less than IS. The right subtree of IS / left subtree of NO contains elements that are greater than IS but less than NO. The right subtree of NO contains elements that are greater than NO.

Because of the arrangement of elements in a B-tree, and because a B-tree is always balanced, B-tree search, insertion, and deletion all have guaranteed $O(\log n)$ time complexity, as we shall see.

We are now ready for a precise definition. A *k-ary B-tree* (or *B-tree of order k*) is a tree with the following properties:

- The root node contains at least 1 and at most $k - 1$ elements. Every other node contains at least $(k - 1)/2$ and at most $k - 1$ elements.
- A non-leaf node that contains e elements ($1 \le e < k$) also has links to exactly $e + 1$ child nodes. Each element sits between a pair of child links, which are links to its left child and right child, respectively.
- All leaf nodes lie at the same depth. A leaf node has no children.
- The elements in each node are arranged in ascending order. For each element *elem* in a non-leaf node, all elements in *elem*'s left subtree are less than *elem*, and all elements in *elem*'s right subtree are greater than *elem*.

The *size* of a *B-tree* is the total number of elements in that B-tree. The *size* of an individual *node* is the number of elements in that node.

The *empty B-tree* has size zero. It has no nodes and no elements.

The *arity* of a B-tree is the maximum number of children per node, i.e., k.

In Java, we can represent a B-tree by an object of class `Btree`, and each B-tree node by an object of class `Btree.Node`, both classes being shown in Program 16.15. Figure 16.16 shows the detailed structures of `Btree` and `Btree.Node` objects.

This data structure is simple and clear, but rather wasteful of space. Every node contains an array of child links, but in a leaf node these child links are all null. An alternative would be to distinguish between leaf and non-leaf nodes, and let only a non-leaf node contain an array of child links. (See Exercise 16.8.)

16.2.2 Search

B-tree search is quite straightforward. Figure 16.17 illustrates searches in a 5-ary B-tree:

(a) To search the B-tree for NO, we first look among the elements of the root node (DK, IS, NO). We find NO there, so the search is successful.

(b) To search the B-tree for IT, we first look among the elements of the root node (DK, IS, NO). We do not find IT there, but we see that IT is greater than IS and less than NO, so we proceed to the right child of IS / left child of NO. Now we look among the elements of that node (IT, LU, NL). We do find IT there, so the search is successful.

(c) To search the B-tree for DE, we first look among the elements of the root node (DK, IS, NO). We do not find DE there, but we see that DE is less than DK, so we proceed to the left child of DK. Now we look among the elements of that node (BE, CA, DE). We do find DE there, so the search is successful.

(d) To search the B-tree for SE, we first look among the elements of the root node (DK, IS, NO). We do not find SE there, but we see that SE is greater than NO, so we proceed to the right child of NO. Now we look among the elements of that node (PT, TR, UK, US). We do not find SE there, so we proceed to the left child of TR. But there is no such child, so the search is unsuccessful.

These examples illustrate an advantage of a B-tree over a BST: the average search path is shorter, since the B-tree is shallower. This advantage is, however, offset by the need to search the elements within each B-tree node on the search path.

```java
public class Btree {

    // Each Btree object is a B-tree header.

    // This B-tree is represented as follows: arity is the maximum number
    // of children per node, and root is a link to its root node.

    // Each B-tree node is represented as follows: size contains its size; a
    // subarray elems[0...size-1] contains its elements;and a subarray
    // childs[0...size] contains links to its child nodes. For each element
    // elems[i], childs[i] is a link to its left child, and childs[i+1] is a
    // link to its right child. In a leaf node, all child links are null.

    // Moreover, for every element x in the left subtree of element y:
    //      x.compareTo(y) < 0
    // and for every element z in the right subtree of element y:
    //      z.compareTo(y) > 0.

    private int arity;
    private Btree.Node root;

    public Btree (int k) {
    // Construct an empty B-tree of arity k.
        root = null;
        arity = k;
    }

    ...    // Other Btree methods (see below).

    /////////////// Inner class for B-tree nodes ////////////

    private static class Node {

        // Each Btree.Node object is a B-tree node.
```

Program 16.15 Java class representing B-tree headers and nodes (*continued on next page*).

```
private int size;
private Comparable[] elems;
private Node[] childs;

private Node (int k, Comparable elem,
                Node left, Node right) {
// Construct a B-tree node of arity k, initially with one element, elem,
// and two children, left and right.
   this.elems = new Comparable[k];
   this.childs = new Node[k+1];
   // ... Each array has one extra component, to allow for possible
   // overflow.
   this.size = 1;
   this.elems[0] = elem;
   this.childs[0] = left;
   this.childs[1] = right;
}

private Node (int k, Comparable[] elems,
                Node[] childs, int l, int r) {
// Construct a B-tree node of arity k, with its elements taken from the
// subarray elems[l...r-1] and its children from the subarray
// childs[l...r].
   this.elems = new Comparable[k];
   this.childs = new Btree.Node[k+1];
   this.size = 0;
   for (int j = l; j < r; j++) {
      this.elems[this.size] = elems[j];
      this.childs[this.size] = childs[j];
      this.size++;
   }
   this.childs[this.size] = childs[r];
}

private boolean isLeaf () {
// Return true if and only of this node is a leaf.
   return (childs[0] == null);
}

...   // Other Btree.Node methods (see below).

}

}
```

Program 16.15 (*continued*)

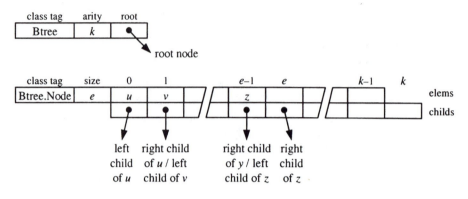

Figure 16.16 Detailed structures of `Btree` and `Btree.Node` objects representing a *k*-ary B-tree.

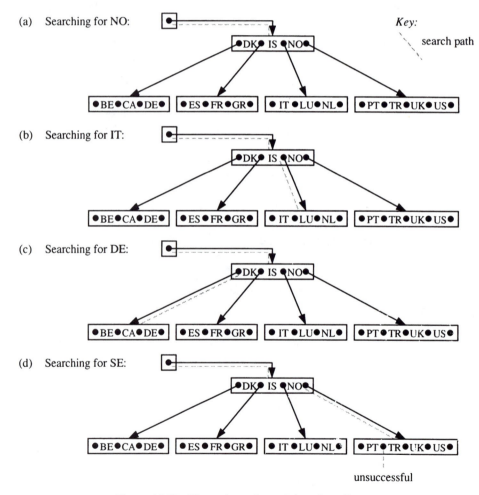

Figure 16.17 Illustrations of search in a 5-ary B-tree.

To find which if any node of a B-tree contains an element equal to *target*:

1. If the B-tree is empty, terminate with answer *none*.
2. Set *curr* to the B-tree's root node.
3. Repeat:
    3.1. Search for *elem* in node *curr*.
    3.2. If *elem* was found in node *curr*, terminate with answer *curr*.
    3.3. If *elem* was not found in node *curr*:
        3.3.1. If *curr* is a leaf node, terminate with answer *none*.
        3.3.2. If *curr* is a non-leaf node:
            3.3.2.1. Set *curr* to the left child of the least element in node *curr* greater than *elem* (or equivalently the right child of the greatest element less than *elem*).

Algorithm 16.18   B-tree search algorithm.

```
public Btree.Node search (Comparable target) {
// Find which if any node of this B-tree contains an element equal to target.
// Return a link to that node, or null if there is no such node.
    if (root == null)
        return null;
    Btree.Node curr = root;
    for (;;) {
        int pos = curr.searchInNode(target);
        if (target.equals(curr.elems[pos]))
            return curr;
        else if (curr.isLeaf())
            return null;
        else
            // Continue the search in childs[currPos], which is the left
            // child of the least element in node curr greater than target.
            curr = curr.childs[pos];
    }
}

//////////// In inner class Btree.Node ... ////////////

private int searchInNode (Comparable target) {
// Return the index of the least element in this node that is not less than
// target.
    ...   // See code on the companion Web site.
}
```

Program 16.19   Implementation of the B-tree search algorithm as a Java method (in class `Btree`), with an auxiliary method (in class `Btree.Node`).

Algorithm 16.18 captures the idea of B-tree search. It can be seen as a generalization of BST search (Algorithm 10.10).

Program 16.19 shows an implementation of the B-tree search algorithm. The `search` method belongs to the `Btree` class (Program 16.15). The auxiliary `searchInNode` method belongs to the `Btree.Node` inner class. It searches a node for the target element, using the array binary search algorithm. (Binary search might seem excessive for a 5-ary B-tree, whose nodes contain at most 4 elements, but it is fully justified in practical applications where we use high-arity B-trees.)

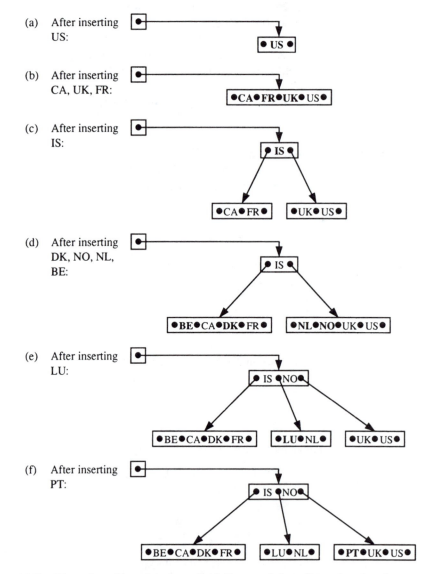

(a) After inserting US:

(b) After inserting CA, UK, FR:

(c) After inserting IS:

(d) After inserting DK, NO, NL, BE:

(e) After inserting LU:

(f) After inserting PT:

Figure 16.20 Illustration of insertions in an (initially empty) 5-ary B-tree (*continued on next page*).

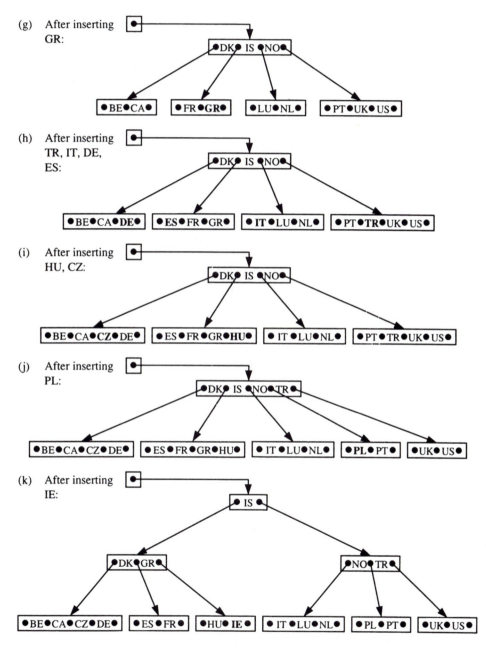

(g) After inserting GR:

(h) After inserting TR, IT, DE, ES:

(i) After inserting HU, CZ:

(j) After inserting PL:

(k) After inserting IE:

Figure 16.20 (*continued*)

16.2.3 Insertion

Now let us consider the problem of inserting a new element into a B-tree. We start with a complete illustration.

EXAMPLE 16.1 *B-tree insertions*

Figure 16.20 illustrates the effects of successfully inserting country-codes into a 5-ary B-tree. Initially, the B-tree is empty, i.e., its header contains a null link. Let us study this illustration in detail.

(a) To insert US into the B-tree, we create a root node containing only US. (This root node is also a leaf node.)

(b) To insert CA, UK, and FR into the B-tree, we insert these elements in the root node, keeping it sorted.

(c) To insert IS into the B-tree, we first attempt to insert it in the root node. But this makes the node ***overflow***, since it now contains too many elements (CA, FR, IS, UK, US). (See below left, where the overflowed node is highlighted.) So we identify the median of these five elements (IS), and ***split*** the leaf node into a pair of siblings: one containing the elements less than the median (CA, FR) and one containing the greater elements (UK, US). We move the median itself up to the parent node. Since in this case there is no parent node (we are splitting the root node), we must create a new parent node and move the median up to it. (See below right.)

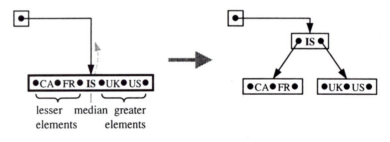

(d) To insert DK into the B-tree, we first look among the elements of the root node. Since DK is less than IS, we proceed to the first child node. Since the latter is a leaf node, we insert DK in it. Similarly, to insert NO, NL, and BE into the B-tree, we insert them in the second, second, and first child nodes, respectively.

(e) To insert LU into the B-tree, we first look among the elements of the root node. Since LU is greater than IS, we proceed to the second child node. Since the latter is a leaf node, we attempt to insert LU in it. But this makes the leaf node overflow. (See below left.) So we identify the median element (NO), and split the leaf node into a pair of siblings: one containing the lesser elements (LU, NL) and one containing the greater elements (UK, US). We move the median itself up to the parent node, which now contains two elements (IS, NO). (See below right.)

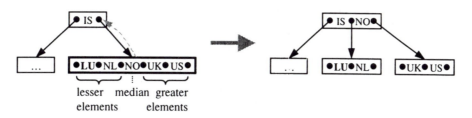

lesser   median   greater
elements   elements

(f) To insert PT into the B-tree, we straightforwardly insert it in the third child node.

(g) To insert GR into the B-tree, we attempt to insert it in the first child node. But this makes the node overflow. So we split it into a pair of siblings, one containing BE and CA, the other containing FR and GR, and we move the median DK up to the parent node.

(h) To insert TR, IT, DE, and ES into the B-tree, we straightforwardly insert them in the fourth, third, first, and third child nodes, respectively.

(i) To insert HU and CZ into the B-tree, we straightforwardly insert them in the second and first child nodes, respectively.

(j) To insert PL into the B-tree, we attempt to insert it in the fourth child node. But this makes the node overflow. So we split it into a pair of siblings, one containing PL and PT, the other containing UK and US, and we move the median TR up to the parent node.

(k) To insert IE into the B-tree, we attempt to insert it in the second child node. But this makes the node overflow:

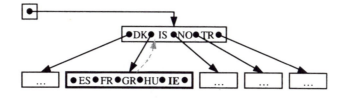

So we split this node into a pair of siblings, one containing ES and FR, the other containing HU and IE, and we move the median GR up to the parent node. But this makes the parent node itself overflow:

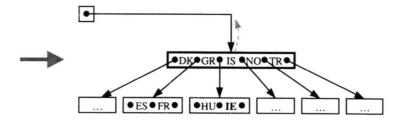

So we split the parent node likewise into a pair of siblings, one containing DK and GR, the other containing NO and TR, and we move the median IS up to a newly-created grandparent node, which we make the root node:

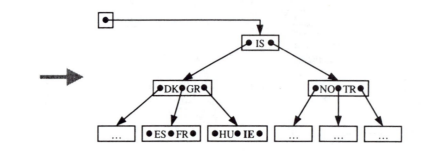

The ideas illustrated in Example 16.1 are captured by Algorithms 16.21 and 16.22. The main algorithm searches the tree in much the same way as the B-tree search algorithm. When the algorithm reaches a leaf node, it inserts the new element in that leaf node (step 4). If that leaf node has overflowed (i.e., it now has k elements), the auxiliary algorithm is called to split that node (step 5).

The auxiliary algorithm splits a given node. It first determines the median of that node's elements (step 1). Then it splits node *curr* into two siblings: *left-sib* takes the elements less than the median, with their children (step 2); and *right-sib* takes the elements greater than the median, with their children (step 3). Finally, the algorithm moves the median itself, and its children *left-sib* and *right-sib*, up to the parent node. If there is no parent node, the algorithm creates one (step 4.1). If a parent node already exists, the algorithm inserts the median into the parent node (step 5.1), and then if necessary it splits the parent node by a recursive call to itself (step 5.2).

Program 16.23 shows a Java implementation of B-tree insertion. The `insert` and `splitNode` methods belong to the `Btree` class. They closely follow Algorithms 16.21 and 16.22, respectively, with one important extra detail. Whenever `insert` moves down the tree from parent to child, it stacks the parent node. Thereafter, if `splitNode` has to move an element up from child to parent, it finds the parent node at the top of the stack. Moreover, since `insert` has already searched the parent node in order to decide which child link to follow, it also stacks the child link's position, for that is exactly where `splitNode` must insert any element moved up from child to parent.

The second auxiliary method, `insertInNode`, belongs to the `Btree.Node` inner class. It inserts a given element, with its children, at a given position in the node.

Note that `splitNode` creates two new nodes, `leftSib` and `rightSib`, and discards the node that is being split. This makes the code elegant and readable. However, it would be more efficient to create only one new node, and reuse the node that is being split. (See Exercise 16.10.)

To insert element *elem* into a B-tree:

1. If the B-tree is empty:
   1.1. Make the B-tree's root a newly-created leaf node containing one element, *elem*.
   1.2. Terminate.
2. Set *curr* to the B-tree's root node.
3. Repeat:
   3.1. Search for *elem* in node *curr*.
   3.2. If *elem* was found in node *curr*:
         3.2.1. Terminate.
   3.3. If *elem* was not found in node *curr*:
         3.3.1. If *curr* is a leaf node, exit the loop.
         3.3.2. If *curr* is a non-leaf node:
                 3.3.2.1.   Set *curr* to the left child of the least element in node *curr* greater than *elem* (or equivalently the right child of the greatest element less than *elem*).
4. Insert *elem* into leaf node *curr*, keeping its elements sorted.
5. If node *curr* has overflowed, split node *curr*.
6. Terminate.

Algorithm 16.21   B-tree insertion algorithm.

To split an overflowed node, *node*, in a B-tree:

1. Let *med* be the median of *node*'s elements.
2. Make *left-sib* a newly-created node, containing all of *node*'s elements to the left of *med*, with all their children.
3. Make *right-sib* a newly-created node, containing all of *node*'s elements to the right of *med*, with all their children.
4. If *node* is the B-tree's root node:
   4.1. Make the B-tree's root a newly-created node containing one element, *med*, with children *left-sib* and *right-sib*.
5. If *node* has a parent node:
   5.1. Insert *med*, with children *left-sib* and *right-sib*, into *node*'s parent, keeping its elements sorted.
   5.2. If *node*'s parent has overflowed, split the parent node.
6. Terminate.

Algorithm 16.22   B-tree insertion: auxiliary algorithm to split an overflowed node.

```
    public void insert (Comparable elem) {
    // Insert element elem into this B-tree.
       if (root == null) {
          root = new Btree.Node(arity, elem, null, null);
          return;
       }
       Stack ancestors = new LinkedStack();
       Btree.Node curr = root;
       for (;;) {
          int currPos = curr.searchInNode(elem);
          if (elem.equals(curr.elems[currPos]))
             return;
          else if (curr.isLeaf())
             break;
          else {
             // Continue the search in childs[currPos], which is the left
             // child of the least element in node curr greater than elem.
             ancestors.addLast(new Integer(currPos));
             ancestors.addLast(curr);
             curr = curr.childs[currPos];
          }
       }
       curr.insertInNode(elem, null, null, currPos);
       if (curr.size == arity)   // curr has overflowed
          splitNode(curr, ancestors);
    }
```

Program 16.23   Implementation of the B-tree insertion algorithm as a Java method, with auxiliary methods (in class `Btree`) (*continued on next page*).

16.2.4 Deletion

Now let us consider the problem of deleting an element from a B-tree. We start with a complete illustration.

EXAMPLE 16.2   *B-tree deletions*

Figure 16.24 illustrates the effects of successfully deleting country-codes from a 5-ary B-tree. Let us study this illustration in detail.

(a) To delete GR from the B-tree, we first search for it and find it in a leaf node. We simply delete GR from that leaf node.

(b) To delete IS from the B-tree, we first search for it and find it in a non-leaf node. We take the least element in IS's right subtree, namely IT, and move it up to replace IS in the non-leaf node.

(c) To delete ES from the B-tree, we first search for it and find it in a leaf node. We delete ES from the leaf node. But this causes the leaf node to ***underflow***, containing fewer

```
private void splitNode (Btree.Node node,
                  Stack ancestors) {
// Split the overflowed node in this B-tree. The stack ancestors contains
//  all ancestors of node, together with the known insertion position in each of
//  these ancestors.
   int medPos = node.size/2;
   Comparable med = node.elems[medPos];
   Btree.Node leftSib = new Btree.Node(arity,
       node.elems, node.childs, 0, medPos);
   Btree.Node rightSib = new Btree.Node(arity,
       node.elems, node.childs, medPos+1, node.size);
   if (node == root)
     root = new Btree.Node(arity, med, leftSib,
         rightSib);
   else {
     Btree.Node parent =
         (Btree.Node) ancestors.removeLast();
     int parentIns = ((Integer)
         ancestors.removeLast()).intValue();
     parent.insertInNode(med, leftSib, rightSib,
         parentIns);
     if (parent.size == arity)   // parent has overflowed
       splitNode(parent, ancestors);
   }
}

///////////// In inner class Btree.Node ... /////////////

private void insertInNode (Comparable elem,
                  Btree.Node leftChild,
                  Btree.Node rightChild,
                  int ins) {
// Insert element elem, with children leftChild and rightChild, at
//  position ins in this node.
   for (int i = node.size; i > ins; i--) {
     elems[i] = elems[i-1];
     childs[i+1] = childs[i];
   }
   size++;
   elems[ins] = elem;
   childs[ins] = leftChild;
   childs[ins+1] = rightChild;
}
```

Program 16.23 (*continued*)

than 2 elements. (See below left, where the underflowed node is highlighted.) So we must try to **restock** the underflowed node by moving an element from one of its nearest siblings. The right sibling cannot lose any elements without itself underflowing. Fortunately, the left sibling contains more than enough elements. So we move the left sibling's righmost element DE up to the parent node, replacing DK, and move DK itself down to the underflowed node:

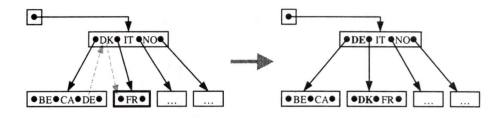

(d) To delete DK from the B-tree, we first search for it and find it in a leaf node. We delete DK from the leaf node. But this causes the leaf node to underflow. Moreover, we cannot restock the leaf node by moving an element from either of its left or right siblings, without making that sibling underflow. However, we can **coalesce** the underflowed node with either of its siblings. Suppose that we choose to coalesce it with its right sibling. We move all that sibling's elements (LU, NL) into the underflowed node, together with the intermediate element from the parent node (IT):

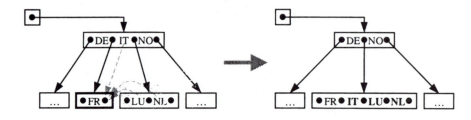

Deleting an element in a leaf node is easy. Deleting an element in a non-leaf node needs a little more work: we must replace it by the least element in its right subtree. The latter element is always in a leaf node.

Every deletion therefore causes some leaf node (not necessarily the node containing the element to be deleted) to contract. If that node underflows, it must be restocked.

Restocking an underflowed node always involves that node's nearest sibling (or one of its nearest siblings, if it has two). Restocking is straightforward if a nearest sibling has at least one spare element, which it can give up without underflowing.

Restocking is less straightforward if neither sibling has spare elements. But in these circumstances it is always possible to coalesce the underflowed node with one of its nearest siblings. The sibling must contain $(k - 1)/2$ elements (the minimum), and the underflowed node $(k - 1)/2 - 1$ elements (one less than the minimum). In total they contain at most $k - 2$ elements. That leaves at least one spare slot for the intermediate element to be moved down from the parent node to the coalesced node.

(If k is odd, the underflowed node and its sibling together contain exactly $k - 2$ elements. If k is even, they actually contain $k - 3$ elements, since in $(k - 1)/2$ we discard the remainder.)

All these ideas are captured by Algorithms 16.25 and 16.26. The main algorithm should be easy to understand. The auxiliary algorithm, which restocks an underflowed node, breaks down into three cases. Step 1 deals with the case of an underflowed root node, which contains no elements at all, and so can simply be discarded. Step 2 deals with the case of an underflowed node that has a nearest sibling with a spare element. Step 3

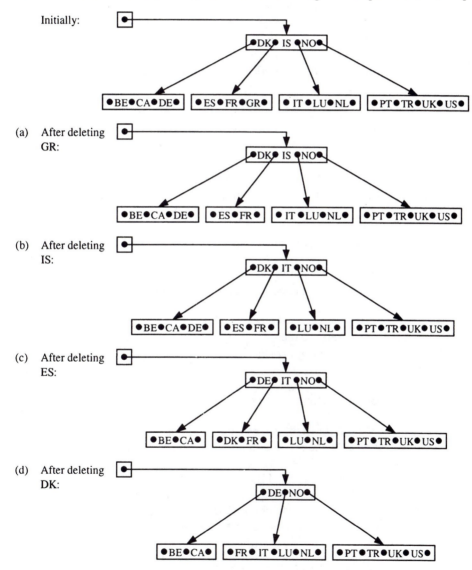

Figure 16.24 Illustration of deletions in a 5-ary B-tree.

To delete the element *elem* from a B-tree:

1. Find which if any node *curr* of the B-tree contains an element equal to *elem*.
    2. If there is no such node, terminate.
    3. If *curr* is a leaf node:
        3.1. Remove *elem* from node *curr*.
        3.2. If node *curr* has underflowed, restock *curr*.
    4. If *curr* is not a leaf node:
        4.1. Let *leftmost-node* be the leftmost leaf node in the right subtree of *elem*.
        4.2. Let *next-elem* be the leftmost element in *leftmost-node*, and remove *next-elem* from *leftmost-node*.
        4.3. Replace *elem* in node *curr* by *next-elem*.
        4.4. If *leftmost-node* has underflowed, restock *leftmost-node*.
    5. Terminate.

Algorithm 16.25   B-tree deletion algorithm.

To restock an underflowed node, *node*, in a B-tree:

1. If *node* is the root of the B-tree (and so has 0 elements and 1 child):
    1.1. Replace the root of the B-tree by *node*'s only child.
    1.2. Terminate.
2. If *node* has a nearest left (or right) sibling with more than the minimum number of elements:
    2.1. Let *sib* be that nearest sibling.
    2.2. Let *parent-elem* be the element in *node*'s parent whose children are *node* and *sib*.
    2.3. Let *spare-elem* and *spare-child* be the rightmost (leftmost) element and child in *sib*, and remove them from *sib*.
    2.4. Insert *parent-elem* and *spare-child* as the leftmost (rightmost) element and child of *node*.
    2.5. Replace *parent-elem* by *spare-elem* in *node*'s parent.
3. If *node* has no nearest sibling with more than the minimum number of elements:
    3.1. Let *sib* be the left (or right) nearest sibling of *node*.
    3.2. Let *parent-elem* be the element in *node*'s parent whose children are *node* and *sib*.
    3.3. Insert all *sib*'s elements and children, followed (preceded) by *parent-elem*, as the leftmost (rightmost) elements and children of *node*.
    3.4. Remove *parent-elem* and the child *sib* from *node*'s parent.
    3.5. If *node*'s parent has underflowed, restock *node*'s parent.
4. Terminate.

Algorithm 16.26   B-tree deletion: auxiliary algorithm to restock an underflowed node.

deals with the case of an underflowed node that must be coalesced with a nearest sibling. In the last case the parent node contracts and might itself underflow; if that happens, the algorithm calls itself recursively to restock the parent node.

We leave the implementation of B-tree deletion to Exercise 16.11.

16.2.5 Analysis

Search

Let us analyze the B-tree search algorithm.

First consider searching a *full* k-ary B-tree, i.e., one in which every node has size $k - 1$. From equation (16.6), this B-tree has size $n = k^{d+1} - 1$. Conversely, if we know n, we can determine the B-tree's depth:

$$d = \log_k(n + 1) - 1$$

Algorithm 16.18 starts by visiting the root node, and each subsequent iteration visits a child of the current node. We can immediately deduce that:

$$\text{Maximum no. of nodes visited} = d + 1$$
$$= \log_k(n + 1)$$
$$= \log_2(n + 1)/\log_2 k \tag{16.7}$$

(See Section B.2 for an explanation of the mathematics used here.) Assuming binary search of the $k - 1$ elements in each visited node, the number of comparisons at each node is about $\log_2(k - 1)$. Therefore:

$$\text{Maximum no. of comparisons} \approx \log_2(k - 1)\log_k(n + 1)/\log_2 k$$
$$\approx \log_2 n \tag{16.8}$$

Now consider searching a *half-full* k-ary B-tree, i.e., one in which every node has size $(k - 1)/2$. Such a B-tree is similar to a full B-tree of order $(k + 1)/2$. On reworking the above analysis we obtain:

$$\text{Maximum no. of nodes visited} = \log_2(n + 1)/\log_2((k + 1)/2)$$
$$= \log_2(n + 1)/(\log_2(k + 1) - 1) \tag{16.9}$$

$$\text{Maximum no. of comparisons} \approx \log_2 n \tag{16.10}$$

Both these analyses lead to the same conclusion: the time complexity of B-tree search is $O(\log n)$. The actual maximum number of comparisons for searching a B-tree is about the same as for searching a balanced BST. Remarkably, the maximum number of comparisons depends neither on the B-tree's arity nor on how full it is. Thus B-tree search is *guaranteed* to be as fast as searching a balanced BST.

Insertion

The B-tree insertion algorithm, by the same reasoning, needs about $\log_2 n$ comparisons to find the node where the new element will be inserted. There is the added complication of node splitting, but the maximum number of nodes to be split is $\log_2(n + 1)/\log_2 k$ (since at most one node is split at each level). In terms of either comparisons or splits, the B-tree insertion algorithm's time complexity is $O(\log n)$.

Deletion

Similarly, the B-tree deletion algorithm needs about $\log_2 n$ comparisons to find the node containing the element to be deleted. Here the added complication is node restocking, but the maximum number of nodes to be restocked is $\log_2(n + 1)/\log_2 k$. In terms of either comparisons or restockings, the B-tree deletion algorithm's time complexity is $O(\log n)$.

16.2.6 Application

A typical application of B-trees is for indexing relational databases. Each table of a relational database consists of a (potentially very large) number of tuples, each tuple having a unique key. The tuples are stored on disk. Retrieving the tuple with a particular key is potentially very time-consuming, in terms of both the number of key comparisons and the number of disk transfers.

Retrieval can be speeded up by *indexing* the table. The index is a map consisting of (*key, addr*) pairs, where *addr* is the disk address of the tuple whose key is *key*. We can represent the index by a high-arity B-tree whose elements are these (*key, addr*) pairs.

Since the number of elements could be very large, the B-tree's guaranteed $O(\log n)$ search time is a major advantage. It is very important to avoid the risk of $O(n)$ search time, which could happen with a BST if it becomes ill-balanced.

Since the index is itself stored on disk, the actual search time is dominated not by comparisons but by disk transfers. Typically, each B-tree node occupies a whole disk block, so the number of disk transfers is just the number of nodes visited. We saw in equations (16.7) and (16.9) that the number of nodes visited when searching a k-ary B-tree is reduced by a factor of between $\log_2(k + 1) - 1$ and $\log_2 k$, compared to searching a BST. If we choose a 128-ary B-tree, the number of nodes visited is reduced by a factor of 6–7.

Summary

In this chapter:

- We have studied two kinds of search trees that are always balanced, guaranteeing $O(\log n)$ search, insertion, and deletion times.
- We have studied AVL-trees, a special kind of binary search tree whose insertion and deletion operations are adapted to restructure the tree locally, whenever necessary to restore height-balance.
- We have studied B-trees, a special kind of k-ary search tree whose insertion and deletion operations keep the tree perfectly balanced, splitting and coalescing nodes when necessary.
- We have seen that B-trees are well suited for indexing large database tables.

Exercises

16.1 Consider the following sentence:

African aardvarks and antelopes are all adapted to their environment.

(a) Starting with an empty AVL-tree, draw diagrams to show the effects of inserting each word of that sentence, in turn. (Treat corresponding upper-case and lower-case letters as equivalent.)
(b) Starting with that AVL-tree, show the effects of deleting the following words, in turn: environment, aardvarks, African, adapted, antelopes.
(c) Compare your answer with the effects of inserting and deleting the same words, in the same order, in an initially empty BST.

16.2 Draw diagrams, similar to Figures 16.4 and 16.5, showing AVL-tree insertion and rotation in cases (3) and (4). In both cases, verify that nodes a, b, and c are height-balanced after the rotation, and that the subtree as a whole is restored to its initial height.
(*Hint:* Cases (3) and (4) are mirror-images of cases (1) and (2), respectively.)

16.3 Draw a diagram, similar to Figure 16.10, showing AVL-tree deletion and rotation in case (1) when the height of *T3* is h rather than $h + 1$. Verify that nodes a, b, and c are height-balanced after the rotation, but that the height of the subtree as a whole is one less than its initial height.

Draw diagrams, similar to Figures 16.10 and 16.11, showing AVL-tree deletion and rotation in cases (3) and (4). In both cases, verify that nodes a, b, and c are height-balanced after the rotation, and that the height of the subtree as a whole is either the same as or one less than its initial height.

16.4 Write a Java instance method, to go in class BST (Program 10.6), that determines whether the BST is height-balanced.

** **16.5** Write a Java implementation of AVL-trees (Section 16.1).
(*Hint:* You will find it convenient to store balance factors in nodes. When a new leaf node is created by BST-insertion the balance factors of the new node's ancestors change: each ancestor's balance factor increases (decreases) by one if the new node is in the ancestor's left (right) subtree. Likewise, when a node is deleted by BST-deletion, the balance factors of that node's ancestors change in the opposite sense. After rotation, the balance factors change again.)

After testing your implementation, add code to count the number of comparisons on each search, insertion, and deletion. Verify that the numbers are consistent with equations (16.2), (16.3), and (16.4).

16.6 Suppose that a large set is to be represented by a B-tree stored on disk. Assume that a disk block is 1024 bytes, and that each node of a k-ary B-tree occupies $8k$ bytes. What value of k will cause each node to occupy a complete disk block? How much disk space will be occupied by a B-tree of 2 097 151 elements? On average, how many disk transfers and how many comparisons will be needed to search the B-tree? (*Note:* 2 097 152 = 2^{21}.)

16.7 Repeat Exercise 16.1 using a 5-ary B-tree.

16.8 The representation of B-trees in Program 16.15 wastes some space: every node contains an array of child links, even a leaf node whose child links are all null. Modify the implementation such that only non-leaf nodes contain arrays of child links.

16.9 Consider iterating over the elements of a B-tree.
(a) Write an instance method, to go in class `Btree` (Program 16.15), that prints all the elements in ascending order.
(b) Write an instance method, also to go in class `Btree`, that returns an iterator that will visit all the elements in ascending order.

16.10 Modify the `splitInNode` method (Program 16.23) to create only one new node, `rightSib`. After copying the appropriate elements and child links into `rightSib`, it should simply delete these elements and child links (and the median element) from `node`, and thereafter use `node` instead of `leftSib`.

* **16.11** Write a Java implementation of the B-tree deletion algorithm (Algorithms 16.25 and 16.26).

** **16.12** Write an `AVLTreeSet` class that implements the `Set` interface of Program 9.4. You may omit some or all of the ...`All` methods.

* **16.13** Modify the spell-checker of Section 9.8 to use your `AVLTreeSet` class of Exercise 16.12, and run the spell-checker using a large vocabulary. Is it noticeably faster?

** **16.14** Write a `BtreeSet` class that implements the `Set` interface of Program 9.4. You may omit some or all of the ...`All` methods.

17

Conclusion

In this chapter we shall study:

- the relationship between abstract data types and object-oriented design (Section 17.1)
- the importance of abstract data types as reusable software components (Section 17.2)
- the distinction between homogeneous and heterogeneous collections (Section 17.3)
- parameterized classes in an extension of Java (Section 17.4)
- a case study using parameterized classes (Section 17.5).

17.1 Abstract data types and object-oriented design

Software design is difficult. It is a delicate balancing act between, on the one hand, producing a highly-efficient solution to the current problem and, on the other hand, producing a more general but possibly less efficient solution to a range of problems. Moreover, software design is of central importance in software development, having a major influence on whether the software system meets its requirements, is reliable, and is maintainable. Many software systems available today fail to satisfy all of their requirements, contain faults ('bugs') in both their design and their implementation, and are difficult to maintain.

Object-oriented design and object-oriented programming aim to solve some of the problems with developing large, complex software systems. Note that object-oriented *design* does not necessarily mandate object-oriented *programming*: an object-oriented design can often be implemented successfully in an ordinary imperative language such as Pascal or C. Nevertheless, it is more convenient to implement an object-oriented design directly in an object-oriented language such as Java or C++, and the resulting code is more likely to be maintainable.

In designing a software system, we should always aim to decompose the system into components (or modules) that are *cohesive* and *loosely-coupled* to one another.

A component *C* is ***cohesive*** ('single-minded') if *C* has a single, clearly-defined purpose, and if all parts of *C* make an essential contribution to that purpose. Conversely, *C* is ***uncohesive*** ('scatter-brained') if it has more than one purpose, or if parts of *C* are not essential to that purpose. A system composed of cohesive components tends to be easier to implement and to maintain: if every component has its own distinct purpose, it is easier to locate any necessary changes (e.g., to correct faults or to meet changing requirements).

Coupling is a measure of the sensitivity of components to changes in one another. Given a component *C*, another component is ***loosely-coupled*** ('insensitive') to *C* if a change in *C* is unlikely to entail significant changes in the other component. Conversely, the other component is ***tightly-coupled*** ('sensitive') to *C* if a change in *C* is likely to entail significant changes in the other component. A system composed of loosely-coupled components tends to be easier to implement and to maintain: if a component *C* has to be changed, other components loosely-coupled to *C* will probably not have to be changed too. (On the other hand, any components that are tightly-coupled to *C* would probably have to be changed, and components tightly-coupled to *them* would probably have to be changed in turn; thus a 'chain reaction' could start.)

Object-oriented design is important because it greatly helps us to design cohesive loosely-coupled components. These components are typically classes.

What makes a class *C* cohesive? Each object of class *C* should be a single logical entity. The contract for class *C* should specify methods that are *necessary* and *sufficient* to perform all required operations on objects of the class.

Given a class *C*, what makes other classes loosely-coupled to *C*? The other classes should not depend on any part of *C* that is likely to change. The parts of *C* that are most likely to change are its instance variables, its auxiliary methods (if any), and the algorithms used to implement its contractual methods. The parts of *C* that are least likely to change are the names, parameter types, result types, and observable behavior of its contractual methods. Other classes are loosely-coupled to *C* if they confine themselves to calling *C*'s contractual methods. This can easily be guaranteed, if we make only the contractual methods public. If *C*'s instance variables (which define the objects' data representation) and auxiliary methods are private, any attempt by other classes to access them will be rejected by the Java compiler.

There is clearly a close relationship between object-oriented design and the ADT concept. (Revisit Section 5.3, where you will find definitions of *necessary* and *sufficient* operations.) The ADT concept is older and more fundamental. An ADT is easily expressed in object-oriented terms as a class, with public instance methods providing the ADT's operations, private instance variables providing the ADT's data representation, and private auxiliary methods if needed.

We have demonstrated repeatedly in this book that designing an application using ADTs ensures that the application code is loosely-coupled to the ADT's implementation. Completely different implementations of the ADT (perhaps with very different time and space complexities) can be used interchangeably, with at most minor changes to the application code. See, for example, the use of the date ADT in Examples 5.2 and 5.3, and the use of the various collection ADTs in case studies throughout this book.

However, object-oriented design is more general than the ADT concept. In object-oriented design we are free to decide which parts of a class are public and which are private. We can equip a class with class variables and class methods as well as instance variables and instance methods. We can organize classes into a hierarchy of superclasses and subclasses, with inheritance. These features are all valuable, but it is important to understand that their use has implications for the quality of the design.

Making an instance or class variable public is a decision that should never be taken lightly. A public instance or class variable can be directly accessed by the application code, making the latter tightly-coupled to the class. As a general rule, instance and class variables should be private, unless they are constants (**final** in Java terminology). Accessing a constant does not result in tight coupling.

If a class has subclasses, they may inherit any or all of their superclass's methods. A subclass that does inherit methods is not entirely cohesive, since it does not itself provide sufficient methods for its intended purpose, relying instead on its superclass to help it. The subclass therefore cannot be completely understood in isolation from its superclass. Moreover, the subclasses may have direct access to the superclass's instance variables, in which case they will be tightly-coupled to the superclass. We can avoid this by denying the subclasses direct access to the superclass's instance variables, restricting the subclasses (just like all other classes) to calling the superclass's public methods.

It is always important that we make changes to a superclass carefully, as these changes might be inherited by all of its subclasses. In Java, this point applies to not only a class extended by another class, but also an interface extended by another interface, and an interface implemented by a class. For example, changing the Set interface (Program 9.4) would force changes in all its implementations (Programs 9.7, 9.11, and 10.41).

17.2 Abstract data types as reusable software components

In the past, software engineers typically paid little or no heed to the work of their predecessors. Each new software system was designed and implemented from scratch. Demand for ever more varied and more complex software systems have made such attitudes untenable. This demand can be met only if new software projects reuse some of the components designed and implemented in previous projects. This is what we mean by *software reuse*.

Reuse of previously designed and implemented components is commonplace in other branches of engineering. A mechanical engineer designs a new car model, not by rede-signing every single component of the car, but instead by designing some new compo-nents and reusing others that are already known to be satisfactory. (In this case the components are engines, carburetors, gear boxes, and so on.) A computer engineer designs a new computer likewise. (In this case the components are processors, memories, disk drives, screens, keyboards, and so on.) The benefits of reuse are clear: the engineer saves time by not having to redesign every component; the engineer can be confident that the reused components are tried and tested; and the engineer can concentrate on design-ing, implementing, and testing the new components.

In the context of software reuse, what is a component? There are several conflicting definitions in common use. A component may be taken to be a class, or a group of classes, or a class with special properties. Here, for simplicity, we will consider a component to be a single class.

A component of a software system is most likely to be reusable if it is cohesive and loosely-coupled to other components of that system. Since object-oriented design tends to lead to a system of cohesive, loosely-coupled classes, these classes are likely to be good candidates for reuse in other systems.

This simple idea, however, hides several problems with software reuse. The fact that components *can* be reused does not guarantee that they *will* be reused.

First, a component will be reused only if its existence is known to other software engineers. This implies some kind of catalog of reusable components, with facilities to allow a software engineer to search for components that meet his or her requirements.

Second, a component will be reused only if it is well understood. To be understood, the component must be accompanied by a 'contract', documenting the operations it supports and the characteristics of its implementation.

Third, a component might need to be adapted for reuse in a new context. In object-oriented design, this adaptation can be achieved through inheritance. A new component can be derived in the form of a subclass that provides additional functionality while preserving the desirable features of the original component.

EXAMPLE 17.1   *Reusable collection classes*

The collection ADTs introduced in this book – Stack, Queue, List, Set, Map, PriorityQueue, Tree, and Graph – are all reusable. Each ADT has a contract that documents the values of the ADT and the observable behavior of its operations. Their various implementations are also reusable. Each ADT implementation documents the characteristics of that implementation, by describing the data representation and/or by stating the time and space complexities of each operation.

The java.util collection classes (summarized in Appendix C) are also reusable, as indeed are all the Java library classes.

17.3 Homogeneous and heterogeneous collections

In this book we have studied a variety of collections: stacks, queues, lists, sets, maps, trees, and graphs. In general, a collection contains zero or more elements, and is equipped with operations to add and remove elements. When we design a collection ADT, we must decide whether the collection is to be homogeneous or heterogeneous.

A *homogeneous collection* may contain only elements of some pre-determined type. For example: a set of integers may contain only integers; a set of strings may contain only strings.

A *heterogeneous collection* may contain elements of different types. For example, a set of objects may contain (for instance) strings only; dates only; or a mixture of strings, dates, and objects of any other classes.

In the Java Collections framework, all of the collection classes are designed to be heterogeneous. The elements in such a collection are arbitrary objects (i.e., objects of class Object or any subclass thereof). This design places few restrictions on the elements that can be contained in such a collection. However, such a collection cannot contain primitive values (such as booleans, integers, and real numbers), since these are not objects. In Java, the only way to support collections of primitive values is to provide a separate homogeneous collection class for each primitive type. For example, as well as a class supporting heterogeneous lists of objects, we might have to provide a class supporting homogeneous lists of booleans, a class supporting homogeneous lists of integers, and so on.

This inconsistent treatment of object and primitive types is obvious elsewhere in the Java class libraries. For example, the java.util.Arrays class provides methods for filling, comparing, searching, and sorting arrays. Program 17.1 shows part of this class. There are *nine* definitions of the overloaded sort method: one for each of Java's seven primitive arithmetic types, and two for objects (one using compareTo to compare objects, the other using a Comparator object given as an argument). The class similarly provides nine definitions of a fill method that fills a given array with a given value; nine definitions of a fill method that fills a given subarray with a given value; nine definitions of an equals method that compares two given arrays; nine definitions of a binarySearch method that searches a given array for a given value; and nine definitions of a sort method that sorts a given subarray!

We have seen that the Java collection classes are designed to be heterogeneous. A collection can contain arbitrary objects (of class Object or any subclass thereof). There can be no guarantee that these objects have anything in common, other than the properties shared by all objects. In practice, however, most collections are actually homogeneous. For example, an application might be designed to use a set of strings; the application code

```
public class Arrays {
    ...    // Methods for filling arrays and subarrays.
    ...    // Methods for comparing arrays.
    ...    // Methods for searching arrays.
    public static void sort (byte[] a)      { ... }
    public static void sort (char[] a)      { ... }
    public static void sort (short[] a)     { ... }
    public static void sort (int[] a)       { ... }
    public static void sort (long[] a)      { ... }
    public static void sort (float[] a)     { ... }
    public static void sort (double[] a)    { ... }
    public static void sort (Object[] a)    { ... }
    public static void sort (Object[] a,
                    Comparator c)           { ... }
    ...    // Methods for sorting subarrays.
}
```

Program 17.1   The class java.util.Arrays (excerpt).

would create a set, then add string objects to it, then remove objects from it in the expectation that the removed objects are strings. In most of the case studies in this book, the collections are actually homogeneous.

However, there are difficulties in using a heterogeneous collection class to implement what is actually a homogeneous collection. Since we have no means in Java to declare the precise class of objects that will be contained in a given collection, it is up to the programmer to remember this important information. In practice the programmer might forget, and the likely consequence is faulty code. Such faults are often difficult to find, since the program might continue after executing the faulty code, eventually failing somewhere else entirely.

EXAMPLE 17.2 *Using a heterogeneous map*

Consider an application that includes the following code fragment:

```
Map register;   // ... maps student identifiers to Student objects.
...
Student newStudent = new Student(...);
register.put("2000-0123-CS", newStudent);
...
Student student1 =
        register.get("2000-0123-CS");   // ILLEGAL!
```

The programmer believes that only Student objects have been added to the map register, so register.get(...) must retrieve a Student object. Nevertheless, the Map interface states only that the get operation returns an Object. So the retrieved object must be cast to the class Student before it can be assigned to the variable student1:

```
Student student1 =
        (Student) register.get("2000-0123-CS");
```

But how can the programmer be certain that only Student objects have been added to the map register? No check takes place when an object is added to the map. Suppose that our application also includes the following code fragment:

```
Staff newProf = new Staff(...);
register.put("2000-9999-CS", newProf);
...
Student student2 =
        (Student) register.get("2000-9999-CS");
```

The application will fail with a ClassCastException when the last statement retrieves an object of unexpected class from the map and casts it to the expected class Student. But the real fault is not in the last statement, but in the statement that previously added an object of unexpected class to the map. (We are assuming here that Staff is not a subclass of Student.) In this tiny example, the failure occurs close to the location of the fault. In a large application, however, the failure and the fault might be in different methods belonging to completely different classes, perhaps written by different programmers.

EXAMPLE 17.3 *Using a homogeneous map*

An alternative design for the application of Example 17.2 would be to write a customized homogeneous StudentMap class, with its own put and get methods:

```
public class StudentMap {
    // A StudentMap object is a map from student ids to Student objects.
    public void put (String id, Student s)  { ... }
    public Student get (String id)          { ... }
    ...  // Other methods and constructors.
}
```

Then the code fragments of Example 17.2 would be rewritten as follows:

```
StudentMap register;
...
Student newStudent = new Student(...);
register.put("2000-0123-CS", newStudent);
...
Student student1 = register.get("2000-0123-CS");
```

Note that there is no need for a cast on retrieving a Student object from register.

```
Staff newStaff = new Staff(...);
register.put("2000-9999-CS", newStaff);   // ILLEGAL!
...
Student student2 = register.get("2000-9999-CS");
```

The faulty statement that tries to add a Staff object to register will now be rejected by the Java compiler, because the second argument's type, Staff, is incompatible with the corresponding parameter's type, Student.

Of course, there is a major objection to this design: it forces us to design and implement the StudentMap class, which is like re-inventing the wheel.

Let us summarize. For an application that actually needs a homogeneous collection, the major objections to using a *generic heterogeneous* collection class (such as Map) are:

- When an element is added to the collection, there is no check that the new element has the same class as the existing elements.

- When an element is retrieved from the collection, it must be explicitly cast to the appropriate class (which only the programmer knows).

The major objection to using a *specific homogeneous* collection class (such as StudentMap) is:

- The collection class must be custom designed and implemented. It might be possible to adapt an existing implementation, but only if its source code is available.

In Java 2 it is impossible to write a *generic homogeneous* collection class (or interface). To be generic, the collection class must be written in terms of the class Object; to be homogeneous, it must be written in terms of the specific class of the elements.

The only possible solution to this conundrum is an extension to the Java language. We shall study such an extension in the next section.

17.4 Extending Java with parameterized classes

What is lacking in Java is the concept of a ***parameterized class***, written in terms of one or more ***class parameters***. We could then ***instantiate*** the parameterized class, to give a normal class, by providing an actual class for each of the class parameters.

For example, consider a parameterized List class with a class parameter Element. We would write this class in the usual way, on the assumption that all the list's elements are of class Element. We could then instantiate the parameterized List class by providing an actual class, say String, in place of the class parameter, Element; the result of the instantiation would be an ordinary class that supports homogeneous lists of strings. We could equally easily instantiate the parameterized List class to support homogeneous lists of dates (say). The parameterized List class would be written once and thereafter could be reused as often as desired; there would be no need to re-invent any wheels.

At the time of writing, several research projects are investigating such extensions to Java, and Sun Microsystems are considering adding parameterized classes to a future version of the Java language.

The ***Generic Java*** project extends Java with parameterized classes (and interfaces), using syntax borrowed from C++. The compiler translates Generic Java source code directly into byte-code. Generic Java also provides a parameterized version of the Java Collections framework. In Generic Java, a parameterized class can be instantiated only with object types, not with primitive types. For details see: www.cis.unisa.edu.au/pizza/gj/.

The ***PolyJ*** project also extends Java with parameterized classes (and interfaces), but using different syntax. PolyJ source code is first translated into normal Java code, which is then compiled by a normal Java compiler into byte-code. In PolyJ, a parameterized class can be instantiated with any Java types, not only object types but also primitive types such as **int** and **boolean**. For details see: www.pmg.lcs.mit.edu/polyj/.

In this and the next sections, we shall present several examples of parameterized classes and interfaces, expressed in Generic Java.

Program 17.2 shows a contract for a set ADT, in the form of a Generic Java parameterized interface named Set. (Compare this contract with the one given in Program 9.4.) This interface has a single class parameter, named Element. Some of the operations have parameters or results of class Element. For example, the add method takes an argument of class Element; this ensures that it can add a member only of class Element. Other operations have parameters or results of class Set <Element>. For example, the addAll method takes an argument of class Set <Element>; this ensures that it can unite this set only with another set whose members are also of class Element. The net effect of this contract is that a Set<*C*> object really does contain only members that are objects of class *C*, and any application code that attempts to violate this contract will be rejected by the Generic Java compiler.

Note that the iterator method returns an object of class Iterator <Element>. This is because the Iterator interface is itself parameterized, as shown in Program 17.3. In particular, the next method returns an object of class Element, rather than Object as in the Java 2 unparameterized Iterator interface (Program 8.41).

Program 17.4 shows a contract for a map ADT, in the form of a Generic Java parameterized interface named Map. (Compare this contract with the one given in Program 11.3.) This interface has two class parameters, named Key and Value. Some of the operations have parameters or results of class Key or Value. For example, the get method takes an argument of class Key, and returns a result of class Value. The class parameters of one class can also be used as parameters of a different class. For example, the keySet method returns a result of class Set <Key>, i.e., a set of keys. The net effect of this contract is that a Map<*K*, *V*> object really does contain only keys of class *K* and values of class *V*, and any application code that attempts to violate this contract will be rejected by the Generic Java compiler.

17.5 Case study: a student record system revisited

In this section, we revisit the student record system that was presented as a case study in Section 11.9. We modify the program to use Generic Java parameterized classes. In particular, we use the parameterized set and map ADTs given in Programs 17.2 and 17.4.

In the original student record system (Program 11.21), we used three maps to store the data. These maps were declared as objects of the heterogeneous collection interface Map:

```
// The system contains three maps: students records all of the students
// by student id; degrees records all of the degree programs by degree
// program id; courses records all of the courses by course id.
private Map students, degrees, courses;
```

However, all three maps were actually intended to be homogeneous, with String keys. The intention was that students would contain only Student values, degrees would contain only Degree values, and courses would contain only Course values.

Using the parameterized Map interface of Program 17.4, we can rewrite the declarations of the three maps in Generic Java as follows:

```
public interface Set<Element> {
```

// Each Set<Element> object is a homogeneous set whose members are
// objects of the class Element.

/////////// Accessors ////////////

```
public boolean isEmpty ();
```
// Return true if and only if this set is empty.

```
public int size ();
```
// Return the cardinality of this set.

```
public boolean contains (Element elem);
```
// Return true if and only if elem is a member of this set.

```
public boolean equals (Set<Element> that);
```
// Return true if and only if this set is equal to that.

```
public boolean containsAll (Set<Element> that);
```
// Return true if and only if this set subsumes that.

/////////// Transformers ////////////

```
public void clear ();
```
// Make this set empty.

```
public void add (Element elem);
```
// Add elem as a member of this set.

```
public void remove (Element elem);
```
// Remove elem from this set.

```
public void addAll (Set<Element> that);
```
// Make this set the union of itself and that.

```
public void removeAll (Set<Element> that);
```
// Make this set the difference of itself and that.

```
public void retainAll (Set<Element> that);
```
// Make this set the intersection of itself and that.

/////////// Iterator ////////////

```
public Iterator<Element> iterator();
```
// Return an iterator that visits all members of this set, in no particular
// order.

```
}
```

Program 17.2 A contract for a set ADT as a Generic Java interface.

```
public interface Iterator<Element> {
```

    // Each `Iterator` object represents an iterator over an collection
    // whose elements are of class `Element`.

```
public boolean hasNext ();
```

    // Return true if and only if this iterator has a next element.

```
public Element next ();
```

    // Return the next element in this iterator, or throw a
    // `NoSuchElementException` if there is no such element.

    ...

```
}
```

Program 17.3   A Generic Java `Iterator` interface.

```
private Map<String,Student> students;
private Map<String,Degree> degrees;
private Map<String,Course> courses;
```

The `Key` class parameter of the parameterized `Map` interface is instantiated with the class `String` in all three cases. The `Value` class parameter is instantiated with a different class in each of the three cases. These declarations make it clear that `students` will contain `Student` values, `degrees` will contain `Degree` values, and `courses` will contain `Course` values.

Now recall the `select` method of Program 11.19:

```
private Map select (Map map, Set keys)  { ... }
```

    // Return the map obtained by selecting only those entries from `map` whose
    // keys are in `keys`.

We cannot tell from this code (but only from the comment) that the result map contains keys and values of the same classes as those in the argument map. Nor can we tell that the argument set is expected to contain members of the same class as the argument map's keys (in this case strings).

Program 17.5 shows the Generic Java version of the `select` method. This is an example of a ***parameterized method***. The phrase $<Value>$ in the first line specifies that the method has a class parameter named `Value`. `Value` is then used to specify both the argument map's type Map $<String, Value>$ and the method's result type Map $<String, Value>$.

For example, consider the method call `select(courses, courseIds)`, where `courses` is of type Map $<String, Course>$ and `courseIds` is of type Set $<String>$. We can make the argument types match the corresponding parameter types in Program 17.5 if we replace `Value` by `Course`; we can also tell that the method call's result type will be Map $<String, Course>$.

```
public interface Map<Key,Value> {
```

// Each Map object is a homogeneous map in which the keys are objects of
// class Key and the values are objects of class Value.

/ / / / / / / / / / / Accessors / / / / / / / / / / /

```
public boolean isEmpty ();
```
// Return true if and only if this map is empty.

```
public int size ();
```
// Return the cardinality of this map, i.e., the number of entries.

```
public Value get (Key key);
```
// Return the value in the entry with key in this map, or null if there is no
// such entry.

```
public boolean equals (Map<Key,Value> that);
```
// Return true if this map is equal to that.

```
public Set<Key> keySet ();
```
// Return the set of all keys in this map.

/ / / / / / / / / / / Transformers / / / / / / / / / / /

```
public void clear ();
```
// Make this map empty.

```
public Value remove (Key key);
```
// Remove the entry with key (if any) from this map. Return the value
// in that entry, or null if there was no such entry.

```
public Value put (Key key, Value val);
```
// Add the entry ‹key, val› to this map, replacing any existing entry
// whose key is key. Return the value in that entry, or null if there was no
// such entry.

```
public void putAll (Map<Key,Value> that);
```
// Overlay this map with that, i.e., add all entries of that to this map,
// replacing any existing entries with the same keys.

}

Program 17.4 A contract for a map ADT as a Generic Java interface.

Similarly, consider the method call `select(degrees, degreeIds)`, where degrees is of type `Map <String, Degree>` and degreeIds is of type `Set <String>`. Using the same logic, we can tell that this method call's result type will be `Map <String, Degree>`.

Finally, recall the `getAllStudents` method of Program 11.20:

> **private** Set getAllStudents (Map map)   { ... }
> // Return the set of all student identifiers contained in the given map of
> // StudentCollection objects.

We cannot tell from this code (but only from the comment) that the argument map is expected to contain values of a class that implements the `StudentCollection` interface (Program 11.20). Nor can we tell that the result set will contain members of the same class as the argument map's keys.

Program 17.6 shows the Generic Java version of the method `getAllStudents` method. Again this is a parameterized method. The phrase `<Value **implements** StudentCollection>` in the first line specifies that the method has a class parameter named `Value`, and moreover that `Value` must be a class that implements the `StudentCollection` interface. Any method call that attempts to instantiate `Value` with a class that does not implement `StudentCollection` would be rejected by the Generic Java compiler.

Note that Programs 17.5 and 17.6 contain no casts. In fact, the whole student record system contains no casts when written in Generic Java.

```
private <Value>
        Map<String,Value> select
                    (Map<String,Value> map,
                     Set<String> keys) {
// Return the map obtained by selecting only those entries from map whose
// keys are in keys.
   Map<String,Value> result =
       new TreeMap<String,Value>();
   Iterator<String> iter = keys.iterator();
   while (iter.hasNext()) {
     String key = iter.next();
     Value val = map.get(key);
     if (val != null)
       result.put(key, val);
   }
   return result;
}
```

Program 17.5   The `select` method in Generic Java.

```
      private <Value implements StudentCollection>
              Set<String> getAllStudents
                          (Map<String,Value> map) {
// Return the set of all student identifiers contained in the given map of
// StudentCollection objects.
      Set<String> result = new TreeSet<String>();
      Iterator<String> iter = map.keySet().iterator();
      while (iter.hasNext()) {
        String key = iter.next();
        Value record = map.get(key);
        result.addAll(record.getStudentIDs());
      }
      return result;
}
```

Program 17.6   The getAllStudents method in Generic Java.

Summary

In this chapter:

- We have discussed the relationship between ADTs and object-oriented design, show-ing that ADTs are more fundamental but object-oriented design is more general.
- We have discussed the importance of ADTs as reusable software components.
- We have studied the distinction between homogeneous and heterogeneous collec-tions, exposing a deficiency in Java 2 that makes it impossible to write generic homo-geneous collection classes.
- We have studied a possible extension of Java with parameterized classes, which eliminates that deficiency.
- We have revisited an earlier case study using sets and maps, showing how the imple-mentation can be improved using parameterized classes.

Exercises

17.1   Say whether each of the following classes and packages is likely to be reusable, and explain your answer:
(a) a date class
(b) a money class, which supports sums of money expressed in dollars and cents
(c) a matrix class, which supports two-dimensional arrays of real numbers
(d) an employee class, which supports Microserf Inc's employee records
(e) a text package, which supports sequences of characters divided into lines
(f) a word-bag class, which supports sets of words each with an attached frequency (and could therefore represent the frequencies of words found in a document)
(g) a generic bag class, which supports sets of objects each with an attached frequency

(h) a family tree class

(i) a transportation network class

(j) a text input-output package

(k) a graphics package, which supports lines, polygons, ellipses, and other graphical elements, together with drawings composed of such elements

(l) a database management package.

17.2 Say whether each of the following collections is homogeneous or heterogeneous:

(a) a list of characters, each of type **char**

(b) a stack of numbers, each of type **int** or **float**

(c) a stack of integers, each of type **short**, **int**, or **long**

(d) a list of objects, each of class Date

(e) a set of objects, each of class Comparable

(f) a set of objects, each of class Student

(g) a set of objects, each of class Student or Staff

(h) a set of objects, each of class Student or Staff or Visitor.

Assume that Person is an abstract class, with concrete subclasses Student, Staff, and Visitor. In (d–h), if the collection is heterogeneous, identify the smallest class (or interface) that includes all the possible elements, and state whether that class includes *only* the possible elements.

17.3 Suppose that your program needs each of the following collections:

(a) a list of **char** values

(b) a set of **char** values

(c) a list of arbitrary objects

(d) a list of Date objects.

Would you choose one of the Java heterogeneous collection classes, or would you use a customized homogeneous collection class? Explain your choice, stating the advantages and disadvantages of any alternative choices.

* **17.4** [For readers who have access to a suitable compiler.] Re-implement the entire student records system (Section 11.9) in a language with parameterized classes, such as C++, Generic Java, or PolyJ.

* **17.5** [For readers who have access to a suitable compiler.] Re-implement the videotape manager (Section 8.8) in a language with parameterized classes.

* **17.6** [For readers who have access to a suitable compiler.] Re-implement the interactive spell-checker (Section 9.8) in a language with parameterized classes.

Appendix A

Summary of Mathematics for Algorithm Analysis

This appendix summarizes some mathematics that we need to analyze the time and space efficiency of algorithms. These mathematical techniques are quite straightforward, and should be well within the capability of an average computer science undergraduate.

- Sections A.1 and A.2 cover powers and logarithms. These are fundamental topics that must be understood before reading Chapter 2.
- Section A.3 covers summation of arithmetic series. This is background material that is desirable (but not essential) to understand the analysis of array algorithms in Chapter 3.
- Section A.4 covers recurrences and shows how to solve them. Again, this is background material that is desirable (but not essential) to understand the analysis of recursive algorithms in Chapter 3 and elsewhere.
- Section A.5 covers the O-notation. This material complements Section 2.3 (complexity of algorithms), and can be read at any time.

For each section, a selection of exercises may be found at the end of the appendix.

A.1 Powers

Given a nonnegative integer n, the n'th *power* of a number b, written b^n, is defined by:

$$b^n = b \times \cdots \times b \tag{A.1}$$

(i.e., the product of n copies of b). In particular:

$$b^3 = b \times b \times b \tag{A.2a}$$
$$b^2 = b \times b \tag{A.2b}$$
$$b^1 = b \tag{A.2c}$$
$$b^0 = 1 \tag{A.2d}$$

It might not be obvious that $b^0 = 1$, but we shall soon see why.

The basic law of powers is:

$$b^{n+m} = b^n \times b^m \tag{A.3}$$

This holds because b^n is the product of n copies of b and b^m is the product of m copies of b, so $b^n \times b^m$ is the product of $n + m$ copies of b. A useful special case of (A.3) is:

$$b^{n+1} = b^n \times b \tag{A.4}$$

Another law of powers is:

$$b^{n-m} = b^n / b^m \tag{A.5}$$

This holds because b^n / b^m is the product of $n - m$ copies of b. A useful special case of (A.3) is:

$$b^{n-1} = b^n / b \tag{A.6}$$

From this, by taking $n = 1$ we can deduce that $b^0 = b^1 / b = 1$.

EXAMPLE A.1

How many different bit strings of length n exist?

Let us first consider some simple cases:

- There are 2 different bit strings of length 1 (0 and 1).
- There are $2 \times 2 = 2^2 = 4$ different bit strings of length 2 (00, 01, 10, and 11).
- There are $2 \times 2 \times 2 = 2^3 = 8$ different bit strings of length 3 (000, 001, 010, 011, 100, 101, 110, and 111).

We can easily generalize from these cases: there are 2^n different bit strings of length n.

Characters are represented in a computer by bit strings. The 7-bit ASCII character set has 2^7 different characters. The 8-bit ISO-LATIN-1 character set has 2^8 different characters. The 16-bit Unicode character set has 2^{16} different characters.

Powers of 2 are ubiquitous in computing, as a consequence of the binary representation of data. The first few powers of 2, shown in Table 1, are well worthwhile memorizing. By a happy coincidence, $2^{10} \approx 1$ thousand, $2^{20} \approx 1$ million, and $2^{30} \approx 1$ billion.

(*Note:* The symbol '$\approx$' means 'is approximately equal to'.)

Table A.1 Powers of 2.

n	0	1	2	3	4	5	6	7	8	9	10
2^n	1	2	4	8	16	32	64	128	256	512	1024

A.2 Logarithms

The logarithm of a number y to the base 2, written $\log_2 y$, is the number of copies of 2 that must be multiplied together to give y. Thus $\log_2 2 = 1$, $\log_2 4 = 2$ (since $2^2 = 4$), $\log_2 8 = 3$ (since $2^3 = 8$), and so on. All powers of 2 have integer logarithms to the base 2, but other numbers have fractional logarithms. Thus $\log_2 5 \approx 2.322$, $\log_2 6 \approx 2.585$, and $\log_2 7 \approx 2.807$.

More generally, the **logarithm** of a number y to the base b (where $b > 1$), written $\log_b y$, is the number of copies of b that must be multiplied together to give y.

From this definition it follows immediately that:

$$\log_b(b^n) = n \tag{A.7}$$

Two important special cases of (A.7) are:

$$\log_b 1 = 0 \tag{A.8}$$
$$\log_b b = 1 \tag{A.9}$$

The basic law of logarithms states that the logarithm of the product of two numbers is the sum of their logarithms:

$$\log_b(y\,z) = \log_b y + \log_b z \tag{A.10}$$

A useful special case of (A.10) is:

$$\log_b(b\,y) = \log_b b + \log_b y = 1 + \log_b y \tag{A.11}$$

To verify (A.10), suppose that $y = b^m$ and $z = b^n$ (so $m = \log_b y$ and $n = \log_b z$). Then $\log_b(yz) = \log_b(b^m \times b^n) = \log_b(b^{m+n}) = m + n = \log_b y + \log_b z$.

A second law states that the logarithm of the quotient of two numbers is the difference of their logarithms:

$$\log_b(y/z) = \log_b y - \log_b z \tag{A.12}$$

A useful special case of (A.12) is:

$$\log_b(y/b) = \log_b y - \log_b b = \log_b y - 1 \tag{A.13}$$

A third law relates logarithms to the base b and logarithms to the base 2:

$$\log_b y = \log_2 y / \log_2 b \tag{A.14}$$

They are related by a constant factor, $\log_2 b$.

The logarithm of an integer is not, in general, an integer. The following functions therefore turn out to be useful in conjunction with logarithms. The **floor** of x is the largest integer not greater than x, and is written floor(x) (or $\lfloor x \rfloor$ in some textbooks). For example, floor(7) = floor(7.1) = floor(7.5) = floor(7.9) = 7. Likewise, the **ceiling** of x is the smallest integer not less than x, and is written ceiling(x) (or $\lceil x \rceil$). For example, ceiling(7.1) = ceiling(7.5) = ceiling(7.9) = ceiling(8) = 8.

EXAMPLE A.2

If n is a positive integer, how many times must we halve the value of n (discarding any remainders) to get down to 1?

We need to ask this question whenever we analyze a divide-and-conquer algorithm (such as binary search, merge-sort, or quick-sort). Such an algorithm solves a problem of size n by dividing it into one or more problems of size $n/2$.

First suppose that n is a power of 2. If $n = 8$, repeated halving gives us 4, 2, 1; thus we need to halve n's value 3 times. If $n = 16$, repeated halving gives us 8, 4, 2, 1; thus we need to halve n's value 4 times. More generally, if $n = 2^m$, we need to halve n's value m times.

Now suppose that n is not a power of 2. If $n = 15$, repeated halving gives us 7, 3, 1; thus we need to halve n's value 3 times. This is the same number of times as for $n = 8$, but one less than for $n = 16$. More generally, if $2^m < n < 2^{m+1}$, we need to halve n's value m times.

Putting these cases together, if $2^m \leq n < 2^{m+1}$, we need to halve n's value m times. If we apply $\log_2$ to all three comparands, we get $\log_2(2^m) \leq \log_2 n < \log_2(2^{m+1})$, which simplifies to $m \leq \log_2 n < m + 1$. In other words, m is the largest integer not greater than $\log_2 n$, i.e., $m = \text{floor}(\log_2 n)$. Thus:

No. of times n's value must be halved to get down to $1 = \text{floor}(\log_2 n)$ (A.15)

Note that halving 1 gives us 0, discarding the remainder. Therefore:

No. of times n's value must be halved to get down to $0 = \text{floor}(\log_2 n) + 1$

(A.16)

A.3 Series summations

An ***arithmetic series*** is a sequence of numbers in which each number differs from its predecessor by a fixed amount. Two examples of arithmetic series are «1, 2, 3, 4, 5, 6, 7» and «10, 9, 8, 7, 6, 5, 4, 3, 2, 1, 0». Here we are primarily interested in summing arithmetic series.

We need to do this when we analyze certain sorting algorithms, such as selection sort and insertion sort, which work in such a way that the length of the sorted subarray increases by one on each iteration.

EXAMPLE A.3

Sum the series consisting of the first n positive integers, i.e., $1 + 2 + 3 + \cdots + (n - 1) + n$.

The easiest way to tackle this problem is to observe that the average of an arithmetic series is the average of its first and last numbers, here $(n + 1)/2$. Since there are n numbers, their sum is n times their average:

$$1 + 2 + 3 + \cdots + (n - 1) + n = n(n + 1)/2$$
$$= (n^2 + n)/2 \qquad \text{(A.17)}$$

We can easily test (A.17). With $n = 2$, it gives $(4 + 2)/2 = 3$, which is correct. With $n = 3$, it gives $(9 + 3)/2 = 6$, which is also correct.

We can also verify (A.17) formally by the technique known as *induction*. With $n = 0$, (A.17) gives $(0 + 0)/2 = 0$, which is correct. If we assume that (A.17) is correct for a nonnegative integer $n = m - 1$, i.e.:

$$1 + 2 + 3 + \cdots + (m - 1) = ((m - 1)^2 + (m - 1))/2$$
$$= (m^2 - 2m + 1 + m - 1)/2$$
$$= (m^2 - m)/2$$

then we can deduce:

$$1 + 2 + 3 + \cdots + (m - 1) + m = (m^2 - m)/2 + m$$
$$= (m^2 + m)/2$$

i.e., (A.17) is correct for $n = m$ also. Since (A.17) is correct for $n = 0$, it must also be correct for $n = 1$; therefore it must also be correct for $n = 2$; therefore it must also be correct for $n = 3$; and so on. In other words, it must be correct for all nonnegative integers n.

We can similarly sum other arithmetic series, for example:

$$1 + 2 + 3 + \cdots + (n - 1) = (n^2 - n)/2 \tag{A.18}$$
$$2 + 3 + \cdots + (n - 1) + n = (n^2 + n - 2)/2 \tag{A.19}$$

A.4 Recurrences

A **recurrence** is a group of equations in which a function $f(n)$, where n is a nonnegative integer, is defined in terms of f itself.

For a recurrence to be meaningful, $f(n)$ must be defined in terms of f applied to nonnegative integers less than n. Moreover, $f(0)$ at least must be defined directly.

In general, we want to *solve* the recurrence by finding a direct definition of $f(n)$, i.e., a definition in terms of n, but not in terms of f itself.

Recurrences arise naturally when we analyze recursive algorithms. Since a recursive algorithm contains calls to itself, its time requirement $T(n)$ must be expressed in terms of T itself.

EXAMPLE A.4

Solve the following recurrence:

$$f(n) = 0 \qquad \text{if } n \leq 1 \tag{A.20a}$$
$$f(n) = f(n - 1) + n \qquad \text{if } n > 1 \tag{A.20b}$$

We can use (A.20a–b) to compute $f(1)$, $f(2)$, $f(3)$, $f(4)$, …:

$$f(1) = 0$$

$$f(2) = f(1) + 2 = 2$$
$$f(3) = f(2) + 3 = 2 + 3$$
$$f(4) = f(3) + 4 = 2 + 3 + 4$$

It seems that $f(n)$ is the arithmetic series sum $2 + 3 + \cdots + n$. Using (A.19) we can derive our hypothesis:

$$(n) = (n^2 + n - 2)/2 \qquad \text{if } n > 0 \tag{A.21}$$

We can verify (A.21) by induction. With $n = 1$, (A.21) gives $f(1) = (1 + 1 - 2)/2 = 0$, which is correct. If we assume that (A.21) is correct for a positive integer $n = m - 1$, i.e.:

$$\begin{aligned} f(m - 1) &= ((m - 1)^2 + (m - 1) - 2)/2 \\ &= (m^2 - 2m + 1 + m - 1 - 2)/2 \\ &= (m^2 - m - 2)/2 \end{aligned}$$

then we can deduce from (A.20b):

$$\begin{aligned} f(m) &= f(m - 1) + m \\ &= (m^2 - m - 2)/2 + m \\ &= (m^2 + m - 2)/2 \end{aligned}$$

i.e., (A.21) is correct for $n = m$ also. It must therefore be correct for all positive integers n.

EXAMPLE A.5

Solve the following recurrence:

$$f(n) = 0 \qquad\qquad\;\; \text{if } n \leq 1 \tag{A.22a}$$
$$f(n) = b\, f(n/b) + n \qquad \text{if } n > 1 \tag{A.22b}$$

We can use (A.22a–b) to compute $f(1)$, $f(b)$, $f(b^2)$, $f(b^4)$, …:

$$\begin{aligned} f(1) &= 0 \\ f(b) &= b\, f(1) + b &= b \\ f(b^2) &= b\, f(b) + b^2 &= 2b^2 \\ f(b^3) &= b\, f(b^2) + b^3 &= 3b^3 \\ f(b^4) &= b\, f(b^3) + b^4 &= 4b^4 \end{aligned}$$

The pattern is clear:

$$f(b^k) = k\, b^k$$

Setting $n = b^k$, whence $k = \log_b n$, we have our hypothesis:

$$f(n) = n \log_b n \tag{A.23}$$

We can verify (A.23) by induction. With $n = 1$, (A.23) gives $f(1) = 1 \times 0 = 0$, which is correct. If we assume that (A.23) is correct for a positive integer $n = m/b$, i.e.:

$$f(m/b) = (m/b) \log_b(m/b)$$
$$= (m/b) (\log_b m - 1)$$

then we can deduce from (A.22b):

$$f(m) = b\, f(m/b) + m$$
$$= b\, (m/b) (\log_b m - 1) + m$$
$$= m\, (\log_b m - 1) + m$$
$$= m\, \log_b m$$

i.e., (A.23) is also correct for $n = m$. It must therefore be correct for all powers of b.

We must still generalize (A.23) to values of n that are not powers of b. This is more difficult, but it turns out that an approximate solution to (A.22) is:

$$f(n) \approx n\, \text{floor}(\log_b n) \qquad \text{if } n > 0 \tag{A.24}$$

EXAMPLE A.6

Solve the following recurrence:

$$f(n) = 0 \qquad\qquad\quad \text{if } n \leq 1 \tag{A.25a}$$
$$f(n) = 2\, f(n/2) + n \qquad \text{if } n > 1 \tag{A.25b}$$

This is just a special case of the recurrence (A.22a–b). By specializing (A.24) we get the following approximate solution:

$$f(n) \approx n\, \text{floor}(\log_2 n) \tag{A.26}$$

A.5 O-notation

Consider a function $T(n)$ that measures the amount of time taken by an algorithm, where n is typically the algorithm's input or the size of the algorithm's input. Frequently we are interested, not so much in the actual value of $T(n)$, but more in the *growth rate* of $T(n)$, i.e., the rate at which $T(n)$ grows as n grows. This is the easiest way to predict whether an algorithm will use a feasible amount of time even when n gets large.

Or consider a function $S(n)$ that measures the amount of space used by an algorithm. Again we are interested primarily in the growth rate of $S(n)$.

In ***O-notation***, we express the growth rate of a function $f(n)$ by $O(g(n))$, where $g(n)$ is the fastest-growing term of $f(n)$, shorn of any constant factors. We simply discard all slower-growing terms in $f(n)$, and any constant factors in the fastest-growing term. Table A.2 shows some examples.

(*Note:* Throughout this section, a, b, c, d, and e are constants.)

Note that we conventionally write $O(\log n)$ rather than $O(\log_2 n)$ or $O(\log_b n)$. From (A.14) we have $\log_b n = \log_2 n / \log_2 b$. Here $1/\log_2 b$ is a constant factor and can be discarded. In other words, in O-notation the base of a logarithm does not matter. This fact can be expressed succinctly as follows:

$$O(\log_b n) = O(\log_2 n) = O(\log n) \qquad \text{for all } b > 1 \qquad (A.27)$$

From Section 2.3 we know that 2^n grows faster than n^3, which grows faster than n^2, and so on. This fact can be expressed succinctly as follows:

$$O(2^n) > O(n^3) > O(n^2) > O(n \log n) > O(n) > O(\log n) > O(1) \qquad (A.28)$$

Table A.2   Some functions and their growth rates.

$f(n)$	$O(g(n))$
c	$O(1)$
$b \log_2 n + c$	$O(\log n)$
$b\, n + c$	$O(n)$
$a\, n \log_2 n + b\, n + c$	$O(n \log n)$
$a\, n^2 + b\, n + c$	$O(n^2)$
$a\, n^3 + b\, n^2 + c$	$O(n^3)$
$a\, 2^n + b\, n^{10} + c$	$O(2^n)$

EXAMPLE A.7

Suppose that an algorithm consists of two steps, performed in sequence. Step 1's time complexity is $O(n^2)$, and step 2's time complexity is $O(n)$. What is the algorithm's time complexity?

We can immediately give the answer as $O(n^2)$, i.e., the greater of $O(n^2)$ and $O(n)$.

To see this, note that the actual time requirements of steps 1 and 2 must be something like the following:

$$T_1(n) = a\, n^2 + b\, n + c$$
$$T_2(n) = d\, n + e$$

(Actually, $T_1(n)$ could contain an $n \log n$ term, and $T_2(n)$ could contain a $\log n$ term, but these would not affect the argument.) The algorithm's total time requirement is therefore:

$$T(n) = T_1(n) + T_2(n) = a\, n^2 + (b + d)n + (c + e)$$

So its time complexity is $O(n^2)$, since the fastest-growing term is $a\, n^2$.

Indeed, an algorithm could consist of 100 steps, of which one is $O(n^2)$ and all the others are $O(n)$, but the algorithm as a whole is still $O(n^2)$.

What we observed in Example A.7 can be expressed succinctly as follows:

$$O(n^2) + O(n) = O(n^2) \qquad (A.29a)$$

Similarly:

$$O(2^n) + O(n^3) \qquad = O(2^n) \qquad\qquad\qquad\qquad\qquad \text{(A.29b)}$$
$$O(n^3) + O(n^2) \qquad = O(n^3) \qquad\qquad\qquad\qquad\qquad \text{(A.29c)}$$
$$O(n^2) + O(n \log n) = O(n^2) \qquad\qquad\qquad\qquad\qquad \text{(A.29d)}$$
$$O(n \log n) + O(n) \quad = O(n \log n) \qquad\qquad\qquad\qquad \text{(A.29e)}$$
$$O(n) + O(\log n) \qquad = O(n) \qquad\qquad\qquad\qquad\qquad \text{(A.29f)}$$
$$O(\log n) + O(1) \qquad = O(\log n) \qquad\qquad\qquad\qquad \text{(A.29g)}$$

More generally:

$$O(g(n)) + O(h(n)) = O(g(n)) \qquad \text{if } O(g(n)) \geq O(h(n)) \qquad \text{(A.30)}$$

The intuition here is simple. Just as a chain is no stronger than its weakest link, an algorithm is no more efficient than its least efficient step.

EXAMPLE A.8

Suppose that an algorithm consists of a loop. The loop body's time complexity is $O(\log n)$, and the loop is performed $c\, n$ times. What is the algorithm's time complexity?

We can immediately give the answer as $O(n \log n)$, i.e., the 'product' of $O(n)$ and $O(\log n)$.

To see this, note that the actual time requirement of the loop body must be something like this:

$$T_1(n) = a \log n + b$$

The algorithm's total time requirement is therefore:

$$T(n) = (c\, n)\, T_1(n) = a\, c\, n \log n + b\, c\, n$$

So its time complexity is $O(n \log n)$, since the fastest-growing term is $a\, c\, n \log n$.

What we observed in Example A.8 can be expressed succinctly as follows:

$$O(n) \times O(\log n) = O(n \log n) \qquad\qquad\qquad\qquad \text{(A.31a)}$$

Similarly:

$$O(n) \times O(1) \quad = O(n) \qquad\qquad\qquad\qquad\qquad \text{(A.31b)}$$
$$O(n) \times O(n) \quad = O(n^2) \qquad\qquad\qquad\qquad\qquad \text{(A.31c)}$$
$$O(n) \times O(n^2) = O(n^3) \qquad\qquad\qquad\qquad\qquad \text{(A.31d)}$$

More generally:

$$O(g(n)) \times O(h(n)) = O(g(n)\, h(n)) \qquad\qquad\qquad \text{(A.32)}$$

Exercises

The exercises in this appendix are grouped by section.

A.1.1   Use a spreadsheet to reproduce Table A.1. Make it also show the first few powers of 3. If your spreadsheet system has graphic capabilities, make it produce graphs of 2^n and 3^n.

A.1.2   Suppose that a computer uses the 8-bit ISO-LATIN-1 character set. How many different character strings of length n exist?

A.1.3   A Java **int** value is represented by a 32-bit twos-complement word. How many different **int** values exist? How many of these are positive? negative? Express your answers (i) exactly, in terms of powers of 2, and (ii) approximately, in terms of thousands, millions, or billions.

A.1.4   (a) Show that $(b^2)^n = b^{2n} = (b^n)^2$.
   (b) Show that $(b^m)^n = b^{mn}$.

A.2.1   Tabulate $\log_2 y$ against y, for $y = 1, 2, 4, 8, 16, \ldots$.
   Now use a spreadsheet to reproduce your table. Make it also show $\log_{10} y$ for the same values of y. If your spreadsheet system has graphic capabilities, make it produce graphs of $\log_2 y$ and $\log_{10} y$.
   There is a simple relationship between $\log_2 y$ and $\log_{10} y$. What is it?

A.2.2   Test (A.16) for $n = 1, 2, 3, \ldots, 10$.

A.2.3   Verify (A.12). Use the technique that was used to verify (A.10).

A.2.4   Verify (A.14). Use the technique that was used to verify (A.10).

A.2.5   (a) Show that $\log_b(y^2) = 2 \log_b y$.
   (b) Show that $\log_b(y^n) = n \log_b y$.

A.3.1   Test (A.18) and (A.19) for $n = 2, 3, \ldots, 6$.

A.3.2   Sum the series «$m, m + 1, \ldots, n - 1, n$». The answer should be zero if $m > n$.
   (A.17), (A.18), and (A.19) are all special cases of this series. Verify that they can be derived from your answer.

A.3.3   Write down a formula for the sum of the series «$2, 4, \ldots, n - 2, n$», where n is even.
   Verify your formula by induction.

* **A.3.4**   A *geometric series* is a sequence of numbers in which each number has a fixed ratio to its predecessor. An example is the series consisting of the first n powers of 2, i.e., «$1, 2, 4, \ldots,$ $2^{n-2}, 2^{n-1}$». Write down a formula for the sum of this series.
   (*Hint:* The sum of this series bears a simple relationship to 2^n. You should be able to see this by computing $1 + 2$, $1 + 2 + 4$, $1 + 2 + 4 + 8$, and so on.)
   Verify your formula by induction.

A.4.1   Test (A.21) for $n = 2, 3, \ldots, 6$.

A.4.2   Using (A.25a–b), tabulate $f(n)$ against n, for $n = 1, 2, 3, \ldots, 10$. Also tabulate the approximate solution (A.26), $n \operatorname{floor}(\log_2 n)$. Is it a good approximation?

A.4.3   Solve the following recurrence:

$$f(n) = 0 \qquad\qquad \text{if } n = 0$$
$$f(n) = f(n - 1) + c\,n \qquad \text{if } n > 0$$

A.4.4   Solve the following recurrence:

$$f(n) = 0 \qquad\qquad \text{if } n = 0$$
$$f(n) = f(n - 1) + n + d \qquad \text{if } n > 0$$

A.4.5   Solve the following recurrence:

$$f(n) = 0 \qquad\qquad \text{if } n = 0$$
$$f(n) = b\,f(n/b) + c\,n \qquad \text{if } n > 0$$

A.4.6   Solve the following recurrence:

$$f(n) = 0 \qquad\qquad \text{if } n = 0$$
$$f(n) = b\,f(n/b) + n + d \qquad \text{if } n > 0$$

A.5.1   Confirm your intuition that $O(n^2) > O(n \log n) > O(n)$ as follows. Consider three different algorithms that solve the same problem. Their time requirements on a particular processor are:

$$T_1(n) = 0.02\,n^2 \text{ seconds}$$
$$T_2(n) = 0.2\,n\,\log_2 n \text{ seconds}$$
$$T_3(n) = 2\,n \text{ seconds}$$

Use a spreadsheet to tabulate these time requirements against n, for $n = 10, 20, \ldots, 100$. What do you observe?

What difference does it make if all three algorithms are run on a processor that is twice as fast?

A.5.2   Suppose that an algorithm consists of three steps, which are performed in sequence. Step 1's time complexity is $O(n^2)$, step 2's time complexity is $O(n \log n)$, and step 3's time complexity is $O(n^3)$. What is the algorithm's time complexity?

A.5.3   Suppose that an algorithm consists of two steps, which are mutually exclusive. (Exactly one of them will be performed, depending on some condition.) Step 1's time complexity is $O(n^2)$, and step 2's time complexity is $O(n \log n)$. What is the algorithm's time complexity?

Generalize your answer, along the lines of (A.30) or (A.32), to the situation where the two steps have time complexities $O(g(n))$ and $O(h(n))$.

A.5.4   Suppose that an algorithm consists of two steps, which are mutually exclusive, inside a loop. Step 1's time complexity is $O(1)$, step 2's time complexity is $O(n)$, and the loop is iterated n times. What is the algorithm's time complexity?

A.5.5   Suppose that an algorithm consists of ten steps, which are performed in sequence. Steps 1–9 all have time complexity $O(n)$ or $O(1)$. Step 10 has time complexity $O(n \log n)$, but is skipped if some condition is satisfied. (The condition does not depend on n.) What is the algorithm's time complexity?

Appendix B
Summary of Java

This appendix summarizes the more advanced features of the Java language used in this book. We assume sufficient knowledge of Java to write at least simple programs involving expressions, statements, and predeclared classes. (Other books introduce this basic material: see Further Reading.)

- Section B.1 very briefly summarizes the basic features of the Java language.
- Section B.2 covers classes and subclasses, objects and methods, inheritance and overriding.
- Section B.3 covers interfaces, which are used to express contracts used for abstract data types in this book.
- Section B.4 covers packages, which are used to group classes and interfaces into a single library.
- Section B.5 covers exceptions, which are used to signal and handle abnormal situations.
- Section B.6 covers inner classes and inner interfaces, which are subsidiary to their enclosing classes and interfaces.

B.1 Basics

Most Java programs are developed using Sun Microsystems' Java software development kit (SDK), and make use of the extensive class libraries provided with the SDK. The SDK also provides development tools including a Java compiler, `javac`, which translates Java source code into Java byte-code, and a Java virtual machine (JVM), `java`, which executes Java byte-code. (*Note:* Early versions of the SDK were also known as the Java development kit or JDK.)

There are two distinct kinds of Java program: applications and applets.

An **application** is a stand-alone program. It is typically executed by a JVM installed on the user's local machine. The application can interact with the user using multiple windows, communicate with other machines via a network, and access files held on the local machine.

An *applet* is a program that is 'contained' in a Web page held at some (possibly remote) Web site. It is usually downloaded by a Web browser from the Web site to the user's local machine, and then executed by a JVM integrated into the browser. An applet usually interacts with the user through a part of the Web page that contains it, but it may create additional windows if required. For security reasons, an applet has restricted access rights to the resources of the local machine: it may communicate with the machine hosting the Web site, but it may not access files held on the local machine.

Alternatively, an applet may be executed directly on the user's machine using the `appletviewer` tool provided by the SDK. In this case, the security restrictions may be relaxed, allowing the applet access rights similar to those of an application.

Most of the programs in this book are applications, but some of the case studies are applets. Many of the programs have a graphical user interface that is implemented using the Java Swing user interface components. Some familiarity with the Java Swing components is needed to understand these programs fully and to modify them.

The Java language, like most programming languages, includes statements, expressions, and primitive types of data. Most of Java's basic features are based on the older language C. Tables B.1 and B.2 summarize the syntax of a subset of Java statements and expressions, respectively. Table B.3 summarizes the primitive data types of Java.

We assume that you are already familiar with these simple statements, expressions, and types. The statements and expressions required to support more advanced language features (such as exceptions) are discussed in the following sections.

Table B.1 The syntax of statements in Java (subset).

Statement	Syntax
block statement	{ *Statement*$_1$ ... *Statement*$_n$ }
expression statement	*Expression* ;
	where *Expression* must be an assignment expression, a unary $++$ or $--$ expression, a method invocation expression, or an instance creation expression
declaration statement	*Type Identifier* ; or
(simplified)	*Type Identifier* = *Expression* ;
	where *Type* is a class name, a primitive type, or an array type
if statement	**if** (*Expression*) *Statement*
if-else statement	**if** (*Expression*) *Statement* **else** *Statement*
switch statement	**switch** (*Expression*)
	{ *Labels*$_1$ *Statements*$_1$ ... *Labels*$_n$ *Statements*$_n$ }
	where *Label* is '**case** *Expression* :' or '**default** :'
while statement	**while** (*Expression*) *Statement*
do statement	**do** *Statement* **while** (*Expression*) ;
for statement	**for** (*Expression*$_1$, ... , *Expression*$_m$; *Expression* ;
	Expression$_1$, ... , *Expression*$_n$) *Statement*
	where *Expression*$_1$, ... , *Expression*$_m$ may also contain variable declarations of the form *Type Identifier* = *Expression*
return statement	**return** ; or
	return *Expression* ;

Table B.2 The syntax of expressions in Java (subset).

Expression	Syntax
literal expression	*Literal* or **true** or **false** or **null** where *Literal* is an integer, floating-point, character, or string literal
variable expression	**this** or *Variable-Name*
instance creation expression	**new** *Class-Name* (*Expression*$_1$, ... , *Expression*$_n$)
array creation expression	**new** *Type-Name* [*Expression*$_1$] ... [*Expression*$_n$] where *Type-Name* is a class name or primitive type
field access expression	*Expression* . *Identifier* or **super** . *Identifier*
method invocation expression	*Method-Name* (*Expression*$_1$, ... , *Expression*$_n$) or *Expression* . *Identifier* (*Expression*$_1$, ... , *Expression*$_n$) or **super** . *Identifier* (*Expression*$_1$, ... , *Expression*$_n$)
array access expression	*Expression* [*Expression*]
unary postfix expression	*Expression* ++ or *Expression* --
unary prefix expression	++ *Expression* or -- *Expression* or (*Type-Name*) *Expression* or *Prefix-Operator Expression* where *Prefix-Operator* is one of +, -, ~, !
binary expression	*Expression Infix-Operator Expression* where *Infix-Operator* is one of +, -, *, /, %, &, ^, |, &&, | |, <<, > ., ..., =¼, !=, <, >, <=, >=.
conditional expression	*Expression* ? *Expression* : *Expression*
assignment expression	*Variable Assignment-Operator Expression* where *Variable* is a variable expression, field access expression, or array access expression; and *Assignment-Operator* is one of =, +=, -=, *=, / = , %=, &=, ^=, | =, <<=, >>=, >>>=.

Table B.3 The primitive data types in Java.

Primitive type	Representation
boolean	byte
char	16-bit unsigned integer
byte	8-bit twos-complement signed integer
short	16-bit twos-complement signed integer
int	32-bit twos-complement signed integer
long	64-bit twos-complement signed integer
float	32-bit single-precision floating point
double	64-bit double-precision floating point

Java differs from most programming languages in that an arithmetic operation never overflows. For example, 32-bit integer arithmetic operations simply take the least significant 32 bits of the result; thus adding or multiplying two large positive integers might produce a negative result. Integer division by zero throws an exception, but floating-point division by zero does not.

B.2 Classes

B.2.1 Single classes

The fundamental building block of a Java program is the ***class***. A class encapsulates data and the operations used to manipulate these data. The ***members*** of a class are ***fields*** (the data) and ***methods*** (the operations). A field is also sometimes known as a *variable* or an *attribute*.

Declaring a class

A class declaration consists of a heading and a body. The heading gives the class a name and specifies its relationship to other classes. The body consists of declarations of fields and methods.

An ***object*** is an instance of a class, and has its own copy of the fields. The data stored in the fields of an object constitute the ***state*** of that object. The object shares its methods with other objects of the same class.

A class may also contain one or more ***constructors***. When a new object is created, a constructor is invoked to initialize the state of the object. Every constructor has the same name as the class to which it belongs.

The fields of a class may be grouped into ***instance variables***, which belong to individual objects, and ***class variables***, which belong to the class itself. A single copy of each class variable is shared by all objects of the class. A class variable is distinguished from an instance variable by including the keyword **static** in its declaration.

Similarly, the methods of a class may be grouped into ***instance methods***, which can be applied to individual objects, and ***class methods***, which can be applied only to the class itself. A class method is distinguished from an instance method by including the keyword **static** in its declaration.

Table B.4   Access modifiers in Java.

Access modifier	Kind of access	Meaning
public	public access	Visible from this class and from all other classes.
protected	protected access	Visible from this class, from all subclasses of this class, and from all other classes in the same package.
private	private access	Visible only from this class (*not* from subclasses).
(none)	default access	Visible from this class (*not* from subclasses) and from all other classes in the same package.

When an instance method is invoked, it receives a reference to a particular ***target object***. Thus it can inspect and/or update the state of the target object directly, by accessing the fields of the object. In the body of an instance method, the target object is identified by the keyword **this**. An instance method may also access the class variables belonging to the class of the target object.

On the other hand, a class method does *not* receive a target object when it is invoked. It can access the class variables but not the instance variables of the class to which it belongs. Indeed, a class method can be invoked even when no instances (objects) of the class have been created.

The declaration of a class member contains an ***access modifier***, which controls access to the member by other classes. The access modifiers in Java are summarized in Table B.4. For the moment, we shall concern ourselves only with public and private access. We shall discuss protected and default access in Section B.4.

A field may be declared as **final**, and such a field is known as a ***constant***. A constant field is given its value when it is initialized, and may not be updated.

EXAMPLE B.1   A bank account class

Program B.5 gives a Java class, Account, representing a simple bank account. A bank account object has two instance variables named id and balance (money amounts are expressed in cents), a constructor named Account, and three instance methods named getBalance, withdraw, and deposit. The instance variables are private, so they can be accessed only from inside the Account class. The constructor and instance methods are all public, so they can be invoked by a method in any class.

EXAMPLE B.2   A savings account class

Let us extend Example B.1 as follows. A savings account pays interest at a given variable interest rate (expressed as a percentage). Periodically, as long as the account is in credit, the balance is increased using the current interest rate.

We must record the current interest rate for the savings account. Since the interest rate may vary, and all savings accounts use the same interest rate, we introduce a class variable named interestRate. We add two class methods, named getRate and setRate, to get and set the interest rate, respectively. We also add an instance method, named payInterest, to pay the interest due. The modifications are shown in Program B.6.

Creating objects and invoking methods

A new object is created by an instance creation expression using the keyword **new**. For example, we can create a new Account object by the following declaration:

```
Account myAccount = new Account("1234-567X");
```

This declares a new variable, myAccount, and invokes the Account constructor to initialize its account identifier to "1234-567X" and its balance to zero.

We can now deposit and withdraw amounts by invoking the instance methods as follows:

```
myAccount.deposit(10000);   // Deposit $100.
myAccount.withdraw(2500);   // Now withdraw $25.
```

An instance method is invoked by giving a target object (e.g., myAccount), the instance method name (e.g., deposit), and the argument(s) it requires (e.g., 10000).

Using the SavingsAccount class from Program B.6, we can set and then get the interest rate as follows:

```
//  Set the interest rate to 4.5%...
SavingsAccount.setRate(4.5);
System.out.println("The current interest rate is "
        + SavingsAccount.getRate() + "%");
```

```java
public class Account {

    // Each Account object represents a bank account.

    // This account consists of an account identifier and a balance.

    private String id;
    private long balance;

    public Account (String id) {
    // Create a new account with identifier id and an opening balance of zero.
        this.id = id;   this.balance = 0;
    }

    public long getBalance () {
    // Return the balance of this account.
        return balance;
    }

    public void withdraw (long amount) {
    // Withdraw amount from this account. The new balance may be negative.
        balance -= amount;
    }

    public void deposit (long amount) {
    // Deposit amount in this account.
        balance += amount;
    }

}
```

Program B.5 A Java class representing simple bank accounts.

A class method is invoked by giving the class name (e.g., `SavingsAccount`), the class method name (e.g., `setRate`), and the argument(s) it requires (e.g., 4.5).

We can go on to create a new `SavingsAccount` object, and pay the interest due, as follows:

```
SavingsAccount mySavingsAccount =
        new SavingsAccount("1234-5678");
mySavingsAccount.deposit(100000);   // Deposit $1000.
mySavingsAccount.payInterest();
```

```
public class SavingsAccount {

    // Each SavingsAccount object represents a savings account, which
    // pays interest when in credit.

    // This savings account consists of an account identifier and a balance. The
    // current interest rate is the same for all savings accounts.

    private String id;
    private long balance;

    private static float interestRate;

    public static float getRate () {
    // Return the current interest rate.
        return interestRate;
    }

    public static void setRate (float newRate) {
    // Set the current interest rate to newRate.
        interestRate = newRate;
    }

    public void payInterest () {
    // Calculate the interest due on this savings account, and update its balance.
        if (balance > 0) {
            long interest =
                (long) (balance * interestRate / 100.0);
            balance += interest;
        }
    }

    ... // Other instance methods as in Program B.5.

}
```

Program B.6   A Java class representing savings accounts.

Method overloading

Sometimes it is useful to provide several versions of an operation, with different types of arguments. For example, consider printing strings, integers, and floating-point numbers. We must declare a separate method for each version, as follows:

```
public void printString (String s)   { ... }
public void printInt (int i)         { ... }
public void printFloat (float f)     { ... }
```

It would be more convenient, however, if all three versions could all have the same name, `print`. We can do this by using a feature called ***method overloading***. Several different methods may have the same name, provided that they have different numbers and/or types of parameters. We can make our printing methods overloaded, as follows:

```
public void print (String s)   { ... }
public void print (int i)      { ... }
public void print (float f)    { ... }
```

We must still write three different method declarations, but they all have the same name.

Constructors can also be overloaded. Indeed, this is essential if a class is to have more than one constructor. For example, the `Account` class of Program B.5 has a constructor that always initializes the balance to zero. We can provide a second constructor that initializes the balance to a given amount, as follows:

```
public Account (String id, long amount) {
// Create a new account with identifier id and an opening balance of
// amount.
   this.id = id;   this.balance = amount;
}
```

The two `Account` constructors are overloaded.

B.2.2 Classes and subclasses

Inheritance

Inheritance is a fundamental concept in object-oriented programming. It allows classes to represent 'is-a-kind-of' relationships. For example, an employee is a kind of person; a rectangle is a kind of shape; and a savings account is a kind of bank account.

With inheritance, the fields and methods of one class may be inherited by other classes, rather than duplicated. For example, if the `Employee` class is a subclass of the `Person` class, an `Employee` object will contain all of the fields and methods of a `Person` object (and perhaps additional ones).

If class *S* inherits from class *C*, we say that *S* is a ***subclass*** of *C*; conversely, *C* is a ***superclass*** of *S*.

Java supports ***single inheritance***: every class has exactly one superclass (except the `Object` class, which has no superclass). However, a class may have any number of subclasses.

A class declaration may specify its direct superclass by an extends clause, as in '**class** `Employee` **extends** `Person`'. By default, the superclass is `Object`. All classes (except `Object` itself) are direct or indirect subclasses of `Object`.

A class may be declared as **final**, which means that it cannot be extended by a subclass. An example of a final class is `String`. The Java compiler will reject any attempt to extend a final class.

We can check the class of a particular object using the **instanceof** operator. The expression '*x* **instanceof** *C*' returns true if the object *x* is an instance of the class *C* (or a subclass of *C*), and false otherwise.

The class of an object can be asserted by using a ***cast***. The expression ' `(C)` *x*' casts the object *x* to class *C*, i.e., asserts that *x* really is an instance of *C* (or a subclass of *C*). If *x* is not, the expression throws an exception.

EXAMPLE B.3   An improved savings account class

The `SavingsAccount` class of Program B.6 duplicates all of the fields and methods of the `Account` class of Program B.5.

A much better solution is to declare `SavingsAccount` as a subclass of `Account`, as shown in Program B.7.

One further modification is required. In the `Account` class of Program B.5, the instance variables `id` and `balance` are declared as private. This prevents a subclass like `SavingsAccount` from accessing them directly. For Program B.7 to work (in particular, to allow `balance` to be accessed directly by the `payInterest` method), we must alter their declarations to make `id` and `balance` *protected*:

```
protected String id;
protected long balance;
```

Assume that `accountsFile` contains records of all the bank's ordinary and savings accounts. The following application code reads all the account records, and pays interest into the savings accounts only:

```
for (;;) {
    Account acc = accountsFile.getAccount();
    if (acc instanceof SavingsAccount)
        ((SavingsAccount)acc).payInterest();
}
```

Note that a method invocation `acc.payInterest()` would be rejected by the Java compiler: `acc` is of type `Account`, and the `Account` class has no method named `payInterest`. In the above code, however, we can confidently assert that `acc` actually refers to a `SavingsAccount` object, because we have just tested it using the **instanceof** operator.

Note also that the code would be faulty if we omitted the **instanceof** check. The cast `(SavingsAccount)acc` would throw an exception if `acc` does not actually refer to a `SavingsAccount` object.

Method overriding

When we introduce a subclass, we sometimes need to modify the behavior of some of the superclass's instance methods. This can be achieved using ***method overriding***. In the subclass, we declare an overriding method that has exactly the same name and parameters as the superclass's method. Java ensures that, when we invoke a method of that name with a target object of the subclass, it is the overriding method that is executed.

```
public class SavingsAccount extends Account {

   // Each SavingsAccount object represents a savings account, which
   // pays interest when in credit.

   // This savings account consists of an account identifier and a balance. The
   // current interest rate is the same for all savings accounts.

   private static float interestRate;

   public static float getRate () {
   // Return the current interest rate.
      return interestRate;
   }

   public static void setRate (float newRate) {
   // Set the current interest rate to newRate.
      interestRate = newRate;
   }

   public void payInterest () {
   // Calculate the interest due on this savings account, and update its balance.
      if (balance > 0) {
        long interest =
            (long) (balance * interestRate / 100.0);
        balance += interest;
      }
   }

}
```

Program B.7   A Java class representing savings accounts (using inheritance).

Only instance methods can be overridden. Moreover, an instance method can be declared as final, which means that it cannot be overridden. The Java compiler will reject any attempt to override an instance method by a class method, or to override a final instance method.

The Object class declares three instance methods that are intended to be overridden by other classes:

```
public boolean equals (Object that);
// Return true if and only if this object is equal to that.

public int hashCode ();
// Return the hash-code value of this object.

public String toString ();
// Return a string rendering of this object.
```

The equals method in the Object class returns true if and only if this object and that are in fact the same object. A subclass must override equals if it is required to compare the states of the two objects. For example, the String class overrides equals with a method that compares the two strings character-by-character.

The hashCode method is used by hash-table data structures, and is discussed in Section 12.1.1.

The toString method in the Object class renders this object by its class name composed with its memory address. A subclass must override toString if it is required to render the object's actual state.

The toString method is invoked implicitly in expressions such as:

```
"The object is " + obj + "."
```

which is equivalent to:

```
"The object is " + obj.toString() + "."
```

The toString method is also used by the JVM to produce formatted debugging information when a program terminates abnormally. For this reason, if no other, the toString method should be overridden by all application classes.

B.2.3 Abstract classes

An *abstract class* is a class that cannot be instantiated. An abstract class is identified by including the **abstract** modifier in its heading. The Java compiler will reject any attempt to create an instance of an abstract class.

EXAMPLE B.4   An abstract bank account class

Suppose that we want to represent two different types of bank account: savings accounts (which pay interest) and checking accounts (which have an overdraft facility). We will declare two classes, `SavingsAccount` and `CheckingAccount`. But we do not want these classes to be unrelated, because both types of account have common properties: the ability to deposit and withdraw money.

Instead, we declare an abstract class, named `AbstractAccount`, that captures these common properties. Then we declare both `SavingsAccount` and `CheckingAccount` as subclasses of `AbstractAccount`. See Program B.8.

The `deposit` method in the `AbstractAccount` class is inherited by both subclasses.

The `withdraw` method in the `AbstractAccount` class is an example of an *abstract method*, which has no body. Each of the subclasses provides a body for `withdraw`. Note that the bodies are different, reflecting different properties of the two types of accounts.

The `SavingsAccount` subclass has one specific method, `payInterest`. The `CheckingAccount` subclass has no specific methods. (But it could be modified to have specific methods, such as `setOverdraftLimit`.)

Since the `AbstractAccount` class is abstract, we cannot instantiate it. We can, however, create `SavingsAccount` and `CheckingAccount` objects by invoking their respective constructors.

An ***abstract method*** is one whose declaration specifies its name, parameters, and result type, but not its body. Its declaration includes the **abstract** modifier, and the method body '{ ... }' is replaced by ';'. An abstract method is permitted only in an abstract class. It is left to each subclass to provide a method body appropriate for that subclass.

B.3 Interfaces

A Java ***interface*** is a special kind of abstract class that consists entirely of constant fields and abstract methods. An interface specifies methods that must be provided by every class that *implements* the interface. All members of an interface must be public. Note that an interface may not contain a constructor.

In this book, we use an interface to specify the contract for each abstract data type (ADT). For example, the `List` interface (Program 8.2) specifies the methods that must be provided by every implementation of the list ADT. Each such implementation is a class declared using an implements clause, such as '**class** `ArrayList` **implements** `List`' in Program 8.9.

A class may implement any number of interfaces (although it may extend only one superclass).

An interface may also extend one or more other interfaces using an extends clause. If interface *K* extends interfaces *I* and *J*, we say that *K* is a ***subinterface*** of *I* (or *J*), and that *I* (or *J*) is a ***superinterface*** of *K*.

Since an interface is abstract, the Java compiler will reject any attempt to create an instance of an interface.

```
public abstract class AbstractAccount {

    // Each AbstractAccount object represents a bank account.

    // This account consists of an account identifier and a balance.

    protected String id;
    protected long balance;

    public abstract void withdraw (long amount);
    // Withdraw amount from this account, if permitted.

    public void deposit (long amount) {
    // Deposit amount in this account.
        balance += amount;
    }

}

//////////////////////////////////////////////////////////////

public class SavingsAccount extends AbstractAccount {

    // Each SavingsAccount object represents a savings account, which
    // pays interest and must always be in credit.

    // This savings account consists of an account identifier and a balance. The
    // interest rate is fixed at 3%.

    private static final float INTEREST_RATE = 3.0;

    public SavingsAccount (String id) {
    // Create a new savings account with identifier id and an opening balance
    // of zero.
        this.id = id;   this.balance = 0;
    }

    public void withdraw (long amount) {
    // Withdraw amount from this savings account, if it remains in credit.
        if (balance >= amount)
            balance -= amount;
    }

    public void payInterest () {
    // Calculate the interest due on this savings account, and update its balance.
        long interest =
              (long) (balance * INTEREST_RATE / 100.0);
        balance += interest;
    }
```

Program B.8 Java classes representing savings and checking accounts (using an abstract class) (*continued on next page*).

```
public class CheckingAccount extends AbstractAccount {

   // Each CheckingAccount object represents a checking account, which
   // pays no interest but has a limited overdraft facility.

   // This checking account consists of an account identifier, a balance, and an
   // overdraft limit.

   private long overdraftLimit;

   public CheckingAccount (String id, long limit) {
   // Create a new checking account with identifier id, an opening balance
   // of zero, and an overdraft limit of limit.
      this.id = id;   this.balance = 0;
      this.overdraftLimit = limit;
   }

   public void withdraw (long amount) {
   // Withdraw amount from this checking account, if its overdraft limit is
   // not exceeded.
      if (balance >= amount - overdraftLimit)
         balance -= amount;
   }

}
```

Program B.8 (*continued*)

EXAMPLE B.5   An interest-paying bank account interface

The SavingsAccount class of Program B.7 represents a particular kind of bank account that pays interest. In a banking application, however, we might want to declare classes representing several different kinds of bank account that pay interest. Each such class should provide a parameterless method named payInterest.

There is only one way to enforce this requirement: introduce an interface that specifies an abstract method, named payInterest. This interface is shown in Program B.9. Note that the payInterest method is abstract by default.

Other bank account classes can now, if required, be declared as implementing this interface:

```
public class SavingsAccount extends AbstractAccount
        implements InterestPayingAccount {

    ...   // Class body as before.

}
```

The Java compiler will ensure that such a class actually implements the interface's `payInterest` method.

B.4 Packages

A *package* is a group of classes and interfaces. The Java class libraries (such as `java.lang`, `java.io`, and `java.util`) are packages.

A class or interface intended to be part of a package *P* must be preceded by a package declaration of the form '`package P;`'.

A class or interface can *import* (use) the contents of a package by naming that package in an import declaration. We can import either a single class or interface, e.g.:

```
import java.util.List;
```

or the entire contents of a package, e.g.:

```
import java.io.*;
```

Alternatively, a class can import a class or interface simply by using its *fully-qualified name*, as in the declaration '`java.util.Set employees;`'.

Every Java class and interface implicitly imports the entire contents of the `java.lang` package. In other words, every class and interface declaration is implicitly preceded by '`import java.lang.*;`'.

A package is typically held in a separate folder whose name reflects the package name (with each '`.`' replaced by '`/`' or '`\`'). For example, the package named `java.util` is typically held in a folder named `java/util`.

This does not imply that packages are related to one another in a hierarchical sense. For

```
public interface InterestPayingAccount {

    // Each InterestPayingAccount object represents a bank account
    // that pays interest.

    public void payInterest ();
    // Calculate the interest due on this account, and update its balance.

}
```

Program B.9   A Java interface specifying interest-paying bank accounts.

example, `java.awt.event` is not a sub-package of `java.awt`, and there is no special relationship between the classes in `java.awt.event` and those in `java.awt`. A subclass may be placed in any package, not necessarily the same package as its superclass.

Two access modifiers are relevant to packages. A class member with protected or default access may be accessed directly by other classes in the same package. (See Table B.4.)

In this book, we typically omit the package and import declarations preceding a class or interface declaration, provided that it is clear what packages contain the imported classes and interfaces. Of course, the source code on the companion Web site does contain these declarations.

B.5 Exceptions

An *exception* is an abnormal situation detected while a program is running. After an exception is detected, it may be *handled* by a special piece of code that takes some remedial action, after which the program can continue running.

In more detail, the operation where the abnormal situation arises is said to *throw* the exception. The executing method then has two options. It can opt to handle the exception itself, after which it continues executing. Alternatively it can opt to throw the exception to its calling method, in which case the executing method is abandoned. The calling method then has the same options: handle the exception itself, or throw it to its own caller. The exception might be thrown all the way up to the program's top-level method. If the latter opts to throw the exception, the program terminates abnormally.

In Java, an exception is just a special kind of object. In fact, every exception is an object of a subclass of the `java.lang.Exception` class. In this book, we use two kinds of exception: runtime exceptions and input/output exceptions.

A runtime exception represents a program error, which should normally be avoided. For example, an `ArrayIndexOutOfBoundsException` is thrown when an array index is out of range; it can be avoided by first checking the index. For another example, a `NullPointerException` is thrown when a null reference is given when invoking an instance method; it can be avoided by first checking that the reference is not null.

An input/output exception (an object of class `IOException`) represents an error in performing an input/output operation. In general, such errors cannot be avoided. For example, a `FileNotFoundException` is thrown when the program attempts to open a nonexistent file. The program could try to anticipate this by first checking that the file exists, but (in a multiprogramming context) some other program could intervene by deleting the file. For another example, an `EOFException` is thrown when the program attempts to read data beyond the end of a file. The program could try to anticipate this by first checking for end-of-file, but some other program could intervene by overwriting the file.

Any method that might throw an exception (other than a runtime exception) must declare this by listing the possible class(es) of exception in its throws clause. If one method calls another method that may throw an exception, then the calling method must either handle or throw that exception. If it throws the exception, the calling method must list the exception in its own throws clause.

For example, the following method (from Program 7.1) calls `java.io` methods that might throw an `IOException`, but does not itself handle such an exception. So it declares that it might throw an `IOException`:

```
public static Person readPerson (BufferedReader input)
               throws IOException  { ... }
```

An exception is created using an instance creation expression (using **new**), and then thrown using a throw statement. For example, the following statement both creates and throws a new `FileNotFoundException`:

```
throw new FileNotFoundException();
```

Exceptions are handled by try-catch statements (see Table B.10). The try block (following **try**) is executed first. If the try block throws an exception, the first catch-clause capable of handling that exception is executed next. A catch-clause can handle any exception of the class named in the catch-clause.

For example, the following try-catch statement attempts to read and process a line from the text file `input`, but displays an error message if an `IOException` is thrown instead:

```
try {
    String line = input.readLine();
    ...  // Process line.
} catch (IOException e) {
    System.out.println(e.getMessage());
}
```

Note that the thrown exception object is available to the body of the catch-clause (being identified by the variable `e` above). The `getMessage` method returns a formatted string describing the exception and where it occurred.

Table B.10   The syntax of statements in Java (for throwing and handling exceptions).

Statement	Syntax
throw statement	**throw** *Expression* ;
try-catch statement	**try** *Block Catch-Clause*$_1$ ... *Catch-Clause*$_m$
	where *Block* is '{ *Statement*$_1$ ... *Statement*$_n$ }'
	and *Catch-Clause* is '**catch** (*Class-Name Identifier*) *Block*'

EXAMPLE B.6   Copying a file of persons

Program B.11 shows a simple application, `PersonsCopier`, that copies a sequence of person records from one file to another. The input and output filenames are provided as command-line arguments.

```java
public class Person {

  public String surname, forename;
  public boolean female;
  public int yob;   // year of birth

  public Person (String surname, String forename,
                 boolean female, int yob) {
    this.surname = surname;
    this.forename = forename;
    this.female = female;
    this.yob = yob;

  }

}
```

///

```java
public class PersonsCopier {

  private static Person readPerson
                    (BufferedReader input)
                    throws IOException {
  // Read a single person record from input. Assume that each person
  // record occupies a single line, in which the surname, forename,
  // gender ('F'/'M'), and year-of-birth are separated by single spaces.
  // Return null if no person record remains to be read.
    String line = input.readLine();
    if (line == null)  return null;
    int i1 = line.indexOf(' ');
    int i2 = line.indexOf(' ', i1+1);
    int i3 = line.indexOf(' ', i2+1);
    String surname = line.substring(0, i1);
    String forename = line.substring(i1+1, i2);
    boolean female =
          line.substring(i2+1, i3).equals("F");
    int yob = Integer.parseInt(line.substring(i3+1));
    return new Person(surname, forename,
          female, yob);
  }
```

Program B.11   A program to copy a file of person records (*continued on next page*).

```
private static void writePerson
                (BufferedWriter output, Person p)
              throws IOException {
   String line = p.surname + " " + p.forename +
       " " + (p.female ? "F" : "M") + " " + p.yob;
   output.write(line + "\n");
}

private static void copyPersons
                (BufferedReader input,
                 BufferedWriter output)
              throws IOException {
   for (;;) {
      Person p = readPerson(input);
      if (p == null)  break;
      writePerson(output, p);
   }
}

public static void main (String[] args) {
  try {
     BufferedReader input =
         new BufferedReader(
             new InputStreamReader(
                 new FileInputStream(args[0])));
     BufferedWriter output =
         new BufferedWriter(
             new OutputStreamWriter(
                 new FileOutputStream(args[1])));
     copyPersons(input, output);
     input.close();
     output.close();
  } catch (IOException e) {
     System.out.println(e.getMessage());
  }
 }
}
```

Program B.11 (*continued*)

The auxiliary methods, readPerson and writePerson, read and write a single person record. Either might throw an IOException, as indicated by its throws clause. The calling copyPersons method could handle this exception. Instead it opts to throw the exception further, as indicated by its own throws clause.

The `main` method contains a try-catch statement that handles any `IOException`. Such an exception may occur either when opening the input and output files, or when copying the person records. Therefore all of this processing is inside the try block. If an `IOException` is thrown, the catch clause is executed, and simply displays a suitable error message.

B.6 Inner classes and inner interfaces

Java 1.1 introduced the concepts of *inner classes* and *inner interfaces*. An inner class (or interface) is one that is a member of another class or interface.

Like other class members, an inner class (or interface) can have private, public, protected, or default access. Private access prevents the inner class (or interface) from being visible outside the class that contains it.

In this book, we use private inner classes to implement auxiliary classes of abstract data types, such as the class representing the nodes of a tree or graph (Program 14.10 or 15.12), or the class representing iterators over a list or set (e.g., Program 10.42).

Since an inner class is 'inside' the outer class, it can access private members of the outer class.

An inner class can be either static or non-static. An object of a non-static inner class has an implicit link to an object of the outer class, and it can access the instance variables and instance methods of that object. An object of a static inner class has no such link, so a static inner class can access only the class variables and class methods of the outer class.

EXAMPLE B.7 A person class using an inner class

Program B.11 uses a very simple class, `Person`, to represent persons. It is a simple wrapper for the instance variables and provides no encapsulation.

A better implementation of a class to represent persons is given in Program B.12. In this `Person` class, we have made all of the instance variables private, thus preventing other classes from accessing them directly. Moreover, rather than inappropriately using **true** to represent female and **false** to represent male, we have introduced an auxiliary class to represent genders.

The `Gender` class is a good candidate for an inner class: it is auxiliary to the `Person` class, and makes little sense on its own. We have made it a static inner class, since it does not require access to the fields of any `Person` object.

In fact, the `Gender` class also illustrates another feature of object-oriented programming in Java. Since there are precisely two genders, we declare constant objects `MALE` and `FEMALE` to represent them. Every female person record will contain a reference to the constant `FEMALE`, and every male person record will contain a reference to the constant `MALE`.

Inside the `Person` class, the constants of the inner `Gender` class are referred to as `Gender.MALE` and `Gender.FEMALE`. Outside the `Person` class, they would be referred to as `Person.Gender.MALE` and `Person.Gender.FEMALE`, reflecting the fact that the `Gender` class is an inner class of the `Person` class.

Program B.12 also shows a modified `PersonsCopier` class that uses the improved `Person` class. Apart from a minor modification to the `Person` constructor, the major changes are the introduction of `toString` methods to render `Person` and `Gender` objects, and a `parse` method to convert "F" or "M" to a `Gender` object. The `write-Person` method no longer needs direct access to the instance variables of the `Person` class.

```java
public class Person {

    private String surname, forename;
    private Gender gender;
    private int yob;    // year of birth

    public Person (String surname, String forename,
                   Gender gender, int yob) {
        this.surname = surname;
        this.forename = forename;
        this.gender = gender;
        this.yob = yob;
    }

    public String toString () {
        return surname + " " + forename + " "
            + gender + " " + yob;
    }

    ///////////// Inner class representing genders ////////////

    public static class Gender {

        public static final Gender
                FEMALE = new Gender(),
                MALE = new Gender();

        public String toString () {
            return (this == FEMALE ? "F" : "M");
        }

        public static Gender parse (String s) {
            return (s.equals("F") ? FEMALE : MALE);
        }

    }

}
```

Program B.12 An application to copy a file of person records using a `Person` class and an inner class (*continued on next page*).

```
public class PersonsCopier {

    private static Person readPerson
                    (BufferedReader input)
                        throws IOException {
    // Read a single person record from input. Assume that each person
    // record occupies a single line, in which the surname, forename,
    // gender ('F'/'M'), and year-of-birth are separated by single spaces.
    // Return null if no person record remains to be read.
        String line = input.readLine();
        if (line == null)  return null;
        int i1 = line.indexOf(' ');
        int i2 = line.indexOf(' ', i1+1);
        int i3 = line.indexOf(' ', i2+1);
        String surname = line.substring(0, i1);
        String forename = line.substring(i1+1, i2);
        Person.Gender gender = Person.Gender.parse(
            line.substring(i2+1, i3));
        int yob = Integer.parseInt(line.substring(i3+1));
        return new Person(surname, forename,
            gender, yob);
    }

    private static void writePerson
                    (BufferedWriter output, Person p)
                        throws IOException {
        output.write(p + "\n");
    }

    ... // Other methods as in Program B.11.
}
```

Program B.12 (*continued*)

Appendix C_____

Summary of the Java Collections Framework

This appendix summarizes the main features of the Java Collections framework. It concentrates on the interfaces and classes most closely related to this book's contents. (For a comprehensive treatment of the framework, consult the Java 1.2 or later API Specification, or see Further Reading.)

- Section C.1 covers the `Collection` interface, and provides an overview of the framework as a whole.
- Section C.2 covers the `List` interface, and the `ArrayList` and `LinkedList` classes that implement that interface. It also shows how to use the `LinkedList` class to support stacks and queues.
- Section C.3 covers the `Set` and `SortedSet` interfaces, and the `HashSet` and `TreeSet` classes that respectively implement these interfaces.
- Section C.4 covers the `Map` and `SortedMap` interfaces, and the `HashMap` and `TreeMap` classes that respectively implement these interfaces.
- Section C.5 covers the auxiliary `Comparable` and `Comparator` interfaces.
- Section C.6 covers the auxiliary `Iterator` and `ListIterator` interfaces.

C.1 Collections

C.1.1 Overview of the Java Collections framework

A *collection* contains zero or more elements. Elements can be added and removed.

In the Java Collections framework, the elements of a collection are always objects (never primitive values).

There are several kinds of collection, which are distinguished by:

- whether duplicate elements are allowed or not
- whether the elements have a defined order or not.

The Java Collections framework supports five kinds of collection: lists, sets, sorted sets, maps, and sorted maps. The framework comprises a `Collection` interface, an interface for each kind of collection, and a number of classes. Each interface (except `Collection`) is implemented by one or more classes, and each class represents the collection by a suitable data structure.

The class diagram of Figure C.1 summarizes the inheritance relationships among the principal interfaces and classes of the framework. All these interfaces and classes belong to the `java.util` package, and are summarized in this appendix.

(*Note:* Our `List` interface of Chapter 8, our `Set` interface of Chapter 9, and our `Map` interface of Chapter 11 are very similar to the similarly-named interfaces of the Java Collections framework. Our interfaces omit a few operations, and there are one or two other minor differences. Any application code that runs against our interfaces should also run against the framework's interfaces without change, except possibly for renaming of constructors.)

C.1.2 The `Collection` interface

The `Collection` interface (Program C.2) specifies the operations common to all collections in the framework.

The `add` and `addAll` operations each returns false if no element was actually added (i.e., if the new element would be a duplicate and the collection disallows duplicate elements). The `remove` and `removeAll` operations each returns false if no element was actually removed (i.e., if the collection contains no matching element to remove).

The `addAll` operation makes it possible to add the elements of any collection to any

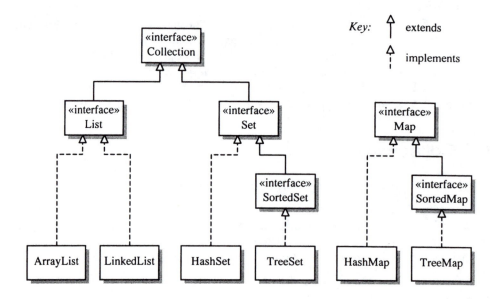

Figure C.1   Class diagram for the Java Collections framework (simplified).

```
public interface Collection {
```

// Each `Collection` object is a collection whose elements are objects.

/////////// Accessors ///////////

```
public boolean contains (Object obj);
```
// Return true if and only if this collection contains `obj`.

```
public boolean containsAll (Collection that);
```
// Return true if and only if this collection contains all elements of `that`.

```
public boolean equals (Object that);
```
// Return true if and only if this collection is equal to `that`.

```
public int hashCode ();
```
// Return the hash-code value of this collection.

```
public boolean isEmpty ();
```
// Return true if and only if this collection contains no elements.

```
public int size ();
```
// Return the number of elements of this collection.

```
public Object[] toArray ();
```
// Return an array containing all elements of this collection.

```
public Object[] toArray (Object[] a);
```
// Return an array containing all elements of this collection, which must be
// storable in a. If a is long enough, store the elements in a itself, otherwise
// create a new array of the same type as a.

/////////// Transformers ///////////

```
public boolean add (Object obj);
```
// Ensure that this collection contains `obj`. Return true if and only if an
// element is actually added.

```
public boolean addAll (Collection that);
```
// Ensure that this collection contains all elements of `that`. Return true if
// and only if at least one element is actually added.

```
public void clear ();
```
// Make this collection contain no elements.

```
public boolean remove (Object obj);
```
// Remove from this collection a single instance of `obj`, if one is present.
// Return true if and only if an element is actually removed.

Program C.2   The `Collection` interface (*continued on next page*).

```
public boolean removeAll (Collection that);
// Remove from this collection all elements that are also elements of that.
// Return true if and only if at least one element is actually removed.

public boolean retainAll (Collection that);
// Remove from this collection all elements that are not also elements of
// that. Return true if and only if at least one element is actually
// removed.

//////////// Iterator ///////////

public Iterator iterator();
// Return an iterator that will visit all elements of this collection.

}
```

Program C.2 (*continued*)

other collection. The removeAll, retainAll, and containsAll operations simi-larly operate on any pair of collections, not necessarily of the same kind.

The iterator operation returns an iterator that will visit all elements of a collection. If the collection is one whose elements have a defined order, the iterator must visit the elements in that order, otherwise it may visit them in any order.

The equals operation is inherited from the Object class, so its argument may be any object. When applied to a collection, equals must return false if its argument is not a collection of the same kind.

C.2 Lists

A *list* is a collection that allows duplicate elements and whose elements have a fixed order.

If a list has n elements, its elements (in order) have indices 0, 1, ..., $n - 1$.

C.2.1 The List interface

The List interface (Program C.3) extends the Collection interface. It provides several operations specific to lists, and it specifies more precisely the behavior of certain operations inherited from Collection.

The inherited add operation adds the given element at the *rear* of the list (and always returns true). The list-specific add operation adds the given element at a given index (and thus increases the indices of the elements following the added element). For each add operation there is a corresponding addAll operation.

The inherited remove operation removes the *first* occurrence of the given element (if any). The list-specific remove operation removes the element at a given index. (Both decrease the indices of the elements following the removed element.)

The inherited equals operation tests whether two lists are equal (i.e., they have the same number of elements, and they have equal elements at each index).

The list-specific `get` and `set` operations respectively inspect and update the element at a given index.

The list-specific `indexOf` operation searches the list in the defined order (left-to-right) for an element that equals the given element. The list-specific `lastIndexOf` operation likewise searches the list in the opposite order (right-to-left).

```
public interface List extends Collection {
    // Each List object is an indexed list (sequence) whose elements are
    // objects.

    ///////////// Accessors /////////////

    public Object get (int i);
    // Return the element with index i in this list. Throw an
    // IndexOutOfBoundsException if i is out of range.

    public int indexOf (Object obj);
    // Return the index in this list of the first element that is equal to obj, or
    // -1 if this list contains no such element.

    public int lastIndexOf (Object obj);
    // Return the index in this list of the last element that is equal to obj, or
    // -1 if this list contains no such element.

    ///////////// Transformers /////////////

    public void add (int i, Object obj);
    // Add obj as the element with index i in this list. Throw an
    // IndexOutOfBoundsException if i is out of range.

    public void addAll (int i, Collection that);
    // Add all the elements of that as the elements with indices i, i+1, ... in
    // this list. Throw an IndexOutOfBoundsException if i is out of
    // range.

    public Object remove (int i);
    // Remove and return the element with index i in this list. Throw an
    // IndexOutOfBoundsException if i is out of range.

    public void set (int i, Object obj);
    // Replace by obj the element at index i in this list. Throw an
    // IndexOutOfBoundsException if i is out of range.

    public List subList (int i, int j);
    // Return a list view of the portion of this list consisting of the elements at
    // indices i, ..., j-1. Throw an IndexOutOfBoundsException if i
    // or j-1 is out of range.
```

Program C.3 The `List` interface (*continued on next page*).

```
///////////  Iterators  ///////////

public Iterator listIterator ();
// Return a list iterator that will visit all elements of this list, in the defined
// order.

public Iterator listIterator (int i);
// Return a list iterator that will visit the elements with indices i, i+1, ... in
// this list, in the defined order.

}
```

Program C.3 *(continued).*

The list-specific `subList` operation returns a list view of part of the list. This view shares the structure and elements of the original list, so any change to the view (by adding, removing, or updating elements) is reflected in the original list, and vice versa.

(In general, a ***view*** derived from a collection *c* shares the structure and elements of *c*, so any change to the view is reflected in *c* itself, and vice versa.)

```
public class ArrayList
      implements List, Cloneable, Serializable {

// Each ArrayList object is an indexed list (sequence) whose elements
// are objects.

// This list is represented by an array, with a variable capacity.

///////////  Constructors  ///////////

public ArrayList ()  { ... }
// Construct an empty list.

public ArrayList (int cap)  { ... }
// Construct an empty list, whose initial capacity is cap.

public ArrayList (Collection that)  { ... }
// Construct a list containing the elements of that, in the order they would
// be visited by that's iterator.

///////////  Transformers  ///////////

public void ensureCapacity (int cap);
// Make this list's capacity at least cap.

public void trimToSize ();
// Make this list's capacity exactly equal to its number of elements.

...    // Other accessors and transformers specified by the above interfaces.

}
```

Program C.4 The `ArrayList` class.

The inherited `iterator` operation returns an iterator that will visit the elements of the list in the defined order. The list-specific `listIterator` operations are similar, but each returns a *list* iterator.

```
public class LinkedList
       implements List, Cloneable, Serializable {

    // Each LinkedList object is an indexed list (sequence) whose elements
    //   are objects.

    //   This list is represented by a doubly-linked list.

    /////////////// Constructors ///////////////

    public LinkedList ()   { ... }
    //   Construct an empty list.

    public LinkedList (Collection that)   { ... }
    //   Construct a list containing the elements of that, in the order they would
    //   be visited by that's iterator.

    /////////////// Accessors ///////////////

    public Object getFirst ();
    //   Return the first element of this list.

    public Object getLast ();
    //   Return the last element of this list.

    /////////////// Transformers ///////////////

    public void addFirst (Object obj);
    //   Add obj as the first element of this list.

    public void addLast (Object obj);
    //   Add obj as the last element of this list.

    public Object removeFirst ();
    //   Remove and return the first element of this list.

    public Object removeLast ();
    //   Remove and return the last element of this list.
    ...    //   Other accessors and transformers specified by the above interfaces.

}
```

Program C.5   The `LinkedList` class.

C.2.2 The `ArrayList` class

The `ArrayList` class (Program C.4) implements the `List` interface. The list is represented by an array, whose length defines the current *capacity* of the list. The capacity is increased automatically whenever necessary. Since this is time-consuming, however, application code should use the `ArrayList(int)` constructor or the `ensureCapacity` operation to anticipate future expansion of the list.

This representation guarantees that the `get` and `set` operations have $O(1)$ time complexity. The `remove` operation has $O(n)$ time complexity. The `add` operation is said to have $O(1)$ *amortized* time complexity, meaning that adding n elements takes $O(n)$ time.

C.2.3 The `LinkedList` class

The `LinkedList` class (Program C.5) implements the `List` interface. The list is represented by a doubly-linked list.

This representation implies that the `get`, `set`, `add`, and `remove` operations all have $O(n)$ time complexity.

The `LinkedList` class provides `addFirst`, `addLast`, `getFirst`, `getLast`, `removeFirst`, and `removeLast` operations. These operations allow a `Linked-List` object to be used as a stack, queue, or doubly-ended queue, as summarized in Table C.6. (*Note:* It is unclear why the designers did not include these operations in the `List` interface: they are generally useful and they can be implemented efficiently whether an array or linked-list representation is chosen.)

C.3 Sets

A *set* is a collection that disallows duplicate elements. In general, the elements of a set have no defined order.

C.3.1 The `Set` interface

The `Set` interface (Program C.7) extends the `Collection` interface. It provides no operations specific to sets, but it specifies more precisely the behavior of certain operations inherited from `Collection`.

Table C.6 Use of `LinkedList` operations to emulate stacks, queues, and doubly-ended queues.

Operation	Stack	Queue	Doubly-ended queue
`addFirst`	–	–	add element at front
`addLast`	add element at top	add element at rear	add element at rear
`getFirst`	–	inspect front element	inspect front element
`getLast`	inspect top element	–	inspect rear element
`removeFirst`	–	remove front element	remove front element
`removeLast`	remove top element	–	remove rear element

The inherited `add` operation returns false if the set already contains the given object. The inherited `remove` operation returns false if the set does not contain the given object.

The inherited `equals` operation tests whether two sets are equal (i.e., they have the same elements, regardless of order).

The inherited `containsAll` operation tests whether one set subsumes another, `addAll` computes a set union, `removeAll` computes a set difference, and `retainAll` computes a set intersection.

```
public interface Set extends Collection {

    // Each Set object is a set whose members are objects.

}
```

Program C.7   The `Set` interface.

```
public interface SortedSet extends Set {

    // Each SortedSet object is a sorted set whose members are objects.

    ///////////// Accessors /////////////

    public Comparator comparator ();
    // Return the comparator associated with this sorted set, or null if it uses its
    // elements' natural ordering.

    public Object first ();
    // Return the first (least) element of this sorted set. Throw a
    // NoSuchElementException if this sorted set is empty.

    public SortedSet headSet (Object obj);
    // Return a set view of the portion of this sorted set whose elements are
    // less than obj.

    public Object last ();
    // Return the last (greatest) element of this sorted set. Throw a
    // NoSuchElementException if this sorted set is empty.

    public SortedSet subSet (Object obj1, Object obj2);
    // Return a set view of the portion of this sorted set whose elements are
    // greater than or equal to obj1 and less than obj2. Throw an
    // IllegalArgumentException if obj1 is greater than obj2.

    public SortedSet tailSet (Object obj);
    // Return a set view of the portion of this sorted set whose elements are
    // greater than or equal to obj.

}
```

Program C.8   The `SortedSet` interface.

C.3.2 The `SortedSet` interface

A *sorted set* is a set whose elements are held in ascending order.

The `SortedSet` interface (Program C.8) extends the `Set` interface. It provides a few operations specific to sorted sets, and it specifies more precisely the behavior of one operation inherited from `Set`.

The inherited `iterator` operation returns an iterator that will visit the sorted set's elements in ascending order. The fact that the set is sorted has no effect on the behavior of the other inherited operations.

The sorted-set-specific `first` and `last` operations return the least and greatest elements, respectively, of the sorted set.

The sorted-set-specific `tailSet`, `headSet`, and `subSet` operations each returns a set view of part of the sorted set, defined respectively by a given least object, a given greater object, or both.

By default, the sorted set's elements must all be `Comparable` objects, and are sorted in their natural ordering. If the sorted set has an associated comparator, however, its elements are sorted in the ordering imposed by that comparator.

```
public class HashSet
    implements Set, Cloneable, Serializable {

    // Each HashSet object is a set whose members are objects.

    // This set is represented by an open-bucket hash table, with a variable
    // capacity and a fixed maximum load factor.

    //////////// Constructors ////////////

    public HashSet ()  { ... }
    // Construct an empty set.

    public HashSet (int cap)  { ... }
    // Construct an empty set, whose initial capacity is cap, and whose
    // maximum load factor is 0.75.

    public HashSet (int cap, float maxLoad)  { ... }
    // Construct an empty set, whose initial capacity is cap, and whose
    // maximum load factor is maxLoad.

    public HashSet (Collection that)  { ... }
    // Construct a set containing the same elements as that.

    ...  // Accessors and transformers specified by the above interfaces.

}
```

Program C.9 The `HashSet` class.

C.3.3 The `HashSet` class

The `HashSet` class (Program C.9) implements the `Set` interface. The set is represented by an open-bucket hash table, whose number of buckets defines the current *capacity* of the set. The capacity is increased automatically whenever a predetermined maximum load factor (0.75 by default) is reached. The implementation uses a hash function expressed in terms of the elements' `hashCode` operation.

This representation implies that the `contains`, `add`, and `remove` operations have $O(1)$ time complexity, provided that the hash function distributes the elements evenly and thinly over the buckets.

C.3.4 The `TreeSet` class

The `TreeSet` class (Program C.10) implements the `SortedSet` interface. The sorted set is represented by a red-black tree, which is a binary search tree equipped with insertion and deletion algorithms that keep it well-balanced.

This representation guarantees that the `contains`, `add`, and `remove` operations have $O(\log n)$ time complexity.

```
public class TreeSet
      implements SortedSet, Cloneable, Serializable {

   // Each TreeSet object is a sorted set whose members are objects.

   // This set is represented by a red-black tree.

   //////////// Constructors ////////////

   public TreeSet ()   { ... }
   // Construct an empty sorted set.

   public TreeSet (Comparator comp)   { ... }
   // Construct an empty sorted set, which will be sorted according to comp.

   public TreeSet (Collection that)   { ... }
   // Construct a sorted set containing the same elements as that, sorted
   // according to these elements' natural order.

   public TreeSet (SortedSet that)   { ... }
   // Construct a sorted set containing the same elements as that, sorted
   // according to the same ordering as that.

   ...   // Accessors and transformers specified by the above interfaces.

}
```

Program C.10   The `TreeSet` class.

C.4 Maps

A *map* contains zero or more entries, where each entry is a pair consisting of a *key* and a *value*. No two entries in the same map are allowed to have the same key. In general, the entries of a map have no defined order.

Maps are *not* Collection objects. Nevertheless, maps belong to the Java Collections framework.

C.4.1 The Map interface

The Map interface (Program C.11) does not actually extend the Collection interface.

```
public interface Map {

    // Each Map object is a map whose keys and values are objects.

    ///////////// Accessors /////////////

    public boolean containsKey (Object key);
    // Return true if and only if this map contains an entry whose key is key.

    public boolean containsValue (Object val);
    // Return true if and only if this map contains an entry whose value is val.

    public Set entrySet ();
    // Return a set view of all entries in this map.

    public boolean equals (Object that);
    // Return true if and only if this map is equal to that.

    public Object get (Object key);
    // Return the value in the entry whose key is key in this map, or null if
    // there is no such entry. Throw a ClassCastException if this map
    // cannot contain a key with the class of key.

    public int hashCode ();
    // Return the hash-code value of this map.

    public boolean isEmpty ();
    // Return true if and only if this map is empty.

    public Set keySet ();
    // Return a set view of all keys in this map.

    public int size ();
    // Return the number of entries in this map.

    public Set values ();
    // Return a collection view of all values in this map.
```

Program C.11   The Map interface (*continued on next page*).

However, many of its operations are similar to the operations of the `Collection` interface, such as `equals`, `isEmpty`, `size`, `clear`, and `remove`.

The `get`, `put`, and `remove` operations each acts on the (unique) entry with a given key. They respectively return the value in the entry, replace the value in the entry, and remove the entry.

The `putAll` operation overlays one map with a second map. Its result is a map containing all entries from both maps, except that where two entries have the same key the entry from the second map is preferred.

The `equals` operation tests whether two maps are equal (i.e., they have the same entries, regardless of order).

The `containsKey` and `containsValue` operations test whether the map contains a given key and a given value, respectively.

```
/////////// Transformers ///////////

public void clear ();
// Make this map contain no entries.

public Object put (Object key, Object val);
// Add to this map an entry whose key is key and whose value is val,
// replacing any existing entry whose key is key. Return the value in that
// entry, or null if there was no such entry. Throw a
// ClassCastException if this map cannot contain a key with the
// class of key.

public void putAll (Map that);
// Overlay this map with that, i.e., add to this map all entries of that,
// replacing any existing entries with the same keys.

public Object remove (Object key);
// Remove the entry whose key is key (if any) from this map. Return the
// value in that entry, or null if there was no such entry.

/////////// Inner interface for map entries ///////////

public static interface Entry {

    // Each Entry object is a map entry, consisting of a key and a value.

    public Object getKey ();

    public Object getValue ();

    public Object setValue (Object val);

}

}
```

Program C.11 (*continued*)

The `entrySet` operation returns a set view of all entries in the map. Similarly, the `keySet` operation returns a set view of all keys in the map. Finally, the `values` operation returns a *collection* view of all values in the map (not a set view, because a map may contain duplicate values). In each case, the view shares the structure and entries of the original map, so any change to the view (by adding or removing entries) is reflected in the original map, and vice versa.

The elements of the set view returned by the `entrySet` operation are guaranteed to be `Map.Entry` objects. The `Map.Entry` inner interface is shown in Program C.11. Its operations are self-explanatory.

C.4.2 The `SortedMap` interface

A *sorted map* is a map whose entries are held in ascending order by key.

The `SortedMap` interface (Program C.12) extends the `Map` interface. It provides a few operations specific to sorted maps, and it specifies more precisely the behavior of one operation inherited from `Map`.

```
public interface SortedMap extends Map {

    // Each SortedMap object is a sorted map whose keys and values are
    // objects.

    /////////////// Accessors ///////////////

    public Comparator comparator ();
    // Return the comparator associated with this sorted map, or null if it uses
    // its keys' natural ordering.

    public Object firstKey ();
    // Return the first (least) key in this sorted map.

    public SortedMap headMap (Object key);
    // Return a map view of the portion of this sorted map whose entries are
    // less than key.

    public Object lastKey ();
    // Return the last (greatest) key in this sorted map.

    public SortedMap subMap (Object obj1, Object obj2);
    // Return a map view of the portion of this sorted map whose entries are
    // greater than or equal to obj1 and less than obj2.

    public SortedMap tailMap (Object key);
    // Return a map view of the portion of this sorted map whose entries are
    // greater than or equal to key.

}
```

Program C.12   The `SortedMap` interface.

The inherited `iterator` operation returns an iterator that will visit the sorted map's entries in ascending order by key. The fact that the map is sorted has no effect on the behavior of the other inherited operations.

The sorted-map-specific `firstKey` and `lastKey` operations return the least and greatest keys, respectively, of the sorted map.

The sorted-map-specific `tailMap`, `headMap`, and `subMap` operations each returns a map view of part of the sorted map, defined respectively by a given least key, a given greater key, or both.

By default, the sorted map's keys must all be `Comparable` objects, and are sorted in their natural ordering. However, if the sorted map has an associated comparator, its keys are sorted in the ordering imposed by that comparator.

C.4.3 The `HashMap` class

The `HashMap` class (Program C.13) implements the `Map` interface. The map is represented by an open-bucket hash table, whose number of buckets defines the current *capacity* of the map. The capacity is increased automatically whenever a predetermined maximum load factor (0.75 by default) is reached. The implementation uses a hash function expressed in terms of the keys' `hashCode` operation.

```
public class HashMap
        implements Map, Cloneable, Serializable {

    //  Each HashMap object is a map whose keys and values are objects.

    //  This map is represented by an open-bucket hash table, with a variable
    //  capacity and a fixed maximum load factor.

    /////////////  Constructors  /////////////

    public HashMap ()  { ... }
    //  Construct an empty map.

    public HashMap (int cap)  { ... }
    //  Construct an empty map, whose initial capacity is cap, and whose
    //  maximum load factor is 0.75.

    public HashMap (int cap, float maxLoad)  { ... }
    //  Construct an empty map, whose initial capacity is cap, and whose
    //  maximum load factor is maxLoad.

    public HashMap (Map that)  { ... }
    //  Construct a map containing the same entries as that.

    ...  //  Accessors and transformers specified by the above interfaces.

}
```

Program C.13   The `HashMap` class.

This representation implies that the containsKey, get, put, and remove operations have $O(1)$ time complexity, provided that the hash function distributes the entries evenly and thinly over the buckets.

Note that the HashSet class (Section C.3.3) uses exactly the same data representation as the HashMap class. This makes the view operations (keySet, valueSet, and values) very efficient: each simply returns the hash table representing the original map.

C.4.4 The TreeMap class

The TreeMap class (Program C.14) implements the SortedMap interface. The sorted map is represented by a red-black tree.

This representation guarantees that the containsKey, get, put, and remove operations have $O(\log n)$ time complexity.

Note that the TreeSet class (Section C.3.4) uses exactly the same data representation as the TreeMap class. This makes the view operations (keySet, valueSet, and values) very efficient: each simply returns the tree representing the original map.

```
public class TreeMap
      implements SortedMap, Cloneable, Serializable {
   // Each TreeMap object is a sorted map whose keys and values are
   // objects.

   // This map is represented by a red-black tree.

   /////////////// Constructors ///////////////

   public TreeMap ()  { ... }
   // Construct an empty sorted map.

   public TreeMap (Comparator comp)  { ... }
   // Construct an empty sorted map, which will be sorted according to comp.

   public TreeMap (Map that)  { ... }
   // Construct a sorted map containing the same entries as that, sorted
   // according to their keys' natural order.

   public TreeMap (SortedMap that)  { ... }
   // Construct a sorted map containing the same entries as that, sorted
   // according to the same ordering as that.

   ...   // Accessors and transformers specified by the above interfaces.
}
```

Program C.14 The TreeMap class.

C.5 Orderings

Consider a collection of values equipped with an *is equal to* operation and an *is less than* operation. These values are said to be ***totally ordered*** if all the following conditions are met for any values x, y, and z:

- either x is equal to y, or x is less than y, or y is less than x
- x is equal to x
- if x is equal to y, then y is equal to x
- if x is equal to y, and y is equal to z, then x is equal to z
- if x is less than y, and y is less than z, then x is less than z.

If y is less than x, we also say that x is greater than y.

We can sort values if and only if they are totally ordered.

Here are two examples and a counter-example:

(a) The integers are totally ordered if we define 'i is equal to j' as '$i == j$' and 'i is less than j' as '$i < j$'.

(b) The strings are totally ordered if we define 's is equal to t' and 's is less than t' in the sense of lexicographic comparison.

(c) The activities someone plans for next week might depend on one another to some extent. Let us define 'activity A is less than activity B' to mean that A must be completed before B is started. These activities are *not* totally ordered, because there might be two distinct activities C and D such that neither C is less than D nor D is less than C.

C.5.1 The `Comparable` interface

The `Comparable` interface (Program C.15) specifies a comparison operation, `compareTo`. If class C implements `Comparable`, class C's `compareTo` operation must impose a total ordering on the objects of class C: we define 'x is equal to y' as 'x.`compareTo`(y) == 0' and 'x is less than y' as 'x.`compareTo`(y) < 0'.

The total ordering imposed by class C's `compareTo` operation is called the ***natural ordering*** of class C.

```
public interface Comparable {

    // Each Comparable object is equipped with a comparison operation that
    // imposes a total ordering on this object and others of the same class.

    public int compareTo (Object that);
    // Return a negative integer if this object is less than that,
    // or zero if this object is equal to that,
    // or a positive integer if this object is greater than that.
    // Throw a ClassCastException if the objects cannot be compared.

}
```

Program C.15 The `Comparable` interface.

```
public interface Comparator {
```

>   // Each `Comparator` object provides a comparison function that imposes
>   // a total ordering on some collection of objects.

```
    public int compare (Object obj1, Object obj2);
```

>   // Return a negative integer if `obj1` is less than `obj2`,
>   // or zero if `obj1` is equal to `obj2`,
>   // or a positive integer if `obj1` is greater than `obj2`.

```
    public boolean equals (Object that);
```

>   // Return true only if this comparator imposes the same ordering as `that`.

```
}
```

Program C.16   The `Comparator` interface.

A class's natural ordering should be consistent with that class's `equals` operation. In other words, 'x.`compareTo`(y) `==` 0' should yield the same value (false or true) as 'x.`equals`(y)'.

C.5.2 The `Comparator` interface

Sometimes the natural ordering of a class is not what is required in a particular application. For example, we might want to sort strings in length order, rather than in their natural (lexicographical) order.

The `Comparator` interface (Program C.16) specifies a comparison operation, `compare`. If c is a `Comparator` object (also known as a ***comparator***), c.`compare` must impose a total ordering on the objects to which it may be applied: we define 'x is equal to y' as 'c.`compare`(x, y) `==` 0' and 'x is less than y' as 'c.`compare`(x, y) $<$ 0'.

The total ordering imposed by a comparator should be consistent with the `equals` operation. In other words, 'c.`compare`(x, y) `==` 0' should yield the same value as 'x.`equals`(y)'.

(*Note:* The major difference between `compareTo` and `compare` is that we can define only one `compareTo` method per class, whereas we can define as many different `compare` methods as we need. A minor difference is that `compareTo` is an instance method of one of the objects to be compared, whereas `compare` is an instance method of a comparator.)

C.6 Iterators

An ***iterator*** over a collection c allows the elements of c to be visited one by one. There is no requirement for an iterator to visit every element of c, nor is there a requirement to visit the elements in any particular order.

An iterator may be viewed as a sequence of elements, together with a *place-marker* (or *cursor*) that lies between the *previous* element and the *next* element. Normally the previous element is the one last visited, and the next element is the one about to be

```
public interface Iterator {

    // Each Iterator object represents an iterator over some collection,
    // allowing the elements of that collection to be visited.

    public boolean hasNext ();
    // Return true if and only if this iterator has a next element.

    public Object next ();
    // Return the next element in this iterator and move its place-marker
    // forward. Throw a NoSuchElementException if there is no
    // next element.

    public void remove ();
    // Remove from the underlying collection the previous element of this
    // iterator. Throw an IllegalStateException if there is no previous
    // element, or if remove has already been called since next was last
    // called.

}
```

Program C.17 The Iterator interface.

visited. Initially there is no previous element. When the last element is visited, there is no next element.

Like a view, an iterator over a collection *c* shares the structure and elements of *c*, so any change to the iterator is reflected in *c* itself, and vice versa.

(*Note:* Iterators are more general than, and supersede, the Java 1.1 enumerations.)

C.6.1 The **Iterator** interface

The Iterator interface (Program C.17) specifies the operations with which every iterator is equipped.

The next operation can be called repeatedly to visit every element in turn:

```
Iterator iter = c.iterator();
while (iter.hasNext()) {
    Object elem = iter.next();
    ...   // Visit the element elem.
}
```

The *next* and *remove* operations can be called repeatedly to visit and then remove every element in turn:

```
Iterator iter = c.iterator();
while (iter.hasNext()) {
    Object elem = iter.next();
    ...                     // Visit the element elem.
    iter.remove();   // Remove the element just visited.
}
```

C.6.2 The `ListIterator` interface

A *list iterator* allows the elements of a list to be visited in both directions.

The `ListIterator` interface (Program C.18) extends the `Iterator` interface. It specifies several operations specific to list iterators.

The `previous` operation can be called repeatedly to revisit elements already visited, or it may be combined with calls to `next` to go backwards and forwards.

The `add` and `set` operations, like `remove`, can be used to change the underlying list.

```
public interface ListIterator extends Iterator {
    // Each ListIterator object represents an iterator over some list,
    // allowing the elements of that list to be visited in both directions.

    public void add (Object obj);
    // Add obj to the underlying list immediately before the next element of
    // this iterator.

    public boolean hasPrevious ();
    // Return true if and only if this iterator has a previous element.

    public int nextIndex ();
    // Return the index of this iterator's next element, or –1 if there is no next
    // element.

    public int previousIndex ();
    // Return the index of this iterator's previous element, or –1 if there is no
    // previous element.

    public Object previous ();
    // Return the previous element in this iterator and move its place-marker
    // backward. Throw a NoSuchElementException if there is no
    // previous element.

    public void set (Object obj);
    // Replace the last element returned by this iterator by obj in the
    // underlying list. Throw an IllegalStateException if there is no
    // such element, or if add or remove has been called since next or
    // previous was last called.
}
```

Program C.18   The `ListIterator` interface.

Further Reading ___

Bibliographic notes

This book is intended to equip you with a working knowledge that will enable you to select abstract data types suitable for use in a particular application, and to implement each abstract data type in terms of efficient data structures and algorithms. Nevertheless, there is always more to learn. Because of the introductory nature of this book, and space limitations, some of the more advanced and theoretical topics have had to be omitted.

There are several classic and comprehensive textbooks on the topics of algorithms and data structures, notably Aho, Hopcroft, and Ullman (1974), and Knuth (1998).

The following notes, organized chapter-by-chapter, contain pointers to further reading on more advanced and theoretical topics.

Chapter 1

This book focuses on algorithms applicable to collections of data, typically insertion, deletion, searching, merging, and sorting algorithms. Other important classes of algorithms have had to be omitted. For a comprehensive (but demanding) treatment of all the main classes of algorithms, see Sedgewick and Lindholm (2000). Goodrich and Tamassia (1998) also cover string and geometric algorithms.

Chapter 2

Algorithm analysis is a complex topic, and only a basic treatment is possible in this book. The *O*-notation is explained particularly well in Standish (1998). For a more comprehensive treatment of algorithm analysis, see Bentley (1986), Goodrich and Tamassia (1998), Sahni (2000), or Weiss (1998).

Chapter 3

Searching and sorting algorithms have been studied in depth throughout the history of computer science. The classic (originally published in 1973) and most comprehensive text is Knuth (1998). For a treatment using Java, see Goodrich and Tomassia (1998) or Standish (1998).

Merge-sort and quick-sort are examples of algorithms developed using the divide-and-conquer design technique. Also important are the greedy, dynamic programming, backtracking, and branch-and-bound techniques. For a full treatment of algorithm design techniques, see Goodrich and Tamassia (1998) or Sahni (2000).

Quick-sort alone has been subject to extensive study, because its performance depends in a complex way on the characteristics of the data and the partitioning algorithm adopted. The seminal paper is Hoare (1962); this describes a partitioning algorithm different from the one in this book.

Chapter 12

The design of hash tables is a rich topic, because the performance of their searching, insertion, and deletion algorithms depends in a complex way on the characteristics of the data, the hash function, and the load factor. This is particularly so for open-bucket hash tables, where clustering has a major impact on performance. For a fuller treatment of hash tables, see Knuth (1998) or Standish (1998).

Chapter 15

Graph theory is a major topic in its own right. This book presents only the most fundamental graph algorithms. For a fuller treatment, see Goodrich and Tamassia (1998), Sahni (2000), or Weiss (1998).

Chapter 16

Many kinds of balanced search trees have been invented. Apart from the AVL-trees and B-trees covered in this book, other important kinds are red-black trees (used in the `java.util.TreeSet` and `java.util.TreeMap` classes), 2-3-4 trees, and splay trees. For a full treatment, see Goodrich and Tamassia (1998), Sahni (2000), or Weiss (1998).

Chapter 17

There are many good texts on object-oriented design, including Booch *et al.* (1998), Gamma *et al.* (1994), and Meyer (1997).

Appendix B

A number of good introductory textbooks on Java are now available. We recommend Bailey and Bailey (2000).

If you are already familiar with a related programming language such as C or C++, a quicker introduction to Java is provided by Flanagan (1999). This also includes a comprehensive overview of the Java class libraries.

Appendix C

For a comprehensive summary of the Java Collections framework, see Flanagan (1999).

Bibliography

A.V. Aho, J.E. Hopcroft, and J.D. Ullman (1974) *The Design and Analysis of Computer Algorithms*, Addison Wesley, Reading, MA, USA.

D.A. Bailey and D.W. Bailey (2000) *Java Elements: Principles of Programming in Java*, McGraw-Hill, Singapore.

J.L. Bentley (2000) *Programming Pearls in Java*, ACM Press, New York, USA.

G. Booch, I. Jacobson, and J. Rumbaugh (1998) *The Unified Modeling Language User Guide*, Addison Wesley Longman, Reading, MA, USA.

D. Flanagan (1999) *Java in a Nutshell*, 3rd edition, O'Reilly, Cambridge, MA, USA.

E. Gamma, R. Helm, R. Johnson, and J. Vlissides (1994) *Design Patterns*, Addison Wesley Longman, Reading, USA.

M.T. Goodrich and R. Tamassia (1998) *Data Structures and Algorithms in Java*, Wiley, New York, USA.

C.A.R. Hoare (1962) Quicksort, *Computer Journal* 5, pp. 10–15.

D.E. Knuth (1998) *The Art of Computer Programming: Sorting and Searching*, 2nd edition, Addison Wesley, Reading, MA, USA.

B. Meyer (1997) *Object-Oriented Software Construction*, Prentice Hall, Englewood Cliffs, NJ, USA.

S. Sahni (2000) *Data Structures, Algorithms, and Applications in Java*, McGraw-Hill, Singapore.

R. Sedgewick and T. Lindholm (2000) *Algorithms in Java*, Addison Wesley, Reading, MA, USA.

T.A. Standish (1998) *Data Structures in Java*, Addison Wesley, Reading, MA, USA.

M.A. Weiss (1998) *Data Structures and Algorithm Analysis in Java*, Addison Wesley, Reading, MA, USA.

Index

Notes on this index
- A page number set *thus* indicates where a term is defined.
- Names of classes and interfaces introduced in this book are unqualified (e.g., List).
- Names of classes and interfaces provided by the Java class library are fully qualified (e.g., java.util.List).

abstract data type (or ADT), 7–8, 103–122, 469–472
    accessor, *113*–114
    applicative transformer, *113*–114
    constructor, *113*–114
    contract, *104*, 105, 111
    data representation, 7–8, 103–104, 106, 111, 116, 117–119
    design, 111–114
    immutable value, *113*
    implementation, 106–111
    mutable value, *113*
    mutative transformer, *113*–114
    necessary and sufficient operations, *111*–113
    observable behavior, *104*
    operation, 103
    processor, 12
    requirements, 104, 114
    separation of concerns, 8
    specification, *see* contract
    transformer, *113*–114
    value, 103
    see also Graph, List, Map, Priority-Queue, Queue, Set, Stack, Tree
accessor, *see* abstract data type
add, 176, 182–183, 188, 208, 213, 219, 222, 266, 340, 343, 519, 521, 536

addAll, 176, 183, 188, 208, 266, 519, 521
addChild, 373
addEdge, 404
addFirst, 523
addLast, 130, 133, 135, 155, 159, 523
addNode, 404
Adel'son Vel'skii, G. M., 437
ADT, *see* abstract data type
Al Khwarizmi, Muhammad abu Ja'far ibn Musa, 3
    quadratic-equation algorithm, 3
algorithm, 1–6, 11–*12*–31, 106, 537, 538
    analysis, 16–17, 25, 29, 39, 41–42, 44, 48–49, 50–51, 53–55, 59–60, 244, 261–262, 314, 325–326, 349, 352, 445–447, 465–466, 537
    feasible, *23*
    history, 1–6
    infeasible, 23
    notation, 6, 13–14
    processor, *12*
    recursive, *24*–31
    step, 6, 12, 15
    termination, 12, 24–25
    vs program, 6
    see also complexity, efficiency, problem
AMDigraph, 415–416
    .Edge, 416
    .Node, 416